Dubai
EXPLORER

Kicking Boredom's Butt Since 1785...

EXPLORER

Editorial

Senior Editor & Photographer	Pamela Grist
	Pamela@Explorer-Publishing.com
Editor	Katie Hallett-Jones
	Katie@Explorer-Publishing.com
Food Editor	Christopher Brown
	Christopher@Explorer-Publishing.com
Proofreader	Linda Peterson
	Linda@Explorer-Publishing.com

Sales & Advertising

Advertising Manager	Hema Kumar
	Hema@Explorer-Publishing.com
Advertising Executive	Wendy Menzies
	Wendy@Explorer-Publishing.com
Corporate Sales	Nadine Laurent
	Nadine@Explorer-Publishing.com

Production & Design

Production Manager	Cathy McKernan
	Cathy@Explorer-Publishing.com
Designer	Pete Maloney
	Pete@Explorer-Publishing.com
Research	Nadia D'Souza
	Nadia@Explorer-Publishing.com
Research	Wendy D'Souza
	Wendy@Explorer-Publishing.com
Layout	Jayde Fernandes
	Jayde@Explorer-Publishing.com
IT & Layout	Derrick Pereira
	Derrick@Explorer-Publishing.com

Distribution

Distribution Manager	Ivan Rodrigues
	Ivan@Explorer-Publishing.com
Distribution Executive	Abdul Gafoor
	Gafoor@Explorer-Publishing.com
Distribution Executive	Mannie Lugtu
	Mannie@Explorer-Publishing.com

Administration

Publisher	Alistair MacKenzie
	Alistair@Explorer-Publishing.com
Administration Manager	Yolanda Rodrigues
	Yolanda@Explorer-Publishing.com

Front Cover Photograph	Paul Thuysbaert
Printer	Emirates Printing Press
Website	Internet Solutions

Explorer Publishing & Distribution

Dubai Media City   Phone (+971-4) 391 8060 Fax 391 8062
PO Box 34275, Dubai   info@explorer-publishing.com
United Arab Emirates   www.explorer-publishing.com

Seventh Edition 2003   ISBN 976-8182-33-4
Copyright © 2003 Explorer Group Ltd

Dear Reader,

Welcome to the ***completely revised*** 2003 *Dubai Explorer*, our 7th edition of the essential (and the original) guide to all things cool here in Dubai. Our tireless Professors of Pleasure here at Explorer Publishing have taken a fresh look at our beloved adopted hometown and all it has to offer. Yes, once again we've combed its streets and sites to provide you with the latest and greatest places to dine, shop, sip and socialise, then worked like madmen (and women) to present it in this fabulous package you are now holding.

As usual, you'll find the customary informative reviews and insights that you've come to expect from our guides, but this year we've taken it a step further to include a whole new section on all things business, and a comprehensive look at the expansive five-star hotels that seem to grow naturally here. What's more, our newly appointed Food Editor (who's terribly truthful, tactful and talented) has revamped our Going Out section.

While we're on the subject of what's new, we'd like to give you a heads up on what to expect in the new year. We've been hard at work on the *A-Z Explorer (Dubai)*, a comprehensive map guide, and the (ahem) handy *Hand-Held Explorer* (our complete guide book for your PDA), as well as two spectacular image books to complement our award-winning original, *Images of Dubai and the United Arab Emirates*. Look for *Dubai: Tomorrow's City Today* and *Sharjah's Architectural Splendour* very soon.

Finally, we'd like to once again thank our fabulous advertisers and tireless team of researchers and writers who toiled without complaint to put together what we feel is our best edition yet. Also, thanks to those of you who called or wrote in to let us know about new and exciting events and activities for this year's edition. We'd love to hear from you too, so log on and become part of our Explorer Community and tell us about your Explorer experiences – good, bad or ugly.

If you love our books, tell your friends about us, and if you seek out a service or outlet on our recommendation, please let them know where you heard about them.

Now, go have some fun on us!

The Explorer Team

Kicking Boredom's Butt Since 1785...

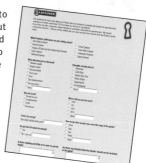

ON-LINE EXPLORER

Web Updates

A tremendous amount of research, effort, and passion go into making our guidebooks. However, in this dynamic and fast-paced environment, decisions are swiftly taken and quickly implemented. As your loyal publisher, we will try to provide you with the most current updates on those things which have DRAMATICALLY changed.

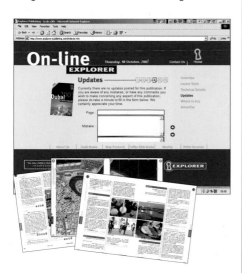

1. To view any changes visit our Website: **www.explorer-publishing.com**

2. At the bottom, go to **Guide Books -> Dubai Explorer -> Updates** and see whether there are any updates you are interested in

3. All updates are in Adobe PDF format*. You may print in colour or black & white and update your guidebook immediately

4. If you are aware of any mistakes, or have any comments concerning any aspect of this publication, please fill in our on-line reader response form... we certainly appreciate your time and feedback.

If you do not have Adobe Reader, free reader versions may be downloaded from (www.adobe.com) or use the link from our site.

Who Are You?

We would love to know more about you... We would equally love to know what we have done right, wrong, or if we accidentally mislead you somewhere...

Please take ONE whole minute to fill out our **Reader Response Form** on our Website.

1. Visit **www.explorer-publishing.com**

2. At the top right, click on **RESPONSE FORM**

3. Fill it out and let us know more about you

Explorer Community

Whether it's an idea, a correction, an opinion or simply a recommendation - we want to hear from you. Log on and be part of the Explorer Community - let your opinions be heard, viewed, compiled and printed... **www.explorer-publishing.com**

Hand-Held Explorer (Dubai)

The *Hand-Held Explorer* for Dubai is the first of Explorer Publishing's travel guides that can be downloaded onto your PDA. Now all the information available in the *Dubai Explorer* can be accessed with the push of a button. Interactive, informative and innovative... the *Hand-Held Explorer* is easy to install, a breeze to use and packed with useful information.

Available from all good electronic stores, selected bookshops or directly from us at Explorer Publishing (391 8060).

ISBN 976-8182-40-7

NOTHING MATCHES UP TO OUR STRIKING VARIETY OF RESTAURANTS.

Explorer's Latest Products

Off-Road Explorer (UAE)

20 Adventurous Off-Road Routes...

With clear and easy to follow instructions, this is an invaluable tool for exploring the UAE's 'outback'. Satellite imagery of every stage of the route

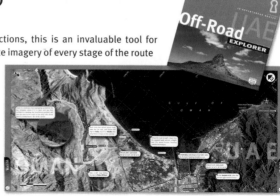

is superimposed with the correct track to follow. For each route, points of interest are highlighted, along with distances and advice on driving the more difficult parts. Remarkable photography peppers this guide, and additional information on topics such as wildlife and archaeology complement the off-road routes.

Images of Dubai & the UAE

A stunning collection of images of Dubai and the United Arab Emirates

Images of Dubai is a visual showcase, sharing the secrets of this remarkable land and introducing newcomers to the wonders of Dubai and the United Arab Emirates. Journey along golden beaches under a pastel sunset, or deep into the mesmerising sands of the desert. View architectural details of one of the most visually thrilling urban environments in the world, and dive undersea to encounter the reef creatures who live there. This book is for all those who love this country as well as those who think they might like to...

Underwater Explorer (UAE)

58 Spectacular Dives

Packed with the top 58 dive sites covering both coastlines and the Musandam, this dedicated guidebook is ideal for divers of all abilities. Detailing dive sites around the UAE, this guide contains suggested dive plans, informative illustrations, shipwreck circumstances and marine life photographs. Written by avid divers who want to share their passion and local knowledge with others, the **Underwater Explorer** includes all the crucial information diving enthusiasts need to know about diving in the UAE.

Sharjah's Architectural Splendour

A striking photographic exploration into the architectural splendour of Sharjah

Take a guided tour of the beauty of Sharjah's architecture and some of the highlights of this remarkable city. From small aesthetic details to grand public compounds, from mosques to souks, the photographs contained within will amaze and delight. Whether you are a long-term resident or a brief visitor, this volume will undoubtedly surprise and delight.

Family Explorer (Dubai & Abu Dhabi)

This is the only family handbook to Dubai and Abu Dhabi

Catering specifically to families with children between the ages of 0-14 years, the easy to use Explorer format details the practicalities of family life in the northern Emirates, including information on medical care, education, residence visas and hundreds of invaluable ideas for indoor and outdoor activities for families and kids.

Zappy Explorer (Dubai)

A complete step-by-step guide for getting things done, the Zappy Explorer leads you through all the procedures involved in settling into life, home or business in Dubai – in a zap!

This authoritative guide contains over 100 well thought-out, clear and easy to follow procedures, and tips and advice for everything from obtaining visas and permits to telecommunications, housing, transportation, licences, banking, education and health, making it your best chance for navigating through Dubai's administrative mysteries.

For a complete list of Explorer Products, please refer to the back of this guidebook

IF IT ISN'T THE GRAND CANYON,
IT ISN'T THE GRAND CANYON.

There's only one. One Grand Canyon. Nothing else is quite the same. Similarly, there's only one Jeep® brand. Only one line of vehicles rugged enough and capable enough to carry the Jeep® name. One line that offers a full range of choices

 **trading enterprises**

An **Al-Futtaim group** company

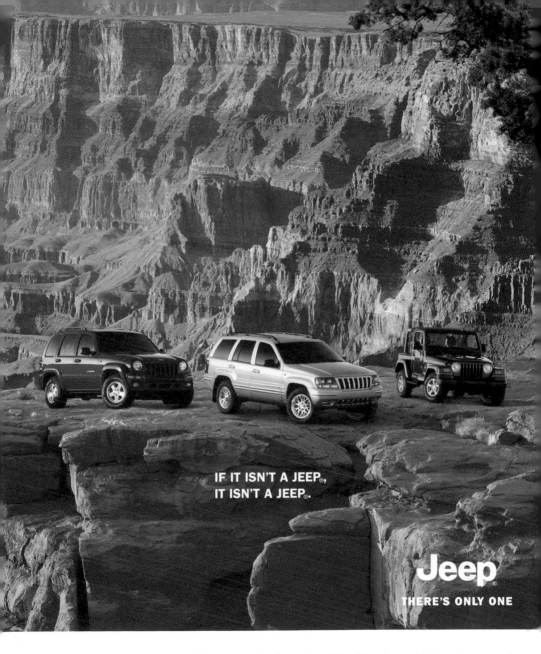

**IF IT ISN'T A JEEP®,
IT ISN'T A JEEP®.**

Jeep®

THERE'S ONLY ONE

- from the head-for-the-hills driving fun of Wrangler to the advanced capabillity of Cherokee and the luxurious power of Grand Cherokee. Nothing else is quite the same. Nothing else is a Jeep®.

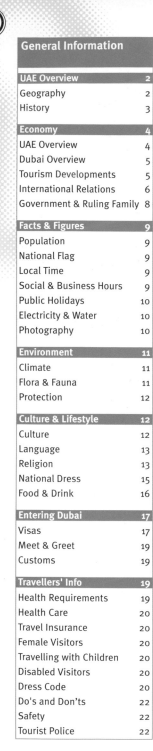

Introduction

Table of Contents

Home Theatre
(circa 1832)

_2003

X-treme your life.

X-TRAIL will take you wherever you want to go. From the rugged yet economical 2.5 litre DOHC engine, to the chilled drink holders, from the advanced ALL MODE 4x4 system, to the washable rear luggage board, the Nissan X-TRAIL is more than great set of wheels, it's a way of life.

www.nissan-me.com

SHIFT_the future

X-TRAIL

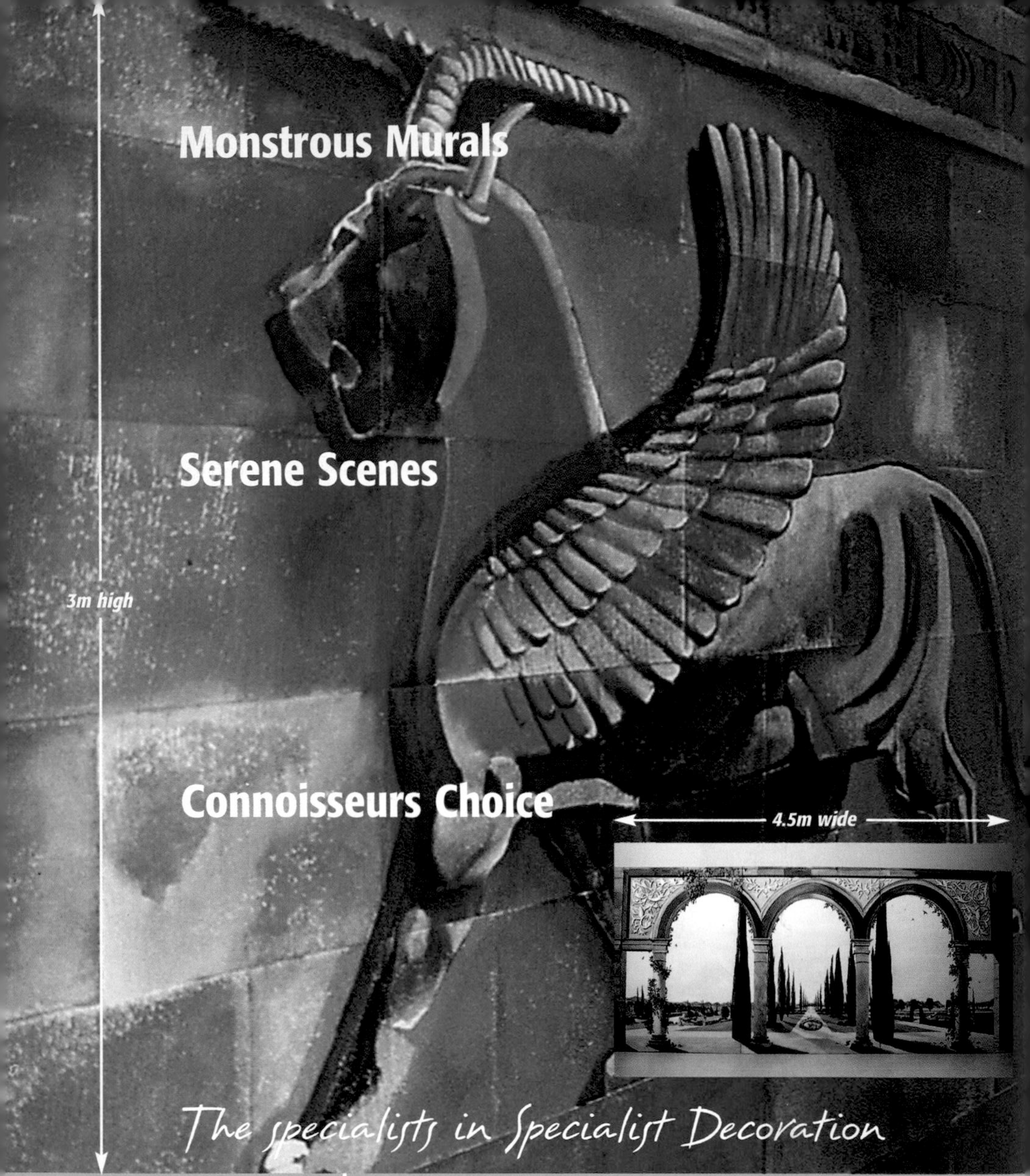

Monstrous Murals

Serene Scenes

3m high

Connoisseurs Choice

4.5m wide

The specialists in Specialist Decoration

Mackenzie Associates

TROMPE L'OEIL, MURALS AND CREATIVE COMMISSIONS

PO Box 34275, Dubai, United Arab Emirates
Tel: +(971 4) 396 2698 Fax +(971 4) 3422812 email: mackenziea1@yahoo.co

General
Information
EXPLORER

General Information

UAE OVERVIEW

Geography

Lying at the north-eastern part of the Arabian Peninsula, the United Arab Emirates (UAE) is bordered by the Kingdom of Saudi Arabia to the south and west, and the Sultanate of Oman to the east and north. The UAE shares 457 kilometres of border with Saudi Arabia and 410 kilometres with Oman. It has a coastline on both the Gulf of Oman and the Arabian Gulf, and is south of the strategically important Strait of Hormuz. The geographic co-ordinates for the UAE are 24 00 N, 54 00 E.

The country is made up of seven different emirates (Abu Dhabi, Ajman, Dubai, Fujairah, Ras Al Khaimah, Sharjah and Umm Al Quwain), which were formerly all independent sheikhdoms. The total area of the country is about 83,600 square kilometres, much of which lies in the Abu Dhabi emirate. With an area of 3,885 square kilometres, Dubai is the second largest emirate.

Golden beaches dot the country's 1,318 kilometres of coastline, of which 100 kilometres are on the Gulf of Oman. The Arabian Gulf coast is littered with coral reefs and over 200 islands, most of which are uninhabited. Sabkha (salt-flats), stretches of gravel plain, and desert characterise much of the inland region.

Dubai itself and the surrounding area consist of flat desert and sabkha. However, to the east, rise the Hajar Mountains (the word *'hajar'* is Arabic for rock). Lying close to the Gulf of Oman, they form a backbone through the country, from the Mussandam Peninsula in the north, through the eastern UAE and into Oman. The highest point is Jebel Yibir at 1,527 metres.

Emirs or Sheikhs?

While the term emirate comes from the ruling title of emir, the rulers of the UAE are called sheikhs.

Most of the western part of the country lies in the Abu Dhabi emirate and is made up of the infamous Rub Al Khali or Empty Quarter desert, which is common to the Kingdom of Saudi Arabia and the Sultanate of Oman. The area consists of arid, stark desert with spectacular sand dunes, broken by an occasional oasis. It is the largest *sand* desert in the world, covering nearly a quarter of the Arabian

Peninsula and has dunes rising in places to well over 300 metres!

Visitors to Dubai will find a land of startling contrasts, from endless stretches of desert to rugged mountains and modern towns. The city of Dubai is situated on the banks of a creek, a natural inlet from the Gulf that divides the city neatly into two. For more details on Dubai's geography, see Exploring [p.132].

Maps

The Dubai Tourist Map (Dubai Municipality) and the Dubai *A-Z Explorer* (Explorer Publishing) are available from all good bookstores around Dubai.

History

Dubai's growth over the last fifty years has been astonishing – it's difficult to imagine the transformation from an undeveloped, although flourishing town, to today's modern metropolis. Until 1830, it was an unremarkable backwater whose people existed from fishing, pearling and small-scale agriculture. At that time, it was taken over by a branch of the Bani Yas tribe from the Liwa oasis to the south, in what is the modern day Abu Dhabi emirate. The Maktoum family, whose descendants still rule the emirate today, led the takeover.

However, nothing much changed for Dubai until the late 1800s, when the then ruler, Sheikh Maktoum bin Hasher Al Maktoum, granted tax concessions to foreign traders, encouraging many of them to switch their base of operations to Dubai from Iran and Sharjah. By 1903, a British shipping line had been persuaded to use Dubai as its main port of call in the area, giving traders direct links with British India and other important trading ports in the region. Encouraged by the farsighted and liberal attitudes of the rulers, Indian and Persian traders settled in the growing town, which

Dubai Creek in the early days

Modern day Dubai Creek

soon developed a reputation as the leading commercial market in the region.

Dubai's importance was further helped by Sheikh Rashid bin Saeed Al Maktoum, father of the current ruler of Dubai, who recognised the importance of Dubai's Creek and improved facilities to attract more traders. The city came to specialise in the import and re-export of goods, mainly gold to India, and trade is the foundation of the wealth of the modern day emirate.

In the broader perspective, Dubai and the other emirates had accepted the protection of the British in 1892 in the culmination of a series of maritime truces. The British regarded the Gulf region as an important communication link with its empire in India, and wanted to ensure that other world powers, in particular France and Russia, didn't extend their influence in the region. In Europe, the area became known as the Trucial Coast (or Trucial States), a name it retained until the departure of the British in 1971.

In 1968, Britain announced its withdrawal from the region and began work to try to create a single state consisting of Bahrain, Qatar and the Trucial Coast. The ruling sheikhs, particularly of Abu Dhabi and Dubai, realised that by uniting forces they would have a stronger voice in the wider Middle East region. Negotiations collapsed when Bahrain and Qatar chose to become independent states. However, the Trucial Coast remained committed to forming an alliance and in 1971, the federation of the United Arab Emirates was created.

The new state was composed of the emirates of Dubai, Abu Dhabi, Ajman, Fujairah, Sharjah, Umm Al Quwain and, in 1972, Ras Al Khaimah (each emirate is named after its main town). Under the agreement, the individual emirates each retained a certain degree of autonomy, with Abu Dhabi and Dubai providing the most input into the federation.

The UAE flag

The leaders of the new federation elected the ruler of Abu Dhabi, His Highness Sheikh Zayed bin Sultan Al Nahyan, to be their president, a position he has held ever since.

However, the creation of what is basically an artificial state hasn't been without its problems, mainly caused by disputes over boundaries between the different emirates. At the end of Sheikh Zayed's first term as president in 1976, he threatened to resign if the other rulers didn't settle the demarcation of their borders. The threat proved an effective way of ensuring co-operation; however, the question of the degree of independence of the various emirates has never been fully determined. The position still isn't settled, but there seems to be more focus on the importance of the federation as a whole, led by Abu Dhabi, whose wealth and sheer size makes it the most powerful of the emirates.

The formation of the UAE came after the discovery of huge oil reserves in Abu Dhabi in 1958 (Abu Dhabi has an incredible 10% of the world's known oil reserves). This discovery dramatically transformed the emirate from one of the poorest states into the richest. In 1966, Dubai, which was already a relatively wealthy trading centre, also discovered oil. The oil revenue allowed the development of an economic and social infrastructure, which is the basis of today's modern society. Education, healthcare, roads, housing, and women's welfare were all priorities. Much of the credit for this development can be traced to the vision and dedication of the late Ruler, HH Sheikh Rashid bin Saeed Al Maktoum, who ensured that Dubai's oil revenues were deployed to maximum effect. His work has been continued by the present Ruler, HH Sheikh Maktoum bin Rashid Al Maktoum. While the modern story of the UAE is still a short one, history really is being made on a daily basis.

ECONOMY

UAE Overview

Today the UAE has an open economy with one of the world's highest per capita incomes (estimated at US $19,000 in 2002), although this is far from being spread evenly amongst the population. Its wealth, once chiefly based on the oil sector, now sees an oil contribution of only around 34% of the country's gross domestic product (GDP). The GDP for 2002 was approximately Dhs.255 billion. Abu Dhabi and Dubai contribute most to the country's GDP - the figures for 2002 put these at 55% and 26% respectively.

Over 90% of the UAE's oil reserves lie in Abu Dhabi, and there is enough at the current rate of production (just over 2.5 million barrels per day) to last a further 100 years. However, although there is a heavy dependence on the oil and gas industry, trade, manufacturing, tourism and construction also play an important part in the national economy. Investment in infrastructure and development projects exceeded an estimated Dhs.250 billion in 2001. The UAE's main export partners are Saudi Arabia, Iran, Japan, India, Singapore, South Korea, and Oman. Last year, the UAE's trade outflow was Dhs.39.4 billion. The main import partners are Japan, USA, UK, Italy, Germany and South Korea.

The situation in the Emirates is radically different from that of 30 - 40 years ago, when the area consisted of small, impoverished desert states. Visitors will find a unified and forward-looking state with a high standard of living and a relatively well-balanced and stable economy. Current reports note that the country's economy is roughly 36 times larger than it was in 1971, a mere 31 years ago! With an annual growth rate of 13.2%, the UAE has one of the fastest GDP growth rates in the world and the UAE's credit rating was ranked first in the Middle East for 2001; at the global level, the UAE sits in 26th place.

Dubai Overview

Other options ➜ Business [p.116]

While oil has been crucial to Dubai's development since the late 1960s, the non-oil sector currently contributes some 88% of the total gross domestic product and is continuing to expand in importance. Because of this, Dubai has been less affected by the recent ups and downs in crude oil prices than other countries in the region. Manufacturing and tourism are both growing at a steady rate, helping to create a well-balanced and diverse economy.

Trade remains the lifeblood of Dubai's business life, as it has for generations. This long trading tradition, which earned Dubai the reputation within the Middle East as 'the city of merchants', continues to be an important consideration for foreign companies looking at opportunities in the region today. It is reflected, not just in a regulatory environment that is open and liberal, but also in the local business community's familiarity with international commercial practices and the city's cosmopolitan lifestyle.

Really Tax Free?

Taxes? Do they exist in Dubai? Well, yes and no. You won't pay income or sales tax, unless you purchase alcohol from a licensed liquor store, and then you'll be hit with a steep 30% tax. The main taxes that you'll come across are a municipality tax, in the form of a 5% rent tax and 10% on food, beverages and rooms in hotels. The rest are hidden taxes in the form of 'fees', such as your car registration renewal and visa/permit fees.

The relative buoyancy of Dubai's economy is reflected most obviously in the many building programmes around the city. New shops, offices and apartment blocks seemingly appear overnight. Likewise, the growth in new hotels is considerable and the main chains are all well represented.

However, don't be blinded by the healthy economy to believe that the average expat coming to work in Dubai will necessarily be on a huge salary. The wealth isn't spread and except for highly skilled professionals, the salaries for most types of work are dropping. This downward trend is attributed in part to the willingness of workers to accept a job at a very low wage. While GDP per capita income was estimated at approximately Dhs.69,000 in 2001, this figure includes all sections of the community and the average labourer can expect to earn as little as Dhs.600 (US \$165) per month.

Unemployment levels in the national population are high, due partly to the desire of nationals to work in the public sector (where salaries and benefits are better), and to their qualifications not matching skills required in the private sector. However, the Government is trying to reverse unemployment with a 'nationalisation' or 'emiratisation' programme (this is common to countries throughout the region). The aim is to rely less on an expat workforce by putting the local population to work. This is being achieved by improving vocational training and by making it compulsory for certain categories of company, such as banks, to hire a determined percentage of Emiratis. Another step the Government has made to make employment in the private sector more attractive to nationals is to implement a pension scheme; private companies are now required to provide a pension for their national employees.

Tourism Developments

Other options ➜ Annual Events [p.53]

With tourism contributing 40% to Dubai's economy, the emirate is well ahead of other countries in the Middle East, which all seem to be playing a losing game of catch-up. Over 3.4 million tourists visited Dubai in 2001 and this figure is expected to grow to six million by 2010. Good infrastructure, a practically crime-free environment, government regulated public transport, etc, all add to the draw of sun, sand and shopping. Revenue generated from the tourism sector stood at approximately Dhs.3 billion last year. Almost all leading hotel chains are represented in Dubai. There are currently 280 hotels with over 23,000 hotel rooms, and more coming on the market on what seems to be a daily basis. The *Grand Hyatt*, opening in the 1st quarter of 2003, will add another 674 rooms and 18 food and beverage outlets to Dubai!

Investment in tourism is truly phenomenal. With the upcoming Dubai 2003 - World Bank and IMF summit of governors, focus is on the construction of a new Dhs.850 million, 11,500 square metre convention centre and hall, as well as a drive to complete current development projects. Attendance is expected to be around 20,000! Government officials are hoping that the new facilities currently under construction will boost meetings, incentive, conference and exhibition (MICE) tourism. Dubai already hosts over 50 international exhibitions each year. See [p.53] for a listing of this year's main events.

One of the most impressive ongoing projects is *Dubai Palm Island* - the world's two largest man-made islands, to be created in the shape of palm trees stretching out 5 km from the Jumeira coastline. When completed, the islands will be visible by the naked eye from the moon and will add 120 km to Dubai's coastline, effectively doubling it! Each 'island' will be 5 km in diameter, consist of 17 'fronds' and will be protected by a barrier reef. On the Jebel Ali Palm, the Middle East's first marine park will complement 2,200 villas, 1,500 apartments and 40 luxury hotels. The Jumeira Palm's villas and townhomes sold out within days of release to the market!

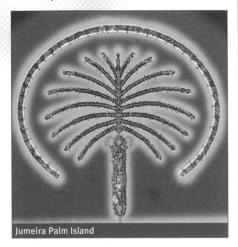

Jumeira Palm Island

Launched in 1996, the month-long *Dubai Shopping Festival* (www.mydsf.com) alone attracts over 2.5 million visitors each year, with shopping bargains to be found all over the city and attractions such as the *Global Village*, where people can visit pavilions from various countries, learn more about each culture and purchase traditional items, plus some real junk! The Dubai Shopping Festival's 2002 ad campaign stretched world-wide and apparently cost Dhs.7.65 million. *Dubai Summer Surprises*, held annually during July and August, brings in large numbers of mostly GCC visitors to enjoy ice-cold fun indoors, along with numerous other events that focus on children and the family.

Inaugurated in 2001, the *cruise ship terminal* at Port Rashid brings thousands of cruise passengers to the city during the mild winter season. *Dubai International Airport* handled almost 14 million passengers as well as 400 flights a day in 2001. Dubai Duty Free's sales target for 2002 is Dhs.1,000,000 - there is little doubt it will be

achieved! Construction of Terminal 3 and Concourses 2 and 3 has begun in order to accommodate a projected 30 million passengers by 2010.

The construction boom is ongoing, with *Dubai Festival City* completion planned for fall 2006. Festival City, to be comprised of six concentric bands of buildings following the curve of the Creek, will house apartments, offices, restaurants and hotels, and will be the new focal point for the Dubai Shopping Festival.

And then there is *Souk Al Nakheel* on Sheikh Zayed Road; by 2004, it will offer 60,000 square metres of retail space and 45,000 square metres of entertainment and leisure facilities, including a 320 metre ski slope!

Opening early 2004, *The Gardens Shopping Centre* will feature the world's largest maze, encompassing over 1,200 metres.

In addition to the construction boom, steps are continually being taken to ensure that Dubai's image remains spotless. It is now rare to find street vendors hawking Russian army binoculars or woodcarvings, and you'll no longer see newspaper vendors at the traffic lights. Car washing without permission and begging are also illegal. What you may find these days though are vendors with a very temporary 'stall' set up on the sidewalk selling pirated DVD's and VCD's from the far east. The Dubai Police are making a concerted effort to stop this trade, but the vendors seem to multiply faster than they can be thrown in jail or deported!

Dubai is not yet targeting or catering to the backpacker crowd, but instead has kept its sights on the more upscale travel market. This might change with time, but for the moment, we have not heard of any development plans that would entice backpackers to this region, although there is one youth hostel offering cheap accommodation.

International Relations

In its foreign relations, the UAE's stance is one of non-alignment, but it is committed to the support of Arab unity. The country became a member of the United Nations and the Arab League in 1971. It is a member of the International Monetary Fund (IMF), the Organisation of Petroleum Exporting Countries (OPEC), the World Trade Organisation (WTO) and other international and Arabic organisations, including the Arab Gulf Co-operation Council (AGCC), also known as the GCC), whose other members are Bahrain, Kuwait, Oman, Qatar and Saudi Arabia. The UAE, led by Sheikh Zayed bin Sultan Al Nahyan, had

a leading role in the formation of the AGCC in 1981 and the country is the third largest member in terms of geographical size, after Saudi Arabia and Oman. All major embassies and consulates are represented either in Dubai or in Abu Dhabi, or in both.

Government & Ruling Family

The Supreme Council of Rulers is the highest authority in the UAE, comprising the hereditary rulers of the seven emirates. Since the country is governed by hereditary rule, there is little distinction between the royal families and the Government. The Supreme Council is responsible for general policy matters involving education, defence, foreign affairs, communications and development, and for ratifying federal laws. The Council meets four times a year and the Abu Dhabi and Dubai rulers have effective power of veto over decisions.

The seven members of the Supreme Council elect the chief of state (the President) from among its members. The President of the UAE is HH Sheikh Zayed bin Sultan Al Nahyan who is also Ruler of Abu Dhabi. He has been President since independence on 2 December 1971, and ruler of Abu Dhabi since 6 August 1966. The Supreme Council also elects the Vice President, who is HH Sheikh Maktoum bin Rashid Al Maktoum, Ruler of Dubai. The President and Vice President are elected and appointed for five year terms. The President appoints the Prime Minister (currently HH Sheikh Maktoum bin Rashid Al Maktoum) and the Deputy Prime Minister.

The Federal Council of Ministers is responsible to the Supreme Council. It has executive authority to initiate and implement laws and is a consultative assembly of 40 representatives who are appointed for two years by the individual emirates. The council monitors and debates government policies, but has no power of veto.

HH Sheikh Zayed bin Sultan al Nahyan

The individual emirates still have a degree of autonomy, and laws that affect everyday life vary between the emirates. For instance, if you buy a car in one emirate and need to register it in a different emirate, you will first have to export and then re-import it! All emirates have a separate police force, with different uniforms and cars. Additionally it is possible to buy alcohol in Dubai, but not in Sharjah. However, while there are differences between the emirates, the current move is towards greater inter-dependence and the increasing power of the federation.

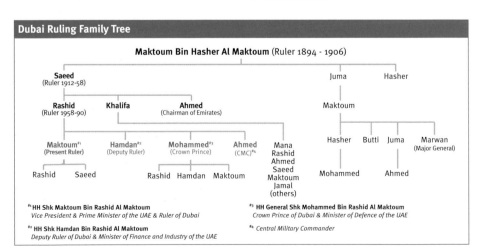

Dubai Ruling Family Tree

Maktoum Bin Hasher Al Maktoum (Ruler 1894 - 1906)

- **Saeed** (Ruler 1912-58)
  - **Rashid** (Ruler 1958-90)
    - **Maktoum**[1] (Present Ruler)
      - Rashid
      - Saeed
    - **Hamdan**[2] (Deputy Ruler)
    - **Mohammed**[3] (Crown Prince)
      - Rashid
      - Hamdan
      - Maktoum
    - Ahmed (CMC)[4]
    - Mana
      Rashid
      Ahmed
      Saeed
      Maktoum
      Jamal
      (others)
  - Khalifa
  - **Ahmed** (Chairman of Emirates)
- Juma
  - Maktoum
    - Hasher
      - Mohammed
    - Butti
    - Juma
      - Ahmed
    - Marwan (Major General)
- Hasher

[1] **HH Shk Maktoum Bin Rashid Al Maktoum**
Vice President & Prime Minister of the UAE & Ruler of Dubai

[2] **HH Shk Hamdan Bin Rashid Al Maktoum**
Deputy Ruler of Dubai & Minister of Finance and Industry of the UAE

[3] **HH General Shk Mohammed Bin Rashid Al Maktoum**
Crown Prince of Dubai & Minister of Defence of the UAE

[4] Central Military Commander

Population

A national census is taken every ten years and the following figures are based on the last one taken in 1995, as well as Ministry of Planning figures for 2001. According to the Ministry, the population of the UAE stood at 2,377,453 in 1995. The end of year count for 2001 put the total number of UAE nationals and expat residents at 3,488,000.

Dubai's population stood at 276,301 in 1980 and 674,101 in 1995, while the end of year figures for 2001 put the population at just over 1,000,000. The growth rate is estimated at around 6% a year, and there are 2.4 men to every woman in Dubai. A recent Dubai Municipality statistical survey revealed that the average size of a UAE national household is 7.6 members, while that of the expat is 3.7.

According to the United Nations Development Program (UNDP), the UAE has the highest life expectancy in the Arab world at 72.2 years for males and 75.6 years for females.

National Flag

In a nation continually striving for world records, when 30 year anniversary celebrations were marked on National Day 2001, the world's tallest flagpole was erected in Abu Dhabi and the world's largest UAE flag was raised at Union House in Jumeira, Dubai. The flag consists of three equal horizontal bands: green at the top, white in the middle, and black at the bottom. A thicker vertical band of red runs down the hoist side.

Local Time

The UAE is four hours ahead of UCT (Universal Co-ordinated Time - formerly known as GMT). There is no summer time saving when clocks are altered. Hence, when it is 12:00 midday in Dubai, it is 03:00 in New York, 08:00 in London, 13:30 in Delhi, and 17:00 in Tokyo (not allowing for any summer time saving in those countries).

Population by Emirate

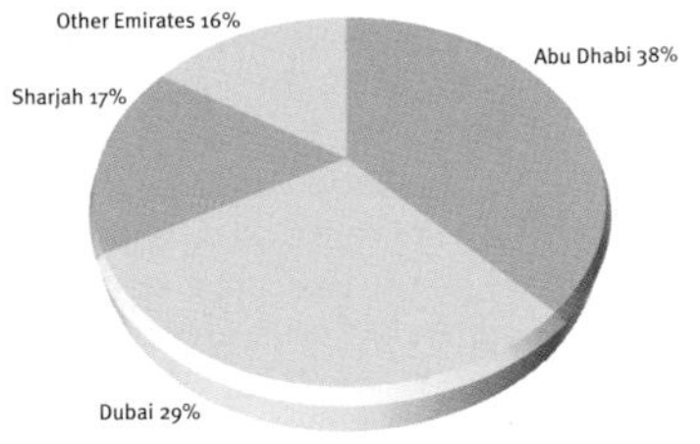

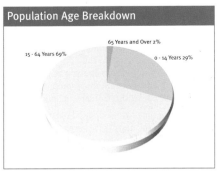

Other Emirates 16%
Sharjah 17%
Abu Dhabi 38%
Dubai 29%

Population Age Breakdown

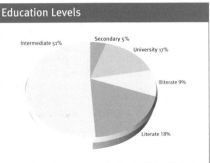

65 Years and Over 2%
15 - 64 Years 69%
0 - 14 Years 29%

Education Levels

Intermediate 51%
Secondary 5%
University 17%
Illiterate 9%
Literate 18%

Source: Ministry of Planning

Social & Business Hours

Other options ➜ Business [p.116]

Social hours are very Mediterranean in style - in general, people get up early, often have an afternoon siesta and eat late in the evening. The attitude to time, especially in business, is often very different from the 'time is money' approach in other parts of the world. So, don't get frustrated if your business meeting happens a day late - the 'Inshallah' (God willing) attitude prevails!

General Info

Facts & Figures

Traditionally there is no concept of the weekend, although Friday has always been the holy day. In the modern UAE, the weekend has established itself on different days, generally according to your company. Until recently, Government offices had Thursday afternoon and Friday off, however, a 1998 ruling established a five day week for Government offices and schools, which are now closed all day Thursday and Friday. Some private companies still take a half-day Thursday and Friday, while others take Friday and Saturday as their weekend. Understandably, these differences cause difficulties, since companies may now be out of touch with international business for up to four days, plus families do not necessarily share weekends.

Government offices are open from 07:30 – 13:30, Saturday to Wednesday. In the private sector, office hours vary between split shift days, which are generally 08:00 – 13:00, re-opening at either 15:00 or 16:00 and closing at 18:00 or 19:00; or straight shifts, usually 09:00 – 18:00, with an hour for lunch.

Shop opening times are usually based on split shift hours, although outlets in many of the big shopping malls now remain open all day. Closing times are usually 22:00 or 24:00, while some food shops and petrol stations are open 24 hours a day. On Fridays, many places are open all day, apart from prayer time (11:30 – 13:30), while larger shops in the shopping malls only open in the afternoon from either 12:00 or 14:00.

Embassies and consulates open from 08:45 - 13:30. They are closed on Fridays and in most cases on Saturdays, but generally leave an emergency contact number on their answering machines.

During Ramadan, work hours in most public and some private organisations are reduced by two to three hours per day, and business definitely slows during this period. Many offices start work an hour or so later and shops are open much later at night. The more popular shopping malls are crowded at midnight and parking at that time is tough to find!

Public Holidays

Other options → Annual Events [p.53]

The Islamic calendar starts from the year 622 AD, the year of Prophet Mohammed's (Peace Be Upon Him) migration (Hijra) from Mecca to Al Madinah. Hence the Islamic year is called the Hijri year and dates are followed by AH – After Hijra.

The Hijri calendar is based on lunar months; there are 354 or 355 days in the Hijri year, which is divided into 12 lunar months, and is thus 11 days shorter than the Gregorian year.

Public Holidays - 2003	
New Year's Day (1)	Jan 1[Fixed]
Eid Al Adha (4)	Feb 12[Moon]
Islamic New Year's Day (1)	Mar 5[Moon]
Prophet Mohammed's Birthday (1)	May 13[Moon]
Accession of H.H Sheikh Zayed (1)	Aug 6th[Fixed]
Lailat Al Mi'Raj (1)	Sept 23[Moon]
Ramadan begins	Oct 27[Moon]
Eid Al Fitr (3)	Nov 25[Moon]
UAE National Day (2)	Dec 2[Fixed]

As some holidays are based on the sighting of the moon and not fixed dates on the Hijri calendar, the dates of Islamic holidays are notoriously imprecise, with holidays frequently being confirmed less than 24 hours in advance. Some non-religious holidays are fixed according to the Gregorian calendar.

The different emirates also have some different fixed holidays, such as the accession of HH Sheikh Zayed, which is only celebrated in Abu Dhabi. The number of days a holiday lasts is in brackets in the table shown above. However, this applies to the public sector only, since not all the listed holidays are observed by the private sector and often the public sector gets a day or two more.

Electricity & Water

Other options → Utilities & Services [p.88]

Electricity and water services in Dubai are excellent and power cuts or water shortages are almost unheard of. Both of these utilities are provided by Dubai Electricity & Water Authority (known as DEWA).

The electricity supply is 220/240 volts and 50 cycles. The socket type is the same as the three point British system. Most hotels and homes have adapters for electrical appliances.

The tap water is heavily purified and safe to drink, but most people prefer to drink the locally bottled mineral waters, of which there are several different brands available. Bottled water is usually served in hotels and restaurants.

Photography

Normal tourist photography is acceptable, but like anywhere in the world, it is courteous to ask permission before photographing people, particularly women. In general, photographs of government buildings, military installations, ports and airports should not be taken.

There is a wide choice of films available and processing is usually cheap and fast, although the quality of reproduction can vary. Ultra-violet filters for your camera are advisable. APS, 35mm negative and slide film can all be processed, although the cost of processing and developing APS is still high, and very few places around town deal with slide film. UCF (336 9399) and Prolab (347 7616) are your best bets for processing slide film, as well as medium or large format film.

ENVIRONMENT

Climate

Dubai has a sub-tropical and arid climate, and sunny blue skies and high temperatures can be expected most of the year. Rainfall is infrequent and irregular, falling mainly in winter: November to March (13 cm per year). Temperatures range from a low of around 10° C (50° F) in winter, to a high of 48° C (118° F) in summer. The mean daily maximum is 24° C (75° F) in January, rising to 41° C (106° F) in August.

During the winter there are occasional sandstorms (the wind is known as the *'shamal'*), when the sand is whipped up off the desert. More surprisingly, winter mornings can be foggy, although the sun invariably burns the cloud away by mid-morning. The most pleasant time to visit is in the cooler winter months, since summer humidity can be a killer - approaching 100% - prepare to sweat!

Flora & Fauna

Other options ➜ Arabian Wildlife [p.148]

As you would expect in a country with such an arid climate, the variety of flora and fauna in the Emirates isn't as extensive as in other parts of the world. However, a variety of creatures and plant life have managed to adapt themselves to life with high temperatures and little rainfall.

In the city of Dubai, as in all cities in the Emirates to a greater or lesser extent, the Municipality has an extensive 'greening' programme underway. Areas along the roads are incredibly colourful for a desert environment, with grass, palm trees and

flowers being constantly maintained by an ar[...] workers and round the clock watering. The c[...] also boasts a large number of attractive and well-[...] kept parks - refer to Parks [p.149].

The region has about 3,500 endemic plants – amazing considering the high salinity of the soil and the harsh environment. The date palm is the most obvious of the indigenous flora, and this provides wonderful seas of green, especially in the oases. Heading towards the mountains, flat topped Acacia trees and wild grasses give a feel of an African 'savannah'. The deserts, in places, are often surprisingly green, even during the dry summer months, but it takes an experienced botanist to get the most out of the area.

Indigenous fauna includes the Arabian Leopard and the Ibex, but sightings of them are extremely rare. Realistically, the only large animals you will see are camels and goats (often roaming dangerously close to roads). Other desert life includes the Sand Cat, Sand Fox and Desert Hare, plus gerbils, hedgehogs, snakes and geckos.

Birdlife in the city is limited - this isn't a place for hearing a dawn chorus, unless you're lucky with where you live. However, recent studies have

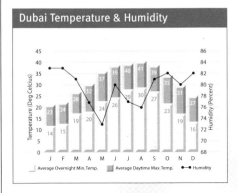
Dubai Temperature & Humidity

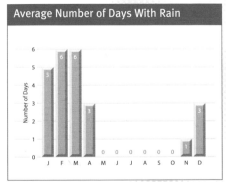
Average Number of Days With Rain

umber of species of birds is rising part to the increasing lushness of ...ost apparent in the parks, and in ..., the country benefits from lying ...irds migrating between Central ...1. You can even see flamingos at ... Sanctuary at the southern end ...

Off the coast, the seas contain a rich abundance of marine life, including tropical fish, jellyfish, coral, the dugong ('sea cow') and sharks. Eight species of whales and seven species of dolphins have been recorded in UAE waters. Various breeds of turtle are also indigenous to the region, these include the loggerhead, green and hawksbill turtles, all of which are under threat from man. These may be seen by divers off both coasts, or if you are lucky, near the East Coast at Kalba. See Khor Kalba [p.172] The best-known local fish is hammour, which is a type of grouper and can be found on most restaurant menus.

Protection

The UAE's, and specifically Sheikh Zayed's, commitment to the environment is internationally recognised. At the Environment 2001 Conference and Exhibition in Abu Dhabi, a statement was made that the UAE would invest US $46 billion on projects related to the environment over the next ten years. Sheikh Zayed set up the Zayed International Prize for the Environment, and has himself been awarded the World Wildlife Fund's Gold Panda Award.

Various organisations have been formed to protect the environment, as well as to educate the population on the importance of environmental issues. The Environmental Research and Wildlife Development Agency (ERWDA) was established in 1996 to assist the Abu Dhabi Government in the conservation and management of the emirate's natural environment, resources, wildlife and biological diversity (02 681 7171). There is also an active branch of the World Wide Fund for Nature in Abu Dhabi (02 693 4510). Sir Bani Yas Island in Abu Dhabi has an internationally acclaimed breeding programme for endangered wildlife. The Arabian Wildlife Centre in Sharjah also has a successful breeding programme for endangered wildlife, particularly the Arabian Leopard.

The UAE is party to international agreements on biodiversity, climate change, desertification, endangered species, hazardous wastes, marine dumping and ozone layer protection. In addition to

emirate-wide environmental controls, Dubai has strictly enforced laws governing the use of chemical insecticides. In 2001, the Dubai government banned any further development along the coast without prior government permission.

Despite all the efforts being made, there are still some serious environmental issues facing the UAE. With no rainfall to speak of for the past few years, the water table is at record low levels and

The Hajar Mountains

desalination plants work overtime to satisfy a thirsty population and keep the numerous parks and verges green. Desertification and beach pollution from oil spills are other areas of worry; one large spill off the coast in 2001 had hundreds of municipality employees and volunteers cleaning up Gulf beaches for weeks afterwards.

See also: *Environmental Groups [p.288]*

CULTURE & LIFESTYLE

Culture

Other options ➔ Business [p.116]

Dubai's culture is firmly rooted in the Islamic traditions of Arabia. Islam is more than just a religion; it is a way of life that governs even the minutiae of everyday events, from what to wear to what to eat and drink. Thus, the culture and heritage of the UAE is tied to its religion. In parts of the world, Islamic fundamentalism has given the 'outside' world a very extreme, blanket view of the religion. However, in contrast to this image, the UAE is very tolerant and welcoming; foreigners are free to practice their own religion, alcohol is served in hotels and the dress code is liberal. Women face little discrimination and, contrary to the policies of Saudi Arabia and Iran, are able to drive and walk around unescorted. Among the most highly prized virtues are courtesy and hospitality, and visitors are sure to be charmed by the genuine warmth and friendliness of the people.

Connected!

'*Wasta*' means connections. If you've got them, all power to you - they'll take you far! However, most people in Dubai don't have wasta - it's reserved for the select few who have somehow managed to establish the 'right' contacts, either through family or friends. It's pretty much the same as in any other country (very much like an old boys' network); however, here it's more pronounced, as rules and regulations aren't always set in stone.

The rapid economic development over the last 30 years has changed life in the Emirates beyond recognition in many ways. However, the country's rulers are very aware of the danger that their traditional heritage will be eroded by the speed of development and increased access to outside cultures and material goods. Hence, they are keen to promote cultural and sporting events that are representative of their past, such as falconry, camel racing and traditional dhow sailing. (Although ironically a large proportion of local entertainment focuses less on traditional pastimes and more on shopping and shopping festivals!) However, traditional aspects of life are still apparent, most obviously in the clothes (see National Dress [p.15]). Arabic culture in poetry, dancing, songs and traditional art is encouraged, and weddings and celebrations are still colourful occasions of feasting and music.

In an attempt to give visitors a clearer appreciation of the Emirati way of life, the Sheikh Mohammed Centre for Cultural Understanding has been established to help bridge the gap between cultures.

See also: *Sheikh Mohammed Centre for Cultural Understanding [p.161].*

Language

The official language of the country is Arabic, although English, Urdu and Hindi are spoken and, with some perseverance, understood! Arabic is the official business language, but English is widely used and most road and shop signs, restaurant menus, etc, are in both languages. The further out of town you get, the more Arabic you will find, both spoken and on street and shop signs. See [p.14] for a quick list of useful Arabic phrases to get you around town.

Arabic isn't the easiest language to pick up... or to pronounce! But if you can throw in a couple of words of Arabic here and there, you're more likely to receive a warmer welcome or at least a smile. Most people will help you out with your pronunciation - people are happy you're putting in the effort, so just give it a shot! Certainly won't hurt to try, and definitely helps when dealing with officials of any sort!

Religion

Other options ➜ Annual Events [p.53]

Islam is the official religion of the UAE, but other religions are respected. Dubai has a variety of Christian churches: the Evangelical Community Church, Holy Trinity, International Christian Church, St Mary's (Roman Catholic) and St. Thomas Orthodox Church. There is also a Hindu temple in Bur Dubai.

Ramadan

In Islam, Ramadan is the holy month in which Muslims commemorate the revelation of the Holy Koran (the holy book of Islam, also spelt Quran). It is a time of fasting when Muslims abstain from all food, drinks, cigarettes and unclean thoughts between dawn and dusk. In the evening, the fast is broken with the Iftar feast. Iftar timings are found in all the daily newspapers.

The Jumeira Mosque

Basic Arabic

General

Yes	na'am
No	la
Please	min fadlak (m) / min fadliki (f)
Thank you	shukran
Please (in offering)	tafaddal (m) / tafaddali (f)
Praise be to God	al-hamdu l-illah
God willing	in shaa'a l-laah

Greetings

Greeting (peace be upon you)	as-salaamu alaykom
Greeting (in reply)	wa alaykom is salaam
Good morning	sabah il-khayr
Good morning (in reply)	sabah in-nuwr
Good evening	masa il-khayr
Good evening (in reply)	masa in-nuwr
Hello	marhaba
Hello (in reply)	marhabtayn
How are you?	kayf haalak (m) / kayf haalik (f)
Fine, thank you	zayn, shukran (m) / zayna, shukran (f)
Welcome	ahlan wa sahlan
Welcome (in reply)	ahlan fiyk (m) / ahlan fiyki (f)
Goodbye	ma is-salaama

Introduction

My name is	ismiy ...
What is your name?	shuw ismak (m) / shuw ismik (f)
Where are you from?	min wayn inta (m) / min wayn inti (f)
I am from ...	anaa min
America	ameriki
Britain	braitani
Europe	oropi
India	al hindi

Questions

How many / much?	kam?
Where?	wayn?
When?	mata?
Which?	ayy?
How?	kayf?
What?	shuw?
Why?	laysh?
Who?	miyn?
To/ for	ila
In/ at	fee
From	min
And	wa
Also	kamaan
There isn't	maa fee

Taxi / Car Related

Is this the road to ...	hadaa al tariyq ila
Stop	kuf
Right	yamiyn
Left	yassar
Straight ahead	siydaa
North	shamaal
South	januwb
East	sharq
West	garb
Turning	mafraq
First	awwal
Second	thaaniy
Road	tariyq
Street	shaaria
Roundabout	duwwaar
Signals	ishaara
Close to	qarib min
Petrol station	mahattat betrol
Sea/ beach	il bahar
Mountain/s	jabal / jibaal
Desert	al sahraa
Airport	mataar
Hotel	funduq
Restaurant	mata'am
Slow Down	schway schway

Accidents

Police	al shurtaa
Permit/ licence	rukhsaa
Accident	Haadith
Papers	waraq
Insurance	ta'miyn
Sorry	aasif (m) / aasifa (f)

Numbers

Zero	sifr
One	waahad
Two	ithnayn
Three	thalatha
Four	araba'a
Five	khamsa
Six	sitta
Seven	saba'a
Eight	thamaanya
Nine	tiss'a
Ten	ashara
Hundred	miya
Thousand	alf

Islam

The basis of Islam is the belief that there is only one God and that Prophet Mohammed (Peace Be Upon Him) is his messenger. There are five pillars of the faith, which all Muslims must follow: the Profession of Faith, Prayer, Charity, Fasting and Pilgrimage. Every Muslim is expected, at least once in his/her lifetime, to make the pilgrimage or 'Hajj' to the holy city of Mecca (also spelt Makkah) in Saudi Arabia.

Additionally, a Muslim is required to pray to Mecca five times a day. The times vary according to the position of the sun. Most people pray at a mosque, although it's not unusual to see them kneeling by the side of the road if one is not close by. It is not considered polite to stare at people praying or to walk over prayer mats.

The modern day call to prayer, through loudspeakers on the minarets of each mosque, ensures that everyone knows it's time to pray! In Dubai, the plan is to build enough mosques so that residents do not have to walk more than 500 metres to pray. Friday is the holy day.

Daily prayer at a Bur Dubai mosque

All over the city, festive Ramadan tents are filled to the brim each evening with people of all nationalities and religions enjoying shisha and traditional Arabic mezze and sweets. In addition to the standard favourite shisha cafés and restaurants around town, the five-star hotels erect special Ramadan tents for the month.

The timing of Ramadan is not fixed in terms of the western calendar, but each year it occurs approximately 11 days earlier than the previous year, with the start date depending on the sighting of the moon (see Public Holidays [p.10]). In 2002, Ramadan will begin around November 5th. In 2003, Ramadan should commence around October 27th. Non-Muslims are also required to refrain from eating, drinking or smoking in public places during daylight hours as a sign of respect. The sale of alcohol is restricted to after dusk, and office hours are cut, while shops and parks usually open and close later. In addition, entertainment such as live music is stopped and cinemas limit daytime screenings of films.

Ramadan ends with a three day celebration and holiday called Eid Al Fitr, or 'Feast of the Breaking of the Fast'. Seventy days later is another Eid holiday and celebration called Eid Al Adha, or 'Feast of the Sacrifice' and this marks the end of the pilgrimage season to Mecca. For Muslims, Eid has similar connotations as Diwali for Hindus and Christmas for Christians.

National Dress

On the whole, the national population still chooses to wear their traditional dress. For men this is the 'dishdash(a)' or 'khandura' - a white full length shirt-dress, which is worn with a white or red checked headdress, known as a 'gutra'. This is secured with a black cord, 'agal'. Sheikhs and important businessmen may also wear a thin black or gold robe or 'mishlah', over their dishdasha at important events, equivalent to the dinner jacket in Western culture.

Arabic Family Names

Arabic names have a formal structure that traditionally indicated the family and tribe of the person. Names usually start with that of an important person from the Koran or someone from the tribe. This is followed by the word 'bin' (son of) for a boy or 'bint' (daughter of) for a girl, and then the name of the child's father. The last name indicates the person's tribe or family. For prominent families, this has 'Al', the Arabic word for 'the', immediately before it. For instance, the President of the UAE is HH Sheikh Zayed bin Sultan Al Nahyan. When women get married, they do not change their name. Family names are very important here, and extremely helpful when it comes to differentiating between the thousands of Mohammeds, Ibrahims and Fatimas!

In public, women wear the black 'abaya' - a long, loose black robe that covers their normal clothes, plus a headscarf, called the 'sheyla'. The abaya is

National Weddings

Weddings in the UAE are a serious and very large affair. Homes are lit from top to bottom with strings of white lights and the festivities last up to two weeks. Men and women celebrate separately, normally in a hotel ballroom or convention centre, depending on the number of guests. High dowries and extravagant weddings may be a thing of the past though, as the Government has placed a ceiling of Dhs.50,000 on dowries, and lavish weddings can result in a prison sentence or Dhs.500,000 fine!

The Government-sponsored Marriage Fund, based in Abu Dhabi, assists nationals in everything to do with marriage - from counselling and financial assistance (long-term loans up to Dhs.70,000 to UAE national men marrying UAE national women), to organising group weddings to keep costs down. While marriage between a national man and a non-national woman is legally permissible (but frowned on), national women are not allowed to marry non-national men. One of the marriage fund's main aims is to promote a reduction in the rate of foreign marriages by UAE nationals.

often of very sheer, flowing fabric and may be open at the front. Some women also wear a thin black veil hiding their face and/or gloves, while older women sometimes still wear a leather mask, known as a 'burkha', which covers the nose, brow and cheekbones. Underneath the abaya, women traditionally wear a long tunic over loose, flowing trousers ('sirwall'), which are often heavily embroidered and fitted at the wrists and ankles.

However, these are used more by the older generation and modern women will often wear trousers or a long skirt beneath the abaya.

Sharjah has recently implemented a Decency Law that penalises those who do not abide by a certain dress code and moral behaviour. "Indecent dress" includes anything that exposes the stomach, back or legs above the knees. Tight-fitting, transparent clothing is also not permitted, nor are acts of vulgarity, indecent noises or harassment. If you are deemed to have offended the law, you will initially be given advice by the police on what decency is, and warned to abide by the law in future. If the police find you breaking the law again, a more severe penalty will be imposed.

Food & Drink

Other options → Eating Out [p.302]

Dubai offers pretty much every type of international cuisine imaginable. While most restaurants are located in hotels and are thus able to offer alcohol, some of the best places to eat are the small street-side stands around town. Refer to the **Going Out** section for more details on everything available to quench both hunger and thirst.

Arabic Cuisine

Modern Arabic cuisine is a blend of many types of cooking, from Moroccan, Tunisian or Iranian to

Shisha Pipes

Egyptian or Afghani, but in Dubai, modern Arabic cuisine invariably means Lebanese food. Sidewalk stands selling *'shawarma'* (lamb or chicken sliced from a spit and served in pita bread) and *'falafel'* (small savoury balls of deep-fried beans), are worth a visit at least once. Fresh juices, especially the mixed fruit cocktail, are another highlight not to be missed.

Pork

Pork is not included on the Arabic menu. Do not underestimate how taboo this meat is to a Muslim. It is not just in eating the meat, but also in the preparation and service of it. Thus to serve pork, restaurants need a separate fridge, equipment, preparation and cooking areas, etc, while supermarkets need a separate pork area in the shop and separate storage facilities. Images of pigs can also cause offence.

Additionally, in Islam it is forbidden to consume the blood or meat of any animal that has not been slaughtered in the correct manner. The meat of animals killed in accordance with the Islamic code is known *'halaal'*.

Alcohol

Alcohol is only served in licensed outlets that are associated with hotels (ie, restaurants and bars), plus a few clubs (ie, golf) and associations. Restaurants outside of hotels that are not part of a club or association are not permitted to serve alcohol.

Permanent residents who are non-Muslims may obtain alcohol for consumption at home without difficulty under a permit system.

See also: *Liquor Licence [p.66]; Alcohol Outlets [p.182]*

Shisha

Throughout the Middle East, smoking the traditional 'shisha' (water pipe) is a popular and relaxing pastime, usually savoured in a local café while chatting with friends. They are also known as hookah pipes or hubbly-bubbly, but are properly called a *'nargile'*. Shisha pipes can be smoked with a variety of aromatic flavours, such as strawberry, grape or apple, and the experience is unlike normal cigarette or cigar smoking. The smoke is 'smoothed' by the water, creating a much more soothing effect. They are one of those things in life that should at least be tried once, and more so during Ramadan, when festive tents are erected throughout the city and filled with people of all nationalities and the fragrant smell of shisha tobacco.

See also: *Shisha Cafes [p.388].*

ENTERING DUBAI

Visas

Other options ➜ Residence Visa [p.58]
Entry Visa [p.58]

Visa requirements for entering Dubai vary greatly between different nationalities, and regulations should always be checked before travelling, since details can change with little or no warning.

All visitors except Arab Gulf Co-operation Council nationals (Bahrain, Kuwait, Qatar, Oman and Saudi Arabia) require a visa, however, citizens of the countries listed below will be granted a *free visit visa* on arrival.

Expat residents of the AGCC who meet certain criteria may obtain a non-renewable 30 day *visa on arrival*. Oman visitors of certain nationalities may enter Dubai on a *free-of-charge entry permit*. The same criteria and facilities apply to Dubai visitors entering Oman.

"No Visa Required"

Citizens of Andorra, Australia, Austria, Belgium, Brunei, Canada, Denmark, Finland, France, Germany, Greece, Hong Kong (with the right of abode in the United Kingdom), Iceland, Ireland, Italy, Japan, Liechtenstein, Luxembourg, Malaysia, Monaco, The Netherlands, New Zealand, Norway, Portugal, San Marino, Singapore, South Korea, Spain, Sweden, Switzerland, United Kingdom (with the right of abode in the UK), United States of America and Vatican City now receive an automatic, free visit visa on arrival in Dubai.

Tourist nationalities (such as Eastern European, Chinese, South African and members of the former Soviet Union) may obtain a 30 day, non-renewable *tourist visa* sponsored by a local entity, such as a hotel or tour operator, before entry into the UAE. Other visitors may apply for an *entry service permit* (for 14 days exclusive of arrival/ departure days), valid for use within 14 days of the date of issue, or for a 60 day *visit visa* (renewable once for a total stay of 90 days) sponsored by a local company. This visit visa costs Dhs.120, plus DNATA (Dubai National Airline Travel Agency) visa delivery fee. Urgent visit visas, delivered in less than four days, can be obtained for Dhs.220, plus DNATA visa delivery fee.

For those travelling onwards to a destination other than that of original departure, a special *transit visa* (up to 96 hours) may be obtained free of charge through any airline carrier operating in the UAE.

A *multiple entry visa* is available for business visitors who have a relationship with a local business. It is valid for visits of a maximum 30 days each time, for six months from date of issue. It costs Dhs.1,000 and should be applied for after entering the UAE on a visit visa.

The Airport

If you're lucky enough to have friends or family collect you from the airport, you'll avoid the hassles of fighting for a taxi with all the other passengers who have just arrived in Dubai. If not, find the curb and, along with everyone else, shove your way into the first available cab. You'll face a stiff Dhs.20 pick up charge, but there's nothing you can do about it (unless you don't mind hiking out of the airport with all your bags to hail a non-airport licensed taxi).

If you're concerned about finding your friends or relatives when you arrive, have no fear. They have a bird's-eye view of you as you stand in line waiting to go through Immigration (look up!), and there's only one narrow exit from the airport once you clear customs.

You'll have a bit of a trek before then, however, as the new terminal is huge. Apparently, it takes six escalators, two moving sidewalks and 3,446 steps to get from the aircraft door to a taxi at the main entrance ... and no baggage trolleys are provided!

Need cash? There are ATM machines dotted around the airport in both arrivals and departures. Currency exchanges are all over the departures area and outside the customs area in arrivals.

Airlines may require confirmation (a photocopy is acceptable) that a UAE visa is held before check-in at the airport. If you have sponsorship from a UAE entity, ensure that they fax you a copy of the visa before the flight. The original is held at Dubai International Airport for collection before passport control. Your passport should have a minimum of three months validity left. Israeli nationals will not be issued visas.

Costs: companies may levy a maximum of Dhs.50 extra in processing charges for arranging visas. The DNATA visa delivery service costs an extra Dhs.10.

Note: Visit visas are valid for 30 or 60 days, not one or two calendar months. If you overstay, there is a Dhs.100 fine for each day overstayed.

Visa Renewals

Visit visas may be renewed for a total stay of up to 90 days. Renewals are usually made by paying for a month's extension (Dhs.500) at the Department of Immigration and Naturalisation (398 1010), Karama, near Dubai World Trade Centre roundabout (Map ref 10-A2).

After the third month, you must either leave the country and arrange for a new visit visa from overseas or, for certain nationalities, fly out of the country on a 'visa run' (see below).

'Visa Run'

The 'visa run' (or 'visa change' flight) basically involves exiting and re-entering the country to gain an exit stamp and new entry stamp in your passport. Unfortunately driving over the border into Oman is not an option, since you will not receive a UAE exit stamp in your passport. Hence the visa run is a flight to a neighbouring country and back to Dubai.

The flight is invariably to Doha, Muscat or Kish Island and it returns an hour or so later. Passengers remain in transit and hence do not need a visa for the country they fly to. There are several flights daily and the cost is about Dhs.400 for a return flight, depending on the season. The low price is only offered for the visa flight and is not available if you want to spend any time in the country to which you are. Flights are offered by Emirates (214 4444), Gulf Air (271 3222) and Qatar Airways (229 2229). See also Travel Agents [p.155].

These flights are the cheapest option for those whose residency application has been approved by the Immigration department and who need to change their visa status for their application to proceed.

The visa run is also an opportunity to stock up on good value duty free, and there are sales outlets in both the departure and arrival halls of Dubai Airport.

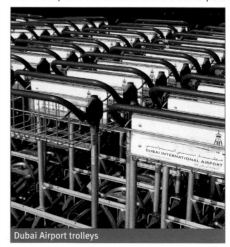
Dubai Airport trolleys

Holders of passports that are allowed a visit visa on arrival at the airport currently have the option of making a visa run indefinitely.

Until 2000, the visa run was an option for all nationalities who had a Dubai sponsor willing to arrange for a new visit visa. Now, unless the situation reverts, a visa run is only possible for nationalities who can gain a visa stamp on arrival at Dubai International Airport. This was implemented in a crackdown on people working in the country illegally without sponsorship or residency.

E-Gate Service

In 2002, a new rapid passenger clearing service was unveiled by the Dubai Naturalisation and Residency Department and the Department of Civil Aviation. The 'E-Gate Service' allows UAE and GCC nationals and residents, and nationals of the 33 countries permitted entry to the UAE without a visa (see [p.17]) to pass through both the departures and arrivals halls of Dubai International Airport without a passport. Swipe your smart card through an electronic gate and through you go, saving a great deal of time otherwise spent in long queues! Applications are processed within minutes in the registration office at the Dubai Airport; you'll need your passport, then you'll be fingerprinted and photographed. The smart card costs Dhs.150 and is valid for two years.

Meet & Greet

Two reception services are offered at the airport to assist people with airport formalities - ideal for children, the disabled and the elderly. The Marhaba Service (224 5780) is run by DNATA and operates mainly at Terminal 1 (plus a few airlines at Terminal 2), while Ahlan Dubai (602 5515) is run by the Civil Aviation Authority and is at Terminal 2. (Both 'marhaba' and 'ahlan' are Arabic for 'welcome'.)

Marhaba provides staff to greet new arrivals and guide them through Immigration and baggage collection, and also gives general information and help with visas. To use Marhaba, a booking has to be made at least 24 hours in advance and passengers are met in the arrivals hall, before passport control. The cost varies according to the service required, but is usually Dhs.75 for one passenger and Dhs.50 each for 2 - 9 passengers. The cost for children between the ages of 2 - 12 years is Dhs.35. Ahlan Dubai is more limited, only offering help with visas for Dhs.10.

Customs

No customs duty is levied on personal effects entering Dubai. It is forbidden to import drugs and pornographic items.

At Dubai International Airport, after collecting your bags in the arrivals hall, they are x-rayed before you enter the city. Videos, DVD's, CD's books and magazines are sometimes checked and suspect items, usually movies, may be temporarily confiscated for the material to be approved. Unless it is offensive, it can be collected at a later date. The airport duty free has a small sales outlet in the arrivals hall.

There has been talk of restrictions on the import or export of large amounts of any currency since the events of 11 September 2001. We recommend that you check this out before you try it! In addition, a new anti-money laundering law is soon to come into effect, which will not only penalise individuals who violate the law, but also financial institutions. The penalty for money laundering will be a prison sentence of up to seven years or a maximum fine of Dhs.300,000. The Central Bank is also due to set a limit for the amount of undeclared cash that can be brought into the country.

Duty Free allowances:

- *Cigarettes - 2,000*
- *Cigars - 400*
- *Tobacco - 2 kg*
- *Alcohol (non-Muslim adults only) - 2 litres of spirits and 2 litres of wine*
- *Perfume - a 'reasonable amount'*

TRAVELLERS' INFO

Health Requirements

No health certificates are required for entry to the Emirates, except for visitors who have been in a cholera or yellow fever infected area in the previous 14 days. However, it is always wise to check health requirements before departure as restrictions may vary depending upon the situation at the time.

Malarial mosquitoes are not really a problem in the cities, although they do exist, mainly around the wadis and pools in the mountains where it is wet. Long-term residents rarely take malaria tablets, but short-term visitors who plan to visit the countryside during mosquito season may be advised to take them. Check requirements a month or so before leaving your home country.

Health Care

The quality of medical care in the Emirates is generally regarded as quite high and visitors should have little trouble in obtaining appropriate treatment if they need it, whether privately or from the government-run hospitals in an emergency. Tourists and non-residents are strongly recommended to arrange private medical insurance before travelling since private medical care can become very expensive.

There are no specific health risks facing visitors, although the climate can be harsh, especially during the summer months. It's advisable to drink plenty of water (and to replace lost salts with energy drinks or salty snacks), and to cover up when out in the sun and use the appropriate factor sunscreen - sunburn, heat-stroke and heat exhaustion can be very unpleasant.

Travel Insurance

All visitors to the Emirates should have travel insurance - just in case. Choose a reputable insurer and a plan that suits your needs and the activities you plan to do while in Dubai. Make sure this insurance also covers 'blood money' (see [p.33]) in case you are involved in an accident involving a death and are found at fault.

Female Visitors

Women should face few, if any, problems while travelling in the UAE. Thanks to a directive by Sheikh Mohammed, men who are caught harassing women have their photo published in the local newspaper. Single female travellers who don't want extra attention should avoid wearing tight fitting clothing and should steer clear of lower end hotels in Deira and Bur Dubai. No matter what, most females receive some unwanted stares at some time or another, particularly on the public beaches. If you can ignore it, you'll save yourself some aggravation! The Dubai Police are very helpful and respectful - call them if you face any unwanted attention or hassles.

Travelling with Children

Dubai is a great place for kids of all ages! Parks and amusement centres abound, and if those aren't interesting enough for the little ones, annual festivals such as the Dubai Shopping Festival and Dubai Summer Surprises offer all sorts of fun-filled activities for the whole family. The Activities section will give a better idea of what there is to do with kids, as will the *Family Explorer*. Hotels and shopping malls are well geared up for children, offering everything from babysitting services to kids activities. Restaurants, on the other hand, have children's menus but tend not to have many high chairs; it's best to ask when making reservations. Discounted rates for children are common - just ask.

Disabled Visitors

Most of Dubai's five star hotels have wheelchair facilities, but in general, facilities for the disabled are very limited, particularly at tourist attractions. Wheelchair ramps are often really nothing more than delivery ramps, hence the steep angles. When asking if a location has wheelchair access, make sure it really does - an escalator is considered "wheelchair access" to some! The Dubai International Airport is equipped for disabled travellers (see also: Meet & Greet [p.19]), and Dubai Transport has a few specially modified taxis. As for parking, good luck! Handicapped parking spaces do exist, but they are often used by ignorant drivers who don't need the facility.

Hotels with specially adapted rooms for the disabled include: the Burj al Arab, City Centre Hotel, Crowne Plaza, Emirates Towers Hotel, Hilton Dubai Creek, Hilton Dubai Jumeirah, Hyatt Regency, Jebel Ali Hotel, Jumeirah Beach Hotel, JW Marriott, Oasis Beach Hotel, Ritz-Carlton Dubai, Renaissance Hotel, Royal Mirage and the Sheraton Jumeirah.

Dress Code

With its liberal attitude there isn't much that visitors to Dubai can't wear, however, as in all countries, a healthy amount of respect for the local customs and sensibilities doesn't go amiss. Short or tight clothing may be worn, but it will attract attention - most of it unwelcome. Like anywhere in the world, attitudes in the rural areas are more conservative than in the cities.

Lightweight summer clothing is suitable for most of the year, but something slightly warmer may be

needed in the evening for the winter months. In winter and summer, be sure to take some sort of jacket or sweater when visiting hotels or the cinema, as the air conditioning can be pretty fierce! In the evenings, restaurants and clubs usually have a mixture of styles; Arabic, Asian or Western - and anything goes. During the day, as in any place with loads of sun, good quality sunglasses, hats and buckets of sunscreen are needed to avoid the lobster look!

Beachwear

Do's and Don'ts

Do make the most of your stay in Dubai - have fun! But don't break the law. It's a simple and easy rule, and common sense will keep you out of trouble while in the UAE. Drugs are illegal and carry a normally lengthy jail sentence. If you are caught bringing drugs into the country, you will be charged with trafficking, which can result in a life sentence. Pornography of any sort is also illegal and will be confiscated immediately.

The best rule of thumb is to respect the local laws, culture and Muslim sensibilities of the UAE; remember you are a visitor and treat the local population with the same respect you'd expect back home.

Safety

While the crime rate in Dubai is very low, a healthy degree of caution should still be exercised. Keep your valuables and travel documents locked in your hotel room or in the hotel safe. When in crowds, be discreet with your money and wallet; don't carry large amounts of cash on you and don't trust strangers offering to double your money with magic potions. Money and gem-related scams run by confidence tricksters are on the increase - be warned!

With the multitude of driving styles converging on Dubai's roads, navigating the streets either on foot or in a vehicle can be a challenge. Quick tips to make your experience on Dubai's streets safer: if your taxi driver is driving too aggressively, tell him to slow down. Cross roads only at designated pedestrian crossings, and make sure all cars have actually stopped for you before crossing. Learn the rules of the road before getting behind the wheel, and drive defensively. Make sure you have insurance!

Tourist Police

In an effort to better serve Dubai's visitors, the Dubai Police have launched the Department for Tourist Security. The role of this department is twofold: to assist visitors through educating them on safety in Dubai, as well as offering quick assistance if visitors face problems of any sort. They act as a liaison between you and the Dubai Police, and offer personal assistance.

Toll-free number: 800 4438.

In general, Dubai police officers are extremely helpful, calm and understanding, and speak a multitude of languages to better serve Dubai's international population.

Their Website: www.dubaipolice.gov.ae is easy to navigate, helpful, and even lists Dubai's top ten most wanted criminals – always an interesting read!

Lost/Stolen Property

To avoid a great deal of hassle if your personal documents go missing, make sure you keep one photocopy with friends or family back home, and one copy in a safe place such as your hotel room safe.

If your valuables do go missing, first check with your hotel, or if you've lost something in a taxi, call the taxi company lost and found department. There are a lot of honest people in Dubai who will return found items. If you've had no luck, then call the Dubai Police or the Department for Tourist Security (see above) to report the loss or theft; you'll be advised on the next steps to follow. If you have lost your passport, your next stop will be your embassy or consulate. For a list of all embassies and consulates in Dubai, see [p.122].

Dubai Tourist Info Abroad

The Dubai Department of Tourism and Commerce Marketing (223 0000) operates 15 offices overseas which promote Dubai to both travellers and businesses.

DTCM Overseas Offices		
Australia & New Zealand	Sydney	+61 2 995 6620
East Africa	Nairobi	+25 4 224 6909
Far East	Hong Kong	+85 2 2827 5221
France	Paris	+33 1 4495 8500
Germany	Frankfurt	+49 69 7100 020
India	Mumbai	+91 22 2283 3497
Italy	Milan	+39 02 8691 3952
Japan	Tokyo	+81 3 3379 9311
Nordic Countries	Stockholm	+46 8 411 1135
North America - East and Central	Philadelphia	+1 215 751 9750
North America - West Coast	Santa Monica	+1 310 752 4488
Russia, CIS & Baltic States	Moscow	+7 95 933 6717
South Africa	Johannesburg	+27 11 785 4600
Switzerland & Austria	Zurich	+41 43 255 4444
UK & Ireland	London	+44 207 839 0580

PLACES TO STAY

Visitors to Dubai will find an extensive choice of places to stay, from hotels to hotel apartments, a youth hostel, and even an eco-tourist hotel, the Al Maha resort, located amongst the dunes on the road to Al Ain.

The growth in the number of hotels and hotel apartments over the last few years has been phenomenal. In the past nine years, the number of hotels has risen from 70 to nearly 400, with many more planned. With so many rooms (over 23,000 at the last count!) needing to be filled, it's not surprising that visitors can expect excellent service and facilities - at least at the higher end of the market.

One service that the larger hotels and hotel apartments offer is to act as a sponsor for those needing a visit visa. This service should cost about Dhs.180 (including mark up) for a regular, and Dhs.280 for an urgent visa, and the visa is deposited at the airport for collection on arrival. However, the visitor is then expected to stay at the accommodation.

Hotels

Hotels range from those costing under Dhs.100 a night to those with a published price, or rack rate, of over Dhs.6,000 a night! While the hotels at the higher end of the market offer superb surroundings and facilities, those at the cheaper end vary - you pay for what you get. Refer to the Index for a list of outlets (including restaurants and bars) that can be found at each hotel.

Hotels in Dubai can be split into 'beach hotels', which are grouped along the coast to the south of the Creek entrance, and 'city hotels'. Most are located within a maximum 30 minute journey from Dubai International Airport. The larger hotels all offer an airport shuttle service, as well as a minibus service to the main tourist spots around the city. A taxi ride from the airport to most hotels will cost around Dhs.40 - 50. Road transport in Dubai is usually quite fast and the majority of journeys will only be of 15 - 20 minutes duration, costing about Dhs.20 - 25.

The Dubai Department of Tourism and Commerce Marketing (DTCM) oversees a hotel classification system which gives an internationally recognised star rating system to hotels and hotel apartments so that visitors can judge more easily the standard of accommodation they will receive.

The DTCM also operates an Internet reservation system for Dubai's hotels at their site: http://dubaitourism.co.ae. This enables guests to reserve rooms online, as well as allowing them a virtual tour of the hotel before they book. Alternatively, the DTCM Welcome Bureau at the airport offers instant hotel reservations, often at a greatly discounted rate.

Refer to the Club Facilities table [p.276] for the list of facilities offered at each hotel. Remember that, as is the case the world over, a discount on the rack rate or published price is usually given.

Hotel Apartments

A cheaper alternative to staying in a hotel is to rent furnished accommodation. This can be done on a daily/weekly/monthly or yearly basis and there are a number of agencies offering this service. One advantage is that the place can feel far more like home than a hotel room. Usually the apartments come fully furnished, from bed linen to cutlery, plus maid service. Additionally there may be sports facilities, such as a gym and swimming pool in the building.

Burj Al Arab (7 star hotel) Map ref ➔ 4-A2

This hotel is very James Bond - all glitz, gold and glamour. This very exclusive seven star hotel (the only one in the world) is built on its own man-made island. It's 321 metres high and houses five restaurants and 202 duplex suites with a host of butlers to look after your every need!

Al Bustan Rotana Map ref ➔ 14-D3

Located near Dubai International Airport, this hotel is best known for its excellent steakhouse, and Italian and Thai restaurants. Opened in 1997, it has a visually impressive but cold lobby, a few small upscale retail outlets, and 275 modern rooms overlooking either the pool area or a busy road.

Crowne Plaza Dubai Map ref ➔ 9-D2

Another of Dubai's entertainment-focused hotels, the older 560 room Crowne Plaza places a good deal of emphasis on its food and beverage outlets - all seven of them. Convenience is key here - not only is it located on Sheikh Zayed Road, but there is a shopping mall beneath this hotel/serviced apartment complex.

Dubai Marine Beach Resort Map ref ➔ 6-D2

Better known as 'Dubai Marine', this independent hotel is best known for its wide variety of restaurants and bars (11) packed into its compact area. The property also includes a small private beach, three swimming pools, a spa and a well-outfitted health club. The 195 villa-style rooms are nestled in gardens located off the central area.

Dusit Dubai Hotel Map ref ➔ 9-A2

This architecturally inspired, modern building on Sheikh Zayed Road comprises four restaurants, including a Thai restaurant and bar – both quite popular, 174 guestrooms, and serviced apartments. With a Far East flavour, much of the emphasis is on luxury amenities combined with Thai hospitality to meet the needs of business travellers.

Emirates Towers Map ref ➔ 9-C2

At 305 metres high and housing 400 rooms, this is the third tallest hotel in the world. Sophisticated and elegant, with a shopping arcade and consistently popular restaurants on the ground level, this hotel on the Sheikh Zayed Road is twinned with an office block. The entrance lobby is impressive, and a ride in the glass-fronted lifts recommended.

Fairmont Hotel Map ref ➔ 9-E1

With four glowing pyramids on top at night, this new hotel across from the Dubai World Trade Centre is hard to miss. The interior (particularly the funky lobby) is much more inspired than the exterior, and besides 394 rooms and serviced apartments, the Fairmont houses some of the trendiest restaurants in town.

Grand Hyatt Hotel Map ref ➔ 13-E3

With 674 of the largest, most tech-smart rooms and suites, Grand Hyatt Dubai introduces a new concept in business/leisure travel, offering top-level conference facilities in a resort environment. Facilities include ten restaurants, a fitness centre and spa, indoor lap pool, treatment rooms, tennis and squash courts, and outdoor pools.

Hilton Dubai Creek Map ref ➔ 11-C2

With very flash yet understated elegance, this new ultra minimalist, centrally located business hotel was designed by Carlos Ott and features interiors of wood, glass and chrome. There are 154 guestrooms plus exclusive Gordon Ramsay restaurants for the super cool. As the name suggests, this hotel is on the Creek, and overlooks the Arabian dhow trading posts.

Hilton Dubai Jumeirah Map ref ➔ 2-D2

This two year old beachfront hotel has 330 guestrooms and 57 luxury suites, most with sea views. Some of Dubai's best restaurants (and in-house entertainers) are housed here, and each outlet features stunning views as well. Located on the 'Golden Mile' Jumeira beach strip, this hotel is family-friendly and buzzing with tourists, especially on the beach.

Holiday Inn Bur Dubai
Map ref → 10-D4

Located near Lamcy Plaza and Wafi City, this business hotel isn't quite as 'five star' as the other five star hotels in town. With 230 rooms, a coffee shop and a few restaurants serving mostly hotel guests, the main reason Dubai residents will visit this quiet venue is to dine at Fakhreldine, one of Dubai's best Lebanese restaurants.

Hyatt Regency Dubai
Map ref → 8-D2

One of Dubai's older hotels, the recently refurbished Hyatt Regency features 400 guestrooms and serviced suites, each with a sea view and some of Dubai's finer, long-standing popular restaurants. While there's no beach nearby, it's within walking distance of the gold, fish and vegetable souks.

Inter-Continental Dubai
Map ref → 8-C4

This dated hotel is best known for its top-notch restaurants ranging from seafood to Italian to Japanese to one of Dubai's latest and trendiest restaurant/bars, all oozing with atmosphere. Facing the Creek in Deira, traffic and parking can be a hindrance in reaching the hotel, but the food's worth the hassle of getting there.

Jebel Ali Hotel & Golf Resort
Map ref → 1-A1

This resort, opened in 1981, has enough activities and facilities to keep guests busy for their entire stay. The 406 roomed hotel is situated amongst acres of secluded beach, landscaped gardens, and one of the region's original golf courses. Guests can also enjoy horse riding and a variety of watersports here.

Jumeirah Beach Club
Map ref → 5-D1

In a city that prides itself on knowing how to deliver first class and exclusive, this place stands out. 48 secluded suites (each with their own balcony or garden) and 2 luxury villas are nestled among the club's manicured gardens and private beach, along with a full range of facilities including tennis, spa, gym, restaurants, bars and swimming pools.

Jumeirah Beach Hotel
Map ref → 4-B2

Part of the Jumeirah Beach Resort, along with the Burj Al Arab, and the Wild Wadi Water Park, this exclusive hotel is one of Dubai's landmarks. The main building, built in the shape of an ocean wave with a colourfully dynamic interior, features 618 sea view rooms, and 25 restaurants along with a host of cafes, bars and shopping outlets.

JW Marriott
Map ref → 12-A3

Located on the edge of bustling Deira and conveniently close to the airport, the Marriott boasts 305 rooms, 39 suites, and 13 bars and restaurants. A grand staircase, detailed marble floors and natural lighting provided by "the Middle East's largest skylight" create a charming lobby, while a landscaped indoor town square provides a relaxing atmosphere.

Le Meridien Dubai
Map ref → 14-E3

Le Meridien's ultra-convenient location, just across from the Dubai airport and a stone's throw from the Aviation Club Tennis stadium, and its very fine array of restaurants, including those of the Meridien Village, are its main assets. One of Dubai's first five-star hotels, none of the 383 rooms has an exquisite view, but all feature superlative luxury and service.

Le Meridien Mina Seyahi
Map ref → 3-A2

Not to be confused with the nearby Le Royal Meridien, this hotel focuses on water-bound fun, from hobie cats to fishing charters. There are 211 rooms, with seaside rooms offering excellent vistas of the well-landscaped grounds, beach and Gulf. The clincher for families is the "Penguin Club", which allows parents to chill while the kids are entertained with supervised activities.

Le Royal Meridien
Map ref → 2-C2

A bit further out in the Mina Seyahi area is Le Royal Meridien. 500 rooms and 13 bars/restaurants, some of which could be considered the finest in Dubai, leave guests begging for fresh superlatives. Among many highlights is the Caracalla Spa, which offers all of the amenities one would expect from a Roman-themed spa.

Dubai City 5 Star Hotels

Metropolitan Palace Hotel
Map ref → 11-D2

An elegant lobby, 212 tasteful rooms and a nice rooftop swimming pool are this hotel's assets. Additionally, the convenient location, a block from the Creek in bustling Deira, merits a thumbs up. The gem in this hotel's crown, though, is the Tahiti restaurant, one of Dubai's premiere restaurants for groups looking for a good time.

Renaissance Dubai
Map ref → 12-A3

A little bit off the beaten path in Dubai's northern Deira (Hor Al Anz) section, this hotel features some of the more popular dining spots in Dubai, Spice Island and Harry's Place. Though not as central as some of the city's other 5-star accommodations, the Renaissance is one of the better values around.

Ritz-Carlton Dubai
Map ref → 2-C2

With stunning Mediterranean architecture and 138 guest rooms all enjoying a view of the Gulf and their own private balcony or patio, you'll be spending a lot of time just enjoying the setting. Match that with Ritz-Carlton's exacting international standards, and you are virtually guaranteed to get plenty of quality for the money you are sure to spend here.

Royal Mirage
Map ref → 3-A2

Aside from the opulent extravagance of the Burj al Arab, this hotel is, if not Dubai's finest, surely its most unique. Traditional Arabian architecture and unparalleled dining and service give one the impression of spending the night in a palace. At the very least, a nighttime tour of the grounds and a trip to Tagine or the fabulous Kasbar are highly recommended.

Sheraton Deira
Map ref → 12-A3

This hotel is probably more attractive to the business traveller or heavy-duty shopper due to its location - close to the airport and souqs. While it might not be one of the city's highlights, with 230 rooms, a host of respectable dining outlets and relatively reasonable rates, this might be one of Dubai's better five star deals.

Sheraton Dubai Creek Hotel
Map ref → 11-C1

Located right on Dubai's creek, this 255 room hotel has just undergone massive renovations, designed to provide the ultimate in comfort and convenience. Complementing one of Dubai's best Japanese restaurants (Creekside) are two Japanese-style Creek-view rooms. Creekside views are stunning, the location is prime, and the interior now stunning.

Sheraton Jumeirah Beach Resort
Map ref → 2-C2

The 255 delightfully decorated rooms are airy and bright here. The hotel offers a full range of sporting facilities, and is very close to the Emirates Golf Club. Along with 12 quality restaurants, a stunning beachfront location and a children's club, this is another good choice for families.

Sofitel City Centre Hotel
Map ref → 14-D1

Adjoining the Middle East's largest shopping centre - Deira City Centre, this hotel is great if you're in town for a shopping holiday. Some of the 327 rooms have a stunning view over the Dubai Creek Golf & Yacht Club. The hotel also features good conference facilities, serviced apartments, four restaurants and an English pub.

Taj Palace Hotel
Map ref → 11-D2

Centrally located in the heart of Deira, this exquisite hotel pulls out all the stops. Boasting the largest rooms in the city, extraordinary service and magnificent interiors, the Taj Palace has created a niche for itself as the only 5 star hotel in Dubai to adopt a "no alcohol" policy in respect of Islamic traditions.

World Trade Centre Hotel
Map ref → 10-A2

Part of the World Trade Centre Complex, this Hotel is ideal for convention goers. As one of Dubai's older 5 star establishments, the lobby feels a bit dated, and some of the 333 rooms are a little on the dark side, but all still offer comfortable accommodation. Additionally, hotel guests have unlimited access to the facilities of The Jumeirah Beach Club.

A Stunning Photographic Collection...

Images of Dubai is a visual showcase, sharing the secrets of this remarkable land and introducing newcomers to the wonders of Dubai and the United Arab Emirates. Journey with our team of photographers along golden beaches under a pastel sunset, or deep into the mesmerising sands of the desert. View architectural details that make the UAE one of the most visually thrilling urban environments in the world, and dive undersea to encounter the reef creatures who live there. Join us in marvelling at the diversity of astounding locations throughout the seven emirates.

With a refreshingly artistic view of the region, striking images are accompanied by inspired text, further capturing the magic of the varied subject matter. This book is for all those who love this country as well as those who think they might like to...

Available from leading bookstores, hotels, supermarkets or directly from Explorer Publishing. Customised copies and bulk orders ensure generous discounts

Explorer Publishing & Distribution • Dubai Media City • Building 2 • Office 502 • PO Box 34275 • Dubai • UAE
Phone (+971 4) 391 8060 **Fax** (+971 4) 391 8062 **Email** info@explorer-publishing.com **Web** www.explorer-publishing.com

EXPLORER

Hotels

Five-Star	Beach Access	Phone	Map	Double	Email
Burj Al Arab (7 Star)	✔	301 7777	4-A2	5,400	reservations@burj-al-arab.com
Al Bustan Rotana		282 0000	14-D3	1,100	albustan.hotel@rotana.com
Al Maha Desert Resort		303 4224	UAE	3,000	almaha@emirates.com
Crowne Plaza Dubai		331 1111	9-D2	1,200	cpdxb@cpdxb.co.ae
Dubai Marine	✔	346 1111	6-D2	960	dxbmarin@emirates.net.ae
Dusit Dubai		343 3333	9-A2	1,000	dddresv@dusit.com
Emirates Towers		330 0000	9-C2	1,300	eth@emirates-towers-hotel.com
Fairmont Hotel		332 5555	9-E1	900	dubai.reservations@fairmont.com
Hilton Dubai Creek		227 1111	11-C2	1,500	hiltonck@emirates.net.ae
Hilton Dubai Jumeirah	✔	399 1111	2-D2	1,450	hiltonjb@emirates.net.ae
Holiday Inn Bur Dubai		336 6000	10-D4	550	hiburdxb@emirates.net.ae
Hyatt Regency Dubai		209 1234	8-D2	675	hyattregency@hytdubai.co.ae
Inter-Continental Dubai		222 7171	8-C4	1,120	interconti_bc@incdubai.com
Jebel Ali Hotel & Golf Resort	✔	883 6000	1-A1	1,872	hoteluae@emirates.net.ae
Jumeirah Beach Club	✔	344 5333	5-D1	2,700	info@jumeirahbeachclub.com
Jumeirah Beach Hotel	✔	348 0000	4-B2	1,700	business.centre@thejumeirahbeachhotel
JW Marriott		262 4444	12-A3	760	marriott@emirates.net.ae
Le Meridien Dubai		282 4040	14-E3	1,200	reservation@le-meridien-dubai.com
Le Meridien Mina Seyahi	✔	399 3333	3-A2	1,100	res.agent1@lemeridien-minaseyahi.com
Le Royal Meridien	✔	399 5555	2-C2	2,200	business@leroyalmeridien-dubai.com
Metropolitan Palace		227 0000	11-D2	1,200	metpalac@emirates.net.ae
Renaissance Dubai		262 5555	12-A3	1,200	rendubai@emirates.net.ae
Ritz-Carlton Dubai	✔	399 4000	2-C2	1,560	rcdubai@emirates.net.ae
Royal Mirage	✔	399 9999	3-A2	1,800	royalmirage@royalmiragedubai.com
Sheraton Deira		268 8888	12-A3	650	sheratondeira@sheraton.com
Sheraton Dubai Creek Htl & Towers		228 1111	11-C1	948	sheradxb@emirates.net.ae
Sheraton Jumeirah Beach Resort	✔	399 5533	2-C2	850	sherjum@emirates.net.ae
Sofitel City Centre Hotel		294 1222	14-D1	950	cityhotl@emirates.net.ae
Taj Palace Hotel		223 2222	11-D2	1,000	tajdubai@emirates.net.ae
World Trade Centre Hotel		331 4000	10-A2	900	info@theworldtradecentrehotel.com

Four-Star	Beach Access	Phone	Map	Double	Email
Airport		282 3464	14-D3	624	apothotl@emirates.net.ae
Al Khaleej Palace Hotel		223 1000	11-D1	880	kpalace@emirates.net.ae
Ascot		352 0900	7-E3	660	info@ascothoteldubai.com
Avari Dubai		295 6666	11-D3	950	sales@avari-dubai.co.ae
Best Western Dubai Grand		263 2555	15-C3	720	dxbgrand@emirates.net.ae
Capitol Hotel		346 0111	7-A2	825	caphotel@emirates.net.ae
Carlton Tower		222 7111	8-C4	480	carlton@emirates.net.ae
Dubai Park		399 2222	3-A3	690	dxbprkht@emirates.net.ae
Four Points Sheraton		397 7444	8-A4	800	fpshrdxb@emirates.net.ae
Golden Tulip Aeroplane		272 2999	8-D3	480	aeroplan@emirates.net.ae
Holiday Inn Downtown		228 8889	11-E2	1,120	hidowtwn@emirates.net.ae
Jumeira Rotana Dubai		345 5888	6-E3	750	jumeira.hotel@rotana.com
Marco Polo		272 0000	8-E4	650	marcohot@emirates.net.ae
Metropolitan Beach Resort	✔	399 5000	2-E2	1,160	metbeach@emirates.net.ae
Metropolitan Deira		295 9171	11-D3	720	metdeira@emirates.net.ae
Metropolitan Dubai		343 0000	5-C4	1,040	methotel@emirates.net.ae
Oasis Beach	✔	399 4444	2-D2	1,008	oasisbeachhotel@dutcohotels.com
Ramada		351 9999	7-E4	900	rhddxb@emirates.net.ae
Ramada Continental		266 2666	12-B4	550	ramadadb@emirates.net.ae
Regent Palace		396 3888	10-A1	560	rameedxb@emirates.net.ae
Riviera		222 2131	8-C3	340	riviera@emirates.net.ae
Rydges Plaza Dubai		398 2222	7-A4	700	rydges@emirates.net.ae
Sea View		355 8080	7-A4	800	seaviewh@emirates.net.ae
Towers Rotana Hotel		343 8000	9-B2	850	towers.hotel@rotana.com

Hotels

Three-Star	Phone	Map	Double	Email
Admiral Plaza	393 5333	7-E2	550	admplaza@emirates.net.ae
Al Khaleej Holiday	227 6565	11-D2	800	kpalace@emirates.net.ae
Ambassador	393 9444	8-A2	365	ambhotel@emirates.net.ae
Astoria	353 4300	8-A2	230	astoria@emirates.net.ae
Claridge	271 6666	8-E4	480	claridge@emirates.net.ae
Comfort Inn	222 7393	11-D2	440	comftinn@emirates.net.ae
Dubai Palm	271 0021	8-E4	144	palmhtl@emirates.net.ae
Gulf Inn	224 3433	11-D1	200	gulfinn@emirates.net.ae
Imperial Suites (suites only)	351 5100	7-E3	288	imphotel@emirates.net.ae
King's Park	228 9999	11-E2	240	kingspark@emirates.net.ae
Lords	228 9977	11-D2	240	lords@emirates.net.ae
Lotus	227 8888	11-D1	260	lotusdbx@emirates.net.ae
Nihal	295 7666	11-D2	360	nihalhtl@emirates.net.ae
Palm Beach Rotana Inn	393 1999	7-E2		palmbhtl@emirates.net.ae
Princess Flamingo	263 5500	15-C3	880	princhtl@emirates.net.ae
Quality Inn Horizon	227 1919	11-D2	520	qualityinn@hotmail.com
Seashell Inn	393 4777	7-E2	280	seashellinnhotel@yahoo.com
Vendome Plaza	222 2333	11-D3	144	vphotel@emirates.net.ae

Two-Star	Phone	Map	Double	Email
Deira Park	223 9922	8-C3	200	deirapak@emirates.net.ae
New Penninsula	393 9111	8-A2	432	pennin@emirates.net.ae
Phoenicia	222 7191	8-C3	264	hotphone@emirates.net.ae
President	334 6565	10-D1	240	presiden@emirates.net.ae
Ramee International	224 0222	8-D4	200	rameedxb@emirates.net.ae
San Marco	272 2333	8-D3	144	smhtldxb@emirates.net.ae

One-Star	Phone	Map	Double	Email
Dallas	351 1223	6-E2	120	sivash2@emirates.net.ae
Middle East	222 6688	8-D3	144	mehgroup@emirates.net.ae
Vasantam	393 8006	8-A2	128	vhdubai@emirates.net.ae
West	271 7001	8-D3	120	westwest@emirates.net.ae

Opening in 2003:
Grand Hyatt, Shangri-La

Note: The above prices are the hotels' peak season published rack rates. Many hotels offer a discount off the rack rate if asked. Peak or high season is from October - April (except during Ramadan, refer to Ramadan & Public Holidays [p.10], for further details).

For more one-star hotels, contact the One Stop Information Centre (223 0000), Department of Tourism & Commerce Marketing, www.dubaitourism.com. For more hotels outside Dubai, refer to the Weekend Break table [p.176].

Classification is based on the DTCM hotel rating in accordance with By-law No. (1) of 1998 concerning Licensing and Classification of Hotels, Guesthouses and Hotel Apartments in Dubai.

Hotel Apartments

Deluxe	Phone	Map	One B/room Apts (Weekly)	One B/room Apts (Monthly)	Two B/room Apts (Weekly)	Two B/room Apts (Monthly)	Email
Al Bustan Residence	263 0000	15-C2	2,993	8,500	6,237	12,500	albustan@emirates.net.ae
Al Faris 3	336 6566	7-E2	3,000	8,000	2,000	7,000	afarisre@emirates.net.ae
City Centre Residence	294 1333	14-D1	5,000	12,500	8,000	16,000	cityhotl@emirates.net.ae
Golden Sands X	355 5553	7-E4	3,150	9,000	4,900	14,000	gldnsnds@emirates.net.ae
Imperial Residence	355 3555	7-E4	2,800	8,250	4,550	10,500	impres@emirates.net.ae
Oasis Court	397 6666	11-A1	2,426	6,750	3,465	7,740	oasis@gtfs-gulf.com
Pearl Residence	355 8111	7-E4	1,781	7,031	-	-	pearles@emirates.net.ae
Rayan Residence	224 0888	11-D1	2,450	9,000	2,450	11,000	-
Rihab Rotana Suites	294 0300	14-D1	3,850	13,500	6,300	20,250	rihab@emirates.net.ae
Rolla Residence	359 2000	7-E3	1,575	4,800	2,275	7,500	rollabus@emirates.net.ae
Wafi Residence (annual rental only)	324 7222	13-D1	-	-	-	-	mkm@waficity.com

Standard	Phone	Map	One B/room Apts (Weekly)	One B/room Apts (Monthly)	Two B/room Apts (Weekly)	Two B/room Apts (Monthly)	Email
Al Awael	271 1211	8-E3	3,240	4,050	1,575	6,750	alawael@hotmail.com
Al Deyafa	228 2555	11-D2	-	-	2,772	9,000	defuap55@emirates.net.ae
Al Faris 1	393 3843	10-D3					afarisre@emirates.net.ae
Al Faris 2	393 5847	7-E2					afarisre@emirates.net.ae
Al Harmoody	273 5222	12-A2	1,008	3,510	-	-	mohdaarh@emirates.net.ae
Al Hina	355 5510	7-E4	1,309*	3,825*	-	-	hinarest@emirates.net.ae
Al Mas	355 7899	7-E4	1,575	4,950	2,772	8,100	almasfur@emirates.net.ae
Al Muraqabat Plaza	269 0550	12-A3	1,540	4,950	3,080	9,900	muraqabt@emirates.net.ae
Al Nakheel	224 1555	11-E1	1,575	4,455	2,079	n/a	alnakhel@emirates.net.ae
Atrium Suites	266 8666	12-C4	-	-	-	-	atrium@emirates.net.ae
Baisan Residence	355 4545	7-E4	2,205*	4,455*	-	-	baisan@emirates.net.ae
Blanco	227 3400	8-D4	1,040	n/a	1,580	-	sacham@emirates.net.ae
Corniche	272 2555	8-D2	1,135	4,860	1,575	5,400	-
Embassy Suites	269 8070	11-D3	1,819	3,150	1,450	4,050	suites@emirates.net.ae
Galleria Dubai	209 6785	8-D2	-	11,500	-	12,500	galleria@hytdubai.co.ae
Golden Sands III	355 5551	7-E4	2,695	8,500	4,000	13,800	gldsands@emirates.net.ae
Premiere	359 9545	7-E4	1,925	7,000	2,625	8,000	preapts@emirates.net.ae
Richmond	398 8456	7-E4	1,732	5,400	2,835	8,100	rchmdhtl@emirates.net.ae
Rimal Rotana Suites	268 8000	11-E3	-	-	5,600	12,000	rimalres@emirates.net.ae
Savoy Residence	355 3000	7-E4	1,733*	4,950*	-	-	savoy@emirates.net.ae
Tower No. One	343 4666	9-B2	2,070	5,940	6,480	17,550	sales@numberonetower.com
Winchester Grand	355 0222	7-e4	3,920	-	5,040	-	wingrand@emirates.net.ae
Winchester Residence	355 0111	8-A4	2,522	10,800	-	-	winchest@emirates.net.ae

Listed	Phone	Map	One B/room Apts (Weekly)	One B/room Apts (Monthly)	Two B/room Apts (Weekly)	Two B/room Apts (Monthly)	Email
Al Shams Plaza	355 1200	7-E4	2,240	5,500	2,310	7,000	anbmr@emirates.net.ae
London Crown II	351 8888	7-E4	1,800	6,750	-	-	info@londoncrowndubai.com
Sky	273 3344	8-D2	1,040	4,500	-	-	skydubai@hotmail.com

Note   The above prices are the hotel apartment's peak season published rack rates and are inclusive of tax and service charge. Many hotels offer a discount off the rack rate if asked. Peak or high season is from October - April (except during Ramadan, refer to Ramadan & Public Holidays, General Information, for further details).

For more listed hotel apartments, contact the One Stop Information Centre (223 0000), Department of Tourism & Commerce Marketing, www.dubaitourism.com.

Key: * marked rates for studio apartments

Youth Hostel

The Dubai Youth Hostel (298 8161), located on Qusais Road, near the Al Bustan Centre, provides the cheapest accommodation in town. A new four-star wing was added to the hostel in 2002, almost tripling the number of rooms. In the old wing, there are 53 beds, available for Dhs.45 per night (YHA members) or Dhs.60 (non-members) in one of 20 clean two-bed dormitory rooms, including breakfast. Beds in the new wing are Dhs.65 for members and Dhs.80 for non-members, including breakfast. Check-in is always open.

Accommodation is available for men, women and families. Single women especially should check availability, since the management reserves the right to refuse bookings from single women when the hostel is busy with men. The hostel is well served by a cheap, regular bus service into the centre of Dubai and reasonably priced taxis are plentiful. The hostel is about 15 minutes from airport Terminal 1 by car.

There are also hostels in Sharjah, Fujairah and Ras Al Khaimah, and one planned in Abu Dhabi.

Camping

Other options ➜ Sports [p.225]

There are no official campsites in the UAE, but there are plenty of places to camp outside the cities. Near Dubai, options include the desert dunes on the way to Hatta, or the Jebel Ali beach, where, in the cooler months, if you get there early enough, you can have your own shelter and shower right on the beach!

While you will find people camping, the majority are UAE residents; it's rare for someone to show up at the airport, camping gear in hand, ready to set off on a camping holiday in the Emirates.

Pick up a copy of the *Off-Road Explorer (UAE)* (Explorer Publishing) for further information on camping - everything from where to go and how to get there, to what to bring and how to prepare, and where to buy what you'll need for your camping trip.

GETTING AROUND

Other options ➜ Maps [p.420]
Exploring [p.132]

The car is the most popular method of getting around Dubai and the Emirates as a whole, either by private vehicle or by taxi. There is a reasonable public bus service, but walking and cycling are limited and there are no trains or trams (see Bus, Car and Taxi entries below). The use of motorcycles is limited to a few brave (foolhardy?) souls. Alternative proposals for transport include a high-speed ferry linking Dubai and Abu Dhabi, and a monorail alongside Sheikh Zayed Road, from Defence Roundabout to just before Interchange Two (construction to begin in 2003).

Lane Discipline?

Lane discipline is yet another challenge to the overall UAE driving experience. As so many different nationalities converge on Dubai's roads, there are bound to be some major differences in driving styles, and lane discipline is a particular annoyance of ours! On the Sheikh Zayed Road for example, the majority of drivers seem to believe that the two far right lanes are reserved for trucks and the two left lanes are for cars. This means that on a highway with a posted speed limit of 120 km per hour, and drivers flying down the fast lane at sometimes over 200 km per hour, you will find a small car plodding along in the next lane over at far below the speed limit! Now, if you have someone coming up on you very, very fast, flashing their headlights and swerving dangerously, where do you go?!

The city's road network is excellent, and the majority of roads are two, three or four lanes. They are all well signposted to different areas and Dubai is probably the best emirate in this respect. Blue or green signs indicate the main areas or locations out of the city and brown signs show heritage sites, places of interest, hospitals, etc.

Once here, the visitor should find Dubai a relatively easy city to negotiate, however, a bit of insider knowledge will help get you from A to B. The Creek divides Bur Dubai to the south from Deira, to the north. These are further divided into several different areas, such as Satwa in Bur Dubai and Al Hamriya in Deira. There are three main crossing points on the Creek - Al Shindagha Tunnel, Maktoum Bridge and Garhoud Bridge. The Creek can also be crossed by a pedestrian foot tunnel near Shindagha, or by boat (these water taxis are known locally as 'abras').

To ease the pressure on inner city roads, a new ring road or bypass called the Emirates Road 311 has been built at a cost of Dhs.150 million. This connects Abu Dhabi directly to Sharjah and the Northern Emirates. Although the hope was to ease the flow of traffic in Dubai, so far there has been no noticeable improvement. Further steps to reduce traffic congestion were taken in summer 2002, with a ban on all trucks on main routes such as Sheikh Zayed Road and the Garhoud Bridge between 06:00 and 22:00.

Roads are named with white road signs, however these are not, with a few exceptions, referred to regularly. People generally rely on landmarks to give directions or to get their bearings and these are usually shops, hotels, petrol stations or notable buildings. Similarly, while there is a new numbered address system, few people actually use it. Thus an accommodation 'address' may read something like; Al Hamriya area, behind the Abu Hail Centre, near Happyland supermarket in the pink building, rather than Building XX, Road XX, Al Hamriya.

To confuse matters further, places may not be referred to by their 'official' name. For instance, Al Jumeira Road is often known as the Beach Road and Bu Kidra roundabout is invariably called Country Club roundabout.

Recently, Sheikh Hamdan bin Rashid Al Maktoum ordered certain streets around Dubai to be given the names of prominent Arab cities. Thus, various streets are now named 'Amman Road', 'Cairo Road', 'Marrakech Road', etc, to demonstrate the strong ties that exist between the UAE and other Arab nations.

Car

Other options → Transportation [p.107]

Over the past two decades Dubai has built, and is still building (so lots of roadworks!), an impressive network of roads. The Municipality estimates that in the last ten years the number of roads in Dubai has literally doubled. There are two bridges and a road tunnel linking the two main districts on either side of the Creek and the roads to all major towns and villages are excellent. An eight lane highway heads south from the city to Abu Dhabi, which takes about 1 - 1½ hours to reach.

Driving Habits & Regulations

Whilst the infrastructure is superb, the general standard of driving is not. Apparently the UAE has one of the world's highest death rates per capita due to traffic accidents. According to the Dubai Police, one person is killed in a traffic-related accident every 48 hours, and there is one injury every four hours - not most positive statistics! Drivers often seem completely unaware of other cars on the road and the usual follies of driving too fast, too close, swerving, pulling out suddenly, lane hopping or drifting, happen far too regularly.

One move to help the situation on the roads was a ban in Dubai on using handheld mobile phones whilst driving. Predictably the sales of hands free systems rocketed, before people went back to their old bad habits.

Driving is on the right and it is mandatory to wear seatbelts in the front seats. Children under ten years of age are no longer allowed to sit in the front of a car, and this ban is now countrywide, though you'll still see people driving with their children on their lap.

Driving & Alcohol

The Dubai Police exercise a strict zero tolerance policy on drinking and driving. This means that if you have had ANYTHING to drink, you are much better off taking a taxi home or having a friend who has consumed nothing drive you home. If you are pulled over and found to have consumed alcohol, you are likely to find yourself enjoying the hospitality of the police station overnight - at least!

Also note that if you are involved in an accident, whether it is your fault or not, your insurance is automatically void if you are found to have been drinking and driving. Penalties are severe, so the simple message is to be safe: if you are going to drink, don't even think of driving.

Fines for any of the above violations are Dhs.100, plus one 'black' point on your licence. Speeding fines are Dhs.200 and parking fines start at Dhs.100. Most fines are paid when you renew your annual car registration. However, parking tickets appear on your windscreen and you have a week or two to pay - the amount increases if you don't pay within the time allotted on the back of the ticket.

Try to keep a reasonable stopping distance between yourself and the car in front. Ultimately it also helps to have eyes in the back of your head and to practice skillful defensive driving at all times.

If you wish to report a traffic violation, call the Traffic Police's toll free hotline (800 4353). The Dubai Police Website: www.dubaipolice.gov.ae

offers all information relevant to driving, such as traffic violations, road maps and contact numbers, etc. The Traffic Police generally provide an excellent service, however, for some reason, they don't seem to bother about speeding cars or reckless drivers.

Speed Limits

Speed limits are usually 60 - 80 km around town, while roads to other parts of the Emirates are 100 – 120 km. The speed is clearly indicated on road signs and there is no leeway for breaking the limit. Both fixed and movable radar traps, and the Dubai Traffic Police, are there to catch the unwary violator! In 2001, 361,500 fines were given for speeding – that number amounted to 64% of all traffic violations. On the spot traffic fines for certain offences have been introduced, but in most cases you won't know you've received a fine until you check on the Website, or renew your vehicle registration.

Driving Licence

Visitors to Dubai have two options for driving. You can drive a rental vehicle with an international driving licence or a licence from your country of origin if you are from one of the countries listed on the transfer list (see [p.64]).

If you wish to drive a private vehicle, you must first go to the Traffic Police to obtain a temporary licence. Please note that unless you have a Dubai driving licence, either permanent or temporary, you are not insured to drive a private vehicle.

Accidents

If you are involved in a traffic accident, however minor, you must remain with your car at the accident scene and report the incident to the Traffic Police, then wait for them to arrive. In Dubai, as long as no one is injured, you must move your vehicle so that it is not blocking traffic. Unfortunately, when you have an accident in this part of the world, you become the star attraction as the passing traffic slows to a crawl and everyone has a good gawk.

Apparently, a recent move to lessen the number of traffic jams caused by accidents was to allow those involved in a non-injury accident to move their cars to the side of the road and deal with the other driver without having to wait for the police. Insurance companies were to supply accident forms to all drivers to comply with this change in regulation; however, we have yet to see one almost

two years on. Better to be safe and call 999 if you have an accident.

Blood Money

If you are driving and cause someone's death, even in an accident that is not your fault, you are liable to pay a sum of money, known as 'blood money', to the deceased's family. The limit for this has been set at Dhs.100,000 per victim and your car insurance will cover this cost (hence the higher premiums). However, insurance companies will only pay if they cannot find a way of claiming that the insurance is invalid (ie, if the driver was driving without a licence or, for example, under the influence of alcohol). The deceased's family can, however, waive the right to blood money if they feel merciful.

Stray animals (mostly camels) are something else to avoid on the roads in the UAE. If the animal hits your vehicle and causes damage or injury, the animal's owner should pay compensation, but if you are found to have been speeding or driving recklessly, you must compensate the owner of the animal - this can be expensive.

See also: *Traffic Accidents [p.113].*

Non-Drivers

In addition to dealing with the nutters in cars, you will find that pedestrians and cyclists also seem to have a death wish! The few cyclists who do brave the roads will often be cycling towards you on the wrong side of the road, invariably without lights if it is night-time. Pedestrians often step out dangerously close to oncoming traffic, and a lack of convenient, safe crossings makes life for those on foot especially difficult. However, the numbers of pedestrian footbridges and pedestrian operated traffic lights are gradually (slowly) increasing.

Parking

In most areas of Dubai, parking is readily available and people rarely have to walk too far in the heat. Increasing numbers of pay and display parking meters are appearing around the busier parts of the city. The areas are clearly marked and range from Dhs.1-2 for an hour. Try to have loose change with you since there are no automatic change machines available. Meters operate between 08:00 - 13:00 and 16:00 - 21:00 Saturday – Thursday. If you haven't purchased a ticket, you may be unlucky enough to receive one from the police for the bargain price of Dhs.100.

Petrol/Gas Stations

Petrol stations in the Emirates are numerous and run by Emarat, Emirates, EPPCO and ENOC. Most offer extra services, such as a car wash or a shop selling all those necessities of life that you forgot to buy at the supermarket.

Emarat Petrol Station

The majority of visitors will find petrol far cheaper than in their home countries - prices range from Dhs.3.75 per gallon for Regular and Dhs.4 for Premium (leaded gasoline), to Dhs.4.2 for Ultima (unleaded). The UAE must be one of the few countries in the world where diesel fuel actually costs more than other fuels!

Car Hire

All the main car rental companies, plus a few extra, are in Dubai and it is best to shop around as the rates vary considerably. It's worth remembering that the larger, more reputable firms generally have more reliable vehicles and a greater capacity to help in an emergency (an important factor when handling the trying times following an accident). Depending on the agent, cars can be hired with or without a driver, and the minimum hire period is usually 24 hours. Prices range from Dhs.70 a day for smaller cars, up to Dhs.1,000 for limousines.

Car Rental Agencies	
Autolease	282 6565
Avis Rent a Car	224 5219
Budget	282 3030
Diamondlease Rent a Car	881 4645
Hertz Rent a Car	282 4422
Thrifty Car Rental	224 5404
United Car Rentals	266 6286

Comprehensive insurance is essential (and make sure that it includes personal accident coverage).

The rental company will also arrange temporary local driving licences for visitors. To rent a car, you are usually required to produce your passport, two photographs and either a valid international driving licence or a national licence from one of the following countries: Austria, Belgium, Canada, Denmark, Finland, France, Germany, Greece, Holland, Ireland, Italy, Japan, Norway, Spain, Sweden, Switzerland, Turkey, UK and USA.

See also: *Vehicle Leasing [p.107].*

Taxi

If you don't have a car, taxis are the most common way of getting around. Currently, visitors have the choice of metered taxis operated under franchise from Dubai Transport Corporation (DTC).

In 2000, the DTC cleverly decided to take over the entire taxi business in Dubai and private taxis were phased out by the end of the year. The days of being ripped off by non-metered taxi drivers were suddenly a thing of the past, but then again, so was choice! In addition to DTC cabs, three taxi firms operate in Dubai with a fixed fare structure – competition at its best!

Metered taxis are run by Dubai Transport Corporation (sand/ camel coloured cars), Cars Taxis (white with blue and red stripes), Metro Taxis (sand coloured) and National Taxis (silver). Eventually all taxis will be the same colour as DTC cabs. Global Positioning System (GPS) equipment is fitted in all 2,000 DTC taxis, giving the car's location with pinpoint accuracy; useful for letting the control point know which is the closest vehicle for your pick-up.

Taxi Companies	
Cars Taxis	269 3344
Dubai Transport Company	208 0808
Gulf Radio Taxi	223 6666
Metro Taxis	267 3222
National Taxis	336 6611
Sharjah: Delta Taxis	06 559 8598

The fare is Dhs.3 for pickup (Dhs.3.50 between 22:00 - 06:00), followed by Dhs.1.25 per kilometre. The starting fare inside the airport area is an extortionate Dhs.20 and only Dubai Transport vehicles are allowed to pick up here. The journey to the town centre from the airport costs around Dhs.30 - 35. You can also hire a taxi for Dhs.500 for 12 hours, or Dhs.1,000 for 24 hours. Van service is Dhs.50 per hour.

Towards the end of 2002, three non-metered taxi companies were once again permitted to work Dubai's roads. Under Dubai Transport franchise as well, these non-metered cabs allow customers the option of bargaining the fare down. Dubai Taxi, Khaibar Taxi and Palestine Taxi all have their prices fixed by Dubai Transport, and from there, it's bargaining time. A word of warning: determine the fare before the ride, and try to find out what the normal cab fare should be first.

Cabs can be flagged down by the side of the road, or you can make a Dubai Transport taxi booking by calling 208 0808. Alternatively, if you drop Dhs.1 into one of the 15 electronic booking machines dotted around town, a taxi is immediately despatched to the machine's location. If you make a booking, you will pay a Dhs.4 starting fare.

To make life a little more confusing, taxi drivers in Dubai occasionally lack any knowledge of the city, and passengers may have to direct them! Start with the area in the city of the destination and then choose a major landmark, such as a hotel, roundabout or shopping centre. Then narrow it down as you get closer. If you are going to a new place, try to phone for instructions first - you will often be given a distinctive landmark as a starting point. It's also helpful to take the phone number of your destination with you, in case things get too desperate! If your taxi driver is well and truly lost, ask him to radio his control point for instructions.

Airport Bus

The Dubai Municipality, in conjunction with the Dubai Department of Civil Aviation, operates airport buses departing from and arriving at Dubai International Airport every 30 minutes, 24 hours a day. Currently there are two loop routes: Route 401 services Deira, while Route 402 services Bur Dubai. The fare is Dhs.3 and is paid when boarding the bus. Airport bus route maps are available at Dubai International Airport.

Dubai Municipality Bus Information (800 4848)

Bus

Dubai Municipality's Transport section operates over 30 bus routes for the emirate, serving the main residential and commercial areas, from Al Qusais in the north-east to Jebel Ali in the south-west and some destinations out of the city. The service is gradually being extended, with more buses covering more routes. Efforts are also being made to display better timetables and route plans at bus stations to encourage people to use this inexpensive method of transport. The majority of passengers tend to be lower income workers.

The main bus station in Deira is near the Gold Souk and in Bur Dubai on Ghubaiba Road, near the Plaza Cinema. Buses run at regular intervals from 6am to around 11pm and fares are cheap at Dhs.1 - 3 per journey. Fares are paid to the driver when you board, so try to have the exact change ready. Also available are monthly discount tickets. Buses also go from Dubai to Al Khawaneej, Al Awir and Hatta for very reasonable prices; a one way ticket to Hatta, 100 km away, is Dhs.10.

Dubai Transport Corporation offers a mini bus service in addition to their taxis. These buses run to Sharjah, Ajman, Umm Al Quwain, Ras Al Khaimah, Fujairah, Al Ain and Abu Dhabi. The minibuses are modern, air conditioned and offer a good value service to the cities of the UAE. Unfortunately, at present these services only carry passengers on the outward journeys. Anyone wishing to return to Dubai by public transport must make alternative arrangements.

- *Dubai Transport - Northern Emirates* (286 1616 or 227 3840)
- *Dubai Municipality* bus information (800 4848) and lost & found (285 0700).

Air

Other options → Airlines [p.118]
Meet & Greet [p.19]

Dubai's location at the crossroads of Europe, Asia and Africa makes it easily accessible. London is seven hours away, Frankfurt six, Hong Kong eight, and Nairobi four. Most major cities have direct flights to Dubai, many with a choice of operator.

Dubai International Airport is currently ranked fourth amongst the world's top international airports, handling almost 14 million passengers in 2001. An ambitious US $540 million expansion programme has transformed the already excellent airport into a state-of-the-art facility ready to meet the needs of passengers for the next 30 years. Work has already started on an even larger third terminal due to service all Emirates flights.

Currently more than 90 airlines take advantage of Dubai's open skies policy, operating to and from over 120 destinations. The UAE's award winning national airline, Emirates, is based here and operates scheduled services to 58 destinations.

General Info

Getting Around

There are two terminals, which are located on different sides of the airport (a 15 - 30 minute taxi ride, depending on the traffic). Both Terminals 1 and 2 offer comprehensive car rental, hotel reservations and bureau de change services.

Terminal 2 was opened in April 1998 and has the capacity to handle 2.5 million passengers annually. Most of the better-known airlines are currently still using Terminal 1, but a fine selection of over 20 airlines operate from the new terminal. Primarily focused on the former Soviet countries, airlines include Chelyabinsk Airlines, Nizhegorodsky and Zitotrans - yes, they do exist. Happy flying!

Duty Free shops are located in both the arrival and departure halls, although the arrivals hall outlet is limited. All travellers have the opportunity to enter the prestigious raffle to win a luxury car, which will be shipped anywhere in the world (tickets Dhs.500 each).

Dubai National Airline Travel Agency (DNATA) (316 6666), is home to most of the main airline offices in Dubai. Here you can make enquiries, collect tickets, etc. DNATA is located in the new Airline Centre building on Sheikh Zayed Road (Map ref 5-C4).

A new amphibious aircraft service links Abu Dhabi and Dubai - the round trip costs Dhs.550. For further information, call Emarat Link (800 2445).

Boat

Opportunities for getting around by boat in the Emirates are limited ... unless you wish to travel by dhow, and then your opportunities are limitless. Crossing the Creek in low wooden boats (known locally as abras) is a very common method of transport for many people in Dubai. Future possibilities for travel by boat include a high-speed ferry linking Dubai and Abu Dhabi, but this is presently only a proposal. There is a cruise ship terminal at Port Rashid, currently the only dedicated complex in the region. It is comprised of a 335 metre quay, with simultaneous berthing capacity for two ships, and a 3,300 square metre terminal.

It is also possible to travel from Dubai and Sharjah to several ports in Iran by boat. There are different companies providing this service and prices vary. A hydrofoil operates from Dubai and costs Dhs.215 for the four hour trip. From Sharjah, the boat takes 10 - 12 hours and costs Dhs.130. All prices are for one-way tickets. There is also a Dhs.20 port tax. For more information, contact the Oasis Freight Co. (06 559 6325).

Walking & Biking

Other options ➔ Cycling [p.231]
Hiking [p.247]
Mountain Biking [p.254]

Cities in the Emirates are generally very car orientated and not designed to encourage either walking or cycling. In addition, the heat in summer months, with daytime temperatures around 45° C, makes either activity a rather sweaty experience!

However, in the winter months, especially in the evening, temperatures are perfect for being outside. At this time of year, walking is a popular evening pastime, especially in the parks, along the seafront in Deira and Jumeira or on the pedestrian paths along both sides of the Creek.

Abras on Dubai Creek

Something to reveal?

Cycling can be an enjoyable way to explore the city; you can cover more ground than on foot and see more than from a car. However, a lot of care is needed when cycling in traffic, since drivers often seem very unaware of this method of transport.

In the quieter areas, many of the roads are wide enough to accommodate cyclists and where there are footpaths, they are often broad and in good repair. There are no dedicated bike lanes, apart from a 1.2 km cycling track along Al Mamzar Corniche (which should take all of 6 minutes to cover!). However, it does at least recognise the need for cyclists to ride without the threat of being mowed down by a speeding car.

MONEY

Cash is still the preferred method of payment in the Emirates, although credit cards are now widely accepted. Foreign currencies and travellers cheques can be exchanged in licensed exchange offices, banks and hotels - as usual, a passport is required for exchanging traveller's cheques.

Exchange Rates

Foreign Currency (FC)	1 Unit FC = x Dhs	Dhs.1 = x FC
Australia	2.05	0.48
Bahrain	9.73	0.10
Bangladesh	0.06	16.67
Canada	2.33	0.43
Cyprus	6.48	0.15
Denmark	0.49	2.04
Euro	3.70	0.27
Hong Kong	0.47	2.13
India	0.07	14.29
Japan	0.03	33.33
Jordan	5.17	0.19
Kuwait	12.15	0.08
Malaysia	0.97	1.03
New Zealand	1.79	0.56
Oman	9.53	0.10
Pakistan	0.06	16.67
Philippines	0.07	14.29
Qatar	1.01	0.99
Saudi Arabia	0.98	1.02
Singapore	2.08	0.48
South Africa	0.37	2.70
Sri Lanka	0.04	25.00
Sweden	0.41	2.44
Switzerland	2.53	0.40
UK	5.82	0.17
USA	3.67	0.27

Rates updated — November 2002

There is more confidence in cheques these days; strict enforcement of laws concerning passing bad cheques has helped. It is a criminal offence to write a cheque with insufficient funds in the bank account, and a jail term will result.

Local Currency

The monetary unit is the 'dirham' (Dhs.), which is divided into 100 'fils'. The currency is also referred to as AED (Arab Emirate Dirham). Notes come in denominations of Dhs.5, Dhs.10, Dhs.20, Dhs.50, Dhs.100, Dhs.200, Dhs.500 and Dhs.1,000. Coin denominations are Dhs.1, 50 fils and 25 fils, but be warned, there are two versions of each coin and they can look very similar. Because 5 and 10 fil coins are rarely available, you will often not receive the exact correct change.

The dirham has been pegged to the US dollar since the end of 1980, at a mid-rate of US $1 ~ Dhs.3.6725. Exchange rates of all major currencies are published daily in the local newspapers.

Banks

The well-structured and ever growing network of local and international banks, strictly controlled by the UAE Central Bank, offers the full range of commercial and personal banking services. Transfers can be made without difficulty as there is no exchange control and the dirham is freely convertible.

For further information on opening a bank account in the UAE, refer to the *Zappy Explorer (Dubai)*.

Banking hours: *Saturday to Wednesday 08:00 - 13:00 (some are also open 16:30 - 18:30). Thursday 08:00 - 12:00.*

Main Banks

ABN AMRO Bank	351 2200
Abu Dhabi Commercial Bank	295 8888
Abu Dhabi National Bank	666 6800
Bank of Sharjah	282 7278
Barclays Bank Plc	335 1555
Citibank	352 2100
Emirates Bank International	225 6256
HSBC Bank Middle East	353 5000
Lloyds TSB Bank Plc	342 2000
Mashreq Bank	222 9131
Middle East Bank	800 4644
National Bank of Dubai	222 2111
Standard Chartered	800 4949
Union National Bank	800 2600

In the banking game, there's only one club to consider.

Lloyds TSB Dubai has a full range of services to meet all your personal and business banking needs.

Personal Banking

- Current, Savings and Loan accounts
- Visa Credit and Debit Cards
- Telephone Banking

Business Banking

- Multi-currency Accounts
- Treasury Services
- Trade Finance Services
- Electronic Banking

You can also take advantage of offshore banking through the Lloyds TSB Overseas Club.

OVERSEAS *Club*

- Choice of Dollar, Sterling or Euro denominated accounts
- Free money transfers from Dubai
- Credit & Debit Cards
- Internet Banking
- Telephone Banking
- Personal Club Manager & team
- Independent investment advice

For more information, please contact us at:
Lloyds TSB Bank plc, P.O. Box 3766, Dubai, United Arab Emirates
Tel: 04 3422 000 Fax: 04 3422 660, e-mail: ltsbbank@emirates.net.ae

The opening of an account and all credit is subject to status. Lloyds TSB Bank plc conditions apply. Lloyds TSB Bank plc. Registered Office: 71 Lombard Street, London EC3P 3BS. Registered in England and Wales No. 2065

HSBC Bank

ATM's

Most banks operate ATMs (Automatic Teller Machines, also known as cashpoints or service tills), which accept a wide range of cards. For non-UAE based cards, the exchange rates used in the transaction are normally extremely competitive and the process is faster and less hassle than traditional travellers cheques.

Common systems accepted around Dubai include: American Express, Cirrus, Global Access, MasterCard, Plus System and VISA. ATMs can be found in all shopping malls, at the airport, at petrol stations and at various street-side locations.

Money Exchanges

Money exchanges are available all over Dubai, offering good service and reasonable exchange rates, which are often better than the banks. Additionally, hotels will usually exchange money and travellers cheques at the standard hotel rate (ie, poor!).

Exchange house hours: *08:30 – 13:00 and 16:30 – 20:30*.

Credit Cards

Most shops, hotels and restaurants accept the major credit cards (American Express, Diners Club, MasterCard, Visa). Smaller retailers are sometimes less keen to accept credit cards and you may have

Exchange Centres	
Al Ansari Exchange	335 3599
Al Fardan Exchange	228 0004
Al Ghurair Exchange	351 8895
First Gulf Exchange	351 5777
Orient Exchange Company	226 7154
Thomas Cook Al Rostamani Exchange	222 3564
Wall Street Exchange Centre	800 4871

to pay an extra five percent for processing (and it's no use telling them that it's a contravention of the card company rules - you have to take it or leave it!). You can, however, call your local credit card company to lodge a complaint if you are charged this five percent 'fee'. Conversely, if you are paying in cash, you may sometimes be allowed a discount - it's certainly worth enquiring!

Tipping

Other options → Tipping [p.40]

Tipping practices are similar to most parts of the world. An increasing number of restaurants include service, although it is unlikely to end up with your waiter. Otherwise, ten per cent is usual.

MEDIA & COMMUNICATIONS

Newspapers / Magazines

The *Gulf News*, *Khaleej Times* and *The Gulf Today* (all Dhs.2 and Dhs.3 on Fridays), are the daily English language newspapers of Dubai and the Northern Emirates. Arabic newspapers include *Al Bayan*, *Al-Ittihad* and *Al-Khaleej*.

Foreign newspapers, most prominently French, German, British and Asian, are readily available in hotel bookshops and supermarkets, although they are more expensive than at home (about Dhs.8 - 12) and slightly out of date. There are also good supplies of hobby magazines, such as computing, photography, sports, and women's magazines (expect to find censored portions, or even occasionally whole pages or sections missing). They are expensive, usually costing two or three times more than at home (between Dhs.30 - 50).

Newspapers and magazines are available from bookshops, supermarkets and hotel shops. Newspapers used to be sold at major road junctions,

Everlastingbonds...

built by need-based solutions for every requirement.

- Remittances through Demand Draft, Mail Transfer, Telex Transfer and Electronic Transfer
- Moneygram (Money-A-Minute Service) remittances to 50,000 destinations in 150 countries
- US Dollar transfers to any bank anywhere in the world within 24 hours
- Commission-free electronic fund transfer system for corporate or individual funds
- Extensive network of correspondent banks
- Buying and selling of banknotes
- Travellers cheques
- Cash advance against credit cards
- Special rates and charges on large amounts
- Free financial market information

Correspondent banks in India
- Canara Bank
- South Indian Bank
- Indian Overseas Bank
- State Bank of Travancore
- ICICI Bank
- HDFC Bank

Al Fardan Exchange
It's About Service

but this practice was stopped in late 2001 as it was deemed too dangerous for the vendors.

Further Reading

Visitors will find a variety of books and magazines available on the Emirates, from numerous coffee table books to magazines with details of aerobics classes. Monthly publications range from the free *Out & About* and *Scene* magazine, to *Connector* and *Aquarius*, both focusing on health and beauty, to the event-focused *Time Out* and *What's On* magazines. Many magazines here seem to almost merge into one; they have no clear-cut identity and the audience always seems the same, no matter which magazine you pick up.

Guides to the region include the Lonely Planet series, as well as Explorer Publishing's *Abu Dhabi Explorer* and *Oman Explorer* (formerly Muscat Explorer). *Sharjah The Guide* and the *Spectrum Guide to the United Arab Emirates* also offer more information on the region.

For the finer points on life in Dubai, books to refer to include: the *Family Explorer* (formerly Kids Explorer), a family guide to life in the UAE; the *Zappy Explorer* (Dubai), a step by step guide to getting things done in Dubai (including how to set up a business); the *Off-Road Explorer* (UAE), the UAE's ultimate outdoor guide; and the *Underwater Explorer* (UAE), a detailed guide to scuba diving in the area. These can be found in all good bookstores around town.

Post & Courier Services

Other options ➔ Postal Services [p.92]

Empost, formerly known as the General Postal Authority (GPA), is the sole provider of postal services in the UAE. In addition, plenty of courier companies operate both locally and internationally, such as Aramex, DHL, Federal Express, etc. Empost also operates an express mail service, Mumtaz Express.

Post within the UAE takes 2 - 3 days to be delivered. Mail takes 7 - 10 days to reach the USA and Europe, 8 - 10 days to reach Australia and 5 - 10 days to reach India. Airmail letters cost Dhs.3 - 6 to send, depending on weight, and postcards cost Dhs.1 - 2. Letters are a dirham cheaper if they are posted unsealed. Aerogrammes can be bought for Dhs.2 each from post offices, and save the bother of buying a stamp before posting.

Stamps can be bought from post offices and certain shops - card shops often sell a limited range of stamps. Deira City Centre and Lamcy Plaza shopping malls both have full postal facilities, and some Emarat petrol stations now have postal facilities. Red postal boxes for outbound mail are located at post offices and near shopping centres. Hotels will also handle your mail if you are staying there.

Main Courier Companies	
Aramex	286 5000
DHL	800 4004
Empost	286 0000
Federal Express	331 4216
TNT	285 3939
UPS	339 1939

There's no house address based postal service; all incoming mail is delivered to a PO Box at a central location and has to be collected from there.

Radio

The UAE has a number of commercial radio stations broadcasting in a range of languages, from Arabic and English to French, Hindi, Malayalam or Urdu. Daily schedules can be found in the local newspapers.

Operating 24 hours a day, everyday, the English language stations, Dubai FM (92 FM), Free FM (96.7 FM) and Ajman's Channel 4 FM (104.8 FM), play modern music. Operating throughout the UAE, Emirates 1FM (99.3, 100.5 FM) plays modern music for a 'younger' audience, while Emirates 2FM (90.5, 98.5 FM) broadcasts a mixture of news, talk shows and modern music. Sadly, while there are some current affairs programs in English, most are sorely lacking in depth.

Ras Al Khaimah's Radio Asia (1152 khz) has programmes in Hindi, Urdu and Malayalam, while Umm Al Quwain's Hum FM (106.2 FM) broadcasts mainly in Hindi with a bit of English.

If you want to hear Arabic music, tune in to 93.9 FM. The BBC World Service can also be picked up with the right equipment.

Television/Satellite TV

Other options ➔ Television (Residents) [p.92]
Satellite TV [p.92]

Local television offers four channels: Dubai 2, 10 and 41 show Arabic programmes, and Dubai 33

When every second counts,
you can count on us.

...atever your express delivery needs, DHL won't let you down. With import and export services delivering to over ...,000 destinations in more than 220 countries, a worldwide staff of over 70,000, state-of-the-art systems and an extensive air and road network, you can rest assured DHL will get there on time - every time.
For more information on how DHL can help your business call 800 4004 toll-free in the UAE
or visit www.dhluae.com

every second counts

broadcasts mainly in English. Emirates Dubai Television broadcasts by satellite throughout the world in Arabic and English.

There is also a great variety of services available via satellite. Most hotels and hotel apartments have satellite television available for residents and many apartment blocks have dishes installed, ready for residents to acquire a decoder. Satellite programmes that can be received range from news programmes, international entertainment or films to sports, cartoons and current events.

Telephones

Other options ➜ Telephone (Residents) [p.89]

Telecommunications are very good, both within the UAE and internationally. All communication is provided by the monopoly Emirates Telecommunications Corporation, commonly known as Etisalat. Calls from a landline to another landline within Dubai are free of charge, and direct dialling is possible to over 170 countries. GPRS and WAP services are now available in the UAE.

Telephone Codes			
UAE Country Code	+971	Directory Enquiries	180
Abu Dhabi	02	Operator	100
Ajman	06	Etisalat Information	144
Al Ain	03	Fault Reports	170
Dubai	04	Billing Information	142
Fujairah	09	Etisalat Contact Centre	121
Hatta	04	Speaking Clock	140
Jebel Ali	04		
Ras al Khaimah	07		
Sharjah	06	To dial a typical Dubai	
Umm Al Quwain	06	number from overseas it is	
Mobile Telephones	050	00 **971** 4 391 8060	

Public payphones are all over the city, a few accept coins, but most require phone cards, which are available from many shops and supermarkets. They come in a variety of values, although for international calls beware: the units vanish at a truly amazing rate! Etisalat has a new generation of prepaid phone cards called 'Smart Cards', which are available for Dhs.30.

Mobile phones are very popular and widely used – there are more than 1.7 million subscribers in the Emirates. Etisalat has a reciprocal agreement with over 60 countries for a GSM international roaming service, allowing visitors whose countries are part of the

agreement to use their mobile in the UAE. However, if your country is not on the list or you don't have a GSM phone, Etisalat offers a useful service called 'Wasel'. It is possible to bring the phone with you (or buy it here) and to purchase a SIM card from Etisalat, which enables you to make and receive calls while in the UAE. A local number is supplied and calls are charged at the local UAE rate.

Internet

Other options ➜ Internet Cafés [p.308]
The Internet (Residents) [p.90]

With around one third of the population using the Internet, the UAE is among the top twenty countries in the world in terms of Internet use. Internet or cyber cafés around town provide easy and relatively cheap access.

Etisalat is the sole provider of Internet services within the UAE and in order to maintain the country's moral and cultural values, all sites are provided via Etisalat's proxy server. This occasionally results in frustrated users being unable to access perfectly reasonable sites. If you come across such a site, you can report it to Etisalat. Please see [p.90] for helpful sites and numbers.

Most organisations that are connected have an eight-character email address. Typical email syntax is: user@emirates.net.ae

You can also surf the Internet without being a subscriber. All that's needed is a computer with a modem and a regular phone line. To dial 'n' surf, simply call 500 5555. For information on charges, see Dial 'n' Surf on [p.90].

Websites

There are numerous Websites on Dubai and the Emirates in general, and new ones are going live all the time. Some are more interesting, successful and relevant than others. The table on page 46 lists those that the Explorer team has found to be the most useful - let us have your suggestions about others to include in the next edition of the book.

DUBAI
FM 92
THE GULF'S #1

Websites

Dubai Information

www.arabiaonline.com	News of the Arab world
www.crazyspin.com	Lists current and upcoming events
www.diningindubai.com	Make reservations online after consulting the Dubai Explorer
www.doctorelite.com	24 hour doctor/pharmacy/medical service
www.dubai.com	Online newspaper-type site - Dubai and international news
www.dubaicityguide.com	Updated daily, lists upcoming and current events
www.dubailocator.com	A superb interactive map site for Dubai
www.dubailook.com	Lists current and upcoming events
www.dubaishoppingmalls.com	List of major shopping centres around Dubai
www.expatsite.com	Find out what's going on back home
www.explorer-publishing.com	Our site!
www.godubai.com	Covers all the events and news of Dubai
www.gulf-news.com	Local newspaper
www.khaleejtimes.com	Local newspaper
www.roomservice-uae.com	Deliveries from your favourite restaurants
www.sheikhmohammed.co.ae	His Highness Sheikh Mohammed Bin Rashid Al Maktoum's site
www.sheikhzayed.com	His Highness Sheikh Zayed Bin Sultan Al Nahyan's site
www.uaemall.com	Shop online in the UAE
www.weather.com	Weather in the UAE

Business/Industry

www.dcci.org	Dubai Chamber of Commerce & Industry
www.dm.gov.ae	Dubai Municipality
www.dubai2003.ae	Dubai 2003 IMF site
www.dubaiairport.com	Dubai International Airport
www.dubaipolice.gov.ae	Dubai Police
www.dubaitourism.co.ae	Department of Tourism & Commerce Marketing (DTCM)
www.dwtc.com	Dubai World Trade Centre
www.dxbtraffic.gov.ae	Dubai Traffic Police - great for viewing traffic fines
www.emirates.net.ae	Emirates Internet - Dubai's Internet service provider
www.etisalat.co.ae	Etisalat - Dubai's telephone service provider

Embassies

www.dwtc.com/directory/governme.htm	Embassies in Dubai
www.embassyworld.com	Embassies abroad

Hotels/Sports

Hotel details listed in **General Information** [p.28], and sporting organisations in **Activities**	

Wheels

www.4x4motors.com	A little more sand than tar
www.diamondlease.com	Car leasing/rental
www.motorhighway.com	Buy a vehicle online
www.valuewheels.com	Buy a vehicle online

UAE ANNUAL EVENTS

Throughout the year Dubai hosts a number of well-established annual events, some of which have been running for years. The events described below are the most popular and regular fixtures on Dubai's social calendar.

Camel Racing

A traditional sport, the sight of these ungainly animals, ridden by young boys, is an extraordinary spectacle. Racing camels can change hands for as much as ten million dirhams! Morning races start very early during the winter months - be there by 07:00, and the races are over by 08:30. Otherwise, it's possible to watch the camels being trained every morning at around 10:00. Free admission.

Desert Rallies

The UAE provides the ideal location for desert rallying and many events are organised throughout the year by the Emirates Motor Sports Federation (EMSF) in Dubai. The highest profile event is the *Desert Challenge*, which is the climax of the World Cup in Cross Country Rallying. It attracts top rally drivers from all over the world and is held the first week of November.

Other events throughout the year include the Spring Desert Rally (4 WD); Peace Rally (saloons); Jeep Jamboree (safari); Drakkar Noir 1000 Dunes Rally (4 WD); Shell Festival Parade; Audi Driving Skills (driving challenge); Federation Rally (4 WD).

For 2003 event details, call EMSF (282 7111). For information on the UAE Desert Challenge call (282 3441).

See also: *Emirates Motor Sports Federation - Rally Driving [p.256].*
UAE Desert Challenge [p.52]

Dhow Racing

The traditional wooden dhows look very atmospheric when racing. The vessels are usually 40 - 60 ft in length and are either powered by men (up to 100 oarsmen per dhow) or by the wind. As well as fixed races throughout the year, there are often events on special occasions, such as National Day. Most events are held at Dubai International Marine Club. See also Dhow Charters [p.163].

Dog Show, The

An event not just for competitors and proud owners, the Dog Show is a popular family outing and the only show of its kind in the Middle East.

You are guaranteed to see both pedigree and crossbreed dogs of every shape, size and colour imaginable. One of the most popular events is the Dog Most Like its Owner competition - the likenesses are uncanny!

Dubai Desert Classic (Golf)

Incorporated into the European PGA Tour in 1989, this popular golfing tournament attracts growing numbers of world-class players. The 2003 return appearance of Tiger Woods is an indication of the prestige associated with this event.

Dubai Marathon

The Dubai Marathon now offers a full marathon along with a 10 km and a 3 km fun run. Attracting all types of runners, the emphasis here is more on fun and participation.

Dubai Raft Race

On the weekend of the Raft Race, the marina comes alive with a carnival atmosphere as teams turn out in a fever of competitiveness to battle against each other on their coloured rafts. Landlubbers can enjoy the spectacle at sea, as well as land based activities such as beach games and music by live bands.

Dubai Rugby Sevens

This two day event is a very popular sporting and spectator fixture. With alcohol freely available at the stadium, the party atmosphere carries on until the small hours! Top international teams play and the competition also provides a rare opportunity for local teams from all over the Gulf to try their luck in their own games, which run alongside some of the big names in sevens rugby.

Dubai Shopping Festival

A combination of festival and shopping extravaganza, DSF, as it is popularly known, is hard to miss as buildings and roads are decorated with

Traditional Dhow Racing

Dhs.100 ~ € 28

Looking for a book distributor in the GCC?

Distributing to the GCC and beyond...

Explorer Publishing & Distribution • Dubai Media City • Building 2 • Office 502 • PO Box 34275 • Dubai • UAE
Phone (+971 4) 391 8060 Fax 391 8062 Email info@explorer-publishing.com Web www.explorer-publishing.com

coloured lights and there are bargains galore in participating outlets. Highlights include a spectacular firework show over the Creek each evening, the international wonders of Global Village and numerous raffles. Other attractions include music, dance and theatrical entertainment from around the world, plus animal shows and a huge funfair. Hotels are at 100% occupancy during this month (January 15 - February 15) and it's cynically dubbed 'Dubai Traffic Festival' due to its success and the resulting traffic congestion in the evenings.

Dubai Summer Surprises

Similar to DSF, but smaller, Dubai Summer Surprises is held to attract visitors during the hot and humid summer months. Aimed at the family, DSS offers fun-packed activities, which are generally held in climate controlled facilities, such as shopping malls, specially constructed areas and hotels. Events are often based on food, heritage, technology, family values, schools, etc.

Alongside DSS, the dramatically reduced summer room rates at hotels have proved a strong attraction for tourists, especially from GCC countries.

Dubai Tennis Open

Held in the middle of February, the US $1,000,000 Dubai Duty Free Tennis Open is a popular and well-supported event. It is firmly established on the international tennis circuit and offers the chance for fans to see top seeds, both male and female, in an intimate setting, battling it out for game, set and match.

Dubai World Cup

The Dubai World Cup is billed as the richest horseracing programme in the world - last years total prize money was over US $15,000,000. The prize for the Group 1 Dubai World Cup race alone was a staggering US $6,000,000. It is held on a Saturday to ensure maximum media coverage in the West, and with a buzzing, vibrant atmosphere, is a great opportunity to dress up and bring out your best hat.

Eid Al Adha

Meaning 'Feast of the Sacrifice', this four day Islamic holiday marks the end of the annual period of pilgrimage to Mecca. Many animals are killed to celebrate this holiday 70 days after the first Eid.

Eid Al Fitr

This Islamic holiday lasts for three days and celebrates the 'Feast of the Breaking of the Fast'. It is held at the end of Ramadan.

Dubai Shopping Festival Opening Ceremony

Exhibitions

With the increasing importance of MICE (Meetings, Incentives, Conferences, Exhibitions) tourism to Dubai, there are currently two large state-of-the-art exhibition spaces showcasing a variety of exhibitions each year. These are the Airport Expo (Map ref 15-A4) and the exhibition halls (presently being expanded) at the Dubai World Trade Centre (Map ref 10-A2). For details of exhibitions in Dubai, contact Dubai Tourism and Commerce Marketing (223 0000). See [p.53] for -a monthly listing of annual events and exhibitions.

Fun Drive

If your idea of fun is venturing through the wilderness of the UAE with 750 other 4 wheel drives, then this is for you. Spread over two days, the Fun Drive is a popular and very sociable, guided off-road jamboree. The first night is spent at a campsite in the desert where catering and entertainment are provided, as well as large Arabic tents for sleeping (although most people take their own tents). The second day ends in a hotel with more activities. Early booking is advised: contact Gulf News Promotions Department for more information.

Great British Day

With a village fête atmosphere, cream teas and fish and chips, Great British Day guarantees a good family day out. It is organised by the British Business Group and held on a Friday in mid-April. Thousands of people of all nationalities attend the event and enjoy competitions, bouncy castles, live music, handicraft stalls, etc, and the finale of a terrific fireworks display.

Horse Racing (Dubai Racing Club)

Nad Al Sheba racecourse is one of the world's leading racing facilities, with top jockeys from Australia, Europe and USA regularly competing

World-class horse racing, Range of
international cuisine, Chances to
win Dhs50,000, Car raffle, Exclusive
ambience - are just some of the
highlights of racing with us.

To plan your evening of entertainment, please contact Dubai
Racing Club for full details of the racing calendar.
Tel: +9714 336 3737, Fax: +9714 336 3727, www.drc.co.ae

نادي دبي لسباق الخيل
DUBAI RACING CLUB

throughout the season (November - April). Racing takes place at night under floodlights and there are usually 6 - 7 races each evening, held at 30 minute intervals. The start time is 19:00 (except during Ramadan when it is 21:00).

The clubhouse charges day membership on race nights of Dhs.85, which allows access to the Members Box. Everyone can take part in various free competitions to select the winning horses, with the ultimate aim of taking home prizes or cash. Hospitality suites, with catering organised on request, can be hired by companies or private individuals. The dress code to the public enclosures is casual, while race-goers are encouraged to dress smart/casual in the clubhouse and private viewing boxes.

General admission and parking are free and the public has access to most areas with a reserved area for badge holders and members.

Islamic New Year's Day

Islamic New Year's Day, marks the start of the Islamic Hijri calendar. It is based on the lunar calendar and should fall on March 14 this year.

See also: *Public Holidays [p.10]*.

Lailat Al Mi'raj

This day celebrates the Prophet's ascension into heaven and is expected to occur on September 23 this year.

Powerboat Racing

The Emirates is well established on the world championship powerboat racing circuit; in Abu Dhabi with Formula I (Inshore) and in Dubai and Fujairah with Class I (Offshore). These events make a great spectacle - take a picnic and settle in with family and friends to be an armchair sports fan for the day. The Dubai Creek also provides a stunning setting for national events in Formulas 2 and 4,

Powerboat Racing at DIMC

which become more competitive every year. The local Victory Team continues to compete in Class I and is ranked the best in the world. Events in Dubai are held at Dubai International Marine Club (DIMC), Al Mina Al Siyahi (399 4111).

Terry Fox Run

Last year thousands of individuals ran, jogged, walked, cycled, wheeled and even roller bladed their way around an 8.5 km course for charity; over Dhs.400,000 was raised in donations. The funds raised will go to cancer research programmes at approved institutions around the world. Check the local media for contact details nearer the time.

UAE Desert Challenge

This is the highest profile motor sport in the country and is often the culmination of the cross-country rallying world cup. Following prestigious events, such as the Paris - Dakar race, this event attracts some of the world's top rally drivers and bike riders who compete in the car, truck and moto-cross categories. The race is held on consecutive days over four stages, usually starting in Abu Dhabi and travelling across the harsh and challenging terrain of the deserts and sabkha to finish in Dubai. For more details, check out www.mid-east-offroad.com.

Horse Racing at Nad Al Sheba

Main Annual Events – 2003

January

1	New Year's Day (Fixed)
3	Dubai Traditional Rowing Race (Heat 1)
9	"Emirates Cup" Traditional Dhow Sailing Race - 60ft
15	Dubai Shopping Festival begins
19-21	Sign & Graphic Imaging ME 2003
19-22	ME Electricity Exhibition
23	Maktoum Challenge I
24-31	Dubai International Sailing Week Regatta 2003
26-29	Arab Health Exhibition
30	Al Shindagha Sprint

February

3-6	Dubai Ideal Home Exhibition
3-6	Gulf Light Exhibition
3-6	Kitchens & Bathrooms Exhibition
3-6	Arablab Exhibition
7	Dubai Traditional Dhow Sailing Race 22ft (Heat5)
11-14	Eid Al Adha (Moon)
13	Maktoum Challenge II / UAE 2000 Guineas
13-14	UAE National Sailing Championship (Series 3)
15	Dubai Shopping Festival ends
16-18	Glass & Ceramics Man. Equipment Trade Show
15	Great British Day
17	Dubai Tennis Open commences
20	Moonshell Mile
21	Dubai Tri Club Olympic Distance Triathalon
24	Dubai City of Gold, Burj Nahaar
27	Kaas El Deheb (at Nad Al Sheba)
27-28	UAE Int Offshore Class II & III 6ltr Championship (Heat 2)
28	Dog Show

March

1	Terry Fox Run (date to be confirmed)
2	Dubai Tennis Open concludes
4-6	8th ME Int Cable, Satellite, Broadcast & Tele Ex.
5	Islamic New Year's Day (Moon)
6	Pearls of Dubai Stakes
6	Dubai Jet Ski Race (Heat 4 - UAE)
6-9	Dubai Desert Classic
8	Al Maktoum Challenge III / Al Bastakiya
11-13	Water, Energy Technology & Environment Exhibition
13	UAE 1000 Guineas
17-19	ME Toy Fair
19-22	ME International Boat Show
20	Godolphin 7 Stars
20-23	Agriflor ME 2003
20-23	Agri-Business Expo ME 2003
26-28	Dubai International Kite-Surfing Challenge
29	Dubai World Cup

April

3	UAE Oaks
6-9	Child Expo

April cont'd

6-9	Gulf Tex-Styles
6-9	Motexha Spring
8-11	Gulf Education & Training
10	Jumeirah Trad. Dhow Sailing Race 43ft (final heat)
10	Nad Al Sheba Gold Cup, UAE Arabian Derby
11	Dubai Wooden Powerboat Race (Heat 3 - UAE)
13-16	Bride 2003
18	Dubai Traditional Dhow Sailing Race 22ft (Heat 7)
22-26	International Jewellery Dubai
24-25	UAE Int Offshore Class II & III 6ltr Powerboat Championship (Heat 3)
27-29	Theme Parks & Fun Centres Show 2003

May

2	"Maktoum Cup" Traditional Rowing Race - 30ft
4-9	International Spring Trade Fair
5-8	Sportex ME 2003
6-9	Arabian Travel Market
8	Dubai Jet-Ski Race (7th and final Heat - UAE)
13	Prophet Mohammed's Birthday (Moon)
16	Dubai Wooden Powerboat Race (Final Heat - UAE)
19-21	The Hotel Show
19-21	The ME Office Interiors & Facilities Man. Exhibition
26-28	Gulf Beauty
29	Sir Bu Naa'ir Trad Dhow Sailing - 60ft (Final Heat)

June

19	Dubai Summer Surprises commences

August

6	Accession Day of His Highness Sheikh Zayed

September

22-25	Motexha Autumn
23	Lailat Al Mirage (Moon)
29-2	Arab Hunting Exhibition commences

October

7-11	Arabshop/ Index
18-22	Gitex
18-24	UAE Desert Challenge (date to be confirmed)
27	Ramadan begins (Moon)

November

25	Eid Al Fitr (Moon)
29-5	Big Five Exhibition Commences

December

2	UAE National Day
6	Dubai Rugby Sevens (date to be confirmed)
7-11	Dubai Airshow
11-15	The ME International Motorshow

Your perfect property is only this far away.

Finding the right property in the UAE for your home or business can be a daunting task. With over 25 years experience in the region (Not to mention over 270 years in the UK), one can always rely on those awfully nice people at Cluttons to look after all your requirements; not only in helping you find your ideal property, but more importantly ensuring your ongoing comfort and convenience throughout your stay.

04 334 8585

Property Management – Residential and Commercial leasing – Valuations and Feasibility Studies
Offices in Sharjah, Oman, Bahrain, Saudi Arabia, London and throughout the U.K.

Fax: 04 334 8362   E-mail: simon@cluttons-uae.com

New
Residents

New Residents

OVERVIEW

Dubai is one of the Gulf's top destinations to which expatriates come for work. The emirate of Dubai is by far the most relaxed within the UAE, but whilst life here can definitely be fun, getting things done can be a headache. People here love paperwork and red tape, and to become an official resident of Dubai you will need plenty of paper, plenty of patience and a sense of humour!

However, attempts are continually being made to streamline processes, and government departments are being encouraged to be more efficient and creative, especially with the use of the Internet for the issue of documents such as trade licences or health cards. In fact, 'e-government' is the buzzword everywhere these days, but that said, don't expect to find everything online, and don't expect the general public's paperwork load and woes to be at all reduced! This government directive is taking time

(years) to filter through to the individual departments and you can still expect to be sent from counter to counter with your documents. This can be confusing, however wherever you are, people are invariably ready to help and will point you in the right direction if you are well and truly lost.

The following information is meant only as a guide to what you will have to go through to become a car owning, phone owning, Internet connected, working resident. For step by step instructions on all procedures and formalities related to living in Dubai, pick up the Zappy Explorer (Dubai). Remember, requirements and laws change regularly, often in quite major ways. Changes are generally announced in the newspapers and can be implemented literally overnight - so be prepared for the unexpected, if that's at all possible!

Remember also that the following applies only to Dubai, and that while Sharjah and Dubai are close geographically and share many rules and regulations, there are many differences between the two emirates.

The Beginning...

To be resident in Dubai you need a sponsor, someone to legally vouch for you – this is usually your employer. Once you have residency, you may then be in a position to sponsor your spouse, parents or children.

The first step to acquiring residency is to enter the country on a valid entry visa (see : Documents - Entry Visa, Residence Visa [p.58]). The *Zappy Explorer (Dubai)* will also guide you step by step through the visa application process.

Your employer in Dubai will usually provide your visa. If you do not already have a job secured, you may obtain a visit visa to enter the UAE for a short time (see also: Visas - Entering Dubai [p.17]). If you are already in Dubai and are applying for a family member or friend, the application form may be collected from the Immigration Department, near Trade Centre roundabout (Map ref. 10-B1).

The original entry visa documentation must be presented to airport Immigration on arrival and your passport will be duly stamped.

Once you have entered the country on the correct visa, the next step is to apply for a health card, which includes a medical test, after which you can apply for residency. This should be done within 60 days of entering the country, or else a fine will be incurred. To legally work, you also require a labour card. Your employer will usually take care of processing all required documentation for you, and sometimes for your family as well.

Labour cards and residence visas are valid for three years and can be renewed (this does not apply to elderly parents or maids) (see: Residence Visa [p.58], and Domestic Help [p.86]). Health cards are valid for one year. If you are a qualified professional with a university degree or have an established employment history, there should be few difficulties in obtaining the necessary paperwork to become resident in Dubai.

Useful Advice

When applying for a residence visa, labour card, driving permit, etc, you will always need a handful of Essential Documents (see below), and you will need to complete countless application forms - invariably typed in Arabic. Don't panic! At most government offices, such as the Immigration Department, Labour Office, Traffic Police, Ministry of Health, government hospitals, etc, there are small cabins full of typists offering their services in English and Arabic, for Dhs.10-15. Most also offer photocopying services and some even take instant passport sized photos.

If you want to expedite the visa application process, you may pay an additional Dhs.100 ('urgent visa' fee) when you apply for the visa at the Immigration Department.

Essential Documents

To save repetition throughout the following section, Explorer has compiled a list of essential documents for you. These are standard items that you will invariably need to produce when processing documentation. Additional documents will be referred to in the appropriate paragraph.

- Original passport (for inspection only)
- Passport photocopies (personal details)
- Passport photocopies (visa/visit visa details)
- Passport sized photographs

You will need countless photographs over the next few months. Usually two passport photocopies and two photographs will be required each time. To save time and money, ask for the original negative when you order your first set of photos. Duplicate photos can then be made easily. There are many small photo shops that offer this service; look in your local area.

In addition, you will often have to produce what is commonly known as an NOC, a 'no objection certificate' (or letter) from your employer or sponsor. This confirms who you are and says that they have no objection to you renting a house, getting a driving licence, etc. It should be on company letterhead paper, signed and then stamped, stamped again (and again!) with the company stamp, to make it 'official'. Remember to take a photocopy of this document.

e-Dirhams

Introduced in late 2001, the credit card-sized e-Dirham card, a pre-paid 'smart card', is an electronic payment tool replacing the use of cash payment for procedures done within various federal ministries. Ministries you will visit requiring e-Dirham usage are the Ministry of Labour & Social Affairs, and the Ministry of Health. Private users may purchase fixed value cards from e-Dirham member banks (see [p.38]). Currently, available denominations are Dhs.100, 200, 300, 500, 1000,

3000, and 5000. Cash is no longer accepted at these ministries; come armed with your e-Dirham card or you will be sent away to purchase one.

DOCUMENTS

Entry Visa

Other options ➜ Entering Dubai [p.17]

You must enter Dubai on the correct entry visa in order to initiate your residence visa application process. This is either a residence or an employment visa. The other two kinds of visa (visit and transit) only allow you to remain here temporarily, as the names imply.

If you enter the country on a visit visa, you can remain in the UAE up to 60 days, after which you can extend your stay once for a further 30 days. The cost for renewal is Dhs.500 - apply through the Immigration Department. Nationalities that can obtain a visit visa on arrival at Dubai International Airport can stay initially for 60 days and renew once through the Immigration Department or take a 'visa run' indefinitely (see also: Entering Dubai [p.17]).

If you manage to secure work whilst on a visit visa, you will have to transfer to an employment visa in order to apply for your residence visa and labour card. You can transfer your visa status through the Immigration Department. You will need the relevant application form (obtainable from the Immigration Department) typed in Arabic, Essential Documents (see [p.57]), a copy of your original labour contract from your new employer and a copy of your sponsor's original passport, plus Dhs.100. Alternatively, you can fly out of the country and re-enter on the correct visa.

Health Card

Once you have the correct visa status (see above), the next step to becoming a resident is to apply for a health card, which is valid for one year. This entitles residents to cheap medical treatment at public hospitals and clinics, (charges are Dhs.20 per visit including medicine; Dhs.50 for a specialist; urgent cases are free). Some employers provide additional private medical insurance and, as in most countries, this is regarded as preferable to state care, although the usual hospital horror stories apply to both sectors.

The current process to apply for a health card is to collect an application form from any public hospital (generally Iranian, Al Baraha (Kuwait), Maktoum or Rashid Hospitals), the Ministry of Health or any First Health Care Centre, whichever is in your local area. Submit the application form (typed in Arabic), along with Essential Documents, employment letter and Dhs.300 (e-Dirham). If you are a dependant and are not employed, you need your tenancy contract, electricity and phone bills (original and photocopy of all documents), instead of your employment letter. In return, they will issue you with a temporary health card and a receipt for Dhs.300.

Then you can go for your medical test - it's best to go to Al Baraha (Kuwait) Hospital for this. Children under 18 do not need to have a medical test; all you need do is apply for a health card and you can then directly submit their residence visa application.

You will need your temporary health card, a copy of the receipt for Dhs.300, and two passport photos. The test fee is Dhs.205; this includes Dhs.5 for typing the application form in Arabic (done by the hospital). The medical test includes a medical examination, a chest X-ray and a blood test for AIDS, Hepatitis, etc. If you are processing a health card for a maid, you will need to pay an additional Dhs.100 to have him or her vaccinated against Hepatitis, and an additional Dhs.10 for typing out the form (refer to Domestic Help [p.86]).

Your temporary health card will be returned to you, and after one to two working days you can collect your medical certificate. The temporary health card will have a date on it stating when to collect your permanent health card. This can take anywhere from a week up to a few months; in the meantime the temporary health card can be used at hospitals should you require treatment.

Office locations:

- *Al Baraha (Kuwait) Hospital*, near Hyatt Regency Dubai hotel, Deira (Map ref. 12-A2)
- *Iranian Hospital*, Al Wasl Road, Jumeira (Map ref. 6-D3)
- *Maktoum Hospital*, near Al Ghurair City, Deira (Map ref. 8-D4)
- *Rashid Hospital*, near Maktoum Bridge, Bur Dubai (Map ref. 11-A4)

Residence Visa

Other options ➜ Visas – Entering Dubai [p.17]

There are basically two types of residence visa: when you are sponsored for employment and when

Moving: From A to B

Relocating: From A to Z

Relocating is about more than moving boxes and changing time zones.
It's about starting over. New home. New school. New neighbours. Perhaps even a new country.
Only a company with offices worldwide can make this transition easier
by offering staff to help you on both ends of your move.
Crown Relocations. A single source for all your relocation needs, here and abroad.
When it comes to beginning life's next chapter, Crown wrote the book.

Helping you begin life's next chapter.

CROWN
RELOCATIONS

Contact Crown Relocations at (971) 4 289 5152 or visit our website: www.crownrelo.com.

you are sponsored by a family member for residency only. As stated, the first step to gaining a residence visa is to apply for a health card.

Once a resident, you must not leave the UAE for more than six months without revisiting, otherwise your residency will lapse. This is not relevant to children studying abroad who are on their parent's sponsorship here, as long as proof of enrollment with the educational institution overseas is furnished.

Office location: Immigration Department, near Trade Centre roundabout (Map ref. 10-B1)

1. Sponsorship by Employer

Your employer should handle all the paperwork, saving you a lot of hassle. After arranging for your residency, they should then apply directly for your labour card (see below).

You will need to supply Essential Documents and education or degree certificates. You must have your certificates attested by a solicitor or public notary in your home country and then by your foreign office to verify the solicitor as bona fide. The UAE embassy in your home country must also sign the documents. Of course, it makes life much simpler if you can do all of this before you come to Dubai, rather than trying to deal with the bureaucracy of your home country from afar!

2. Family Sponsorship

If you are sponsored and are arranging sponsorship for family members since your employer will not do so, you will have a lengthy and tedious process ahead (see below). Good luck!

Note: it is very difficult for a woman to sponsor her family. There are some exceptions to this rule: those women employed as a doctor, lawyer, teacher etc earning a minimum stipulated salary may be permitted to sponsor family members. In most cases though, the husband/father will be the sponsor.

To sponsor your wife or children, you will need a minimum monthly salary of Dhs.3,000 plus accommodation, or a minimum all-inclusive salary of Dhs.4,000. Only what is printed on your labour contract will be accepted as proof of your earnings.

For parents to sponsor children, difficulties arise when sons (not daughters) become 18 years old. Unless they are enrolled in full time education in the UAE, they must transfer their visa to an independent sponsor or the parents may pay a Dhs.5,000 security deposit (once only) and apply for an annual, renewable visa. If they are still in

education, they may remain under parental sponsorship, but again, only on an annual basis.

When sponsoring parents, there are certain constraints depending on your visa status; ie, you should be in a certain category of employment, such as a manager, and earning over Dhs.6,000 per month. In addition, a special committee meets to review each case individually - usually to consider the age of parents to be sponsored, health requirements, etc. Even when a visa is granted, it's only valid for one year and is reviewed for renewal on an annual basis.

If you are resident under family sponsorship and then decide to work, you will need to apply for a labour card, and you will also need a second medical test - this should be paid for by your employer.

The Process

To become a resident, collect a residency application form from the Immigration Department and have it typed in Arabic. Then submit the application, along with Essential Documents, medical certificate and Dhs.100 (e-Dirham).

It is essential that you fill out the names of your parents (including your mother's maiden name) in the specified section. Once the application is approved (this may take up to a month), you will be issued with a permit of entry for Dubai and you must exit and re-enter the country, submitting the entry permit on re-entry to Immigration (ie, passport control), who will then stamp your passport. You should then submit your original passport to the Immigration Department, the original passport of your nominated sponsor, along with your medical certificate, four passport photos and Dhs.300 (e-Dirham) in order to get your permanent residency stamp. This can take anywhere from ten days to 1 - 2 months, or longer. Then you can relax!

Once you have your residency stamped, your sponsor or employer may insist that they need to keep your passport. This seems to be the accepted practice amongst many local sponsors, however, unless you work in Jebel Ali, there are currently no legal requirements under UAE law for you to hand over your passport. If you aren't comfortable with them keeping it, don't let them! Other sponsors will keep your labour card in return for you keeping your passport.

As a fully-fledged resident, you are now welcome to take out a bank loan, buy a car, rent an apartment in your own name, get a liquor licence, etc.

See also: Visa Run – Entering Dubai [p.17]; Zappy Explorer (Dubai).

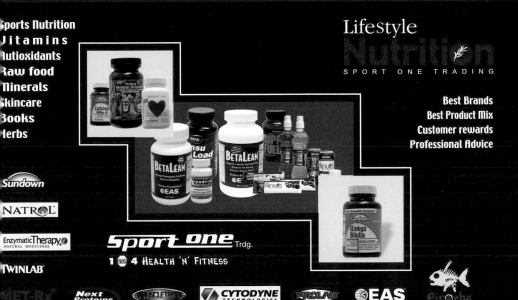

Labour Card

To work in the UAE you are legally required to have a labour card. This can only be applied for once you have residency.

If your employer is arranging your residency, the labour card should be processed directly after residency has been approved. You should not need to supply any further documentation. Before your labour card is issued, you will need to sign your labour contract, which is printed in both Arabic and English. It's a standard form issued by the labour authorities and completed with your details. Unless you read Arabic, it may be advisable to have a translation made of your details, since the Arabic is taken as the legal default if there is any dispute, (refer to Employment Contracts [p.70]).

If you are on family residency and decide to work, your employer, not your sponsor, will need to apply for a labour card. Your sponsor will need to supply a letter of no objection (also known as an NOC or no objection certificate).

Documents to supply include: Essential Documents, NOC, education certificate/s (if appropriate) and usually a photocopy of your sponsor's passport - they may also require the sponsor's original passport.

Expat students on their parent's visa, who wish to work in Dubai during the summer vacation, should apply to the Department of Naturalization & Residency for a permit allowing them to work legally.

Location: Labour Department – nr Galadari roundabout, (269 1666, Map ref. 12-C4).

Free Zones

Other options → **Free Zones [p.62]**
Business [p.126]

Employees of companies in free zones have different sponsorship options, depending on the free zone. For example, in Jebel Ali you can either be sponsored by an individual company or by the free zone authority itself. Whether the Jebel Ali Free Zone, Dubai Internet or Media City, or the Dubai Airport Free Zone, the free zone authorities will handle the processing of your visa through the Immigration Department, and generally, they are able to process your visa very quickly. Once Immigration has stamped your residence visa in your passport, the free zone will issue your labour card - this also acts as your security pass for entry to the free zone (your passport will be retained in

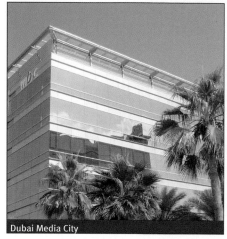
Dubai Media City

Jebel Ali, but not in the other free zones). Your visa is valid for three years, and the labour card either one or three years, depending on the free zone.

CERTIFICATES & LICENCES

Driving Licence

Other options → **Transportation [p.107]**

Taking to the roads in Dubai is taking your life in your hands! The standard of driving certainly leaves much to be desired.

Until you acquire full residency, you can drive a hire car provided you have a valid driving licence from your country of origin, or an international licence (this only applies to those countries on the transfer list [p.64]) Make sure your driving licence details are registered with the car hire company.

Zappy Explorer

For detailed information on all procedures related to obtaining certificates and/or licences in Dubai, pick up a copy of the *Zappy Explorer* from any good bookstore around town.

To drive private vehicles, you must first apply to the Traffic Police for a temporary Dubai licence. You will need to fill out the application form and take Essential Documents and Dhs.10 to obtain a temporary licence that is valid for one month (longer periods are also available).

A TRADITION OF HOSPITALITY

Dubai Country Club is an idyllic retreat, offering you an atmosphere of warm hospitality whilst you enjoy the impressive range of facilities. Whatever your pleasure may be - golf, tennis, squash & keeping fit for the energetic, to chilling out by the pool or just experiencing a superb range of restaurants, bars and events for those who enjoy a more leisurely pace - Dubai Country Club has it all. There is more happening, more often than anywhere else - and it is much less expensive than you would think.

The Dubai Country Club is for everyone to enjoy and if you are looking for a warm, friendly atmosphere with plenty of social activity, then this is the club for YOU!

THE DUBAI COUNTRY CLUB

P.O.BOX: 5103, DUBAI, UAE TEL: +971 4 3331155 FAX: +971 4 3331409
E-mail: dcc@emirates.net.ae - Website: www.dubaicountryclub.com

Once you have your residence visa, you must apply for a permanent UAE licence. Nationals of certain countries can automatically transfer their driving licence, providing the original licence is valid. These countries are:

Licence Transfers

Australia, Austria, Belgium, Canada, Cyprus, Czech Republic, Denmark, Finland, France, GCC member countries, Germany, Greece, Iceland, Ireland, Italy, Japan, Luxembourg, Netherlands, New Zealand, Norway, Poland, Portugal, Singapore, Slovakia, South Africa, South Korea, Spain, Sweden, Switzerland, Turkey, United Kingdom, United States.

Some of the above licences will need an Arabic translation by your consulate – check with the Traffic Police. You may also be required to sit a short written test on road rules before the transfer will take place.

If you aren't from one of the above countries, you will need to sit a UAE driving test. To apply for a permanent driving licence, submit the following documents (see below) to the Traffic Police, plus your valid Dubai residence visa and Dhs.100.

Always carry your Dubai driving licence when driving. If you fail to produce it during a police spot check, you will be fined. Driving licences can be renewed at the Traffic Police, as well as at other sites around Dubai, including Al Safa Union Co-operative (394 5007, Map ref. 5-B2), Al Tawar Union Co-operative (263 4857, Map ref. 15-C2) and Jumeira Plaza (342 0737 Map ref. 6-C2). The licence is valid for ten years, and if you manage to drive on the UAE roads for this long without going crazy, you deserve a medal!

No UAE Licence?

You cannot drive a privately registered vehicle on an international or foreign driving licence, as the vehicle is only insured for drivers holding a UAE driving licence.

Driving Licence Documents

- Relevant application form from the Traffic Police typed in Arabic
- Essential Documents
- A copy of your sponsor's passport or a copy of the company's trade licence
- NOC from your sponsor/ company in Arabic
- Your original driving licence (and photocopy) (and translation, if requested by the Traffic Police).

Sometimes your sponsor's original passport is asked for, as well as a copy. However, this seems to depend on whim more than anything concrete.

Office locations:
- Traffic Police HQ - near Galadari roundabout, Dubai - Sharjah Road (269 2222, Map ref. 15-C1)
- Bur Dubai Police Station - Sheikh Zayed Road, Junction 4 (398 1111 Map ref. 4-A4).

Driving Test

If your nationality isn't on the automatic transfer list above, you will need to sit a UAE driving test in order to be legally eligible to drive in Dubai, regardless of whether you hold a valid driving licence from your country of origin. If you haven't driven in your country of origin and need to obtain a driving licence, the following information will apply to you as well.

The first step is to obtain a learning permit - apply at the Traffic Police for the application form. You will also need Essential Documents, Driving Licence Documents, Dhs.40 and you will be given an eye test at the Traffic Police. Then find a reputable driving school - check the Yellow Pages or try:

- Al Hamriya Driving School (269 9259)
- Dubai Driving School (271 7654)
- Emirates Driving Institute (263 1100)

Some driving institutions insist that you pay for a set of pre-booked lessons. In some cases, the package extends to 52 lessons and can cost up to Dhs.3,000! The lessons must be taken on consecutive days and usually last 30 - 45 minutes. Other companies offer lessons on an hourly basis, as and when you like, for Dhs.35 per hour. Women are required to take lessons with a female instructor, at a cost of Dhs.65 per hour, as opposed to male instructors who charge Dhs.35 per hour. If a woman wants to take lessons with a male instructor, she must first obtain NOC's from her husband/sponsor and the Traffic Police. That said, if she has previous driving experience, she will have to sit a test with an instructor (who could be male) before signing up for lessons (no NOC's required for this one!).

When your instructor feels that you are ready to take your test, you will be issued with a letter to that effect and can now apply for a test date. You will need to fill out the necessary application form at the Traffic Police, and also hand in your Essential Documents, Driving Licence Documents, Dhs.35, and again you must take an eye test elsewhere and bring them the certificate the optician supplies you. The time between submitting your application and the test date can be as long as two months.

Are you relocating Your manager, Executive or CEO ?

As their Dubai HR Manager, you are probably wondering how you are going to find the time to assist with this move?

You don't have to.

At In Touch Relocations, we know the in's and out's of settling newcomers into Dubai.

We can assist with their home-find, utilities hook up, drivers licence, school enrolment, shopping mall guide etc. The list is extensive and guaranteed to save a family from the stress, frustrations and hassles such a move generates.

At In Touch Relocations we can tailor-make a relocation package that will suit your company and your employees.

So, as their HR Manager, you can focus on inducting your new manager and get them started on the job they were employed to do.

Using In Touch Relocations is a proven cost effective solution to your senior management relocation needs.

• City orientation • Settling in Dubai • Homefind assistance • Education service • Departure service • Help desk assistance

Give your senior management a positive feeling about being in Dubai and working for your company – contact In Touch Relocations, Dubai's only truly dedicated relocation experts

Call Kim Lindsay
for a free consultation
Tel +971 4 332 88 07
Fax +971 4 332 83 93
mobile +971 50 6535793

In Touch
R E L O C A T I O N S

intouch@emirates.net.ae - www.intouchdubai.com

You will be given three different tests on different dates. One is a highway code test, another an 'internal' test which includes garage parking, etc, and the third is a road test. Once you pass all three tests, you will be issued with a certificate (after about five days), which you should take to the Traffic Police to apply for your permanent driving licence. Before you are issued with your permanent driving licence, you will have to attend two compulsory hour-long road safety lectures, the cost of which is incorporated into the price of your lessons.

Liquor Licence

Other options ➜ Alcohol [p.182]

Dubai has the most liberal attitude towards alcohol of all the emirates. If you wish to buy alcohol for consumption at home, you will need a special liquor licence to buy from a liquor shop (not the local supermarket). In public, only four and five-star hotels are licensed to serve alcoholic drinks in their bars and restaurants, as well as some private sports clubs. You won't need a liquor licence to drink at a hotel or club.

The licence allows you to spend a limited amount on alcohol per month - this amount is based on your monthly salary. While no minimum salary level is stated, Dhs.3,500 is generally felt to be the minimum for an application to be accepted. Only non-Muslims with a residence visa may obtain a licence, and for married couples, only the husband may apply.

To apply, collect an application form from the Dubai Police HQ. Your employer must sign and stamp the form, then submit it (in both Arabic and English), to CID at the Dubai Police HQ along with Essential Documents, your labour contract (stating your salary), your spouse's passport copy, and Dhs.105. It should be processed in under two weeks. Alternatively, check with either MMI or A&E, the two licensed liquor store chains in Dubai, to see if you can yet apply for your liquor licence in store, saving you the hassle of visiting the Police HQ.

Buying alcohol from liquor shops can be expensive, as you have to pay an additional tax of 30% on all items. However, the range of alcohol for sale is excellent. Cheaper, unlicensed alternatives for buying alcohol include Ajman's 'Hole in the Wall' (near the Ajman Kempinski) and Umm al Quwain's Barracuda Resort, next to Dreamland Aqua Park. It is illegal to transport alcohol around the Emirates without a liquor licence; this is particularly enforced in Sharjah.

Office location: Liquor Licensing Section, CID, Dubai Police HQ, Dubai - Sharjah road, near Al Mulla Plaza. (Map ref. 15-C1)

Office hours: Saturday - Wednesday 07:30 - 12:00.

Birth Certificates & Registration

Every expat child born in the UAE must be registered with a residence visa within 40 days of birth. Without the correct documentation, you may not be able to take your baby out of the country.

The hospital that the baby is delivered at will prepare the official 'notification of birth' certificate in English or Arabic upon receipt of hospital records, photocopies of both parents' passports and marriage certificate, and a fee of Dhs.50. Take the birth certificate for translation into English to Dubai Hospital's Preventative Medicine Department (behind Al Baraha (Kuwait) Hospital) where you will be issued with an application form, which must then be typed in English (Dhs.50 fee). You should also take the certificate to be attested at the Ministry of Health (Dhs.10 fee) and the Ministry of Foreign Affairs (Dhs.50 fee).

Once this is done, ensure you register your child's birth at your embassy or consulate. To do this you will require the local notification of birth certificate, both parents' birth certificates, passports and marriage certificate. In addition, you may want to arrange a passport for your baby. Then you must apply for a residence visa through the normal UAE channels.

Before the birth, it is worth checking the regulations of your country of origin for citizens born overseas. (See [p.122] for the list of embassies and consulates in Dubai.)

Marriage Certificates & Registration

Most people prefer to return to their country of origin to get married, but if you are planning to marry in Dubai you have a number of options.

1. Muslims

As a Muslim marrying another Muslim, you should apply at the marriage section of the Sharia Court (Dubai Court), next to Maktoum Bridge. You will need two male witnesses, and the bride should ensure that either her father or brother attends as a witness. You will require your passports and copies, proof that the groom is Muslim, and the fee of Dhs.50. You can marry there and then.

Opening hours: 07:30 - 14:00 & 17:30 - 20:30.

where can I buy...

..read the label

ALL STORES OPEN- Thursday & Saturday: 10.00am-9.00pm
Monday to Wednesday: 10.00am-2.00pm, 5.00pm-9.00pm
(Dnata Wednesday: 10.00am-9.00pm)

For more information on obtaining your license call 04-3872909

For a Muslim woman marrying a non-Muslim man, the situation is more complicated as the man must first convert to Islam. For further information, the Dubai Court (334 7777) or the Dubai Court Marriage Section (303 0406) can advise. This can be an incredibly long and complicated process (up to six months before the paper work is completed) and many couples end up returning to their country of origin to marry there.

2. Atheists

Atheists should contact their local embassy or consulate to arrange a local civil marriage.

3. Christians

Christians can choose to have either a formal church ceremony with a congregation or a small church ceremony and a blessing afterwards at a different location, such as a hotel.

At the official church ceremony, you will need two witnesses to sign the marriage register - the church then issues a marriage certificate (you will also need to take copies of your passport and residence visa). You can then take the certificate and your Essential Documents to your embassy in order to attest the document.

Catholics must also undertake a Marriage Encounter course, which usually takes place at St Mary's Church (337 0087) on a Friday. You will need to fill out a standard form and at the end of the course you are presented with a certificate. You should then arrange with the priest to undertake a pre-nuptial ceremony and again you are asked to fill out a form. You will need to take your birth certificate, baptism certificate, passport and passport copies, an NOC from your parish priest in your home country and a Dhs.250 donation. If you are a non-Catholic marrying a Catholic, you will need an NOC from your embassy/consulate stating that you are legally free to marry. A declaration of your intent to marry is posted on the public noticeboard at the church for three weeks, after which time, if there are no objections, you can set a date for the ceremony.

Anglicans should contact the Chaplain at Holy Trinity Church (337 4947) for an appointment. You will need to fill out a number of forms, basically stating your intention to marry, that you aren't a Muslim and confirming that you are legally free to do so. Documents required are your original passport and photocopies, passport sized photos and a letter from both sets of parents stating that you are legally free to marry. If you have previously been married, you will need to produce either your divorce certificate or the death certificate of your previous partner. You will also need Dhs.520, plus Dhs.50 for the marriage certificate. If you wish to hold the ceremony outside the church, an additional Dhs.500 will be charged.

These marriages are recognised by the government of the UAE, and the chaplain's or priest's signature may be authenticated by taking an Arabic translation of the marriage certificate to the Dubai Court after the ceremony. Filipino citizens are required to contact their embassy in Abu Dhabi before the Dubai Court will authenticate their marriage certificate.

4. Hindus

Hindus can be married through the Hindu Temple and the Indian Embassy - contact the marriage section for further details (397 1222). The department publishes a booklet with guidelines on how to get married, and you will have to fill out an application form on the premises. Formalities take a minimum of 45 days.

Death Certificates & Registration

In the unhappy event of a death of a friend or relative, the first thing to do is to notify the police of your district. On arrival, the police will make a report and the body will be taken to hospital, where a doctor will determine the cause of death. A post-mortem examination/inquest is not normally performed, unless foul play is suspected or the death is a violent one. Contact the deceased's embassy or consulate for guidance.

The authorities will need to see the deceased's passport and visa details. The hospital will issue a death certificate declaration on receipt of the doctor's report, for a fee of Dhs.50. Make sure that the actual cause of death is stated. Then take the declaration of death and original passport to the police, who will issue a letter addressed to Al Baraha (Kuwait) Hospital. The letter, plus death declaration and original passport and copies should be taken to Al Baraha Hospital, Department of Preventative Medicine, where an actual death certificate will be issued for a small fee. If you are sending the deceased home, you should also request a death certificate in English (an additional Dhs.100), or for other languages, apply to the legal profession.

You should then take the certificate to the Ministry of Health and the Ministry of Foreign Affairs for registration. Notify the relevant embassy/consulate for the death to be registered in the deceased's country of origin. They will also issue their own death certificate. Take the original passport and death certificate for the passport to be cancelled.

The deceased's visa must also be cancelled by the Immigration Department. Take the local death certificate, original cancelled passport and embassy/ consulate death certificate.

To return the deceased to his/her country of origin, you will need to book a flight through DNATA and get police clearance from airport security to ship the body out of the country, as well as an NOC from the relevant embassy. The body will also need to be embalmed - and you must obtain a letter to this intent from the police. Embalming can be arranged through Maktoum Hospital for Dhs.1,000, which includes the embalming certificate. The body must be identified before and after embalming, after which it should be transferred to Cargo Village for shipping.

The following documents should accompany the deceased: local death certificate, translation of death certificate, embalming certificate, NOC from the police and embassy/consulate death certificate and NOC, and cancelled passport.

A local burial can be arranged at the Muslim or Christian cemeteries in Dubai. The cost of a burial is Dhs.1,100 for an adult and Dhs.350 for a child. You will need to arrange for a coffin to be made, as well as transport to the burial site. Cremation is also possible, but only in the Hindu manner and with the prior permission of the next of kin and the CID.

See also: Support Groups [p.100]

WORK

Working in Dubai

Working in Dubai is very different from working in Asia, Europe or North America. One of the greatest advantages is the general proximity of everything - there are no stuffy trains to catch, no real distances to commute and it's always sunny!

Expat workers basically fall into two categories: those who have been seconded by companies based in their home country, and those who have come to Dubai in search of the expat lifestyle.

Working Hours

Working hours vary quite dramatically within the emirate, and are based on straight-shift and split-shift timings. Split-shift timings allow for an afternoon siesta, and are generally 08:00 - 13:00 and 16:00 - 19:00. Straight-shift timings vary from government organisations' 07:00 - 14:00, to private companies' 09:00 - 18:00. Some companies work a 5½ day week, with the weekend on Thursday afternoon and Friday. However, more companies are adopting a five day working week, with government departments and some private sector companies observing a Thursday/Friday weekend, and other private sector companies observing a Friday/Saturday weekend.

Social Life

Circle of Friends
Try to be open minded and make an effort to get to know people from all backgrounds. Diversity is the spice of life.

The Rumour Mill
Dubai has a very healthy grapevine and quite often you'll know of people before you meet them. In the end everyone knows what's going on! If possible, use it to your advantage but remember... walls have ears!

Live it up!
Get ready to live the high life with five-star hotels and tea at the Ritz. You can do more for less in Dubai, so you've no excuse to stay at home.

Public holidays are set by the government and religious holidays are governed by the moon. During Ramadan, organisations are meant to reduce their working hours for their Muslim employees, with the public sector working a six hour day. (For further details on holidays, refer to Public Holidays [p.10].)

Finding Work

If you do not have employment on arrival, the best way to find a job is to register with the recruitment agencies and to check the small ads and the employment pages in the main newspapers. An employment supplement is published in the Gulf News Sunday, Tuesday and Thursday, and in the Khaleej Times on Sunday, Monday and Wednesday.

A note of caution concerning the use of the words 'UK/US educated' in the papers. As far as we can make out, this is an 'accepted' form of discrimination. Basically, it should read 'white, Western educated'.

Recruitment Agencies

There are a number of recruitment/employment agencies in Dubai. To register, check with the agency to find out if they take walk-ins. Most only accept CVs via email these days, and will then contact you for an interview. You'll need your CV or résumé, and passport photographs for the interview, if you get one. Invariably you will also have to fill out an agency form summarising your CV. The agency takes its fee from the registered company once the position has been filled. It is illegal for a recruitment company to levy fees on candidates for this service.

Main Recruitment Agencies	
BAC	336 0350
Clarendon Parker	391 0460
Job Scan	355 9113
Job Track	397 7751
Kershaw Leonard	343 4606
Nadia	331 3401
Seekers	351 2666
SOS	396 5600
Talent	335 0999

Don't rely too heavily on the agency finding a job for you; more often than not they depend on you spotting a vacancy that they have advertised in the paper and telephoning them to submit your interest. Should you be suitable for the job, the agency will mediate between you and the employer and arrange all interviews. Good luck!

Employment Contracts

Once you have accepted a job offer, you may be asked to sign a copy of your contract in Arabic as well as in English. Be sure to check the Arabic translation before you sign, as this is taken as the legal default if there is a dispute. There have been instances of the Arabic reading differently from the English. You should also refer to a copy of the UAE Labour Law for details of other benefits and entitlements (see below).

If you are sponsored by your spouse and wish to work, you will need to obtain an NOC (No Objection Certificate) from him before signing a contract with your new employer. Your employer will then apply for your labour card.

Labour Law

The UAE Labour Law is a work in progress; the most recent version available is 1980's, though updates and amendments occur from time to time. The Labour Law outlines everything from employee entitlements (end of service gratuity, workers' compensation, holidays etc), to employment contracts and disciplinary rules. The law tends to favour employer rights, but it does clearly outline those employee rights that do exist in the UAE.

Labour unions are illegal, as are strikes. Recent moves have been made by the Ministry of Labour to assist workers (particularly labourers) in labour disputes against their employers. The Ministry now punishes companies who do not comply with the Labour Law - licences are withdrawn if warnings are not heeded. Non-payment of salaries is a common problem - hopefully to be sorted out one day soon!

A copy of this useful publication should be available from your employer or can be obtained through the Ministry of Labour & Social Affairs (269 1666). The UAE Labour Guide, published by the Ministry in 2002, also outlines workers' rights.

'Banning'

However, before you leap in and sign that job contract, make sure it's the job that you really want. In the UAE there is a cunning little law that aims to stop certain people from job hopping; if you resign from a job, you can potentially receive a minimum six month, maximum two year ban from working in the UAE. You can also potentially be banned from entering the country for six months!

People resigning from a job fall into three groups:

• Those who resign to return to their own country. Their residence visa will be cancelled (if they wish to live/work here in the future, they must find a new sponsor and apply for residency, etc, from the beginning).

• Those who resign to look for other work. If they are lucky, their old company will supply an NOC and their residency can be transferred. This is provided that they have been employed by the company for over one year and that they fall into certain categories of employment.

• Those who resign to work for another company. People in this category run the risk of a one year labour ban (possibly two under the new provisions) and residence visa cancellation. They may also risk an immigration ban. This applies where the person was employed under a contract for a specified term. If the contract was for an unlimited period, they only risk an immigration ban if they are not part of an exempt category.

For details of the categories of employee that cannot be banned, refer to the most recent version of the UAE Labour Law.

FINANCIAL & LEGAL AFFAIRS

Other options → **Money [p.38]**

Banks

Dubai is not short of internationally recognised banks that offer standard facilities, such as current, deposit and savings accounts, ATMs (otherwise known as automatic teller machines, service tills or cashpoints), chequebooks, credit cards, loans, etc. There are plenty of ATM machines around Dubai (location details can be obtained from the bank), and most cards are compatible with other Dubai based banks, a few also offer global access links.

To open a bank account in Dubai, you need to have a residence visa or to have your residency application underway. You will need to present the banking advisor with your original passport, copies of your passport (personal details and visa) and an NOC from your sponsor. Some banks set a minimum account limit - this can be around Dhs.2,000 for a deposit account and as much as Dhs.5,000 for a current account.

Opening hours: Saturday - Wednesday 08:00 - 13:00; Thursday 08:00 - 12:00. Some banks, such as Mashreq and Standard Chartered, also open in the evenings from 16:30 - 18:30.

National Bank of Dubai

Cost of Living

Drinks	
Beer (pint/bottle)	Dhs.15
Fresh fruit cocktail	Dhs.10
House wine (glass)	Dhs.20
House wine (bottle)	Dhs.90 - 120
Milk (1 litre)	Dhs.3
Water	
1.5 litres (supermarket)	Dhs.2
1.5 litres (hotel)	Dhs.10 - 18

Food	
Big Mac	Dhs.9
Bread (large)	Dhs.4 - 8
Cappuccino	Dhs.7 - 15
Chocolate bar	Dhs.1.50 - 2
Eggs (dozen)	Dhs.5
Falafel	Dhs.2
Fresh fruit	Dhs.1-19/kg.
Fresh meat	Dhs.6-40/kg.
Sugar	Dhs.3.5/kg.
Shawarma	Dhs.3
Tin of tuna	Dhs.3

Miscellaneous	
Cigarettes (per packet)	Dhs.5
Film	Dhs.7
Film processing (colour, 36 exposures)	Dhs.35 - 45
Hair cut (female)	Dhs.100
Hair cut (male)	Dhs.40
Postcard	Dhs.2

Getting Around	
Abra Creek crossing	50 fils
Car rental (compact)	Dhs.90/day
Private Creek tour	Dhs.50
Taxi (airport to city)	Dhs.40 - 50
Taxi (airport to beach)	Dhs.70 - 80
Taxi (+ Dhs.1.25 every km)	Dhs.3 drop charge
City tour (half day)	Dhs.110
Bus from airport to downtown	Dhs.3
Desert safari (half day)	Dhs.270

Entrance Fees	
Beach club (may include lunch)	Dhs.60 - 200
Cinema	Dhs.25 - 30
Museum	Dhs.2 - 10
Nightclub	Dhs.50 - 100
Park	Dhs.3 - 5

Sports	
Fishing (two hours)	Dhs.100
Go Karting (15 mins)	Dhs.75
Golf (18 holes)	Dhs.80 - 375
Jet ski hire (30 mins)	Dhs.100
Parasailing (1 ride)	Dhs.200

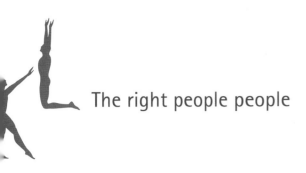 The right people people

Kershaw Leonard is committed to finding 'First Class' people for its 'World Class' clients...

How can we help you?

- Executive Search
- Sales and Marketing
- Human Resource Management
- Supply Chain Management
- Finance
- I.T. and Telecoms
- Construction and Engineering
- Office Management
- Business and Secretarial Support
- Temporary and Contract Staff

Kershaw Leonard – in a class of its own...

Address: Suite 325, Emarat Atrium Building, Sheikh Zayed Road, P.O. Box 71770
Dubai, United Arab Emirates.
Tel: (971-4)3434606 Fax: (971-4) 3438330
E-mail: kershawleonard@kershawleonard.net
Website: kershawleonard.net

Financial Planning

Planning for the financial future - unless you take the head in the sand approach - is an important aspect of modern day life, and especially necessary for expats.

Before you do anything, you should contact the tax authorities in your home country to ensure that you are complying with the financial laws there. Most countries will consider you not liable for income tax once you prove your UAE residence or your non-residence in your home country (a contract of employment is normally a good starting point for proving non-residence). As a non-resident, however, you may still have to fulfil certain criteria (such as only visiting your home country for a limited number of days each year).

Generally, the main reason for accepting an expat posting is to improve your financial situation. It is recommended not to undertake any non-cash investments until you know your monthly savings capacity, even though this may take up to six months to ascertain. In fact, the first steps you should take with your new earnings are to begin paying back as much debt as possible (starting with your credit card/s!).

If you have a short-term contract, stay away from long-term investment contracts. Once you have decided that expat life is for you and that you are ready to plan for the future, you might want to establish the following: emergency cash buffer (3 - 6 months salary), retirement home, retirement income, personal and family protection (life assurance, health coverage), etc.

When selecting a financial planner, use either a reputable name, or at least an institution regulated by the UAE Central Bank. If another authority is 'regulating' your advisor, you cannot expect the principal UAE authority to be of assistance to you, and your chances of recourse in the event of a problem may be severely hampered. For financial planners, we recommend word of mouth or any of the major international companies.

Taxation

The UAE levies no personal income taxes or withholding taxes of any sort. The only noticeable taxes you are obliged to pay as an expat are a 5% municipality tax on rental accommodation and a 30% tax on alcohol bought at liquor stores. In addition, there is a 10% municipality tax and a 15 - 16% service tax in hotel food and beverage outlets (these are no longer shown separately on customers' bills).

Business Groups & Contacts

For information on doing business or setting up a business in Dubai, refer to your local business group or the commercial attaché at your embassy/consulate. The contact numbers may be found in the table below and in the Business section.

Also worth contacting are Dubai Chamber of Commerce (228 0000 Map ref. 11-C2) and the Economics Department (222 9922 Map ref. 11-C1), both located along the Corniche in Deira.

Books:

- *Don't They Know It's Friday* by Jeremy Williams OBE
- *Dubai Commercial Directory*
- *Hawk Business Pages*
- *How to Live & Work in the Gulf* by Hamid Atiyyah
- *UAE: A MEED Practical and Business Guide*
- *Zappy Explorer (Dubai)* by Explorer Publishing

Clubs & Associations

American Business Council	331 4735
Australia New Zealand Association	394 6508
British Business Group	397 0303
British Community Assistance Fund	337 1413
Canadian Business Council	359 2625
Club for Canadians, The	355 6171
Denmark Business Council	222 7699
Egyptian Club	336 6709
French Business Council	335 2362
German Business Council	359 9930
German Speaking Women's Club	332 5797
Indian Association	351 1082
Italian Cultural Association	050-453 5422
Norwegian Centre	337 0062
South African Business Group	050-653 2469
Swiss Business Council	321 1438

Dirhams - the local currency

Legal Issues

For most people, any sort of brush with the 'wrong' side of the law can be a worrying experience, but in a foreign country and with an alien language, this can be particularly unnerving. If you are in really serious difficulties, you should contact your embassy or consulate as soon as possible and follow their advice, plus find yourself a good lawyer.

The UAE is governed by sharia law - this is Islamic canonical law that is based on the traditions of Prophet Mohammed (PBUH) and the teachings of the Koran - and only a graduate of a sharia college can practice in court here. All court proceedings are conducted in Arabic, so you will find it important to hire legal representation that you trust.

Legal Consultants

Afridi & Angell	331 0900
Al Tamimi & Company	331 7090
Berrymans Lace Mawer	359 9939
Clifford Chance	331 4333
Clyde & Company	331 1102
Denton Wilde Sapte	331 0220
James Berry & Associates	351 1020
Stockwell & Associates	228 3194
Towry Law Group	335 3137
Trench & Associates	355 3146
Trowers & Hamlins	351 9201

HOUSING

Housing in Dubai

On the Dubai property market, rental was the name of the game till summer 2002, when freehold property ownership for non-Nationals was finally announced. Most developments offering land ownership are due to be complete at the end of 2003 at the earliest, so for most, rental is still the only option available.

New residents arriving in Dubai on a full expat package may have accommodation included - but don't be fooled by the charm of the expat lifestyle; life here can be very expensive.

Search Tips

A Des. Res.?

Check proximity of potential homes to churchbells, mosques, rubbish bins, schools, and the airport flight path.

New Buildings

Look out for buildings under construction - it's often a good way to find a place you like and be one of the first on the waiting list. The guys on site should be able to give you the name of the real estate agent or landlord.

Noise Control...

In the less built up areas beware that the area around your new home could be ripe for development - few people really appreciate a noisy building site just a few metres from their bedroom window! Construction work starts at about 6am and finishes by 9 or 10pm, with the odd 1am concrete pour, often seven days a week.

Real Estate Glossary

It is generally best to rent from a real estate agent, as they will handle all the paperwork for you. It's worth nothing that single women occasionally have difficulty renting apartments and may need to put their employer's name on the lease.

Abbreviations

BR	Bedroom
Ensuite	Bedroom has private bathroom
Fully fitted kitchen	Includes appliances (oven, refrigerator, washing machine)
L/D	Living/dining room area
W/robes	Built-in wardrobes (closets)
Hall flat	Apartment has an entrance hall (ie. entrance doesn't open directly onto living room)
D/S	Double storey villa
S/S	Single storey villa
C.A/C	Central air-conditioning (usually included in the rent)
W.A/C	Window air-conditioning (often indicates an older building)
S/Q	Servant quarters
ext S/Q	Servant quarters located outside the villa
Pvt garden	Private garden
Shared pool	Pool is shared with other villas in compound

Better Homes...

elping you make better choices

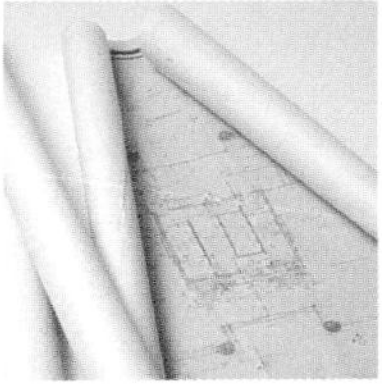

apartments

consultancy

interior decoration

retail

international

showrooms

maintenance

villas

offices

warehouses

property management

Purchasing a Home

While in the past, only GCC Nationals could own residential property, options for expatriate land ownership are on the increase in Dubai. Summer 2002 brought the much-awaited news of freehold property ownership for people of all nationalities. The option of property purchase is yet another method the government is employing in order to encourage foreign investment in the emirate.

With opportunities for long-term visas and mortgages, buyers have been flocking to the various upscale developments, snapping up properties in record times. The Jumeirah Palm Island sold all of its 2,000 villas and townhomes (Dhs.1.7-4.6 million) in just over two weeks, and the Jumeirah Beach Residence sold 3,000 apartments in the first week! The first phase of Emirates Hills (78 villas) sold out in a mere 15 minutes.

Currently, non-GCC nationals are permitted to own land only in certain developments: Emaar Properties' Dubai Marina, Emirates Hills, The Greens, The Meadows, The Lakes and Arabian Ranches, Dubai Palm Developers' two Dubai Palm Islands (Jumeirah and Jebel Ali) and Jumeirah Islands, and Estithmaar's Jumeirah Beach Residence.

For further information on property ownership, contact Dubai Palm Developers (399 1400), Emaar Properties (332 9966), or Estithmaar (399 1114).

Being in its infancy, this area is likely to change radically. Watch the Explorer Website for more information and updates (www.explorer-publishing.com).

Mortgages

Soon after the government announced the granting of freehold status of residential property to foreign nationals, mortgage plans were introduced for investors purchasing property. This is another first in the region and can be seen as an indication of Dubai's seriousness in encouraging foreign investment in real estate. The maximum mortgage granted is Dhs.5 million and financing companies offer up to 90% of the purchase price or valuation to UAE nationals, and up to 80% to GCC and foreign nationals. Mortgages must be paid back in monthly instalments within a maximum of 25 years. The mortgage amount depends on the chosen mortgage plan and is also limited to an amount no greater than 60 times the monthly household (both husband and wife's) income. For more information on mortgages, contact Amlak (800 4337).

New Developments for Purchase			
Development	**Completion**	**Number of Units**	**Unit Cost**
Arabian Ranches	2003	5,500 villas	Not available
Dubai Marina	2003	1,500 apartments	580,000+
Greens, The	2003	600+ apartments	188,888+
Jumeirah Beach Residence	2005	3,000+ apartments	199,000+
Jumeirah Islands	2004	600+ villas	Not available
Meadows, The	2003	147+ villas	999,888+
Palm, Jumeira, The	2005	2,500 townhomes & villas	1,700,000+
Springs, The	2004	1,400 villas	448,888+

Villas on Dubai Palm Island

Renting a Home

The majority of Dubai residents rent their home for the duration of their stay in Dubai. Rents over the past few years have consistently risen, and in general are very high. However, it is expected that accommodation at the higher end of the market (over Dhs.45,000 for apartments and Dhs.100,000 for villas per annum) will drop eventually due to supply exceeding demand and freehold property ownership now being an option for all. Prices at the lower/middle end are expected to remain firm due to heavy demand. Rents are always quoted for the year, unless otherwise stated.

Rent Disputes

The Rent Committee of Dubai Municipality (206 3833) exists to assist both tenants and landlords in rent disputes. Amongst recent cases, the majority of disputes were raised by landlords rather than by tenants, and sadly there were no cases related to extortionate rents. Maybe one day...

Government Apartments and Villas

The Dubai Government owns and manages more than 18,000 residential and commercial properties around Dubai, with rents suitable for all levels of income. Because these properties tend to be very good value for money, many have long wait lists. To find out more or to put your name on a waiting list, contact the Dubai Real Estate Department (398 6666) or look at their Website: www.realestate-dubai.gov.ae.

Dubai Property Group

In 2002, a group of professional real estate companies banded together to work to ensure proper conduct in real estate dealings in Dubai. Examining current real estate industry practices, they make proposals for change that will benefit all concerned. Their goal is to try to make a difference for residents of Dubai, working closely with the Rent Committee and the Government of Dubai (through the Dubai Development Board). (www.dubaipropertygroup.com)

The Lease

To take out a lease personally you need to be a resident. The real estate agent will need a copy of your passport and visa, a no objection letter (NOC) from your company, a copy of your salary certificate and an initial signed rent cheque (plus up to three post-dated cheques covering the remaining period of the lease). Unlike elsewhere in the world, rent cheques have to be paid to the landlord up-front and not on a monthly basis. This can cause problems, as many new residents do not have the cash available to pay this sort of lump sum in advance. Needless to say, banks are quick to offer loans! To rent through your company, you require a copy of the company trade licence, a passport copy of whoever is signing the rent cheque and, of course, the rent cheque/s itself.

Renter's Nightmare!

The majority of leases in Dubai are fixed for one year, and unless you find a really nice landlord who offers you an opt-out clause, you are locked in till the end of the year! Penalty? You might not get your deposit back, and you certainly won't get the remainder of your rent back!

Be careful when you sign your lease as you will have to pay your entire year's rent in either one to three cheques, so make sure the apartment or villa you've just found is really the one you'd like to make your home for the next year!

Main Accommodation Options

1. Apartment/Villa Sharing

For those on a budget, the solution may be to share an apartment or villa with colleagues or friends. Check the noticeboards in supermarkets such as Choithrams, Park N Shop or Spinneys, or sports clubs, for people advertising shared accommodation. Spinneys online at www.Spinneys.com posts details of places to live and people to live with. The classified section in the local newspapers also advertises accommodation.

2. Standard Apartment

There are generally two types of apartments available for rent - those with central air conditioning (A/C) and those with noisier window A/C where the unit is in the apartment wall. Some

Apartments - Annual Rent

B/R	Bur Dubai	Deira
1	33,000 - 45,000	28,000 - 40,000
2	46,000 - 55,000	36,000 - 60,000
3	55,000 - 80,000	44,000 - 80,000
4	70,000 - 110,000	60,000 - 100,000

B/R	Satwa	Sheikh Zayed Rd
1	25,000 - 38,000	40,000 - 46,000
2	40,000 - 70,000	52,000 - 60,000
3	55,000 - 80,000	65,000 - 80,000
4	60,000 - 90,000	75,000 - 120,000

even have central heating too. Central A/C accommodation is always more expensive, although in some buildings the charge for A/C is absorbed into the rent. Top of the range, central A/C apartments often come semi-furnished (cooker, fridge, washing machine), boast 24 hour security, satellite TV, covered parking, gym, pool, etc. Normally, the more facilities that come with the apartment, the more expensive the rent.

3. Villa

The same procedure applies to leasing villas as for apartments. Value for money villas are very hard to find and where you used to be able to find older, cheaper villas in some parts of Jumeira, many are being demolished for redevelopment. As with apartments, villas differ greatly in quality and facilities, such as pool, security, compound, etc.

Villas - Annual Rent	
B/R	**Annual Rent**
2	40,000 - 65,000
3	55,000 - 135,000
4	70,000 - 150,000
5	100,000 - 200,000

4. Hotel Apartment

An alternative option is to rent a hotel apartment - ideal if you require temporary, furnished accommodation, although they are expensive. Apartments can be rented on a daily/weekly/monthly or yearly basis. They come fully furnished (sofas to knives and forks) and serviced (maid service), with satellite TV and are often complemented by sports facilities (pool and gym, etc). Water and electricity are also included in the rent.

Hotel Apartments - Rates			
B/R	**Daily**	**Weekly**	**Monthly**
1	330 - 550	2,300 - 3,080	8,250 - 9,350
2	600 - 800	3,850 - 4,400	11,000 - 12,100
3	770 - 1,050	5,390 - 5,775	13,200 - 14,300

Residential Areas

Other options → Exploring [p.132]

As in all cities, there are obvious areas of desirable residence. The more upmarket areas for villas are Jumeira and Umm Suqeim, with cheaper options in Satwa, Al Garhoud, Mirdif and Rashidiya. The most popular area for apartments tends to be Bur Dubai, behind the Bur Juman shopping mall, and along Sheikh Zayed Road which is lined with modern glass skyscrapers. Cheaper options are in Deira, the old Pakistani Consulate area, Satwa and Karama. However, the odd top of the range building can be found in these cheaper areas, and likewise, the odd bargain can still be found in the more upmarket areas of Jumeira or Umm Suqeim. There's a good mix of nationalities in most places.

A cheaper option is to live in the Gardens near Jebel Ali, or in the nearby emirates of Sharjah or Ajman. Here prices for apartments are generally much cheaper by between ten to twenty thousand dirhams per year, and villas are cheaper still. However, while there are great savings to be made by living in either of these emirates, beware the Sharjah - Dubai highway - renowned for mammoth delays around rush hour. And now beware the new Sharjah Decency Law. If your work or social life is based in Dubai, you could find that living here saves your sanity!

A glance through the property pages in the newspapers will give you an idea of what is available where, and for how much. Check out the following areas, plus the maps at the end of the book to get a feel for the layout of Dubai. Also have a look at the Exploring section [p.132] for further helpful descriptions of the various areas within Dubai.

Al Garhoud   Map ref → 14-D4

- Centrally located
- A fairly quiet, residential part of town. However, close to the airport; depending on the direction of the wind, aircraft noise can be heard
- Villas with less expensive rents than other central areas; very few apartments
- Mix of nationalities - mainly Nationals, Arab and Western expats.

Al Mina Al Seyahi (Al Sufouh)   Map ref → 2-D1

- Prime property (once it's built!): Dubai Marina, Palm Island and the various Emaar developments (The Lakes, The Meadows, The Greens, Arabian Ranches etc) should be stunning
- Being hailed as Dubai's new downtown (not there yet though)
- Beautiful beaches nearby
- Mainly upmarket villas; very high rents, but your neighbours are five-star hotels and royalty!

Al Qusais   Map ref → 15-D2

- Characterless area located on the border of Dubai and Sharjah

- Some of the lowest rents in town, but noise can be overwhelming and the commute into Dubai similar to that from Sharjah
- Mainly Asian residents in four storey blocks.

Bur Dubai (two main residential areas)

1. Creek   Map ref ➜ 8-A2

- Lots of hustle and bustle
- Area has character, but limited parking
- Apartments with low rents; low income district
- Mainly Asian residents; 95% of people on the streets are male.

2. Golden Sands (Mankhoul)   Map ref ➜ 7-E4

- Great name, but it's really just a concrete jungle with no green spaces and plots of sand between apartment buildings up to eight storeys high
- Apartments with high rents, yet it's still a popular area
- Limited access to the area results in traffic congestion at certain times of day
- Good mix of nationalities; great if you're female (any age) and like being chatted up on the street by guys in cars.

Golden Sands apartments

Deira   Map ref ➜ 8-E2

- One of Dubai's older districts, now mostly a concrete jungle with little neighbourhood feel
- Terrible traffic problems all day
- Lower rent apartment blocks. However, alongside the Creek some upmarket apartment buildings catering to higher income expats (Twin Towers, etc)

- Mostly Arab expats and Asian residents.

Jebel Ali Village/Gardens   Map ref ➜ 2-A3

- Pleasant atmosphere amongst the older villas as there are trees; however, new villas are concrete and brick compounds with virtually no green spaces
- Bit of a commute, unless you work at Jebel Ali or Dubai Media or Internet Cities
- Mix of bungalows and villas; rents are reasonable to expensive for new villas, and very reasonable for older villas
- Popular with oil company expats, many Westerners
- 'The Gardens' is a new community of 3,800 apartments plus villas with the main attraction being the low rents. We're hoping this will spark a much needed rent reduction all-around in Dubai!

Jumeira   Map ref ➜ 5-D2

- Wide, quiet and leafy streets; close to the beach
- Mainly large, walled villas with established gardens; high rents
- A suburban feel; many Nationals, Arab and Western expats.

Jumeira modern villas

Karama   Map ref ➜ 10-D2

- Convenient central location, but little green space; more of a concrete jungle again
- 'Calvin Karama' - the nearby souk sells just about everything
- Mostly four storey apartments with mostly inexpensive rents
- Predominantly Asian community feel.

Mirdif   Map ref → 16-B4

- Up and coming area of Dubai, but no local supermarkets or shops and located a ways out of town
- Under the airport flight path - beware!
- Costa del Sol feel with single villas and villa compounds; much cheaper rents than other areas
- Residents are mainly Nationals, Arab and Western expats; lots of families, many with children.

Oud Metha   Map ref → 13-E1

- Another up and coming, centrally located area
- A fair amount of construction ongoing, but rents are better value for money than other areas
- Convenient access, one of Dubai's largest malls and lots of restaurants nearby
- 4 storey apartment buildings with mostly Arab and Western expats.

Satwa   Map ref → 6-D3

- Older, established and atmospheric part of town; located between trendy Sheikh Zayed Road and prestigious Jumeira
- Mix of housing and rents, plus some great inexpensive villas
- Mix of nationalities; possibly not the best place for a single female to live.

Real Estate Agents	
Alpha Properties	228 8588
Arenco Real Estate	337 2402
Asteco	269 3155
Better Homes	344 7714
Cluttons	334 8585
Property Shop, The	345 5711
Real Estate Specialists, The	331 2662
Rocky Real Estate	353 2000
Union Properties	294 9490

Sheikh Zayed Road   Map ref → 9-C2

- No community feel - mostly office workers in the vicinity
- Extremely noisy, although apartments facing away from the road are slightly quieter
- Residential apartments in skyscrapers; very high rents
- Trendy location with a good mix of nationalities and sexes.

Umm Sequim   Map ref → 4-C2

- Quiet suburban feel
- Great established compounds; mix of old and new, with lots of individual villas. Lower rents than Jumeira, but higher than Mirdif
- Mix of nationalities, but mostly Nationals and Western expats.

Real Estate Websites	
Al Futtaim Real Estate	www.afrealestate.com
Alpha Properties	www.alphaproperties.com
Arenco	www.arencore.com
Asteco	www.astecoproperty.com
Better Homes	www.bhomes.com
Cluttons	www.cluttons.com
Dubai Gov't real estate	www.realestate-dubai.gov.ae
Dubai Property Group	www.dubaipropertygroup.com
Real estate in Dubai	www.ikaar.com
Sherwoods	www.sherwoodsproperty.com
Union Properties	www.unionproperties.com

Other Rental Costs

Extra costs to be considered are:

- Water and electricity deposit (Dhs.2,000 for villas, Dhs.1,000 for apartments) paid directly to Dubai Electricity & Water Authority (DEWA) and fully refundable on cancellation of lease
- Real estate commission 5% of annual rent (one-off payment)
- Maintenance charge 5% of annual rent
- Municipality tax 5% of annual rent
- Fully refundable security deposit (Dhs.2,000 - 5,000)
- Some landlords also require a deposit against damage (usually a fully refundable, one-off payment).

If you are renting a villa, don't forget that you may have to maintain a garden and pay for extra water, etc. To avoid massive water bills at the end of every month, many people prefer to have a well dug in their backyard for all that necessary plant and grass watering. Expect to pay around Dhs.1,500 - 3,000 to have a well dug and a pump installed.

Some of the older villas may also need additional maintenance, which the landlord may not cover. Often the more popular accommodation has waiting lists that are years long. To secure an immediate tenancy many people offer the landlord 'key-money', a down payment of several thousand dirhams to secure the accommodation.

Moving Services

Two main options exist when moving your furniture and personal effects either to or from Dubai: air freight and sea freight. Air freight is a better option when moving smaller amounts, but if you have a larger consignment, sea freight is the way to go. Either way, ensure your goods are packed by professionals.

Unless you send your personal belongings with the airline you are flying with, you will need to use the services of a removal company. A company with a wide international network is usually the best and safest option, but more importantly, you must trust the people you are dealing with. Ensure they are competent in the country of origin and have reliable agents in the country to which you are shipping your personal belongings. Most removal companies offer free consultations, plus advice and samples of packing materials - call around.

Moving Tips:

- Book moving dates well in advance
- Don't forget insurance and purchase additional insurance for irreplaceable items
- Make an inventory of the items you want moved (keep your own copy!)
- Ensure everything is packed extremely well and in a way that can be checked by customs and repacked with the least possible damage; check and sign the packing list
- Keep a camera and film handy to take pictures at each stage of the move (valuable in case of a dispute)
- Do not pack restricted goods of any kind
- If moving to Dubai, ensure videos, DVD's and books are not offensive to Muslim sensibilities

When your belongings arrive in Dubai, you will be called to Customs to be present while the authorities open your boxes to ensure nothing illegal or inappropriate is brought into the country. Assisting in this process can be exhausting; the search may take place outdoors over a few hours, with your belongings thrown on the floor. After this, depending on the agreement you have with the removal company, either their representative in Dubai will help you transport the boxes to your new home, or you can make the arrangements locally.

Relocation Experts

Relocation experts offer a range of services to help you settle into your new life in Dubai as quickly as possible. Practical help ranges from finding accommodation or schools for your children to connecting a telephone or information on medical care. In addition, they will often offer advice on the way of life in the city, putting people in touch with the social networks to help them establish a new life.

Moving Services	
Relocation Companies	
In Touch Consultants	332 8807
The Real Estate Specialists	331 2662
Elite Lifestyle Services	304 7118
Global Relocations	352 3300
Removal Companies	
Allied Pickfords	338 3600
Crown Worldwide Movers	289 5152
Gulf Agency Company (GAC)	345 7555

Furnishing Accommodation

Other options → Furniture & Household Items [p.196]
Second-hand Items [p.205]

Good quality furniture and household items can be found at reasonable prices here. The most popular furniture outlets in Dubai are Habitat, ID Design, IKEA, Marlin, THE One, and Home Centre and Pan Emirates (both located in Dubai and Sharjah). Other favourites for Indian teak and wrought iron are Khans (06 562 1621), Pinkies and Luckys (06 534 1937) in Sharjah, and Indian Village in Dubai.

For cheap second-hand furniture visit Karama. You can often buy furniture from the previous tenant, through 'garage' sales or small ads in the newspapers, or from supermarket noticeboards. Karama also has plenty of shops selling inexpensive, basic furniture, pots, pans and ironing boards, etc.

Household items

WE HANDLE WITH CARE

At GAC Removals we make sure that every move is wrapped with the utmost care and professionalism. So whether you're moving your home, around

the block or around the world, make sure you make the right move, with GAC Removals.

 Gulf Agency Company

Gulf Agency Company (Dubai) LLC P.O. Box 2404, Dubai, U.A.E. Telephone +971 4 3457555 Fax +971 4 3457202

Garage Sales

If you're leaving the Emirates and have some items that you don't want to ship back home, hold a garage sale. It's a great way to earn some cash while getting rid of all the junk that you couldn't fob off on friends! Ask your neighbours if they have some unwanted treasures to dispose of, and then advertise the sale on local supermarket noticeboards and place ads in the daily newspapers classifieds section. If permitted, post some easy to follow direction signs with arrows in prominent locations. Clearly mark the goods with prices, then on the day have plenty of plastic bags, old newspapers for wrapping glass items and loads of change... then simply be prepared to haggle hard!

If you're on your way to becoming a full-fledged resident of Dubai and would like to check out the various garage sales around town, have a look at the above listed locations... happy shopping!

Household Appliances

Carrefour, Jashanmal, Jumbo Electronics and Plug Ins have decent selections of heavy household appliances. Make sure that your purchases come with a warranty! All the main brands are found in the UAE, but the fittings are made for the European market, and thus North American makes can be harder to find.

Prices are quite reasonable for new appliances, but if you would prefer to buy second-hand, have a look at the noticeboards at the various supermarkets around town. Of course, there is no guarantee with second-hand goods, so beware!

Household Insurance

No matter where you live in the world and how 'safe' a place appears to be, it's always wise to insure the contents of your home. There are many internationally recognised insurance companies operating in Dubai - check the Yellow Pages, or Hawk Business Pages for details.

General information insurance companies need when forming your policy is your home address in Dubai, a household contents list and valuation, and invoices for items over Dhs.2,500. Cover usually extends to theft, storm damage, fire, etc. For an additional fee you can insure personal items outside the home, such as jewellery, cameras, etc.

Laundry Services

Whilst there are no self-service launderettes in Dubai, there are hundreds of small outlets, plus larger supermarkets and some hotels, offering laundry and dry-cleaning services at reasonable rates and next day delivery. You can also take clothes for ironing only, at approximately Dhs.1 per item. It's always a good idea to speak to the laundry man himself if you have a preference on how you want an item ironed (or if you would like to avoid the 'shiny' look!).

Domestic Help

Other options ➔ Entry Visa [p.58]

Although you may never have considered hiring a domestic helper before, many people in Dubai do, as the service is comparatively cheap and easy to arrange. For the busy or the lazy, it means the house is spotless and shirts are always pressed.

To employ the services of a full-time live in domestic helper, you must have a minimum monthly salary of Dhs.6,000. The helper cannot be related to you, nor of the same nationality as you. As the employer, you must sponsor the person and deal with all residency papers, including the medical test, etc. Singles and families in which the wife isn't working may face difficulties sponsoring a helper. It's normally best to find someone through an agency dedicated to hiring domestic helpers. You will be asked to sign a contract stating that you will pay your employee a minimum salary of about Dhs.750 each month with an airfare home once a year. There may also be a small fee if you are hiring via an agency.

The residence visa for a maid will cost around Dhs.5,000 (Dhs.4,800 for the government fee, Dhs.100 for the residence visa and Dhs.100 for the labour card). Residency is only valid for one year. You can obtain a residence visa card through the normal channels, after which some embassies (eg, the Philippines) require to see the labour contract of your newly appointed maid. This is to ensure that all paperwork is in order and that the maid is receiving fair treatment. It is illegal to share a maid with another household.

An alternative and cheaper option is to have part-time home help and there are a number of agencies that offer domestic help on an hourly basis. The standard rate is about Dhs.20 - 25 per hour, with a minimum of two hours per visit. The number of hours required will obviously depend on the size of your accommodation and the level of mess. The service includes general cleaning, washing, ironing and sometimes babysitting.

Domestic Help Agencies

Domestic Help Agencies	
Helpers	395 6166
Home Help	355 5100
Maids to Order	393 0608
Molly Maid	398 8877
Ready Maids	272 7483

Pets

Bringing Your Pet Here

There are currently no restrictions on bringing pets with you to Dubai. However, to do so, you will first require an import permit from the Ministry of Agriculture and Fisheries (295 8161). The permit normally takes about a week to process.

You will need the following documents:

• Copy of your pet's vaccination certificate

• Copy of a government health certificate from your country of origin (not from a private vet)

• Copy of your passport.

Dubai Kennels & Cattery (285 1646), The Doghouse (347 1807) or the Ajman Pet Resort (06 743 1629) can help you obtain an import permit, customs clearance and collection from the airport, delivery and/or boarding of your pet, if required. If you choose not to use their services, either your local vet or the airline you are travelling with should be able to advise you of the necessary requirements. There is no quarantine for pets brought into the UAE.

Pet Services

Pet Services		
Ajman Pet Resort	06 743 1629	Grooming, boarding
Dogsbody	349 9879	Grooming
Dubai Kennels & Cattery	285 1646	Boarding kennels
Pets At Home	331 2186	Pet sitting
The Doghouse	347 1807	Grooming, boarding

Taking Your Pet Home

The regulations for 'exporting' your pet depend on the laws of the country to which you are moving. Basic requirements are:

• A valid vaccination card, not older than 1 year, but not less than 30 days.

• A health certificate issued by the Municipality or the Ministry of Agriculture and Fisheries, normally issued one week before departure.

• A travel box, normally wooden or fibreglass, that meets airline regulations.

Your local vet, kennels or the airline that you are travelling with can inform you of the specific regulations pertaining to your destination, such as quarantine rules, etc.

Cats & Dogs

Your pet must be vaccinated regularly and wear the Municipality ID disc (supplied on vaccination) on its collar at all times. The Municipality controls Dubai's huge stray population by trapping and euthanasing animals. If your pet is trapped without an ID disc, it will be treated as a stray.

All pets should also be sterilised and kept safely on your premises. Once sterilised, they will wander less and will therefore be less exposed to the dangers of traffic and disease. If you feed the stray population around your home, you will simply create a problem for yourselves and your neighbours with a burgeoning stray population. To do something proactive to help, or if you see an injured cat and need assistance, contact Feline Friends (050 451 0058). For help with stray or injured dogs, call K9 Friends (347 4611).

Veterinary Clinics

Veterinary Clinics	
Ajman Pet Resort	06 7431629
Dr Matt's Clinic	349 9549
Elite Veterinary Clinic	339 1137
European Veterinary Clinic	343 9591
Jumeirah Veterinary Clinic	394 2276
Modern Veterinary Clinic	395 3131
Veterinary Hospital	344 2498

Pet Shops

Though regulations governing the sale of animals in pet shops exist, they are rarely actively enforced. Animals are often underage (although their papers state differently), sometimes sick or even pregnant, and the conditions in which they are kept leave a lot to be desired. Rather than encouraging this trade, you would do better to give a home to one of the many stray animals in Dubai. Contact Feline Friends or K9 Friends to see who needs a home.

Animal Souks

It is a shame that animal souks still operate and thrive here. There is a large animal souk in Sharjah

New Residents

Housing

which is not to be visited by the faint-hearted. One of a number dotted around the country, it supplies falcons, eagles, exotic parrots, primates ... the list goes on, with a promise of "if you want it, we'll get it for you".

The CITES protected list is disregarded in these souks. Animals are kept in cramped, overcrowded cages, and are often diseased. For a place that sells itself as a clean, regulated tourist destination, little seems to be done to curb what appears to be a sickeningly successful trade.

Help!

If you see a cat or dog which is stray, injured or in distress, then please try to get it to the nearest vet (see table [p.87]). Most have 24hr mobiles or pagers. If you need further assistance, call either Feline or K9 Friends... but remember that they are both run by volunteers and would very much appreciate if others would also be "animal responsible" and help out. Call Feline (050 451 0058) or K9 (347 4611) if you'd like to offer time, assistance or support.

UTILITIES & SERVICES

Electricity & Water

These utilities, along with sewerage, are provided by Dubai Electricity & Water Authority (commonly known as DEWA). The authority provides an excellent service, with extremely rare electricity or water shortages/stoppages.

When you sign up, you will have to pay a water and electricity deposit (Dhs.2,000 for villas; Dhs.1,000 for apartments) directly to DEWA. This is fully refundable on cancellation of your lease.

Monthly bills can be paid at any DEWA office, through various banks, or even on the Internet. Those offering this service are listed on the reverse of the bill. Bills are assessed one month and the meter read the next month.

Main office: next to Wafi Shopping Mall, Bur Dubai (324 4444, Map ref. 13-D1).

Opening hours: Saturday - Wednesday 07:30 - 21:00 bill payments and 07:30 - 14:30 enquiries. Thursday 07:30 - 21:00 bill payments only, and telephone enquiries 08:30 - 14:00.

Electricity

There's plenty of it! The electricity supply in Dubai is 220/240 volts and 50 cycles. Socket type is identical to the three point British system. Adaptors can be purchased at any grocery or hardware store.

Water

More expensive than oil! The tap water is safe to drink, but not always pleasant, and visitors generally prefer the locally bottled mineral water, which is widely available. Bottled water is usually served in hotels and restaurants.

Buying 20 litre water bottles, rather than small 1½ litre bottles, is more environmentally friendly and can make a considerable cost saving for drinking

Water Suppliers	
Culligan	800 4945
Desert Springs	800 6650
Oasis Water	800 5656

water. The bottle deposit is usually Dhs.25 - 35, and refills Dhs.5 - 7. These large bottles can be used with a variety of methods for decanting the water. Choices include a hand pump, available from supermarkets and costing about Dhs.3. A fixed pump can be bought for about Dhs.60, or a variety of refrigeration units are also available. Prices vary depending on the model, but on average are about Dhs.400. Water suppliers will deliver to your door, saving you some backache.

One of the slightly crazy aspects of life in the Emirates is that during the summer months, if your water tank is on the roof, you won't need to heat water, since it's already hot when it comes out of the cold tap! Indeed the only way to have a cold(ish) shower is to keep the immersion heater off and to use the hot tap.

Gas

Gas mains don't exist in Dubai, but there is the option of buying individual gas canisters for cooking if required. These can be connected to a gas oven and generally cost about Dhs.230 per new canister and Dhs.28-50 for a refill. There are numerous companies around town supplying gas canisters.

Gas Suppliers	
New City Gas Distributors	351 8282
Oasis Gas Suppliers	396 1812
Salam Gas	344 8823
Union Gas Co	266 1479

Telephone

Emirates Telecommunications Corporation (known as Etisalat) is the sole telecommunications provider in the Emirates - Dubai headquarters are in the groovy glass building near the Creek with a large ball on the top. They are responsible for telephones, both landlines and mobiles, and the Internet (through its sister company Emirates Internet & Multimedia).

Etisalat is generally an efficient and innovative company, continuously introducing new services and even cutting bills to the consumer from time to time. You should have few problems in processing paperwork, receiving services or rectifying problems. Recent public mutterings about whether it is healthy for Etisalat to maintain its monopoly position don't seem to be getting any sort of official response.

Opening hours: Saturday - Wednesday 07:00 - 13:00, and 15:00 - 17:00 (bill payments only); Thursday 08:00 -13:00 (bill payments only). The main office in Deira, opposite the Sheraton Hotel & Towers is open the same Saturday - Wednesday timings, but 24 hours for bill payments and pre-paid SIM cards. Jebel Ali Free Zone office: Saturday - Thursday 09:00 - 17:00.

Landline Phones

To install a regular landline phone connection in your home, you need to apply directly to Etisalat with the following: Etisalat application form in English (handwritten is acceptable), copy of passport and residence visa, NOC from your employer, Dhs.250, and a copy of your tenancy agreement.

Once you have submitted the application, it takes between 2 - 3 days until a phone connection is installed. Even if you have your own phone handset, Etisalat will provide one, and it's usually bright pink, green or blue. If you require additional phone sockets, order them at the same time, and pay a further Dhs.50 for the first socket and then Dhs.15 per socket thereafter. The procedure is usually extremely efficient and streamlined.

Etisalat offers many additional services, such as call waiting, call forwarding, a 'follow me' service - for more information contact you nearest Etisalat branch, check the Etisalat home page (www.etisalat.co.ae) or have a look at the *Zappy Explorer (Dubai)*.

Quarterly rental: standard landline (for all sockets) - Dhs.45. All calls made locally within Dubai on and to a landline are free. For international and mobile rates, check the phone book.

Discount long distance rates: standard landline: all day Friday and government-declared national public holidays. Weekdays (outside GCC): 21:00 - 07:00; Weekdays (GCC only): 19:00 - 07:00.

Mobile Phones

Most people in Dubai seem to own a mobile phone, if not two! Etisalat puts the number of GSM subscribers in the UAE at well over 1.7 million. Mobiles can be purchased from Etisalat, specialised telecommunications shops, most electronics shops and large supermarkets, such as Carrefour.

Etisalat GSM assistance telephone service - dial 101 for enquiries.

Missing Mobile

If you lose your mobile or have it stolen, call 101 to disconnect your number temporarily. You might need to know your passport number for security.

Non-resident

(ie, visa not fully processed/visit visa)

If your visa is not fully processed, or if you are visiting the country and want to use your mobile, currently your only option is Wasel GSM service.

This is a popular variation of GSM service, available to both non-residents and residents, allowing you to decide on the amount of outgoing calls that can be made on your phone, but allowing unlimited incoming calls. For residents, this includes while you are abroad (you will be charged the international rate).

The subscription is for one year and payment for outgoing calls needs to be made in advance. The cost is Dhs.185 for one year's subscription and you can apply at any branch office. The annual renewal charge is Dhs.100. Fill out the application form and you will also need your Essential Documents, although, as mentioned, you do not need to be a resident to avail of this service. The service includes connection, one year's rental, SIM card charges and Dhs.10 free credit. You may 'recharge' your card for outgoing calls in Dhs.10 units. The minimum amount that you can recharge your card at an Etisalat machine is Dhs.50.

Resident

If you are a resident of Dubai applying for a mobile phone connection, collect an application form from any Etisalat office. Submit the application to any Etisalat branch office, along with your passport and residence visa copy and Dhs.215. This amount includes rental for the first quarter. You should receive your SIM card there and then and once you have it installed, you're ready to dial. An alternative to the standard mobile phone agreement is to apply for the Wasel GSM service (see above).

Rental charges: quarterly rental charge for the standard mobile phone service - Dhs.90.

Local rates: peak rate - 30 fils per minute (06:00 - 14:00 & 16:00 - 24:00); off-peak rate - 21 fils per minute.

International discount rates: all day Friday and government-declared national public holidays. Weekdays (outside GCC): 21:00 - 07:00; weekdays (GCC only): 19:00 - 07:00.

Internet

Other options → Internet Cafes [p.388]
Websites [p.44]

For connection to cyberspace, Etisalat's sister company, Emirates Internet & Multimedia (EIM) is the sole provider of Internet services through its UAE proxy server. With the proxy server in place, some sites are restricted (if you find a blocked site that you believe is perfectly reasonable, you can report it to Etisalat on help@emirates.net.ae).

You can access Emirates Internet from any standard telephone line using an appropriate modem at speeds in excess of 56 Kbps. If you require higher speed access, you can apply for an ISDN line (64 Kbps) or an ADSL line (128 Kbps); for more information contact Etisalat (800 6100).

Numerous Internet sites about the Emirates exist, check out the Website listing [p.44].

To get yourself connected, you will require a landline in your name or your company's name, a copy of your passport and residence visa, and the Internet application form from Etisalat.

Registration charge: Dhs.100 for dial-up or ISDN; Dhs.200 for ADSL (plus optional software installation by Etisalat technician Dhs.100).

Rental: standard Internet connection Dhs.20 per month; ISDN line Dhs.60 quarterly; ADSL line Dhs.250 per month.

User charge: for the standard and ISDN connection, there is an additional user charge: peak rate - Dhs.1.8 per hour (06:00 - 01:00); off-peak - Dhs.1 per hour. With an ADSL line, you are logged on 24 hours a day and pay no further charges.

Dial 'n' Surf

This facility allows you to surf without subscribing to Internet service. All that's needed is a computer with a modem and a regular phone (or ISDN) line - no account number or password is required. In theory you then simply dial 500 5555 to gain access. However, in practice it may not be quite so straightforward, since there are different set ups depending on your software. If you have difficulties, contact the helpdesk (800 5244).

Charges: a charge of 15 fils per minute is made for the connection and billed to the telephone line from which the call is made.

Internet Help

abuse@emirates.net.ae for reporting on hacking, illegal use of Internet, spamming etc.

watch@emirates.net.ae for reporting inappropriate sites

custserv@emirates.net.ae for comments, billing disputes and general Internet inquiries

help@emirates.net.ae for technical support

www.emirates.net.ae to visit the Etisalat homepage & for Emirates Internet & Multimedia products and services, billing inquiries, online change of passwords, change of ISDN access speed

Tel 800 6100 for Internet Help Desk

Bill Payment

Bills are mailed monthly and are itemised for international and mobile calls, SMS (short message service) and service charges. For all bill payments it's possible to pay at Etisalat branch offices, on the Internet, as well as at certain banks such as Emirates Bank International and HSBC (details can be obtained through Etisalat). Etisalat also has cash payment machines at several sites around Dubai, saving you the hassle of queuing at Etisalat or the bank; again, details can be obtained from Etisalat. You can also recharge your Wasel service using these machines.

If you don't pay your landline telephone bill within the first ten days of the month, or your GSM bill within 45 days, you will be cut off, although you will still receive incoming calls for up to 15 days afterwards. Before the final disconnection, Etisalat very kindly automatically calls landlines and sends an SMS to mobiles to remind people to pay up.

MEDECINS SANS FRONTIERES

أطبّــاء بـــلا حــدود

nconditional Medical Aid. where needed. when needed.

2002 WINNER OF THE UAE HEALTH FOUNDATION PRIZE

MSF has been counting on you, and millions have been counting on MSF. Your continuous support has helped relieve pain and suffering of thousands of people around the world.

YOUR DONATIONS are actually supplying medicine, aiding war casualties, administrating vaccinations, providing prenatal care, fighting epidemics, and improving water and sanitation practices and facilities.

YOUR DONATIONS help MSF be an aid against, and a witness to all that endanger humanity, where needed and when needed.

PLEASE DONATE. Help us help them.

YOUR DONATION WILL MAKE A DIFFERENCE

OR DONATION OR TO RECEIVE A FREE COPY OF MSF QUARTERLY NEWSLETTER "EMBRACE",
PLEASE SEND YOUR NAME AND ADDRESS TO: MEDECINS SANS FRONTIERES, POBOX: 47226 ABU DHABI, UAE
OR CONTACT OUR OFFICES: ABU DHABI - Tel: 02 631 7645 • Fax: 02 621 5059, DUBAI - Tel: 04 345 8177 • Fax: 04 345 6754

Bill Enquiry Service

Etisalat provides a useful bill enquiry service, enabling customers to obtain the current amount payable on their phone/s up to the end of the last month. The aim is to help customers budget their calls and to facilitate prompt settlement of bills, leading to fewer disconnections.

The information is only available for the phone that the call is made from (in theory) and the cost of the call inquiry is charged at the normal rate. To use the service, dial 142 (English) or 143 (Arabic). You may also use Etisalat cash payment machines for this service, and Etisalat's 'online billing service', to pay Internet bills.

Postal Services

Other options → Post & Courier Services [p.42]

There is no house address based mailing system in the UAE - all mail is delivered to the Central Post Office and then distributed to centrally located post office boxes. While many residents direct mail to a company mailbox, it's also possible to rent a personal PO Box. To apply for one, you require an application form from the Central Post Office and Dhs.160. You can then select a PO Box at a convenient location near to your home (if one is available).

Emirates Postal Service (Empost) will send you notification by email when you receive registered mail or parcels in your PO Box. There is no charge for this service, but you do have to register your email address and details with Empost. They will tell you the origin, arrival date, type of mail and its location, and for Dhs.9, you can have your parcel or registered mail delivered to your door - all you have to do is provide your address in the attached file in your return email.

Location: Central Post Office (337 1500), Za'abeel Road, Karama (Map ref. 10-E2).

Opening hours: Saturday - Wednesday 08:00 - 24:00; Thursday 08:00 - 22:00.

Television

UAE television is divided amongst the emirates with Dubai, Abu Dhabi, Sharjah and Ajman all broadcasting terrestrially and via satellite. Dubai has four channels; Dubai 2, 10 and 41 show Arabic programmes, whilst Dubai 33 broadcasts mainly in English. It offers a mixture of serials, documentaries and films (chiefly American, British and Australian), as well as films from 'Bollywood'. Programme details are published daily in the local press.

Emirates Dubai Television broadcasts by satellite throughout the world in Arabic and English. Abu Dhabi has an English language channel, while Sharjah and Ajman TV transmit mainly Arabic programmes, with some in English.

There are numerous video/DVD rental stores around the cities and the latest releases from Hollywood and Bollywood are widely available, usually in English or Hindi and with Arabic subtitles. Anything that offends the country's moral code is censored - be prepared for some interesting continuity!

The UAE's cable TV network, Emirates Cable TV & Multimedia (E-Vision), is a subsidiary of Etisalat. Subscription currently includes approximately 70 Arabic, Asian and Western channels, though this will rise to 100 channels in the future. The basic subscription fee is Dhs.50 and for an extra charge, you can add pay satellite channels. For further information, contact 800 5500, or log on to www.emiratescatv.co.ae.

Satellite TV

The digital in-home entertainment revolution is sweeping through the Middle East - and Dubai is its epicentre judging by the number of satellite dishes in the city! Satellite TV offers viewers an enormous number of programmes and channels to watch and there is a confusing choice of options available. Most leading hotels offer satellite in their rooms, showing news, sports, movies, documentaries, cartoons, etc.

Considering the diversity of people watching, it's not surprising that programmes of all hues, flavours and tastes are available. Couch potatoes first have to decide what types of programme they want to watch and then whether they are willing to pay for them.

Satellite Main Dealers

Al Gurg	351 2173
Arabtec SIS	286 8002
Bond Communications	800 5400
Eurostar	225 5777
E-Vision	800 5500
Global Direct	339 5585
Orbit Direct	800 4442
Plug Ins	295 0404
SatLink - Showtime	336 5055
Showtime Direct	808 8888

The various channels available can be split into two types:

1. Pay TV Satellite Channels

These are channels that require payment for installation and equipment such as the decoder, dish, etc, followed by a viewing subscription for the channels you choose to watch. Generally, subscriptions can be paid monthly, quarterly or annually. Take your time making the right choice because the Middle East has a competitive pay TV market, with four pay TV networks all offering a range of channels.

2. Free to Air Satellite Channels

These are channels that require payment for the installation and reception equipment, but there is no viewing subscription. There are more than 200 of these types of channels.

Equipment

Equipment can be bought from various locations; directly from the main dealers, electrical shops, second-hand shops or classified ads. The majority of dealers offer installation. For apartment blocks or buildings with a large number of viewing points, a central system is recommended, making it economical as well as offering more choice. Persuade your landlord to install the system if the block does not already come with satellite receiving equipment.

HEALTH

General Medical Care

The quality of medical care in the Emirates is generally regarded as quite high and visitors should have little trouble in obtaining appropriate treatment if they need it, whether privately or from the government-run hospitals in an emergency. Tourists and non-residents are strongly recommended to arrange private medical insurance before travelling since private medical care can become very expensive.

Expatriates are permitted to bring up to three months' supply of medicine (for personal use only) to Dubai. Special permission granting six months' supply of medicine is granted if you have a doctor's prescription stating it is a necessity. Beware

though, if you bring illegal medicine into Dubai, you risk having it confiscated; check with the authorities first!

Hospitals/Clinics	
Hospitals	
Al Amal Hospital	344 4010
Al Baraha Hospital Emergency	271 0000
Al Maktoum Hospital	222 1211
Al Wasl Hospital Emergency	324 1111
American Hospital Emergency	336 7777
Belhoul Intern Hospital Centre	345 4000
Dubai Hospital Emergency	271 4444
International Private Hospital Emergency	221 2484
Iranian Hospital Emergency	344 0250
Rashid Hospital Emergency	337 4000
Welcare Hospital Emergency	282 7788
Private Centres/Clinics	
Al Borj Medical Centre Emergency	345 4666
Al Zahra Private Medical Centre	331 5000
Allied Diagnostic Centre	332 8111
Dr Akel's General Medical Clinic Emergency	344 2773
Dubai London Clinic Emergency	344 6663
Dubai Physiotherapy Clinic	349 6333
General Medical Centre	349 5959
Healthcare Medical Centre	344 5550
Jebel Ali Medical Centre Emergency	881 4000
Manchester Clinic	344 0300
New Medical Centre Emergency	268 3131
Emergency Denotes 24 hour Emergency Service	

There are no specific health risks facing visitors, although the climate can be harsh, especially during the summer months. It's advisable to drink plenty of water (and to replace lost salts with energy drinks or salty snacks), and to cover up when out in the sun and use the appropriate factor sunscreen - sunburn, heat-stroke and heat exhaustion can be very unpleasant.

UAE nationals and expatriate residents are allowed healthcare for a minimal cost at the government hospitals and clinics. In Dubai, the Department of Health and Medical Services runs New Dubai, Rashid, Al Baraha, Maktoum and Al Wasl hospitals.

Diagnostics	
Al Zahra Private Medical Centre	331 5000
Allied Diagnostic Centre	332 8111
American Hospital Dubai	336 7777
Dr. Leila Soudah Clinic	395 5591
Medic Polyclinic	355 4111
Medical Imaging Department	309 6642
Welcare Hospital	282 7788

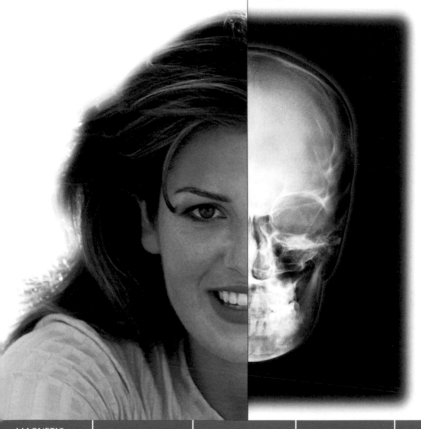

More than skin deep

The Edge

MAGNETIC RESONANCE IMAGING (MRI)	X-RAY	COMPUTERISED TOMOGRAPHY (CT)	ULTRASOUND	MAMMOGRAPHY

For us, a beautiful image
is one that reflects your
good health.

مـركـز آلايـد للتشــخيـص
Allied Diagnostic Centre

P.O.Box 32442 Dubai, United Arab Emirates
Tel: (971 4) 3328111, Fax: (971 4) 3328222
E-mail: adcdxb@emirates.net.ae

Dubai Hospital is one of the best medical centres in the Middle East, with specialised clinics, while Al Wasl is a specialised maternity and gynaecology hospital. The department also operates a number of outpatient clinics.

There are also various private medical hospitals and clinics. All are required to display a price list in Arabic and English for patients.

Each emirate has at least one pharmacy open 24 hours a day. The location and telephone numbers are listed in the daily newspapers and on the Dubai Police Website: www.dubaipolice.gov.ae. The Municipality has emergency numbers (223 2323 or 266 3188), which also give the name and location of open chemists.

Opening times of pharmacies are 08:30 - 13:30 and 16:30 - 22:30 Saturday - Thursday. On Fridays, times are 16:30 - 22:30, although some pharmacies may open on Friday mornings, 09:00 - 13:00.

Dermatologists

Al Zahra Private Medical Centre	331 5000
Belhoul International Hospital Centre	345 4000
Dr Mohamed Al Zubaidy Clinic	227 7533
Dr Simin Medical Clinic	344 4117
International Private Hospital	221 2484
Jebel Ali Medical Centre	881 4000
Medilink Clinic	344 7711
UltraCare Medical Group	223 0033
Welcare Hospital	282 7788

Maternity

Every expatriate child born in the UAE must be registered at the Ministry of Health within two weeks, and hold a residence visa within four months of birth. Without the correct

Gynaecology & Obstetrics

Al Zahra Private Medical Centre	331 5000
American Hospital Dubai	309 6879
Belhoul International Hospital Centre	345 4000
Dr. Leila Soudah Clinic	395 5591
Dubai London Clinic	344 6663
Elixir Medical Centre	343 4090
Fakih Gynecology & Obstetrics Centre	349 2100
General Medical Centre	349 5959
International Private Hospital	221 2484
Jumeirah Family Clinic	344 8844
Manchester Clinic	344 0300
Medilink Clinic	344 7711
Royal Medical Centre	345 6780
Welcare Hospital	282 7788

documentation, you won't be able to take your baby out of the country. The hospital you deliver at will prepare the birth certificate in Arabic upon receipt of hospital records, photocopies of both parents' passports, the marriage certificate and a fee of Dhs.50. Take the birth certificate for translation into English to the Ministry of Health Department of Preventive Medicine (there's one in every emirate). They will endorse and attest it for a fee of Dhs.10. Once this is done, ensure you register your child at your embassy or consulate (you may also want to arrange for a passport for your baby at this time), then you must apply for a residence visa through the normal UAE channels. Before the birth, it's worth checking the regulations of your country of origin for citizens born overseas.

Ante Natal Care

Al Zahra Private Medical Centre	331 5000
American Hospital Dubai	309 6879
Ballet Centre	344 9776
Belhoul International Hospital Centre	345 4000
Dr. Leila Soudah Clinic	395 5591
Dubai London Clinic	344 6663
Fakih Gynecology & Obstetrics Centre	349 2100
General Medical Centre	349 5959
Jumeirah Family Clinic	344 8844
Manchester Clinic	344 0300
Medilink Clinic	344 7711
Royal Medical Centre	345 6780
Welcare Hospital	282 7788

Post Natal Care

American Hospital	309 6879
Ballet Centre	344 9776
Belhoul International Hospital	345 4000
Dr. Leila Soudah Clinic	395 5591
Essensuals Aromatherapy Centre	344 8776
Fakih Gynecology & Obstetrics Centre	349 2100
General Medical Centre	349 5959
Jumeirah Family Clinic	344 8844
Medilink Clinic	344 7711
Royal Medical Centre	345 6780
Welcare Hospital	282 7788

Dentists/Orthodontists

The standard of dentistry in Dubai is generally very high. Practitioners and specialists of all nationalities offer services on a par with or better than those found 'back home'. Prices, however, match the level of service and most health insurance packages do not cover dentistry, unless

it is emergency treatment as the result of an accident. Word of mouth works particularly well for finding a suitable dentist. Alternatively, phone around to find out what methods and equipment, etc, are used.

Private Dentists/Orthodontists	
Al Zahra Private Medical Centre	331 5000
American Dental Clinic	344 0668
British Dental Clinic	342 1318
Clinic for Orthodontics & Aesthetic Dentistry	330 0220
Clinic for Orthodontists &Aesthetic Emergency	050 775 0216
Dr M S Ahmadi Clinic	344 5550
Dr Michael's Dental Clinic	349 5900
Dr Tim Walters	228 3948
Drs Nicolas & Asp Dental Centre	345 4443
Drs Nicolas & Asp Pager Emergency	91941341
Dubai London Clinic Emergency	344 6663
Jumeira Beach Dental Clinic	349 9433
Swedish Dental Clinic	223 1297
Talass Orthodontic & Dental Centre	349 2220
Emergency Denotes 24 hour Emergency	

Alternative Therapies

The UAE has finally permitted the practice of alternative medicine, including homeopathy, Ayurveda, osteopathy, herbal medicine and traditional Chinese medicine. An office of Complementary & Alternative Medicine has been set up at the Ministry of Health, which examines and grants licences to practitioners of alternative medicine before they are able to legally practise here.

With the granting of licences for alternative therapists, Dubai residents now have a range of healing methods

Massage

to choose from in addition to the more conventional approach to medicine. As always, word of mouth recommendation is the best way of establishing who might offer the most appropriate treatment and approach. The following are some of the treatments offered and the main practitioners in Dubai.

Acupressure/Acupuncture

These are two of the oldest healing methods in the world. Acupressure is a system where manual pressure is applied by the practitioner at specific points along the body's energy lines, whereas acupuncture employs needles to stimulate various points along the body's energy lines. Despite the fact that needles are used, this ancient method of healing can be a pleasant experience and can assist with many ailments.

Community Medical Centre	398 5328
Dubai Physiotherapy Clinic	349 6333
Gulf American Clinic	349 8556
House of Chi/House of Healing	397 4446
Jebel Ali Medical Centre	881 4000

Homeopathy

Homeopathy uses natural remedies to help with both physical and emotional problems. It strengthens the body's defence system, helping eliminate many health issues. Currently, Dr. Ludmila Vassilieva is the only licensed homeopath in Dubai.

• *Dr Sergei Clinic* (228 3234).

Massage Therapy/Reflexology

Reflexology is a science based on the premise that zones and reflex areas in the feet and hands correspond to all parts and systems of the body. Pressure applied to these reflex areas results in stress reduction and improved health. While many salons and spas in Dubai offer massage, and some, reflexology as well, the following focus more on holistic healing. For a listing of spas offering massage, see Activities [p.224].

eSSensuals Aromatherapy Centre	344 8776
House of Chi/House of Healing	397 4446

Back Treatment

Without your back, you're nothing! Luckily treatment is widely available in Dubai, with top notch specialists from all around the world practising here.

New Residents

Health

(Chiropractic/Osteopathy/Craniosacral Therapy/Pilates)

The first two treatments concentrate on manipulating the skeleton in a non-intrusive manner to improve the functioning of the nervous system or blood supply to the body. Chiropractic is based on the manipulative treatment of misalignments in the joints, especially those of the spinal column, while osteopathy involves the manipulation and massage of the skeleton and musculature.

Craniosacral therapy aims to relieve pain and tension by gentle manipulations of the skull to balance the craniosacral rhythm.

Pilates is said to be the safest form of neuromuscular reconditioning and back strengthening available.

Canadian Chiropractic & Nat Health Ctr	342 0900
Chiropractic Speciality Clinics	02 634 5162
Clark Chiropractic Clinic	344 4316
General Medical Centre	349 5959
Gulf American Clinic	349 8556
House of Chi/House of Healing (Pilates)	397 4446
Neuro Spinal Hospital	342 0000
Orthosports Medical Centre	345 0601
Osteopathic Health Centre	344 9792
Pilates Studio	343 8252
Specialist Orthopaedic & Rehab Centre	349 5528

Mental Health

Counselling/Psychology

Comprehensive Medical Centre	331 4777
Dr Roghy McCarthy Psychology Clinic	394 6122
Dubai Community Health Centre	344 6700
Welcare Hospital	282 7788

Psychiatry

Al Rashad Psychiatry Clinic	398 9740
Dr Akel's Medical Centre	349 4880
Dubai Community Health Centre	344 6700
Welcare Hospital	282 7788

Support Groups

Even the most resilient of personalities can be affected by culture shock or simply a change in circumstances, whether this is the stress of settling into a new environment and adjusting to new places and faces, or coming to terms with a more personal problem. Dubai can be a challenging place to live and with many residents originating from overseas, there is often a lack of family support that many people are used to. Making the first step of reaching out for help can be tough, however, there are groups out there offering a hand through the difficult patches.

Check out the list below, or any of the monthly health-focussed magazines that are usually available in surgeries, nutrition stores, etc, for updates of support groups. If possible, get personal recommendations first, as standards can vary enormously, especially if a group or workshop are linked to a business. Be wise and use your discretion.

The Dubai Community Health Centre (previously the Childcare and Development Centre) (344 6700) offers pleasant, healing space for support group meetings for no charge, so if your group isn't already in existence in Dubai - be a pioneer and start it!

The following groups do not charge to attend their meetings:

- *Adoption Support Group* (394 6643/394 2387). Meetings held once a month at different locations.
- *Al Anon Family Groups* (AA) (343 0446) Meets Mondays 19:30 at American Hospital Dubai.
- *Alcoholics Anonymous* (AA) (394 9198) (24 hour hotline).
- *Attention Deficit Hyperactive Disorder* (ADHD) (394 6643). Meets second Saturday of the month at the Community Health Centre.
- *Breastfeeding Telephone Support* 08:00-20:00, 7 days (050 453 4670)

American Hospital

The gift of good health

At Al Zahra, we bring you
the promise of good health.
With world-class expertise and
state-of-the-art technology & facilities
that cover all fields of medical science.

Education

- *Diabetic Support Group* (309 6876). Meets every three months on a Wednesday evening at 17:30. Based at the American Hospital Dubai. Contact Nibal.

- *Fertility Support Group* (050 646 5148/050 632 4365/ 050 456 4109). Meets the first Tuesday of every month at 19:00. Based at the Dubai Gynaecological and Fertility Unit, Rashid Hospital. Contact Ram Kumar/Lalitah/Tricia

- *Mother 2 Mother* (050 595 2974). Support, friendship, fun and advice for all mothers, from those who are expecting to those who have already delivered.

- *Pastoral Care* (395 4601). A listening ear from someone who cares.

- *Professional Single Mothers Group* (050 535 6220). Meetings held once a month. Contact Mitra or Amel.

- *Special Families Support* (393 1985). Monthly meetings on a Friday. For the families of special needs children. Contact Ayesha Saeed.

- *Still Birth & Neo Natal Death Society* (SANDS) (884 6309/395 4564). Meetings held approximately once a month. Contact June Young or Angela Scally.

- *Twins, Triplets or More!* (050 654 0079). Baby Circle (for pregnant mothers and mothers with multiples up to one year) meets every Monday. Double Trouble (for those with multiples aged one year and up) meets every other Tuesday. (www.twinsormore.2om.com). Contact Paula.

The following group charges a fee to attend their meetings.

- *Slimmers Support Group* (349 6333). Weekly meetings with Clinical Nutritionist Carol Sadler at the Dubai Physiotherapy Centre. Dhs.30.

Help on the Web

www.doctorelite.com is a Website run by doctors and health professionals in the UAE, containing information on where to find a doctor who speaks your language, health tips, where to find a pharmacy open late at night, etc. Basically, the main function of the Website is to provide a search engine that allows you to look for practitioners in the UAE and internationally. It details their qualifications, specialities, medical degrees, etc - very helpful!

EDUCATION

In Dubai, due to the diverse expat culture, the education system is extremely varied and there are many schools from which to choose, all of which are fee paying for expats. For further information on the education system, schools, fees, etc, refer to the *Family Explorer* (formerly *Kids Explorer*), published by Explorer Publishing.

It's always best to seek advice from friends or colleagues about a school's reputation. Many schools

Welcare Hospital

In pursuit of providing quality healthcare.

Our Care and Commitment: Your Concern, Comfort and Convenience.

Welcare Hospital, in pursuit of providing quality healthcare, offers an environment of compassion, harmony and hope. Without compromising on the patient's mostly-needed factor: comfort and convenience. We care about you; it's our commitment.

Welcare Hospital
Setting New Standards

24-Hour Accident & Emergency Service. Tel: 2829900

ox: 31500, Dubai, UAE. Tel: 04 2827788, Fax: 04 2828226 E-mail: welcare@emirates.net.ae Web: www.welcarehospital.com

operate a waiting list and families are not necessarily able to enrol their child at their preferred school.

School terms: autumn (mid September - mid December); spring (early January - early April); summer (mid April - early July).

Generally, to enrol your child at a school the following information is needed:

- School application form
- Copies of student's and parents' passports - both information page/s and residence visa stamp
- Passport size photos (usually eight)
- Copies of student's birth certificate
- School records for the past two years
- Current immunisation records and medical history
- An official transfer certificate from the student's previous school detailing his/her education
- Some schools also require a student questionnaire to be completed.

Original transfer certificates must contain the following details:

- Date of enrolment
- Year placement
- Date the child left the school
- School stamp
- Official signature

The Ministry of Education also requires the following documentation for any student enrolling at any school in the emirate:

- Original transfer certificate (to be completed by the student's current school)
- Most recently issued original report card.

If the student was attending a school in any country other than the UAE, Australia, Canada, European nation or USA, the transfer certificate and the most recently issued original report card must by attested by the Ministry of Education, Ministry of Foreign Affairs and the UAE embassy in that country.

Nursery & Pre-School

(Age: babies - 4½ years)

Nursery schools usually like to interview a child before accepting him/her. Most nurseries adopt English as their common teaching language and annual fees can vary dramatically, depending on the level of establishment you approach.

Hours: most nurseries run for 4 - 5 hours in the morning.

Fees: approximately Dhs.3,000 - 12,000 per annum.

Nurseries & Pre-schools

De La Salle Montessori International	398 6218
Dubai Gem Private Nursery	337 1463
Dubai Infants School	337 1463
French Children's Nursery House	349 6868
Gulf Montessori Nursery	282 2402
Gymboree Play & Music	345 4422
Jumeira International Nursery	394 5567
Jumeirah International Nursery School	349 9065
Kids Cottage Nursery	394 2145
Kids Island Nursery	394 2578
Ladybird Nursery	344 1011
Little Land	394 4471
Little Star Nursery	398 2004
Palms	394 7017
Safa Kindergarten	344 3878
Small Steps Nursery Mirdiff	288 3347
Small World	345 7774
Smart Children's Nursery	398 0074
Tiny Home Montessori Nursery	349 3201
Yellow Brick Road Nursery	282 8290

Primary & Secondary School

(Age: 4½ - 11 years) (Age: 11 - 18 years)

Most schools require proof of your child's previous school academic records. You will also need an official letter from a school in your home country detailing your child's education to date and some schools even ask for a character reference! The child may also be required to take a short entrance exam and there may even be a physical examination as well as a family interview.

Depending on your nationality and educational requirements, most national curriculum syllabuses can be found in Dubai schools, covering GCSE's, A levels, French and International Baccalaureate and CNEC as well as the American and Indian equivalent.

Standards of teaching are usually high and schools have excellent facilities, with extracurricular activities on offer. The Ministry of Education regularly inspects schools to ensure rules and regulations are being upheld, and most schools insist on a school uniform. Some school fees include books and transport to school by bus, but mostly, fees only cover the basic education.

Hours: most are from 08:00 - 13:00 or 15:00, Saturday - Wednesday.

Fees: Primary: approximately Dhs.10,000 - 20,000 per annum. Secondary: approximately Dhs.15,000 - 45,000 per annum. Other costs may include a deposit or registration.

University & Higher Education

Most teenagers at university or higher education level return to their 'home' country to enrol in further education there. However, for those who wish to stay in Dubai, a few choices exist.

A number of universities and colleges around the UAE with American, Australian and European affiliates offer degree and diploma courses in Arts, Sciences, Business and Management, and Engineering and Technology. Many commercial organisations also offer higher education courses for school leavers, mature students and adults alike. Details of these establishments can be found in the Hawk Business Pages or Yellow Pages. Both the American University of Dubai and the University of Wollongong are accredited, and offer undergraduate and graduate degrees.

Universities

Universities	
American University in Dubai (AUD)	399 9000
American University in Sharjah (AUS)	06 558 5555
University of Wollongong (Australian curriculum)	395 4422
The Higher Colleges of Technology (HCT) and **Zayed University** offer higher national diplomas and under-graduate degrees to UAE national students only.	

Special Needs Education

If you have a child or children with special needs, before embarking on your adventure in the Emirates, we recommend that you first contact one or more of the following schools/centres, as student spaces are limited. All centres are charities, rather than government run, and thus rely on donations, sponsorship, grants and a certain amount of voluntary work from outside helpers. Entry into most is generally between the ages of $3\frac{1}{2}$ to 5, unless the child was in a special needs school previously. Generally, teaching is in English, but Arabic language instruction is also available, and in most cases, each child receives an individual programme. All charge tuition fees.

- The Al Noor Centre for Children with Special Needs (394 6088) provides therapeutic support and comprehensive training to special needs children of all ages. The centre also equips its 220 students with work-related skills, assisting them in functionally integrating into society as young adults.
- The Dubai Centre for Special Needs (344 0966) currently has 119 students, all of whom have an individual programme, including physiotherapy, speech therapy and/or occupational therapy. A pre-vocational programme is offered for older students, which includes arranging work placements.
- Rashid Paediatric (340 0005) includes physical, occupational and speech therapy. In the afternoons, 13:30 - 17:00, therapists see children on an outpatient basis, also working on early intervention,

Primary & Secondary Schools

School	Curriculum	Grades	Location	Telephone
Al Mawakeb School	US	Primary/ Secondary	Al Rashidiya	285 1415
American School of Dubai	US	KG1 - Grade 12	Jumeira	344 0824
Cambridge High School, The	UK	Primary/ Secondary	Garhoud	282 4646
Deira Private School	UK	KG1 - Grade 7	Garhoud	282 4082
Dubai College	UK	Secondary	Al Sufouh	399 9111
Dubai English Speaking School	UK	Primary	Bur Dubai	337 1457
Dubai Infants School	UK	Primary	Karama	337 0913
Emirates International School	UK	Primary/ Secondary	Al Wasl Road	348 9804
English College, The	UK	Secondary	Umm Suqeim	394 3465
Horizon English School	UK	Primary	Jumeria	394 7879
International School of Choueifat	International	Primary/ Secondary	Al Sufouh	399 9444
Jebel Ali Primary School	UK	Primary	Jebel Ali Village	884 6485
Jumeira English Speaking School	UK	Primary	Safa Park	394 5515
Jumeira Primary School	UK	Primary	Jumeira	394 3500
Lycee Georges Pompidou	French	Primary	Al Karama	337 4161
Regent School	UK	Primary	Primary	344 8049
School of Research Science	UK	Primary/ Secondary	Al Qusais	298 8772
St. Mary's Catholic High School	UK	Primary/ Secondary	Al Karama	337 0252

and assisting school children with motor, learning, speech and communication difficulties.

- Additionally, there is a therapeutic horse riding programme for children with special needs - Riding for the Disabled (336 6321)

Note that in general, the UAE is not set up for those with special needs, and you won't find many wheelchair ramps around. Those ramps that we have seen appear to be there to assist with construction rather than wheelchairs, as they all seem to be at a 60 degree angle. When considering employment in the Emirates, check with your future employer whether any medical insurance programme they offer will cover special needs children, as many do not. (See also: Disabled Visitors [p.20])

Learning Arabic

Can you speak the lingo? While it's relatively easy to pick up a few local words of greeting, if you are keen to learn more, there are a number of private institutions that offer very good Arabic language courses. Refer to Language Schools [p.290].

If you want just a few words to help you get by, have a look at the Arabic expressions table on [p.14].

TRANSPORTATION

Other options → Car [p.32]
Car Hire [p.34]
Zappy Explorer

Cars are the most popular mode of transport in Dubai and those who are licensed, and can afford it,

generally have one. The main options if you wish to drive here for any length of time are to buy a vehicle (for which you will need residency), or to lease. Visitors (short or long term) have the option of renting a vehicle from one of numerous rental companies.

The following section covers leasing, buying (new or used vehicles), registration, fines, insurance and traffic accidents.

The Dubai Traffic Police recorded information line (268 5555) or Website: www.dxbtraffic.gov.ae (Arabic and English) tells you all you ever wanted to know about fines, speeding tickets, registering vehicles, applying for driving licences, emergency numbers, suggestions etc.

Office locations:

- Traffic Police HQ - near Galadari roundabout, Dubai - Sharjah Road (269 2222, Map ref. 15-C1)
- Bur Dubai Police Station - Sheikh Zayed Road, Junction 4 (398 1111, Map ref. 4-A4).

Vehicle Leasing

Leasing a vehicle has many advantages over buying. Not only is it a good option financially for shorter periods, but there are also fewer hassles when it comes to breakdowns, re-registration, etc, since the leasing company should deal with everything. All services are provided inclusive of registration, maintenance, replacement, 24 hour assistance and insurance (comprehensive with personal accident is advisable). You may find that your employer has connections with a car hire company and can negotiate better rates for long-term hire than you can on an individual basis.

Used cars for sale

New Residents

Transportation

Leasing is generally weekly, monthly or yearly. Cars typically range from Mitsubishi Lancers or Toyota Corollas to Mitsubishi Pajero 4 wheel drive vehicles. Monthly lease prices range from Dhs.1,500 for a small vehicle to Dhs.1,900 for larger cars and Dhs.3,500 for a 4 wheel drive. As the lease period increases, so the price decreases.

For short term rental there are many companies offering daily services - check the Hawk Business Pages for the most competitive. To hire any vehicle you will need to provide a passport copy, credit card and a valid driving licence from your home country or a valid international driving licence.

Vehicle Leasing Agents

Autolease	282 6565
Diamondlease Rent A Car	331 3172
Fast Rent a Car	224 5040
Super Star Rent A Car	271 5725
United Car Rental	266 6286

Buying a Vehicle

In Dubai, the car rules as the most popular method of getting around, and buying one gives you far greater flexibility than relying on other means of transport. Choosing a car here can be a tough decision as the market is huge - should it be second-hand, a 4 wheel drive, what has a good A/C, what colour's best...?

Only those with a residence visa can own a vehicle in the UAE. Most people will find that cars are far cheaper than in their home countries and that with the low cost of petrol and maintenance, they can afford something a little bit more extravagant than they would otherwise think of buying.

New Vehicles

If you are going to invest in a brand new vehicle, you will find most models available on the market through the main dealers.

Used Vehicles

Where can you go to buy a second-hand vehicle? Due to the relative cheapness of cars and the high(ish) turnover of expats in the Emirates, there is a thriving second-hand market. Dealers are scattered around town, but areas to start with include Sheikh Zayed Road and Garhoud. Expect to pay a premium of about Dhs.5,000 for buying through a dealer, since they also offer a limited warranty, insurance, finance and registration, unlike a less 'official' sale. Sometimes the main dealers will offer good deals on demonstration cars, which are basically new but have been used by the showroom for test drives.

Alternatively, visit Dubai Municipality's Used Car Complex at Al Awir/Ras Al Khor, where all the cars have been checked by EPPCO's Tasjeel service. If you're online, have a look at www.valuewheels.com.

New Car Dealers

Alpha Romeo	Gargash Motors	266 4669
Audi	Al Nabooda Automobiles	347 5111
BMW	AGMC	339 1212
Cadillac	Liberty Automobiles	282 4440
Chrysler	Trading Enterprises	295 4246
Chevrolet	Al Yousuf Motors	339 5555
Daewoo	Al Yousuf Motors	339 5555
Dodge	Trading Enterprises	295 4246
Ferrari	Al Tayer Motors	282 5000
Fiat	Al Ghandi Auto	266 6511
Ford	Al Tayer Motors	282 5000
Galloper	Al Habtoor Motors	269 1110
GMC	Liberty Automobiles	282 4440
Honda	Trading Enterprises	295 4246
Hyundai	Juma Al Majid	269 0893
Isuzu	GENAVCO LLC	396 1000
Jaguar	Al Tayer Group	282 5000
Jeep	Trading Enterprises	295 4246
Kia	Al Majed Motors	268 6460
Land Rover	Al Tayer Group	282 5000
Lexus	Al Futtaim Motors	228 2261
Mazda	Galadari Automobiles	299 4848
Mercedes	Gargash Enterprises	269 9777
Mitsubishi	Al Habtoor Motors	269 1110
Nissan	Arabian Automobiles	295 1234
Opel	Liberty Automobiles	282 4440
Pontiac	Mirage General Trading	266 0062
Porsche	Al Nabooda Automobiles	347 5111
Rolls Royce	Al Habtoor Motors	269 1110
Saab	Gargash Motors	266 4669
Skoda	Autostar Trading	269 7100
Toyota	Al Futtaim Motors	228 2261
Volkswagen	Al Nabooda Automobiles	347 5111
Volvo	Trading Enterprises	295 4246
Wrangler	Trading Enterprises	295 4246

Used Car Dealers

4 x 4 Motors	Opp Al Bustan Rotana	282 3050
Autoplus	Sheikh Zayed Road	339 5400
Boston Cars	Al Awir	333 1010
Car Store, The	Sheikh Zayed Road	343 5245
House of Cars	Sheikh Zayed Road	343 5060
Motor World	Nr Ports & Customs	333 2206
Off Road Motors	Jct 3, Sheikh Zayed Rd	338 4866
Quality Cars	Trading Enterprises	295 4246

For other second-hand deals, check the classifieds section in the newspapers and supermarket noticeboards (mainly Spinneys or Park N Shop).

Before buying a second-hand car it's advisable to have it checked by a reputable garage - just to 'make sure', especially for 4 wheel drives, which may have been driven off-road rather adventurously! Expect to pay around Dhs.300 for this service, and it's best to book in advance.

All transactions for vehicles must be directed through the Traffic Police. A Dhs.3,000 fine is imposed on both buyer and seller for cars sold unofficially.

Ownership Transfer

To register a second-hand ('pre-owned') car in your name, you must transfer vehicle ownership. You will need to submit an application form, the valid registration card, the insurance certificate, the original licence plates and Dhs.20 to the Traffic Police, plus an NOC from the finance company, if applicable. The previous owner must also be present to sign the form.

Vehicle Import

In the first half of 2002, over 100,000 vehicles were imported into Dubai. A requirement for cars imported by individuals or private car showrooms that were manufactured after 1997/98, is an NOC from the official agent in the UAE or from the Ministry of Finance and Industry (if no official agent exists). This is to ensure that the car complies with GCC specifications (or rather that the local dealers are not outdone by the neighbouring competition!).

Additionally, believe it or not, if you are buying a vehicle from another part of the Emirates, you have to export and import it into Dubai first! This means lots of paperwork and lots of hassle. You will need to take your Essential Documents, the sale agreement, current registration and Dhs.60. You will then be issued with a set of temporary licence plates, which are valid three days - enough time to submit a new registration application in Dubai.

Vehicle Insurance

Before you can register your car, you must have adequate insurance, and many companies offer this service. The insurers will need to know the year of manufacture and may need to inspect the vehicle. Take along a copy of your Dubai driving licence, passport copy and copy of the existing vehicle registration card.

Annual insurance policies are for a 13 month period (this is to cover the one month grace period that you are allowed when your registration expires). Rates depend on the age and model of your car and your previous insurance history. The rates are generally 4 - 7% of the vehicle value or 5% for cars over five years old. Fully comprehensive with personal accident insurance is highly advisable. For more adventurous drivers, insurance for off-roading accidents is also recommended. Norwich Winterthur is one of the few insurers who will cover off-road accidents. For details on all insurance companies, look in the Yellow Pages or Hawk Business Pages.

It's wise to check whether insurance covers you for the Sultanate of Oman, as within the Emirates you may find yourself driving through small Omani enclaves (especially if you are off-road, for example near Hatta, through Wadi Bih and on the East Coast in Dibba). Insurance for a visit to Oman can be arranged on a short-term basis, usually for no extra cost.

Registering a Vehicle

All cars must be registered annually with the Traffic Police. In an effort to shorten queues and save time, this has been farmed out to sites other than the Traffic Police, namely EPPCO. Facilities include vehicle testing and full registration with the police; contact EPPCO Tasjeel (267 3940).

If you don't wish to do it yourself, some companies offer a full registration service for a fee, which includes collecting your car, testing and registering it and delivering it back to you all in the same day. EPPCO Tasjeel offers a service called Al Sayara, which costs Dhs.200, plus the testing and registration fees.

There is a one month grace period after your registration has expired in which to have your car re-registered (hence the 13 month insurance period).

Be aware that some second-hand dealers may sell you a car that under normal circumstances would not pass the annual vehicle testing. However, with 'friends' at the test centre they are able to get the car 'passed', leaving you stuck when you come to do it yourself the following year.

The following charge a fee for undertaking registration, in addition to normal registration costs.

Registration Service	
AAA	285 8989
Al Sayara Tasjeel	800 4258
Midland Cars	396 7521/2
Protectol	285 7182

Norwich Union rewards claim free driving with competitive rates

The reputation Norwich Union Insurance has earned for prompt, efficient and professional service has encouraged us to take a fresh look at private Motor insurance.

Norwich Union insurance brings new standards of simplicity, service and value for money to provide you with more freedom to drive your expectations and enjoy your adventures.

For more information on how the Norwich Union Motor Insurance Policy can protect your car, call Norwich Union Insurance today between:

0800 hrs to 2000 hrs (Sat-Wed) and 0800 hrs to 1600 hrs (Thursday).

800 4845

Quite simply the best motor insurance protection in the Middle East.

or • Home • Travel

The Process

In order to obtain licence plates for the vehicle, the car must first be tested then registered with the Dubai Traffic Police.

If you have purchased a new vehicle from a dealer, the dealer will register the car for you. You do not need to test a new vehicle for the first two years, though you must re-register it after one year. In some cases, second-hand dealers will register the car for you.

The test involves a technical inspection, checking lights, bodywork, fire extinguisher, emissions, etc. Once the car has been 'passed' you will receive a certification document.

Remember to take Essential Documents, insurance documents valid 13 months, the proof of purchase agreement, the vehicle transfer or customs certificate (if applicable), and Dhs.330. Before the registration procedure can be completed, all traffic offences and fines against your car registration number must be settled - a potentially expensive business!

Traffic Fines & Offences

If you are caught by the police driving or parking illegally, you will be fined (unless the offence is more serious). You can also be fined Dhs.50 on the spot for being caught driving without your licence. If you are involved in an accident and don't have your licence with you, you will be given a 24 hour grace period in which to present your licence to the police station. If you don't, you risk having your car impounded and may have to go to court.

There are a number of police controlled speed traps, fixed cameras and mobile radar around Dubai (speed cameras only operate in one direction). There is no leeway for breaking the speed limit - not that it seems to bother many people! The fine for speeding is Dhs.200. Parking tickets are Dhs.100 and up. In addition, a black point penalty system operates for certain offences.

The Dubai Traffic Police Information Line (268 5555, Arabic & English), or Website: www.dxbtraffic.gov.ae enables you to check the fines you have against your vehicle or driving licence - a handy thing to know rather than being faced with an unexpectedly large bill when you renew your car registration!

Office location: for payment of traffic fines, Traffic Fines section, Traffic Police HQ - near Galadari roundabout, Dubai - Sharjah Road (269 2222, Map ref. 15-C1).

It is also possible to pay road fines at other locations around Dubai. These include Al Safa Union Co-operative, Al Tuwar Union Co-operative and Jumeira Town Centre. Payment of fines online using a credit card at www.dxbtraffic.gov.ae is also possible for a small fee.

Black Points

In addition to a system of fines for certain offences, a black points penalty system operates. If you have a permanent licence and receive 12 black points four times in one year, your licence is taken away and your car impounded. The first time you hit 12 points, you receive a fine and your licence is revoked for anything between two weeks and a month. For the next set of 12 points, the penalty is more severe, and so on.

If you are on a probationary licence and aged between 18 - 21, and receive 12 points within 12 months, your licence is revoked and you have to start the whole process of obtaining a licence from the beginning.

However, it seems that there are no hard and fast rules or amounts when it comes to black points ... if you do something serious, your licence can be taken away immediately. If you run a red light, you receive nine black points instantly.

Breakdowns

In the event of a breakdown you will usually find that passing police cars stop to help, or at least to check your documents! We recommend that you keep water in your car at all times - the last thing you want is to be stuck with your car in the middle of summer with no air conditioning, nothing to drink, and lots of time to waste waiting for help.

The Arabian Automobile Association (AAA) (285 8989) offers a 24 hour roadside breakdown service for an annual charge. This includes help in minor mechanical repairs, battery boosting, or help if you run out of petrol, have a flat tyre or lock yourself out. The more advanced service includes off-road recovery, vehicle registration and a rent a car service. It's a similar concept to the RAC or AA in Britain, or AAA in the States.

Recovery Services/Towing (24 hour)	
AAA Services	285 8989
Ahmed Mohammed Garage	333 1800
Dubai Auto Towing Services	359 4424
IATC Recovery	800 5200
Jay International	050 652 0021

Traffic Accidents

Other options → **Accidents [p.33]**

Bad Luck! If you have an accident dial 999 in serious cases, or in less critical cases, call Deira (266 0555), Bur Dubai (398 1111), or Sharjah (06 538 1111). The Dubai Traffic Police Information Line (268 5555, Arabic & English) gives the numbers of police stations around the emirate.

You must wait for the police to arrive. They will assess the accident and apportion blame on site (and tough if you disagree with their judgement!). In this part of the world, if you have an accident, you are then the star attraction of a million rubberneckers. Sadly, the norm seems to be to let your car block as much traffic as possible till the Police tell you to move it.

If there is minor damage, move the vehicles to the side of the road. However, if there is any doubt as to who is at fault or if there is an injury (however slight) do not move the cars, even if you are blocking the traffic. Apparently, if you help or move anyone involved in an accident, the police may hold you liable if anything then happens to that person.

Having assessed the accident and apportioned blame, the police document the necessary details and give you a copy of the accident report. Submit the paper to your insurance company to get the vehicle repaired. A pink accident report means you are at fault, and green means you are not to blame. The police may retain your driving licence until you obtain the necessary documentation from the insurance company to say the claim is being processed. Your insurers will then give you a paper that entitles you to retrieve your licence from the police.

Repairs

By law, no vehicle can be accepted for repair without an accident report from the Traffic Police. Usually your insurance company has an agreement with a particular garage to which they will refer you. The garage will carry out the repair work and the insurance company will settle the claim.

And Finally...

Oh the follies of Dubai...

The final amount paid for the number 2 on a vehicle license plate bought in 2001 was Dhs.1,240,000. Auctioned off over two days initially, personalised license plates brought in a staggering Dhs.44,000,000 of revenue! Check out the Traffic Police's website for current auction details www.dxbtraffic.gov.ae/en.

Transportation

Twin Towers on Dubai Creek

Slider design

Small & compact

Enhanced processor

Dual expansion

Voice memo button

Bluetooth technology

Ultra-sharp colour display

You can turn your Tungsten T™ handheld virtually into anything from a video player, photo album, ebook reader or why not carry the whole Dubai Explorer guide in your Palm!

Zire

Great value

Extra security

Hassle-free

Infrared port

Lots of space

A trendy handheld

Two application buttons

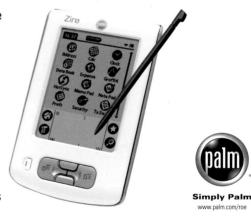

Simply Palm
www.palm.com/roe

Palm handhelds can be purchased from retailers and electronic shops, including branches of Jumbo, CompuME, Axiom Telecom, Plug-Ins, Virgin Megastore, Jacky's Electronics, Dubai Duty Free, Al-Andalus Electronics, Jarir Bookstore and SMB Computers

Business
EXPLORER

Business

BUSINESS

General Information

Other options → Economy [p.4]

Strategically located between Europe and the Far East, Dubai is clearly the city of choice for both multinational and private companies wishing to tap the lucrative Middle Eastern, Indian, and African markets, which have a combined population of 1.4 billion people. Annual domestic imports exceed $17 billion, and Dubai is the gateway to over $150 billion (annual) in trade.

While there are many reasons why Dubai has become such an attractive location for businesses, the single most important factors driving Dubai's economy are the government's planned yet innovative approach to business, and continual investment in developing the city's soft and hard infrastructure to make Dubai very 'business and investment friendly'.

Looking to the future, Dubai is targeting for the economy to become totally non-oil driven by 2010, when it is reported that the emirate's reserves may run out. One of the key planks in this strategy has been the development of a high-end tourist industry. Whereas any detailed discussion of Dubai's economy 5-10 years ago would have only made a cursory mention of tourism, today it is one of the most important factors driving the economy of the city.

Business Climate

Other options →History [p.3]
Dubai Overview [p.5]
International Relations [p.6]

The pace of economic growth in Dubai over the past 20 years has been incredible - trade alone has grown at over 9% per annum over the past 10 years - and the emirate stands poised for future strong growth, with the development of the multi-billion dollar *Palm Island* project and multitudes of new business and financial ventures. With the vision of the rulers of Dubai and the UAE, both the legislation and government institutions have been designed to minimise bureaucracy and create a business-friendly environment.

Government officials take an active role in promoting investment in the emirate, and decisions are taken (and implemented) swiftly. Government departments have also in recent years placed increasing importance on improving customer service levels.

The commitment of Dubai's rulers to economic development is pioneering in the Middle East, and is seen by many as a best practice model for other governments in the region. While Dubai is probably the most expensive business location in the Middle East, companies are ready to pay this premium to reap the rewards offered, namely: no tax collection and low business fees, a high degree of political stability, steady, strong economic growth rates, excellent infrastructure, and a high quality of life for expatriate residents.

Trade & Trading Partners

While Abu Dhabi is the political capital of the UAE, Dubai is firmly entrenched as the commercial capital. Dubai emirate accounts for about 75% of the UAE's entire imports, and about 85% of non-oil exports; Dubai also enjoys about 80% of the lucrative re-export market to other Gulf, African and Indian-subcontinent countries. Overall, trade represents approximately 16% of Dubai's GDP.

Strategically located between Asia and Europe, Dubai counts countries such as Japan, South Korea, China, India, the UK and the US amongst its most important trade partners for both imports and exports. In terms of re-exports, Iran, India, the other Gulf countries, and the former CIS states are amongst the most important markets for Dubai.

Both the government and the business community in Dubai have displayed a repeated ability to exploit business opportunities in the region. Such responses are possible due to the excellent infrastructure, flexible rules and regulations (Dubai has one of the most open foreign trade policies in the region), and the huge expatriate community that has a collective ear tuned to the needs of their home countries.

Infrastructure

Dubai has used its (limited) oil revenues - 90% of Dubai's GDP is non-oil - to maximum benefit by investing heavily in basic and advanced infrastructure required to make the city attractive to both foreign investors and visitors. Equally important, the government maintains low tariffs (no departure taxes, road tolls, etc), which further stimulates demand.

Both the airport and ports in Dubai have achieved international recognition as regional hubs, and offer passenger and freight connections to almost every destination in the world. Connecting these key facilities and other points in the city is an extensive road network which is constantly being expanded and upgraded to meet future requirements.

International banks such as HSBC, Citibank, Standard Chartered Bank and Lloyds TSB offer advanced financial products for trade and commerce, while the government-controlled Etisalat offers a full range of advanced voice and data telecommunication services. Each Dubai Government department has a web site, and a large number of government services are available online.

Dubai International Financial Centre

The finance sector is perhaps the sole area of the economy in which Dubai lags behind another Gulf state, namely Bahrain, which has traditionally been considered as the financial hub for the region.

That, however, is expected to change with the inauguration of the Dubai International Financial Centre (DIFC), which was unveiled in 2002, and is expected to start operations later in 2003. Situated on a huge property running from Emirates Towers to Interchange 1 behind Sheikh Zayed Road, the project will include an estimated 9 million square feet of commercial and residential real estate.

DIFC is expected to become the regional hub for corporate financing activities and share trading in the Middle East, and is hoping to become a mid-way time zone bridge between the markets of Asia and Europe. Deutsche Bank and Moody's are expected to be some of the initial participants, while NASDAQ has been tipped as a possible operator of the planned stock exchange. The project will receive a key publicity boost with the planned World Bank and International Monetary Fund Annual Meeting, which will be held in Dubai, late 2003.

Dubai International Airport

Dubai International Airport has quickly established itself as the key regional air hub in the Middle East - over 100 airlines operate out of the airport, and offer direct links to upwards of 140 cities. Aside from American carriers who have yet to tap the market, almost every other major airline (and a lot that you have probably never heard of), operates regular flights. Major cities such as London are served non-stop by Emirates (thrice daily), British Airways (twice daily), as well as carriers such as Cathay Pacific and Royal Brunei. Because Dubai operates under an "open skies" policy, there are very few restrictions on foreign airlines' ability to pick up passengers in Dubai and carry them to a third country.

Dubai Airport	
Flight Enquiry	206 6666
Dubai Airport	224 5555
DNATA	316 6666

The ultra-modern Rashid Terminal, constructed in 2000, is being joined by an adjacent twin sister terminal that will be dedicated to Emirates Airlines flights, and which should be ready by late 2003 or early 2004. With a fleet of over 35 planes serving over 60 destinations, Emirates Airlines has already become the carrier of choice in the Middle East. While Emirates is seldom the cheapest option, they offer a high level of service on exceptionally modern, well-maintained planes. Emirates has more planes on order, and expects to increase their fleet size to at least 100 planes by 2010.

For the business traveller, this means that Dubai enjoys direct connections on reputable airlines to almost any destination in the world (direct flights to North America on Emirates are expected to commence in 2003). The recently introduced E-Gate card, available for Dhs.150 (for 2 years) allows UAE residents to avoid Immigration line-ups with a quick swipe of the card and fingerprint scan. For those travelling without checked-in luggage, it is now possible to be out of the airport within 15 minutes from arrival at the gate, including a quick stop at the duty-free shop in the arrivals hall.

Dubai International Airport

Dozens of airlines, including Emirates, Air France, Cathay Pacific, and Singapore Airlines, operate regular freight services out of Dubai, taking advantage of the Airport Free Zone and well-established air-sea cargo trade moving through Jebel Ali Port. Courier companies such as Aramex, DHL, UPS and Fedex offer fast connections through their airport hubs.

Airlines

Airline	Number
Air France	294 5899
Air India	227 6787
Air Malta	331 9990
Alitalia	224 2256
American Airlines	393 5792
British Airways	307 5555
Cathay Pacific	800 4343
Cyprus Airways	221 5325
Emirates	214 4444
Gulf Air	271 3222
KLM	335 5777
Lufthansa	343 2121
Malaysia Airlines	397 0221
Oman Air	351 8080
Qatar Airways	229 2229
Royal Brunei	351 4111
Royal Nepal	294 5138
South African	397 0766
Sri Lankan	294 9119
Swissair	294 5051
United Airlines	203 3878

Dubai Ports Authority

While Port Rashid, located next to the mouth of the Creek, was historically considered the main trading entry port for the emirate, the future is clearly focused on *Jebel Ali Port*, which is the largest man-made harbour in the world. The two terminals handle a combined annual throughput of over 4 million TEU (twenty equivalent units) of containers in 2002, which ranks the port within the top 20 container terminals in the world. All of the major shipping lines have regular weekly services connecting Dubai with Europe, the Far East and North America.

Jebel Ali is also the key transhipment centre for containers and other general cargoes destined for the Arabian Gulf - this trade has been driving up Dubai's traffic by upwards of 15% per annum over recent years. The wooden dhows calling at the Creek and Hamriya Port also play a pivotal role in the Dubai economy; demand for these smaller ships, which can discharge almost anywhere along the coast, is largely driven by restrictions and unavailability of the latest consumer goods in other regional countries.

In early 2002, Dubai Ports Authority (DPA) and the Jebel Ali Free Zone Authority (JAFZA) were merged with Dubai Customs, resulting in a single corporation controlling virtually the entire importation process, from discharging goods (DPA), through warehousing and final processing

Trench & associates
LEGAL CONSULTANCY

specialise in:

AE Company and Commercial Law, especially with
ard to Dubai Internet City establishments

AE and International Litigation

tellectual Property Registration and Protection,
uding Website developments

, Union National Bank Bldg., Dubai. Tel: 3553146, Fax: 3553106 • www.trenchlaw.com • E-mail: trench@emirates.net.ae

(JAFZA), and finally, entry into the local market (Customs). The result has been a more business-orientated approach to Customs, and the introduction of modern, integrated electronic data processes for the arrival and importation of goods into the Dubai market.

Dubai Ports & Customs

Government Departments in Dubai	
Department of Civil Aviation	224 5333
Department of Economic Development	222 9922
Department of HH the Ruler's Affairs & Protocol Affairs	353 1060
Department of Health & Medical Services	337 0031
Department of Ports & Customs	345 9575
Department of Tourism and Commerce Marketing	351 1600
Development Board	228 8866
Dubai Chamber of Commerce & Industry	228 0000
Dubai Courts	334 7777
Dubai Drydocks	345 0626
Dubai Duty Free	206 6444
Dubai Electricity & Water Authority	334 8888
Dubai Government Workshop	334 2999
Dubai Municipality	221 5555
Dubai Police Headquarters	229 2222
Dubai Ports Authority	881 5000

Dubai business community. It promotes commerce through various means, both locally as well as internationally.

Among other activities, the Chamber compiles all business-related data for the emirate, issues certificates of origin of commodities and other goods, nominates experts for goods surveying, receives commercial complaints, states and sets standards, defines commercial usage and terminology, and holds economic and commercial conferences.

Every commercial, professional and industrial company must register with the Chamber (very small businesses may be excepted).

Government Departments

Various departments and ministries - both federal and local - are key to setting up and doing business in Dubai. From the Chamber of Commerce, which offers business-related services, to the Ministry of Labour, which issues all labour-related permits, to the Ministry of Economy, the federal ministry that oversees and regulates all business activity, each now follows recent government mandates to offer advanced e-government services (often Web-based) and improved customer service.

Dubai Chamber of Commerce & Industry

The Dubai Chamber of Commerce & Industry (DCCI), located in a modern glass building on the Deira side of the Creek, was set up by the Dubai Government to provide a variety of services to the

Dubai Department of Economic Development

This department, also known as the Economic Department, is the first office to visit if you are planning on opening an office. It is a key institution when setting up as it is the authority that issues the ever-important and necessary trade licence. Therefore, those setting up a company outside a free zone will have to deal with this organisation, and will continue to do so as long as they are doing business/operating.

Reflecting the bustling local economy, this office, located in a modern building in Deira, is always extremely busy.

To learn more about the DED's responsibilities or for trade licence-related issues, visit their comprehensive Website: www.dubaided.com or www.dubaided.gov.ae, or visit the information counter to collect material. For more specific advice, speak to the Corporate Relations Department.

Dubai Municipality

The Municipality is another key government department to deal with when setting up a business outside of a free zone. All companies must gain approval from the Municipality for their premises before setting up; zoning regulations are both devised and enforced here.

Responsible for Dubai's overall structure, the Municipality approves and monitors all construction in this emirate. Besides creating and maintaining urban landscaping, from public parks to 'greened' roundabouts and medians, the department also provides Dubai residents and companies with all municipal services (transportation infrastructure etc) as well as environmental protection and regulation, and public health services.

The Dubai Municipality is comprised of numerous departments, each located in a different area within the city; the head office is located in Deira, near Etisalat.

Ministry of Economy & Commerce

The Ministry of Economy is the federal institution overseeing all economic activity in Dubai. It plays a supervisory and regulatory role in setting up all commercial companies.

Foreign companies wanting to set up a branch in Dubai, as well as insurance companies, agents and brokers, must obtain approval from this Ministry.

The Ministry of Economy also handles the registration of commercial agents/agencies. Other responsibilities include issuing certificates of origin for National exports and the protection of trademarks.

Ministry of Labour & Social Affairs

This Ministry is a federal institution and is responsible for labour issues and approval of all labour-related permits (with the exception of some free zones). Only official representatives of companies deal directly with this Ministry, which is particularly strict on who is allowed to enter the building and submit documents. Only an officially authorised person, such as the company owner, sponsor or PRO (public relations officer), may perform the labour-related procedures for each company.

This Ministry also issues the *UAE Labour Law* (see p.124).

Doing Business

Aside from Agency Law (see p.124), which is in many cases avoidable by establishing in one of the various free zones, Dubai is an enjoyable and rewarding place to live and do business. There are many exciting business opportunities for companies and entrepreneurs to serve an increasingly sophisticated and growing market.

The sheer scope of public-sponsored projects currently being implemented throughout Dubai, including *Palm Island* (over US$2 billion), *Festival City* (over US$2 billion), *Healthcare City* (US$1.8 billion) and the *Dubai Airport* expansion (approx. US$2.5 billion) will virtually ensure sustained economic growth over the next 5-10 years. When combined with huge private sector investments in commercial, manufacturing, distribution, and residential facilities, there are countless opportunities in the trade, retail and service sectors of the economy.

Multinational corporations have also recognised the rewards of setting up a base in Dubai, particularly in the various free zones. The top 10 Fortune 500 firms have a regional office or base in Dubai, along with numerous others, usually conducting international trade in the Middle East and Africa region.

Business Groups & Contacts

In addition to the various government departments specifically responsible for providing commercial assistance to enterprises in Dubai, there are various chambers of commerce and other business groups that help facilitate investments, and provide opportunities for networking with others in the community. Some groups provide information on trade with their respective country, as well as on business opportunities both in Dubai and internationally. Most also arrange social and networking events on a regular basis.

Embassies or consulates can also be a good business resource and may be able to offer contact lists for the UAE and the country of representation.

Business

Trade Centres and Commissions

Australian Trade Commission	331 3444
British Embassy - Commercial Section	397 1070
Canadian Trade Commission	352 1717
Cyprus Trade Centre	228 2411
Danish Trade Centre	222 7699
Egyptian Trade Centre	222 1098
Export Promotion Council of Norway	353 3833
French Trade Commission	222 4250
German Office of Foreign Trade	352 0413
Hong Kong Trade Development	223 3499
Indian Trade Centre	393 5208
Indian State Trading Corporation	227 1270
Italian Trade Commission	331 4951
Japan External Trade Organisation	332 8264
Korean Trade Centre	222 0643
Malaysian Govt. Trade Centre	331 9994
Philippine Embassy - Commercial Section	223 6526
Polish Trade Centre	223 5837
Romanian Trade Representation	394 0580
Singapore Trade Centre	222 9789
Spanish Commercial Office	331 3565
Sultanate of Oman Office	397 1000
Taiwan Trade Centre	396 7814
Thailand Trade Centre	228 4553
Trade Representative of the Netherlands	352 8700
USA Consulate General - Commercial Section	331 3584

Embassies/Consulates

Country	Phone	Map ref
Australia	321 2444	5-D3
Bahrain	02 665 7500	UAE-A4
Canada	352 1717	8-A4
China	398 4357	10-C1
Denmark	222 7699	11-D1
Egypt	397 1122	11-B1
France	332 9040	9-E1
Germany	397 2333	11-A1
India	397 1222	11-B1
Iran	344 4717	6-C3
Italy	331 4167	9-E2
Japan	331 9191	9-E2
Jordan	397 0500	11-A1
Kuwait	397 8000	11-B1
Lebanon	397 7450	11-B1
Malaysia	335 5528	10-D3
Netherlands	352 8700	8-A4
Norway	353 3833	8-A2
Oman	397 1000	11-B1
Pakistan	397 0412	11-A1
Qatar	398 2888	10-C1
Saudi Arabia	397 9777	11-B1
South Africa	397 5222	11-A1
Sri Lanka	398 6535	7-B3
Switzerland	329 0999	9-E2
Thailand	349 2863	5-D2
UK	397 1070	8-B4
USA	311 6000	9-E2

Business Councils

American Business Council	331 4735
Australian Business in the Gulf (ABIG)	395 4423
British Business Group	397 0303
Canadian Business Council	359 2625
Denmark Business Council	222 7699
French Business Council	335 2362
German Business Council	359 9930
Iranian Business Council	344 4717
Pakistan Business Council	337 2875
South African Business Group	050 653 2469
Swedish Business Council	337 1410
Swiss Business Council	321 1438

BUSINESS CULTURE

Other options ➔ Culture [p.12]

Customs

Despite its cosmopolitan outward appearance, Dubai is an Arab city in a Muslim country, and people doing business in Dubai must remember this fact. Even if your counterpart in another company is an expatriate, the head decision-maker may be a UAE National, who might take a different approach to business matters. Your best bet when doing business in Dubai for the first time is to observe closely, have lots of patience, and make a concerted effort to understand the culture and respect the customs. Once you understand the customs and culture, follow them, and keep ahold of that patience!

Although women have not made significant inroads into the mainstream of business, there are both National and expatriate women in Dubai who have risen to positions of prominence.

Etiquette

Tea and coffee are a very important part of Arabic life, and it may be considered rude to refuse this offer of hospitality during a meeting. Tilting the small Arabic coffee cup back and forth several times with your fingers will signal that you do not want another refill.

Although proper dress is important for all business dealings, the local climate has dictated that a shirt and tie (for men) is sufficient for all but the most important of business encounters;

Dhs.100 ~ € 28

women usually choose a suit or a skirt/blouse that are not excessively revealing.

In Arabic society, a verbal commitment, once clearly made, is ethically if not legally binding; reasonable bargaining is an important part of reaching any such agreement. And finally, it is important to remember that Dubai is still a relatively small business community, and so confidentiality and discretion are of the utmost importance in all business dealings.

Meetings

A strong handshake should not only start off each meeting, but also end the encounter - a longer handshake at the end is an indication that the meeting has gone well. It is always preferable to start a meeting with a non-business discussion, but avoid enquiring about somebody's wife, even if you know the wife - general enquiries about the family are more appropriate.

Don't be surprised if other people walk in and out during the meeting to discuss unrelated matters, and be prepared that the meeting may run longer than expected.

While meeting agendas might be important to ensure that all relevant matters are discussed, they are better used as a checklist (at the end) instead of a schedule for discussions during the meeting.

Time

While punctuality for meetings is very important, the visitor must always remember to be patient if the host is delayed, due to an unforeseen (and possibly more important!) other visitor. Remember, traffic accidents on Sheikh Zayed road are a very predictable event (they happen every day), so plan ahead, and don't be forced to use them as an excuse for being late.

Business Hours

Other options → **Social & Business hours [p.9]**
Ramadan [p.13]
Working Hours [p.69]

Dubai has no set in stone business hours, or even fixed working days for that matter. Government departments generally work between 07:00-14:00 Sat-Wed, although departments providing services to the public sometimes offer extended hours. Many multinational companies prefer the Sun-Thurs work week, which provides greater overlap with other international offices, while other companies work a straight 6 day week (Sat-Thurs). Private sector offices normally work 08:00-17:00 or a 09:00-18:00 day, though some take advantage of the Labour Law guidelines and make the most of their employees' time with a 08:00-18:00 work day.

Banks remain open until about 13:30 on weekdays, but close early on Thursdays, while large supermarkets generally maintain hours between 09:00 and 22:00 throughout the week. Shopping malls are open for about 12 hours, starting from 10:00 (later on Friday), while other shops in the city generally close between 13:00 and 16:30.

During the holy month of Ramadan, working hours for government and some private sector companies are reduced by 2 or more hours, while shops and malls open later in the day and stay open much later in the evening - call ahead to avoid frustration.

LAWS

Laws & Regulations

As with many countries in the Middle East, UAE law requires that companies have a local (UAE National) participant holding at least 51% of the shares. While there has been discussion of easing or even removing these ownership restrictions, no change in the regulations is imminent. 100% foreign ownership is permitted for the following:

- a company located in a UAE free zone (see page 126)
- a company with activities open to 100% GCC ownership (Gulf Co-operation Council: Saudi Arabia, Oman, Kuwait, Qatar)
- a company in which wholly owned GCC companies enter into partnership with UAE Nationals
- a branch or representative office of a foreign company registered in Dubai
- a professional or artisan company practising business activities that allow 100% foreign ownership

Agency Law

By law, foreign nationals intending to set up a company such as a sole proprietorship, a branch of a foreign company, or a professional company must find a National agent and sign a local (national) service agency agreement with him. The local agent is usually referred to as a 'sponsor'.

The sponsor does not have any responsibility for the business, but he is obliged to assist with all government-related procedures such as obtaining government permits, trade licenses, visas, and labour cards. His signature will be required for most application forms.

A sponsor may be a UAE National or a company fully owned by UAE Nationals. The choice of a sponsor can be of significant importance, particularly for a larger company. Appointing a sponsor who is considered prominent and influential can open many doors that might otherwise be extremely difficult to access. Local sponsors may be paid a lump sum and/or a percentage of the profits or turnover.

A foreign national looking to establish a business in Dubai must place a lot of trust in this system - before choosing an agent, it is highly advisable to first investigate his reputation in the market, and agree on each party's rights and responsibilities. Once established, it is very difficult to break an agency agreement, except in the case of cessation of activity.

Commercial Agent

If a foreign company wants to supply goods and/or services from abroad without establishing a physical presence in Dubai, it can appoint a commercial agent as a distributor for its goods and/or services in the UAE. The agent is entitled to exclusive rights to distribute and market specific products and services within a specific territory. The company is not allowed to distribute these products in that territory. If the company does assist in a sale, its commercial agent is entitled to a commission.

Such a commercial agency also covers franchises, distributorships and commission arrangements. The agent must register the agency agreement with the Ministry of Economy.

Legal Consultants

Afridi & Angell	331 0900
Allen & Overy	332 3190
Al Owais & Manfield	221 9000
Al Tamimi & Co	331 7090
Barahim	228 4399
Clifford Chance	331 4333
Clyde & Co	331 1102
Denton Wilde Sapte	331 0220
Emirates Advocates	330 4343
Hill Taylor Dickinson	331 7788
James Berry & Associates	351 1020
Key & Dixon	359 0096
Nabulsi Legal Consultants	222 3004
Naji Beidoun & Associates	222 5151
Simmons & Simmons	02 627 5568
Stockwell & Associates	228 3194
Towry Law Group	335 3137
Trench & Associates	355 3146
Trowers & Hamlin	351 9201

Labour Law

Other options → Banning [p.70]

The UAE Labour Law is very employer friendly. Labour issues are administered by the Federal Ministry of Labour and Social Affairs. The law is loosely based on the International Labour Organisation's model and deals with employer/employee relations such as working hours, termination rights, benefits, and repatriation. Little recourse for employees exists and exploitation does occur, particularly amongst blue collar workers and labourers. Trade unions do not exist and strikes are forbidden.

Government workers and employees of quasi-government institutions are not necessarily subject to the UAE Labour Law. Some free zones, including the Jebel Ali Free Zone Authority, have their own labour rules, and disputes are settled by the Authority, without recourse to the Federal Ministry. A copy of the UAE Labour Law can be obtained from the Dubai offices of the Ministry of Labour (269 1666).

Copyright Law

Introduced in 1993, the UAE Copyright Law was most recently updated in 2002 with the development of Federal Copyright Law No.7. This law, which is overseen by the Ministry of Information and Culture, protects the rights of creators, performers, producers of audio recordings, as well as broadcasting and recording corporations.

Trademark Law

The UAE Federal Government first introduced its trademark law in 1974, then updated it in 1993. Throughout, the government has continually improved its efforts to protect registered trademark owners. Trademark registration in the UAE is done through the Ministry of Economy and Commerce. The entire registration process can take anywhere from 12 to 18 months. Under the UAE trademark law, trademark owners can now protect their marks and count on government assistance to penalise those infringing upon their trademark.

SETTING UP

It is difficult to provide 'hard and fast' rules to those wishing to set up a company in Dubai. The main difficulty in providing this information is the amount of variables involved. Rules depend on nationality, business activity, capital amounts, partners, products etc, and the laws and/or regulations change on a regular basis. Check with the relevant government department(s) before proceeding.

After obtaining a trade licence, there are generally five set up options for non-GCC nationals. These are: setting up a branch of a foreign company, a limited liability company (LLC), a sole proprietorship, a professional company, and setting up in a free zone.

Trade Licence

After having read the *Zappy Explorer (Dubai)*, visit the Department for Corporate Relations and the Investment Promotion Centre at the Dubai Economic Department (DED). In an effort to promote investment, and in particular, foreign investment, this friendly and efficient department will assist with the paperwork involved in obtaining a trade licence, which is the first step in setting up. The Dhs.200-500 fee is worthwhile, and will save numerous headaches. The office is located in the DED head office on the first floor.

Branch or Representative Office

Established foreign companies may set up a branch or a representative office of their firm in Dubai. The branch will be considered a part of the parent company, and not a separate legal entity. Unlike a branch office, a representative office is permitted to practice promotional services for the company and products, and also facilitate contacting potential customers.

For the complete branch or representative office setting up procedure, including costs, timing, tips and advice, pick up a copy of the *Zappy Explorer (Dubai)*.

Limited Liability Company (LLC)

An LLC is a business structure that is a hybrid of a partnership and a corporation. Its owners are shielded from personal liability; the liability of the shareholders is limited to their shares in the company's capital.

This company type suits organisations interested in developing a long-term relationship in the local market. Responsibility for the management of an LLC can be vested in either the national or foreign partners, or in a third party.

For the complete LLC setting up procedure, including costs, timing, tips and advice, pick up a copy of the *Zappy Explorer (Dubai)*.

Sole Proprietorship

A sole proprietorship by definition means 'one owner'. This is the most basic company form where the owner has a trade licence in his name and is personally held liable for his accounts, i.e. he is responsible for the company's financial obligations. The proprietor can conduct business in the commercial, professional, industrial, agricultural or real estate industry.

Nationals and GCC nationals are permitted to set up a sole proprietorship with few restrictions. Stricter conditions apply for non-GCC nationals.

A non-GCC national setting up a sole proprietorship is restricted in the type of activities he may perform. The company should be in a service or knowledge-based industry.

For the complete sole proprietorship setting up procedure, including costs, timing, tips and advice, pick up a copy of the *Zappy Explorer (Dubai)*.

Business

Setting Up

Professional Company

Also referred to as a business partnership, professional business company, or consultancy business, this company type falls under the civil code, rather than under commercial law. This differentiation is unique to the UAE. Such firms may engage in professional or artisan activities, but the number of staff members that may be employed is limited and a UAE national must be appointed as local service agent.

An important part in applying for the licence is showing evidence of the credentials and qualifications of the employees and partners.

For the complete professional company setting up procedure, including costs, timing, tips and advice, pick up a copy of the *Zappy Explorer (Dubai)*.

Free Zones

Other options ➜ Free Zones [p.62]

Jebel Ali Free Zone Authority (JAFZA), established in 1985 at an estimated cost of over US$2 billion, has become a runaway success, and today is home to almost 2,500 companies from about 100 different countries. The signboards dotting the free zone are a who's who of both Fortune 500 companies and local business houses. The original area between the port and Sheikh Zayed Road is almost full, and massive efforts are underway to develop the desert on the other side of the road. JAFZA offers investors 100% control of their business, duty-free import of products (for manufacturing/transit/export), lease-hold

Dubai Media City

land ownership, and guaranteed freedom from corporate taxation.

Free Zones	
Ajman Free Zone Authority	06 742 5444
Dubai Airport Free Zone Authority	299 5555
Dubai Media City	391 4615
Dubai Internet City	391 1111
Fujairah Free Zone Authority	09 222 8000
Hamriya Free Zone Authority – Sharjah	06 526 3333
Jebel Ali Free Zone Authority	881 5000
RAK Free Zone	07 228 0889
Sharjah Airport Free Zone Authority	06 557 0000
Umm al-Quwain Ahmed Bin Rashid Free Zone Authority	06 765 5882

The success of JAFZA has spawned competing facilities in Sharjah, Ajman, Fujairah, Abu Dhabi and Ras al Khaimah. Although these other free zones offer lower fees, JAFZA still remains the preferred choice for many companies, due to the excellent infrastructure and relatively easy administrative procedures.

Dubai has also inaugurated other innovative free zones in recent years. *Dubai Internet City* (DIC) is home to over 450 companies operating in the high-tech sector, while *Dubai Media City* (DMC) has 300 tenants in six categories ranging from publishing and broadcasting to production and post-production. Companies in this free zone are not subject to censorship within the broad guidelines of the country's moral code. The *Dubai Airport Free Zone* and the newly announced Dubai International Financial Centre round out the free zone offerings in Dubai. Each of these free zones also offers investors 100% control of their business.

For details on setting up in any of the UAE's free zones, have a look at their respective Websites. For the setting up procedure for JAFZA, DIC or DMC, pick up a copy of the *Zappy Explorer (Dubai)*.

Selecting an Office or Warehouse

When applying for a trade licence, the rent agreement is normally required as part of the documentation. Ensure you select a location for your premises in an area in which you are permitted to perform your business activity. Dubai has strict zoning rules which restrict where a company may open up an office or warehouse. Approval must be gained from the Dubai Municipality and will depend on the business activity.

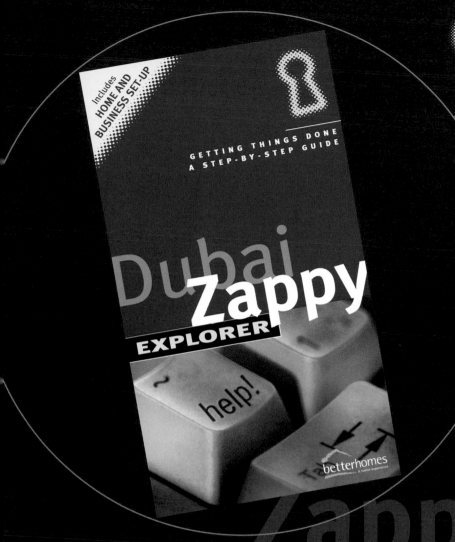

GETTING THINGS DONE
A STEP-BY-STEP GUIDE

Includes
HOME AND
BUSINESS SET-UP

Dubai
Zappy
EXPLORER

help!

Tai betterhomes

Zappy

Making Your Life in Dubai Easier...

A complete step-by-step guide for getting things done... the **Zappy Explorer** leads you through procedures on all aspects of life, whether business or personal – in a ap! This authoritative guide contains over 100 well thought-out, clear and easy to ollow procedures, and tips and advice for everything from obtaining visas and ermits to telecommunications, housing, transportation, licences, banking, ducation and health, making it your best chance for navigating through Dubai's dministrative mysteries.

- Immigration
- Residence
- Communications
- Transportation
- Personal Affairs
- Business
- Maps

Available from leading bookstores, hotels, supermarkets, or directly from Explorer Publishing

Don't sign a tenancy agreement for a warehouse or office before the Dubai Economic Department (DED) has contacted the Municipality and approved it. If the property is leased from or granted by the Government of Dubai, you will also need a sub-lease no objection letter from the Real Estate Department.

Office Rents

Office rents in Dubai compare with those of most international cities. Rents are usually calculated by the square foot and vary depending on location. Certain areas, such as Sheikh Zayed Road and Dubai Internet and Media City tend to have much higher rents than other areas due to their prime location and high demand. Building facilities vary from none, to those including a health club, restaurants, retail outlets and assigned parking. Leases are on an annual basis and must be paid up front or with up to four post-dated cheques.

Serviced Offices

As an alternative to the hassle and expense involved in finding and leasing office space, fully serviced offices are now being offered by a number of companies in Dubai. A good option if you are starting up a small business, normally the facilities and services offered are top quality. Serviced offices are fully furnished and are complete with high speed Internet connection, telephone lines, business support services etc.

The *Gulf Business Centre* (332 8850) offers fully serviced apartments between 12-34 m² within the

Crowne Plaza complex on Sheikh Zayed Road. The international corporation, *Regus*, (211 5100) has serviced offices plus gym facilities in the Union House Building across from the Deira City Centre shopping mall. The *Signature BusinessClub* (332 8990) also offers fully serviced offices at the Fairmont Hotel for a single monthly charge.

Land Ownership

Currently, foreign companies and non-Nationals are not permitted to own commercial land in the UAE other than in free zones, where leasehold ownership is offered. Commercial property must be either rented or leased, and rates are high.

The year 2002 has witnessed significant changes in land ownership rules for residential properties, where leasehold and freehold ownership opportunities have emerged for non-Nationals - it remains to be seen if this trend will spill over into the commercial market.

Work Permits

Other options → **Visas [p.17]**
Residence Visa [p.58]
Labour Card [p.62]

The employer is responsible for all work permits and related immigration procedures; this can be quite a tedious endeavour, so be warned, and start the process early. If setting up in a free zone, the free zone authority will handle all immigration-related procedures, which simplifies the process dramatically, but costs slightly more.

Sheikh Zayed Road

The company must cover all costs (visa, medical test, etc) involved in hiring an employee. Costs for family members are the employee's responsibility, unless otherwise stated in the employment contract.

Labour Contracts

Other options → **Employment Contracts [p.70]**

When applying for a work permit, the Ministry of Labour provides a model labour contract in Arabic. It is advisable to draft an additional contract with further employment and benefit details, particularly for senior staff. The employment contract is enforceable in a court of law (except in the case of some free zones) as long as it does not contravene the Labour Law. The Arabic version of the contract will prevail in a court of law.

Staffing

Other options → **Finding Work [p.69]**

For companies operating outside the free zones, the Ministry of Labour will set a maximum number of expatriate staff that may be hired, according to the size of the business and the business activity. In some cases, such as banks, the Ministry will state the minimum percentage of employees that must be UAE Nationals.

Recruitment of staff is an entirely separate challenge. Various agencies can assist with the recruitment of labourers from overseas, while other local recruiters specialise in searches for professional and managerial positions. In reality, many positions are filled through word of mouth between friends and business colleagues, and also through 'wasta' (connections).

Customs

Other options → **Customs [p.19]**

Imports to Dubai (and the UAE) are subject to 4% customs duty, which is applied at the time of delivery at the port or airport; there are no duties on the import of personal effects. No customs duties are payable on goods that do not leave the various free zones.

The Gulf Co-operation Council (GCC) has announced plans for a GCC Customs Union to take effect from 2003. Under the terms of this agreement, all six GCC countries would apply a rate of 5% to import.

Taxation

Although UAE law provides for taxation, no personal income taxes or corporate taxes are actually levied and collected, either in the city or the free zones; the free zones offer additional guarantees to companies concerning their future tax free status. The UAE has double-taxation treaties with various countries, although the effectiveness of these treaties is limited given that the effective tax rates in the UAE are nil. The only corporations subject to income taxes in the UAE are courier companies, oil companies, and branches of foreign banks.

Exchange Controls

Other options → **Money [p.38]**
Banks [p.38]

The UAE Dirham (AED or Dhs.) is pegged to the US Dollar at the rate of about 3.67 dirhams per dollar, and never fluctuates significantly from this level. Due to the strength of the local economy, the large foreign currency reserves, the lack of advanced financial currency products, and restrictions on foreign share ownership, the dirham has not been attacked by foreign speculators, and is perceived to be a safe currency.

There are no foreign exchange controls, and there are generally no restrictions on repatriating capital and/or earnings. In an attempt to control problems of money laundering, banks are supposed to report all transactions in excess of Dhs.40,000 to the government, although pre-approval is not required.

White Collar Crime

Like everywhere in the world, there are instances of white collar crime, so companies must establish proper audit controls. However, companies exert a greater level of control over their employees because most are expatriates, with some employers even holding passports.

In the UAE, it is considered a crime to issue a cheque for which insufficient funds exist in the bank account - penalties for this offence range from a fine to imprisonment. The authorities tend to favour the more extreme punishment for this crime - be warned!

Business

Setting Up

What kind of adventure will you have today?

Discover Dubai and the UAE with our exciting range of tours, safaris and activities. Cruise Dubai Creek, dine among the dunes, or get an aerial perspective. Take a city tour, go deep sea fishing, desert driving or explore the *wadis*. We'll even tailor-make a package just for you – from scuba diving to sand-skiing.

Call us on Dubai 303 4888 or Abu Dhabi 633 8111.

Arabian Adventures

www.arabian-adventures.com

Dubai: Tel: +971 4 343 9966
Abu Dhabi: Tel: +971 2 633 8111
Fujairah: Tel: +971 4 303 4888
E-mail: arabian.adventures@emirates.com

Exploring

EXPLORER

Exploring

DUBAI AREAS

Exploring

This section of the book is aimed at the bewildered newcomer to Dubai or the resident who wants a better feel for the various areas of the city.

What there is to see and do ranges from visiting museums and heritage sites, relaxing at parks and beaches, to enjoying various tour and sightseeing opportunities. Spend a couple of hours driving around and you will find that this is a bustling modern city with few old buildings or historical sites. However, a huge effort is being made to preserve and restore the traditional Arabic heritage, and the city has a variety of attractions, both old and new, that are worth visiting.

Also covered are places out of Dubai, although for more information on Abu Dhabi, the Sultanate of Oman and off the beaten track in the UAE, refer to the *Abu Dhabi Explorer*, the *Oman Explorer* (formerly *Muscat Explorer*) and the *Off-Road Explorer (UAE)*.

Dubai originally grew around the Dubai Creek, however, it is now developing into a linear coastal settlement, mainly spreading south-west towards Abu Dhabi. The 15 km long Creek is only about 500 metres wide, and has three main crossing points — Al Shindagha Tunnel nearest the sea, then Al Maktoum Bridge and furthest inland, Al Garhoud Bridge.

For each of the main geographical areas of Dubai, we have described the key activities and landmarks. Dubai Creek divides the city into two areas — to the south is known as Bur Dubai and to the north as Deira.

On the Bur Dubai side of the city are Oud Metha (a recreational and commercial area), Satwa, and Karama (both original suburbs of old Dubai), plus Jumeira and Umm Suqeim (originally fishing settlements) further along the coast away from the Creek. Further past Umm Suqeim, on the way to Abu Dhabi, is Jebel Ali, which is the most southerly point of the city, and famous for its port and free zone. The road that takes you to Jebel Ali and Abu Dhabi is the Sheikh Zayed Road, an eight-lane highway lined with skyscrapers housing both businesses and residents. Areas north of the Creek include Al Garhoud, the district close to the airport, and the newer residential development of Mirdif.

Dubai Creek

The Creek has played a pivotal role in the development of Dubai, and it neatly divides the modern city into two distinct areas (Bur Dubai to the south and Deira to the north). In Arabia, like anywhere in the world, a creek or waterway made a natural environment to build a community around. The earliest Dubai settlement was near the mouth of the Creek, but when it was dredged to create a larger anchorage and encourage trade, the growing town gradually crept further inland.

Dubai Creek has three main crossing points — Al Shindagha Tunnel nearest to the sea, then Al Maktoum Bridge and furthest inland, Al Garhoud Bridge. Both bridges can be raised to allow boats through to the boatyard inland, but this usually only happens late at night. There is also a pedestrian foot tunnel near Al Shindagha.

The layout of the roads and the heat, especially in summer, do not make Dubai the easiest city to explore on foot, however, many parts are well worth the effort of walking around. In particular, these include the souks and the corniche areas on both sides of the Creek, which can be combined with an atmospheric 'abra' (water taxi) crossing. The term 'corniche' is used to refer to any walkway by a stretch of water — in the UAE, this can be along the seafront or around one of the creeks or lagoons. A useful guide is the *Town Walk Explorer (Dubai)* (Dhs.10), which outlines two routes through the most interesting parts of the city. It is available from all good bookshops or directly from Explorer Publishing.

Whilst there are three main crossing points of the Creek, a more exciting way of crossing it is by boat. Known locally as abras, these water taxis ply between the two banks as they have done for decades. The abra crossing takes about fifteen minutes and can be made in either direction from the dhow wharfage area on the Deira side, and the Al Seef Road part of Bur Dubai.

The basic wooden boats seat about 30 people and are used as a convenient and cheap method of transport. For visitors, they are a great way to see the modern towers of Deira, the older Arabic architecture of Bur Dubai and to get a real feel of the city. At 50 fils, it's probably the cheapest tour in the world! The steps down to the Creek are steep, so be careful when stepping across to your boat. Alternatively, for Dhs.50, you can hire a boat and driver for a private river tour for half an hour.

For a more luxurious tour of the Creek, consider an organised boat trip. For further details, refer to Creek Tours [p.160].

Bur Dubai

Once a flat, sandy area with a sprinkling of palm trees and barasti (palm) houses, this area of the city is nowadays very much the bustling business hub of Dubai, with modern buildings and plenty of shops selling textiles and electronics. It is also a heavily residential part of the city, and popular with expats of all nationalities. Most live in 8 storey apartment blocks in an area known as Golden Sands (between Al Mankhool Road and Trade Centre Road), which seems very popular, despite the concrete jungle feel and high rents. Except for near the Creek, as there's not much to see, this is not a great district to explore on foot, and women in Western dress can attract a lot of attention from cruising cars.

South of the Creek mouth is Port Rashid. The Dubai Ports Authority building (a large glass and chrome construction imaginatively designed to represent a paddle steamer) indicates its proximity, and all the paraphernalia of a port can be glimpsed over the surrounding fence.

Bur Dubai

Dubai Areas

Exploring

The area near the mouth of the Creek, known as Al Shindagha, is a good starting point to explore Bur Dubai. Here you can visit Sheikh Saeed Al Maktoum's House and the Heritage & Diving Village (a two minute walk from each other), before following the Creek inland to Dubai Museum. For further information, see Museums & Heritage [p.143].

Near the Astoria Hotel, is the busy Al Faheidi Street, see [p.220]. Its narrow, bustling streets are a paradise for electrical goods. Close by are the wooden shaded walkways of the Textile Souk, where every type of fabric, from printed and plain silk or linen to cotton, can be found.

Facing Dubai Museum is the Diwan, the Ruler's office, where the business of Dubai emirate's administration is undertaken. The Diwan is the highest administrative body of the Dubai government. Built in 1990, the low white building is surrounded by black railings and combines modern materials with a traditional design, including examples of traditional windtowers.

Located near the Diwan, the Grand Mosque was recently renovated at an estimated cost of fifteen and a half million dirhams. It can accommodate 1,200 worshippers, and has 54 domes and a 70 metre minaret — presently the tallest in the city.

It is possible to walk inland along the edge of the Creek past the Diwan to the Bastakiya district of the city. The relaxed atmosphere of this walkway is popular with residents and tourists in the know. Refer to the *Town Walk Explorer (Dubai)* for further details. An outdoor restaurant in this area is a great place to enjoy Arabic fare and shisha pipes while watching the river traffic.

Bastakiya (also Bastakia) is one of the oldest heritage sites in Dubai. This intriguing neighbourhood dates back to the early 1900s when traders from Bastak in southern Iran were granted tax concessions by the then ruler of Dubai and encouraged to settle there. Here you can view one of the earliest forms of air conditioning in the shape of windtowers ('barajeel' in Arabic), which are distinctive rectangular structures on top of the traditional flat roofed buildings. These were built to catch the slightest of breezes and funnel them down into the rooms and courtyards of the houses below. Amble down alleyways, step into a converted house, which is now an art gallery, Majlis Gallery, (see [p.186]), and picture yourself living in a bygone era.

An ongoing reconstruction project is gradually turning the area into a pedestrian conservation area, with over 50 houses due for restoration by

2004. Eventually there will be a museum, a cultural centre and a restaurant.

Numerous embassies are in this area, and further inland from the Creek is the popular BurJuman Shopping Centre, see [p.209]. Located near the Golden Sands area, on a busy crossroads on Khalid bin Waleed Road (or Bank Street, as it is popularly known), this already huge mall is currently being extended and looks like it will be tripling in size.

Deira

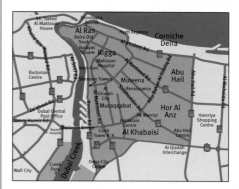

Arrive at the Deira side of the Creek by abra for an atmospheric feel of the place, or arrive by road for a more hair-raising experience! Narrow convoluted streets bustle with residential and commercial activity, and gold, spices, perfumes and general goods beckon from the numerous souks. Rents are generally less expensive on this side of the Creek and the streets are mainly full of people in the evenings.

Take a stroll along the dhow wharfage to experience the hustle and bustle of wooden dhows being unloaded — excellent for a feel of old and new Dubai, side by side. Marvel at the trust that is evident from the piles of goods left on the wharfage and take in the incongruous sight of fruit, vegetables, electronics and even cars being offloaded from the same vessel. This is a real visual treat and an excellent photo opportunity.

Bordering the Creek are some wonderful buildings; the large sphere on top of a high rise pinpoints the Etisalat telecommunications building — you can't miss it! The glass building housing the National Bank of Dubai (known locally as the 'pregnant lady') is an amazing feat of engineering and has an almost sculptural feel. For the best view of the contrast of ancient trading dhows moored in front of modern Dubai, try to be on the opposite side of the Creek at dusk (near the British Embassy). As

Dhs.100 ~ € 28

Exploring Dubai Areas

in the UAE since 1976

MAPSgeosystems

Survey & Mapping from Ground, Air & Space

- Aerial Photography
- Satellite Image Processing
- Ground Survey
- Utility Mapping
- Geodetic Network Rehabilitation
- Terrain Modelling
- T3D Vector Mapping
- Orthoimage Production
- Geographic Data Acquisition
- Spatial Data Integration
- GIS Implementation
- Application Service Provision

Master Reseller for **DIGITALGLOBE**™
highest resolution QuickBird satellite imagery

MAPS (UAE), Corniche Plaza 1, P.O. Box 5232, Sharjah, UAE,
Tel : +971 6 5725411, Fax : +971 6 5724057

www.maps-geosystems.com
info@maps-geosystems.com

Operations throughout Europe, Middle East and Africa, with
regional offices in: Munich, Sharjah, Beirut, Lisbon, Bucharest,
Dubai, Abu Dhabi, Conakry, Dakar

Deira

the sun goes down behind you, it creates dramatic reflections in both the glass and water.

Take the pedestrian underpass to the left of the abra station steps to enter the oldest market in Dubai, now mainly selling houseware items. Close by is the Spice Souk, where a lot of the stores look half closed with only a few items in the window or on a table outside. That's all a trader needs to see to order dozens, hundreds or tonnes of the goods on offer. Produce such as loose frankincense and other perfumed oils are available, along with dried herbs and twigs, which are sold for medicinal purposes. The souk spreads over a large area between Al Nasr Square and the Creek area at the Gold Souk.

If you are interested in carpets, Deira Tower on Al Nasr Square is the place to go. Around 40 shops offer a colourful profusion of carpets from Iran, Pakistan, Turkey and Afghanistan, to suit everyone's taste and pocket.

Dubai, the 'City of Gold', is famed for its gold shopping, and one of the most popular places to shop for it is the Gold Souk. Here there are streets and streets of gold – the volume is so overwhelming that a second, or even third, visit may be required before making a final purchase. Bargaining is expected, and discounts depend on the season and the international gold rate. Dubai Shopping Festival and Dubai Summer Surprises are the main periods for low prices; at these times huge discounts attract gold lovers from around the world. Be sure to haggle hard to get the 'best price'. Individual designs and pieces can be made, or copies to your own specifications done within a few days.

Take time to look up at the wooden covered walkway, erected to make shopping more bearable under the hot sun, and wander through the alleyways discovering antiques amongst the silver and gold on offer. Even if you aren't buying, an evening wander through the gold souk in Deira is one of Dubai's unique, not-to-be-missed experiences.

In this part of town the earliest school in the city, Al Ahmadiya School, has been turned into the Museum of Education and is located next to the Heritage House. For further information on Al Ahmadiya School, refer to Museums & Heritage [p.143].

Also worth a visit in terms of atmosphere is the Fish Market. This is the largest and busiest of Dubai's fish markets, and is visited by numerous tourists and city residents.

A fish museum is being created at Deira Fish Market as part of a two and a half million dirham facelift. The aim is to give shoppers and tourists alike a better idea about the types of fish available in the Arabian Gulf, the history of the fishing trade in the UAE in general and Dubai in particular, and the types of fishing boats and equipment used by fishermen.

The Fruit & Vegetable Market is a visual treat. You'll find an astounding range of shapes and colours and produce from many countries. As in the Fish Market, you can pay a 'wheelbarrow man' to follow you around; while you buy, he carries your shopping. Prices are unbelievably cheap — you can end up paying the same for a box of fruit or vegetables, as you'd pay for a small bag in the supermarkets. However, be prepared to work for it — as in any souk, haggling is the name of the game!

Nearby is the weekly Friday Market, which operates between September and April. Stalls sell everything from varied foodstuffs, such as Yemeni spices and honey, to traditional crafts, pets, plants and household commodities. Children can enjoy

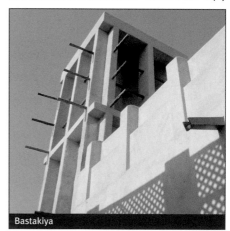

Bastakiya

donkey and cart rides, adding to the family day out feel. Look for the road signs to the Hamriya fruit and vegetable markets.

Being Dubai, development plans are in the offing to reclaim land from the sea and transform the Deira seafront by building residential and commercial units, as well as public utilities and tourist attractions. The aim is to complete these by 2005.

For further information on carpets and gold, refer to the Shopping section of the book [p.180].

Al Garhoud

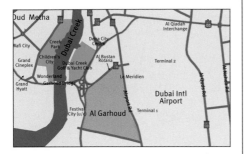

The area known as Al Garhoud lies to the north of Al Garhoud Bridge (the most inland of the two bridges that cross the Creek), on the Deira side of the Creek. It is primarily a commercial district, which quietens down at night, although there are residential pockets. There are places by the Creek that offer escape — near the bridge is a popular spot for fishing.

Close to the bridge is space allocated for Dubai Festival City — one of the city's latest shopping and entertainment extravaganzas. It is being developed at an estimated cost of six billion dirhams over the next three years. The first phase, which is due to open in 2003, will include a marina, a 3.2 km waterfront promenade, 40 water view restaurants and an amphitheatre. Subsequent phases will include hotels, restaurants, family entertainment venues, a 'global village', residential and office space, plus indoor and outdoor shopping.

Almost in the middle of Garhoud is the Dubai Tennis Stadium, which doubles as a concert venue since Dubai presently has no other public stadium. Concerts seem to take place more frequently than sporting events. A couple of locations in Garhoud have al fresco licensed bars and restaurants overlooking pleasant landscaped courtyards. Two are Century Village and the Irish Village, which are

built into the side of the tennis stadium, and another is at Le Meridien Dubai hotel near the airport.

One of the more visually interesting buildings in Garhoud is the one shaped like the front half of an airplane, which rather appropriately is the training centre for the national airline, Emirates.

Deira City Centre Mall is the largest shopping mall in the Gulf, and is probably one of the most popular with visitors and residents alike. It is a linear mall with a light airy feel and plenty of underground parking, plus two multi storey car parks adjacent to the mall. Usually referred to as City Centre, it is always busy and gets particularly crowded at weekends and in the evenings.

Opposite City Centre and bordering the Creek for 1½ km is a large and enticing stretch of carefully landscaped greenery, home to the Dubai Creek Golf & Yacht Club. The club boasts an imaginative clubhouse based on the shape of dhow sails — the image of the famous buildings is found on the Dhs.20 note. This is a peaceful retreat from the bustle of the city and the course is floodlit allowing evening play. Non-members are welcome to visit the clubhouse and relax at one of the popular bars or restaurants.

Oud Metha/Umm Hurair

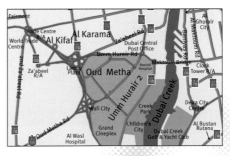

The Oud Metha Road cuts diagonally through this part of Dubai and is bordered by the Creek to the north, and Za'abeel road to the west, and Al Quta'eyat Road to the south. Within this residential area, you'll find recreational, social and educational facilities, as well as Lamcy Plaza, one of Dubai's larger shopping malls, with a maze-like layout that virtually forces you around the whole store.

Just off Oud Metha Road are various countries' social clubs and two of Dubai's churches. Close by are Rashid Hospital, the American Hospital, and Al Nasr Leisureland. This leisure complex offers a variety of facilities, including bowling and an indoor ice rink.

Dubai Areas

Exploring

Near the Al Maktoum Bridge, which was the first bridge built across the Creek, are the Dubai Courts and Creekside Park. The manicured lawns of the park run for 3 km alongside the Creek to Garhoud Bridge. An entrance fee is charged to visit and facilities include an amphitheatre, mini 'falaj' (traditional irrigation system) and a children's play area. For an aerial view of your surroundings, travel high above in one of the silver cable cars.

The latest attraction at Creekside Park is Children's City, the world's fifth largest 'infotainment' facility, comprising 77,000 square metres. Exhibits target children between the ages of 5 - 15 and are science and learning focused. There is also a planetarium inside.

WonderLand Theme & Water Park is at the Garhoud Bridge end of Creekside Park, and is a popular amusement park offering various rides, from bumper cars to a hot air balloon. There's even a roller coaster and a log flume ride.

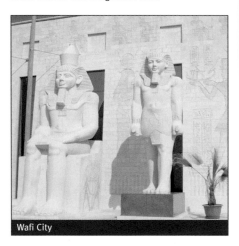
Wafi City

Next to WonderLand and near Garhoud Bridge is Al Boom Tourist Village, which is popular mainly with local couples who hire the hall for wedding functions. Tourists visit to sample the local cuisine and to enjoy an evening cruise of the Creek on one of the beautifully illuminated dhows.

Opposite Al Boom Tourist Village is a patch of land where, if you are lucky, you can glimpse a traditional wooden dhow being built. Mainly used for trade, these distinctive high bowed vessels take months to construct, but their lifespan is reckoned to be over a century.

Wafi City consists of several complexes, including a shopping mall, numerous popular restaurants, a nightclub and a health club and spa with an ancient Egyptian theme. The health club and mall exteriors are impressive, with huge mock Egyptian statues and a row of crouching sphinxes guarding the entrances. Wafi Mall specialises in upmarket quality items from established names. This site is also home to Planet Hollywood, hard to miss, as it is housed in a giant blue globe.

Near Wafi City is the Grand Cineplex, an 11-screen cinema, and the Grand Hyatt Hotel with its 18 food and beverage outlets, opening early 2003.

Al Karama

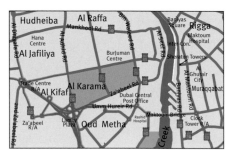

Al Karama is primarily a residential area, consisting of 3-4 storey apartment blocks and street level shops. It is very built up, but unusually for Dubai, the layout of the pavements and streets encourages pedestrians.

The open air Al Karama Shopping Centre consists of two central streets lined with lots of small shops with their produce spilling out onto the pavements. This is a great area for buying cheap and cheerful items such as funky clothes, suitcases, T-shirts, sunglasses and souvenirs, and for watching the cosmopolitan hotchpotch of nationalities that comes to shop here. There are always tourists in this part of town haggling hard for items.

Many of the goods are cheap imitations, if not counterfeit copies, of designer labels (usually easy to spot, although some of the fakes aren't too bad). Recently, the Dubai Municipality has been strict in clamping down on the sale of such items, but that said, you're still likely to have a guy sidle up to you asking if you want to buy a 'Rolex'!

The Fruit and Vegetable Market is worth a visit for the atmosphere and some good cheap produce. If you are looking for second-hand or inexpensive furniture, a street virtually devoted to furniture can be found near the Fruit and Vegetable Market, parallel to the main shopping drag. More expensive furniture can be found in the very upscale interior design showrooms that line the busy Za'abeel Road.

Sheikh Zayed Road

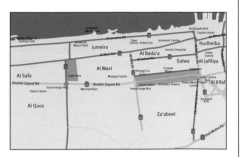

Another important area in Dubai stretches southwest from Trade Centre roundabout, parallel with the coast along the infamous eight lane Sheikh Zayed Road (known for its crazy drivers!) towards Abu Dhabi. The initial stretch after the roundabout is lined with modern high-rise office and apartment blocks, hotels and shopping malls. It is truly amazing to see this forest of stunning buildings that has sprung up.

At the start of the Sheikh Zayed Road 'business district' is the landmark Dubai World Trade Centre (illustrated on Dhs.100 banknotes) and exhibition halls. The 39 storey tower was once the tallest building in Dubai and remains an instantly recognisable point on the skyline, although it has now been surpassed in terms of size and grandeur by several other buildings in the city. For a great view, especially in winter when it is less hazy, there is a guided tour to the observation deck. This starts at 9:30am and 4pm from the information desk in the lobby and costs Dhs.5. The new conference and exhibition centre, will be complete in time for the IMF Conference in fall 2003.

Alongside the Sheikh Zayed Road and towering above every other building in the city, the Emirates Towers look set to replace the Trade Centre as the No.1 address for international businesses in Dubai. At 355 metres, the tower housing offices is the tallest building in the Middle East. The smaller tower, at 305 metres and with 'only' 53 storeys houses the Emirates Towers five star hotel.

Interchange One is also known locally as Defence Roundabout, and near here is an interesting skyscraper, which looks like a good chunk in the centre is missing. Apparently, the design of the Dusit Dubai Hotel is based on the image of hands praying.

The area to the north of the Sheikh Zayed Road is mainly residential with a mix of villas and apartment towers. To the south of the road, off Interchange Two, is an industrial and commercial area known as the Al Quoz Industrial Estate.

Tucked away in Al Quoz is the Courtyard. This building is home to a variety of retail outlets, and art exhibitions are held on a regular basis, however, the main attraction is the courtyard itself, surrounded by different façades, which combine a variety of building styles from around the world.

If you head inland from Interchange Two for about 5 km, you will arrive at the Dubai Camel Racecourse. First thing in the morning, you can watch the camels and their young trainers being put through their paces. A large floral roundabout proclaims the entrance to Nad Al Sheba, which has a golf course, but is mainly known for horseracing, including the richest horse race in the world, the Dubai World Cup.

Al Satwa

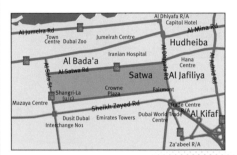

One of the more atmospheric and 'Arabic feeling' areas of Dubai, Al Satwa has plenty of low 4-5 storey apartment blocks with small shops on the ground floor. In Arabic, Al Satwa means 'hold up' referring to its more adventurous past.

The focal point of Al Satwa is Al Diyafah Street where residents can dodge the traffic and wander up the broad palm lined street checking out the shops, inexpensive restaurants and cafés.

At the western end of Al Diyafah Street, nearest the sea, is the Dar Al Ittehad (Union House) building. This is where the treaty to create the Arab world's first federation of states, the United Arab Emirates, was signed on 2 December 1971. This is also the site of the UAE's largest flag at 40 x 20 metres on top of a 120 metre reinforced column. This is floodlit at night and is noticeable from quite a distance.

At the other end of Al Diyafah Street is the permanently busy Al Satwa Road. Along here are numerous small shops selling mainly textiles, inexpensive clothes and general household items. You'll also find tailors here who have a good reputation for copying designs very inexpensively.

Between Al Satwa Road and Al Wasl Road is a street with wider pavements and shops selling plants and flowers. The aptly named Plant Street is where you can buy fir trees in December, unusual artificial trees all year round, and all sorts of fresh flowers. It also has numerous pet shops, with exotic birds, fish and animals for sale. Alongside this mini 'jungle' area are art shops selling original paintings, drawings and prints. Many offer framing facilities at very reasonable rates.

On Al Wasl Road is the beautiful and intricate Iranian Mosque, with distinctive blue tiles, arches and pillars mirroring the similarly patterned Iranian Hospital opposite.

In Arabic, Jumeira means 'burning embers'. The public beach, Jumeira Beach Corniche, quickly fills with tourists and people gawping at other people — if you want some peace, try one of the beach parks. The nearest is the Jumeira Beach Park, which is off Beach Road in a beautiful tropical paradise setting.

A poignant sight can sometimes be seen along the Beach Road — the head of a giraffe peeking over the perimeter wall of the Dubai Zoo. This was originally a private collection of animals housed in a large private garden, but it is now owned by the Municipality. The animals are in small, limiting cages. Attempts have been made to send some of the animals to other zoos around the world to increase the space for the remaining inmates. Over recent years there has been talk about building a new zoo for the animals at Mushrif Park near the airport. Sadly, at the moment, it seems that this is just talk and those with a more 'modern' approach to animals may prefer to pass on a visit here.

Jumeira

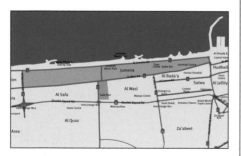

On the Bur Dubai side of the city, stretching south for about 10 km along the coast from Satwa's borders towards Umm Suqeim, is the area of Jumeira. This was once a fishing village, but is now a desirable residential area. The expression, 'Jumeira Jane', has even entered the local lingo, referring to a stereotyped well-heeled female resident of this district. There are lots of medical practices, dentists, beauty salons, etc, catering to the needs of the local resident population along the two main roads in the district — Jumeira Beach Road (also known as the Beach Road) and Al Wasl Road.

There is a very small town feel to the shopping strip on either side of the road near the Jumeira Mosque. This is easily the most beautiful mosque in the city, as well as the best known, and it features on the Dhs.500 bank note. Constructed from a distinctive creamy/pink stone, it is especially lovely at night when it is lit up.

Mirdif

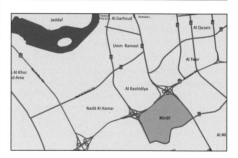

On the eastern outskirts of the city, Mirdif is one of Dubai's newer residential areas. It's popular for its villas, which are fairly inexpensive due to their location beneath the airport's flight path. Although villas have sprung up quickly here, local amenities, such as shops and parks, haven't kept pace with expansion – in fact, they don't exist!

Umm Suqeim

Stretching from Jumeira towards Al Mina Al Siyahi is the mostly residential area of Umm Suqeim. Two main roads border this district, running parallel with the coast; the continuation from Jumeira of the Jumeira Beach Road, and the Al Wasl Road.

Interestingly, Umm Suqeim was hit by the plague at the beginning of the 20th century when most of

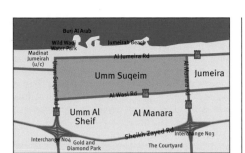

the residents died, hence its rather unpleasant name 'mother of all sicknesses'. However, the modern day residents seem healthy enough taking their children to the various schools, walking their pets in the afternoons or just strolling around the neighbourhood.

Running between Al Wasl Road and Sheikh Zayed Road is the green oasis of Safa Park. Facilities here include a big wheel, various games pitches and plenty of barbecue sites. The tennis courts are generally busy and it's a popular place in the early evening with joggers who jog around the perimeter to avoid paying the entrance fee.

Off Al Wasl road is Park N Shop, a small outdoor shopping parade with stores that are much frequented by local residents, giving a sense of community.

Souk Al Nakheel is another shopping complex that has just started development on the other side of the Sheikh Zayed Road. It will eventually be the location of the largest shopping mall in Dubai, with its own indoor ski hill!

On the borders of Umm Suqeim and Jumeira is Majlis Ghorfat Um Al Sheef, which is a small park with an excellent museum of how life used to be. It was built in 1955 and used as a summer residence by the late Sheikh Rashid bin Saeed Al Maktoum.

The largest landmark in the area is the 321 metre Burj Al Arab, which stands on its own specially constructed island 280 metres offshore. A globally recognised landmark, it is quite simply unique and the atrium alone is large enough to fit the Dubai World Trade Centre inside! Its name translates into English as the 'Tower of the Arabs', and its sail shaped design is seen on all new car number plates.

The outside of the minimalist blue and white structure is dramatically transformed in the evening when a kaleidoscope of lights makes it look like a giant video screen (or UFO!). It also paves the way for the almost kitsch opulence of the interior, where abundant gold and saturated colours dominate.

The 'sail' of the Burj Al Arab towers over the breaking wave shape of the Jumeirah Beach Hotel

alongside, which even at 25 storeys high is dwarfed by the tower. On the same site is the Wild Wadi Water Park — one of the world's most advanced water adventure parks with many exhilarating rides set amongst dramatic landscaping.

Further expansion is due along this coastline. Madinat Jumeirah will be a new district with restaurants, cafés and a traditional souk. Waterways will enable visitors to travel around by abra and the main hotel will be designed like a summer palace amidst landscaped gardens.

Al Sufouh/Al Mina Al Siyahi

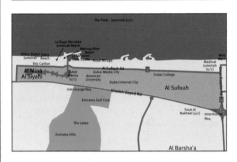

The Al Mina Al Siyahi stretch of coastline extends from Black Palace Beach (named after one of the palaces visible from the road), up to the borders of Jebel Ali Port. Living up to its name of 'touristic port', the coastline here has seen a huge amount of luxury development over the last few years, with much more to come in the future — these will certainly be high prestige residential addresses. Due to the amount of construction along these beaches, access has been greatly curtailed.

The new growth has included numerous five-star beach hotels, such as the conventionally designed Sheraton Jumeira, Le Meridien Mina Seyahi and Le Royal Meridien Jumeira Beach to the imaginative, themed Royal Mirage and Ritz-Carlton. There are also numerous business developments, most notably the innovative Dubai Media and Internet Cities. They are the world's first free zones for information technology, e-business and media.

Next to the Royal Mirage hotel will be the entrance to the Jumeira Palm Island. This is the first of the two new man-made islands off the coast of Dubai, the other to be located south-west of the Jebel Ali Hotel. The islands will add 120 kilometres to Dubai's coastline. Each will be shaped like a palm tree, surrounded by a barrier reef. The Jumeira Palm sold all of its 2,000 villas and townhomes within weeks of release. These will be built amidst tropical vegetation and buyers can choose from a range of architectural styles, from Arabic to Portuguese or Chinese. About 40 hotels, shopping malls, and cinema complexes are planned for this island.

Further along, the first phase of the Dubai Marina development can be seen, which is due for completion by mid 2004. This site will be primarily a residential area with high rises, restaurants, coffee shops and boutiques lining a marina.

Nearby, on the Sheikh Zayed Road, you will spot two large electric guitars and the 'Empire State Building' — this is the Dubai branch of the Hard Rock Café. The American theme continues at the nearby American University of Dubai, which unusually, is a mixed campus. The building looks like a miniature White House or Senate building, complete with dome and columns.

On the other side of the highway is the landscaped greenery of the Emirates Golf Club. A serene retreat from the bustle of the city, this golf club boasts a clubhouse based on the image of Bedouin tents. Non-members are welcome to visit for a round of golf or to relax at one of the bars or restaurants in the clubhouse.

Nearby are the various prestigious Emaar residential developments – The Meadows, The Lakes, The Hills, The Greens and Arabian Ranches. The area is aiming to be a 'city within a city' with villas, townhouses, apartments, lakes, parks, entertainment facilities, restaurants and shops.

Jebel Ali

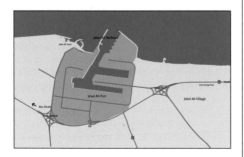

Lying to the south of the city, Jebel Ali is chiefly known for its free zone and port, which provide manufacturing and trade facilities in an environment that is attractive to foreign investors. The free zone now has around 2,000 companies from 92 countries located here.

Although 'jebel' means mountain in English, it seems a little dramatic to refer to this slight rise in the land as anything approaching even a hill! If you ignore the large port and industries associated with the free zone, the 'mountain' does, however, offer attractive views of the Gulf. One of the most pleasant places to visit in this area is the Jebel Ali Hotel & Golf Resort, as well as the public beach beyond the hotel (refer to Beaches [p.150] for details).

Visitor's Checklist

The following is our list of 'must do's' for a visit to Dubai, which we have included to help you plan a schedule of things to see and do. While the city isn't over-endowed in the cultural and heritage stakes, there are plenty of options to keep most people busy in between relaxing by the pool!

Arabic Food

Try Al Koufa or Al Areesh restaurants, go for a dune dinner, buy a shawarma from any roadside restaurant, eat dates and smoke a shisha pipe for a true 'local experience'.

Museums/Historic/Shopping

After visiting Dubai Museum take a walk through Bastakiya, stop at the Majlis Gallery, then shop for souvenirs in Karama. Alternatively visit some of Sharjah's many fine museums and souks.

Dubai Creekside

Start at the Heritage & Diving Village, drop into Sheikh Saeed's House, take an abra ride over the Creek for a walk along Deira's Dhow Wharfage then on to the Spice Souk and the Gold Souk.

Sightseeing Tours

A desert trip is a must while in Dubai to experience the beauty and the fun of the desert. Ride a camel, climb a sand dune, watch the stars, eat your fill, and learn how to belly-dance!

Out of Dubai

Head for the East Coast or the Hajar Mountains near Hatta - both drives take you through great desert and mountain scenery with small towns, forts and mosques. The East Coast has excellent beaches and water sports, while Hatta has spectacular scenery and freshwater pools. Have a look at the Friday Market, on the way - you might find the deal of a lifetime!

In Dubai

Other options → **Art [p.185]**
Children's City [p.295]
Mosque Tours [p.161]

For residents and visitors alike, a visit to one of the museums or heritage sites is a great opportunity to discover something more about the culture and history of the UAE, as well as to catch a glimpse of a quickly disappearing way of life.

Entrance fees are minimal and information is given in both Arabic and English. Note that opening times often change during the summer months, Ramadan, Eid, and public holidays, so check before leaving home to avoid disappointment.

Refer also to Dubai Areas [p.132] for information on what there is to do that can be combined with a visit to a museum or heritage site.

Al Ahmadiya School & Heritage House

Location → Al Khor St, Al Ras · Deira | **226 0286**
Hours → 08:00 - 14:00 Closed Thu & Fri
Web/email → www.dubaitourism.co.ae | **Map Ref →** 8-C2

Al Ahmadiya School, or the Museum of Education, was the earliest regular school in the city and a visit here is an excellent opportunity to see the history of education in Dubai. It was established in 1912 by Mr Ahmadiya and instruction was given by some of the leading teachers of the day to Dubai's elite, including the late ruler of Dubai, Sheikh Rashid bin Saeed Al Maktoum. With the opening in the 1950s of more modern schools, Al Ahmadiya was neglected until its restoration and conversion into a museum in March 2000.

The school is located next to the Heritage House, the former home of Mr Ahmadiya, which dates back to 1890. Guides and touch screens take you through the tour of the two museums. Admission is free.

Dubai Museum

Location → Al Faheidi Fort · Bastakiya, Bur Dubai | **353 1862**
Hours → 08:30 - 20:30 Fri 14:30 - 20:30
Web/email → www.dubaitourism.co.ae | **Map Ref →** 8-B3

This is no stuffy museum and is well worth a visit, even if the museum 'thing' isn't your scene. Built

in 1787 as a fort for sea defence and residence of the ruler of Dubai, Al Faheidi Fort was renovated in 1970 to house the museum. The site has been expanded to include a large area under the courtyard of the old fort.

Everything is represented in an original and highly creative way. Step off a dhow unloading its wares to enter a souk of the 1950s and walk through a labyrinth of shops and craftsmen's dwellings ... you can even peek into an Islamic school. Then enter the world of life at an oasis, the desert at night, a tribute to the sea and archaeological finds from the area. *Highly recommended.*

Entrance fees: *adults Dhs.3; children under ten Dhs.1.*

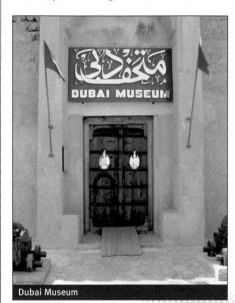

Dubai Museum

Godolphin Gallery

Location → Nad Al Sheba Racecourse · Nad Al Sheba | **336 3031**
Hours → Timings on request
Web/email → www.godolphin.com | **Map Ref →** 17-A3

A great location for horse racing fans, the Godolphin Gallery celebrates the Maktoum family's private racing stable, and houses the world's finest collection of horse racing trophies. The Gallery was refurbished in 2002 and incorporates interactive touch-screen consoles, action photographs, video presentations and memorabilia from the first nine years of the Godolphin racing stable. Adjacent to the Nad Al Sheba Club, the gallery is open from January to April.

Museums & Heritage

Exploring

Godolphin Gallery

Gold & Diamond Museum

Location → Gold & Diamond Park · Shk Zayed Rd |**347 7788**
Hours → 10:00 - 22:00 16:00 - 22:00 Fri
Web/email → www.goldanddiamondpark.com **Map Ref** → 4-B4

An interesting feature of the Gold & Diamond Park is the visitors' centre, which includes a museum and a themed café. Showcases display traditional Arabian jewellery and give its history, and there are guided tours of the manufacturing plant to see how jewellery is made. Then of course, there's the chance to flex your plastic and buy some beautiful works of art from the numerous retail outlets in the complex. Alternatively, you can watch your own design being made on the spot.

The tour takes approximately 30 minutes. Entrance is free.

Heritage & Diving Village

Location → Nr Al Shindagha Tunnel · Al Shindagha |**393 7151**
Hours → 08:00 - 22:00
Web/email → www.dubaitourism.co.ae **Map Ref** → 8-B1

Situated near the Creek mouth, the Heritage & Diving Village provides a glimpse of Dubai's traditional culture and lifestyle. Focusing on the Emirates maritime past, pearl diving traditions and architecture, the centre offers storybook displays, including a tented Bedouin village and ancient armoury. Camel and pony rides are available some afternoons. Several shops sell handicrafts and there is a cafeteria. Ideal for family visits, the village is close to Sheikh Saeed Al Maktoum's House.

Plans are underway to re-establish Al Shindagha with its traditional windtower houses and narrow *sikkas* (alleyways), and to rebuild 32 traditional houses, as well as creating modern promenades along the Creek with cafés and souks. Work is scheduled for completion in 2003.

Majlis Ghorfat Um Al Sheef

Location → Beach Rd · Jumeira |**394 6343**
Hours → 08:30 - 13:30 15:30 - 20:30 Fri 15:30 - 20:30
Web/email → www.dubaitourism.co.ae **Map Ref** → 5-A2

Located on the boundaries of Jumeira and Umm Suqeim, this tiny park was constructed in 1955 and used by the late Sheikh Rashid bin Saeed Al Maktoum as a summer residence. The word *majlis* is Arabic for 'meeting place'.

This is a simple two storey building made from coral, stone and gypsum, with doors and windows of teakwood *(saaj)*. The ground floor is an open veranda (called *leewan* or *rewaaq)*. On the second floor, the majlis is decorated with carpets, pillows, lanterns, rifles and Arabic coffee pots. The roof terrace was used for sleeping – ideal to catch the slightest breeze – and originally it offered an uninterrupted view right to the sea.

Dubai Municipality has added a garden, which includes the traditional channel irrigation system *(falaj)*. A barasti palms shelter occupies a corner of the property, complete with windtower.

> *Location: Look for the brown Municipality historical places signposts for Majlis Al Ghoraifa, off Jumeira Beach Road, past Jumeira Beach Park, next to Valuemart supermarket and Al Hamur Marine Sports.*

Sheikh Saeed Al Maktoum's House

Location → Nr Al Shindagha Tunnel · Al Shindagha |**393 7139**
Hours → 08:30 - 21:00 Fri 15:00 - 22:00
Web/email → www.dubaitourism.co.ae **Map Ref** → 8-A1

The modest home of Dubai's much-loved former ruler is the original site from which Dubai grew. Originally it was strategically situated at the mouth of Dubai's lifeline, the Creek, but this carefully restored house-turned-museum now lies close to the Bur Dubai side of Al Shindagha Tunnel.

Dating from 1896, the house is built in the traditional manner of the Gulf coast, from coral covered in lime and sand coloured plaster. There are different sections of the house showing aspects of Dubai life pre-oil, as well as some rare and wonderful photographs of old Dubai, and an

lorious, victorious, breathtaking

he Godolphin Gallery

...where dreams become reality!

nore information on Gallery opening times please contact us by telephone
rough **www.godolphin.com**
Al Sheba Racecourse, Dubai. Telephone: + 971 4 336 3031

Godolphin

old currency and stamp collection. This interesting museum is worth combining with a visit to the nearby Heritage & Diving Village.

Entrance fees: Dhs.2 adults; Dhs.1 children; under fives free.

Out of Dubai

Other options → Out of Dubai [p.165]

Ajman Museum

Location → Opp Etisalat · Ajman Town Centre | **06 742 3824**
Hours → 09:00 - 13:00 16:00 - 19:00 Fri 16:00 - 19:00 Closed Sat
Web/email → n/a   **Map Ref** → UAE-C2

Ajman Museum, like most museums in the Emirates, is interesting and well arranged, with displays described in both English and Arabic. The fort guide is well worth the Dhs.4 charged.

The museum has a variety of exhibits, including a reconstruction of rooms from a traditional home, a street in a souk, weapons, crafts, manuscripts and archaeological finds. Also on display is a collection of passports (Ajman used to issue its own). It is housed in a former residence of the ruler of Ajman – a fortress dating back to around 1775. In 1970, it became the main police station, before becoming the museum in the early 1980s.

Entrance fees: adults Dhs.4, children under 6 years Dhs.2 and Dhs.1 for students.

Evening Timings: 17:00 - 20:00 summer; 16:00 - 19:00 winter.

Al Hisn Fort/Heritage Museum

Location → Al Hisn Ave, Bank St · Sharjah | **06 568 5500**
Hours → 09:00 - 13:00 17:00 - 20:00 Closed Mon & Fri am
Web/email → sdci@sdci.gov.ae   **Map Ref** → UAE-C2

Built in 1820 this fort was originally the home of Sharjah's ruling family, the Al Qassimi. It was renovated in 1996-97 and displays a range of information and artefacts from the region, with an introductory video (English and Arabic) covering Sharjah's history. One of the most interesting collections is of old photographs, which illustrate just how much Sharjah has changed over the years.

The fort is built in the traditional courtyard style with three towers on the surrounding walls. Enclosed by modern buildings, it is hard to imagine it as it once was – a more isolated building on the edge of the Creek. The fort links Sharjah's main heritage and arts areas.

Timings: 09:00 - 13:00 & 17:00 - 20:00; Closed Mon, Fri am.

Discovery Centre

Location → Opp Sharjah Airport · Sharjah | **06 558 6577**
Hours → See timings below
Web/email → www.shj.gov.ae   **Map Ref** → UAE-C2

This really is the latest and greatest centre for children, from toddlers to under 13s. Opened in March 1999, this colourful scientific centre provides everything children love to see and do in safe, supervised surroundings. Based on themed areas, children can touch, experiment, run and have fun. Of course, the underlying aim is to teach youngsters about the biological, physical and technological worlds in a practical way.

There's a lot to do and learn in this active environment. A soft play area is available for the very young. Pushchair access is good and the centre has a mosque, café, toilets and a shop, as well as ample parking. *Excellent.*

Costs: *children under 2 years free; ages 2 - 12 mornings Dhs.4, evenings Dhs.7; 13 years and above mornings Dhs.5, evenings Dhs.10. For families (maximum two adults, three children) mornings Dhs.15, evenings Dhs.30.*

Timings: *Wednesday, Thursday and Friday general public 15:30 - 20:30. July and August evening hours 16:30 - 20:30.*

School groups only: Saturday and Monday 09:00 - 14:00 (mixed groups). Sunday and Tuesday 09:00 - 14:00 (girls only).

Fujairah Heritage Village

Location → Nr Fujairah Fort · Fujairah | **09 222 6662**
Hours → 07:00 - 13:30 Closed Fri
Web/email → n/a   **Map Ref** → UAE-E2

Opened in 1996 close to the ruins of an old fort, this 6,000 square metre heritage village depicts life in the UAE as it was before the discovery of oil. The large walled area displays original houses, fishing boats and simple dhows, all of which were constructed from palm leaves (barasti), as well as clay, stone and bronze implements and pots, hunting and agricultural tools.

The heritage village is close to Ain Al Madhab Gardens. These gardens are situated in a valley in the foothills of the Hajar Mountains just outside Fujairah City and are fed by mineral springs. This warm sulphur-laden water is also used in two swimming pools available for ladies and men. Ain Al Madhab has chalets for private use with large wooded gardens. On public holidays, an outdoor theatre is used for festivals that include traditional singing and folklore dances.

Entrance fees: Dhs.5.

Fujairah Museum

Location → Opp Ruler's Palace · Fujairah **na**
Hours → 08:30 - 13:30 16:30 - 18:30 Fri 14:00 - 18:30 Closed Sat
Web/email → n/a   **Map Ref** → UAE-E2

Situated near Fujairah Fort, this museum offers an insight into Fujairah's history and heritage. It has displays of the traditional way of life and of archaeological artefacts found in excavations throughout the Emirate. Work by local and foreign archaeologists has yielded items dating back over 4,500 years, including Bronze and Iron Age weapons, finely painted pottery, delicately carved soapstone vessels and pre-Islamic silver coins.

The museum was enlarged during the summer of 1998 to permit more finds to be displayed.

Entry fee: adults Dhs.3; children Dhs.1.

Heritage Area

Location → Corniche Rd · Sharjah **06 569 3999**
Hours → 09:00 - 13:00 17:00 - 20:00 Closed Mon & Fri am
Web/email → n/a   **Map Ref** → UAE-C2

The beautifully restored Heritage Area in Sharjah is a great place for individuals with an interest in local history. The area includes a number of old buildings; Al Hisn Fort (Sharjah Fort), Sharjah Islamic Museum, Sharjah Heritage Museum (Bait Al Naboodah), the Majlis of Ibrahim Mohammed Al Midfa and the Old Souk (Souk Al Arsah). Here you will see traditional local architecture and artefacts, and home life depicted as it was over 150 years ago.

Be prepared to park your car and walk – the round trip is less than 1½ km. Toilets can be found in each venue. The Arabic coffee shop in the shaded courtyard of Souk Al Arsah, serves hot and cold drinks.

The Majlis of Ibrahim Mohammed Al Midfa is situated between the souk and the waterfront. This peaceful majlis is famous for its round windtower, the only one of its kind in the UAE. The owner, Mr Al Midfa, was secretary to four rulers of Sharjah until he died in 1983. One of the first writers in the UAE, he also initiated the beginnings of a library in Sharjah.

See also: Souk Al Arsah [p.169], Al Hisn Fort (Sharjah Fort) [p.170], Sharjah Islamic Museum [p.148], Sharjah Heritage Museum (Bait Al Naboodah) [p.148]

National Museum of Ras Al Khaimah

Location → Behind Police HQ · Ras Al Khaimah **07 233 3411**
Hours → 08:00 - 12:00 16:00 - 19:00 Closed Tue
Web/email → www.rakmuseum.gov.ae   **Map Ref** → UAE-D1

Located in the old fort, a former home of the present ruler of Ras Al Khaimah, this museum mainly has natural history and archaeological displays, many of which were found in RAK. Other rooms exhibit a variety of everyday paraphernalia from life before the discovery of oil, including weaving looms, agricultural tools, jewellery, clothing and guns. Upstairs you can see an account of the British expedition against Ras Al Khaimah in 1809, as well as a model of a '*baggala*', a typical craft used in the early 1800s. Look out for fossils set in the rock strata of the walls of the fort -- these date back 190 million years!

Entrance fees: adults Dhs.2; children Dhs.1. To enter with your camera Dhs.5.

Location: behind Police Headquarters in the old town close to the bridge. From Dubai, turn left at the second roundabout after the Clock roundabout and the museum is 100 metres to your right.

Sharjah Archaeological Museum

Location → Nr Cultural R/A · Sharjah **06 566 5466**
Hours → 09:00 - 13:00 17:00 - 20:00 Closed Sun & Fri am
Web/email → n/a   **Map Ref** → UAE-C2

Opened in May 1997, this hi-tech museum offers an interesting display of artefacts and antiquities from this part of the world. Linked to a conference centre and used as an educational venue for local schoolchildren, the museum has installed computers in each display hall to provide in-depth information on the archaeological pieces displayed.

Sharjah Al Hisn Fort

Segregated into separate interconnecting halls by subject matter and chronology, you are guided by a series of films explaining what is on display. A designated area is for seasonal displays of the latest discoveries from excavation sites in the Emirates. *Well worth a visit for archaeology and history lovers.*

Entry fee: no charge.

Timings: Note: Wednesday pm ladies and children only.

Sharjah Art Museum

Location → Sharjah Arts Plaza Area · Sharjah | **06 568 8222**
Hours → 09:00 - 13:00 17:00 - 20:00 Fri 16:30 - 20:30 Closed Mon
Web/email → n/a **Map Ref →** UAE-C2

Opened in April 1997, the three storeys of Sharjah Art Museum dominate the arts plaza area. It was purpose-built in a traditional style, chiefly to house the personal collection of over 300 paintings and maps of the ruler, HH Dr Sheikh Sultan.

Permanent displays include the work of 18th century orientalists and artists, with oil paintings and watercolours depicting life from all over the Arab world. Other exhibits in the 72 small galleries change frequently, often with exhibitions by local artists and students, or foreign artists. The museum also hosts lectures and various cultural activities. There's also an art reference library, bookshop and coffee shop.

Entry fee: no charge.

Timings: Note: Wednesday pm ladies and children only.

Sharjah Heritage Museum (Bait Al Naboodah)

Location → Sharjah Arts Plaza Area · Sharjah | **06 569 3999**
Hours → 09:00 - 13:00 17:00 - 20:00 Closed Mon & Fri am
Web/email → folklory.emirates.net.ae **Map Ref →** UAE-C2

This two-storey building is a reconstruction of how a typical family lived about 150 years ago – usually with several generations and different branches of the family all under one roof. Originally it was the home of the Al Naboodah family (three generations of the family lived here until 1972), and is built with a traditional courtyard structure. The museum shows the various rooms of a home, and displays items such as clothing, weapons, bronze cooking pots and goatskin water bags. Note the traditional games in the children's room, in particular the camels made from starfish – no computer games here!

Sharjah Islamic Museum

Location → Nr Cultural R/A · Sharjah | **06 568 3334**
Hours → 09:00 - 13:00 17:00 - 20:00 Closed Mon & Fri am
Web/email → n/a **Map Ref →** UAE-C2

Housed in a renovated, 200 year old building, Sharjah Islamic Museum displays an unrivalled collection of rare Islamic masterpieces and manuscripts, representing the cultural lifestyle of Muslims over 1,400 years. Examples of Islamic arts and crafts such as crockery, ceramics, glass and metalwork are on show, in addition to gold and silver jewellery and textiles. There's also an impressive collection of scientific instruments, gold plated Korans and a replica of the curtain that covers the famous Ka'aba Stone at Mecca. This display, which is from HH Dr Sheikh Sultan's private collection, is exhibited in the former residence of Saeed bin Mohammed Al Shamsi.

The museum is open during holy days and public holidays.

Sharjah Natural History Museum

Location → Nr Sharjah Int Airport · Jct 8, Sharjah | **06 531 1411**
Hours → 09:00 - 19:00 Thu 12:00 -19:00 Fri 14:00 - 22:00 Closed Sun
Web/email → www.shjmuseum.gov.ae **Map Ref →** UAE-C2

Combining entertainment and learning in the most dynamic of atmospheres, this fascinating museum unfolds through five exhibit halls to expose you to the earth's secrets. Exhibits include a 35 metre diorama of the UAE's natural habitats and wildlife; a stunning geological UV light display with samples from all over the world; a hall showing the interaction between man and his environment – including the museum's best-known exhibit ... a mechanical camel; a botanical hall; and the marine hall, where replicas of Gulf and Indian Ocean sea creatures can be viewed as if from the bottom of the sea.

The site also incorporates the *Arabian Wildlife Centre* (06 531 1999), which is a breeding centre for endangered species – most famously, the Arabian leopard, and the *Children's Farm* (06 531 1127), where animals, such as donkeys, camels and goats can be fed and petted.

The facilities are state-of-the-art and offer an enjoyable, interactive and educational day out. Picnic areas are available, plus cafés and shops. The headquarters of the *Arabian Leopard Trust* is also located here. Great fun for all ages, and a place that you will want to visit again and again.

Entrance fees: adults Dhs.5; children Dhs.2. School classes by appointment.

Timings: Sat - Wed 09:00 - 19:00; Thu 12:00 - 19:00; Fri 14:00 - 20:00.

Location: about 28 km outside Sharjah on the Al Dhaid highway.

Sharjah Science Museum

Location ➜ Halwan, nr TV station · Sharjah | **06 566 8777**
Hours ➜ See timings below
Web/email ➜ www.shj.gov.ae   Map Ref ➜ UAE-C2

This museum offers visitors hands-on exhibits and demonstrations, covering subjects such as aerodynamics, colour and physiology, with demonstrations on electricity and cryogenics. There's also a children's area where the under fives and their parents can learn together. Trained staff are available.

Those who are inspired to learn more about science can book a seat in the Learning Centre. This offers more in-depth programmes on many of the topics presented in the museum and includes a science lab, computers, technology lab, multimedia production centre, discovery area and a reference library. There is also a café and a gift shop, and school groups are welcome.

Entrance fees: adults Dhs.3 morning, Dhs.5 afternoon; ages 2 - 12 Dhs.1 morning, Dhs.2 afternoon; under two free; families Dhs.8 morning, Dhs.15 afternoon.

Timings: Sat - Tue 09:00 - 14:00; Wed - Fri and public holidays 15:30 - 20:30. June, July, August evening opening at 16:30.

PARKS

Other options ➜ **Beach Parks [p.152]**

Dubai has a number of excellent parks, and visitors are certain to be pleasantly surprised by the expanses of green lawns and the variety of trees and shrubs — a perfect escape from the concrete jungle of the city.

In the winter months, the more popular green parks are very busy at weekends. Most have a kiosk or café selling snacks and drinks, alternatively take a picnic or use the barbecue pits that many parks provide (remember to take your own wood or charcoal, and food!). Creekside Park has an amphitheatre, and often holds concerts on public holidays or special occasions. Details are announced in the newspapers 2 - 3 days before.

Regulations vary, with some banning bikes and roller blades, or limiting ball games to specific areas. Pets are not permitted and you should not take plant cuttings, nor should you leave the remnants of your picnic behind — others won't appreciate and neither would you. Most parks have a Ladies Day, when entry is restricted to women, girls and young boys (check the individual entries). All parks open at 8am and close at varying times over 12 hours later. During Ramadan, park timings change, usually opening and closing later in the day.

Entrance to the smaller parks is free, while the larger ones charge Dhs.5 per person, except for Safa and Mushrif parks, which cost Dhs.3 per person.

Creekside Park

Location ➜ Nr Wonderland · Creekside, Umm Hurair 2 | **336 7633**
Hours ➜ 08:00 - 23:00 Thu & Fri 08:00 - 23:30
Web/email ➜ dm@gov.ae   Map Ref ➜ 14-A1

Here you can enjoy a day in the country with acres of gardens, as well as fishing piers, jogging tracks, BBQ sites, children's play areas, restaurants and kiosks. There's also a mini falaj (the traditional irrigation system) and a large amphitheatre.

Running along the park's 2.3 km stretch of Creek frontage is a cable car system, the first of its kind in the Emirates. Opened in April 2000, it allows visitors an unrestricted view of the area from 30 metres in the air. Alternatively, near gate 1 visit the amazing Children's City, a new interactive museum for children.

From gate 2, four wheel cycles can be hired for Dhs.20 per hour (you can't use your own bike in the park). Roller blading is allowed. Wednesdays are for women and children only (boys up to the age of six years).

Entrance fee: Dhs.5. Cable car: adults, Dhs.25; children Dhs.15. Children's City: adults Dhs.15; children Dhs.10.

Mushrif Park

Location ➜ 9 km past Dxb Airport · Al Khawaneej Rd | **288 3624**
Hours ➜ 08:00 - 23:30
Web/email ➜ n/a   Map Ref ➜ 16-D4

The largest park in Dubai, Mushrif Park is a little out of town, but popular with families owing to its unusual features and extensive grounds (you may prefer to take your car in to get around). Wander around the miniature houses from different countries or take the train, which tours the park regularly in the afternoons for Dhs.2 a ride. Visit the camel and pony areas and have a ride in the

Parks

Exploring

afternoons for Dhs.2, or swing and slide in the children's play areas.

Separate swimming pools are available for men and women. No bikes or roller blades are allowed and there are no ladies only days.

Entrance fee: Dhs.3 per person; Dhs.10 per car.

Swimming pools: Dhs.10 per adult; Dhs.5 per child (a membership scheme is available).

Rashidiya Park

Location ➜ Past Dubai Intl. Airport · Rashidiya   **285 1208**
Hours ➜ 08:00 - 23:00   Thu & Fri 08:00 - 23:30
Web/email ➜ n/a   Map Ref ➜ n/a

This is a surprisingly clean and pretty park with attractive flowerbeds and brightly coloured children's play areas. It is mainly used by local residents, although it would also suit mothers with pre-school children. Shaded grassy areas are ideal for picnics. Saturdays to Wednesdays are for ladies and children only.

Safa Park

Location ➜ Nr Union Co-op & Choithrams · Al Wasl Rd   **349 2111**
Hours ➜ 08:00 - 22:30
Web/email ➜ parks@dm.gov.ae   Map Ref ➜ 5-C3

Spot the giant Ferris wheel opposite Jumeira Library and you've found Safa Park. Artistically divided into sections and play areas, this large park offers an electronic games parlour for teenagers, bumper cars and the big wheel, which operates at weekends. It also has three tennis courts (first come first served, especially busy in the evenings), volleyball, basketball and football pitches, obstacle course, a lake and waterfall, over 20 barbecue sites and massive expanses of grassy areas.

Although there is a jogging track within the grounds, many people simply jog or walk around the outside of the park during the cooler hours of the day. Two and four wheel bicycles can be hired inside (the use of personal bikes is not allowed). Roller blading is allowed and Tuesday is ladies day, with boys aged up to about seven admitted.

Entrance fee: Dhs.3 per person, free for children under three years. Bike hire: Dhs.100 deposit; Dhs.20 - 30 for one hour.

BEACHES

Other options ➜ **Parasailing [p.255]**
Swimming [p.263]

Lovers of the seaside who want to swim or enjoy the beach will find a number of options in Dubai. Choose between the public beaches which usually have limited facilities but no entrance charge, and the beach parks which charge for entrance, but have a variety of facilities, including changing rooms and play areas. If none of these appeal try the beach clubs, which are normally part of a hotel or resort. For further information on beach clubs, refer to [p.268].

If you want to explore by yourself, map pages 2-6 clearly show Dubai's south-western coastline where there are several beaches, although access to the public is restricted in some areas.

Options for public beaches include the lagoon at Al Mamzar (Map 12-D3), which has a roped-off swimming area, chalets and jet skis for hire. Travelling south, you'll come to Jumeira Beach Corniche (Map 6-C2), which is a great favourite with tourists for soaking up the sun, swimming and people watching. Facilities include shaded picnic tables, small play areas for children, showers and sheltered swimming areas. A tree-planting programme will eventually screen the beach from the road and provide more shade. The jetty here is a popular spot for fishing.

Moving further south brings you to the small beaches near the Dubai Offshore Sailing Club (Map 4-E2), Wollongong University (immensely popular with the kite surfers) and the Jumeira Beach Hotel (Map 4-B2).

Running between the Metropolitan Resort & Beach Club (Map 2-E2) and the Sheraton Jumeira Beach (Map 2-C2) hotels, is another stretch of beach that is a pleasant spot for walking and people watching. This busy beach is popular with hotel guests and residents, although the sand is compact and rough.

Die hard beach lovers frequent the beach past the Jebel Ali Hotel, where there is a 10 km expanse of beach (Map 1-A1). This is a great spot for barbecues and camping, with occasional shade and showers that never seem to work!

Regulations for the public beaches are gradually becoming stricter. Currently dog owners are banned from walking their dogs on the beaches. There is also a ban on 4 wheel driving on the beach, but this is often ignored. Daily clean ups and Dubai

Police and Municipality patrol units roam beaches looking for any sort of offender. Officially, other banned beach activities include barbecues on sand, camping and holding large parties. Contact the Public Parks and Recreation Section (336 7633) for clarification. Regulations don't appear to be strictly enforced on the more open beaches, such as at Jebel Ali.

New regulations with far more restrictions on what you can and cannot wear operate in Sharjah; so if you are planning a trip there ensure that you are aware of the latest rules. Refer to the Decency Law [p.16].

Warning Although the waters off the coast of Dubai generally look calm and unchallenging, rip tides can carry swimmers away from the shore very quickly. Fatalities have occurred in the past. Take extra care when swimming off the public beaches where there are no lifeguards.

Beach Parks

Other options ➜ **Parks [p.149]**

A visit to one of Dubai's beach parks is an enjoyable way to spend the day and a perfect break from city life. Here you can enjoy that tropical paradise experience, with an oasis of lush greenery and stretches of sandy beach and palm trees!

Both of Dubai's beach parks are very busy on weekends, especially in the cooler months, although Al Mamzar Park covers such a large area that it rarely feels overcrowded. They both have a Ladies Day when men are not admitted (except for young boys with their family). Dresswise, it is fine to wear swimsuits, bikinis (top and bottom halves please!) or swimming trunks, but only on the beach. Like the green parks, the beach parks open at 8am and close over 12 hours later. During Ramadan, opening times change.

Al Mamzar has an amphitheatre, and often stages concerts on special occasions or public holidays — look out for details in the newspapers 2 - 3 days in advance.

Both of the beach parks have lifeguards on duty during the day. A raised red flag means that it is unsafe to swim, and you are strongly advised to heed the warning. Although the waters off Dubai's coast generally look calm and unchallenging, rip tides can carry swimmers away from the shore very quickly. Fatalities have occurred in the past.

Al Mamzar Beach Park

Location ➜ Past Al Hamriya Port · Al Hamriya | **296 6527**
Hours ➜ 08:00 - 10:30 Thu & Fri 08:00 - 23:30
Web/email ➜ n/a   Map Ref ➜ 12-E2

For an away from it all feel, it's hard to beat Mamzar. Four beaches, open grassy spaces and plenty of greenery create a tranquil haven. It's always popular, especially on Fridays, but its 90 hectares of grounds rarely feel overcrowded. A large amphitheatre is located near the entrance and paths wind between plenty of picnic areas and children's playgrounds.

The well-maintained beaches have sheltered areas for swimming, as well as changing rooms with showers, and kiosks selling food and the small necessities you left at home. Chalets complete with barbecue area, can be hired for Dhs.150 - 200. There are also two swimming pools, and lifeguards patrol the beaches and pool areas. Wednesdays are for women and children only (boys up to the age of about eight).

Entrance fees: Dhs.5 per person; Dhs.30 per car, including all occupants. Pool fees: Dhs.10 per adult; Dhs.5 per child. Under 12's must be accompanied by an adult.

Jumeira Beach Park

Location ➜ Nr Jumeirah Beach Club · Jumeira | **349 2555**
Hours ➜ 08:00 - 22:30 Thu & Fri 08:00 - 23:00 Sat & Sun ladies and children only
Web/email ➜ n/a   Map Ref ➜ 5-C2

Looking like something from an exotic 'Bounty' advertisement, with azure seas, palm trees and a long, narrow, shady stretch of beach, this is a popular and well-used park. The trees and gardens are well established and there are plenty of grassy areas for all ages to run around on. Barbecue pits are available for public use, as well as a volleyball area for ball games.

Lifeguards are on duty along the beach between 08:00 - 18:00 and swimming is not permitted after sunset. Saturday is for women and children only, including boys up to the age of about five years. No adult bicycles or roller blades are allowed in the park.

Entrance fee: Dhs.5 per person, Dhs.20 per car.

There are many companies in Dubai offering an exciting variety of city and safari tours. An organised tour can be a great way to discover the UAE, especially if you are only here for a short time or do not have ready access to a vehicle. The following information is not exhaustive, but covers the most popular tours given by the main operators. Refer to the Tour Operators table on [p.155] for a list of the largest and most respectable companies operating out of Dubai.

Tours range from a half-day city tour to an overnight safari visiting the desert or mountains and camping in tents. On a full-day, evening or overnight tour, meals are generally provided, while on a half-day city tour you will usually return in time for lunch. Check what is included when you book, as sometimes there may be an extra charge for meals. Generally, all tours include soft drinks and water as part of the package. Expect to pay anything from Dhs.50 for a half hour tour of the Creek to Dhs.110 for a half-day city tour, and about Dhs.350 for an overnight desert safari.

Most trips require a minimum of four people for the tour to run. Companies usually take couples or individuals if there is a group already booked that they can join. If you want a tour or car to yourself, you will probably have to pay for four people, even if there are less of you.

It is advisable to book three or four days in advance, although in some cases less notice is not a problem. A deposit of up to 50% is normal, with the balance payable when you are collected. Cancellation usually means loss of your deposit, unless appropriate notice is given; this differs from company to company.

On the day of the tour you can be collected from either your hotel, residence, or from a common meeting point if you are part of a large group. Tours usually leave on time — no-shows do not get a refund, so don't be late! It's advisable to wear cool, comfortable clothing, plus a hat and sunglasses. Desert or mountain tours require strong, flat-soled shoes if there is the possibility of walking. The temperature can drop considerably in the desert after sunset, especially in winter, so take warm clothing. Other necessities include sunscreen and camera with spare films and batteries.

The desert safaris are a must for anyone who hasn't experienced dune driving before, especially

Mina Seyahi Beach

good for friends and relatives visiting the Emirates. Most companies will take an easier route if there are young children, the elderly, those prone to carsickness, or anybody who doesn't want to experience extreme dunes.

Most companies have excellent safety records, but there is an element of risk involved when driving off-road. Remember, you are the client and if the driver is going too fast for your group, tell him to slow down — there shouldn't be any wheels leaving the ground! Accidents have happened in the past, but with a good driver you should have total confidence and you'll be in for a thrilling ride.

The following descriptions of the main tours are intended simply to give an idea of what's most commonly included. Obviously each tour operator has their own style, so the content and general quality may differ from one company to another.

City Tours — In Dubai

Dubai by Night

This is a tour around the palaces, mosques and souks of the city, whilst enjoying the early evening lights. See the multitude of shoppers in their national costumes and streets heaving with character, then enjoy dinner at one of Dubai's many restaurants. (half day)

Dubai City Tour

This is an overview of the old and new of Dubai. The souks, the fish market, mosques, abras,

Tours & Sightseeing

Exploring

Bastakiya windtower houses and thriving commercial areas with striking modern buildings are some of the usual inclusions. (half day)

City Tours — Out of Dubai

Abu Dhabi Tour

The route from Dubai passes Jebel Ali Port, the world's largest man-made seaport, on the way to Abu Dhabi, capital of the United Arab Emirates. Founded in 1761, the city is built on an island. Visit the Women's Handicraft Centre, Heritage Village, Petroleum Exhibition and Abu Dhabi's famous landmark — the Corniche. (full day)

Ajman & Sharjah Tour

Ajman is the place to visit if you want to see wooden dhows being built today just as they were hundreds of years ago. Take in the museum before driving to the neighbouring emirate of Sharjah, where you can visit the numerous souks. Finish with a wander around the restored Bait Al Naboodah house to see how people lived before the discovery of oil. (half day)

Al Ain Tour

Known as the 'Garden City', Al Ain was once a vital oasis on the caravan route from the Emirates to Oman. Here there are many historical attractions, from one of the first forts to be built by the Al Nahyan family over 175 years ago, to prehistoric tombs at Hili, said to be over 5,000 years old. Other attractions include Al Ain Museum, the camel market, the falaj irrigation system, which is still in use, and the quaint souk. (full day)

Ras Al Khaimah Tour

Drive up country along the so-called Pirate Coast through Ajman and Umm Al Quwain. Explore ancient sites and discover the old town of Ras Al Khaimah and its museum. The return journey passes natural hot springs and date groves at Khatt, via the starkly beautiful Hajar Mountains. (full day)

Shopping Tour

Known as the 'shopping capital of the Middle East', Dubai is a shopper's paradise! From almost-designer clothes at incredibly low prices to electronics, watches or dazzling bolts of cloth in the Textile Souk, everything is available at prices to suit every budget — don't forget to bargain your way through the day! Then there are the malls... ultra modern and air conditioned, and selling everything you'd expect, plus a lot more! (half day)

See also: Bargaining [p.182], Shopping Malls [p.207].

Safari Tours

Dune Dinners

Late afternoons are ideal for enjoying the thrill of driving over golden sand dunes in a 4 wheel drive vehicle. Departing at around 4pm, the route passes camel farms and fascinating scenery, which provide great photo opportunities. At an Arabic campsite enjoy a sumptuous dinner and the calm of a starlit desert night, then return around 10pm. (half day)

East Coast

Journey east to Al Dhaid, a small oasis town known for its fruit and vegetable plantations. Catch glimpses of dramatic mountain gorges before arriving at Dibba and Khorfakkan on the East Coast. Have a refreshing swim, then visit the oldest mosque in the UAE nestling below the ruins of a watchtower. This tour usually visits the Friday Market for a browse through carpets, clay pots and fresh local produce. (full day)

Full-Day Safari

This day-long tour usually passes traditional Bedouin villages and camel farms in the desert, with a drive through sand dunes of varying colours and heights. Most tours also visit Fossil Rock and the striking Hajar Mountains, the highest mountains in the UAE. A cold buffet lunch may be provided in the mountains before the drive home. (full day)

Hatta Pools Safari

Modern highways, soft undulating sand dunes and a kaleidoscope of colours lead the way to Hatta, in the foothills of the Hajar Mountains. Swim in the Hatta Pools and see the hidden waterfall inside a gorge.

The trip generally includes a stop at the Hatta Fort Hotel, where you can relax and enjoy the swimming pool, landscaped gardens, archery, clay pigeon shooting and 9-hole golf course. Not every tour has lunch at the hotel, some have it in the mountains, especially in the cooler winter months. (full day)

Mountain Safari

Travelling north along the coast and heading inland at Ras Al Khaimah, the oldest seaport in the region, you enter the spectacular Hajar Mountains at Wadi Bih. Rumble through rugged canyons onto steep winding tracks, past terraced mountainsides and old stone houses at over 1,200 metres above sea level. It leads to Dibba where a highway quickly returns you to Dubai, stopping at Masafi Market on the way. Some tours operate in reverse, starting from Dibba. (full day)

Tours & Sightseeing. · Exploring

Tour Operators & Travel Agents

Company	Phone	Fax	Email
Africa Connection	339 0232	339 1112	africa@emirates.net.ae
Arabian Adventures	303 4888	343 9977	aadops@emirates.co.ae
Arabianlink Tours	06 572 6666	06 572 1440	arablink@emirates.net.ae
Charlotte Anne Charters	09 222 3508	222 3508	seatrips@emirates.net.ae
Columbus Tours	224 2555	222 5622	columbus@emirates.net.ae
Creek Cruises	393 9860	393 7123	malika@emirates.net.ae
Creekside Leisure	336 8406	336 8411	creeksideleisure@inuae.com
Danat Dubai Cruises	351 1117	351 1116	danatdxb@emirates.net.ae
Desert Rangers	340 2408	340 2407	rangers@emirates.net.ae
DTTS	343 2221	343 3363	dttsdxb@emirates.net.ae
East Adventure Tours	355 5677	-	tourism@emirates.net.ae
Emirates Holidays	343 9999	343 9888	emirates.holidays@emirates.com
Escapades By Mohebi Aviation	353 4444	353 3393	aviation@mohebi.com
Gulf Ventures	209 5509	209 5503	gulfventures@mmi.co.ae
Kanoo Holidays	334 1 444	336 6626	kanoohly@emirates.net.ae
Khasab Tours	266 9950	268 6857	khaztour@emirates.net.ae
Lama Tours	273 2240	273 5575	lamatour@emirates.net.ae
Leisure Time Tourism & Cargo	332 7226	331 0738	lesrtime @emirates.net.ae
Net Tours	266 6655	266 8662	nettours@emirates.net.ae
North Star Expeditions LLC	332 8702	332 8703	norstar@emirates.net.ae
Off-Road Adventures	343 2288	343 7472	ora@emirates.net.ae
Orient Tours	06 568 3838	06 552 5077	otshj@emirates.net.ae
Planet Travel Tours & Safaris	282 2199	282 6867	planet@emirates.net.ae
Quality Tours	297 4000	297 3339	dxbtours@emirates.net.ae
Relax Tourism	345 0889	345 1886	relaxdxb@emirates.net.ae
Royal Tours	223 1274	223 1679	royaltou@emirates.net.ae
SNTTA Travel & Tours	282 9000	282 9988	sntta@emirates.net.ae
Soul of Stars	050 6942960	399 5672	dimcdxb@emirates.net.ae
Thomas Cook Al Rostamani	349 0408	349 0823	tcartdr@al-rostamani.co.ae
Turner Travel and Tourism	345 4504	345 1426	sales@turnertraveldubai.com
Voyagers Xtreme	345 4504	345 1426	sales@turnertraveldubai.com

Overnight Safari

This 24 hour tour starts at about 3pm with a drive through the dunes to a Bedouin style campsite. Dine under the stars, sleep in the fresh air and wake to the smell of freshly brewed coffee, then head for the mountains. The drive takes you through spectacular rugged scenery, along wadis (dry riverbeds), before stopping for a buffet lunch and then back to Dubai. (overnight)

ACTIVITY TOURS

In addition to the city and safari tours, some companies offer more specialised activities. From the adrenaline buzz of a desert driving course, a dune buggy desert safari, mountain biking or hiking to a peaceful canoe tour of Khor Kalba, these tours combine fun and adventure.

Note that a basic level of fitness may be required. Refer also to the Activities section of the book for other activities that you can enjoy in the Emirates.

Arabian Adventures

Location → Emirates Holidays Bldg, Shk Zayed Rd | **303 4888**
Hours → 09:00 - 18:00 Closed Thu, Fri
Web/email → www.arabian-adventures.com   **Map Ref →** 5-C4

Arabian Adventures offers the chance to venture into the desert or to explore the rugged peaks and wadis of the Hajar Mountains with experienced guides. Their tours cover the whole of the UAE and are a perfect opportunity to discover the richness of Arabian culture and heritage.

The company also arranges sporting activities, such as golf, fishing or scuba diving, as well as special interest activities, such as horse racing. Alternatively, ask them to create an itinerary just for you.

Arabian Adventures also organises overland explorer programmes to Bahrain, Iran, Oman, Qatar and Yemen. For further information, call the above number or Abu Dhabi (02 633 8111).

Tours & Sightseeing

Exploring

Desert Rangers

Location → Dubai Garden Centre · Shk. Zayed Rd   **340 2408**
Hours → 09:00 - 18:00   Closed Fri (office)
Web/email → www.desertrangers.com   **Map Ref →** 6-E3

Desert Rangers are one of only a few companies in the country offering outdoor adventure activities. In addition to the standard range of desert and mountain tours, they offer something a little different, visiting locations that you are unlikely to see with another company.

From the adrenaline buzz of a dune buggy desert

Dune Buggying with Desert Rangers

safari, to the peaceful canoe tour of Khor Kalba, there are plenty of opportunities to try some more unusual activities.   With camel riding, sand boarding, canoeing, raft building, initiative tests and team building, camping, hiking, mountain biking or dune buggying to choose from, your weekends should never be dull! They also specialise in multi-activity trips for children, especially schools and youth groups.

East Adventure Tours

Location → In Pyramid Centre · Al Karama   **355 5677**
Hours → 09:00 - 19:00
Web/email → www.holidayindubai.com   **Map Ref →** 10-E1

If you're new to Dubai and would like to discover the city and its surroundings, East Adventure Tours can provide a personal guide/driver as an escort.

Trips can include a Bedouin desert safari, a dhow dinner cruise and camel safari, as well as activities such as horse riding and golf.

The escort service extends to after dark and can accompany you to restaurants, or even suggest where to go. This unique chauffeur/escort service is available 24 hours a day. For further information, visit the Website or contact Mr Ali (050 644 8820).

Voyagers Xtreme

Location → Dune Centre · Al Satwa   **345 4504**
Hours → 09:00 - 18:00
Web/email → www.turnertraveldubai.com   **Map Ref →** 6-E3

Operated by a dedicated team of professionals who specialise in helping people make the most of their leisure time in the UAE, Voyagers Xtreme (VX) offers a range of unique and adventurous activities over land, air and sea. On offer is everything from hot air ballooning, dune driving, a Mussandam cruise, dive charters, Cessna air tours, skydiving, sailing, rock climbing, plus outdoor team building programmes. They also offer a unique two day self-drive desert expedition to the Empty Quarter – the world's largest sand desert.

In addition to local adventures, VX offer a selection of overseas adventure holidays – from easy to xtreme!

Birdwatching

Other options → **Falconry Shows [p.160]**
Khor Kalba [p.172]
Environmental Groups [p.288]

As a destination for birdwatchers, Dubai's reputation has grown considerably over the years. The increasing lushness of the area attracts more and more birds, many of which are not easily found anywhere in Europe or elsewhere in the Middle East. Over 80 species breed locally, while during the spring and autumn months over 400 species have been recorded on their migration between Africa and Central Asia.

In the city, the best bird watching sites include the many parks and golf clubs, where parakeets, Indian rollers, little green bee-eaters and hoopoe can easily be spotted. Other species found in the Emirates include the Socotra cormorant, striated scops owl, chestnut-bellied sandgrouse, crab plover, Saunders' little tern and Hume's wheatear.

At the end of Dubai Creek, the Khor Dubai Wildlife Sanctuary is the only nature reserve within the city.

Discover the best in you... Go outward bound with...

Desert Rangers.

Desert Rangers is an exiting and innovative company that offers a variety of outward-bound activities and adventure safaris, providing exclusive opportunities for you when in the UAE to try something totally different.

Overnight Safari	**Sandboarding Safari**	**Dune Buggy Safaris**
Mountain Safari	**Tailor-made Packages**	**Canoe Expeditions**
Hatta pool Safari	**Trekking**	**Dune Dinner Safari**
Mountain Biking		**Camel Trekking**

Desert Rangers
TOURS & ADVENTURE SPORTS

PO Box 37579, Dubai, UAE · Tel (+971 4) 3402408 · Fax (+971 4) 3402407

rangers@emirates.net.ae

DESERT GROUP

It's a great place to see the greater flamingo, as well as other shore birds and waders. Entrance to the reserve is prohibited, however, you can easily spot the flamingos from the road, as you drive from Bu Kidra roundabout to the Wafi junction, with the Creek on your right, or as you drive towards Al Awir from Bu Kidra roundabout.

Other excellent places for birding around the Emirates include the mangrove swamps in Umm al Quwain and Khor Kalba on the East Coast. Khor Kalba is the only place in the world where you can spot the rare white-collared kingfisher. Birdwatching tours in a canoe to the mangroves can be arranged through Desert Rangers.

In addition, falconry, the sport of sheikhs, has a deep-rooted tradition here. The best opportunity for enjoying these beautiful and powerful birds is on an organised tour when you can see the birds in flight.

Birdwatching Tours

Location → Various locations | **882 0655**
Hours → Timings on request
Web/email → www.birding-arabia.com | Map Ref → n/a

Colin Richardson, author of *The Birds of the United Arab Emirates*, has been organising birdwatching trips since 1993. Tours include a visit to Khor Dubai, where thousands of Arctic shore birds and flamingos winter; Umm Al Quwain with its crab plovers and Socotra cormorants; Khor Kalba, where the rare and threatened white-collared kingfisher is found and irrigated fields where Indian rollers and bee-eaters are abundant.

The tours are easy-going and there's always time to relax and take photos. Trips can be custom-made and it's wise to book in advance. Prices start at Dhs.200 per person. Some previous birdwatching experience is an advantage.

Emirates Bird Records Committee

Location → n/a | **050 642 4358**
Hours → Timings on request
Web/email → www.uaeinteract.com | Map Ref → UAE-A4

The Emirates Bird Records Committee collates information about the country's birds and maintains the UAE checklist. A weekly round up of sightings and a monthly bird report are available via email. For further details, contact the Committee Chairman, Simon Aspinall.

Bus Tours

Other options → **Walking Tours [p.162]**

Big Bus Company, The

Location → Behind Citibank, Office 315 · Oud Metha | **324 4187**
Hours → Various timings
Web/email → www.bigbus.co.uk | Map Ref → 13-D2

It's not a mirage, there really are eight open air London double-decker buses roaming the streets of Dubai! Operating since May 2002, the buses leave from Wafi City (outside Biella restaurant) on the hour and half hour – climb on board for an interesting and informative tour.

City tours on the Big Bus

The aerial view from the bus makes for a visually interesting treat, but it's wise to break the tour at their recommended stops (the seats aren't very comfortable) and then hop on the following bus once you've finished exploring. There's a live commentary in English on every trip, with little known facts such as in 1968 there were only 13 cars in Dubai! Overall, an entertaining and professional tour.

Prices: adults Dhs.75; children Dhs.45 (ages 5 - 15); free for under 5s; families Dhs.195 (two adults and two children).

Camel Rides

Other options → **Camel Racing [p.48]**

A visit to Arabia is hardly complete without a close up experience with the 'ship of the desert', the camel. Many of the tour operators incorporate a short camel ride on their desert

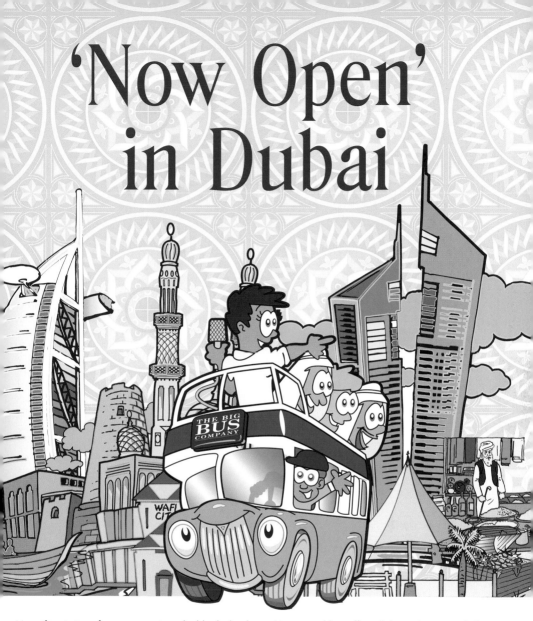

'Now Open' in Dubai

- Magnificent views from an open-top, double decker bus • Hop-on and hop-off at all the major sites in Dubai
Live English commentary on every tour • Buses operate 7 days a week from outside the main entrance of Wafi City
- No advance booking necessary • Free entry to Dubai Museum and Sheikh Saeed Al Maktoum's House
Pay by Visa Card and receive 10% discount • Free Wafi Advantage Card, offering discounts at selected outlets.

THE BIG BUS COMPANY.
now in Dubai

For further information or bookings, please contact us on +971 4 324 4187

safaris, alternatively for a unique adventure, try a camel ride into the spectacular sand dunes. Your guide will lead you to a Bedouin camp, where you can enjoy a rest and some refreshments. Along the way there are stops for photos, so that you can remember this unique experience long after the aches subside! Prices are from Dhs.200 per person.

Al Ain Golden Sands Camel Safaris

Location → Hilton Al Ain · Al Ain | **03 768 8006**
Hours → 10:00 - 13:00 17:30 - 20:00   Closed Fri
Web/email → alcamels@emirates.net.ae   Map Ref → UAE-D4

For something a bit more adventurous, Al Ain Golden Sands Camel Safaris offers a selection of tours that include a camel ride over the dunes of Bida Bint Saud. The rides usually last 1 - 2½ hours, and all the tours include transfers from Al Ain, as well as Arabic coffee and dates.

Creek Tours

Other options → **Dubai Areas [p.132]**
Boat, Dhow & Yacht Charters [p.162]
Dinner Cruises [p.379]

For a more luxurious tour of the Creek than by abra, an organised Creek Tour is a wonderful way to see new and old Dubai side by side, while enjoying a peaceful and relaxing journey. Prices per adult range from about Dhs.35 for a daytime trip to Dhs.260 for an evening cruise with dinner. Many of the tours are in a traditional wooden dhow (often with air conditioned decks to avoid the heat in summer).

Creekside Leisure

Location → Opp Dubai Municipality HQ · Creekside, Deira | **336 8406**
Hours → Timings on request
Web/email → www.tour-dubai.com   Map Ref → 11-C1

Creekside Leisure specialises in daily Creek tours on a traditional dhow. All tours last for one hour and are one of the most informative ways to view the city, plus a great photo opportunity. The company uses pre-recorded headsets (Arabic, English, German and Russian), which include a 45 minute history of Dubai and a perspective on places of interest, not only along the banks of the Creek, but throughout the Emirates. Hot and cold refreshments are available.

The company is due to launch Floating Majlis,

which will be a two hour dinner cruise, with licensed bar and music, on Saturdays and Wednesdays. The cost per person will be Dhs.150; children aged 5 - 12, half price.

Timings: 11:30, 13:30, 15:30, 17:30, 19:30.

Cost: Dhs.35 for adults; Dhs.20 for children over 5 years.

Danat Dubai Cruises

Location → Nr British Embassy · Bur Dubai | **351 1117**
Hours → 08:00 - 18:30
Web/email → www.danatdubaicruises.com   Map Ref → 8-C4

Boasting a top speed of 18 knots, this 34 metre state-of-the-art catamaran offers a variety of great cruises – ideal for that special occasion. Operating daily, these scenic cruises are a relaxing way to start or end the evening and to enjoy the bustle of Dubai's famous waterway.

Three separate decks allow passengers to choose their favourite seating area. The top deck is outside and covered by a protective awning, while the other two are enclosed and air conditioned. Being twin-hulled, the vessel has the added advantage of stability, ensuring customer comfort. Danat Dubai is also available for charter (see Boat & Yacht Charters).

Royal Tours

Location → Nr Sheraton Htl · Creekside, Deira | **223 1567**
Hours → Timings on request
Web/email → www.royaltours-dubai.com   Map Ref → 11-C1

Short and sweet sightseeing tours of Dubai Creek on board Royal Tours air conditioned dhow depart every hour between 10am and 6pm. There are also daily evening cruises, which depart hourly from 18:00 - 24:00.

Prices for the hour long tour (including soft drinks) are Dhs.35 for adults and Dhs.20 for kids aged 4 - 12. For the evening cruise, prices are Dhs.50 for adults and Dhs.25 for kids.

Falconry Shows

Other options → **Birdwatching [p.156]**

Falconry, the sport of sheikhs, has a deep-rooted tradition in the UAE and is still practised today. At one time, falcons were used to catch wild prey, such as hares, so that the family would not have to kill any of their valuable livestock for meat.

Nowadays, Sheikh Zayed has declared the UAE a conservation zone to protect depleted wildlife.

However, the keeping of falcons is still popular and it's not unusual to see these beautiful and valuable birds being transported around the Emirates — even at the airport (where of course they fly first class!). In general, it's not possible to watch them being flown, unless personally invited, although it is possible to see these impressive birds on some tours.

Feathers of Arabia

Location ➜ Throughout the UAE | 050 643 0990
Hours ➜ Timings on request
Web/email ➜ dandaman@emirates.net.ae   Map Ref ➜ n/a

Dan Daman gives falconry displays throughout the UAE, showing not only falcons, but also birds indigenous to the country such as buzzards, kites, owls and eagles. Usually he flies the birds and gives a short talk about the art, and then, under close supervision, visitors may have the chance to fly the birds themselves. Demonstrations are often part of an Arabian desert evening arranged by the tour operators (an excellent photo opportunity!).

Dan operates chiefly between October 1 and May 31, as the summer months are too hot to fly the birds, although sometimes he will display them and give lectures. Dan can converse in English, Flemish, French and German. Private bookings cost approximately Dhs.1,000 for the evening and require two week's notice.

Feathers of Arabia also install falconariums for hotels and individuals and will give advice on falcon breeding.

Helicopter Tours

Other options ➜ **Plane Tours [p.162]**

Aerogulf Services Company

Location ➜ Dubai Int Airport · Al Garhoud | 282 3157
Hours ➜ 07:00 - 20:00
Web/email ➜ aerogulf@emirates.net.ae   Map Ref ➜ 15-A2

What better way to view the sights of Dubai than from the air? This is an ideal opportunity for residents and visitors alike to experience the UAE from a unique perspective – see traditional fishing dhows, windtower houses, the impressive parks, the winding creek, the port, fishing villages, beaches and much more. Aerogulf offers short sightseeing tours by helicopter of Dubai and other

parts of the Emirates, as well as passenger transport to and from selected hotel locations. Flight times can be anytime between 10:30am and before sunset. Contact Captain Peter Spoor or the operations staff for further information.

Flight location: Oilfields Supply Centre, near Al Maktoum Bridge, opposite Deira City Centre Mall.

Hot Air Ballooning Tours

Other options ➜ **Plane Tours [p.162]**

Voyagers Xtreme

Location ➜ Dune Centre · Al Satwa | 345 4504
Hours ➜ 09:00 - 18:00
Web/email ➜ www.turnertraveldubai.com   Map Ref ➜ 6-E3

The adventure that takes you higher than the rest! This is a great way to celebrate anything from a birthday or anniversary to a product launch.

Daily flights for up to 12 people operate every morning from Fossil Rock with a fully certified pilot. Enjoy breakfast as the balloon is prepared, although you're more than welcome to give the set-up team a hand. Once the balloon is ready, it's up, up and away! You'll enjoy a one hour flight over the desert and mountains that will take your breath away (don't forget your camera). It's just one morning, but the experience will last a lifetime!

Mosque Tours

Other options ➜ **Museum & Heritage Tours [p.143]**

Shk Mohammed Centre for Cultural Understanding

Location ➜ Beach Centre, Beach Rd, Jumeira | 344 7755
Hours ➜ 09:00 - 17:00   Closed Fri
Web/email ➜ smccu@emirates.net.ae   Map Ref ➜ 6-B2

This non-profit making organisation was established to bring down the barriers between different nationalities and to help visitors and residents understand the customs and traditions of the UAE. To achieve this a variety of activities are organised, such as mosque visits, usually to Jumeira Mosque on Sunday and Thursday mornings. These are conducted by a guide, who explains the process and procedure of prayer. Remember that visitors are expected to dress conservatively and to cover up to enter the mosques.

Tours & Sightseeing

Exploring

There are also home visits, offering the opportunity to visit the home of a UAE national for a traditional lunch. Visits by school groups can be arranged and courses in Arabic are offered.

Plane Tours

Other options → **Helicopter Tours [p.161]**
Hot Air Ballooning [p.161]

Fujairah Aviation Centre

Location → Fujairah Int Airport · Fujairah | 09 222 4747
Hours → Timings on request
Web/email → www.fujairahaviationcentre.com   **Map Ref** → UAE-E2

A bird's-eye view of the mixture of coastline, rugged mountains, beautiful valleys, villages and date plantations is available from the Fujairah Aviation Centre. Flights can last from 30 minutes to four hours, which will enable you to see almost the entire Emirates. The 'discovery flight' is a 30 minute flight over the East Coast and Oceanic Hotel. At Dhs.100 per person, it's an excellent way to see the coast from a different perspective. A longer tour for 1 - 3 people costs Dhs.480 per hour.

The following are some suggested itineraries, although the pilots can prepare other routes especially for you.

Scenic Flight 1: Fujairah - Dibba - Masafi - Fujairah; Scenic Flight 2: Fujairah - Hatta - Al Dhaid - Masafi - Fujairah; Scenic Flight 3: Fujairah - Al Ain - Abu Dhabi - Dubai - Sharjah - Ajman - Umm Al Quwain - Ras Al Khaimah - Dibba - Fujairah.

Stable Tours

Other options → **Horse Riding [p.248]**
Polo [p.256]

Nad Al Sheba Club

Location → Nr Bu Kidra R/A · Nad Al Sheba | 336 3666
Hours → Various
Web/email → www.nadashebaclub.com   **Map Ref** → 17-A3

An early morning visit to the world's top racehorse training facilities at Nad Al Sheba is inclusive of a cooked breakfast, a behind-the-scenes glimpse of the jockey's facilities and a view over the racecourse from the Millennium Grandstand, plus the chance to see horses training. The tour ends with a visit to the Godolphin Gallery where the Dubai World Cup is on display. Please call for timings and prices.

Note: the Gallery closes for 4-6 weeks in November/December for refurbishment.

Walking Tours

Other options → **Bus Tours [p.158]**

Whilst the layout of the roads and the heat, especially in summer, do not make Dubai the easiest city to explore by foot, there are many areas that are well worth the effort of walking around. In particular, these include the souks and the corniche areas, on both the Bur Dubai and Deira sides of the Creek, which can be combined with an atmospheric abra (water taxi) crossing. The term 'corniche' is used to refer to any walkway by a stretch of water — in the Emirates these can be along the seafront or around one of the creeks or lagoons.

A useful and informative guide is the *Town Walk Explorer (Dubai)* (Dhs.10), which outlines two routes through the most interesting parts of the city. It is available at all good bookshops, or directly from Explorer Publishing (Web/email - www.explorer-publishing.com).

BOAT, DHOW & YACHT CHARTERS

Boat & Yacht Charters

Other options → **Creek Tours [p.160]**
Dinner Cruises [p.379]
Dhow Charters [p.163]

Charlotte Anne Charters

Location → Dibba · Fujairah | 09 222 3508
Hours → Timings on request
Web/email → www.charlotteannecharters.com   **Map Ref** → UAE E1

Charlotte Anne is a twin-masted Baltic schooner made of 200 tonnes of solid Swedish oak. The yacht is captained by Chris Hurndall and his wife Renate who have welcomed hundreds of guests to cruise the coast of the Mussandam. Charters range from a day (up to 35 passengers), to overnight, three-day cruises (sleeps ten), or longer. Ideal for birthdays or team building – in fact, any excuse to get away from city life!

For divers a trip aboard the *Charlotte Anne* is a must, but snorkelling and swimming are also a great way to enjoy the ocean. The *Charlotte Anne* is fully air conditioned and all meals are provided. Charters leave from Dibba port. Omani visas are not required.

Danat Dubai Cruises

Location → Nr British Embassy · Bur Dubai | **351 1117**
Hours → 08:00 - 18:30
Web/email → www.danatdubaicruises.com **Map Ref** → 8-C4

This 34 metre state-of-the-art catamaran is available to host group charters, product launches, seminars, wedding receptions ... the options are endless! The boat can operate regular charters into and out of all the popular marinas along the coast.

Danat Dubai has a capacity of 300 passengers (for sit down functions this is limited to 170 people). Onboard facilities include a dance floor, music system, video monitors, large screen projection, sun deck and two enclosed air conditioned decks. Catering, live entertainment or a DJ can be provided as part of the charter. Danat Dubai also offers a range of scheduled cruises (see Creek Tours).

El Mundo

Location → DIMC · Al Sufouh | **343 4709**
Hours → Various
Web/email → www.elmundodubai.com **Map Ref** → 3-A2

Dubai has an exciting new tourism venture, the sailing vessel *El Mundo*. The company caters to most requests, from watching the dhows and abras crossing Dubai's Creek to live entertainment, business lunch cruises and special charters. Alternatively, why not enjoy a two or three day sail to snorkel, dolphin watch and hike in the Mussandam? Choose from a range of activities from 'fun in the sun', 'sun and sea cruise' to 'castaway cruise' or 'sole charter'.

Le Meridien Mina Seyahi Beach Resort & Marina

Location → Le Meridien Mina · Al Sufouh | **399 3333**
Hours → Various
Web/email → www.lemeridien-minaseyahi.com **Map Ref** → 3-A2

Le Meridien Mina Seyahi operates a variety of charters from their marina. A number of boats are available for trips of different lengths, numbers of people and for a variety of activities, such as deep-sea fishing, bottom fishing, trawling, sightseeing or full-day cruises. Prices are available on request and depend on the package required (all rates include a skipper and equipment). The *Soul of Stars* operates from the marina and bookings can be made through the hotel.

Soul of Stars

Location → Le Meridien Mina · Al Sufouh | **050 694 2960**
Hours → On request
Web/email → dimcdxb@emirates.net.ae **Map Ref** → 3-A2

Built in 1995, *Soul of Stars* is a traditional 65 ft clipper. The yacht can be chartered and can cater for up to 35 people. Facilities include three double cabins, a grand piano, a semi-rigid rubber outboard boat and the opportunity to snorkel or fish. Skipper and crew are provided.

Alternatively, enjoy one of their scheduled tours, which run all year-round. The two hour morning cruise leaves at 10am, while the sunset cruise leaves at 4pm. Both trips include soft drinks and light snacks (Dhs.175 per person, free for children under 14 years). There's also a two night trip to the Mussandam leaving every Thursday afternoon at 6pm and returning on Saturday at 7am (Dhs.1,700 per person, full board, for a maximum of eight people).

Yacht Solutions

Location → Jumeirah Beach Htl · Umm Suqeim | **348 6838**
Hours → Timings on request
Web/email → www.yacht-solutions.com **Map Ref** → 4-B2

Yacht Solutions promises to satisfy your charter cruising requirements. They can arrange anything from a short exciting blast aboard a high-speed sports rib, to an exclusive overnight stay on their 20 metre *Princess* motor yacht: a myriad of cruising options are available and they provide full catering options. Corporate enquiries are especially welcome.

Dhow Charters

Other options → **Boat & Yacht Charters [p.162]**
Creek Tours [p.160]
Dinner Cruises [p.379]

Travelling up and down the Creek or along the coast by traditional wooden dhow can be a wonderfully atmospheric and memorable experience. For charters, contact one of the following companies.

Alternatively, large independent groups can try chartering a dhow from the fishermen at Dibba to travel up the coast of the Mussandam.

Boat, Dhow & Yacht Charters

Exploring

Be prepared to haggle hard in the Mussandam — knowing a bit of Arabic may smooth things along. Expect to pay around Dhs.2,500 per day for a dhow large enough to take 20 - 25 people, or Dhs.100 per hour for a smaller one.

You'll need to take your own food and water, etc, as nothing is supplied except ice lockers that are suitable for storing supplies. Conditions are pretty basic. However, you will have freedom to plan your own route and to see the beautiful fjord-like scenery of the Mussandam from a traditional wooden dhow.

If you leave from Dibba (or Dabba), Omani visas are not required, even though you enter Omani waters. It is also possible to arrange stops along the coast and it's probably best to take camping equipment for the night, although you can sleep on board.

The waters are crystal clear, although the weather can seriously reduce visibility for divers, and turtles and dolphins can be seen from the boat. It's ideal for diving, but hire everything before reaching Dibba (try the Sandy Beach Diving Centre, [p.236]). Alternatively, spend the day swimming, snorkelling and lazing, and for an extra Dhs.500 hire a speedboat.

Al Boom Tourist Village

Location ➜ Nr Al Garhoud Bridge · Umm Hurair 2 |**324 3000**
Hours ➜ 20:30 - 22:30
Web/email ➜ abt@emirates.net.ae   Map Ref ➜ 14-A3

Al Boom Tourist Village is the biggest operator of dhow boats on the Creek. They currently have seven dhows, ranging in capacity from 20 - 280 passengers. Along with each private charter, they offer a range of enticing menus, such as sea paradise, international delicacies, local delights, Far Eastern feast and Indian cuisine.

Another highlight of this location is Al Areesh Restaurant, which is situated on the bank of the Creek, and offers an Arabic and international buffet.

Prices: range from Dhs.500 per hour for Al Taweel (single deck, 20 passenger capacity), to Dhs.3,000 for Kashti (double deck, 150 passenger capacity).

Al Marsa Charters

Location ➜ Musandam, Dibba · Oman/UAE |**+968 836 550**
Hours ➜ Timings on request
Web/email ➜ info@musandamdiving.com   Map Ref ➜ n/a

Providing dhow, diving, live-aboard, and cruising charters, Al Marsa is a great way to get away.

Operating out of Daba Al-Mina fishing harbour on the East Coast, they have access to some of the most exhilarating seascapes along the Musandam Peninsula. Relax on the spacious Dhow's sundeck for a one-day cruise and discover some of the charming fisherman's villages only accessible by sea. Alternatively, try an overnight cruise and explore remote and sheltered Dawhat (Fjords) by day and enjoy the peace and tranquillity of a secluded Khawr (bay) anchorage by night.

Creek Cruises

Location ➜ Creekside, Deira |**393 9860**
Hours ➜ 09:00 - 18:00   Closed Fri
Web/email ➜ www.creekcruises.com   Map Ref ➜ 11-C2

The magnificent dhows *Malika Al Khor* and *Zomorrodah* are the largest of their kind on the Creek. They can be chartered for any kind of occasion and are suitable for groups of between 20 and 200 people. Facilities include an air conditioned deck, an Arabic style majlis, a professional sound system and dance floor.

For an extra charge, Creek Cruises can arrange a DJ or magician, etc, to liven up your party. Alternatively, join the air conditioned dhow *Jamila* for a pleasant two hour dinner cruise of the Creek (20:00 - 22:00).

For further information, contact the above number or (050 624 3793).

Charters: Dhs.1,500 per hour (minimum two hours). Catering can be provided from Dhs.80 per person upwards.

Location: far end of Quays 1 and 2.

Creekside Leisure

Location ➜ Opp Dubai Municipality HQ · Deira |**336 8406**
Hours ➜ Timings on request
Web/email ➜ www.tour-dubai.com   Map Ref ➜ 11-C1

Creekside Leisure (formerly Coastline Leisure) was one of the first companies to be established on the Creek. They are well known in Dubai for offering a complete service, hence their large amount of repeat business.

They have two boats available and offer private charters for any occasion, from a romantic dinner for two to corporate hospitality for up to 50 guests. The dhows are fully licensed and have a professional sound system. Catering, live entertainment and business facilities can be arranged for an extra cost.

The company is due to launch Floating Majlis, which will be a two hour dinner cruise on Saturdays and Wednesdays. The cost per person will be Dhs.150; children aged 5 - 12, half price.

Khasab Travel & Tours

Location ➜ Mezanin, Warba centre · Deira	**266 9950**
Hours ➜ Timings on request	
Web/email ➜ www.khasab-tours.com	**Map Ref** ➜ n/a

Visit the spectacular Mussandam Peninsula on a dhow, with the chance of seeing dolphins, going swimming and snorkelling or just enjoying the scenery of the area known locally as the 'Norway of Arabia'. Sailing north from Dibba on the East Coast, the cruise follows the stunning coastline where rocky cliffs rise straight out of the sea, and pass small fishing villages accessible only by boat.

With Dibba only two hours drive from Dubai, a dhow cruise can easily be done in a day. The company can also arrange flights to the Mussandam, weekend breaks or longer holidays in Khasab where you can go diving.

> *Costs: adults Dhs.150 for a half-day, four hour cruise with refreshments; Dhs.250 full-day, including lunch. At some times of the year children under 12 are free and there are special rates for groups. The cruises depart from Dibba harbour and there is no minimum number per trip. Although the Mussandam is part of Oman, no visas are required for this trip.*

Royal Tours

Location ➜ Nr Sheraton Htl · Creekside, Deira	**223 1567**
Hours ➜ Timings on request	
Web/email ➜ www.royaltours-dubai.com	**Map Ref** ➜ 11-C1

Royal Tours have two dhows available for charter on Dubai Creek, which are suitable for parties, functions or just a cruise for a group. A variety of entertainment can be provided, with options including magicians, one man shows, traditional Lebanese folk dancing, belly dancing, as well as music from an Indian, Arabic or Filipino band.

Programmes can be tailored to suit your requirements and meals or refreshments are also available. The charter price depends on the type of entertainment and catering required.

OUT OF DUBAI

Other options ➜ **Weekend Breaks [p.176]**

If you have access to a car, it's worth spending some time exploring places outside the city. To the east of Dubai lies the town of Hatta — just over an hour's drive away, it is the only town of any notable size in the emirate of Dubai, apart from the capital itself.

South of Dubai is Abu Dhabi, the largest of all the emirates, covering 87% of the total area of the country and with a population close to one million. The capital is Abu Dhabi, which is also capital of the UAE. Al Ain is the second most important city in this emirate.

North of Dubai are the other emirates which form the northern part of the UAE. As you travel north of Dubai these are Sharjah, Ajman, Umm Al Quwain and Ras Al Khaimah.

Also covered in this section is the East Coast of the peninsula — a mix of rugged mountains and golden beaches, it's one of the most interesting areas in the country to explore.

For further information on exploring the UAE 'outback', refer to the *Off-Road Explorer (UAE)*, published by Explorer Publishing.

Hatta

Other options ➜ **Weekend Breaks [p.176]**

About 100 km from Dubai and 10 km from the border with Oman, but within the emirate of Dubai, is the town of Hatta. Nestling at the foot of the Hajar Mountains, the town is the site of the oldest fort in the emirate (built in 1790), and there are several watchtowers on the surrounding hills.

The town has a sleepy, relaxed feel about it and beyond the ruins and the Heritage Village, there is little to see or do here. However, past the village and into the mountains are the Hatta Pools, where you can see deep, strangely shaped canyons carved out by rushing floodwater.

As you come to Hatta, left at the fort roundabout on the main Dubai - Oman road, is the Hatta Fort Hotel. It is a popular weekend destination for many people, either for a meal, to enjoy the range of activities or for a longer stay. On the main Dubai - Hatta road is the Big Red sand dune, which is over 100 metres high. It's a popular spot for practising

Out of Dubai

Exploring

dune driving in 4 wheel drives or dune buggies, as well as trying sand skiing. Alternatively, take a walk to the top (it takes about 20 minutes), for a sense of achievement and a great view.

For further information on the area around Hatta, refer to the *Off-Road Explorer (UAE)* by Explorer Publishing.

See also: *Dune Buggies [p.238]; Sand Boarding [p.259]; Tour Operators [p.155].*

Hatta Heritage Village

Location → Hatta town · On road to Hatta Pools   **na**
Hours → 08:00 - 17:00 Closed Fri am
Web/email → n/a   **Map Ref** → UAE-D3

Hatta Heritage Village is a recreation of a traditional mountain village set in an oasis. Constructed around an old settlement, you can explore the narrow alleyways and discover traditional life in the mud and barasti houses. There is a large central fort and further up the hill, past the place for grinding coffee and overlooking the village, is the South Tower. Beyond the children's playground is a falaj, a tranquil oasis of running water and shaded seating areas.

Opposite the entry to the village, a house displays traditional products and handicrafts.

Abu Dhabi Emirate

Other options → **Weekend Breaks [p.176]**

For a lot more information on the emirate of Abu Dhabi, refer to the *Abu Dhabi Explorer*, published by Explorer Publishing.

Abu Dhabi

Only 50 years ago Abu Dhabi consisted of little more than a fort, surrounded by a modest village of just a few hundred date palm huts. However, with the discovery of oil in 1958 and with exports starting five years later, the situation changed dramatically. The income enabled the growth of a modern infrastructure — visitors will find a city of skyrise buildings, a large port, numerous hotels, hospitals and all the latest facilities. The airport is located on the mainland, 35 km from the city.

The city lies on an island, which became home to the Bani Yas Bedouin tribe in 1761 when they left the Liwa oasis in the interior. Being an island, it offered security as well as excellent grazing, fishing and fresh water supplies. The descendants of this tribe have, in alliance with other important tribes and families in the region, governed the emirate ever since.

To the south of Abu Dhabi lies the Liwa oasis on the edge of the infamous Rub Al Khali or Empty Quarter desert. With fertile oases and incredible sand dunes, it is a fascinating area to explore in a 4 wheel drive vehicle.

Al Ain

Al Ain is the second most important city in the Abu Dhabi emirate. It lies on the border with Oman and shares the Buraimi Oasis with the Sultanate. The shady oasis is a pleasant stretch of greenery amidst the harsh surroundings, and the palm plantations have plenty of modern examples of the ancient 'falaj' irrigation system.

As well as being the birthplace of the ruler of the UAE, HH Sheikh Zayed bin Sultan Al Nahyan, Al Ain has a variety of sights to interest visitors, including a museum, fort, livestock and camel souks. Outside

Camel rides on the beach

Take a trip down memory lane.

Remember Hatta Fort Hotel, nestling amidst the scenic Hajar Mountains, is an oasis of luxury, tranquillity, relaxation and exciting sporting facilities, including golf, archery, tennis and clay pigeon shooting. Don't forget it's only an hour's drive from Dubai and the ideal location to unwind in a spacious chalet-style room.

Enjoy the view, the cuisine, the peace and the memories.

P.O.Box 9277, Dubai
Tel: +971 4 852 3211 Fax: +971 4 852 3561
Email: HFH@jaihotels.com
Website: www.jebelali-international.com
Sales & Marketing Office
Tel: +971 4 315 4350/4351 Fax: +971 4 399 2625

فنادق جبل علي انترناشيونال
JEBEL ALI INTERNATIONAL
HOTELS
تقاليد الضيافة والإكرام
A TRADITION OF HOSPITALITY AND EXCELLENCE

the central city, visits to Jebel Hafeet and Hili Fun City and archaeological site are also worthwhile.

If you are a fan of off-road driving and would like to explore this area further, the *Off-Road Explorer (UAE)* gives details of four stunning trips around Al Ain/Buraimi.

Ajman

Other options → Weekend Breaks [p.176]
Museums & Heritage [p.143]

The smallest of the seven emirates is Ajman, the centre of which lies about 10 km from Sharjah, although the buildings of the two towns merge along the beachfront. Ajman is not merely a coastal emirate, but also has two inland enclaves, one at Masfut on the edge of the Hajar Mountains and one at Manama in the interior between Sharjah and Fujairah. Ajman has one of the largest dhow building centres in the UAE, which offers a fascinating insight into this traditional skill.

Investment in this small emirate is growing, with the opening of the Ajman Kempinski Hotel & Resort and a popular shopping complex, Ajman City Centre, sister to the busy Dubai mall. Outlets include Carrefour hypermarket, Magic Planet amusement centre, many small shops and a six screen CineStar cinema complex.

Ras Al Khaimah

Other options → Weekend Breaks [p.176]
Museums & Heritage [p.143]

The most northerly of the seven emirates, Ras Al Khaimah (RAK) is one of the most fertile and green areas in the UAE, with possibly the best scenery of any city in the country. It lies at the foot of the Hajar Mountains, which can be seen rising into the sky just outside the city. Some areas of the town are even built on slightly elevated land with a view — rare when compared to other cities in the UAE, which are as flat as the proverbial pancake!

Like all coastal towns in the region, it traditionally relied on a seafaring existence and had an important port for pearling, trading and fishing. It is really two towns; the old town (Ras Al Khaimah proper) and across the creek, the newer business district (Al Nakheel). Visit the souk in the old town and the National Museum of Ras Al Khaimah, which is housed in an old fort, a former residence of the Sheikh.

The RAK Free Trade Zone is a five year development plan designed to accelerate economic growth in the emirate. A large shopping and leisure complex known as Manar Mall provides a one-stop shop for everyday needs, a cinema complex, family entertainment centre and water sports area.

The town is quite quiet and relaxing and it is a good starting point for exploring the surrounding countryside and visiting the ancient sites of Ghalilah and Shimal. Alternatively, visit the hot springs at Khatt or the camel racetrack at Digdagga.

One town in the emirate, Masafi, is home of the country's favourite bottled spring water; the UAE's (far superior!) answer to Evian!

RAK is the starting or finishing point for a spectacular trip through the mountains via Wadi Bih to Dibba on the East Coast and is also the entry point to the Mussandam Peninsula, Oman. Refer to the *Off-Road Explorer* (UAE) for further information on the trip through Wadi Bih, and also for exploring the Mussandam.

See also: *Wadi & Dune Bashing [p.264].*

Sharjah

Other options → Art [p.185]
Museums & Heritage [p.143]
Weekend Breaks [p.176]

Historically, Sharjah was one of the wealthiest towns in the region, with settlers earning their livelihood from fishing, pearling and trade, and to a lesser extent from agriculture and hunting. It is believed that the earliest settlements date back over 5,000 years. Today Sharjah is still a centre for trade and commerce, although its importance in this respect has been overshadowed by Dubai. The city grew around the creek or lagoon, which is still a prominent landmark in the modern city.

Sharjah is only a 20 minute drive from Dubai (depending on the infamous Dubai - Sharjah highway which can be extremely congested during rush hour), and is worth a visit, mainly for its various museums. In 1998, UNESCO named this emirate the cultural capital of the Arab world due to its commitment to art, culture and preserving its traditional heritage. Opposite Sharjah Natural History Museum, on the Al Dhaid road, past Sharjah Airport, a monument has been built to commemorate this award.

Sharjah is the only emirate with a coastline on both the Arabian Gulf and the Gulf of Oman. A visit from the city of Sharjah to its territory on the East Coast heads through the spectacular Hajar Mountains and takes 1½ - 2 hours (obviously depending on whether you're a speed demon).

Out of Dubai   Exploring

The towns of Dibba, Khorfakkan and Kalba are all part of Sharjah.

A useful guidebook to refer to for further information on this emirate is *Sharjah The Guide*.

Decency Law

Visitors should be aware that a decency law has been implemented in Sharjah. Leaflets were distributed in all public places to make people aware of the codes of moral behaviour and dress sense. This essentially means that there is now little freedom in this emirate for men and women who are not related or married to interrelate, or even be in a car together. In addition, to avoid offence (and attracting the interest of the police) you should dress much more conservatively than in Dubai. Basically, avoid wearing tight or revealing clothing in Sharjah, and that goes for guys as well as ladies!

Sharjah Creek

Sharjah is built around Khalid Lagoon, which is popularly called the Creek, with a walkway around it known as Sharjah Corniche. The Corniche is a popular spot for a stroll in the cool of the evening, especially with families, and there are various places for coffee along the way. In the middle of the Creek is a huge fountain, or jet of water, allegedly the second highest in the world.

From three points on the lagoon, small dhows can be hired for a trip around the Creek to see the lights of the city from the water. It is also a great photo opportunity during daylight hours. Prices are fixed and cost Dhs.30 for a 15 minute trip for a party of ten, while a tour of the lagoon to the bridge and back takes about 30 minutes and costs Dhs.60.

Majaz Canal

Over the last couple of years an eighty million dirham project has linked the Khalid Lagoon with the Al Khan Lagoons and the Mamzar Park area via the new 1,000 metre-long Majaz Canal.

The aim was to create a 'Little Italy' tourist attraction along the canal, complete with boat rides between the two lagoons. While the Venice-like touches for the canal might not be quite as impressive as the original, facilities include a restaurant/coffee shop for now. The development is in keeping with the Sharjah Government's desire to develop the tourism industry on a cultural and educational basis. Three bridges have been built over the canal near Khalid Lagoon, on Al Khan Road, and near Al Khan Lagoon as part of the project.

Al Dhaid

Al Dhaid is a green oasis town on the road from Sharjah to the East Coast. It is the second most important town in the Sharjah emirate and was once a favourite retreat from the deserts and coasts during the scorching summer months. Years ago, an extensive falaj (irrigation system) was built, both above and below ground to irrigate the land. The area is fertile and agricultural produce includes a wide range of fruit and vegetables from strawberries to broccoli and, of course, a large date crop.

On the outskirts of Al Dhaid, shoppers will find roadside stalls selling local pottery, carpets, fruit and vegetables.

During the winter months camel racing is held at the racetrack on the road to Mileiha.

Sharjah New Souk

Location → Nr Corniche · Sharjah   **na**
Hours → 09:00 - 13:00 16:00 - 22:00 Closed Fri am
Web/email → n/a   **Map Ref →** UAE-C2

Consisting of two long, low buildings running parallel to each other and connected by footbridges, Sharjah New Souk (or Central Souk) is a haven for bargain hunters. Inside it's new looking and functional, but from the outside it is intricately decorated and imaginatively built in an 'Arabian' style. Each building is covered, but open to the elements. The site has about 600 shops. Upstairs small shops sell furniture, carved wood, souvenirs and a fabulous range of carpets from a variety of countries. The shops downstairs sell modern items, such as clothing, small electrical goods, shoes, textiles, gold jewellery and toys.

Souk Al Arsah

Location → Nr Bank St · Sharjah   **na**
Hours → 09:00 - 13:00 16:30 - 21:00 Closed Fri am
Web/email → n/a   **Map Ref →** UAE C2

This is one of Sharjah's oldest souks, which has been renovated in the style of a traditional market place using shells, coral, African wood and palm leaves. There are about 50 small shops set in a maze of peaceful alleyways and selling items such as traditional silver jewellery, perfumes, spices, coffee pots and wedding chests, plus numerous other items, old and new.

Umm Al Quwain

Other options → **Weekend Breaks [p.176]**

Lying further north along the coast from Dubai, between Ajman and Ras Al Khaimah, is the emirate of Umm Al Quwain. The town is based around a large lagoon or creek and has a long seafaring tradition of pearling and fishing. On a superficial level, not much has changed here over the years and it gives an idea of life in the UAE in earlier times. The emirate has six forts that still exist and there are a few old watchtowers around the town, but otherwise there is not a lot else to see or do in the town itself.

However, the lagoon, with its mangroves and birdlife, is a popular weekend spot for boat trips, windsurfing and other water sports, since it is sheltered and free of dangerous currents. Just north of Umm Al Quwain, the area near the Barracuda Hotel (and grey-market liquor store) is a growing fun park. Dreamland Aqua Park, UAQ Flying Club, UAQ Shooting Club and the opportunity to try karting and paintballing make this the 'activity centre' of the Northern Emirates. With more resorts and facilities planned, this area can only get better!

East Coast

Other options → **Museums & Heritage [p.143]**
Weekend Breaks [p.176]

A trip to the East Coast of the Emirates is well worth taking, even if you are only in the UAE for a short time. The coast can be reached in 1½ - 2 hours and the drive takes you through the rugged Hajar Mountains and down to the Gulf of Oman. Take the road through the desert to Al Dhaid and Masafi (source of the local bottled water). At Masafi, you can do a loop round, either driving north to Dibba and then along the coast to Fujairah and Kalba and back to Masafi, or the other way round.

The mountains and East Coast are popular for camping, barbecues and weekend breaks, as well as various sporting activities. Snorkelling is excellent, even close to the shore and locations such as Snoopy Rock are always popular. In addition, the diving on this coastline is usually excellent, with plenty of flora and fauna to be seen on the coral reefs. Check out the *Underwater Explorer (UAE)*, published by Explorer Publishing, for further information.

For fans off-road driving, the route to the East Coast has a number of interesting diversions, check out the *Off-Road Explorer (UAE)*, published by Explorer Publishing, for further information.

See also: Camping[p.31]; Diving[p.234]; Snorkelling [p.261].

Al Hisn Fort

Location → Kalba, Nr Fujairah · East Coast | **09 277 4442**
Hours → 09:00 - 13:00 17:00 - 21:00   Closed Mon & Fri am
Web/email → n/a | **Map Ref →** UAE-E2

As you drive along the coast road in Kalba town, you come to the restored house of Sheikh Sayed Al Qassimi, overlooking the sea. It is located at the end of a large grassy expanse with swings and small rides for children. On the opposite side of the road is Kalba's Al Hisn Fort, which houses the town's museum. It includes a limited display of weapons and admission is free.

Note: Wed afternoon ladies and children only.

Badiyah

Probably best known as the site of the oldest mosque in the UAE, Badiyah is roughly located half way down the East Coast, north of Khorfakkan.

The mosque stands next to the coast road and is made from gypsum, stone and mud-bricks. It is officially called Al Masjid Al Othmani and is thought to date back 1,400 years, having been built in the year 20 Hijra in the Islamic calendar, or 640 AD in the Roman calendar. The small whitewashed building, which is surrounded by a 1½ metre wall, is still used for prayer, so non-Muslim visitors will have to satisfy themselves with a photo from the outside. The mosque is built into a low hillside with several ruined watchtowers on the hills behind. It has just been repaired and re-whitewashed.

The village of Badiyah itself is one of the oldest settlements on the East Coast and is believed to have been inhabited since 3000 BC.

Bithna

Set in the mountains about 12 km from Fujairah, the village of Bithna is notable chiefly for its fort and archaeological site. The fort once controlled the main pass through the mountains from east to west and is still impressive, probably more so than the fort at Fujairah. It can be reached from the Fujairah - Sharjah road where the village of Bithna is signposted. The fort is through the village and wadi.

The archaeological site is known as the Long Chambered Tomb or the T-Shaped Tomb, and was probably once a communal burial site. It was excavated in 1988 and its main period of use is thought to date from between 1350 and 300 BC,

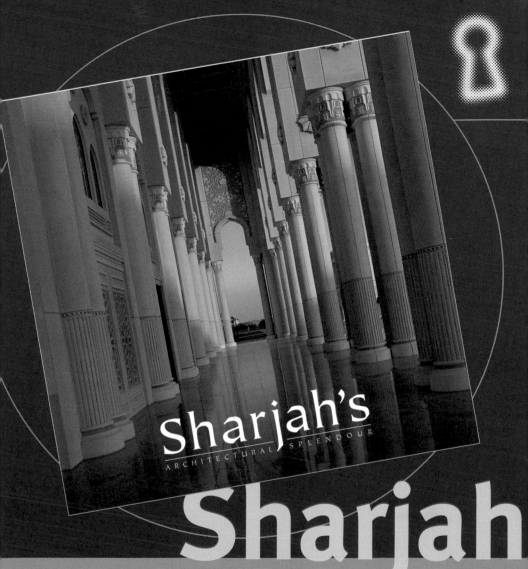

A striking photographic exploration into the architectural splendour of Sharjah

Take a guided tour of the beauty of Sharjah's architecture and some of the highlights of this remarkable city. From small aesthetic details to grand public compounds, from mosques to souks, the photographs contained within will amaze and delight. With striking images linked with text that is at once analytical and informative, this volume provides education as well as delight. Whether you are a long-term resident or a brief visitor, this volume will undoubtedly surprise and delight.

Available from leading bookstores, hotels, supermarkets or directly from Explorer Publishing. Customised copies and bulk orders ensure generous discounts.

Explorer Publishing & Distribution • Dubai Media City • Building 2 • Office 502 • PO Box 34275 • Dubai • UAE
Phone (+971 4) 391 8060 Fax (+971 4) 391 8062 Email info@explorer-publishing.com Web www.explorer-publishing.com

although the tomb itself is older. Fujairah Museum has a detailed display of the tomb that is worth visiting since the site itself is fenced off and covered against the elements. The tomb can be found by taking a right, then left hand turn before the village, near the radio tower.

Dibba

Located at the northern most point of the East Coast, on the border with the Mussandam, Dibba is made up of three fishing villages. Unusually each part comes under a different jurisdiction: Dibba al Hisn is Sharjah, Dibba Muhallab is Fujairah and Dibba Bayah is Oman! However, there is no sign of this when you visit the town, which is relaxed and friendly.

The area is very historical and there are various burial sites throughout the

region. In particular, rumour has it that a vast cemetery with over 10,000 headstones can still be seen (although we have yet to hear of anyone actually finding it!). This is the legacy of a great battle fought in 633 AD, when the Muslim armies of Caliph Abu Baker were sent to suppress a local rebellion and to re-conquer the Arabian Peninsula for Islam.

The Hajar Mountains provide a wonderful backdrop to the village, rising in places to over 1,800 metres. Dibba is the starting or finishing point for the stunning drive to the West Coast, through the mountains via Wadi Bih.

Tip: For the journey through Wadi Bih, a 4 wheel drive is pretty essential, since the route is often blocked by boulders carried by the floods... so be prepared to rebuild the road, or to turn back.

See also: Khasab Dhow Charters — Dhow Charters [p.163].

Fujairah

Fujairah often seems to be best known as the youngest of the seven emirates, since it was part of Sharjah until 1952. However, there is a lot more to the only emirate located entirely on the East Coast. It is in a lovely area with golden beaches bordered by the Gulf of Oman on one side and the Hajar Mountains on the other. The town is a mix of old and new; worth visiting in particular is the old fort, which is reportedly about 300 years old and overlooks the atmospheric old town.

The surrounding hillsides are dotted with ancient forts and watchtowers, which add an air of mystery and charm. Off the coast, the seas and coral reefs make it a great spot for fishing, diving and water sports. It is also a good place for birdwatching during the spring and autumn migrations since it is

on the route from Africa to Central Asia.

The emirate has started to encourage more tourism by opening new hotels and providing more recreational facilities. Since Fujairah is close to the mountains and many areas of natural beauty, it makes an excellent base to explore the countryside and see wadis, forts, waterfalls and even natural hot springs.

An excellent tourist map has been produced by the Municipality (09 222 7000) and Fujairah Tourism Bureau (09 223 1436). It includes superb hill shading, roads, graded tracks, 4 WD tracks, a decent co-ordinate system and places of interest. On the reverse side is a brief overview of each place of interest, combined with an overview of the city.

Kalba

If you go on an outing to the East Coast don't turn back at Fujairah, for just to the south lies the tip of the UAE's Indian Ocean coastline. Here you will find Kalba, which is part of the Emirate of Sharjah and renowned for its mangrove forest and golden beaches. The village is a pretty, but modern, fishing village that retains much of its charm.

A road through the mountains linking Kalba to Hatta has recently been completed, creating an interesting alternative to returning to Dubai on the Al Dhaid - Sharjah road.

Khor Kalba

South of the village of Kalba is Khor Kalba set in a beautiful tidal estuary (khor is the Arabic word for creek). This is the most northerly mangrove forest in the world, the oldest in Arabia and is a 'biological treasure', home to a variety of plant, marine and birdlife not found anywhere else in the UAE. If you are a birdwatcher or nature lover, try to spend a few days in this surprising and beautiful region of Arabia.

Although it has been proposed to make this a fully protected nature reserve, it is still waiting for Federal protection. The mangroves grow in this area due to the mix of saltwater from the sea and freshwater from the mountains, but they are receding due to the excessive use of water from inland wells.

For birdwatchers, the area is especially good during the spring and autumn migrations, and special species of bird include the reef heron and the booted warbler. It is also home to the rare white-collared kingfisher, which breeds here and nowhere else in the world. There are believed to be only 55 pairs of these birds still in existence.

Le MERIDIEN
AL AQAH BEACH RESORT

the way hotels should be

**FIVE STAR LUXURY
NOW OPEN ON THE
UAE'S EAST COAST**

OVER 200 SEA-FACING

ROOMS. A DIVING &

WATERSPORTS CENTRE.

A HEALTH CLUB

OFFERING CLEOPATRA

BEAUTY TREATMENTS.

RESTAURANTS & BARS. A

KIDS CLUB. THE LARGEST

SWIMMING POOL IN THE

UAE. CONFERENCE &

MEETING FACILITIES. AND

ONE OF THE MOST

PRIVATE STRETCHES OF

BEACH ON THE INDIAN

OCEAN. SO WHAT ARE

YOU WAITING FOR?

Dive right in

Le MERIDIEN
AL AQAH BEACH RESORT

P O BOX 3070
FUJAIRAH UNITED ARAB EMIRATES
TEL +971 (9) 244 9000
FAX + 971 (9) 244 9001
CALL TOLL FREE UAE 800 4041
www.lemeridien.com
www.lemeridien-alaqah.com

IN PARTNERSHIP WITH NIKKO HOTELS

A canoe tour by Desert Rangers is an ideal opportunity to reach the heart of the reserve and you can regularly see over a dozen kingfishers on a trip. There is also the possibility of seeing one of the region's endangered turtles, or a dugong, although sightings are more common for divers than from the shore or boat. The reserve is a unique area so treat it with respect — leave it as you would wish to find it.

See also: Desert Rangers - Canoeing [p.227]; Birdwatching [p.156]; Falconry [p.160].

Khorfakkan

Khorfakkan lies at the foot of the Hajar Mountains half way down the East Coast between Dibba and Fujairah. It is a popular and charming town, set in a bay and flanked on either side by two headlands, hence its alternative name 'Creek of the Two Jaws'. It is a favourite place for weekend breaks or day trips and has an attractive corniche (waterfront) and beach. A new souk sells the usual range of the exotic and the ordinary. There are plenty of things to do including fishing, water sports or a trip to Shark Island, alternatively sit in the shade with a fruit juice and people watch.

Part of the emirate of Sharjah, it has an important modern port; ships discharging their cargo here can save a further 48 hour journey through the Strait of Hormuz to the West Coast. Nearby is the old harbour, which is an interesting contrast to the modern port.

Set in the mountains inland is the Rifaisa Dam. Local legend has it that when the water is clear, a lost village can be seen at the bottom of the dam.

Wahala

This site is inland from Khor Kalba and is notable for a fort, which archaeologists judge to be over 3,000 years old. It is believed that the fort once protected the resources of the mangrove forests for the local population.

Mussandam

Other options → **Weekend Breaks [p.176]**

The Mussandam Peninsula is the Omani enclave to the north of the UAE. It has only been opened to tourists relatively recently and is a beautiful, unspoilt region of Arabia. The capital is Khasab, a quaint fishing port largely unchanged by the modern world. The area is of great strategic importance since its coastline gives control of the

main navigable stretch of the Strait of Hormuz, with Iran only 45 km across the water at the narrowest point. To the west is the Arabian Gulf and to the east the Gulf of Oman.

The region is dominated by the Hajar Mountains, which run through the UAE and the rest of Oman. It is sometimes called the 'Norway of the Middle East', since the jagged mountain cliffs plunge directly into the sea and the coastline is littered with inlets and fjords. The views along the coast roads are stunning. Inland, the scenery is equally as breathtaking, although to explore properly, a 4 wheel drive and a good head for heights are pretty indispensable! Just metres off the coast are beautiful coral beds with an amazing variety of sea life, including tropical fish, turtles, dolphins (a common sight), occasionally sharks, and even whales on the eastern side.

To reach the Mussandam from Dubai, follow the coast road north through Ras Al Khaimah. At the roundabout for Shaam take the exit right and follow the road to the UAE exit post. The Omani entry point is at Tibat, then basically follow the road until it runs out. Note that by car, non-GCC nationals can only enter and exit the Mussandam on the Ras Al Khaimah side of the peninsula, not at Dibba on the East Coast. There are UAE and Omani border posts, so the correct visas are required. Alternatively, it is possible to fly to Khasab from Dibba, although it takes longer than driving from Dubai and is more expensive.

Refer to the *Off-Road Explorer (UAE)* and the *Oman Explorer* (formerly *Muscat Explorer*) for further information on this fascinating part of Arabia.

Sultanate of Oman

Other options → **Weekend Breaks [p.176]**

The Sultanate of Oman is a friendly, laid back and very beautiful place to visit, especially after the hustle and bustle of Dubai. Visitors have two options — either to go east and into Oman proper or north to visit the Omani enclave known as the Mussandam. Both areas can be visited either by plane or car.

If you are driving into Oman, there are two main border crossing points — at Hatta or through the Buraimi Oasis, near Al Ain. At both places your vehicle will be searched, so it's advisable not to include prohibited items (alcohol, etc) in your luggage. The journey from Dubai to Muscat by car takes 4 - 5 hours, although crossing the border at the start or end of a public holiday can sometimes be tediously slow, with a 1 - 2 hour wait.

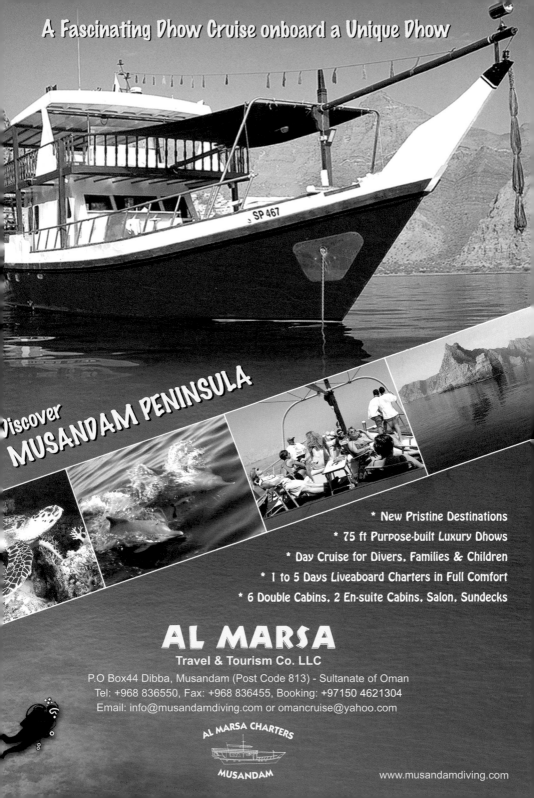

Flying takes about 45 minutes to Muscat. There are flights daily by Emirates and Oman Air, which cost between Dhs.400 - 600, depending on the season.

The local currency is the Omani Riyal (referred to as RO), which is divided into 1,000 baisa (or baiza). The exchange rate is usually about Dhs.10 = RO.1.

Note that talking on hand held mobile telephones whilst driving is illegal in Oman, as is driving a dirty car (yes, seriously)!

For further information on what Oman has to offer both visitors and residents, refer to the *Oman Explorer* (formerly *Muscat Explorer*).

Omani Visas

Visas for Oman are required for most nationalities, whether entering by air or road. Different regulations apply depending on your nationality and how long you want to stay in Oman. In general, a visit visa can be obtained upon arrival at the airport, or upon reaching the border crossing for between Dhs.35 – 50. Remember that regulations in this part of the world often change virtually overnight, so check details before you leave to avoid disappointment.

It is a straightforward procedure to apply at the consulate in Dubai for a visit visa, though this will cost more than just arriving at the border. Alternatively, let your sponsor (hotel, tour operator, Omani company) do the paperwork for you. Certain nationalities in the UAE on a tourist visa may obtain an Omani tourist visa (without sponsorship) on arrival at Seeb International Airport for Dhs.50. If you wish to return to the UAE after your visit to Oman, you will need a new visa.

If you are a UAE resident, a visa can be obtained on arrival at the border for Dhs.35. British and American citizens with UAE residency may consider applying for a two year multiple entry visa (Dhs.100).

For the Mussandam, the standard visit visa is needed, either from the consulate or by applying at the border (if you fulfil the criteria).

WEEKEND BREAKS

Other options → Camping [p.31]
Out of Dubai [p.165]

A great way to escape the hassles of the city and work is to go away for the weekend. This can either be a 'do it yourself' break within the UAE or to Oman, or a special deal arranged through a travel agent to a destination such as Jordan, the Seychelles or Kish Island.

With distances in the UAE being relatively small, it's easy to get well away from home without having to drive for hours — you can even check into a beach hotel minutes from your home and feel that you have entered another world! The alternative to staying in a hotel is to camp, and this is a very popular, well-established pastime in the Emirates.

An alternative option to the standard UAE breaks is to contact the main travel agents in Dubai. These companies often have special offers for people who feel like something a little different — how about a trip to Zanzibar, Bahrain or India? These offers are generally only available to GCC residents. The travel agents listed in the table are some of those that meet the travel needs of people living in Dubai, who want good advice, exciting itineraries and holidays that will not cost the earth. Last minute deals can often be found on the Internet (ie www.emirates.com, www.dnata.com, or www.arabia.msn.com).

If you decide to stay in a hotel and are booking with them direct, remember that (if asked) they will often give a discount on their 'rack' rate or published price. There are also often special promotions running, particularly in the quieter summer months when there are some incredible bargains available at five-star hotels. The cost of breakfast may or may not be included, so check when you book. Typically, for a weekend in the peak season or for corporate rates, expect a 30% discount off the rack rate. Off peak this can be as much as 60% lower.

For a list of places to stay, check out the Weekend Break table. This has a guide to the room costs at the hotels, however, as explained above these may be discounted further. Before choosing a destination, you may like to refer to the information on the other emirates under Out of Dubai or the Sultanate of Oman. For more detailed information on the Emirate of Abu Dhabi and the Sultanate of Oman, refer to the *Abu Dhabi Explorer* and the *Oman Explorer*, both books are part of the Explorer series of guidebooks. For camping options, see the *Off-Road Explorer (UAE)*, while if you're a fan of the marine world, refer to the *Underwater Explorer*.

Weekend Break Summary

United Arab Emirates (+971)

Abu Dhabi Emirate	Hotel	Phone	Email	Rate
Abu Dhabi[(02)] - 180km	Abu Dhabi Hilton	681 1900	auhhitw@emirates.net.ae	900 (+16%)
	Inter-Continental	666 6888	abudhabi@interconti.com	790(+16%,B)
	Khalidia Palace	666 2470	kphauh@emirates.net.ae	450
	Le Meridien	644 6666	meridien@emirates.net.ae	1200(+16%)
	Mafraq Hotel	582 2666	mafraq@emirates.net.ae	500(+16%)
	Sheraton Abu Dhabi	677 3333	sheraton@emirates.net.ae	800(+16%)
Al Ain[(03)] - 130km	Al Ain Hilton	768 6666	alhilton@emirates.net.ae	575(+16%)
	Inter-Continental	768 6686	alain@interconti.com	650(+16%)
Jazira[(02)] - 60km	Al Diar Jazira Beach	562 9100	reservations@jaziraresort.com	750(+16%)
Liwa[(088)] - 365km	Liwa Resthouse	22 075	–	165(B)
Ajman Emirate				
Ajman[(06)] - 20km	Ajman Kempinski	745 1555	ajman.kempinski@kemp-aj.com	850(+20%)
Dubai Emirate				
Dubai[(04)]	Jumeirah Beach	348 0000	reservations@jumeriahbeachhotel.com	1,400(+20%)
	Ritz-Carlton Dubai	399 4000	rcdubai@emirates.net.ae	2,050
	Royal Mirage	399 9999	royalmirage@royalmiragedubai.com	1,850+20%
Hatta[(04)] - 110km	Hatta Fort	852 3211	hfhhotel@emirates.net.ae	525(+20%)
Jebel Ali[(04)] - 50km	Jebel Ali Resort	883 6000	hoteluae@emirates.net.ae	990(+20%)
East Coast Emirates				
Fujairah[(09)] - 130km	Al Diar Siji	223 2000	sijihotl@emirates.net.ae	500(+15%)
	Fujairah Hilton	222 2411	shjhitwsal@hilton.com	700(+15%)
	Sandy Beach Motel	244 5555	sandybm@emirates.net.ae	385
Khorfakkan[(09)] - 160km	Oceanic Hotel	238 5111	oceanic2@emirates.net.ae	460
Ras Al Khaimah Emirate				
RAK[(07)] - 75km	Al Hamra Fort	244 6666	hamfort@emirates.net.ae	550(B)
	Ras Al Khaimah Hotel	236 2999	rakhotel@emirates.net.ae	440
	RAK Hilton	228 8888	rkhilton@emirates.net.ae	550
Umm Al Quwain Emirate				
UAQ[(06)] - 50km	Flamingo Beach Resort	765 1185	flaming1@emirates.net.ae	350

Sultanate of Oman (+968)

	Hotel	Phone	Email	Rate
Barka - 250km	Al Sawadi Resort	895 545	sales@alsawadibeach.com	230(+17%)
Khasab - 150km	Khasab	830 271	–	340
Muscat - 450km	Al Bustan Palace	799 666	albustan@interconti.com	1,290(+17%)
	Crowne Plaza	560 100	cpmct@omantel.net.om	580(+17%)
	Grand Hyatt Muscat	602 888	hyattmct@omantel.net.om	880(+17.4%)
	Holiday Inn Muscat	687 123	mcthinn@omantel.net.om	590(+17%)
	Inter-Continental	600 500	muscat@interconti.com	700(+17%)
	Mercure Al Falaj	702 311	accorsales@omanhotels.com	420(+17%)
	Radisson SAS	685 381	sales@mcdzh.rdsas.com	550(+17%)
	Sheraton Oman	799 899	sheraton@omantel.net.om	650(+17%)
Nizwa - 350km	Falaj Daris	410 500	fdhnizwa@omantel.net.om	295
Salalah - 1,450km	Salalah Hilton Resort	211 234	sllbc@omantel.net.om	660(+17%)
Sohar - 250km	Sohar Beach	841 111	soharhtl@omantel.net.om	350(+17%)
Sur - 650km	Sur Mercure	443 777	reservationssur@omanhotels.com	430(+17%)

Key Rack Rate = Price in dirhams of one double room; +xx% = plus tax; B = inclusive of breakfast.

Note The above prices are the hotel's peak season rack rates. Remember many hotels will offer a discount off the rack rate if asked! Distances are measured from Dubai.

Weekend Breaks

Exploring

ONE MILLION

TITLES.

---

20 CATEGORIES.

ONE GREAT

STORE.

Shopping

EXPLORER

Shopping

SHOPPING

Other options → Exploring [p.132]

There's no doubt that shopping has been elevated to an art form in Dubai and the city basks in its reputation as the 'Shopping Capital of the Middle East'. However, despite its tax-free status, visitors are often surprised, not too mention a little disappointed, to realise that the accolade doesn't necessarily translate into bargains galore in every store. Although prices on speciality goods in the region such as carpets, textiles and of course gold are extremely competitive, many imported goods are generally similar to any other major city in the world. The key to shopping like a pro in Dubai is to bargain where possible since prices, especially in the souks, can drop quite substantially.

What this city does afford avid shoppers, however, is choice and a thousand ways to part with their plastic. The following section provides information on all that is relevant for shoppers — from what to buy to where to buy it, plus a few tips on how to stretch the mighty dirham.

Dubai's glitzy shopping malls, replete with world-renowned shops and adequate parking, are covered in detail. In twenty-first century Gulf living, the shopping mall has become a social centre for residents and visitors alike. Malls have given birth to a new breed of entertainment, totally equipped with air-conditioning, a hotchpotch of nationalities and an unrivalled selection of shops and activities to pass the time.

Check out the coloured boxes; these list the most popular brand names of goods and cover where you can buy them. Don't forget the streets and areas for shopping — they're worth braving the heat, and this is where the intrepid shopper can track down some genuine bargains. The same applies to Dubai's souks (covered in the Exploring section).

Consumers will quickly become aware of the numerous (and endless) promotions and raffles on offer in Dubai from local radio and TV shows, to Dubai International Airport, to the smallest, most insignificant of shopping malls. The majority don't even require you to buy a special ticket, but will simply hand them over with your till receipt. Great fun — especially if you win that Lexus!

Dubai Chamber of Commerce (228 0000) publishes a useful book: The Dubai Commercial Directory, which lists products and services available, and the companies that sell them. There is also a list of brand names and their dealers. All international brands including department stores, designer stores and car dealerships are offered in the UAE on an agency basis, mostly run by a few large national families such as Al Futtaim, Al Ghurair, Al Tayer and Al Nabooda.

Note: Traps for the unwary shopper do exist in Dubai. Some of the international stores sell items at prices

Dhs.100 ~ € 28

that are far more expensive than in their country of origin (you can even still see the original price tags!). This can be as much as 30% higher – beware!

Refunds and Exchanges

Usually faulty goods are more easily exchanged than refunded at the shop of purchase, so always keep receipts and ask to see the manager if there is a problem. If, however, you have simply changed your mind about a recently purchased item, most retailers are not so obliging. Most will only exchange or give credit notes and very few will refund. You may also find that their policy changes for different items.

To be successful at all, unwanted items being returned need to be untouched, unworn, unused and in their original packaging. Always check the refund and exchange policy when buying something, and always keep your receipt somewhere safe. Most retailers will get hot under the collar if you persist; just let them know that the customer is always right! As a last resort, appeal to their need for ongoing patronage by their customers. If you really think you've been duped, see below.

Consumer Rights

Unfortunately there are no laws, codes or regulations in Dubai that protect consumers. Render that into another language and it means stores can do what they please. There is however an excerpt in the UAE Civil and Commercial code that states that the customer is entitled to recover the price which has been paid on faulty goods. But unless you are prepared to take the shop to court, that exchange will have to do.

If you are persistent and have a complaint about a purchased item, and can not get any assistance from the shopkeeper, the Emirates Society for Consumer Protection (394 5132) may be able to help you.

Alternatively, the Consumer Protection division in the Department of Economic Development (222 9922) will assist customers who have a problem with a purchase where the shopkeeper refuses to help. The department also handles cases involving expiry dates and warranties, etc.

Shipping

Shopping is a popular pastime for many of Dubai's residents, and even more so for the numerous visitors who come to shop their hearts out, especially during the Dubai Shopping Festival and Dubai Summer Surprises. Exporting goods can be a tedious task, but there is certainly no shortage of shipping and cargo agencies that offer good value for money. The best plan of action is to contact an agency directly. You will find plenty of listings under 'shipping' in the Dubai Yellow Pages. Most companies operate globally and are quite reliable. For larger items, many shippers will happily make room for odd bits of furniture in containers booked by other customers who haven't quite filled them up – and they give great discounts whilst they're about it.

Quotes can vary quite dramatically, but to give an indication, the average cost per kilo to Australia is Dhs.95, to the UK, around Dhs.85, and to North America, Dhs.180. These prices are inclusive of handling and packing charges. You can expect to pay up to double for door to door service, but half if travelling by boat. You have the option of sending the items by airmail, courier, or sea. For even larger shipments refer to Residents. During the Dubai Shopping Festival and Dubai Summer Surprises quite a few courier and shipping companies have special rates, so if you are planning to embark on a shopping frenzy, check them out.

See Also: New Residents [p.56]

How to Pay

You will have no problem exchanging money, withdrawing money or paying for goods in Dubai. ATM's (otherwise known as automatic teller machines, service tills or cash points) are readily accessible. Most cards are accepted by the plethora of banks in Dubai which offer international access through CIRRUS or PLUS ATM's.

Credit cards are widely accepted, the exception being small traders in the souks and local convenience stores. Accepted international credit cards include American Express, Visa, MasterCard and Diners Club. Discounting the high rates of interest you will have to pay, local banks reward their credit card users with a number of promotions, competitions and discounts. US currency is also widely accepted, even by the ubiquitous local store.

Shopping

Shopping

Since the dirham is pegged to the US dollar, the exchange rate offered is broadly the same throughout Dubai. For the astute shopper though, the best bargains are secured by using the local currency. There are numerous money exchange bureaus in all major shopping areas and the souks. Being equipped with dirhams will make shopping a whole lot quicker, hassle free and potentially translate into some cash discounts for you.

See Also: *New Residents [p.56]*

Bargaining

Other options → **Exploring [p.132]**

Although bargaining is often an alien way of doing business for many, it is a time-honoured tradition in this part of the world. Vendors will often drop the price quite substantially for a cash sale, especially in the souks. So, relax, think something for 'nothing', and remember to take your time – this can be fun!

The key to bargaining is to decide what you are happy paying for the item and to walk away if you don't get it for that. Always be polite and amiable, and never use rudeness or aggression as bargaining tools. Start with a customary greeting, and know the value of the item in negotiation; you can learn this by scouting around in other shops. Ask the shop assistant how much and when he tells you, look shocked, or at least indifferent. In the souk, a common rule is to initially offer half the quoted price.

Once you've agreed to a price, that's it – it's a verbal contract and you are expected to buy. Remember, storekeepers are old pros at this and have an instinct for a moment's weakness! Remember also that you don't have to buy if the price is not right. You can always walk away and return later. It is not uncommon for shop assistants to chase you out of the shop to secure a purchase. The consumer is the one with the power in the bargaining process – use it or lose it.

Away from the souks, bargaining is not common practice, although many stores often operate a set discount system, saying that the price shown is "before discount". It's always worth asking if you can have money off, especially if you are paying by cash — if you don't ask, you don't get. Even pharmacies have a last price system whereby they will reduce what is shown on the price tag, normally by ten percent.

WHAT & WHERE TO BUY

Dubai's stores sell an abundance of goods and you should have few problems finding what you need. The following section covers the main categories of products that can be bought in the city, from carpets to cars, electronics to gold, and where to buy them.

Alcohol

Other options → **Liquor Licence [p.66]**
On the Town [p.391]

Anyone over 21 years of age can buy alcohol at licensed bars, restaurants, and some clubs for consumption on the premises. However, to buy alcohol or liquor for consumption at home requires a liquor licence – it's not just a case of popping into your local supermarket. Only non-Muslim residents can apply for a liquor licence. For information on how to obtain a licence and the restrictions that apply, see p.66 in the New Residents section.

Note that residents who have a liquor licence from another emirate are not permitted to use it in Dubai, (except for old Sharjah licences, which are no longer valid in Sharjah, but which can be endorsed by Dubai Police).

African & Eastern Ltd		
Al Karama	334 8056	Map 9-C3
Bur Dubai	352 4521	Map 7-A3
Deira	222 2666	Map 10-D2
Jumeira	344 0327	Map 5-C2

Maritime & Mercantile Int'l LLC		
Al Karama	335 1722	Map 9-C2
Al Wasl	394 1678	Map 4-A3
Bur Dubai	393 5738	Map 10-D2
Deira	294 0390	Map 10-D2
Jumeira	344 0223	Map 5-C2
Trade Center	352 3090	Map 10-E1
Timings: 10:00 - 14:00 & 17:00 - 21:00; 10:00 - 21:00 Thursdays and Saturdays. Closed Friday.		

Once you have gone to the trouble of acquiring a licence, it's easy enough to purchase alcohol from the special stores that are strategically scattered around Dubai. Especially useful are those located near supermarkets such as Spinneys, so you can do all your shopping in one trip. When you do get your licence, you may find that friends you never knew you had are angling to help you out on shopping trips! There is one trap to be aware of though.

What
you
desire

BurJuman
A BETTER class of SHOPPING.

Tel: 04-3520222
www.burjuman.com

When you get to the checkout, expect to pay 30% more than the sale price. The purchase of liquor attracts a hefty tax here.

There are however known ways of jumping the gun... the Emirates have a few 'hole in the wall' stores selling tax free alcohol to unlicensed patrons. These stores are easy to purchase from if you don't mind the trek. The Barracuda Beach Motel next to Dreamland Aqua Park near Umm Al Quwain is one of the most frequented by Dubai residents. Similarly, there is another store opposite the Ajman Kempinski, which literally is a hole in the wall. Although this sounds like the easy option, you will find the selection not as comprehensive as the licensed outlets scattered throughout the city. Bear in mind it is illegal to transport alcohol over the border of an Emirate, and in particular, through Sharjah. Police often turn a blind eye to this followed practice, but if you get busted with booze in your car, we told you so!

Arabian Souvenirs

Other options → **Carpets [p.190]**
Gold & Diamond Museum [p.144]
Al Karama [p.138]

For visitors and residents alike, many items from this part of the world make novel souvenirs, gifts or ornaments for the home. Historically, this was a Bedouin culture and possessions had to be practical and transportable, reflecting the nomadic lifestyle of the indigenous population. Prices and quality of traditional items vary enormously and these days many come from India or Oman. The souks usually offer the best prices, but there is something to suit all budgets here.

Carpets are a favourite buy. Don't forget to take your time and see as many choices as possible, plus build up a rapport with the carpet seller and haggle, haggle, haggle! Other items to buy with a local theme include the symbol of Arabic hospitality: the coffee pot and cups, worry or prayer beads, plus wooden knick-knacks, such as dhows, falconry accoutrement and wooden canes. Genuine and old traditional items, such as wedding chests, are usually expensive and increasingly difficult to find in the UAE. However, modern 'antiqued' copies are widely available.

Abu Ahmed Antiques	Al Diyafa St., Satwa	345 3021
Al Jaber Gallery	Deira City Centre	295 4545
Creative Arts Centre	Beach Rd , Jumeirah	344 2303
Falcon Gallery	Behind the G.P.O., Bur Dubai	337 5877
Showcase Antiques, Art & Frames	Jumeirah Beach Road	348 8797

Traditional wooden doors are also sought after. These can be used as intended or hung against the wall as a piece of art. Alternatively, it's popular to have them turned into furniture, usually tables with a glass top so the carving can still be seen. Most of the furniture on sale today is from India or Oman.

Ancient looking rifles, muzzle-loading guns and the functional and decorative dagger ('khanjar'), a short curved knife in an elaborately wrought sheath, are also popular buys. However, if you are planning to take them back home as gifts or momentos, check with your airline on procedures, otherwise airport security won't be too impressed.

Arabian Souvenirs

Traditional wedding jewellery made of heavy silver and crafted into simply engraved (and extremely heavy) necklaces, bracelets, earrings and rings are coveted forms of historical art, especially as many of the larger pieces make excellent pictures if they are mounted behind glass in a frame.

Alternatively, if gold is more to your taste then you are in the right city – there is an amazing choice of gold jewellery in Dubai. The Gold Souk (see [p.136]) is well worth a visit and because there are no taxes on top of the international gold rate, it is very reasonably priced. The cost of workmanship is also very competitive, and if you are feeling artistic, you can create your own design.

Once valued more highly than gold, the dried resin from the frankincense tree in southern Oman has been traded for centuries, and makes a charming gift, especially when bought with a small wooden chest and charcoal burner to give off its evocative scent. You will probably either love or hate the smell of incense and the heavy local perfumes, but they are great as authentic gifts that exude the culture of the Middle East. Oud is a popular and expensive oil used in many of the perfumes, while Myrrh and other sweet smelling mixtures are also sold. Ask to smell some burning before deciding to purchase.

Shisha or hubbly bubbly pipes are a fun item to have and can be bought with variously flavoured tobacco, such as apple or strawberry. Both working or ornamental ones are available and some stores sell a protective carrying case – handy if you are taking it into the desert or to the beach.

Foodwise, look out for delicious Lebanese sweets, often made from pastry, honey and ground nuts and dates, or fresh dates supplied by the main producers from around the world. Iranian caviar is widely available and very good value, and is sold without import duty or a valued added tax.

Finally, there are the usual corny tourist souvenirs of the 'I heart Dubai' variety, plus fluffy camels, and sand pictures with glass panels that contain the seven different coloured sands of the seven different emirates (it's a wonder that there's any sand left in the UAE). However, if you are tired of clichés and looking for a more upmarket and easily transported souvenir of the UAE, it is worth picking up a good coffee table book such as *Images of Dubai and the United Arab Emirates*. This artistic, award-winning photographic book, available in all good bookshops, offers a refreshing visual perspective of this part of the world.

Art

Other options → Art Classes [p.287]
Museums & Heritage [p.143]

While there's nowhere like the Tate Gallery or the Louvre in Dubai, there are a number of art galleries that have interesting exhibitions of art and traditional Arabic artefacts. Most simply operate as a shop and a gallery. However, some also provide studios for artists and are involved in the promotion of art within the Emirates.

The Majlis Gallery and The Courtyard are both worth visiting in their own right as examples of traditional or unusual architecture. They provide striking locations in which you can also enjoy a wide range of art, both local and international.

Other places that are definitely worth a visit include the Sharjah Art Museum (06 551 1222) (refer to Museums & Heritage [p.143] for more information), and the Art and Culture Shop in the Hotel Inter-Continental Dubai (222 7171)

The smaller galleries such as Aquarius (349 7251), Artworks Gallery (262 6530), Derby Art Gallery (331 1047), Index (331 9688), Profile Gallery (332 6006) and Sunny Days (349 5275) are also worth having a look at.

Creative Art Centre

Location → Nr Choithrams · Beach Rd, Jumeira	**344 4394**
Hours → 08:00 - 18:00 Closed Fri	
Web/email → arabian@arts.com	Map Ref → 5-E2

Previously a centre for art classes, the Creative Art Centre is now a large art gallery with eight showrooms set in two villas. The gallery has a wide range of fine art, Arabian antiques and gifts, and a team of in-house framers, artists and restorers work on-site.

The gallery provides art for hotels, offices and interior designers, as well as for the general public. The range of antiques includes Omani chests, old doors, weapons and silver. Lynda Shephard, the managing partner, is a well-known artist in both Oman and Dubai.

Location: in two villas set back from Jumeira Beach Road. Take the turning inland between Choithrams supermarket and Town Centre shopping mall.

What & Where to Buy

Shopping

Four Seasons Ramesh Gallery

Location → Karama · Al Karama
Hours → 10:00 - 22:00
Web/email → www.fourseasonsgallery.com
| 334 9090
Map Ref → 10-D2

This large gallery, previously situated in the BurJuman shopping centre, has moved to Karama, near the Main Post Office. Opened in 1970, it is one of the larger galleries in Dubai, exhibiting and selling a mixture of work by local and international artists. There are different exhibitions of art throughout the year, and it's a great place to purchase a gift that will leave a lasting impression. Their range has also been expanded to include furniture now, making this a one-stop home decorating shop; purchase your favourite artwork, have it framed, then find the furniture to match!

Green Art Gallery

Location → St 51332, Beh Dubai Zoo · Jumeira
Hours → 09:30 - 13:30 16:30 - 20:30   Closed Fri
Web/email → www.gagallery.com
| 344 9888
Map Ref → 6-A2

The Green Art Gallery features original art, limited edition prints and handcrafted work by artists from all over the world. In particular, the gallery draws on those influenced and inspired by the heritage, culture and environment of the Arab world and its people. The gallery also encourages local artists by guiding them through the process of exhibiting and promoting themselves. Seasonal exhibitions are held from October to May.

Hunar Art Gallery

Location → Villa 6, Street 49 · Al Rashidiya
Hours → 09:00 - 13:00 16:00 - 20:00   Closed Fri
Web/email → hunarart@emirates.net.ae
| 286 2224
Map Ref → 15-A4

This gallery, located in a modern villa, exhibits fine art by international artists alongside local artists' works. Beautifully decorated Japanese tiles, Belgian pewter and glass pieces fill the spaces between traditional Persian paintings and contemporary art. Often on display is work by the well-known artists Rima Farah and Abdul Quadir Al Rais. Iraqi calligraphy is also featured here from time to time, as well as local watercolours.

Majlis Gallery, The

Location → Al Faheidi Street · Bur Dubai
Hours → 09:30 - 20:00
Web/email → majlisga@emirates.net.ae
| 353 6233
Map Ref → 8-A2

In the quaintest of surroundings in the old Bastakiya area of the city, the Majlis Gallery is situated in an old Arabic house, complete with windtowers and courtyard. Small whitewashed rooms lead off the central garden area and host a variety of exhibitions by contemporary artists. In addition to the fine art collection, there's an extensive range of handmade glass, pottery, fabrics, frames, unusual pieces of furniture and bits and bobs. The gallery hosts, on average, ten exhibitions a year, but is worth visiting year-round for both the artwork and the atmospheric surroundings.

Sharjah Arts Plaza Area

Location → Nr Bazaar, Al Hisn Ave · Sharjah
Hours → 09:00 - 13:00 17:00 - 20:00   Closed Mon
Web/email → n/a
| 06 568 8222
Map Ref → UAE-C2

After careful restoration, this area of Sharjah is home to a rich variety of arts-related ventures. Many of the buildings date from the late 18th century and the setting is peaceful and tranquil — very conducive to the artistic process.

Local pottery on display

What & Where to Buy

Shopping

In addition to Sharjah Art Museum, buildings include Sharjah Arts Centre (Bait Al Sarkal), which is an art school holding classes for boys and girls, and morning classes for women. This fine building was once a hospital and has a rich history. Nearby, are the Arts Cafe (06 537 3993), open 17:00 - 21:00, and Arts Library, while the Very Special Arts building is a studio for disabled artists. Bait Obeid Al Shamsi is a large, carefully restored house where visitors can wander at will. An alley leads to the Emirates Fine Arts Society building and here the work of local artists of all ages and nationalities is exhibited. The work on display changes frequently and exhibits include a variety of media, from oil paintings to photography.

All around the plaza area are studios and exhibitions and visitors are encouraged to wander around freely; occasionally work is for sale.

Total Arts	
Location → Courtyard, The · Al Quoz	**228 2888**
Hours → 10:00 - 13:00 16:00 - 20:00 Closed Fri	
Web/email → www.courtyard-uae.com	Map Ref → 4-D4

Operating since 1996, Total Arts is one of the galleries located in this unique courtyard. The gallery generally exhibits works of art from a variety of cultures and continents, however, there is a bias towards Middle Eastern artists, or to works that have somehow been influenced by Arabian culture. Total Arts occupies two floors of The Courtyard, with over 10,000 square feet of gallery space. It has over 300 paintings on permanent display, and there are regular shows of traditional handicrafts and antique furniture. However, one of the main attractions here must be the cobbled courtyard itself, which is surrounded by different façades combining a variety of building styles from around the world. All provide great photo opportunities and make it well worth the trek from the centre of town. Other outlets here include furniture and antiques, artist studios, photo studios, and a coffee shop.

Art Supplies

Other options → Art Classes [p.285]
Art [p.185]
Museums & Heritage [p.143]

Creative types who like to dabble in arts and crafts can find tools of the trade at any of the below stores. If you're looking anything in particular, try contacting each individual store before embarking

on a wild goose chase. The stores are sprawled throughout the city and you might find yourself shop-hopping if you don't plan ahead.

Al Hathboor General Trading	335 2466
Art Stop	349 0627
Art Source	285 6972
Chinese Trading	266 3384
Dubai International Art Centre	344 4398
Elves and Fairies	344 9485
Emirates Trading Est.	337 5050
Talent Stationery	343 2734

Beach Wear

Other options → Clothes [p.191]

Since many Dubai residents spend their weekends either basking by the pool or catching some sporting action on the emirate's fabulous beaches, it's not perhaps so surprising that people will often spend as much money on a pukka set of swimming togs than on a suit for work!

Generally, prices are extremely high in the specialist beach wear boutiques that stock everything from French and Italian designer wear to achingly hip Californian and Australian surfing labels. Since there is no real 'off' season, these shops often have sales and discounts at strange times of the year - so if labels are a crucial for your beach wear collection, it's worth asking to be put on a mailing list so you'll be first in the queue to snap up the bargains.

Dubai's many sports shops also stock a decent range of swimwear, but these veer towards no-nonsense styles for competitive swimmers rather than die-hard beach babes. For those less bothered about making a fashion statement when they peel off on the beach, head for the department stores in the larger malls such as City Centre and Bur Jurman.

BHS, Woolworth's, Debenhams and Marks & Spencer all sell a good range of fashionable beach wear for women, men and children including all related paraphernalia such as hats and beach bags at prices which won't break the bank.

Al Boom Marine	Jumeria Beach Road	289 4858
Bare Essentials	Jumeria Centre	349 9702
Beyond the Beach	Mercato	346 1780
Heat Waves	Jumeria Plaza	349 7111
Oceano	Palm Srip	346 1861
Westwood	Deira City Centre	295 5900

What & Where to Buy

Shopping

Books

Other options → Libraries [p.291]
Second-hand Shops [p.205]

A good selection of English language books is sold in Dubai, covering a broad range of subjects, from travel or computing, to children's books, the latest best-seller and coffee table books about the Emirates. Most of the larger hotels have small bookshops offering a limited choice, including the latest fiction and travel books on the UAE.

Al Jabre	BurJuman Centre	351 6740
Book Centre, The	Titan Department Store	349 7135
Book Corner	Al Ghurair City	223 2333
	Deira City Centre	295 3266
	Dune Centre	345 5042
	Galleria Shopping Mall	272 7385
	Jumeirah Plaza	344 0323
Book Worm	Park & Shop Complex	
Books Gallery	Al Ghurair City	223 2333
Books Plus	Beach Centre (Jumeira)	344 9045
	Lamcy Plaza	335 9999
	Oasis Centre	339 5459
	Spinneys (UmmSuqeim)	394 1657
Carrefour	Deira City Centre	295 4545
House of Prose	Jumeirah Plaza	344 9021
Kids Plus	Town Centre	344 2008
Magrudy's	Deira City Centre	295 7744
	Magrudy Shopping Mall	344 4193
	Mercato	344 4161
Spinneys	Al Mankhool Rd (Bur Dubai)	355 5250
Titan Bookshop	Al Wasl Rd (Umm Suqeim)	394 1657
	Trade Centre Rd (Bur Dubai)	351 1777
	Crowne Plaza	331 8671
Whitestar	Beach Centre, The	344 9045

You are unlikely to find as extensive a range of books and bookshops as in your home country, although the number and size of outlets is increasing. You will find that foreign newspapers and magazines, which are flown in regularly, are always much more expensive than at home. To all the males out there who enjoy perusing through racy blokes' mags, be warned: due to censorship laws in the UAE, pictures of semi-naked women are always disguised by a giant black pen mark.

Good chains with wide-ranging selections are Book Corner, Books Plus and Magrudy's. Book Corner recently opened the largest bookstore in the UAE, adding a tremendous 25,000 square feet of browsing space for Dubai's book lovers.

House of Prose and BookZone are two second-hand bookshops (good for buying cheap novels or selling unwanted books). Carrefour, Spinneys, Choithrams and Park'n'Shop supermarkets also carry a very reasonable selection of books and magazines.

Cards & Stationery

Other options → Books [p.188]

Most supermarkets carry an ample supply of greeting cards, wrapping paper and stationery. However, there are a number of speciality stores to be found lurking amid the weaving and winding corridors of Dubai's streets and malls. It is at these places you will find the best variety in Dubai, especially for cards, where they offer everything from Christmas and Easter to Mother's Day and Eid cards.

While postcards are a smashing bargain, greeting cards tend to be very expensive, especially those celebrating special occasions or holidays. Locally produced cards are much cheaper, more original, and often better quality – they can be found in most card shops and usually feature local artists' work.

Al Fahidi Stationery	Al Fahidi Street	353 5861
	Murshid Bazaar	226 5508
	Opp Al Khaleej Hotel	222 8641
Book Corner	Al Ghurair City	223 2333
	Deira City Centre	295 3266
	Dune Centre	345 5490
	Galleria Shopping Mall	272 7385
	Jumeirah Plaza	344 0323
Carlton Cards	Deira City Centre	294 8707
	Lamcy Plaza	336 6879
Emirates Trading	Jumeira	349 4874
	Near Al Nasr Cinema	337 5050
Farook International Stationery	Al Fahidi Street	352 1997
Gulf Greetings	Al Bustan Centre	263 2771
	BurJuman Centre	351 9613
	Deira City Centre	295 0079
	Oasis Centre	339 5459
	Spinneys (Umm Suqeim)	394 0397
	Wafi Mall	324 5618
Magrudy's	Deira City Centre	295 0079
	Jumeirah	344 4192
	Mercato	344 4161
Office One	Za'abeel Rd	335 9929
Titan Bookshop	Holiday Centre Mall	331 8671

Wrapping paper? Book Corner, THE One (home furnishings) and Woolworths have some of the most unique and certainly the most reasonable we've found. Similarly, Ikea sells gift-wrapping paraphernalia at a fraction of the price of the more established card and gift-wrap stores.

Dhs.100 ~ € 28

(side tab) Shopping — What & Where to Buy

A Novel Experience

You're never very far from a great bargain at Book Corner. With over 120,000 titles, we are the largest bookseller in the UAE. Buy everything from books on Feng Shui to stationery, from software to toys. You will soon discover that at Book Corner, there are endless things to do and not enough time to do them in.

BOOK CORNER

A novel experience!

Carpets

Other options → **Arabian Souvenirs [p.184]**

Whether you are a regular buyer or just a novice, carpet shopping can be a fascinating experience. In Dubai, countries of origin for carpets range from Iran and Pakistan to China and Central Asia, and there is a truly exquisite array of designs and colours.

However, to ensure that you are buying the genuine article at a good price, it's advisable to find out a bit about carpets before making the final decision. If possible, visit a number of shops to get a feel for price, quality and traditional designs, as well as the range available. As a very rough guide, the higher the number of knots per square inch, the higher the price and quality. Silk is more expensive than wool, and rugs from Iran are generally more valuable than the equivalent from Turkey or Kashmir. Also, check if it is machine or handmade (handmade ones are never quite perfect and the pile is slightly uneven). Salesmen will happily offer plenty of advice, but be sure that it's what you want at a price you want, and don't feel pressured to buy simply because the assistant has just unrolled 30 plus carpets for you. Bargaining is part of the game and is expected in all shops. Prices vary from a few hundred to many thousand dirhams, but are always negotiable.

Deira Tower shopping mall in Al Nasr Square has the largest number of carpet outlets under one roof – the majority of traders are from Iran. As part of the Dubai Shopping Festival, a carpet souk is set up in a large air-conditioned tent at the Airport Exhibition Centre. Here you can find a mind-boggling choice of carpets at excellent prices.

See also: *Dubai Shopping Festival [p.50].*

Afghan Carpets	Airport Road	286 9661
	Oasis Centre	339 5786
Al Orooba Oriental	BurJuman Centre	351 0919
Carpetland	Za'abeel Road	337 7677
Feshwari	Nr Iranian Hospital	344 5426
Kashmir Gallery	Al Ghurair City	222 5271
Khyber Carpets	Galleria Shopping Mall	272 0112
Persian Carpets	Deira City Centre	295 0263
	Jumeirah Beach Hotel	348 0223
	Le Royal Meridien	399 5400
Quem Persian Carpet	Sheraton Dubai	228 1848
Red Sea Exhibition	Beach Centre, Jumeira	344 3949

Cars

Other options → **New Residents [p.56]**

New residents are often pleasantly surprised to find that cars here are much cheaper than in their own country, and with competitive interest rates offered by banks and dealers, buying a new car isn't necessarily for an elite few. All the major car manufacturers are represented and give good discounts towards the end of the year (when next year's model is due in the show room) and during the shopping festival.

Alternatively, the second-hand market thrives here with an abundance of used car dealerships all over town. Here you'll find everything from barely used Porsches and Ferraris to 4x4's ideal for thrashing around in the desert. Prices are never final so stand your ground if you're determined to clinch a deal; remember the dealer has paid its previous owner a fraction of the price he's trying to sell it to you for.

For other good deals, check the newspapers, supermarket notice boards or Websites such as

Persian Carpets

www.valueonwheels.com. It's a good idea to have the vehicle checked out by a reputable garage though, before you take the plunge and buy.

Clothes

Other options → Beach Wear [p.187]
Shoes [p.205]

Dubai is a fashionista's heaven – here you will find everything from the priciest designer shops, to up-to-the-minute boutiques, to pile-it-high-sell-it-cheap bargain basements. Upmarket stores dedicated to designer names are mainly found in the shopping malls and hotel arcades, although many designer names still reside on Al Maktoum Street in Deira.

Most malls have a good selection of inexpensive quality clothing and there is now an increasing trend towards 'global' stores that sell the same clothing items the world over, turning over their stock every four to six weeks. Handily, they also show the retail price in each country on the tag, so it's quite satisfying to know that you are paying no more than anyone else is.

The shopping areas of Satwa and Karama offer a heady mixture of cheap clothing outlets of wildly varying quality. On a good day, you could quite easily kit yourself for a night on the town for the price of a few fruit cocktails. On a not-so-good day, forget it unless there's a bad taste party in the offing.

Trendy Clothing

Amichi	Mercato	344 4161
Armani Jeans	Mercato	344 4161
	Palm Strip	345 9944
Bebe	Al Ghurair City	223 2333
	BurJuman Centre	352 0222
Benetton	Al Ghurair City	221 1593
	BurJuman Centre	351 1331
	Deira City Centre	295 2450
	Jumeirah Centre	349 3613
Bershka	Deira City Centre	295 4545
	Mercato	344 4161
Bhs	Al Ghurair City	227 6969
	BurJuman Centre	352 5150
	Lamcy Plaza	305 9208
Bossini	Beach Centre, The (Jumeira)	349 0749
	BurJuman Centre	351 6917
	Lamcy Plaza	305 9313
	Meena Bazaar (Bur Dubai)	352 4817
Burberry	Deira City Centre	295 0347
Calvin Klein	BurJuman Centre	352 5244
	Deira City Centre	295 0194
Cartoon Fashion	Deira City Centre	295 0413
Cerruti	Twin Towers	227 2789
Chanel	Wafi Mall	324 0464
Christian Lacroix	BurJuman Centre	351 7133
	Wafi Mall	324 0465
Debenhams	Deira City Centre	294 0011
Diesel	Deira City Centre	295 0792
DKNY	BurJuman Centre	351 3788
	Deira City Centre	295 2953
DKNY Jeans	Town Centre	349 7693
Dolce & Gabbana	Deira City Centre	295 0790
Donna Karan	BurJuman Centre	351 6794
Escada	BurJuman Centre	352 9253
Esprit	BurJuman Centre	355 3324
Etoile	Wafi Mall	324 0465
Evans	Deira City Centre	294 0011
G2000	BurJuman Centre	355 2942
Gasoline	Palm Strip Mall	345 0543
Gerry Webber	Deira City Centre	295 4914
	Wafi Mall	324 3899
Giordano	Al Ghurair City	223 7904
	BurJuman Centre	351 3866
	Deira City Centre	295 0959
	Karama Centre	336 8312
	Wafi Mall	324 2852
Givenchy	Wafi Mall	324 2266
Gucci	Al Maktoum Street	221 5444
Guess	BurJuman Centre	355 3324
Hang Ten	Deira City Centre	295 3702
	Karama Centre	337 8191
Hyphen	Deira City Centre	294 0011
In Wear	BurJuman Centre	355 4007
	Deira City Centre	295 0261
Jaeger	Wafi Mall	324 9838
JC Penny	BurJuman	351 5353
	Deira City Centre	295 3988

What & Where to Buy

Shopping

Karen Millen	Deira City Centre	295 5007
	Palm Strip	345 6703
Kookai	Deira City Centre	295 2598
	Wafi Mall	324 9936
Kunooz	Palm Strip	346 1462
Lacoste	Deira City Centre	295 4429
Levis	BurJuman Centre	351 6728
	Deira City Centre	295 9943
Mango	BurJuman Centre	355 5770
	Deira City Centre	295 0182
	Palm Strip	346 1826
Marks & Spencer	Al Futtaim Centre	222 2000
Max Mara	BurJuman Centre	352 1133
Mexx	BurJuman Centre	355 1881
	Deira City Centre	295 4873
	Lamcy Plaza	334 0182
Monsoon	Deira City Centre	295 0725
Mr. Price	Lamcy Plaza	335 9999
MTV Fashions	Palm Strip	345 2991
Next	BurJuman Centre	351 0026
	Deira City Centre	295 2280
Oasis	Deira City Centre	294 0011
	Wafi Mall	324 9074
Oui	Deira City Centre	295 3906
Paris Gallery	Hamarain Centre	268 8122
Part Two	Deira City Centre	295 0261
Pierre Cardin	Twin Towers	224 7774
Polo Ralph Lauren	BurJuman Centre	352 5311
	Deira City Centre	294 1200
Pull & Bear	Deira City Centre	295 3525
River Island	Deira City Centre	295 4413
Rodeo Drive	Al Bustan Rotana Hotel	282 4006
	Galleria Shopping Mall	272 0114
Sana Fashion	Karama	337 7726
Splash	Nr Maktoum Bridge	335 0525
	Oasis Centre	339 0511
Truworths	Deira City Centre	295 2469
Verri	Twin Towers	228 2262
Westwood	Deira City Centre	295 5900
Woolworths	Deira City Centre	295 5900
XOXO	BurJuman Centre	355 3324
YSL	Mercato	344 4161
Zara	BurJuman	351 3332
	Deira City Centre	295 3377

For smart men's suits, jackets and casuals, a number of shops along the Creek in Deira, especially around the Twin Towers area, exist – many offering permanent sales on 'designer' suits.

If you are confused about the sizing system here, ask the shop assistant for help. They usually know each country's sizing equivalent, or they will have a conversion chart for ready reference.

An alternative to buying clothes off the rack is to have them custom-made by a tailor, and there are many places around the city offering this service.

They will make an item from a drawing or photograph, and can copy outfits purchased elsewhere if you can leave the original for a few days. If necessary, they will also advise on the amount of material you should buy. The finished results can be excellent and the prices are very reasonable. Word of mouth is the best method of finding a reliable, switched-on tailor; otherwise, trial and error is the only answer.

For sales, the period around the Dubai Shopping Festival isn't bad, but the best times are the August/September and the January sales when everyone is getting rid of the old and bringing in the new. If you can bear to rummage, discounts of 70% aren't uncommon. Another excellent time for bargains is around the end of Ramadan when the Eid sales begin. However, beware; if the stock in many of the international stores looks like it's been made and shipped in especially to satisfy sales fever – you're right, it has.

Computers

Other options → Electronics & Home Appliances [p.194] Bur Dubai [p.82]

You should have few problems finding the right hardware and software to submerge yourself into the latest technology. Numerous outlets sell the latest merchandise – there are even specialist shopping malls devoted to computers and computer products. Try the Al Ain Centre next to Spinneys Ramada, or the Al Khaleej Centre, across the road. These two malls cater mainly to IT types, selling everything and anything associated with computer gadgets. There is also 'Computer Street', at the other end of Bank Street, which has many small stores that specialise in selling in bulk. The price quoted is often a cash price only.

Al Faris Computer	Bur Dubai	393 3444
Compu Me	Al Garhoud	282 8555
Explorer Computers	Bur Dubai	393 4080
Jumbo Electronics	Shk Zayed Rd	332 8315
Plug-ins	Deira City Centre	295 0404

Each year, around the middle of October, the exhibition halls at the Dubai World Trade Centre hold GITEX, the biggest IT exhibition in the Middle East. If you are really serious about computers and the latest technology, this is the place to visit – every computer company that you can think of, plus a few others, has a stand there. There's also a GITEX Shopper held at the Airport Expo, so when you've cruised the stands and decided what latest

gizmo you can't live without, you can pop along and buy it with a good discount.

The UAE government, together with the BSA (Business Software Alliance) is clamping down heavily on the sale of pirated software. As a result, most computer shops are reputable and offer the usual international guarantees.

However, if you have a legitimate problem with sub-standard computer equipment, and cannot gain a satisfactory outcome after complaining directly to the shop, the Consumer Protection Cell (222 9922) in the Department of Economic Development should be able to give practical assistance to gain a fair outcome. This can include setting up and overseeing meetings between the two parties, implementing fines, and even arranging for the payment of refunds to be made at the Economic Department, leaving 'dodgy' sales practices little room for manoeuvre.

Electronics & Home Appliances

Other options → Computers [p.192]
Al Faheidi St. [p.220]

From well known to not-so-instantly-recognisable brands, Dubai's stores stock a reasonable selection of electronics and home appliances. Prices are often hyped as being lower than in many parts of the world, but it is worth checking things out before leaving home, especially if you are out to buy a major item.

Like most goods, it pays to shop around for the best prices, although shops are generally fairly competitive due to the number of places offering the same or similar items. Bargaining will reduce the price further (often 'apparently' to the level of destroying the store's profit margin).

Warranties, after-sales service, delivery and installation should be finalised before making any purchase. If you intend on returning to your home country with an item, check that you are buying a model that will operate there (for example, manufacturers set the sound frequency on televisions differently in different parts of the world, so what works in Dubai won't necessarily work at home).

Alternatively, if you are happy buying second-hand electronics, check out the Classifieds sections of the daily newspapers (Gulf News and Khaleej Times). A range of items is advertised, often virtually as good as new. It may also be worth going to some of the 'garage' sales that are advertised by people who are usually returning to

their home country and are selling off some of their unwanted possessions. You can buy something for nothing from leaving expats; they usually sell at ridiculously low prices. Their main priority is usually to get rid of everything as quickly as possible, regardless of how much money they lose. Remember, it's a buyer's market, and some great bargains can be found, making these options excellent for people who do not want to part with their hard earned cash.

Aftron	Al Futtaim Electronics	211 9111
	Deira City Centre	295 4545
Aiwa	Al Sayegh Bros	227 4142
Bang & Olufsen	Music Centre	262 2700
Black & Decker	Jashanmal	269 3659
Bosch	Mohd Hareb Al Otaiba	269 1575
Bose	G & M International LLC	266 9000
Braun	The New Store LLC	353 4506
Elekta	Elekta Gulf	883 7108
General Electronics	Juma Al Majid	266 0640
Grundig	Agiv (Gulf)	223 2228
Hitachi	Eros Electricals	266 6216
Ignis	Universal Electricals	282 3443
Jashanmal	Wafi Mall	324 4800
JVC	Oasis Enterprises (LLC)	282 1375
Kenwood	Jashanmal	266 5964
Lenox	Eros Electricals	266 6216
Minolta	Viking Electronics	223 8167
National	Al Zubaidi Electronics	226 3688
	Jumbo Electronics	352 3555
Panasonic	Jumbo Electronics	352 3555
	Viking Electronics	223 8167
Phillips	Agiv (Gulf)	223 2228
	Al Ghandi Electronics	337 6600
Pioneer	Agiv (Gulf)	223 2228
Popular Brands	Carrefour	295 1600
	Jacky's Electronics	282 1822
	Plug-ins	295 0404
	Radio Shack	295 2127
Russel Hobbs	Jashanmal National	266 5964
Samsung	Al Ghurair City	223 2333
	Eros Electricals	266 6216
	Juma Al Majid	266 2340
	Samsung Electronics	222 5747
Sanyo	Agiv (Gulf)	223 2228
	Al Futtaim Electronics	359 9979
Sharp	Agiv (Gulf)	223 2228
	Cosmos	352 1155
Siemens	Scientechnic	266 6000
Simpson	Universal Electrical	282 3443
Sony	Jumbo Electronics	352 3555
Thomson	G & M International	266 9000
Toshiba	Al Futtaim Electronics	211 9111
Whirlpool	Al Ghandi Electronics	337 6600
Yamaha	Agiv (Gulf)	223 2228

The strength of the sun in the Gulf means that for many people, sunglasses are their most important accessory. Consumers will find just about every brand of normal glasses and sunglasses imaginable, from designer names to designer rip-offs and much more in between. While prices range from a few dirhams to many hundreds, it is best to buy sunglasses with a good quality lens. Make sure that they give 100% UVA and UVB protection, and are dark enough (and large enough) to protect the eye from the sun's glare.

Most of the larger shopping malls have an optician who can make up prescription lenses, offer a good range of glasses and contact lenses, and also give eye tests. These are free of charge in most optical shops, as long as you order your glasses there or specify that the glasses are for driving. However, some places charge Dhs.20 - 50 for the eye test.

Al Adasat Opticals	Lamcy Plaza	335 4006
Al Jaber Optical	Deira City Centre	295 4400
Al Sham Optic	Oasis Centre	339 5459
City Optic	Deira City Centre	295 1400
Dubai Opticals	BurJuman Centre	352 0222
	Deira City Centre	295 4303
Fashion Optics	Palm Strip	346 1462
Grand Optics	Carrefour Shindagha	393 6133
	Deira City Centre	295 4699
Grand Sunglasses	Deira City Centre	295 5334
Lunettes	Jumeirah Centre	349 9702
Lutfi Opticals Centre	Wafi Mall	324 1865
Opic Gallery	Deira City Centre	295 3825
Optic Art	BurJuman Centre	352 0222
Sunglass Hut	Deira City Centre	295 0261
Yateem Opticians	Al Ghurair	223 2333
	BurJuman Centre	352 0222
	Emirates Towers Boulevard	330 0000

Flowers

Other options → Plants & Trees [p.204]
Plant Street [p.140]

For those special occasions or for that special someone (or as a desperate last minute present), flowers make a beautiful gift. There is a reasonable selection of florists all over the city and places often sell dried flowers as well as fresh. Excellent flower arrangements can also be bought from Spinneys supermarkets and Carrefour hypermarket in Deira City Centre Mall. The local florist shops also offer superb arrangements at very reasonable prices. It is worth a visit to the local florists even if you don't intend buying, as the skill and adeptness of local florists are well worth seeing first-hand.

Blooms Flowers	Jumeira Beach Road	344 0912
City of Flowers	Jadhaf	324 3525
Desert Flowers	Nr Iranian Hospital	349 7318
Flower Box	Jumeira Centre	344 9484
Gift Express	Jumeira Centre	342 0568
Intraflora	Al Riqqa Street (Deira)	223 1199
Oleander	Jumeira Beach Road	344 0539
Planters	Opp Hamarain Centre	266 6427
Sentiments	Nr Picnic Rest (Satwa)	349 8969

If you are looking for florists who deliver internationally as well as locally, refer to the Dubai Yellow Pages. Interflora signs adorn many of the windows of local shops that offer international deliveries. Prices vary according to the type of arrangement and flowers you choose, but the minimum order for local delivery is usually Dhs.100 per bouquet.

Food

Other options → Health Food [p.198]
Fish Market [p.136]
Fruit & Vegetable Market [p.136]

Food-wise, Dubai has a good range of stores and supermarkets that cater more than adequately to the city's multi-national inhabitants. While there may be some speciality foods you can't buy in Dubai, most items are available.

Prices vary dramatically. Produce is imported from all over the world, and some items are double what they would cost in their country of origin. However, fresh foods, such as fruit and vegetables, can be

Goodies

amazingly cheap, especially if bought from places like the Fruit and Vegetable Market near Hamriya Port, or in Karama.

There are plenty of 'corner' shops in residential areas, good for a pint of milk and much more. Many accept orders over the phone for local home deliveries, saving you the walk. Popular food shops include Spinneys and Choithrams (both have branches all over the city), and Park 'N' Shop, near Safa Park, which is much frequented by the residents of Jumeira and Umm Suqeim.

In Deira City Centre Mall, there's Carrefour (formerly known as Continent), a huge hypermarket, which is part of a large French chain. It sells everything from cheap shoes to toothpaste, as well as a good selection of fruit, vegetables and an excellent selection of fish and seafood. Other branches of Carrefour can be found in Ajman, Abu Dhabi, Al Ain, Sharjah, Ras Al Khaimah, plus the latest new branch in Bur Dubai. The Lulu supermarket chain also offers a variety of goods at reasonable prices. If you are looking for a certain type of food, there are a number of speciality stores... For American food, try Choithrams, Safestway or Park'N'Shop; for Asian/Japanese, head for Lals supermarket; for British and European go to Spinneys, and for French produce, look no further than Carrefour. Pork is sold in a limited number of shops around town. Selected Spinneys stores and Choithrams carry pork. While expensive, it is of high quality.

Furniture & Household Items

Other options → Furnishing Accomodation [p.84]
Za'abeel Road [p.139]

Whether you need kitchenware, bathroom accessories, linens, towels, curtain rods, lampshades or furniture, you will find goods to suit every taste and budget. There are some excellent home furnishing stores in Dubai, but

Al Jaber Gallery	Deira City City Centre	295 4114
	Opp Hamarain Centre	266 7700
Apollo	Sheikh Zayed Rd	339 1358
Bhs	BurJuman Centre	352 5150
Cane Craft	Karama	337 4572
Carre Blanc	Deira City Centre	295 3992
Carrefour	Deira City Centre	295 1600
Chen One	Century Plaza	342 2441
Cottage Furniture	Jumeira Centre	349 9702
Debenhams	Deira City Centre	294 0011
Ethan Allen	Jumeira Beach Road	342 1616
Fauchar	Wafi Mall	324 4426
Grand Stores	BurJuman Centre	352 3641
Guess Home	BurJuman Centre	355 3324
Habitat	Al Wasl Road	344 2002
Harvest Home Trading	Jumeira Centre	349 9702
Home Centre	Oasis Centre	339 5199
Homes R Us	Beach Centre, The	344 9045
ID Design	Al Ittihad Road	266 6751
IKEA	Deira City Centre	295 0434
JC Penny	BurJuman Centre	351 5353
	Deira City Centre	295 3988
Khans	Nr General Post Off.	06 562 1621
La Maison	Holiday Centre Mall	331 2022
Lalique	Wafi Mall	324 2556
Laura Ashley	Deira City Centre	295 1804
Lucky	Industrial Number 11	06 534 1937
Marina Gulf Trdg	Al Barsha Road	347 8940
MFI	Oasis Centre	339 3503
Pier Import	Bin Sougat Centre	286 0030
	Mazaya Centre	343 2002
Sara	Deira City Centre	295 0408
Sara - Villeroy & Boch	Wafi Mall	324 4426
Showcase Antiques	Nr. Dxb Muncipality	348 8797
Tanagra	Al Ghurair City	223 4302
	Deira City Centre	295 0293
	Wafi Mall	324 2340
THE One	Jumeira Beach Road	342 2499
	Wafi Mall	324 1224
Westwood	Deira City Centre	295 5900
Wicker	Zabeel Rd	337 8888
Woolworths	Deira City Centre	295 5900

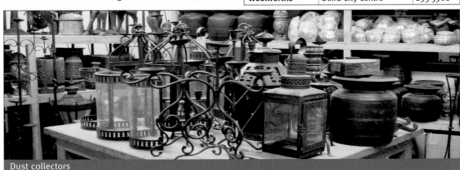

Dust collectors

Shopping — What & Where to Buy

Breakfast in Bed?

Better Homes Interiors
helps you to put first things first...

Soft Furnishings.
Cushions, throws, slip covers...
let us make those 'finishing touches'
in the designs, fabrics and colours
of your choice.

Bed Linen.
Duvet covers, sheets, pillow
cases... have your bedroom
just the way you like it.

Curtains.
Ready-made or made-to-measure.
We also have measurements of
most of our properties, to make
your life that bit easier.

...leaving you to relax in your new home and enjoy breakfast in bed.

el (04) 3447714

eriors@bhomes.com

betterhomes
A better experience

remember that in addition to the above list, many of the supermarkets sell kitchenware and a selection of linen etc.

A number of upmarket stores sell the latest styles in furniture. THE One, Home Centre and Ikea are a few of the many that offer the latest in home decor. Second-hand furniture can often be found through the classified pages in the newspapers or from supermarket noticeboards.

Besides all those shops in Dubai which have recently sprung up offering 'antiqued' Indian furniture, the originals: Khans, Pinkies and Luckys in Sharjah sell an excellent range of Indian teak and wrought iron items at very reasonable prices.

Hardware & DIY

Other options → Outdoor Goods [p.203]

Whilst it is often easier and cheaper in Dubai to get in 'a man who can' to tackle all those niggling domestic jobs, many still prefer to do-it-themselves. As a result of this demand, stores such as Ace Hardware, with branches around Dubai, have become better stocked with each passing year. Customised paints, glazes, special paint effect materials, electronic tools and hardware materials are all easily obtained in Ace, but also check out the smaller stores in downtown Satwa where prices may be cheaper and the choice surprisingly varied.

Ace Hardware	BurJuman Centre	355 0698
	Shk Zayed Road	338 1416
Carrefour	Al Shindagha	393 9395
	Deira City Centre	295 1600
Harley Davidson	Sheikh Zayed Rd	339 1909
Picnico General Trd	Beach Rd (Jumeira)	394 1653
Ulo Diving	Sharjah	06-5314036

Health Food

Other options → Health Clubs [p.270]

Thanks to the health trend finally arriving in Dubai, specialist health food stores, and even regular pharmacies selling a range of supplements are popping up on a regular basis. The major supermarkets sell an ever-increasing (but still very limited) range of organic and gluten-free products, such as organic cornflakes, herbal teas, rice-cakes, oat cakes, gluten-free pasta, etc. Choithrams even makes its own gluten-free bread. A small variety of herbal liver, kidney and blood cleansing products are available on the market, as are some detoxifying products. Note that vitamins, minerals, supplements, organic and health foods are expensive compared to back home, and the selection of brands, while improving, is still limited, so bring vitamins and supplements from home if you can.

An increasing number of sports shops offer products and supplements that are geared to sports performance or slimming, and this area of nutrition is extremely well catered for, with many outlets packed to the brim with all sorts of shakes, meal replacement bars and performance enhancing supplements.

Diet & Delight	Al Hana Centre	398 3826
Healthy Eating	Al Garhoud Road	286 5777
Healthy Living	Mazaya Centre	343 8668
Nutrition Centre	Jumeirah Centre	344 7464
Nutrition Palace	Crowne Plaza	332 8118
Nutrition Zone	Town Centre	344 5888
Planet Nutrition	Deira City Centre Mall	294 5889
	Jumeirah Plaza	342 0969
	Spinneys (Umm Suqeim)	394 4108

Jewellery, Watches & Gold

Other options → Souks[p.218]
Gold & Diamond Museum [p.144]
Deira [p.82]
Bur Dubai [p.82]

When it comes to watches and jewellery, Dubai is almost guaranteed to be able to supply whatever you are looking for. Prices range from a few dirhams to diamond studded watches costing many thousands of dirhams. Don't forget to check out the souks – here you can find all kinds of designs, for all ages and tastes.

Gold

EXPLORE
THE GREAT
INDOORS

Armchairs, beds, candles, desks, easy chairs, fabrics, glassware, halogen lamps, kitchenware, lighting, mats, office furniture, plants, quilts, rugs, sofas, toys, venetian blinds, wall units....
IKEA stores literally cover the A to Z of good living without adding to your cost of living. We have over 12,000 inspiring, yet functional ideas for you to explore, so why not come and discover what best suits your lifestyle.

GMASCO 5100623670/02

Appropriately for the City of Gold, jewellery comes in many forms, with cultured pearls from Japan, or classic, ethnic creations from India. Note that the standards of workmanship can vary so if you are spending a lot of money, it is worth going to a more reputable store.

Al Fardan	Deira City Centre	295 4238
Al Fardan Jewellers	Hamarain Centre	269 9997
Al Fardan Jewels	Twin Towers	222 1222
Al Futtaim Jewellery	Al Ghurair City	223 8320
	Deira City Centre	295 2906
Al Liali	Mercato	344 4161
Bin Hendi Jewellery	Deira City Centre	295 2544
	Jumeirah Beach Hotel	348 7030
Breitling Watches	Deira City Centre	295 4109
Cartier	BurJuman Centre	355 3533
	Emirates Towers	330 0034
Chopard	Wafi Mall	324 1010
Citizen	Al Ghurair City	223 2333
Damas Jewellery	Al Bustan Centre	263 4055
	BurJuman Centre	352 5566
	Deira City Centre	295 3848
	Hamarain Centre	268 8149
	Wafi Mall	324 2425
Fossil	BurJuman Centre	351 9794
	Deira City Centre	295 0108
Gold Souk	Opp Fish Market (Deira)	n/a
	Sharjah	n/a
Golden Ring	Deira City Centre	295 0373
Guess	Deira City Centre	295 2577
Mahallati Jewellery	Mercato	344 4161
Mansoor Jewellery	BurJuman Centre	355 2110
Paris Gallery	BurJuman Centre	351 7704
	Deira City Centre	295 5550
	Hamarain Centre	268 8122
Philippe Charriol	BurJuman Centre	351 1112
Prima Gold	BurJuman Centre	355 1988
	Deira City Centre	295 0497
Pure Gold	Mercato	344 4161
Raymond Weil	Deira City Centre	295 3254
Rivoli	BurJuman Centre	351 2279
	Deira City Centre	295 4496
	Palm Strip	346 1977
	Wafi Mall	324 6675
Rossini	Deira City Centre	295 4977
	Wafi Mall	324 0402
Seiko	Al Ghurair City	227 8036
Silver Art	Deira City Centre	295 2414
Swarovski	Wafi Mall	324 0168
Swatch	BurJuman Centre	359 6109
	Deira City Centre	295 3932
	Wafi Mall	324 0518
Tag Heuer	Wafi Mall	324 3030
Tiffany & Co	BurJuman Centre	359 0101
	Deira City Centre	295 3884
Watch House	BurJuman Centre	352 8699
	Deira City Centre	295 0108

Gold

Dubai is famous throughout this part of the world as the 'City of Gold', since it sells and imports/re-exports a vast amount of this beautiful metal. A walk around the Gold Souk is more than enough to confirm that the title is richly deserved.

Priced according to the international daily gold rate, gold is available in 18, 21, 22 or 24 carats, in every form imaginable, from bracelets, rings and necklaces to gold ingots. In addition to the weight price, a small charge will be added for craftsmanship, which varies according to the intricacy of the design. Dubai's Gold Souk is famed the world over for its low prices and sheer variety on offer – just remember to bargain hard.

If you don't see the particular piece you're looking for, bring in a photo or drawing and the craftsman will make it for you – usually on approval so even if you don't like the finished product, you are not obliged to buy.

Kids' Stuff

Other options → Places to Shop [p.207]
Family Explorer Guidebook

A variety of goods can be found in Dubai for children of all ages, from nursery equipment to the latest computer games, to mini designer fashions. For younger children, it's even possible to hire specialised items, such as car seats or cots. Virtually every conceivable toy or game is available somewhere in Dubai, and you should have few problems buying the more old fashioned games or the latest fashionable 'must have' toys.

Adams 0 - 10	BurJuman Centre	355 2205
Anil Kids Trading	Al Bustan Centre	263 0476
Baby Shop 0 to 9	Abu Hail Centre	266 1519
Baby Shop 0 to 10	Oasis Centre	338 0965
Baby Shop 0 to 11	Za'abeel Road (Karama)	335 0212
Early Learning Centre	BurJuman Centre	359 7709
	Deira City Centre	295 1548
	Spinneys (Umm Suqeim)	394 1204
	Wafi Mall	324 2730
Kids R Us	Oasis Centre	339 1817
Little Me	Palm Strip	345 6424
Mothercare	Al Ghurair City	223 8176
	BurJuman Centre	352 8916
	Deira City Centre	295 2543
	Spinneys (Umm Suqeim)	394 0228
Mummy & Me	Al Maktoum Street	227 3580
Ovo Kids	Deira City Centre	295 0885
Prémaman	BurJuman Centre	351 5353
Toys R Us	Al Futtaim Centre	224 0000

Shopping

What & Where to Buy

You may prefer to buy toys, especially for very young children, from more reputable shops that are less likely to sell sub-standard items.

For a fuller picture on all that Dubai and the Northern Emirates have to offer families with children up to the age of 14 years, refer to the *Family Explorer* (formerly *Kids Explorer*) published by Explorer Publishing. This offers invaluable information on everything from education and medical care to top venues for a birthday party, and both outdoor and indoor activities – perfect for when the temperatures soar.

Leather & Luggage

Other options → Shipping [p.181]
Al Karama [p.138]

Like the memories of Dubai, good leather lasts forever. Imagination and artistry combine in a wide range of fine leather goods, from key rings, gloves or wallets to handbags, shoes, suitcases, etc. A wide range of styles and prices are available, but for cheaper items don't forget to check out Karama.

Aigner	BurJuman Centre	351 5133
	Deira City Centre	295 4149
Aristocrat	BurJuman Centre	355 2395
Francesco Biasia	Deira City Centre	295 5263
	Mercato	344 4161
La Valise	Deira City Centre	295 5509
Leather Palace	Al Ghurair City	222 6770
	BurJuman Centre	351 5251
	Hamarain Centre	266 7176
Louis Vuitton	BurJuman Centre	359 2535
Mohd Shareif	Al Ghurair City	228 1996
	BurJuman Centre	355 3377
Porsche Design	Deira City Centre	295 7652
Sacoche	Deira City Centre	295 0233

Lingerie

Other options → Clothes [p.191]

Emirati ladies have a reputation for being one of the highest consumers of luxury lingerie in the world and, as testament to that, almost every mall houses a proliferation of frilly, frighteningly expensive lingerie boutiques.

Every designer name in lingerie is healthily represented in Dubai. (There's even one lingerie boutique in The Mazaya Centre that is far better known elsewhere for its boudoir 'accessories' but, in this store at least, it sells underwear only). So, if you are on the lookout for a few decent additions to

a bridal trousseau, and money is no object, there surely can be few better places to shop.

However, if you veer towards function rather than glamour, there are several noteworthy alternatives. In the past year or so, lingerie chain La Senza has been opening up branches in shopping malls throughout the Emirates offering an extremely decent range of underwear and nightwear at affordable prices. Woolworth's in City Centre stocks a good range of lingerie at excellent value. Marks & Spencer itself, of course, in Deira and the newly opened branch in Sharjah's Sahara Centre, has a staunch following for its lingerie lines – but expect to pay heavily inflated prices for the privilege of buying the UK's favourite underwear in Dubai.

Bare Essentials	Jumeirah Centre	324 4555
Carrefour	Deira City Centre	262 7061
Charisma	Hamarain Centre	344 9045
	Wafi Mall	355 1251
Debenhams	City Centre	351 3881
In Wear	Deira City Centre	355 2205
Inner Lines	Deira City Centre	294 0011
	Deira City Centre	295 0627
La Perla	BurJuman Centre	345 4119
La Senza	Palm Strip	344 0552
Le Belleamie	Beach Centre, The	343 9910
My Time	BurJuman Centre	295 1600
Outfit	BurJuman Centre	295 4545
Shufoof Lingerie	Mazaya Centre	295 0627
Triumph	Deira City Centre	295 4276
	Mercato	344 4161
Womens Secret	Deira City Centre	295 9665

As long as you don't mind turning up at the cash till with your smalls nestling among the weekly shop, well-regarded European lingerie labels Sloggi and Dim are available in many supermarkets. Larger branches of Choithram's and Park'n'Shop offer a wide range of styles and great value for money

Medicine

Other options → General Medical Care [p.94]

There's no shortage of pharmacies or chemists in Dubai – these are indicated on shop signs by what looks like a snake wrapped around a cocktail glass. Remember to check the expiry date of medicine before purchasing it. Most pharmacies also carry a variety of beauty products, baby care items, sunscreens, perfumes etc.

In the Emirates you are able to buy prescription drugs over the counter. If you are certain what antibiotics or drug you need, it saves the expense and hassle of a doctor, and pharmacists themselves are always quite happy to listen to symptoms and suggest a remedy.

Each emirate has at least one pharmacy open 24 hours a day – the location and phone numbers are listed in the daily newspapers. In addition, a Municipality emergency number (223 2323) will give the name and location of 24-hour pharmacies.

Music & Videos

Although the selection isn't as large or as up to date as in North America, Asia or Europe, there are now Tower Records and Virgin 'megastores' in Dubai selling the latest current releases on CD, DVD and video. From famous international bands, Arabic or classical music to Bollywood and Hollywood releases, Dubai caters for a variety of styles and tastes. However, CD's, DVD's and videos are only released once they have been screened (and censored, if appropriate) to ensure that they do not offend the country's moral code.

Al Mansoor	BurJuman Centre	351 3388
	Wafi Mall	324 4141
Carrefour	Deira City Centre	295 1600
Diamond Palace	BurJuman Centre	352 7671
Music Box	Al Ghurair City	221 0344
Music Room	Beach Centre	344 8883
Plug-Ins	Deira City Centre	295 0404
Spinneys - all branches	Dubai (H.Q)	355 5250
Thomson	Al Ghurair City	223 2333
Tower Records	Palm Strip	345 3030
Virgin Megastore	BurJuman	352 0222
	Deira City Centre	295 8599
	Mercato	344 4161

Videos are in the PAL format, so before you buy or rent a video make sure it has a multi-format capability. There are numerous video rental stores around the city – check one out in your area. Alternatively, Spinneys supermarkets have a good DVD and video section. Blank audio and videotapes are for sale at major grocery stores. Rental prices range from Dhs.4 to Dhs.10 per video and around Dhs.10 (as well as a hefty deposit sometimes) per DVD.

Musical Instruments

Other options → Music Lessons [p.292]

Music lovers will find only a limited number of stores to buy instruments from in Dubai, and if you want to buy a larger instrument, such as a piano,

you will have to place an order. Sheet music is not widely available, and your best bet is probably to order it over the Internet – check out the main search engines and see where they take you.

Fann Al Sout Music	Deira	271 9471
Galleria Music	Karama	334 5468
Golden Guitar	Hamriya	269 5552
House of Guitar	Nr. Lulu Centre (Karama)	334 9968
Mozart Musical Instruments	Karama	337 7007
Zak Electronics	Deira	269 5774
	Za'abeel Rd (Karama)	336 0715

Outdoor Goods

Other options → Camping [p.31]
Hardware & DIY [p.198]

Aside from the humidity, sand, and desert creepy crawlies, the UAE has a fascinating outdoor existence, and off-roading and camping are revered pastimes for many. A weekend away offers a peaceful escape from the hustle and bustle of city, and there are virtually no limitations on where you can pitch your tent and light your fire. For most people, the lack of heat and humidity make the winter months the best time to go. However, if you choose your location carefully – at altitude or by the sea – the summer months aren't always completely unbearable. To get kitted out with the basics for a night under the stars, or just some gear to enjoy a few hours in the great outdoors, check out stores listed below. If you are a more avid outdoor enthusiast and prefer to have specialised equipment, you'll have to either order it online, or bring it from home.

Ace Hardware	BurJuman Centre	355 0698
	Shk Zayed Road	338 1416
Carrefour	Al Shindagha	393 9395
	Deira City Centre	295 1600
Harley Davidson	Sheikh Zayed Rd	339 1909
Picnico General Trd	Beach Rd (Jumeira)	394 1653
Ulo Diving	Sharjah	06-5314036

Party Accessories

Other options → Party Organisers [p.298]

Most major supermarkets and stationery stores sell the basic party paraphernalia, and if you go to the more specialised shops, you'll find an even wider range. From cards, balloons, candles, table settings and room decorations to gift-wrapping and fancy dress outfits, bouncy castles and

What & Where to Buy

Shopping

entertainers, the choice for both children's and adults parties is very comprehensive.

... you can even get a clown!

Balloon Lady, The	344 1062
Card Shop	398 7047
Elves & Fairies	344 9485
Flying Elephant	347 9170
Gulf Greetings	222 6918
Impulse	337 6053
Kids Play	228 4300
Magrudy Book Shop (Jumeira)	344 4193
Papermoon	345 4888
Toys 'R' Us	222 5859

Party Services (MMI)

Everything you need to get your party going! Wine or pint glasses, ice buckets, coasters etc. are available from Maritime & Mercantile International LLC (MMI), which offers this service free of charge (no liquor licence required). Leave a Dhs.500 fully refundable deposit to use all the items listed below. A minimal breakage charge of Dhs.5 per glass will be deducted from the deposit and the balance refunded. Items must be returned within five days of the deposit being paid. A party pack includes 24 pint beer glasses; 24 wine glasses, 2 ice buckets, 2 waiter trays, 3 bar towels, and 24 coasters.

Perfumes & Cosmetics

Other options → Souks [p.218]

Beauty in Dubai is big business, and whether the temperature goes up or down, there's always a busy trade in perfumes and cosmetics. Just about every perfume in the world is available somewhere, and new fragrances are for sale almost as soon as they are launched in their country of origin.

For a more personalised fragrance, look out for the local perfumeries that are in every shopping area and a vital part of the locals' grooming ritual. Fragrances tend to combine a heady mix of aromatic Arabian oils which are individually blended – don't go overboard on application however as one dab can last days.

Ajmal Perfumes	Al Ghurair City	222 7991
	Bur Juman Centre	351 5505
	Deira City Centre	295 3580
	Emirates Tower	330 0000
Areej	Bur Juman Centre	352 2977
	Emirates Towers	330 3340
	Jumeira Beach	348 9001
	Mercato	344 4161
	Oasis Centre	339 1224
Avon	Lamcy Plaza	334 5329
Body Shop	Deira City Centre	295 4110
	Jumeirah Centre	344 4042
Crabtree & Evelyn	Bur Juman Centre	352 5425
Debenhams	Deira City Centre	294 0011
Faces	Al Ghurair City	223 4302
Jashanmal	Wafi Mall	324 4800
Lush	Bur Juman Centre	359 7697
	Deira City Centre	295 9531
MAC	Deira City Centre	295 7704
	Wafi Mall	324 3112
Make Up Forever	Wafi Mall	324 4426
Nature Shop, The	City Tower 1	331 0303
	Deira City Centre	295 4181
Nina Gallery	Beach Centre, Jumeira	342 1166
Paris Gallery	Al Bustan Centre	261 1288
	Bur Juman Centre	351 7704
	Centre, The	269 3155
	Deira City Centre	295 5550
	Hamarain Centre	268 8122
	Lamcy Plaza	336 2000
	Town Centre	342 2555
	Wafi Mall	324 2121
Rasasi	Al Ghurair City	223 2333
	Bur Juman Centre	352 0222
Red Earth	Al Ghurair City	227 9696
	Deira City Centre	295 1887

Plants & Trees

Other options → Flowers [p.195]
Plant Street [p.140]

If you're lucky enough to have a garden, or even a bit of balcony, it is definitely worth planting a few shrubs, trees or bedding plants in pots which are all very good value for money. Having a garden full of foliage is great for keeping the sand at bay, and it's surprising how many varieties of plants can thrive in such arid conditions, although constant watering is vital. Be aware that the extra water will add substantially to your water bills, but the plus side is that if you decide to hire a gardener, it will probably be a great deal cheaper than you imagined. If you can't be bothered to traipse around a nursery, all the larger supermarkets stock a good selection of indoor and outdoor plants, but expect to pay a few dirhams more for convenience.

Garden lovers will be thrilled with Dubai Garden Centre (340 0006) - a new purpose-built centre catering to all your gardening whims and fancies. The grand opening of this two-storey modern glass building will be held during the Dubai Shopping Festival 2003, but the doors unofficially opened in November 2002. It is truly a garden lovers' paradise with unique finds from all around the world. From plants to patio furniture to garden accessories (including fountains and sculptures) and barbecue supplies, the merchandise is of excellent quality. The very first of its kind in Dubai, it's definitely worth a visit.

Dubai Garden Ctr.	Jct 3-4 Shk Zayed Rd	Map 4-B4
Dubai Municipality Nursery	Al Garhoud	Map 13-E4
Satwa	High Street	Map 6-D3/4
Sharjah Creek Rd	Nr. Animal & Bird Market	n/a

Second-hand Items

Rather than throwing out your unwanted clothes, shoes, books, kitchen equipment etc, why not take them to one of the second-hand shops in Dubai? Some of these shops operate on a charity basis, so you are doing a good turn, as well as not being wasteful.

For buying or selling second-hand items, such as furniture, cookers etc, remember to check out the Classifieds section of the newspapers, or the notice boards at the various supermarkets as well as referring to the table below. For clothes, Dubai Charity Shop and notable newcomer In Disguise are worth a visit for their abundant selection of designer items for sale – most in excellent condition and at bargain basement prices.

Al Noor Charity Shop	394 6088
Dubai Charity Shop	337 8246
Holy Trinity Thrift Centre	337 8192
House of Prose (books)	344 9021
In Disguise	342 2752

Shoes

Other options → Beach Wear [p.187]
Clothes [p.191]

Whether your penchant is for Doc Martins, flip-flops or kitten-heeled mules, shoes come in as many shapes and sizes as there are feet. A wide range of styles is available, from high fashion to comfortable casual wear, in a variety of colours, materials and in many sizes smaller and larger than average.

Training shoes tend to be more reasonably priced in Dubai than elsewhere, although addicts may find that their favourite styles are often one season behind. All major brands of shoes are available here, at decent price levels, but be warned: if you're shoe shopping in Karama and think you've just stumbled on the deal of your lifetime, remember this is the area for fakes.

Aldo Shoes	Al Ghurair City	223 8851
	Deira City Centre	295 7885
	Mercato	344 7995
Aqua Shoes	Al Ghurair City	221 3340
Bally	BurJuman Centre	352 0222
	Deira City Centre	295 0240
Canary	Al Ghurair City	222 1673
Chausseria	Deira City Centre	295 2897
Clarks	Deira City Centre	294 8266
Domino Shoes	Al Ghurair City	221 0298
	BurJuman Centre	351 2321
	Mercato	344 4161
Ecco	Al Ghurair City	223 2333
	Mercato	344 4161
Escada	BurJuman Centre	352 9253
Florsheim	BurJuman Centre	351 5353
	Deira City Centre	295 3988
Marelli	Al Ghurair City	227 0933
Milano	Al Ghurair	222 8545
	Deira City Centre	294 0011
	Deira City Centre	295 7492
	Mercato	344 9517
Nine West	Al Ghurair City	221 1484
	BurJuman Centre	351 3214
	Deira City Centre	295 6887
	Lamcy Plaza	336 5994
	Mercato	349 1336
	Oasis Centre	339 1779
	Town Centre	344 0038
Philippe Charriol	BurJuman Centre	351 1112
Rockport	Deira City Centre	295 0261
	Emirates Tower Boulevard	330 0000
Shoe City	Deira City Centre	295 0437
Shoe Mart	Abu Hail Road	262 2125
	Lamcy Plaza	337 9811
	Oasis Centre	339 5459
	Opp Ramada Spinneys	351 9560
Valencia	Al Maktoum Street	223 2772
	Deira City Centre	295 0990
	Jumeirah Centre	344 2032
	Twin Towers	221 6104

What & Where to Buy

Shopping

Sporting Goods

Other options → Underwater Explorer
Off-Road Explorer

Dubai is a great location for a variety of sports, from the popular activities such as tennis, sailing, golf or football to more unusual activities like sand skiing. Try the general sports shops listed below for items like squash racquets or sports clothing. Alternatively there's a range of specialist sports shops around the city. Unless yours is an unusual sport in the Emirates or you require a more specialised piece of equipment, you should have little difficulty in finding what you require.

360 Sports	BurJuman	352 0222
Adidas	Deira City Centre	295 4151
Al Boom Marine	Jumeira	394 1258
Alpha Sports	Deira City Centre	295 4087
Body Glove	Oasis Centre	352 0222
Carrefour	Deira City Centre	295 1600
Emirates Sports	Wafi Mall	324 2208
Future Bikes	Karama	396 6015
Golf House	BurJuman Centre	351 9012
	Deira City Centre	295 0501
	Lamcy Plaza	334 5945
Magrudy's (Kids bikes)	Deira City Centre	295 7744
	Magrudy Mall	344 4193
Sketchers	BurJuman Centre	352 0222
Sport One Trading	BurJuman Centre	352 0222
Studio R	Deira City Centre	295 0261
Sun & Sand	Al Ghurair City	222 7107
	BurJuman Centre	351 5376
	Jumeirah Centre	349 9702
ULO Diving	Sharjah	06 531 4036

See Also: *Canoeing* (ULO Sharjah); *Cycling* (Carrefour, Future Bikes, Magrudy's, Pascal's, Trek, Wheels); *Diving* (see dive centres); *Golf* (Golf House); *Ice Skating* (ice rinks sell some equipment); *Jet Skiing* (Al Boom Marine, ULO Sharjah); *Motor Sports* (various shops on Al Awir Road); *Sailing* (Dubai Offshore Sailing Club, Jebel Ali Sailing Club, ULO Sharjah); *Snorkelling* (dive centres, Carrefour); *Water-skiing* (Al Boom Marine); *Windsurfing* (Al Boom Marine, ULO Sharjah).

Tailoring & Embroidery

Other options → Arabian Souvenirs [p.184]
Textiles [p.206]
Textile Souk [p.134]

With the vast numbers of textile shops in Dubai, it's well worth buying some fabric and having items made up to your specification – whether it's curtains, cushions or an almost designer suit, most items are possible.

When trying a tailor for the first time, it's advisable to order only one item to check the quality of the work. Tailors can copy a pattern that you supply, or copy from an original item if you can leave it for a few days. Most tailors have a range of pattern books in-house that you can browse through; alternatively check out a bookstore for pattern books. Even cuttings from magazines can be used as the basis for a design.

Ali Eid Al Muree	Jumeirah Beach Rd	348 7176
Couture	Deira	269 9522
Eves	Deira	228 1070
First Lady	Al Faheidi Street	352 7019
La Donna	Hamriya, Al Wahida Rd	266 6596
Ma Belle	Nr Hamarain Centre	269 6500
Monte Carlo	Bur Dubai	352 0225
Oasis	Nr Emirates Exchange	334 4227
Regency Tailors	Bur Dubai	352 4732
Sheema	Bur Dubai	353 5142
Vanucci Fashions	Riqqa Road	269 4951

The tailor will also advise on how many metres of material are needed (buy a little extra to be on the safe side). Most tailors provide the notions such as buttons, shoulder pads, cotton and zips. Confirm the price (obviously the more complex the pattern, the pricier it gets), before committing to have it made, and make sure that it includes the cost of the lining, if appropriate.

A good tailor should tack it all together so that you can have a trying on session before the final stitching. When it is finished, try it on again. Don't be bashful about asking them to put something right if you are not completely happy.

In addition to the numerous tailors are specialist embroidery shops catering mainly for the heavily decorated Arabic version of the Western style white wedding dress. Embroidery can create a wonderful effect, especially for a special occasion; however, this intricate work will obviously greatly increase the cost of your item.

Textiles

Other options → Arabian Souvenirs [p.184]
Tailoring & Embroidery [p.206]

On both sides of the Creek you can find plenty of fabric shops selling everything from the cheapest to the finest quality textiles. In particular, Cosmos Lane and Al Faheidi Street in Bur Dubai have an excellent choice of shops. However, if you can't face busy, non-air conditioned areas of the city, most of the shopping malls have textile shops, although prices here are generally higher.

The shops in Bur Dubai's Textile Souk are a treasure

trove of textiles, colours, textures and weaves from all over the world. Shimmering threads adorn thin voile and broderie anglaise, satin and silk tempt, and velvets jostle with peach skin, although good, drill cottons are still difficult to find. Shop around as the choice is virtually unlimited and prices are negotiable. Sales occur quite frequently in this area, particularly around major holidays and the Dubai Shopping Festival.

Abdullah Hussain	Al Ghurair City	221 7310
	BurJuman Centre	351 7253
Al Masroor (gents)	Deira City Centre	295 0832
Damas (ladies)	Al Ghurair City	223 2333
St Tropez	Jumeirah Plaza	349 2216
Yasmine (ladies)	Al Diyafa Street	295 3858

PLACES TO SHOP

The following section on places to shop has been split into two. The first half covers shopping malls, with additional focus on the six largest malls in Dubai, while the second half of the section covers the main shopping streets or areas scattered around the city.

From shoes...

Shopping Malls

The attractive, and often imaginatively designed, modern shopping malls in Dubai are one of the highlights of shopping here. They are generally spacious and fully air conditioned, offering a great escape from the often-searing heat of the city. Here you will find virtually every kind of store that you can imagine, from supermarkets or card shops, to clothes emporiums and specialist perfume shops. However, the popular malls are more than just a place to buy goods; in the evenings and weekends especially, a lively, social buzz ensues as people window shop, meet friends, eat out and people watch as they sip coffee.

During the Dubai Shopping Festival and Dubai Summer Surprises, the larger malls are venues for special events such as dancing or magic shows. These performances are always popular and involve acts from all around the world. The malls also feature numerous raffles during these months – the prize for the lucky few is usually a car.

Most malls have a food court, offering a variety of types of cuisine, from the ubiquitous hamburger, to Arabic mezze, Japanese or Mexican food. Some malls also have children's play areas, arcade games, cinemas and most have convenient, extensive and free parking. The following are the largest and most popular malls in town.

Check out what Dubai's malls have to say about themselves on their Website: www.dubaishoppingmalls.com.

...to designer labels, Dubai has it all

Places to Shop

Shopping

Main Shopping Malls

Al Ghurair City

Location → Al Rigga Rd · Deira
Hours → 10:00 - 22:00 Closed Fri am
Web/email → www.alghuraircity.com

| 223 2333

Map Ref → 11-D1

This was the first purpose built shopping centre in Dubai and although it's a bit out of the way for many residents, it is considered well worth the trek. The mall has over 250 shops on two levels and sells reasonably priced goods compared to similar speciality and designer clothes stores in other malls. The mall's atmosphere is fairly unique, as it is the only shopping centre that opens directly onto the street with cafes on pavements in true European style. Recently opened in Al Ghurair City is Book Corner, the largest bookstore in Dubai, and yet another new branch of Spinneys.

Al Ghurair City

Books, Cards & Gifts

Book Corner
Lifestyle
Tanagra

Clothes

Bebe
Benetton
Bhs
Bossini
Cartoon
Esprit
French Connection (FCUK)
G2000
Giordano
Guess
Mexx
Springfield
United Colours Of Benneton

Department Stores

Bhs
Mohd. Sharief & Bros.

Electronics

Samsung Digital

Eyewear

Al Jaber Opticals
Yateem Optician

Food

Al Safeer (Lebanese)
Chinese Palace (Chinese)
McDonald's
Mrs. Vanellis (Italian)
Nawab (Indian)
Seattle's Best Coffee & Cinnabon
Starbucks Coffee

Jewellery & Gold

Al Haseena Jewellery
Damas Jewellery

Kids' Stuff

Mothercare

Leather & Luggage

Leather Palace

Lingerie

Ann Summer
Lujean Lingerie
My Time Fashion

Medicine

Sultan Pharmacy

Music & Videos

Music Box
Thomson

Perfumes & Cosmetics

Ajmal Perfumes
Faces
Paris Gallery
Rasasi
Red Earth

Services

Al Ghurair International Exchange
Baby Strollers
Free Gift Wrapping (Information Desk)
Postage Stamps (Information Desk)
Rainbow Photolab
Wheel Chairs for the Handicapped
  (Information Desk)

Shoes

Aldo
Ecco
Nine West

Sporting Goods

Sun & Sand Sports

Supermarkets

Al Maya Lals

Watches

Citizen
Rivoli
Seiko
Swatch
Watch House

BurJuman Centre

Location → Trade Centre Rd · Bur Dubai
Hours → 10:00 - 22:00 Fri 14:00 - 22:00
Web/email → www.burjumandubai.com

|352 0222

Map Ref → 11-A1

This is the place to go if designer fashion is what you want. The three-story complex, with parking level shops prides itself on a better class of shopping. The BurJuman centre is fashionable from all angles, from what they actually sell to their classy advertising campaigns. Many of Dubai's haute couture outlets can only be found here. But don't assume everything in this mall is beyond your budget; many popular US and European outlets do a roaring trade with something to suit every pocket.

The Dome Café affords some of the best traffic watching opportunities in Dubai. The food court provides excellent food in pleasant surroundings and Planet Sega and Toby's Jungle Adventure is somewhere to leave the crawler ballers for a while.

BurJuman Centre

Underground parking is plentiful, convenient and sectioned off by the names of animals to make it easier to remember in which area you've parked.

Books, Cards & Gifts

Al Jabre Al Elmiah
  Bookshop
Gulf Greetings
Tanagra
Tiffany & Co

Clothes

Bebe
Benetton
Bhs
Bossini
Calvin Klein
Christian Lacroix
DKNY
Donna Karan
Elle
Escada
Esprit
G2000
Giordano
Guess
In Wear
Levis
Liz Claiborne
Mango
Massimo Dutti
Max Mara
Mexx
Next
Polo Ralph Lauren
XOXO
Zara

Department Stores

Ace Hardware
Bhs
Grand Stores
Guess Home
JC Penny

Mohd Sharief & Bros

Electronics

Jumbo
Oman National Electronics

Eyewear

Dubai Opticals
Optic Art
Yateem Optician

Food

A & W
Al Baiq (Lebanese)
Al Zomorod (Juices)
Chinese Palace (Chinese)
Dome Cafe
Fillings (Sandwiches,
  Soups & Salads)
Fujiyama (Japanese)
Gloria Jeans
La Gaufrette
Mrs. Fields
Pizza Roma
Sala (Thai)
Shamiana (Indian)

Jewellery & Gold

Damas Jewellery
Mansoor Jewellery
Prima Gold

Kids' Stuff

Early Learning Centre
Mothercare
Osh Kosh B'Gosh

Leather & Luggage

Aigner
Aristocrat
Leather Palace
Louis Vuitton

Lingerie

Bhs
Elle
Ines de la Fressange
La Perla
La Senza Lingerie
My Time Fashion
Outfit

Medicine

BurJuman Pharmacy

Music & Videos

Al Mansoor
Diamond Palace
Virgin

Perfumes & Cosmetics

Ajmal Perfumes
Areej
Crabtree & Evelyn
Kenzo
Lush
Paris Gallery
Rasasi

Services

Al Ghurair International
  Exchange
Champion Cleaners
  (Laundry Service)
DNATA (Travel Agent)

Glamour Shots
Mashreq Bank
Rainbow Photo Lab
Seconds (Key Cutting)
Xerox Emirates

Shoes

Bally
Domino Shoes
Escada
Florsheim
Nine West
Philippe Charriol

Sporting Goods

360 Sports
Golf House
Reebok
Sketchers
Sport One Trading
Sun & Sand

Supermarkets

Lals

Watches

Cartier
Fossil
Philippe Charriol
Rivoli
Swatch
Watch House

Places to Shop

Shopping

Deira City Centre Mall

Location → Opp Dubai Creek Golf Club · Al Garhoud | 295 4545
Hours → 10:00 - 22:00 Fri 14:00 - 22:00
Web/email → www.deiracitycentre.com   Map Ref → 14-D1

Deira City Centre

Big, brash and bound to deliver is the best way to describe the Gulf's largest shopping centre. Deira City Centre has everything, which is probably why the place is jam-packed every day with people oozing out of every nook and cranny. You can find anything from a Persian carpet to a designer hair clip here.

With Ikea posted at one end, a Carrefour hypermarket in the middle, and Debenhams at the other, the mall manages to fit as many shops as would make up three ordinary malls into the structure. Miniature courts lie along corridors that lead off the central walkway – each dedicated to a specific range of products which makes it much easier to find what you are looking for. An eleven-screen cinema complex shows the latest releases and the array of restaurants that line the approach to the cinemas has enough choice to tempt even the pickiest diner.

For such a large and bustling mall, City Centre is surprisingly easy to navigate. Parking is plentiful but the 4000 spaces make it very easy to lose the car! If you are one of the few in the mall there to actively shop, the best time to visit is during the morning, when the herds are easily avoided.

Books, Cards & Gifts
Book Corner
Carlton Cards
Gulf Greetings
Magrudy's
Sara
Tanagra
Tiffany & Co

Cinema
Cinestar

Clothes
Benetton
Burberrys
Calvin Klein
Diesel
DKNY
Dolce & Gabbana
Evans
Gerry Webber
Giordano
Guess
Hang Ten
In Wear
Kookai
Lacoste
Levis
Mango
Mexx
Monsoon
Next
Part Two
Polo Ralph Lauren
Pull & Bear
River Island
Truworths
Zara

Department Stores
Debenhams
Westwood
Woolworths

Electronics
Aftron
Al Falak
Plug-Ins
Radio Shack

Eyewear
Al Jaber Optical
City Optic
Dubai Opticals
Grand Optics
Grand Sunglasses

Food
Al Safeer (Lebanese)
Cactus Cabana (Tex-Mex)
Chilis (American)
China Times (Chinese)
Cinnabon
Coco's (American)
Costa Coffee
Fujiyama (Japanese)
Hatam (Persian)
Mrs. Vanelis
Panda Chinese
Pizzeria Uno
Shamiana (Indian)
Subway

Furniture & Household
Al Jaber Gallery

Carre Blanc
Carrefour
IKEA
Laura Ashley

Hypermarket
Carrefour

Jewellery & Gold
Al Futtaim Jewellery
Bin Hendi Jewellery
Damas Jewellery

Kids' Stuff
Early Learning Centre
Mothercare
Ovo Kids

Leather & Luggage
Aigner
Aristocrat
La Valise
Porsche Design
Sacoche

Lingerie
Inner Lines
Triumph
Womans' Secret

Medicine
New Ibn Sina Pharmacy

Music & Videos
Plug-Ins
Virgin Megastore

Perfumes & Cosmetics
Ajmal Perfumes
Body Shop
Debenhams
Lush
MAC
Nature Shop, The
Paris Gallery
Red Earth

Services
Al Futtaim Travel
Al Ghurair Exchange
National Bank Of Dubai

Shoes
Aldo
Bally
Clarks
Milano
Rockport
Shoe City
Valencia

Sporting Goods
Adidas
Alpha Sports
Golf House
Studio R

Watches
Breitling
Fossil
Raymond Weil
Rivoli
Rossini
Swatch

Lamcy Plaza

Location ➔ Nr EPPCO HQ · Oud Metha |335 9999
Hours ➔ 10:00 - 22:00 Fri 10:00 - 22:30
Web/email ➔ lamcydxb@emirates.net.ae   Map Ref ➔ 10-D4

Lamcy Plaza is a huge five-story mall located a stone's throw away from Wafi Centre. The themed mall has the Tower of London as its subject, and is popular among Dubai's Asian and Eastern European residents. The shops are open plan, merging from one to the other with a multitude of fashions, shoes and home wear. The children's play area is always a hit with the kids.

Lamcy is particularly good for children's toys and clothing, as well as a wide range of sports goods. It can, however, become very cramped and confusing. Just don't be in a rush to dash in, buy what you want and dash out – it's not that simple! With sales galore during Eid and the shopping festivals, Lamcy is ideal for bargain shopping for the whole family.

Lamcy Plaza

Books, Cards & Gifts
Books Plus
Carlton Cards
Life Style

Clothes
Bhs
Bossini
G2000
Gasoline
Hang Ten
Indigo Nation
Jeffrey Rogers
Mexx
Mr. Price

Eyewear
Al Adasat Opticals

Food
Arrabiatta (Italian)
Bombay Chowpatty (Indian)
China Grill (Chinese)
Hardees
KFC
Kwality (Indian)
Mongolian BBQ
Pizza Hut
Starbucks Coffee
Taste Buds

Kids' Stuff
Loulou Al Dugong's
Mothercare

Lingerie
Bhs
La Senza

Medicine
Lamcy Pharmacy

Music & Videos
Music City

Perfumes & Cosmetics
Paris Gallery

Services
Al Ansari Exchange
ATM Machines
Digital Photo Express
Emirates Driving Institute
Empost (Postal Services)
Flower Shop
Gift Wrap & Baloon Shop
Telephone Bill Payment
  Machine
Traffic Fine payment
  Machine

Shoes
Aldo
Hush Puppies
Nine West
Shoe Mart

Sporting Goods
Golf House
City Sports

Supermarkets
Lamcy Supermarket

Watches
Rivoli
Watch House

Places to Shop

Shopping

Mercato

Location → Jumeirah Beach Road · Jumeira **344 4161**
Hours → 10:00 - 22:00 Closed Fri am
Web/email → mercato@emirates.net.ae   **Map Ref →** 5-E1

This candy-coloured confection of a mall is the latest shopping mecca for Dubai's ever-restless shopping mall junkies.   Built in the theme of an Italian renaissance city, Mercato has upped the shopping experience several gears in the Jumeira area, and with over 90 up-market outlets including a Spinneys

supermarket and several food and coffee pit stops, it is bound to be an overwhelming success.

The interior of the mall is based around a traditional Italian piazza with little off-shoot walkways crammed with shops, most of which handily have entrances at the front and the back of the store. A large multi-cinema complex is also housed within the mall, yet with its over-the-top décor and many new-to-Dubai stores, a couple of hours wandering round is Mercato is actually enough visual entertainment in itself.

Mercato

Automotive Accessories
BMW Lifestyle

Books, Cards & Gifts
Gulf Greetings
Magrudy's

Cinema
Century Cinema

Clothes
Amichi
Armani Jeans
Bershka
Cotton Fields Jeans
Diesel Jeans
Hip Hop
Kas Australia
Maestro
Mango
Massimo Dutti
Next
Oysho
Polo Jeans Co.
Promod
Pull & Bear
Top Shop
Trussardi

Electronics
Bose, Kenwood, Thompson

Food
Chinese Palace (Chinese)
Cinnabon
Dolce Antico (Italian)
Patchi (Chocolates)
Paul Rustic & Specialty Breads
Starbucks

Home Accessories
Azoo
Home Centre
Susan Walpole

Jewellery & Gold
Al Liali
Argento
Danas
Mahallati Jewellery
Pure Gold

Kids' Stuff
Adams
Armani Junior
Early Learning Centre

Leather & Luggage
Francesco Biasia

Lingerie
Nayomi
Triumph

Music & Videos
Virgin Megastore

Perfumes & Cosmetics
Areej
MAC

Services
The Nail Spa

Shoes
Aldo
Domino
Ecco
Milano
Nine West

Supermarkets
Spinneys

Wafi Mall

Location ➔ Garhoud Bridge Rd · Oud Metha | 324 4555
Hours ➔ 10:00 - 22:00 Fri 16:30 - 22:00
Web/email ➔ www.waficity.com   Map Ref ➔ 13-D2

Look for the three glass pyramids atop the large complex on the road near Al Garhoud Bridge and be prepared not to find Egypt. What you will see, however, is the distinctive roof of the Wafi Mall, Dubai's little piece of stained glass shopping glory.

Possibly the most exclusive mall in Dubai, Wafi houses a wide range of designer outlets, luxury gift shops, coffee shops, designer food stores, home furnishings and the most luxurious ladies toilets in town – at Dhs.10, a visit well worth it for the décor alone.

Encounter Zone is a popular attraction for the kids – not cheap, but offering excellent activities and the children are well looked after if you want to leave them whilst you shop. Wafi is also a haunt for young local men who 'cruise' the mall to look at all the pretty female shoppers.

Wafi Mall

Books, Cards & Gifts
Fauchar
Gulf Greetings
Mont Blanc
Petals
Sara - Villeroy & Boch
Swarovski
Tanagra

Clothes
Betty Barclay
Chanel
Gerry Webber
Giordano
Givenchy
Jaeger
Kookai

Department Stores
Jashanmal
Salam Studio & Stores

Electronics
Jumbo Electronics

Eyewear
Lutfi Opticals Centre
Rivoli

Food
Café Renoir
Goodies
Square, The
Starbucks Café

Furniture & Household
THE One

Jewellery & Gold
Al Mansour Jewellers
Damas Jewellery
G.B. Diamonds LLC.
Kunooz Jewellery

Kids Stuff
Early Learning Centre
Fun City
Osh Kosh B'gosh

Lingerie
Caresse
Charisma
Jashanmal
La Senza
Le Boudoir
Salam Studio & Stores

Medicine
Al Sham Pharmacy

Music & Videos
Al Mansoor
G & M International
Popular Music Institute

Perfumes & Cosmetics
MAC
Make Up Forever
Paris Gallery

Services
Al Ansari Exchange

Sporting Goods
Emirates Sports

Supermarkets
Goodies

Watches
Chopard
Rivoli
Rossini
Swatch
Tag Heuer

Places to Shop

Shopping

Other Shopping Malls

Beach Centre, The

Location ➜ Nr Dubai Zoo · Beach Rd, Jumeira | 344 9045
Hours ➜ 09:30 - 13:00 16:30 - 21:30   Closed Fri am
Web/email ➜ beachctr@hotmail.com   Map Ref ➜ 6-B2

This is a large, airy mall with spacious restaurants, lining the Beach Road frontage. Over 50 outlets sell goods ranging from books and furniture to jewellery, knick-knacks and carpets, plus there is a pharmacy and an optician. There is also an Internet corner called Cyber Cafe - Training Zone (surfing and playing games cost Dhs.7.50 per hour).

The Beach Centre is a good place to meet friends, do some shopping and then sit and chat. The atmosphere is sociable, especially in the central coffee shop area. Look for the blue glass building, to distinguish it from the 'pink' plaza (Jumeirah Plaza) and Jumeirah Centre further up the road.

Emirates Towers Boulevard

Location ➜ Emirates Towers · Shk Zayed Rd | 330 0000
Hours ➜ 10:00 - 22:00 Fri 16:00 - 22:00
Web/email ➜ www.emirates-towers-hotel.com   Map Ref ➜ 9-C2

Emirates Towers Boulevard certainly has the No.1 address in the city; linking two of Dubai's most imposing buildings, Emirates Towers Hotel and the Emirates Towers Offices. Exclusive, spacious and striking, the mall reflects the buildings above it. Its outlets include restaurants and cafes, as well as numerous designer fashion boutiques and expensive jewellers.

Worth a visit if you are looking for good food, but as yet, it's not a major shopping venue. Parking is bountiful, but you just might want to leave the car at home on this occasion since the Boulevard is Dubai's first mall to incorporate several licensed outlets.

Jumeirah Centre

Location ➜ Nr Jumeira Mosque · Beach Rd, Jumeira | 349 9702
Hours ➜ 09:00 - 21:00 Fri 16:00 - 21:00
Web/email ➜ gmggroup@emirates.net.ae   Map Ref ➜ 6-C2

Formerly known as Markaz Al Jumeira, this mall has exclusive ladies boutiques side by side with The Body Shop and a Baskin Robbins ice-cream parlour. It's popular with Jumeira residents and prices are not the cheapest, but not overly expensive either. Stationery Stores are well-stocked and toyshops keep youngsters occupied, while adults can check out the latest watch design, get their camera repaired or choose Persian rugs and unusual art.

Jumeirah Plaza

Location ➜ Nr Jumeira Mosque · Beach Rd, Jumeira | 349 7111
Hours ➜ 09:30 - 13:00 16:30 - 21:30 Fri 16:30 - 21:30
Web/email ➜ parklane@emirates.net.ae   Map Ref ➜ 6-C2

Easily spotted alongside the Beach Road, this pink stone and glass building is a delight to browse around. The shops are full of items for the home; textiles, novelties, specialist tools for craft and needlework, plus electronics and mobile phones. There is also a second-hand bookshop, House of Prose, and a kids' play area, Safe Play.

The cascading fountains, exotic fish and tropical vegetation under the glass-roofed atrium are a perfect foil for painting, sculpture and art exhibitions and Dubai International Arts Centre has an outlet here. You can also arrange license renewals or pay fines to Dubai Police.

Oasis Centre

Location ➜ Nr, Ace Hardware · Jct 2, Shk Zayed Rd | 339 5459
Hours ➜ 10:00 - 22:00 Fri 16:00 - 22:00
Web/email ➜ www.landmarkgroupco.com   Map Ref ➜ 5-A4

This mall has a number of bright airy, good-value superstores. It is best known for Home Centre, Lifestyle, a fantastically-priced giftware store, and Petland. It also possesses a reconstruction of a traditional falaj irrigation system. There is also a number of good quality outlets selling everything from cosmetics and linen to fashions for the family. Splash and Home Centre are open throughout the day (unlike their other branches, which close in the afternoon).

The mall is a good family venue with two excellent children's areas – Fun City for youngsters and Cyborg – a migraine-inducing, cave-like area that houses a ten-pin bowling alley and several karaoke booths among its neon attractions.

Looks good!
Feels good!
Shops great!

- FASHION • WATCHES & JEWELLERY
- SPORTS GEAR • SHADES & SHOES
- ACCESSORIES • LADIES AND MEN'S SALONS
- MUSIC • ICE CREAM • CAPPUCINO
- INTERNET CAFÉ • JAPANESE RESTAURANT
- SERVICES

PalmStrip

The Mall on the Beach, Jumeirah

Tel. Dubai 04-3461462, Visit www.dubaishoppingmalls.com
Timing: 10am to 10pm

INCA/PS/12R

Palm Strip

Location ➜ Opp Jumeira Mosque · Beach Rd, Jumeira | **346 1462**
Hours ➜ 10:00 - 22:00 Fri 13:30 - 22:00
Web/email ➜ www.dubaishoppingmalls.com   Map Ref ➜ 6-D2

Dubai's mall on the beach with an up-market 'Beverly Hills' type atmosphere is built on two levels and is unusually not enclosed by air-conditioning. The shady frontage provides easy access to a range of upmarket shops, which primarily include designer labels and other big names like Tower Records and Starbucks. It also features N-Bar, Dubai's first slick, groovily kitted-out walk-in nail bar. Palm Strip is especially lively in the cooler evenings and winter months. Parking is plentiful - if you know where to go. Around the side, is the entrance to a little-known, rarely used underground car park.

Other outlets include: Mango, My Time Ladies Salon, The Young Designers Emporium, Fashion Optics, Little Me, Rivoli in style in store, Gian Franco Ferre Studio, Escada Sport, Haagen Dazs, Oceano, F1 Net Café, Cote Deco, Beyond the Beach, Rialto, Spaghetti & Co.

Spinneys (Umm Suqeim)

Location ➜ Umm Suqeim | **394 1657**
Hours ➜ 08:00 - 24:00
Web/email ➜ spinbbis@emirates.net.ae   Map Ref ➜ 5-A3

This light and airy shopping centre not only houses a huge Spinneys supermarket, but also has a small range of shops, which expands its appeal. The Disco 2000 music shop offers video and DVD rental, while Petals is an ideal shop for presents and special items for the home. There's also Fun Corner, a kids' play area. If you're after something to eat, the Indian Pavilion restaurant and Cafe Havanna make this mall a pleasant place to linger, as well as somewhere for buying the essentials.

Town Centre

Location ➜ Beach Rd, Jumeira | **344 0111**
Hours ➜ 10:00 - 22:00 Fri 17:00 - 22:00
Web/email ➜ www.towncentrejumeirah.com   Map Ref ➜ 5-E1

This well-planned mall offers a range of stores selling everything from clothes to jewellery. It's busy in the evenings and at weekends, especially with youngsters who are enticed here by the entertainment centre — Fun Town, which houses high-tech computer games. Another draw is the special promotions that are held from time to time

and the foodcourt upstairs. There's also Moka Café, which has 14 TV screens!

Twin Towers

Location ➜ Nr Htl Inter-Continental · Deira | **221 8833**
Hours ➜ 10:00 - 13:00 17:00 - 22:00 Fri 17:00 - 22:00
Web/email ➜ www.twintowersdubai.com   Map Ref ➜ 8-C4

One of Dubai's most elegant malls overlooking the Creek, the refined surroundings of the Twin Towers offers a relaxing and congenial shopping ambience. The towers are home to exclusive designer outlets such as Hugo Boss and Emporio Armani. Jewellery, perfumes, children's clothes and watches round out the shopping selection. There is a variety of cafés and restaurants on the third floor, and the building also has residences, offices and a health club. Free basement parking is available if you leave the complex with a Dhs.20 purchase. Not a place for bargain hunters generally, but great at sale time as discounts tend to be hefty.

Other outlets include: Pierre Cardin, Valencia Class, Umberto Bilancioni, Cerruti 1881, Seddiqi & Sons, Marco Borocco, Brioni, Baumler, Verri, Mini Man, Italian Jewellery LLC, JMB Fashion, Al Sanaji General Trading, China Way - Chinese Dragon Restaurant, Apply Café & Restaurant and Danial Restaurant.

Souks

Other options ➜ Dubai Areas [p.132]
Textile Souk [p.134]
Gold Souk [p.136]
Gold & Diamond Museum[p.144]

Souks are the Arabic markets where all kinds of goods are bought, sold and exchanged. Traditionally, dhows

Spice Souk

**Welcome to
Twin Towers Shopping Centre
Welcome to
the Mall on the Creek**

An exclusive collection of
international fashion, precious
jewellery, designer watches,
accessories, art gallery, services
and friendly restaurants
with a breathtaking view.

The Mall on the Creek **TWIN TOWERS** SHOPPING CENTRE **Deira Creek, Dubai,** Tel: 04 2249222

www.twintowersdubai.com

Timing: 10am to 10pm

Park out front, or in the Basement for Free

from the Far East, China, Ceylon and India would discharge their cargoes, and the goods would be haggled over in the souks adjacent to the docks. Over the years, the items on sale have changed dramatically from spices, silks and perfumes to include electronic goods and the latest kitsch consumer trends.

Although Dubai's souks aren't as fascinating as others in the Arab world, such as Marrakech in Morocco or Mutrah in Oman, they are worth a visit for their bustling atmosphere, the eclectic variety of goods and the traditional way of doing business.

For further information on areas in Dubai such as the Deira Covered Souk, Deira Spice Souk and the Gold Souk, or in Sharjah, Souk Al Arsah and the Sharjah New Souk, refer to Local Areas and Sharjah – Out of Dubai in the Exploring section of the book.

Streets/Areas to Shop

Other options → **Satwa [p.83]**
Bur Dubai [p.82]
Al Karama [p.138]

Al Diyafah Street

Location → Al Satwa	na
Hours → 09:00 - 14:00 16:00 - 21:30 Closed Fri am	
Web/email → n/a	Map Ref → 7-A3

Al Diyafah Street is fondly known as 'uptown Satwa' to residents, as opposed to the cheaper shopping area around the corner ('downtown Satwa'). With many shops facing the street and in the Dune Centre,

Arabian Souvenirs

this is the place to buy everything from silk carpets to beverage cabinets in the shape of a globe. If you've been invited to a last minute black-tie formal and there's no time for a tailor to whip you up a tuxedo, you can hire one at Elegance or Formal Wear.

Be prepared though, this area has a high shop turnover and what was there yesterday may not be there today.

Cooler evenings are a good time to visit this busy area for a quick shop and a bite to eat. Enjoy a sundowner espresso on the pavement tables of one of the numerous cafés, or an ice cream at the Haagen-Dazs Café. There are also Lebanese, Persian and Chinese restaurants, as well as one of the best shawarma restaurants in Dubai. Weekend nights are also ideal for people watching – especially if you enjoy observing testosterone-filled young men driving up and down the strip showing off their flashy cars and revving their engines in the hopes of attracting even more attention.

Al Faheidi Street

Location → Nr Astoria Htl · Bur Dubai	na
Hours → 08:00 - 13:30 16:00 - 21:30 Closed Fri am	
Web/email → n/a	Map Ref → 8-A2

This busy street in Bur Dubai is definitely the place to visit when you're in the market for electronic goods. The multitude of electrical shops offers brand names such as Sony, Panasonic, JVC, Sharp, Phillips, Grundig, GEC, etc at negotiable prices. Don't make your purchase at the first shop you come to; take time to look around and discover the best range and price. It gets busy in the evenings, so you may have difficulty parking.

The Thomson shop has a large choice of cheap original cassettes and inexpensive CD's. Thomas Cook Al Rostamani is the place to go to change your currency or traveller's cheques at a favourable rate, and plenty of restaurants are on hand to replenish you after a hectic session of haggling. These include Talk of the Town for Chinese and Indian food, and Bananas for a decent pizza, as well as the various outlets at the nearby Astoria and Ambassador hotels.

Karama Shopping Complex

Location → Al Karama	na
Hours → 08:30 - 14:00 16:00 - 22:00 Closed Fri am	
Web/email → n/a	Map Ref → 10-D2

The long street running through the middle of Karama has veranda-covered shops on both sides enticing you to "buy, buy, buy" cheap and cheerful goods at below average prices. Plenty of mix n' match ideas direct from the Far East are offered, such as sports apparel, T-shirts, shorts, sunglasses, shoes, gifts, plus all the usual souvenirs – fluffy camels and shisha pipes. The area is also famous as the place to buy fake designer accessories. Stores along the Karama strip are all packed to the gills with copy Gucci, Prada and Chanel, but the best lines are kept away at the back or upstairs, so ask if they have any more to show you to gain entry to the inner-sanctums. Remember to bargain hard.

There are several small restaurants in the area offering Indian, Pakistani, Filipino and Arabic cuisine – good food at amazingly cheap prices. Wander around the fish market to buy locally caught hammour, prawns, crabs, etc, or bargain at the fruit and vegetable shops for bananas, mangoes and a variety of different vegetables, including gourds and mouli.

On Sale!

Shopping Malls - Contact Information

Mall Name	Tel	Webpage	Map Ref
Al Ain Centre	352 1099	n/a	8-A4
Al Bustan Centre	263 0000	www.al-bustan.com	15-C1
Al Ghurair City	223 2333	www.alghuraircity.com	11-D1
Al Hana Centre	398 2229	www.dubaishoppingmalls.com	7-A4
Al Khaleej Centre	355 8590	www.alkhaleejcentre.com	7-E3
Al Manal Centre	227 7701	www.almanalcentre.com	8-D3
Al Mulla Plaza	298 8999	n/a	12-C4
Al Rais Centre	352 7755	n/a	7-E3
Beach Centre, The	344 9045	n/a	6-B2
BurJuman Centre	352 0222	www.burjuman.com	11-A1
Center, The	269 3155	www.astecoproperty.com	12-A3
Century Plaza	349 8062	n/a	6-C2
Deira City Centre Mall	295 4545	www.deiracitycentre.com	14-D1
Emirates Towers Boulevard	330 0000	www.emirates-towers-hotel.com	9-C2
Galleria Shopping Mall	209 6000	www.dubai.hyatt.com	8-E2
Gold & Diamond Park	347 7788	www.goldanddiamondpark.com	4-B4
Hamarain Centre	262 1110	www.dubaishoppingmalls.com	12-A4
Holiday Centre Shopping Mall	331 7755	www.holidaycentredubai.com	9-D2
Jumeirah Centre	349 9702	www.dubaishoppingmalls.com	6-C2
Jumeirah Plaza	349 7111	www.dubaishoppingmalls.com	6-C2
Karama Centre	337 4499	www.bridgewaygroup.com	10-D2
Lamcy Plaza	335 9999	www.dubaishoppingmalls.com	10-D4
Magrudy Shopping Mall	344 4192	www.magrudy.com	6-C2
Mazaya Centre	343 8333	www.mazayacentre.com	5-E3
Mercato	344 4161	n/a	5-E1
Oasis Centre	339 5459	www.landmarkgroupco.com	5-A4
Palm Strip	346 1462	www.dubaishoppingmalls.com	6-D2
Spinneys (Umm Suqeim)	394 1657	www.spinneys.com	5-A3
Town Centre	344 0111	www.towncentrejumeirah.com	5-E1
Twin Towers	221 8833	www.twintowersdubai.com	8-C4
Wafi Mall	324 4555	www.waficity.com	13-D2
Warba Centre	266 6376	n/a	12-A3

Places to Shop

Shopping

Activities

EXPLORER

Activities

ACTIVITIES

Other options ➔ Exploring [p.132]
Going Out [p.302]

It might not seem readily apparent, but life in Dubai is not all shopping malls, restaurants, and 5-star hotels. No matter what season, visitors and residents alike will discover a variety of engaging activities to fulfil almost any interest or hobby. Warm winters provide the perfect environment for a variety of outdoor activities, while a host of diversions are available to take your mind off the extreme heat and humidity of the summer. From rock climbing on an indoor training wall to flower arranging or yoga classes, the fun doesn't have to stop when the tarmac starts melting! However, it's surprising what can actually be done in the heat of the summer, and even in the hottest months you can find dedicated enthusiasts sailing or playing golf when it's 48° C!

Land access is far less of a problem than in many expats' home countries, so it can be easy travelling into the wilderness of the mountains or onto remote beaches. Between Jebel Ali Hotel and Abu Dhabi, however, it is illegal to do certain activities on the beaches, such as 4 wheel driving, horse riding, fishing or water sports. This may not seem to be rigorously enforced in the quieter areas, but is still against the law if you're caught.

Sometimes word of mouth is the best way to learn about your favourite hobby, so if it's not listed here ask around and you may well find that trainspotting really does go on.

As usual, we welcome your suggestions as to what to include or change in the book next year. If you belong to any club, organisation, or group; however, small, large, official or unofficial — we'd like to hear from you. See our Reader Profile Survey on our Website (www.explorer-publishing.com) and give us your comments and details.

For information on where to buy sports equipment, refer to Sporting Goods [p.206].

SPORTS

When the weather starts to cool, Dubai and the surrounding emirates are ideal for athletes and outdoor enthusiasts, making it hard to imagine that there is a sport or activity that isn't being practised at some point in the year. Traditional favourites such as tennis, golf (on beautifully manicured courses), aerobics, rugby, cricket and hashing abound, while for the more adventurous, radical pursuits such as skydiving, rock-climbing, mountain biking, and caving are available.

With its stunning beaches, clear water and world-class water parks, it's no surprise that a variety of water sports are represented in Dubai. Scuba diving is probably the most popular, while less organised but still prevalent ways to have fun getting wet include sailing, surfing, water-skiing, and a rising interest in the eccentric sport of kiteboarding. Keep in mind that while the Gulf waters often seem tranquil, dangers such as stingrays, jellyfish, strong currents and rip tides are lurking, so always be wary. At beach parks, pay attention to the lifeguard's flag (if it's red, stay on the beach), but if you're at one of the public beaches always take a little more care.

One of the original pastimes, and still one of the most popular is getting out into the wilderness. As you spend more time in the area, and the weather starts to cool, you too will feel the lure of the open desert, the dramatic wadis, and the rustic mountains. Whether you decide to partake in camping, hiking, wadi and dune bashing, or some combination of these, we suggest getting a copy of the superb *Off-Road Explorer (UAE)*, published by Explorer Publishing. Included in the guide are stunning photographs and detailed satellite imagery of many routes and hikes. The guide is ideal for discovering the best of the UAE's scenery,

which is reminiscent, in places, of the Australian outback or African savannah. Apart from detailed satellite images, the handy guide also has GPS co-ordinates, information and photos of flora and fauna, and twenty off-road routes to explore. It really is the UAE's definitive outdoor guide!

Abseiling

Please see → **Climbing** [p.228]
Out of Dubai [p.165]

Aerobics

Other options → **Dance Classes** [p.287]
Health Clubs [p.270]

Whether it's step, pump, aqua or straight aerobics, most of the health, beach and sports clubs offer exercise classes on a regular basis. For a complete list of up to date classes, timings and instructors check with individual clubs and book in advance for the more popular sessions. Prices per class are usually Dhs.20 - 25 for club members and Dhs.25 - 30 for non-members.

Al Majaz	
Location → Trade Centre Rd · Al Karama	**335 3563**
Hours → 09:00 - 14:00 16:00 - 21:00	
Web/email → www.goldenfistkarate.com	Map Ref → 10-D1

For further information on Al Majaz, refer to the review under Yoga [p.284].

Ballet Centre, The	
Location → Behind Jumeira Plaza · Jumeira	**344 9776**
Hours → 09:00 - 12:30 15:00 - 18:30 Closed Fri	
Web/email → balletct@emirates.net.ae	Map Ref → 6-C3

The Ballet Centre is a long established dance and fitness centre which offers a wide range of classes in a relaxed and attractive environment. For aerobics fans, there are a variety of sessions at different times and plenty of choice for different levels of fitness. The well equipped studios and coffee shop are popular, and the instructors are friendly and professional.

Sports

Activities

Aikido

Please see → **Martial Arts [p.251]**

Aqua Aerobics

Jumeirah Beach Club

Location → Jumeirah Beach Club, The · Jumeira | **344 5333**
Hours → 08:00 Sat & Wed
Web/email → www.jumeirahbeachclub.com   Map Ref → 5-D1

Aqua Aerobics is a form of exercise that's great for cardiovascular fitness, as well as for toning the body. In particular, it's a good work out for people who suffer from knee to lower back injuries, as the water acts as a cushion around the joints and reduces impact. It has also been known to help slow down the advance of osteoporosis, and is an excellent exercise for pregnant women. Weights can be used to increase the intensity of the workout, which last 45 - 60 minutes.

Archery

Dubai Archery Group

Location → Dubai College · Al Sufouh | **344 2591**
Hours → Thu 15:00
Web/email → linton@emirates.net.ae   Map Ref → 3-C2

Small, friendly and informal, the Dubai Archery Group gathers on the grass playing field at Dubai College on Thursday afternoons (from approximately 3pm until dark). Coaching is available and there's limited club equipment that novices can use. There's a target charge of Dhs.10 per session for adults and Dhs.5 for under 18's.

While no great physical strength is required, archery is not really a sport for children under the age of ten.

Hatta Fort Hotel

Location → 110Km from Dubai · Hatta | **852 3211**
Hours → Timings on request
Web/email → www.dutcohotels.com   Map Ref → UAE-D3

The Hatta Fort Hotel's archery range is 25 metres long and has eight standard target stands. The recurve bow, which is curved forward at the ends and straightens out when the bow is drawn, is suitable for adults and children over the age of 10 years. Archery fans can enter the hotel's annual archery competition and the Dubai Archery Club also holds its annual archery tournament here.

Hotel residents can try archery for a nominal fee of Dhs.10, while visitors are charged Dhs.30 per 30 minute session. Professional assistance is available for this surprisingly challenging sport.

Boules

Other options → **Bowling [p.226]**

Irish Village Boules

Location → Aviation Club, The · Al Garhoud | **282 4750**
Hours → 11:00 - 01:30
Web/email → www.aviationclubonline.com   Map Ref → 14-C3

An unlikely, but very pleasant venue, where the 'village green' can be booked to play boules, or pétânque, in accordance with the rules of boules. For further details, contact the Irish Village on the above number.

Timings: 11:00 - 01:30 weekdays; 11:00 - 02:30 Wed & Thu.

Bowling

Other options → **Boules [p.226]**

Al Nasr Leisureland

Location → Behind American Hospital · Oud Metha | **337 1234**
Hours → 09:00 - 24:00 Open throughout the week
Web/email → www.alnasrleisureland.ae   Map Ref → 10-E4

One of Dubai's original leisure venues, Al Nasr Leisureland is popular with all. The modern eight lane bowling alley is synthetic and thus smarter looking and faster! Shoes, etc, can be hired as usual. Sustenance is provided by various fast food outlets and alcohol is served at the bar. Booking is recommended, since there are regular leagues during the week when the whole alley is busy. Check before you go!

Entrance fees: Dhs.10; plus Dhs.7 per game and free shoe rental.

Thunder Bowl

Location → Nr Defence R/A · Jct 1, Shk Zayed Rd | **343 1000**
Hours → 09:00 - 01:00
Web/email → tb@emirates.net.ae   Map Ref → 5-E3

Thunder Bowl is a complete entertainment experience and the first bowling alley of its kind in the Middle East. It operates 20 computerised Brunswick lanes, a pool and snooker hall, and three food outlets.

Various leagues operate, including one for juniors (ages 7 - 16) every Thursday from 10am, and a ladies league every Monday and Wednesday morning. Thursday afternoons are a not to be missed 'cosmic' bowling experience, with the centre illuminated in ultra-violet and special effect lighting (Dhs.80 per lane, per hour). The centre also has a hall for parties, with packages that include bowling time and the usual party paraphernalia.

Prices: Dhs.10 per game, weekdays; Dhs.15 weekends; shoe rental Dhs.3. There is no longer an entrance fee.

Bungee Jumping

There's nowhere in Dubai where you can bungee jump year-round. However, during the Dubai Shopping Festival, it is one of the attractions on the Bur Dubai side of the Creek, near Creekside Park, and is offered by an organisation from Australia. For more information, keep a look out when DSF approaches and check the daily press for details.

Camping

Other options → Outdoor Goods [p.203]
Tours & Sightseeing [p.153]
Weekend Breaks [p.176]

With the weather rarely anything other than sunny, and some spectacular locations in various parts of the country, the UAE is a great place for camping. For most people, the best time to go is between October and April, as in the summer it can get unbearably hot sleeping outside. Choose between the peace and stillness of the desert or camp amongst the wadis and mountains, next to trickling streams in picturesque oases. Good campsites can be found only short distances away from tarmac roads, so a 4 WD is not necessarily required.

In general, very little rain and warm temperatures mean you can camp with much less equipment and preparation than in other countries. This can be the perfect introduction for first timers or families with children of any age, although a certain amount of care is needed to avoid the occasional insect.

Note Although the UAE has a low rainfall, care should also be taken in and near wadis during the winter months for flash floods, (remember it may be raining in the mountains miles from where you are and when it rains, boy, does it rain!).

For most people, a basic amount of equipment will suffice. This may include:

- Tent (to avoid the creepy crawlies / rare rain shower)
- Lightweight sleeping bag (or light blankets and sheets)
- Thin mattress (or air bed)
- Torches and spare batteries (a head torch is a useful investment)
- Cool box (to avoid food spoiling / away from insects)
- Water (always take too much)
- Food and drink
- Camping stove, firewood or BBQ and charcoal (if preferred)
- Matches!
- Insect repellent and antihistamine cream
- First aid kit (including any personal medication)
- Sun protection (hats, sunglasses, sunscreen)
- Jumper / warm clothing for cooler evenings
- Spade
- Toilet rolls
- Rubbish bags (ensure you leave nothing behind!)
- Navigation equipment (maps, compass, Global Positioning System (GPS))

For the adventurous with a 4 WD, there are endless possibilities for camping in remote locations amongst some of the best scenery in the UAE. The many locations in the Hajar Mountains (in the north near Ras Al Khaimah or east and south near Hatta or Al Ain), and the huge sand dunes of Liwa in the south provide very different areas, each requiring some serious off-road driving to reach, but offering the real wilderness camping experience.

For more information on places to visit, refer to the *Off-Road Explorer (UAE)*.

Canoeing

For those interested in getting up close to the marine and bird life of the UAE, or for a slightly different sport that provides access to hidden places, canoeing is an enjoyable and revealing activity.

Areas for good canoeing include Khor Kalba Nature Reserve, the coastal lagoons of Umm Al Quwain, between the new and old towns of Ras Al Khaimah, north of Ras Al Khaimah before Ramsis and through the mangrove covered islands off the north coast of Abu Dhabi. Many of these areas are on their way to becoming protected reserves, so treat them with respect. Some adventurous kayakers occasionally visit the Mussandam in sea touring canoes. Here it is possible to visit secluded bays and view the spectacular rocky coastline, with its fjord like inlets and towering 1,000 metre cliffs.

For further information, refer to the *Off-Road Explorer (UAE)* and the Hatta to Kalba route.

See also: Khor Kalba [p.172].

Sports

Activities

Canoeing with Desert Rangers

Desert Rangers

Location ➜ Dubai Garden Centre Bldg, Shk Zayed Rd | 340 2408
Hours ➜ 09:00 - 18:00   Closed Fri (office)
Web/email ➜ www.desertrangers.com   Map Ref ➜ 6-E3

Desert Rangers offers trips through the mangroves of the UAE's unique nature reserve at Khor Kalba in 2 - 3 seat Canadian canoes. Initial instruction is followed by hands-on practice to develop skills and confidence, then paddle through the mangrove lagoon and experience the unique scenery and abundant wildlife found nowhere else in the UAE. Enjoy the tranquillity and beauty; all you can hear is the lap of the water and the clicking of crabs' claws.

A guide accompanies you and the cost per person is Dhs.300. Only a basic level of fitness is needed and it is suitable for all ages.

Caving

Other options ➜ Out of Dubai [p.165]

The caving network in the Hajar Mountains is extensive and much of it has still to be explored and mapped. As in any region, caving here varies from the fairly safe to the extremely dangerous. Even with an experienced leader, it is not for the casual tourist or the poorly equipped.

Some of the best caves are near Al Ain, the Jebel Hafeet area and in the Hajar Mountains just past Buraimi, near the Omani border. The underground passages and caves have spectacular displays of curtains, stalagmites and stalactites, as well as pretty gypsum flowers and wool sparkling — all

unimaginably fragile, so don't touch! Unfortunately there are no companies offering guided tours; caving is limited to unofficial groups of dedicated cavers who plumb the depths on a regular basis.

The Hajar Mountain range continues into the Sultanate of Oman, where it is higher and even more impressive. In Oman, the range includes what is believed to be the second largest cave system in the world, as well as the *Majlis Al Jinn Cave* — the second largest known chamber in the world.

It is important to understand the dangers of going underground and the precautions that must be taken. Take at least two torches each and enough spare batteries and bulbs — someone will always drop a torch or one may fail. Other equipment includes: a couple of litres of water (at least), a hard hat and long sleeved overalls to protect you from sharp rocks or knee and elbow pads, a basic first aid kit and twine to mark less obvious parts of the route (remember to take it, and any other rubbish, with you when you leave). In addition, never wander off alone and don't break any of the rock formations to take away as souvenirs. Check the weather forecasts or the local meteorological office to find out about recent rainfalls. Flash floods occur regularly at certain times of the year.

Warning: No mountain rescue services exist, therefore anyone venturing out into mountains should be reasonably experienced, or be with some one who knows the area. Tell someone who is not going with you where you are going and when you will be back. Tragedies have occurred in the past.

Climbing

Other options ➜ Health Clubs [p.270]
Out of Dubai [p.165]
Mountaineering [p.254]
Hiking [p.246]

Excellent rock climbing can be found in a number of locations, despite the shattered appearance of most of the mountains in the UAE. Particular areas to explore include Ras Al Khaimah, Dibba, Hatta and the Al Ain/Buraimi region. By choosing venues carefully, it is possible to climb all year-round — even in summer when daytime air temperatures approach 50°C.

The earliest recorded rock climbs were made in the south east near Al Ain/Buraimi in the late 1970s and, apart from some climbing in the Ras Al Khaimah area, little seems to have been recorded until the mid-1990s. Since then, a small group of climbers have been pioneering new routes and discovering a number of major new climbing areas. To date, more than 200 routes have been climbed

Sports

Activities

and named. These vary from short outcrop routes to difficult and sustained mountain routes of alpine proportions. New routes are generally climbed 'on sight', with traditional protection.

Most routes are in the higher grades — ranging from (British) Very Severe, up to extreme grades (E5). Due to the nature of the rock, some climbs can feel more difficult than their technical grade would suggest. However, there are some excellent easier routes for new climbers, especially in Wadi Bih and Wadi Khab Al Shamis. Many routes, even in the easier grades, are serious propositions with loose rock, poor belays and difficult descents, often by abseil, making them unsuitable for total novices.

Several areas are being developed for sport climbing with a growing number of routes being bolted where protection would otherwise be a problem. Some of the hardest routes in the country (up to French Grade 7c) have been pioneered in Wadi Bih and Wadi Khab Al Shamis by serious climbers from Dubai and Abu Dhabi.

If you want to meet up with like-minded people, there always seems to be someone doing something in Wadi Bih each weekend!

For further information on rock climbing in the UAE, refer to the *Off-Road Explorer (UAE)* published by Explorer Publishing.

For further information on climbs around Buraimi and in the Hajar Mountains in Oman refer to the guidebook Rock Climbing in Oman by RA McDonald (Apex Publishing 1993, London/Oman). Despite being several years old, it still gives a comprehensive overview of the most frequented climbing sites within easy reach of Muscat and in the more remote areas, and provides plenty of practical information. Few new routes have been opened or documented in these areas since the book was published.

Pharaohs Club

Location → Pyramids · Umm Hurair | **324 0000**
Hours → 07:00 - 22:00 Fri 09:00 - 21:00
Web/email → www.uae-climbing.com. Map Ref → 13-D2

This is the only indoor climbing wall in Dubai. Built by one of the leading climbing wall companies from the UK, it comprises a varied set of walls for climbing routes and bouldering, with crash mats for safety during low level climbs and ropes in place on all routes. The difficulty varies, providing a good introduction for complete beginners while also being challenging enough for serious climbers.

Classes run by experienced instructors are available for all ages and levels of ability. During the winter, there are climbing trips to Ras Al Khaimah (some training is needed before going into the mountains). Bi-monthly competitions are also held. The wall is open to everyone, but book in advance as numbers are limited.

Price: Dhs.40 per hour.

Rock Climbing

Location → Various locations | **050 647 7120**
Hours → Timings on request
Web/email → arabex@emirates.net.ae Map Ref → n/a

No formal climbing or mountaineering club exists in the Emirates, but an effective grapevine means that new or visiting climbers can generally be pointed in the right direction.

Some nights of the week have developed into unofficial meetings at Dubai's indoor climbing wall at the Pharaohs Club. While new climbers are welcomed, this group does not run courses for beginners with no equipment or experience. Since there are no mountain rescue services available, it is expected that anyone venturing into the mountains is basically competent, even if they do not climb to a high standard.

If you are interested in learning to climb, refer to the review for the Pharaohs Club.

Contact: for more information contact John Gregory on the above number.

Crab Hunting

Lama Desert Tours

Location → Al Khaleej Road · Deira | **273 2240**
Hours → On Request
Web/email → lamatour@emirates.net.ae Map Ref → 12-A2

This is a more unusual tour for the Emirates. Leaving at 4pm by coach, you head to Umm Al Quwain where you are offered a light dinner before heading out by boat to hunt crabs. This is followed by a BBQ buffet dinner, where your catch of the day is served boiled or grilled, then at 11pm you head back to Dubai. A minimum of six people is required for the tour to go ahead and the charge per person is Dhs.220. For further information, call the above number, 273 1007 or 050 453 3168.

Cricket

Other options ➜ Sporting Goods [p.206]
Annual Events [p.48]

With the large numbers of enthusiastic fans from all over the world, especially India, Pakistan and Sri Lanka, cricket seems to lead even football as the most popular sport in Dubai!

Car parks, rough land and grassy parks all sprout stumps at weekends and evenings, as a mix of ages comes out to play. Many organisations field their own cricket teams for inter-company competitions and it is also very popular in schools. Coaching is widely available.

Major international matches are held regularly in the Emirates, especially at the ground in Sharjah, where it's possible to see some of the world's best teams and to get the chance to cheer your own side on.

Darjeeling Cricket Club

Location ➜ Nr Dubai Country Club · Al Awir Rd | **333 1746**
Hours ➜ See timings below
Web/email ➜ coxoil@emirates.net.ae   Map Ref ➜ 17-B3

Formed in 1969 by a group of expats, the name comes from the Darjeeling Sports Shop in Bahrain which provided the first playing kit. Matches of 25 overs start at 09:00 and 13:30 every Friday, while net practice takes place under floodlights on Tuesday evenings. In early March, there's a six-a-side Gulf tournament and the rest of the year sees matches against visiting test sides when they are competing in Sharjah.

Hockey is played at the same ground and the clubhouse, complete with bar, is open Tuesday to Sunday. The club is available for private functions.

Costs: Membership Dhs.650 per playing member; Dhs.250 per social member. A non-member match fee of Dhs.20 is levied.

InSportz

Location ➜ Nr Gold & Diamond Park, Shk Zayed Rd | **347 5833**
Hours ➜ 09:00 - 22:00
Web/email ➜ insportz@emirates.net.ae   Map Ref ➜ 4-C4

Coaching is in full swing at the InSportz Club. Children have the opportunity to acquire professional help in honing their skills and sharpening their techniques. Over the years there have been several coaches who have lent their support to organising camps for children. This year Noel David, former Indian International Cricketer has joined the group of qualified coaches and will be aiding children in all areas of the game. The resident coach will provide children with the finer details of the game and also assist them with some fitness tips. The focus is on enjoyment and development of the children's skills in the game.

Croquet

A classic croquet lawn is available for a game in the grounds of the Jebel Ali Hotel. For more information, call Club Joumana (283 6000).

Cycling

Other options ➜ Mountain Biking [p.254]
Sporting Goods [p.206]
Out of Dubai [p.165]

Dubai, and the Emirates in general, are not the most bike-friendly of places, but there are plenty of areas to ride, and exploring where you can go and what there is to see is a great way to get to know the city.

Riding in traffic requires a lot of care and attention, as in any country, but more so in the Middle East. Drivers vastly underestimate the speed cyclists are capable of and don't allow enough room, or time for them — be especially careful at junctions and roundabouts. However, there are quieter areas with fewer cars, and some roads have wide footpaths providing traffic free routes for biking around town.

Although bikes are not allowed in most of Dubai's parks, a great way to see them is to hire 2 or 4 wheel bikes in the parks and to do the grand tour — try this at Safa or Creekside Parks. Pleasant places to ride, especially in the evening, include the pedestrian areas on both sides of the Creek. Although helmets are not legally required serious consideration should be given to wearing one.

Outside the city, the roads are fairly flat and boring until you near the mountains. Jebel Hafeet near Al Ain, the Hatta area of the Hajar Mountains and the central area in the mountains near Masafi down to the coast at either Fujairah or Dibba, offer interesting paved roads with better views. The new road from Hatta through the mountains to Kalba on the East Coast, is probably one of the most scenic routes in the country.

Clubs and groups of cyclists generally ride on weekends, early mornings and evenings when the roads are slightly quieter.

Sports

Activities

Dubai Roadsters

Location ➜ Various locations | 344 1980
Hours ➜ Timings on request
Web/email ➜ thesepo@emirates.net.ae   Map Ref ➜ n/a

Dubai Roadsters was born out of a passion for cycling shared by a number of individuals in the Dubai area. The group meets for weekday and Friday morning rides – the only criteria for joining are a safe bike, cycling helmet, pump and spare tubes.

On Fridays the group always ends somewhere for a well-deserved coffee and bagels. The average distance covered on a Friday ride is 65 - 100 km, depending on the weather and heat, while weekly rides are about 30 km. The average speed is a comfortable 30 km/h. There are no membership fees to join and Mario Cippolini wannabees are most welcome! For further details, contact Jeff Yeaton.

Desert Driving Courses

Other options ➜ Fun Drive - Annual Events [p.52]

For those who want to master the art of driving a 4 wheel drive over rolling sand dunes without getting stuck (and getting yourself out when you do!), several organisations offer desert driving courses with instruction from professional drivers. Both individual and group tuition per vehicle is available. Vehicles are provided on some courses, while others require participants to take their own. Alternatively, you may be able to hire a vehicle for an additional cost. Courses vary widely, but expect to pay around Dhs.250 - 300 for the day. Picnic lunches and soft drinks may be included.

Al Futtaim Training Centre

Location ➜ Opp. Municipality Garage · Rashidiya | 285 0455
Hours ➜ 08:00 - 17:00   Closed half day Thu & closed Fri
Web/email ➜ training@alfuttaim.co.ae   Map Ref ➜ n/a

Explore the wild side of the Emirates in your 4 wheel drive in safety and confidence. The desert campus training course gives off-road driving enthusiasts knowledge and experience of venturing into the desert. It starts with a three hour classroom session covering the basics of your vehicle, with tips on protecting it from breaking down, overheating, changing tyres in the sand, negotiating sand dunes and other driving techniques. This is followed by five hours of supervised off-road driving where you take your own 4WD up and down the dunes.

Cost: Dhs.300 per person, which includes an off-road driving manual and snacks.

Desert Rangers

Location ➜ Dubai Garden Centre Bldg, Shk Zayed Rd | 340 2408
Hours ➜ 09:00 - 18:00   Closed Fri (office)
Web/email ➜ www.desertrangers.com   Map Ref ➜ 6-E3

Desert Rangers offers lessons for anyone wanting to learn how to handle a car in the desert. If you are just starting, introductory days teach you the basics of venturing off-road, including how to negotiate easy dunes, how to avoid getting stuck and how to get out of it if you do! While advanced days involve guided drives to more challenging areas of the desert where you can learn how to get yourself out of bigger trouble!

Courses are available for individuals or groups and since programmes are flexible, they can be combined with barbecues and other activities to make your ideal day.

Stuck in the sand - again!

Emirates Driving Institute

Location ➜ Behind Al Bustan Centre · Al Qusais | 263 1100
Hours ➜ 08:00 - 13:00   15:00 - 17:30
Web/email ➜ www.edi-uae.com   Map Ref ➜ 15-D2

The Emirates Driving Institute offers a one day desert driving course for Dhs.200 on working days, Dhs.225 on Thursdays, and Dhs.250 on Fridays, including lunch. Equipment can be supplied, if required. Participants receive a certificate on completion of the course.

Sports

Activities

Jeep UAE Off-Road Driving Academy

Location ➜ Various locations
Hours ➜ Timings on request
Web/email ➜ n/a

| 268 5758

Map Ref ➜ n/a

Jeep owners wanting a fun way to explore the do anything, go anywhere nature of their vehicle can take a specialised full-day driving course. Aimed at novice desert drivers, it can also serve as valuable refresher course for those who have driven off-road previously.

You'll learn the full range of your Jeep's capabilities in a controlled desert environment. The course consists of four modules: know your vehicle, 4x4 systems and selection, deflation; ascent, descent and approach angles, speed and gear selection, stopping in sand; vehicle recovery and towing, use of low ratio gears, digging out your vehicle; orientation, convoy driving, rules for sand driving. Courses are not available during the summer months.

> *Price: Dhs.280 for you and a friend, but strictly for Jeeps and their owners only. New Jeep customers are offered this course for free.*

Off-Road Adventures

Location ➜ Metropolitan Hotel · Jct 2, Shk Zayed Rd
Hours ➜ 08:00 - 20:00
Web/email ➜ www.arabiantours.com

| 343 2288

Map Ref ➜ 5-C4

The great outdoors is an environment that suits Karim Rushdy, the owner of Off-Road Adventures. With 16 years off-road experience in the UAE, he is well equipped to handle the portfolio of thrills generated by his safari tours and focuses on three factors; safety, exclusivity and personnel expertise. The company caters to individuals and small groups, and the range of activities can be stretched even wider, as Karim believes that it is possible to tailor-make a tour to suit any requirement (within reason!).

In addition to off-road driving courses, the company arranges weekly fun drives, treasure hunts, camping and trekking tours, camel safaris and sand boarding.

Voyagers Xtreme

Location ➜ Dune Centre · Al Satwa
Hours ➜ 09:00 - 18:00
Web/email ➜ www.turnertraveldubai.com

| 345 4504

Map Ref ➜ 6-E3

Under the expert guidance of Jochen Neugebauer, Voyagers Xtreme offers lessons for anyone wishing to handle a 4 WD in the desert. The one day introductory course covers all the basic skills required for off-roading; the dos and don'ts, negotiating dunes, how to avoid getting stuck and what to do when you are (recovery techniques). You're given a walkie-talkie to enable you to learn as you drive (don't worry, you won't be the only one saying 'I'm stuck'!). If, like many clients, you're bitten by the off-roading bug, more advanced courses can be arranged.

Courses are available for individuals or groups. Take your own vehicle or hire from Voyagers Xtreme.

Diving

Other options ➜ Snorkelling [p.261]

The coastal waters around the UAE are rich in a variety of marine and coral life as well as shipwrecks, which make diving here a fascinating sport. It's possible to dive all year in the warm seas. As well as exotic fish, such as clownfish and seahorses, it is possible to see spotted eagle rays, moray eels, small sharks, barracuda, sea snakes, stingrays and much more.

The UAE is fortunate to have two coastlines; to the west, covering Abu Dhabi, Dubai, Sharjah etc, and on the East Coast, covering Fujairah, Khorfakkan, Dibba etc. Most of the wrecks are on the western coast, while the beautiful flora and fauna of coral reefs can be seen to the east.

There are many dive sites that are easily accessible from Dubai and provide some great diving. Visibility ranges from 5 - 20 metres. Some of the most popular sites include:

MV Sarraf Three About seven nautical miles offshore lies this 42 metre long barge, a car barge complete with various vehicles and a tugboat rest close by. All these vessels lie upright in 22 metres of water and provide a good opportunity for a limited penetration dive. The wrecks abound with a multitude of fish including barracuda, guitar sharks and spotted eagle rays.

Cement Barge This 25 metre long vessel sits upright in ten metres of water, about 12 minutes off Dubai's coast. It is a relatively easy dive and ideal for newly qualified divers or those seeking the first time thrill of diving. This is an opportunity to see a mixture of reef creatures such as clownfish and parrotfish, together with stingrays.

MV Dara This is perhaps the most historic of the West Coast wrecks. Sunk as the result of an Omani rebel mine, the *MV Dara* constituted the greatest loss of life at sea during peacetime (with 238 lives lost), since

Sports

Activities

the *Titanic*. The vessel lies on her side in 20 metres of water. This dive is classified as an advanced dive due to tidal influences. Having sunk in 1961 the marine life is well established and provides an excellent dive if the conditions are favourable.

Port Rashid Wrecks The breakwater at Dubai Dry Dock is the final resting place for a number of wrecks, including the *LC Beauty Judy*, an 8½ metre landing craft, the MV *Nasser* and the *MV Ant*, a tug boat. These vessels lie in 12-15 metres of water and provide an opportunity for some interesting exploration.

Sheikh Mohammed Barge This is a former working barge that was deliberately sunk approximately 12 nautical miles offshore by order of Sheikh Mohammed bin Rashid Al Maktoum to establish an artificial reef. Close to the barge is another boat and a lifting crane. For advanced divers this site provides an excellent wreck dive among an abundance of large marine life.

Off the East Coast, dive sites include **Martini Rock**, which is a small underwater mountain covered with colourful soft coral, with a depth range of 3 - 19 metres. North of Khorfakkan lies the **Car Cemetery**, a reef that has thrived on a number of vehicles placed in 16 metres of water. Visibility off the East Coast ranges from 5 - 20 metres.

In addition, dive trips are available to the area north of the UAE, known as the **Mussandam**, which is part of the Sultanate of Oman. Often described as the 'Norway of the Middle East', due to the numerous inlets and the way the sheer cliffs plunge directly into the sea, it offers some of the most spectacular and virgin dive sites in the region. Here sheer wall dives with strong currents and clear waters make it a thrilling experience for advanced divers, while the huge bays, calm waters and shallow reefs offer easier dives for the less experienced. Visibility ranges from 10 - 35 metres. Note that if you travel to Khasab, the capital of the Mussandam, you are sometimes not allowed to take your own tanks across the border, but must rent from one of the dive centres there. Omani visas are required.

Alternatively, from Dibba on the East Coast of the UAE, fast dive boats take divers up the coast for a distance of between 5 - 75 km. The cost, for what is normally a two-dive trip, ranges between Dhs.150 - 500. During the winter, whale sharks are sometimes sighted and dolphins normally ride the bow waves of boats.

Experienced divers, intermediates and people wishing to learn how to dive are all well catered for by a plethora of companies in the UAE. These offer all levels of courses, starting from an introductory dive to instructor level and technical diving, under the different international training organisations, such as CMAS, PADI, NAUI, IANTD, HAS, etc.

For further details on diving in the UAE and the Mussandam, refer to the *Underwater Explorer (UAE)*. For more general information on Abu Dhabi and the Sultanate of Oman refer to the *Abu Dhabi Explorer* and the *Oman Explorer* (formerly Muscat Explorer). All these books are published by Explorer Publishing.

See also: The Mussandam — Sultanate of Oman [p.174].

7 Seas Divers	
Location ➜ Nr Khorfakkan Souk · Khorfakkan	**09 238 7400**
Hours ➜ 08:00 - 20:00	
Web/email ➜ www.7seasdivers.com	Map Ref ➜ UAE-E2

This PADI (Professional Association of Diving Instructor) 5-star IDC dive centre offers daily day and night diving trips to a variety of sites in Khorfakkan, the Mussandam in Oman and to Lima Rock. Training is given from beginner to instructor level and lessons can be given in Arabic, English, French, German or Russian. Facilities include four boats and the centre also arranges equipment sale, rental and servicing from their base close to Mashreq Bank and the Khorfakkan Souk.

The company can also arrange accommodation, transport and visas for visitors to the UAE. They have an office at the Oceanic Hotel, as well as in Khorfakkan.

Al Boom Diving	
Location ➜ Opp. Iranian Hospital · Al Wasl Rd	**342 2993**
Hours ➜ 09:00 - 21:00 Fri 14:00 - 21:00	
Web/email ➜ www.alboommarine.com	Map Ref ➜ 6-C3

Al Boom's Aqua Centre is a one-stop dive shop, offering the full range of PADI diving courses around a schedule that suits you. Whether you just want to give diving a go, or are looking for a specific course, this PADI 5-star centre with experienced diving professionals will fulfil your needs.

For those already qualified, they have daily dive trips, equipment maintenance and servicing, as well as air fills and rental of the latest equipment. They offer a complete range of Aqua-Lung, US Divers and Sea Quest diving equipment as well as a wide selection of accessories and clothing.

Sample costs: 'open water course' Dhs.1,200; 'advanced open water' Dhs.700. Trips to the East Coast start at Dhs.200 for a two-tank dive with all equipment included.

Sports

Activities

Emirates Diving Association

Location ➜ Bur Dubai	**393 9390**
Hours ➜ Sat & Wed 08:30-13:00, 17:00-21:00	
Web/email ➜ www.emiratesdiving.com	Map Ref ➜ 8-B1

The main aim of this group is to conserve, protect and restore the UAE's marine resources by understanding and promoting the marine environment and environmental diving. They do this in a variety of ways including promoting research on the marine environment and by holding the annual 'clean-up dive' and 'beach clean-up' campaigns. In the future, Emirates Diving Association hopes to establish a marine park using the artificial reefs technique, which tries to create coral reefs, as well having monitoring stations for research purposes. Contact them for more information on diving in the UAE.

Pavilion Dive Centre

Location ➜ Jumeirah Beach Htl · Umm Suqeim	**406 8827**
Hours ➜ 09:00 - 18:00	
Web/email ➜ www.jumeirahinternational.com	Map Ref ➜ 4-B2

Located in the luxurious hotel grounds, this centre is run by qualified PADI instructors and has received the highest rating for a dive centre. An extensive range of courses is available, from beginner to instructor, plus speciality courses for advanced divers. Courses can be tailor-made to suit your schedule.

Daily dive trips for certified divers leave the hotel marina at 10am, weather permitting. This is generally a two-dive trip, and returns to the marina between 13:00 - 15:00. All diving is on wrecks, which vary in depth from 10 - 30 metres. The centre also organises trips to the Mussandam region of Oman. MARES equipment is available from the retail centre, together with Bodyglove wetsuits and a range of accessories.

Costs: discover scuba Dhs.320; open water Dhs.1,750; adventures in diving Dhs.1,000; two dives full equipment Dhs.250; two dives tank only Dhs.190. For NITROX add Dhs.40 for one tank or Dhs.50 for two.

Sandy Beach Diving Centre

Location ➜ Sandy Beach Motel · East Coast	**09 244 5050**
Hours ➜ 08:00 - 18:00	
Web/email ➜ sbdiving@emirates.net.ae	Map Ref ➜ n/a

This dive centre is now managed by the Sandy Beach Hotel and offers a qualified and dynamic team of dive instructors and support staff. It's open all year-round for diving, accommodation and a retail outlet that stocks the latest diving gear (products from Scubapro, Ikelite and Uwatec, to name a few).

Their famous house reef, Snoopy Island, is alive with hard corals and marine life and is excellent for both snorkelling and scuba diving. The more adventurous can take a trip on one of their dive boats that depart daily to sites around Fujairah and Khorfakkan. Trips to the Mussandam (Oman) offer fascinating dives for the more experienced.

Boat timings: 09:30, 12:00, 02:30.

Location: Al Aqqah, Fujairah – halfway between Dibba and Khorfakkan.

Scuba 2000

Location ➜ Al Badiyah Beach · Fujairah	**09 238 8477**
Hours ➜ Timings on request	
Web/email ➜ www.scuba2000uae.com	Map Ref ➜ UAE-E2

This East Coast dive centre is open all year and provides daily trips to dive sites on both the Dibba and Khorfakkan sides. All sites are easily accessible by boat from the centre; in particular Snoopy and Sharque islands provide excellent diving and snorkelling, with an abundance of colourful fish, coral, turtles and barracuda.

The standard courses are available for everyone from beginners to advanced divers. The centre has one fully qualified PADI instructor and an experienced diver is on hand if a buddy is needed. The resort has a large, secluded beach nestling among palm groves, and also hires out jet skis, canoes and pedal boats.

Costs: range from Dhs.250 for discover scuba; Dhs.1,500 for open water; Dhs.800 for advanced.

Scuba Arabia

Location ➜ World Trade Centre Apts, Shk Zayed Rd	**331 4014**
Hours ➜ 09:00 - 19:00 Closed Fri	
Web/email ➜ scuba@emirates.net.ae	Map Ref ➜ 9-D2

This dive centre teaches PADI courses for all levels, while 'discover scuba' courses are available for those just looking for a taste of the underwater world. Diving is arranged on a daily basis, either from Dubai or Ajman, and there are weekend dhow trips to the Mussandam. For bookings contact Croydon (050 551 8254).

The centre also runs one of the best-stocked scuba diving shops in Dubai (331 7433) and a full-time repair

Add some depth to your lifestyle at
The Pavilion Dive Centre.

- Daily dive trips departing at 10 am. Trips to Musandam also available.
- Dive Dubai's favourite wreck sites.
- Full range of PADI dive courses available.
- Highly qualified PADI instructors.
- Enjoy the pleasant surroundings of The Jumeirah Beach Hotel.
- Retail centre - Mares dive equipment, Bodyglove wetsuits and a range of diving accessories.

Enriched Air Nitrox now available.

For more information and bookings call The Pavilion Dive Centre on 406-8827/28
Open 9 am - 6 pm daily

The Jumeirah Beach Hotel is a trading name of Jumeirah Beach Resort LLC.
Company with Limited Liability. Registration Number 45069. Share Capital Dhs. 300,000 fully paid up.

www.jumeirahinternational.com

workshop. The main brands sold are Scubapro, Uwatec and Ikelite. Qualified divers can rent diving equipment, buy re-breathing equipment or have their air refilled. All equipment is well maintained and rental rates are extremely competitive.

Scuba International

Location ➜ Fujairah | 09 222 0060
Hours ➜ 10:00 - 19:00   Closed Fri
Web/email ➜ www.scubaInternational.net   Map Ref ➜ UAE - E2

The first diving college in Arabia, Scuba International offers facilities for both divers and non-divers, from recreational dive charters and diver training (PADI, DSAT and TDI), to RYA sanctioned boat-handling courses, chamber operating courses, instructor courses or water sports and dive vacation bookings. Two wrecks provide the ideal opportunity for first time and experienced divers. The 'discover scuba' dive costs Dhs.250.

The college is purpose-built to cater to divers' needs, and offers nearby accommodation in Fujairah's hotels, plus an on-site pool, beach, restaurant and bar to open shortly. It operates a recompression chamber with on-call chamber staff who are able to treat any diving emergency 24 hours a day.

Scubatec

Location ➜ Sana Bld · Trade Centre Rd, Al Karama | 334 8988
Hours ➜ 09:00 - 01:30   4:00 - 08:30   Closed Fri
Web/email ➜ www.scubatec.net   Map Ref ➜ 10-C1

Scubatec is a 5-star IDC centre licensed by the Professional Association of Diving Instructor (PADI) and Technical Diving Instructor (TDI). Experienced instructors make the transition from above to below the water a safe and enjoyable one, and instruction can be in Arabic, English, German or Urdu.

The company offers a full range of courses from beginner to instructor and will schedule a course to fit your lifestyle, while enabling you to learn at your own pace. Dubai and East Coast dive trips are available. The cost, including hire of full gear, is Dhs.200 for two wreck dives at a site 10 km offshore from Dubai.

Sharjah Dive Club

Location ➜ Shj Wanderers Sports Club · Sharjah | 050 636 6802
Hours ➜ See timings below
Web/email ➜ www.sharjahwanderers.com   Map Ref ➜ UAE-C2

Sharjah Dive Club is a main member-section of the Sharjah Wanderers Sports Club (SWSC). So, in addition to an energetic and friendly diving club, members get the benefit of the sports and social activities of SWSC.

The diving club is a full member of the British Sub Aqua Club (BSAC branch number 406), and follows its training, certification and diving practices. The clubhouse facilities include a training room, social area, equipment room, compressors, dive gear for hire, two dive boats and on-site pool facilities. Club night is every Tuesday from 20:30 until late, with diving every Thursday and Friday, weather permitting.

Dune Buggy Riding

Exhilarating and fun, dune buggies are not particularly environmentally sound, but are surprisingly addictive.

In particular, every Friday the area around the 'Big Red' sand dune on the Dubai - Hatta Road is transformed into a circus arena for off-road lovers. Future Motor Sports, along with about four other companies, rent out off-road quad bikes and karts, which are available to drive (without a licence) in fenced off areas. Alternatively, if you're in the area on a Friday, hang around to be entertained by the sight of locals driving their Nissan Patrols on two wheels!

Buggy addicts could also contact the tour operators [p.155], since many of them offer the chance to try dune buggies as part of their desert safaris.

Remember, if you fall when you go up and over a dune, these things are heavy!

Al Badayer Motorcycles Rental

Location ➜ Hatta Rd | 050 636 1787
Hours ➜ 09:00 - 18:00
Web/email ➜ n/a   Map Ref ➜ UAE-D3

Also called quad bikes, dune buggies are great fun and extremely exhilarating. Al Badayer Motorcycles Rental has buggies that range in power from 50 or 80cc to 250cc – watch out for the 250 if it's your first time! Prices vary from Dhs.80 -

Sports

Activities

200 per hour. For further details, contact Ahmed Sallam on the above number.

Desert Rangers

Location → Dubai Garden Centre Bldg, Shk Zayed Rd | 340 2408
Hours → 09:00 - 18:00   Closed Fri (office)
Web/email → www.desertrangers.com   Map Ref → 6-E3

Having been given a helmet and a brief talk on safety, you are led to the course to familiarise yourself with the dune buggy. Designed and built in the UK, they are safe and lots of fun. There are single and two seater buggies, allowing ten people to be on the course at one time. It is possible to run relays of participants at intervals of 10 - 15 minutes. All activities are closely monitored by experienced Rangers.

Cost: Dhs.350 per person.

Fishing

Other options → Boat & Yacht Charters [p.162]

The fishing season runs from September/October through to April, although it is still possible to catch sailfish and queenfish in the hot summer months. Fish commonly caught in the waters off Dubai include king mackerel, barracuda, tuna, trevally, bonito, kingfish, cobia and dorado or jacks.

Beach or surf fishing is popular all along the coast of the UAE — even barracuda can be caught from the shore in season. As well as the beaches, Jumeira Beach Corniche is a good place — try the end of the promenade. The creek front in Creekside Park is also a popular spot, though maybe you won't want to put the fish on the barbie! Alternatively, on Fridays hire an abra for the morning (either at the Bur Dubai or Deira landing steps) and ask to be taken out to the mouth of the creek to fish; be sure to agree on a price before you leave.

The more adventurous, with cash to spare, may consider deep-sea fishing.

Bounty Charters

Location → Various locations | 348 3042
Hours → Timings on request
Web/email → -   Map Ref → n/a

Bounty Charters is a fully equipped 36 ft Yamaha Sea Spirit game fishing boat captained by Richard

Forrester, an experienced game fisherman from South Africa.

Fishing charters can be tailor-made to your needs, whether you want a full day trying for the challenging sailfish, or a half-day trawling or bottom fishing for the wide variety of fish found in the Gulf. There is also night fishing or charters of 3 - 5 days to the Mussandam Peninsula (book in advance, since planning takes 7 - 10 days). For prices and more details contact Richard on the above number or on 050 658 8951.

Club Joumana

Location → Jebel Ali Htl · Jebel Ali | 804 8058
Hours → 06:30 - 22:00
Web/email → www.jebelalihotel.com   Map Ref → 1-A1

Departing from one of Dubai's most beautiful marinas, four or eight hour deep-sea fishing trips are available for up to seven people. The opportunity exists to catch sailfish, barracuda, lemonfish, trevally, hammour (groupers) and kingfish, and the captain, all fishing tackle and equipment, soft drinks and snacks are included in the price.

Creek Cruises

Location → Creekside, Deira | 393 9860
Hours → 09:00 - 18:00   Closed Fri
Web/email → www.creekcruises.com   Map Ref → 11-C2

Discovery is a 42 ft yacht that is available for luxury cruising and sports fishing. For fishing trips, it is equipped with professional fishing equipment, fish finder and bottom riggers. The yacht also has an air conditioned cabin, large sundeck, rest room, music system, safety kit and can accommodate a maximum of ten guests. Charter cruises are also available; all prices on request.

Dubai Creek Golf & Yacht Club

Location → Opp Deira City Centre · Al Garhoud | 295 6000
Hours → 06:30 - 22:00
Web/email → www.dubaigolf.com   Map Ref → 14-C2

Take a trip on the club's own boat and experience the adrenalin rush of big game sports fishing. The boat comfortably carries up to six passengers and the rates include everything, from boat, tackle,

Sports

Activities

bait and fuel to a friendly crew that knows how to find great fish. What a day! When your appetite demands attention there's a galley stocked full of your choice of beverages, plus a meal to suit, from breakfast to a gourmet dinner.

Charter costs: Dhs.1,500 for four hours; Dhs.2,200 for eight hours; Dhs.200 per additional hour.

Fun Sports

Location ➜ Various locations, see below
Hours ➜ 09:00 - 17:00 | **399 5976**
Web/email ➜ funsport@emirates.net.ae
Map Ref ➜ n/a

Fun Sports is one of the leading water sports companies in Dubai, offering fishing, sailing, windsurfing, water skiing, wakeboarding, jet skiing, knee boarding, banana rides, kayaking, power boat rides, parasailing and sunset cruising!

Their facilities are available at some of Dubai's main beach hotels, however, you don't have to be a member of the beach clubs to use Fun Sports' equipment. Tuition is available for all levels of ability, with courses in sailing, windsurfing, water skiing and kids surfing. Fun Sports are led by a team of professional instructors and safety is always a priority. For bookings contact Suzette on the above number, fax (399 5796) or 050 453 4828.

Locations: They operate at the following beach clubs: Dubai Marine Beach Resort & Spa, Hilton Dubai Jumeirah, Metropolitan Resort & Beach Club, Oasis Beach Hotel, Ritz-Carlton Beach Club, Royal Mirage, Le Meridien Mina Seyahi and Jumeira Beach Park.

Le Meridien Mina Seyahi Beach Resort & Marina

Location ➜ Le Meridien Mina · Al Sufouh
Hours ➜ 24 hrs | **399 3333**
Web/email ➜ www.lemeridien-minaseyahi.com
Map Ref ➜ 3-A2

Enjoy a full or half-day fishing trip in one of the best fishing grounds of the Arabian Gulf. The experienced skipper will guide you to what could be your most exciting catch ever! Sailfish are the main prize, and Le Meridien Mina Seyahi supports the tag and release scheme.

Trips are made on the custom-built *Ocean Explorer* and *Ocean Luhr*. While you are welcome to take your own gear, the boats are fully equipped with 20, 30 and 50 lb class tackle, as well as fly fishing equipment. Charters can be tailored to suit your requirements.

Prices: Dhs.1,500 for four hours; Dhs.1,700 for six hours; Dhs.2,200 for eight hours; Dhs.2,400 for ten hours.

Oceanic Hotel

Location ➜ Beach Rd, Khorfakkan · East Coast
Hours ➜ 14:30 - 18:00 | **09 238 5111**
Web/email ➜ www.oceanichotel.com
Map Ref ➜ UAE-E2

Round off a trip to the East Coast with a sunset fishing trip. Set off in a speedboat to the local fisherman's favourite fishing spot (apparently a catch is virtually guaranteed!). Then watch the sunset as you return to the hotel. The catch can be cooked by the hotel chef, who will prepare it according to your taste. All equipment is supplied.

Cost: Dhs.100 per person, for 3 - 4 people per boat, for about two hours.

Royal Tours

Location ➜ Nr Sheraton Htl · Creekside, Deira
Hours ➜ Timings on request | **223 1567**
Web/email ➜ www.royaltours-dubai.com
Map Ref ➜ 11-C1

As well as their dhow operations, Royal Tours offer a yacht for rent, mainly for fishing trips. The two bedroom, air conditioned yacht is available for charter for 4 - 7 people, and includes all fishing equipment. Contact the above number for more information and prices.

Soul of Stars

Location ➜ Le Meridien Mina · Al Sufouh
Hours ➜ On request | **050 694 2960**
Web/email ➜ dimcdxb@emirates.net.ae
Map Ref ➜ 3-A2

Soul of Stars, a traditional 65 ft clipper, can be hired for deep-sea fishing trips for groups of 1 - 25 people. The charge per person is Dhs.250 for four hours or Dhs.300 for six hours, minimum six people, and trips include soft drinks and light snacks.

Every Thursday at 6pm the boat departs for a two night fishing/sailing trip to the Mussandam, returning on Saturday morning at 7am (price Dhs.1,700 per person, full board, including Omani permit). The boat can also be hired for private parties for up to 35 people, and during the week there are two hour morning and sunset cruises (Dhs.175 per person, including unlimited soft drinks and light snacks). Skipper and crew are provided.

منتجع جبل علي للجولف واسبا
JEBEL ALI GOLF RESORT & SPA
A member of *The Leading Hotels of the World*

WISH YOU WERE HERE?

A picture speaks a thousand words. There are however 1001 ways to enjoy your stay at Jebel Ali Golf Resort & Spa. From the standard nine-hole championship golf course to the very popular and convenient Peaco children's club, it's no wonder Jebel Ali Golf Resort & Spa is regarded as the premier resort of the region. With excellent restaurants, pristine beaches and superbly landscaped gardens, it's a world of pretty and inviting pictures.

فنادق جبل علي انترناشيونال
JEBEL ALI INTERNATIONAL
HOTELS
تقاليـد الضيافـة والامتيـاز
A TRADITION OF HOSPITALITY AND EXCELLENCE

Tel. +9714 883 6000. Fax +9714 883 5543
Email: JAGRS@jaihotels.com
Website: www.jebelali-international.com

Yacht Solutions

Location → Jumeirah Beach Htl · Umm Suqeim | 348 6838
Hours → Timings on request
Web/email → www.yacht-solutions.com   Map Ref → 4-B2

Fenikia Marine offers the opportunity to experience the thrill of fishing on board one of their sports fishing vessels. With modern tackle and some luck you may even catch one of the prized Gulf sailfish (a tag and release scheme is in operation), while other catches include kingfish, tuna, and barracuda. Experienced skippers guide you to the best fishing grounds and for the less experienced there is plenty of advice to make your fishing experience a memorable one. Shorter charters are available, but prices start from Dhs.65 per person per hour.

Flying

Other options → Helicopter Tours [p.161]
Hot Air Ballooning Tours [p.161]
Plane Tours [p.162]

Dubai Flying Association

Location → Al Garhoud | 351 9691
Hours → Timings on request
Web/email → www.dfa-dxb.com   Map Ref → 14-D3

In 1987 a group of private pilots formed Dubai Flying Association (DFA) by selling Dhs.10,000 debentures to 18 individuals. They raised enough money to buy their first aircraft and within a year had bought a second.

Today, DFA is a registered flying association of qualified pilots and is well known in aviation circles throughout the region. The club is non-profit making, aiming to provide flying to members at cost. 'Fly-ins' at Ras Al Khaimah and Fujairah international airports are annual features, while the DFA Ball is an established event on the Dubai social calendar. Call Evelyn Brey for details.

Membership: Dhs.500 per annum. All holders of UAE private pilot's licences are welcome, and the association can assist in licence conversion from any ICAO recognised licence.

Emirates Flying School

Location → Terminal 2, Dubai Int Airport · Al Twar | 299 5155
Hours → 08:30 - 17:30
Web/email → www.emiratesflyingschool.com   Map Ref → 15-B2

Emirates Flying School, the only approved flight training institution in Dubai, operates six US built Piper aircraft and has been training pilots of all nationalities since 1989. The school offers the basic private pilot's licence and the commercial pilot's licence for those who want to make flying a career, while the instrument rating course allows pilots to fly in restricted visibility. The school offers conversion of international licences to a UAE licence. Gift vouchers costing Dhs.500 are available for those interested in experiencing flying for the first time.

Fujairah Aviation Centre

Location → Fujairah Int Airport · Fujairah | 09 222 4747
Hours → Timings on request
Web/email → www.fujairahaviationcentre.com Map Ref → UAE-E2

This company grew from a hobby into a business: the Fujairah National Group's chairman is a keen aviator and set up the centre. With its high calibre instructors, the centre quickly received accreditation as a flying school from the Civil Aviation Authorities in the UAE and UK.

Facilities include twin and single engine training aircraft, an instrument flight simulator and workshop for repairs. Training is offered for the private pilot's licence, commercial pilot's licence, instrument rating and multi-engine rating. All ages are welcome, but students must be aged 17+ to fly solo and 18 when a licence is issued. Trial lessons and gift vouchers are available. English is the language of civil aviation, so pupils must be conversant in written and oral English.

Costs: trial flying lessons Dhs.240 per half hour, Dhs.480 per hour. Ground training Dhs.50 per hour, flight training Dhs.400 per hour.

Flight training for the new Cessna 172S is Dhs.480 per hour; the Cessna 172P Dhs.400 per hour; and twin engine Dhs.1,200 per hour.

Umm Al Quwain Aeroclub

Location → 17km North of UAQ on RAK Rd · UAQ | 06 768 1447
Hours → 09:00 - 17:30
Web/email → www.uaqaeroclub.com   Map Ref → UAE-C1

This was the first sports aviation club in the Middle East, providing opportunities for aviation enthusiasts to fly and train throughout the year at excellent rates. Activities include flying, skydiving, skydive boogies, paramotors and helicopter training. The modern facilities include a variety of small aircraft, two runways, eight spacious hangars with engineering services, pilot's shop and a briefing room.

Sports

Activities

The club also offers sightseeing tours by Cessna aircraft (Dhs.300 per 30 minutes for three people, plus pilot; or 10 minute tours for Dhs.50 per person). For longer flights, a plane with a professional pilot can be hired for Dhs.600 per hour. A trip by air is the perfect way to view the beautiful lagoons and beaches of UAQ.

Location: 16 km along the road from UAQ roundabout heading in the direction of Ras Al Khaimah, before Dreamland Aqua Park and opposite UAQ Shooting Club, on the left handside of the road ... just look for the big aeroplane by the sea.

Timings: 08:30 - 17:30 winter; 09:00 - 19:00 summer.

Football

Other options → Sporting Goods [p.206]

Like most places on the planet, you don't have to travel far to have a game of football in the Emirates! On evenings and at weekends, parks, beaches and any open areas seem to attract a game, generally with a mix of nationalities taking part. Even villages in the countryside usually have a group knocking a ball around on the local sand and rock pitch — see if you can join in, or join a more formal club. Pitches are available outdoors and indoors in Dubai, while coaching, mainly for kids, is offered at a number of sports centres and health clubs.

Dubai Celts GAA Club

Location → Dubai Exiles · Al Awir Rd | 458 8173
Hours → See timings below
Web/email → www.dubaicelts.com   Map Ref → 17-B3

Dubai Celts GAA Club (Gaelic Athletic Association) holds games and organises training in the sports of men's and ladies' Gaelic football, hurling and camogie. In addition to monthly matches within the UAE, international tournaments are held in Bahrain (November) and Dubai (March) each year. The season runs from September to June and everyone is welcome to join in, regardless of whether they've played the sports before. Social members are also welcome and there is at least one social gathering every month.

Training sessions are held every Saturday and Tuesday at 20:00 at the Dubai Exiles Rugby Club.

Emirates Golf Club

Location → Jct 5, Shk Zayed Rd | 347 3222
Hours → 06:00 - 23:00
Web/email → www.dubaigolf.com   Map Ref → 3-A3

Emirates Golf Club is home to the Reebok Soccer Academy, which was established in September 2000. With 140 juniors enrolled, the academy is aiming for bigger and better things this year with the opening of two polyurethane pitches. These will complement the existing grass pitches that are arguably the best five-a-side pitches in Dubai. The academy operates regular squad coaching, as well as camps during school holidays and half terms.

Golf

Other options → Annual Events [p.48]

The UAE is quite rightly known as the golf destination in the Gulf, with excellent year-round facilities and many important tournaments being held here. Dubai has a range of international courses that are fully grassed, as well as brown (sand) courses, and courses that are a mixture of grass and sand. In an area of the world where rain is so scarce, the green golf courses appear as oases of colour in the middle of the desert!

On the international scene, Dubai Creek Golf & Yacht Club and Emirates Golf Club are the home of the *Dubai Desert Classic*, which is part of the European PGA (Professional Golf Association) Tour. There are also monthly local tournaments and annual competitions which are open to all, such as the *Emirates Mixed Amateur Open*, the *Emirates Ladies' Amateur Open* (handicap of 21 or less) and the *Emirates Men's Amateur Open* (handicap of 5 or less).

Dubai Golf

Dubai Golf operates a central reservation system for individuals or groups who wish to book a round of golf in Dubai. They currently represent Emirates Golf Club, Dubai Creek Golf & Yacht Club and Dubai Golf & Racing Club.

For further information check out their Website at www.dubaigolf.com, contact them on email at booking@dubaigolf.com, or call 347 5201 (fax 347 5377).

Sports

Activities

Club Joumana

Location ➜ Jebel Ali Htl · Jebel Ali
Hours ➜ 06:30 - 22:00
Web/email ➜ www.jebelalihotel.com

| 804 8058

Map Ref ➜ 1-A1

The scenically stunning 9-hole par 36 resort course is a fair and exciting challenge for any level of player. Beautifully landscaped with exotic trees and views of the Arabian Gulf, it is also home to the Challenge Match, curtain raiser to the *Dubai Desert Classic*. Past participants include Tiger Woods, Mark O'Meara, Nick Faldo, Ernie Els, Seve Ballesteros and many more. For tee time reservations and further information, contact Club Joumana reception.

Dubai Country Club

Location ➜ Nr Bu Kidra R/A · Al Awir Rd
Hours ➜ 08:00 - 24:00
Web/email ➜ www.dubaicountryclub.com

| 333 1155

Map Ref ➜ 17-B3

This was the first ever golf club in Dubai, having opened a 9-hole sand course way back in 1971. Since then it has opened its 18-hole Al Awir course, also on sand. If you're wondering how this is possible (aren't you technically always in a bunker?), this is how it works – you carry your own piece of fairway to place under the ball for driving up to the 'browns'. Browns are the sand course equivalent of greens and are regularly brushed to give them a true roll. The club also has a floodlit driving range and a resident golf pro, Kevin Hind.

Costs: Country Club members can play for free; non-members pay Dhs.65 per day.

Dubai Creek Golf & Yacht Club

Location ➜ Opp Deira City Centre · Al Garhoud
Hours ➜ 06:30 - 22:00
Web/email ➜ www.dubaigolf.com

| 295 6000

Map Ref ➜ 14-C2

Venue of the *Dubai Desert Classic* on the PGA European Tour in 1999 and 2000, this golf course is open to all on a 'pay as you play' basis. The beautifully landscaped 18-hole par 72 course is deceptively challenging, snaking between six man-made lakes, rolling green fairways and clusters of palm trees. The clubhouse was nominated 'best clubhouse' in *Golf World's* Best of the Best awards.

There's also a 9-hole par 3 course, three practice holes, driving range, putting green (all floodlit for evening practice) and six PGA qualified golf pros. The par 3 course is ideal for those without a handicap (the cost to play is Dhs.40 per person).

Emirates Golf Club

Location ➜ Jct 5, Shk Zayed Rd
Hours ➜ 06:00 - 23:00
Web/email ➜ www.dubaigolf.com

| 347 3222

Map Ref ➜ 3-A3

The unique clubhouse and buildings are immediately recognisable by their Bedouin tent design, which disguises modern, air conditioned interiors. This club was the first grass course in the Middle East and is a former and future host of the European PGA *Dubai Desert Classic*. Standards throughout are high, with two 18-hole championship courses to choose from; the Majlis and the Wadi.

The club also offers the perfect learning environment at the Emirates Academy of Golf, two driving ranges (one floodlit) and dedicated practice areas. Other facilities include restaurants and a large swimming pool and patio (often the site of concerts and shows).

Fees: Majlis course Dhs.475; Wadi course Dhs.330 - 365. Cart hire Dhs.50; club hire Dhs.80.

Facilities are open to members and non-members alike, although all players must produce a valid handicap certificate (<28 men / <45 women).

Montgomerie, The

Location ➜ Emirates Hills Residential Estate
Hours ➜ 07:00 - 21:00
Web/email ➜ www.themontgomerie.com

| 399 9955

Map Ref ➜ 2-E4

The first thing you notice here is the scale of the course; set in 200 acres it features the sort of dramatic landscapes that are the hallmark of the great Scottish courses. Designed by Colin Montgomerie in association with Desmond Muirhead, the 18-hole par 72 course has some unique characteristics, including the world's largest green in the shape of the UAE. Practice facilities include a golf academy, driving range, short game and putting practice areas, a skill-honing 9-hole par 3 course, plus a swing studio with state-of-the-art swing analysis software. The Academy Restaurant offers dining alternatives from 6:30am through to late evening.

Nad Al Sheba Club

Location ➜ Nr Bu Kidra R/A · Nad Al Sheba
Hours ➜ 07:30 - 24:00
Web/email ➜ www.nadalshebaclub.com

| 336 3666

Map Ref ➜ 17-A3

This Scottish links style golf course with its undulating fairways and pot bunkers is the only floodlit 18-hole golf course in the UAE, with golf being possible until midnight all year. The back nine are situated inside the track of the famous Nad Al Sheba racecourse, home of the *Dubai World Cup*, the world's richest race meeting.

The club has a fully stocked pro shop, a 50 bay floodlit driving range and individual, group and junior coaching by a team of four PGA professionals. The most popular course is the 'learn golf in a week'. A variety of memberships are available from annual or monthly or for those just visiting.

Resort Golf Course, The

Location ➜ Jebel Ali Htl · Jebel Ali	883 6000
Hours ➜ 07:00 till nightfall	
Web/email ➜ www.jebelali-international.com	Map Ref ➜ 1-A1

Situated in beautifully landscaped grounds, this 9-hole par 36 course offers golfers the opportunity to play in the company of peacocks and with panoramic views of the Arabian Gulf. The course has four tee boxes at each hole, giving the opportunity to play either a 9-hole or an 18-hole round. Five of the holes are designed around a saltwater lake and the course is spikeless. Other facilities include a well-stocked pro-shop, floodlit driving range, instruction from PGA professionals, putting green and short game facilities.

The course is home to the *Challenge Match*, curtain raiser to the *Dubai Desert Classic*. Past participants include Tiger Woods, Nick Faldo, Ernie Els, and many more.

Visitors are welcome on a 'pay as you play' basis. Although no handicap certificates are necessary, visitors must have a sound knowledge of golfing etiquette, rules and course experience.

UAE Golf Association

Location ➜ Creek Golf Club · Al Garhoud	295 6440
Hours ➜ 09:00 - 17:00 Closed Fri	
Web/email ➜ www.ugagolf.com	Map Ref ➜ 14-C2

This non-profit organisation is the governing body for amateur golf in the UAE. It is overseen by the General Authority of Youth and Education and is affiliated to the Royal and Ancient Golf Club of St Andrews in the United Kingdom. Its aims are to make golf more affordable and accessible in the UAE, with a programme to support junior players and the development of the national team. Members receive certain benefits and can attain a handicap according to

CONGU (Council of National Union of Golf) or LGU (Ladies Golf Union) rules (Dhs.400).

Affiliate membership: starts at Dhs.200 per year. UGA membership runs from 1 January to 31 December.

Hang Gliding

Please see ➜ Flying [p.242]

Hashing

Other options ➜ Pubs! [p.404]

The Hash House Harriers are a worldwide family of social running clubs, the aim being not to win (which is actually frowned on), but to be there and take part. It was started in Kuala Lumpur in 1938 and is now the largest running organisation in the world, with members in over 180 countries, in approximately 1,600 chapters.

Hashing consists of following a course laid out by a couple of 'hares'. Running, jogging or walking is acceptable and courses are varied and often cross-country. Hashing is a fun way to keep fit and to meet new people, since clubs are invariably very sociable and the running is not competitive.

While it was in Malaysia that the sport first took off, its roots can be traced to the British cross-country sport of 'hare and hounds', and also probably to similar events in other areas of the world. In the 1930s, British servicemen in Malaysia were stationed in the Royal Selonger Club which was known as the 'hash house' due to the quality of its food. After a particularly festive weekend, a hare and hound paper chase was suggested, and so the hash began. After World War II the hash continued, but it wasn't until 1962 that a second chapter was permanently formed in Singapore and from there the sport has spread worldwide.

Barbie Hash House

Location ➜ Various locations	na
Hours ➜ Timings on request	
Web/email ➜ www.deserthash.net	Map Ref ➜ n/a

Meeting on the first Tuesday of every month, this is a girls' only gathering with a Barbie theme – the dress code is pink with a tiara, it helps to be blond and they drink champagne. About 15 to 20 members meet all year-round for a fun social evening that also involves a bit of hashing/walking, a meal and singing their Barbie song. It's open to women of all ages for a monthly

Sports

Activities

fee of Dhs.10. Contact can be made through the Website address.

Creek Hash House Harriers

Location → Various locations | 050 451 5847
Hours → Various
Web/email → www.creekhash.net   Map Ref → n/a

This is a men-only hash that meets at different locations each Tuesday throughout the year. Start times are normally 30 minutes before sunset, with runs lasting 40 - 50 minutes. The concept of hashing is not to race but to follow pre-marked trails and false trails, with the keen runners covering more ground than the social members, who jog and walk their way round at the rear of the pack.

Further information can be obtained from Ian Browning on the above number or Richard Holmes (050 644 4258).

Desert Hash House Harriers

Location → Various locations | 203 2720
Hours → Various
Web/email → www.deserthash.net   Map Ref → n/a

The Desert Hash House Harriers (DH3) is a social running group for men and women. It meets every Sunday evening throughout the year at various locations in Dubai. Runs start an hour before sunset and last about 50 minutes.

For more information, contact the GM, Tony 'Cotn' Redshaw (050 457 1941), Stuart Wakeham (050 454 2635) or On Sec Elise Pobjoy (050 459 1974). For details of where they meet see the *Gulf News* Classifieds on Sunday under the Dubai personal column, or visit their Website.

Cost: per run Dhs.50 per person, inclusive of food and beverages.

Moonshine Hash House Harriers

Location → Various locations | 050 774 1580
Hours → Once a month
Web/email → rayros@emirates.net.ae   Map Ref → n/a

Moonshine Hash House Harriers run once a month on the night of the full moon. A mixed hash that meets at the taverns throughout Dubai, they run, jog, amble or walk around a trail set with checkpoints, 'falsies' and 'on-backs'. This invariably lasts around one hour and creates a thirst, which is then quenched upon return to the aforementioned alehouses for the traditional hash ceremonies.

Go along, find out what hashing is all about and meet 'Wingnut', 'Earlybird', 'Corkscrew' and 'Rhode Island'. Contact, as above, or Maria Cottam (050 774 1580).

Cost: Dhs.10 per hash.

Hiking

Other options → Outdoor Goods [p.203]
Climbing [p.228]
Mountaineering [p.254]
Out of Dubai [p.165]

Although the area around Dubai is mainly flat and uninspiring, an hour's drive will take you to very

Wadi Bih

Sports

Activities

different surroundings, ideal for hiking and far removed from the sprawling, hectic city.

One of the nearest, and easiest, places to reach from the city is the foothills of the Hajar Mountains on the Hatta road, about 100 km from Dubai and near the border with Oman. After passing through the desert and the flat savannah-like plains, stark and rugged outcrops transform the landscape on either side of the road. Explore turnings you like the look of, or the road to the right signposted 'Mahdah 64 km', along which are numerous paths, wadis and scaleable hills.

Hiking

Further into the Hajar Mountains (Hajar is Arabic for rock), the multi-coloured mountains and large wadis provide peace and tranquillity, as well as the famous Hatta Pools. Here there are plenty of excellent walks, with a surprising amount of greenery and refreshing, cool pools.

Other great areas for hiking and exploring in the Hajar Mountains include anywhere near Al Ain, many places in Wadi Bih (the mountainous route from Ras Al Khaimah to Dibba), or the mountains near the East Coast. The mountains here do not disappoint and the further off the beaten track you get, the more likely you are to find interesting villages where the people live much as they have for centuries.

As with any trip into the UAE 'outback', take sensible precautions. Tell someone where you're going and when you should be back, take a map and compass or GPS, and stout walking boots (for the loose rock). Don't underestimate the strength of the sun and take food for energy, sunscreen and, most importantly, loads of water. For most people, the cooler and less humid winter months are the best season for hiking.

Refer also to the *Off-Road Explorer (UAE)* published by Explorer Publishing. Apart from striking satellite images of routes to explore, there are details of interesting hikes with tracks superimposed on photographs. This is a handy manual and includes information on health and safety, flora and fauna, GPS co-ordinates, etc. One of the most important warnings is to be especially careful in wadis (dry riverbeds) during the wet season, as dangerous flash floods can flood a wadi in seconds.

Contacts: *Useful contacts willing to advise like-minded people are: Alistair MacKenzie (alistair@explorer-publishing.com) - Dubai, John Gregory (050 647 7120) - Ras Al Khaimah.*

Desert Rangers

Location → Dubai Garden Centre Bldg, Shk Zayed Rd | **340 2408**
Hours → 09:00 - 18:00 Closed Fri (office)
Web/email → www.desertrangers.com   Map Ref → 6-E3

Guided by experienced Rangers, walk among the majestic mountains of the UAE, ascend rocky summits and enjoy the freedom of rough mountain country with its dramatic sun-baked features.

Desert Rangers can easily handle up to 100 people at once by dividing them into smaller groups and taking different tracks to the summit. A variety of routes can be taken to suit the group's age and level of fitness. Locations include Fujairah, Dibba, Masafi, Ras Al Khaimah and Al Ain.

Cost: *Dhs.275 per person.*

Hiking Frontiers

Location → Various locations | **na**
Hours → See timings below
Web/email → alistair@explorer-publishing.com   Map Ref → n/a

A sister club to *Biking Frontiers* with pretty much the same outdoor-loving members, this group is involved in hiking around the UAE and Oman. A diverse bunch of active hikers and bikers, both male and female. Typical hiking season is from October through to March. Either meet on Friday mornings, or head out camping on Thursday evening and hike Friday. Main requirements are that you are enthusiastic, have proper walking boots, carry enough water and are reasonably fit. You are responsible for your own safety and ensuring that you don't exceed your own capabilities. If you are interested in meeting a fun bunch of like-minded people, or in knowing a bit more, email Alistair on the above address.

Sports

Activities

Hockey

Other options → Ice Hockey [p.250]

Darjeeling Hockey Club

Location → Darjeeling Cricket Club · Al Awir Rd | **333 1746**
Hours → 20:00 - 22:00   Closed Mon
Web/email → darjeelinghockey@hotmail.com   Map Ref → 17-B3

The hockey club shares the facilities of the Darjeeling Cricket Club, which was formed over 30 years ago by a group of British expats. Members range from ex-professional players to complete beginners (coaching is available); all are welcome. The team plays on a mixed sex basis and is a mix of young and old.

Matches are played under floodlights against visiting navy teams and other expat clubs. The club also enters and arranges tournaments (past highlights include tours to Singapore and Hong Kong), and trips to Perth and other GCC countries are planned for the coming year. The English style clubhouse bar is open throughout the week, except Mondays.

Cost: Annual membership of the hockey section is Dhs.650 per playing member; Dhs.250 per social member.

Sharjah Wanderers Hockey Club

Location → Shj Wanderers Sports Club · Sharjah | **06 566 2105**
Hours → Wed 20:00
Web/email → www.sharjahwanderers.com   Map Ref → UAE-C2

This club began life as a small part of the Sharjah Contracts Club in 1976 and from its inception has been very successful. The hockey section became the first mixed side in the Gulf and, while fielding men's and ladies sides, has always retained a strong mixed club atmosphere. With an age range of 16 - 45, it's also a family club.

The main principle here is to play sport within a friendly atmosphere, without losing the competitive challenge, and over the years the club has participated in various international tournaments, playing against teams from the UAE, Bahrain, Cyprus, Hong Kong, Saudi Arabia and the UK. Changing facilities are available at the clubhouse and all are welcome.

Contact: Cormac (tel/fax 06 566 0864).

Horse Riding

Other options → Annual Events [p.48]
Horse Racing [p.50]

Club Joumana

Location → Jebel Ali Htl · Jebel Ali | **804 8058**
Hours → 06:30 - 22:00
Web/email → www.jebelalihotel.com   Map Ref → 1-A1

Approximately 30 minutes drive from central Dubai, Club Joumana is set in the beautiful grounds of the Jebel Ali Hotel. The riding centre has five horses, an outdoor arena and keeps livery on request. Individual half hour lessons and one hour desert rides are available. Keith Brown, the riding instructor, is available for lessons from Tuesday to Sunday, from 1 October to 1 June each year.

Riding is not available during the summer months (June to September). For further information on rates contact Club Joumana reception.

Emirates Riding Centre

Location → Nr Palm Beach Resort · UAQ | **06 766 6644**
Hours → 07:00 - 19:00   Closed Mon
Web/email → n/a   Map Ref → 17-A1

Formerly known as the Dubai Equestrian Centre (DEC), which was formed in 1983 under the patronage of HH Sheikh Maktoum bin Rashid Al Maktoum. The centre has 147 horses and facilities include an international sized floodlit arena, riding school arenas, dressage arenas and lunging ring.

The weekly ridership of adults and children numbers about 600, and includes the national team members. DEC holds at least two competitions and three school shows per month, as well as weekly gymkhanas from October to early May. It is registered with the British Pony Club.

DEC's ten instructors, who are all qualified by the British Horse Society, offer training in showjumping, dressage and musical dressage. Trail rides and hacks are also offered. The centre holds regular clinics and stable management courses.

Sports

Activities

Jebel Ali Equestrian Club

Location → Jebel Ali Village · Jebel Ali
Hours → Timings on request
Web/email → n/a

| 884 5485

Map Ref → 1-E3

'Just like the stables back home' describes the comfortable atmosphere of the Jebel Ali Equestrian Club, with the horsey smell and buzz of equine activities. Both children and adults can learn to ride here and, for the more experienced, hacking, dressage and jumping are options. Group lessons, packages and private lessons are available, and the registration fee per rider is Dhs.120, or Dhs.300 per family. Children can also join stable management courses since the club is an approved branch of the British Pony Club. For those who have their own horse, there's a livery service and air conditioned stables.

Sharjah Equestrian & Racing Club

Location → Jct 6 · Al Dhaid Rd
Hours → 07:00 - 10:00 15:00 - 19:00 Closed Mon
Web/email → www.forsanuae.org.ae

| 06 531 1155

Map Ref → UAE-C2

Located about 20 minutes drive from the centre of Sharjah, this riding centre was built in 1984 under the supervision of HH Sheikh Abdullah bin Majid Al Qassimi. It held its first competition a year later.

Facilities include a big floodlit sand arena, a floodlit paddock, a grass showjumping arena and hacking trails into the desert. The centre keeps 200 horses and regular riders number about 150, plus occasional riders for dressage, showjumping and hacks. The three full-time instructors, and part-time instructors, offer training up to national championship level. Riding here is by prior appointment and approval, so for more information, contact the centre.

Note: summer timings may differ.

Ice Hockey

Dubai Mighty Camels Ice Hockey Club

Location → Al Nasr Leisureland · Oud Metha
Hours → Sat & Tue 09:00 - 11:00
Web/email → www.dubaimightycamels.com

| 208 9470

Map Ref → 10-E4

Ice hockey has been a fixture on the local sports scene ever since Al Nasr Leisureland opened in 1979.

The club's purpose is to provide adult recreational ice hockey with no upper age limit. Currently membership stands at over 40 players, of more than a dozen nationalities. If you have your own equipment, give them a call. There are social get togethers and barbecues from September to May.

The club hosts an annual tournament in March, which in 2003 will be attended by 12 - 15 teams from the Gulf, Europe and the Far East. For more information, contact Jim Kittl or Ron Murphy or visit the Website for the latest news and scores.

Dubai Sandstorms Ice Hockey Club

Location → Al Nasr Leisureland · Oud Metha
Hours → Sat 16:30 - 21:00
Web/email → rproctor@emirates.net.ae

| 344 1885

Map Ref → 10-E4

This club was established to provide boys and girls (6 - 18 years) with the opportunity to learn ice hockey. The emphasis is on participation, teamwork and sportsmanship. No previous experience is necessary since participants are placed in teams based on their age, size and level of skill. The season runs from mid-September to mid-May, with practices held twice a week. Throughout the season, matches are played against Dubai, Abu Dhabi, Al Ain and Oman teams, with an international tournament scheduled for March each year. The registration fee of Dhs.600 includes an ice hockey jersey, and covers all practices and games during the season.

Ice Skating

Al Nasr Leisureland

Location → Behind American Hospital · Oud Metha
Hours → 09:00 - 24:00 Open throughout the week
Web/email → www.alnasrleisureland.ae

| 337 1234

Map Ref → 10-E4

Well, if it's large enough to hold an ice hockey tournament, then it's large enough for an energetic youngster's birthday party or to just skate around to your heart's content. Open to the public, except when rented by clubs, the rink is part of the Leisureland complex, which also houses a bowling alley, fast food outlets, arcade amusements and small shops. Occasionally the rink is used in the evening as a concert venue.

Cost: skating Dhs.10 for two hours, including boot hire.

Timings: the rink is open for two hour sessions starting at 10:00, 13:00, 16:00 and 19:30.

Sports

Activities

Galleria Ice Rink

Location → Hyatt Regency · Deira | **209 6550**
Hours → See timings below
Web/email → www.hyattdubai.com Map Ref → 8-D2

Located in the centre of the shopping mall (which makes the environment a bit chilly!) and next to the Galleria cinema, this is a popular and usually busy ice rink. Fees for public sessions are Dhs.25 per person, including skate hire, or Dhs.15, using your own skates. The use of socks is mandatory in rental boots, so take your own, or buy them for Dhs.5.

Membership rates start at Dhs.300 per month or Dhs.1,200 per year and members are entitled to unlimited skating. Lessons are available for non-members, and cost from Dhs.80 per half hour.

Timings: Sat - Thu 10:00 - 13:30, 14:00 - 17:30 & 18:00 - 21:00. On Fri and public holidays the rink closes at 20:00.

Jet Skiing

Other options → Beach Clubs [p.268]
Beaches [p.150]
Water Skiing [p.265]
Wakeboarding [p.264]

Every afternoon sees trailer loads of jet skis parked at the first lagoon between Dubai and Sharjah, near Al Mamzar Beach Park, or near Al Garhoud Bridge, on the opposite side of the bridge to Dubai Creek Golf & Yacht Club. Most are available for hire at approximately Dhs.100 for half an hour. A new area to hire jet skis is between the Ritz-Carlton and Le Royal Meridien Beach Resort & Spa where locals turn up everyday with trailers carrying 4 - 10 jet skis. Likewise, the beach near the Jumeirah Beach Hotel is a good place to try, and many of the beach clubs offer them for rent.

Note that a 1998 law limits jet skiers to within a 500 metre boundary from the shore, with the threat of legal action for exceeding this limit. With all the aquatic traffic, you may find the waters of Dubai

Creek a little murky, and other locations offer a cleaner environment, as well as stricter controls and better safety records. Recently a Russian man died when his jet ski accidentally collided with that of a British woman on Dubai Creek. The charges against the woman were eventually dropped and she was allowed home, but only after spending time in prison.

In addition, it may be worth checking that your medical insurance covers you for this potentially dangerous sport — apparently, broken legs are not all that uncommon!

Judo

Please see → Martial Arts [p.251]

Karate

Please see → Martial Arts [p.251]

Karting

Dubai Kart Club

Location → Nr Jebel Ali Hotel | **282 7111**
Hours → 14:00 - 19:00
Web/email → n/a Map Ref → 1-A1

Dubai Kart Club runs the 12 round UAE championship at their purpose-built international standard FIA licensed circuit, just 20 minutes from Dubai. Founded over 25 years ago, the circuit has four different configurations with the longest being just under 1 kilometre. The UAE championship runs from January to April and September to December.

Four classes of kart are raced: International 16 years and above, National 12 years and above, Rotax Max Seniors, Cadets 8 - 12 years. The top level of karts raced are capable of speeds of 165kph and spectators will be thrilled by the spectacle of

Jet skiis

Sports

Activities

competitive motor sport, as up to 25 karts race for the chequered flag. The cadet class, if not as fast, is equally entertaining. Entrance is free. Facilities include a grandstand and catering by the Jebel Ali Hotel. Membership is under discussion.

Formula One Dubai

Location → WonderLand · Umm Hurair |338 8828
Hours → 10:00 - 21:00
Web/email → www.formula1karting.com   Map Ref → 14-A3

Formula One Dubai no longer has any indoor circuits but they have an outdoor circuit at Wonderland. They also cater for corporate entertainment, children's parties, individual practice sessions and specialised outdoor functions. No experience is necessary to take part in this exhilarating and entertaining activity.

Cost: Dhs.40 for 10 minutes; children under 10 years Dhs.30. Endurance race, 1 hour, Dhs.140 per person (minimum eight people).

Kayaking

Other options → Tours & Sightseeing [p.153]
Canoeing [p.227]

Beach Hut, The

Location → Sandy Beach Motel · East Coast |09 244 5050
Hours → Timings on request
Web/email → www.sandybm.com   Map Ref → n/a

The Beach Hut offers a variety of water sports equipment. For those who just want to paddle out to Snoopy Island to explore, there are kayaks for hire at Dhs.30 an hour. You can also try windsurfing, and diving and snorkelling equipment is available for rent or sale.

Kitesurfing

Kitesurfing is a fast growing new sport that's gaining loads of publicity, partly because it's so extreme. It's not windsurfing, it's not wakeboarding, it's not surfing and it's not kite flying, but instead is a fusion of all these disciplines with other influences to create the wildest new water sport for years.

Arabian Gulf Kite Club, The

Location → Various locations |880 1010
Hours → Timings on request
Web/email → www.fatimasport.com   Map Ref → n/a

This new club offers the chance to try the sports of kitesurfing, mountain board kiting, power kiting, display kiting and kite buggys.

In particular, kitesurfing is an up and coming extreme sport that involves flying across the water harnessed to a kite and a small windsurfing board – the only downfall is that you have to be fit to even attempt it! A popular meeting place for Dubai kitesurfers is the beach between the University of Wollongong and Umm Suqeim Clinic, off Jumeira Beach Road.

Equipment sale and training courses are available and the club recommends equipment by Naish, Flexifoil and Peter Lynn for use in Arabian Gulf conditions. For further details, contact Fatima Sports (050 455 5216).

Fun Sports

Location → Various locations, see below |399 5976
Hours → 09:00 - 17:00
Web/email → funsport@emirates.net.ae   Map Ref → n/a

A little bit of knowledge of wake boarding and/or windsurfing is helpful to get a handle on this sport. It deals with tackling the forces of nature – specifically the wind. It's even suitable for children above the age of eight, as safety is ensured and stressed upon. A one-to-one session offers you all the attention you need. For those who are taking this sport up for the first time, there's a one-hour session on the sand before you actually face the real thing. Sessions are booked according to your convenience, but classes are preferably conducted in the afternoon.

Martial Arts

Al Majaz

Location → Trade Centre Rd · Al Karama |335 3563
Hours → 09:00 - 14:00 16:00 - 21:00
Web/email → www.goldenfistkarate.com   Map Ref → 10-D1

For further information on Al Majaz, refer to the review under Yoga [p.284].

Sports

Activities

Dubai Aikido Club

Location → Dubai Karate Centre · Al Satwa | **344 4156**
Hours → 17:00 - 20:00
Web/email → dubaiaikidoclub@hotmail.com   Map Ref → 6-A4

Aikido is an effective martial art for self-defence, not only because it teaches how to defend against an attack, but also because it trains the mind. Enthusiasts believe that it makes individuals stronger and more complete human beings, who are better able to diffuse or defend themselves against negative situations.

Dubai Aikido Club was established in 1995 and is affiliated to the Aikikai Aikido world headquarters, Japan and to the Aikido Association International, USA. For further information contact John Rutnam, chief instructor.

They meet at the Trade Centre Apartments Club and the Dubai Karate Centre, Al Wasl Road, Jumeira. Classes are held on Sun and Tue 17:30 - 18:30 for children and families and 19:30 - 21:30 for the general public.

Dubai Karate Centre

Location → Al Wasl Rd, Nr Emirates Bank · Al Satwa | **344 7797**
Hours → See timings below
Web/email → n/a   Map Ref → 6-A4

At Dubai Karate Centre a team of black belt, JKA qualified instructors teach a style of karate called shotokan, the oldest and most popular form of karate, as well as aikido and judo. The club is a member of the Japanese Karate Association (JKA), and has been established in Dubai since 1979. It offers tuition from beginner to black belt for anyone aged six years and above.

Courses are held on Saturday, Monday and Wednesday evenings between 17:00 - 19:00, depending on experience, and the fees include three sessions a week.

Costs: Dhs.100 initial registration fee, then Dhs.200 monthly membership fee. Uniforms cost Dhs.100 from the club.

Golden Falcon Karate Centre

Location → Nr choithram superma4rket, · Al Karama | **336 0243**
Hours → 08:30 - 12:00 16:30 - 22:30
Web/email → www.goldenfalconkarate.com   Map Ref → 10-C3

Established in 1990, this karate centre is affiliated to the Karate Budokan International and the UAE Judo, Taekwondo and Karate Federation. Classes are held according to demand, in judo, taekwondo

and fitness, with certificates awarded to successful students for each upgrading test. Call instructors, Suresh and Satial, for further details.

House of Chi & House of Healing

Location → Musalla Towers · Khalid Bin Walid St | **397 4446**
Hours → Closed Fri
Web/email → www.hofchi.com   Map Ref → 8-A5

For information on House of Chi & House of Healing, refer to the review under Yoga [p.285].

Taekwondo

Location → Ballet Centre, The · Jumeira | **344 9776**
Hours → Sun, Tue 03:30 - 21:00 Thu 10:00 - 13:00 Closed Wed, Fri
Web/email → balletct@emirates.net.ae   Map Ref → 6-C3

The Ballet Centre has Munir Gharwi (7th Dan black belt) teaching taekwondo. This form of martial art teaches children mental calmness, courage, strength and humility, courtesy, integrity, perseverance, self-control and indomitable spirit!

Microlights

Please see → Flying [p.242]

Mini Golf

Other options → Golf [p.243]
Kids' Stuff [p.295]

Aviation Club, The

Location → Nr Tennis Stadium · Al Garhoud | **282 4122**
Hours → 06:00 - 23:00
Web/email → www.aviationclubonline.com   Map Ref → 14-C3

This 9-hole, par 3 pitch and putt course is set in picture postcard surroundings, between the tennis stadium and the clubhouse. With manicured fairways and greens, each hole is a reasonable challenge for beginners and more accomplished golfers. The course offers great variation with the holes differing in distance from 40 to 82 yards.

Open to members only, for further details contact sports reception.

Hatta Fort Hotel

Location → 110Km from Dubai · Hatta	**852 3211**
Hours → Timings on request	
Web/email → www.dutcohotels.com	Map Ref → UAE-D3

With a background of lovely views of the Hajar Mountains, Hatta Fort offers a choice of mini golf or a 9-hole cross-country fun golf course. The mini course is American style crazy golf and lies mostly in the shade of the trees below the hotel. The charge for two people is Dhs.25. The 9-hole course can be played for Dhs.35 per person, per round (including clubs and balls). Each hole is par 3, ranging from 68 to 173 yards. Golf instruction and lessons are available.

Entrance fees: Day visitors on Fri and public holidays purchase a voucher at the entry gate (Dhs.40 for adults, Dhs.20 for children), which is redeemable against hotel facilities.

Hyatt Golf Park

Location → Hyatt Regency · Deira	**209 6741**
Hours → 15:30 - 23:00	
Web/email → www.dubai.hyatt.com	Map Ref → 8-D2

Adjacent to the Hyatt's side car park is a 9-hole pitch and putt grass golf course for the avid golfer to improve their short game. There is also an 18-hole crazy golf course. Clubs are provided and golf balls can be purchased for Dhs.8 each. The park is floodlit in the evenings and the clubhouse in the centre of the park overlooks a small lagoon. Go for golf or simply enjoy a drink at the 19th hole.

Prices: 9-hole pitch and putt – one round Dhs.15, two rounds Dhs.25; 18-hole crazy golf – Dhs.10 per person (ball and club included).

Moto-Cross

Dubai Youth Moto-Cross Club

Location → Various locations	**333 0659**
Hours → Timings on request	
Web/email → www.dubaimotocross.ae	Map Ref → n/a

With a 20 year history in Dubai, this club has recently been revitalised and now over 65 riders of all ages and abilities experience this thrilling sport. The club operates two tracks; a junior and cadet track for riders aged up to ten years, and a senior track for 80cc and 125cc riders. Riders are graded by age and ability, with beginners as young as five competing in the cadet class. Training events are also held.

The tracks are open most Fridays throughout the season (early September to April), with the Dubai Youth Championship running fortnightly from October to March. Newcomers are always welcome, but beware, it's extremely addictive!

For more information contact Shaun Whitley (050 553 7812) or visit the Website.

Motorcycling

Other options → Driving Licence [p.62]

Al Ramool Motorcycle Rental

Location → Big Red Dune Area · Hatta Rd	**050 453 4401**
Hours → Timings on request	
Web/email → desertfun99@hotmail.com	Map Ref → UAE-D3

Al Ramool offers LT50, LT80, 125cc, 350cc and 620cc motorcycles for rent. Crash helmets are provided for safety and prices range from Dhs.20 - 100 for 30 minutes. As an additional service, transport from Dubai is available on request. The company offers a variety of tailor-made packages – contact Mohammad Ali Rashed (050 453 3033) for further details.

UAE Motorcycle Club

Location → Al Muragabat Street · Deira	**266 9002**
Hours → 09:00 - 17:00 09:00 - 13:00 Closed Fri	
Web/email → www.uaedesertchallenge.com	Map Ref → 11-E2

Now in its fifth season, the UAE Motorcycle Club is officially sanctioned by the International Motorcycle Federation, the world governing body of the sport. The club runs a five round off-road endurance championship series, leading to an overall UAE champion. Interest in the club has grown considerably, with an average of 70 competitors per race and an overall membership of 175. The Chairman is Middle East Rally Champion, Mohammed bin Sulayem, and the club is a launching ground for competitors to race in the *UAE Desert Challenge.*

Membership: any riders over the age of 18 who have their own motorcycle and UAE driving licence, are welcome. Races are on Fri mornings, starting on 12 January 2003, and then every four weeks, until early May.

Sports

Activities

Mountain Biking

Other options → Cycling [p.231]
Out of Dubai [p.165]

Contrary to the initial view of the Emirates, the interior has a lot to offer outdoor enthusiasts, especially mountain bikers. The 'outback' is rarely visited, but on a mountain bike it is possible to see the most remote places that are inaccessible even by 4 wheel drive.

For hardcore mountain bikers there is a good range of terrain, from super technical rocky trails, in areas like Fili and Siji, to mountain routes like Wadi Bih, which climb to over 1,000 metres and can be descended in minutes. The riding is mainly rocky, technical and challenging. There are many tracks to follow and, if you look hard, some interesting singletrack can be found.

However, be prepared and be sensible — the sun is strong, you will need far more water than you think and it's easy to get lost. Plus falling off on this rocky terrain can be extremely painful!

For further information on mountain biking in the UAE, including details of possible routes, refer to the *Off-Road Explorer (UAE),* published by Explorer Publishing.

Biking Frontiers

Location → Various locations | 050 552 7300
Hours → See timings below
Web/email → www.bikingfrontiers.com   Map Ref → n/a

So, you're a mountain biking fan? If you don't mind thrashing yourself over seriously rocky trails, up and down big mountains, through wadis and like getting lost once in a while... then give Biking Frontiers a call!

They are a fairly serious group of riders, but any competent mountain bikers are welcome. Your own bike, helmets and proper gear are essential. The group also enjoys camping, hiking and barbecues – there's always something going on. Rides are every Friday, and sometimes Saturdays, as well as city rides in the evenings during the week. Contact Paul on the above number or Pete (050 450 9401).

Desert Rangers

Location → Dubai Garden Centre Bldg, Shk Zayed Rd | 340 2408
Hours → 09:00 - 18:00 Closed Fri (office)
Web/email → www.desertrangers.com   Map Ref → 6-E3

Whether you're a fanatical biker craving challenging terrain, or a complete beginner preferring a gentler introduction to the delights of off-road biking, Desert Rangers will determine a suitable route depending on your requirements and group size. The company is one of only a few outward-bound leisure companies to specialise in more unusual activities in the UAE.

The cost of Dhs.300 per person is inclusive of bike, helmet, guide, pick up and drop off and soft drinks.

Mountaineering

Other options → Out of Dubai [p.165]
Climbing [p.228]

Although the area immediately surrounding Dubai is mostly flat with sandy desert and sabkha (salt-flats), there are areas inland that are a paradise for the more adventurous mountain walker. To the north, the Ru'us Al Jibal Mountains contain the highest peaks in the area, at over 2,000 metres. To the east, the impressive Hajar Mountains form the border between the UAE and Oman; stretching from the Mussandam Peninsula north of Ras Al Khaimah, to the Empty Quarter desert, several hundred kilometres to the south.

The terrain is heavily eroded and shattered due to the harsh climate, and trips range from short easy walks leading to spectacular viewpoints, to all day treks over difficult terrain, with some major mountaineering routes on faces of alpine proportions. Many of the routes follow centuries old Bedouin and Shihuh trails through the mountains and a few are still used today as a means of access to the more remote settlements.

Mountain Biking

Dhs.100 ~ € 28

Some of the terrain is incredible and one can only wonder at the skills of the hardy mountain people who pioneered the trails.

Battered photocopies of a guide written in the mid-1980s exist, and this may form the basis of a dedicated climbing and mountaineering book at some point.

Heat and humidity mean that serious mountain walking is best between the months of November and April.

For further information on possible routes for mountaineering in the UAE, refer to the *Off-Road Explorer (UAE)*, published by Explorer Publishing.

Warning: No mountain rescue services exist, therefore anyone venturing out into mountains should be reasonably experienced, or be with some one who knows the area. Tragedies have occurred in the past.

> *Contacts: Useful contacts willing to advise like-minded people are: Alistair MacKenzie (alistair@explorer-publishing.com) - Dubai, John Gregory (050 647 7120) - Ras Al Khaimah.*

Netball

Dubai Netball League	
Location → Country Club · Al Awir Rd	050 544 7953
Hours → Wed 18:30 - 22:30	
Web/email → n/a	Map Ref → 17-B3

Dubai Netball League was established in the mid-1970s, with six teams vying for the league title. Today there are over 15 teams divided into three divisions. Players range from teenagers to grandmothers, and beginners to experts.

Games are played from September to May on Wednesday nights on the two courts at the Dubai Exiles Rugby ground. Team training is on a Sunday or Monday night. During the season, players are selected for the InterGulf Netball Championships; a competition that brings together teams from Abu Dhabi, Bahrain, Dubai, Kuwait, Oman and Saudi Arabia. In 2003, the competition will be held in Bahrain in early March. For further information, contact Helen Donnachie (050 544 7953).

Paintballing

Other options → Shooting [p.259]

Pursuit Games	
Location → WonderLand · Umm Hurair	324 1222
Hours → Timings on request Closed Sun	
Web/email → wonderld@emirates.net.ae	Map Ref → 14-A3

This is a fun fighting game for teenagers and adults where the bullets are balls of paint! Get a crowd together and they will soon be divided into two teams by the experts, who give a thorough safety demonstration before equipping you with overalls, 'Darth Vader' type facemasks and special guns equipped with paintballs.

This is a strategy game played by shooting balls of paint onto your opponent, thus marking and eliminating them. Stalk your enemies and get them before they get you! If you're hit, you're out until the next game! For further information, contact Kaz (050 651 4583).

> *Cost: Dhs.70 for a typical two hour game with 100 paintballs, gun and gas. An extra 100 paintballs costs Dhs.50.*

Paragliding

Please see → Sky Diving [p.260]
Flying [p.242]

Parasailing

Other options → Tours & Sightseeing [p.153]

Pavilion Marina & Sports Club	
Location → Jumeirah Beach Htl · Umm Suqeim	406 8800
Hours → 06:30 - 22:30	
Web/email → www.jumeirahinternational.com	Map Ref → 4-B2

Experience the thrills of parasailing from a custom-built American parasailing boat. It's worth a try, if only to experience the wonderful views of the coast from a different perspective. Flights last for about eight minutes and there's no need to run down the beach for take off, or landings in the sea. Availability is subject to weather conditions.

> *Costs: eight minute flight Dhs.145 per person for non-members; Dhs.125 for members of the sports club.*

Sports

Activities

Parasailing

Polo

Other options → Horse Riding [p.248]

Dubai Polo Club

Location → Dubai-Al Ain Road · Al Awir |336 3664
Hours → na
Web/email → poloclub@emirates.net.ae   Map Ref → 17-B3

The Dubai Polo Club is under new management (Emaar). As such, club activities are currently on hold and timings and other details will be changing. For further information, please contact the above number.

Ghantoot Polo & Racing Club

Location → Shk Zayed Rd towards Abu Dhabi |02 562 9050
Hours → Timings on request
Web/email → grpc1@emirates.net.ae   Map Ref → UAE-A4

With six polo fields, polo school with floodlights, 2,000 seat racing grandstand, three tennis courts, swimming pool, gym, sauna and restaurant, this club has first class facilities for all the family to enjoy. Membership is available and non-members are welcome to dine at the restaurant or to watch the regular polo matches.

The polo season starts in October and continues until the end of April. The calendar is full with regular chukka tournaments and high profile international games. The quality of play and horses is high and spectators are always welcome. Ghantoot hosts two race meetings on 18 December 2002 and 16 April 2003.

Location: Ghantoot is located half way between Dubai and Abu Dhabi, near Jazira Hotel, about thirty minutes from Dubai by car.

Quad Bikes

Please see → Dune Buggy Riding [p.238]

Rally Driving

Other options → UAE Desert Challenge [p.52]
Desert Rallies [p.48]

Emirates Motor Sports Federation

Location → Nr Aviation Club · Al Garhoud |282 7111
Hours → 09:00 - 17:30 Timings on request Closed Thu, Fri
Web/email → www.emsf.org.ae   Map Ref → 14-D4

For rally enthusiasts in the UAE, the Federation organises a variety of events throughout the year, from the 4 WD 1000 Dunes Rally to the Champions Rally for saloon cars. Other Federation events include road safety awareness campaigns and classic car exhibitions. The driving skill competitions are open to all (separate category for ladies), the only prerequisite being a valid UAE driving licence. This is the official motor sport authority in the UAE and is a non-profit government organisation.

Membership fees: Federation membership for rally enthusiasts is Dhs.750 and a professional competition licence is required to participate in this expensive sport.

Rappeling

Please see → Climbing [p.228]
Out of Dubai [p.165]

Roller Blading

Other options → Parks [p.149]
Creekside Park [p.149]
Sporting Goods [p.206]

Although the experts make it look easy, roller blading is a good challenge and great exercise, as well as being lots of fun. Dubai's many parks provide some excellent locations: try Creekside Park and Safa Park for smooth, wide pathways with few people and enough slopes and turns to make it interesting. Alternatively, check out the seafront near the Hyatt Regency Hotel or the promenade at the Jumeira Beach Corniche, where the view is an added bonus.

Sports

Activities

Rugby

Other options → Annual Events [p.48]
Sporting Goods [p.206]

Dubai Exiles Rugby Club

Location → Nr Dubai Country Club · Al Awir Rd | **333 1198**
Hours → Timings on request
Web/email → exiles@emirates.net.ae | Map Ref → 17-B3

Definitely Dubai's serious rugby club, the Exiles is the Emirates' oldest and best established bastion of the sport. Training sessions are scheduled throughout the week with the 1st and 2nd XVs meeting on Sundays and Wednesdays and veterans on Tuesdays and Saturdays. There's also training for children (mini's) on Mondays and Wednesdays. The 1st XV play in the Arabian Gulf First Division and the 2nds in the Emirates League, so there's plenty of regional travel and competition. There are matches most Friday afternoons and some Wednesdays.

The Exiles also host the annual *Dubai International Rugby Sevens* tournament, which attracts international teams from all the major rugby playing nations. The club also provides facilities for the Emirates Football League, and clubhouse facilities are available for hire.

Dubai Hurricanes

Location → Country Club · Al Awir Rd | **333 1155**
Hours → See timings below
Web/email → www.eteamz.com/dubaiHurricane | Map Ref → 17-B3

Dubai Hurricanes are the latest exciting arrival on the Gulf rugby scene. Originally formed in 1999 as a purely social outfit, the club has competed in the annual Dubai Sevens tournament and its success on both the rugby and social fronts, enabled their entry into the Arabian Gulf League for the 2001/02 season. The progress into this league is a clear reflection of the club's rugby ambitions, although at the same time they remain committed to a strong social spirit – the root of all rugby!

Training is on Sunday and Tuesday evenings from 19:30pm. They also have a ladies team. All new players (whatever their ability) are welcome ... go on, dust off those boots!

Contacts: *Club Captain Chris Govier (050 657 2458); Caroline (050 784 2710); Cecile (050 694 7938).*

Running

Other options → Annual Events [p.48]

For over half the year, the weather couldn't be better for running in the emirates, whilst in the summer, despite the high temperatures and humidity, you'll find dedicated runners out pounding the miles all over the UAE. In the hottest months, the evenings, and the early mornings especially, are the best times to be out.

Clubs and informal groups meet regularly to run together, with some runs being competitive or training runs for the variety of events organised throughout the year.

Regular, short distance races are held, as well as a variety of biathlons, triathlons, duathlons and hashes, which provide a reasonably full and varied schedule. Two of the favourite competitions are the Round the Creek relay race and the epic Wadi Bih Run. For the latter, teams of five run the 70 km from Ras Al Khaimah on the west coast to Dibba on the east, over mountains topping out at over 1,000 metres. Runners take turns to run different stages with a support vehicle and this event, held annually, attracts up to 300 participants. A relatively new event is the *Dubai Marathon*, which will be held on 13 January 2003.

Contacts: *Wadi Bih race, John Gregory (050 647 7120) or arabex@emirates.net.ae. Round the Creek Hash Relay (to be held on 24 January 2003), Ian Colton (050 658 4153) or sukka@emirates.net.ae.*

Dubai Creek Striders

Location → Trade Centre car park · Shk Zayed Rd | **321 1999**
Hours → Fri 06:15
Web/email → malcolmm@murrob.co.ae | Map Ref → 9-E2

This medium to long distance running club was established in 1995 and organises weekly runs on Friday mornings. Distances and routes differ each week, but normally consist of shorter 10 km runs during the summer up to winter marathon training runs of about 32 km, ready for the annual 42.2 km Dubai Marathon in early January.

Scenic running is guaranteed, with most runs visiting the Creek at some stage. It's wise to confirm the start time and place, as special runs are held during the year. There are no joining fees, but take Dhs.5 - 10 for drinks and your email address. Contact Malcolm Murphy for further details.

Sports

Activities

Dubai Road Runners

Location → Safa Park · Al Wasl Rd | **394 1996**
Hours → Sat 18:30
Web/email → www.dubai-road-runners.com   Map Ref → 5-C3

Come rain or shine, 100% humidity and 50ºC temperatures, Dubai Road Runners always meet at Safa Park in the car park by gate number 4. The objective of the meeting is to run either a 3½ km or 7 km track around the park. A Dhs.5 entrance fee is charged, and most people try to run this standard course against the clock. The club also organises competitions and social events throughout the year.

All standards, all ages and all nationalities are welcome. Contact Graham Rafferty for more information by phone, email or visit the Website.

Sailing

Other options → Annual Events [p.48]
Boat & Yacht Charters [p.162]

In winter, the temperatures are perfect for sailing and water sports in general, while in the summer you can escape some of the scorching heat that prohibits some land-based sports. Sailing is a popular pastime in Dubai, with many people being members of one of the sailing clubs on Jumeira Beach and Al Mina Al Siyahi. Membership in the clubs allows you use of the leisure facilities, the club's beach, to join in the activities, rent sailing and water sports equipment, and moor or store your boat (always an extra cost!).

There's quite a healthy racing scene for a variety of classes of boat and there's also the occasional long distance race, such as the annual Dubai to Muscat race, held in March. The traditional dhow races are also a sight to see.

Many companies will take you out on a cruise, either for a couple of hours or for a full day, for pleasure or for fishing. You can also charter your own boat for periods ranging from one morning to several weeks!

See also: Dhow Racing — Annual Events [p.48].

Dubai Offshore Sailing Club

Location → Beach Rd, Jumeira | **394 1669**
Hours → 09:00 - 05:00 09:00 - 12:00
Web/email → www.dosc.org   Map Ref → 4-E2

This is a friendly club that welcomes sailors of all abilities. It's recognised by the Royal Yachting Association (RYA) and runs courses throughout the year. There's an active dinghy and yacht fleet and races are held twice a month. The Thursday and Friday Cadet Club is great for younger sailors who can also enjoy the water sports programmes.

The club provides mooring, storage, launch facilities, sail training and a full yachting and social calendar. The modern clubhouse has full catering facilities. This is a non-profit making organisation, and its success depends on the active support of its members. For further information, contact Carolyn Honeybun or Club Manager, Alfred Hunter (394 2669).

Timings: members only 09:00 - 24:00; public sailing 09:00 - 17:00.

Sailing

Sports

Activities

Fun Sports

Location → Various locations, see below | 399 5976
Hours → 09:00 - 17:00
Web/email → funsport@emirates.net.ae | Map Ref → n/a

Fun Sports offers multi-hull sailing courses to anyone who has been bitten by the sailing bug, with professional sailing instructors available to teach beginners and improvers. Membership of one of the beach clubs is not necessary to sail with Fun Sports. For bookings contact Suzette on the above number, fax (399 5796) or (050 453 4828).

Locations: The company operates at the following beach clubs: Dubai Marine Beach Resort & Spa, Hilton Dubai Jumeirah, Metropolitan Resort & Beach Club, Oasis Beach Hotel, Ritz-Carlton Beach Club Royal Mirage, Le Meridien Mina Seyahi and Jumeira Beach Park.

Jebel Ali Sailing Club

Location → Nr DIMC · Al Sufouh | 399 5444
Hours → 09:00 - 20:00 Thu & Fri 09:00 - 22:00
Web/email → www.jebelalisailingclub.com | Map Ref → 2-E2

This club is fully recognised by the Royal Yachting Association to teach and certify sailing, windsurfing and powerboating, and instruct in kayaking. The membership is very active, making it a lively and friendly organisation, and races are held most weekends for toppers, lasers, catamarans and cruisers. Lessons are available to non-members.

There's a pool to chill off in with an outside barasti bar for refreshment and functions, as well as shaded lawns for relaxing. The main clubhouse and restaurant are open 09:00 - 20:00 Saturday to Wednesday, and 09:00 - 22:00 Thursday and Friday.

Contact: Sharon Allison or Colin Slowey on the above number or h2osport@emirates.net.ae or their Website.

Sand Boarding/Skiing

Other options → Tour Operators [p.155]

OK, so it's rather like skiing through sludge, but it can be great fun! Head into the desert outside Dubai (especially easy if you have a 4 wheel drive, although not essential), find yourself some big dunes and feel the 'rush' of the wind as you take a slow, jerky ride down the sandy slopes. It's a quick sport to learn and it doesn't hurt when you fall. One of the favourite areas is the huge dune affectionately known as 'Big Red' half way to Hatta, on the left by the main road.

The boards are usually standard snowboards but,

as the sand is quite hard on them, they often can't be used for anything else afterwards. Some sports stores sell 'sand boards', which are cheaper and more basic snowboards. As an alternative for children, a plastic sledge or something similar is enough to give a lot of fun.

All the major tour companies take tours to sand board the highest dunes and offer basic instruction on how to stay up, how to surf and how to fall properly! This can be available either as part of another tour or as a dedicated sand boarding tour. A half-day sand boarding tour costs Dhs.175 - 200.

Shooting

Other options → Paintballing [p.255]

Hatta Fort Hotel

Location → 110km from Dubai · Hatta | 852 3211
Hours → Timings on request
Web/email → www.dutcohotels.com | Map Ref → UAE-D3

Clay pigeon shooting is one of the many activities offered at Hatta Fort Hotel, which is less than an hour's drive from Dubai. More frequently visited as an overnight retreat from the hustle and bustle of Dubai, Hatta Fort is a sports fan's playground with the added attraction of superb food and beverage facilities. The hotel has a newly opened rock pool, and offers a Friday barbie for Dhs.85 net, including complimentary pool entry.

Cost: Dhs.95 for 25 shots. Day visitors on Fri and public holidays purchase a voucher at the entry gate (Dhs.40 for adults, Dhs.20 for children), which is redeemable against hotel facilities.

Jebel Ali Shooting Club

Location → Nr Jebel Ali Htl · Jebel Ali | 883 6555
Hours → 13:00 - 22:00 Closed Tue & August
Web/email → www.jebelali-international.com | Map Ref → 1-A2

At the Jebel Ali Shooting Club, members and non-members are welcome. Shooting is done in clay on five different flood lit ranges from Skeet to Ball Trap, American Trap, Olympic Trap and Sporting as well as at the indoor 25 metre long computerised pistol range.

Instructors are available for comprehensive lessons in either pistol or clay shooting.

Prices: non-members lessons - Dhs.100 (clay shooting) Dhs.75 (pistol shooting); members lessons - Dhs.75 (clay shooting) Dhs.50 (pistol shooting).

Sports

Activities

Ras Al Khaimah Shooting Club

Location → Al Dehes · 20 min from RAK Airport | **07 236 3622**
Hours → 15:00 - 20:00
Web/email → n/a   Map Ref → UAE-D1

This club welcomes anyone interested in learning to shoot any type of gun, from 9mm pistols to shotguns and long rifles. There are a variety of ranges, some air conditioned and indoors such as the 50 metre rifle range, while others are outdoors, like the 200 metre rifle range. Archery is also available. A canteen sells snacks and soft drinks, and the club is open on Mondays for women and children only.

Skydiving

Other options → Paragliding [p.255]
Hang Gliding [p.245]

Umm Al Quwain Aeroclub

Location → 17km North of UAQ on RAK Rd · UAQ | **06 768 1447**
Hours → 09:00 - 17:30
Web/email → www.uaqaeroclub.com   Map Ref → UAE-C1

In addition to flying, paramotors and microlights, Umm Al Quwain Aeroclub dropzone operates as a skydive school and boogie centre. You can enjoy an eight level AFF (Accelerated Free Fall) parachute course (price Dhs.5,200, the Dhs.200 is refundable) and train for your international parachute licence. Alternatively, if you are curious to know what jumping out of a plane feels like, try a tandem jump with an instructor from 12,000 feet for Dhs.720. Special rates are available for practice jumps for professional teams and skydivers from all around the world are welcome.

Location: 16 km along the road from UAQ roundabout heading in the direction of Ras Al Khaimah, before Dreamland Aqua Park and opposite UAQ Shooting Club, on the left handside of the road ... just look for the hangars and the big plane by the sea!

Snooker

Dubai Snooker Club

Location → Nr Post Office · Al Karama | **337 5338**
Hours → 09:00 - 02:00 Fri 15:00 - 01:00
Web/email → www.dubaisnooker.com   Map Ref → 10-E2

Snooker and pool for everyone, and you don't need to be a member to have a game. Dubai Snooker Club has 15 snooker tables and eight pool tables, plus three private snooker rooms for families and groups. Five tournaments a year are organised, which anyone can enter.

Cost: Dhs.20 per hour per table.

Location: on the small street joining the road connecting Za'abeel Road with Maktoum Bridge road, opposite the main Post Office. The entrance is on the right side of the building.

Millennium Avenue

Location → Al Safiya Bld, nr Galadari R/A · Deira | **266 6595**
Hours → 10:00 - 02:00 Fri 14:00 - 03:00
Web/email → www.danaclassic.com   Map Ref → 12-B4

This is a pool hall with a difference – the tables are round! For pool, snooker or billiards, the tables are a novelty that seem to have caught on with all nationalities. Round pool follows the rules of the normal game, except there are only three pockets and 13 coloured balls. A raised cushion in the centre of the table makes the game more interesting. Opened in July 2000, Millennium Avenue has 18 billiard tables in spacious surroundings and two private snooker tables. The club organises annual interclub leagues. Other facilities include computer games and an Internet café.

Snooker Point

Location → Nr Al Nasr Cinema · Al Karama | **334 1551**
Hours → 10:00 - 03:00 Fri 14:00 - 03:00
Web/email → n/a   Map Ref → 10-D3

Not your regular pool hall, but a smart venue for an afternoon or evening game in surprisingly salubrious surroundings! Play at one of the eight full size snooker tables or nine pool tables and relax in between shots or games in fine looking chairs.

An attractive bar in the pool room offers fruit cocktails, coffees and teas, and the Arabic music TV adds to the 'pool bar' feel, while the snooker room is quieter, allowing maximum concentration on those important shots. Everyone is welcome.

Price: Dhs.4 per 15 minutes per table.

Location: pass the main entrance of Lamcy Plaza then follow the signs to Snooker Point. Just before you join the slip road onto Umm Hurair Road heading towards Maktoum Bridge, it's on the right, just past Italian Connection restaurant.

Sports

Activities

Snooker

Snorkelling

Other options → Diving [p.234]

A mask and snorkel is a great way to see the varied underwater life of the Gulf or the East Coast, where it is especially good. On the Gulf of Oman coast, popular places include Snoopy Island, near the Sandy Beach Motel, Dibba. There are also good spots further north, such as the beach north of Dibba village, where the coast is rocky or there's coral close to the shore. For somewhere closer to home, the sea off Jumeira Beach has a fair amount of marine life.

Most hotels or dive centres rent equipment — snorkel, mask and fins. Costs vary greatly, so shop around.

Check out the *Underwater Explorer (UAE)* for further information on where and how to go snorkelling in the UAE.

Beach Hut, The

Location → Sandy Beach Motel · East Coast | 09 244 5050
Hours → Timings on request
Web/email → www.sandybm.com Map Ref → n/a

For those who want an exhilarating snorkelling experience, the Beach Hut is the only way to go! Snoopy Island, the 'house' reef, is just off their private beach and is an excellent site to enjoy the underwater world. Equipment is available for sale, alternatively rent a full set for the day for Dhs.50. You can also try kayaks or windsurfing.

Oceanic Hotel

Location → Beach Rd, Khorfakkan · East Coast | 09 238 5111
Hours → 14:30 - 18:00
Web/email → www.oceanichotel.com Map Ref → UAE-E2

An ideal place for snorkelling, the East Coast boasts beautiful clear waters and plenty of fish and coral. The Oceanic Hotel offers a boat ride to Sharque Island and provides snorkelling gear for Dhs.60, alternatively snorkel and swim from the hotel beach to Hidden Beach. Equipment hire is Dhs.30 for one hour. These prices apply to hotel residents, visitors will also have to pay an entrance fee of Dhs.45 per adult and Dhs.25 per child.

Scuba 2000

Location → Al Badiyah Beach · Fujairah | 09 238 8477
Hours → Timings on request
Web/email → www.scuba2000uae.com Map Ref → UAE-E2

This East Coast centre offers snorkelling either directly from the beach or with a boat ride, usually to Snoopy and Sharque Islands, or Al Badiyah Rock. Snorkelling trips to these destinations costs Dhs.50, inclusive of fins, mask, snorkel and boots. The centre also has other water sports facilities, including diving, jet skis, pedal boats and canoes.

Scuba Dubai

Location → Dubai World Trade Ctr Apts · Shk Zayed Rd | 331 7433
Hours → 09:00 - 13:00 16:00 - 20:30 Thu 09:00 - 19:00 Closed Fri
Web/email → info@scubadubai.com Map Ref → 9-D2

For those wishing to arrange their own snorkelling trips, equipment can be rented from Scuba Dubai on a 24 hour basis, collecting one day and returning the next. Rates for Thursday, Friday and Saturday are the same as renting for one day as the shop is closed on Fridays.

Costs: Rental of mask and snorkel is Dhs.10 for 24 hours, boots and fins are an additional Dhs.10.

Underwater fun

Sports

Activities

Softball

Dubai Softball League

Location ➜ Metropolitan Htl , Shk Zayed Rd | 050 650 2743
Hours ➜ Wed & Sat 19:00 - 23:00
Web/email ➜ www.dubaisoftballleague.org   Map Ref ➜ 5-C4

Softball started in Dubai in the early 1970s and was mostly played by Western expats; however, the league now boasts a truly multinational mix. The league runs from mid-September until the beginning of December and again from mid-January to the end of May. The only criteria to play is that you must be aged 16 or over.

Dubai is host to the bi-annual Middle East Softball Championships. Generally held in November and April, these events attract over 500 players from around the Gulf. Everyone is welcome to watch, entrance is free and food and beverages are available. For further information, call Garth Gregory (050 650 2743) or check out the Website.

Speedboating

Fun Sports

Location ➜ Various locations, see below | 399 5976
Hours ➜ 09:00 - 17:00
Web/email ➜ funsport@emirates.net.ae   Map Ref ➜ n/a

For those of you who wish to take a break and let your hair down, or just venture out into the vast blue waters of the Gulf, speed boating will be right up your alley. You can hire a boat that comes along with a captain and go wherever you please, even up close to the Burj al Arab. Future trips will include getting up close to Palm Island as well. Trips are based on prior bookings as well as weather conditions.

Squash

Other options ➜ Beach, Health & Sports Clubs [p.266]

Dubai Squash League

Location ➜ Dubai & Sharjah | 050 646 4596
Hours ➜ Timings on request
Web/email ➜ meshrakh@emirates.net.ae   Map Ref ➜ n/a

The squash league has been active in Dubai and Sharjah since the 1980s and is run by the UAE Squash Rackets Association. Approximately 400 competitors play at over 30 clubs each season. Matches are held every Monday for the Dubai and Northern Emirates Premier Series. A team fields three players and must have five to seven players registered to join in the competition. The Open Squash League also meets on Monday evenings. This involves five divisions with each team fielding five players, and having eight to ten players registered to join in the competition. In addition, mini-tournaments are arranged. For more information, contact Shavan Kumar.

Surfing

Other options ➜ Beaches [p.150]

Surprisingly, Dubai is a respectable surfing location. While it certainly doesn't compare to the hot-spots in Indonesia or Hawaii, and you probably wouldn't come here on a surfin' safari, there are a dedicated group of surfers who watch the weather and tides and from around November to June, get a couple of days of rideable waves a month to satisfy their cravings. Swells are generally on the smaller side (2 to 4 feet),

Surfing

but every now and then, conditions are right and bigger stuff comes through. The sport's popularity has increased in the last few years with new boards becoming available on the market. Check out the Surfers of Dubai web-site (www.surfersofdubai.com) for information on spots, where to buy boards, and when to meet to watch surf videos.

Swimming

Other options → Beaches [p.150]
Beach, Health & Sports Clubs [p.266]

Dubai's location on the Arabian Gulf means easy access to water that's relatively clean and a pleasant temperature for most of the year. During the three hottest months of the summer, the water near the beach is often hotter than a bath!

Most hotels have swimming pools that are open for use by the public for a day entrance fee. This charge varies, but ranges from Dhs.25 - 50 weekdays, rising at weekends (the beach clubs tend to be more expensive). Swimming lessons are widely available from health and beach clubs, as well as from dedicated swimming coaches. Pools are usually cooled for the summer months.

Swimming off the beaches is also possible, whether it's a public beach, beach club or one of the beach parks. Remember to be modest in your choice of costume and on the East Coast especially, keep an eye out for jellyfish, etc.

Warning When swimming in the sea do not underestimate the strength of the tides and currents. Even on the safest looking beaches rip tides have been known to carry people out to sea. In 1999, 100 people drowned off the UAE's coast, due in part to the combination of strong rip tides and lack of swimming ability.

Table Tennis

Other options → Beach, Health & Sports Clubs [p.266]

Please see the list of beach, health and sports clubs. Most offer at least one table tennis table!

Tennis

Other options → Beach, Health & Sports Clubs [p.266]
Dubai Tennis Open [p.50]

Dubai has firmly established itself on the international tennis circuit with the $1,000,000 *Dubai Duty Free Tennis Open*, held each year in the middle of February. However, if playing on the centre court is a little out of your league, you'll find plenty of other opportunities to enjoy this popular game.

For the budding Pete Sampras, outdoor courts are available at most of the health and beach clubs. Many are floodlit, allowing play in the cool of the evening — in the summer this is about the only time you'd want to play outside! The indoor courts at InSportz are a bonus for the summer months (347 5833), which are available for public use at very reasonable rates.

Prices for hiring courts vary between Dhs.25 - 50 weekdays, but you may be charged as much as Dhs.100 at weekends. Group or individual coaching is widely available.

Aviation Club, The

Location → Nr Tennis Stadium · Al Garhoud	282 4122
Hours → 06:00 - 23:00	
Web/email → www.aviationclubonline.com	Map Ref → 14-C3

The Clark Francis Tennis Academy at The Aviation Club offers a variety of courses, lessons and activities for all ages and abilities. The club boasts a range of excellent facilities (probably the best tennis facilities in town), including six floodlit Decoturf tennis courts. Individual classes start at Dhs.150 per person (Dhs.600 for five lessons).

The club hosts *The Aviation Cup* (Dhs.78,000), as well as the annual *Dubai Duty Free Tennis Open* each February, an event that's firmly established on the international tennis circuit.

Dubai Tennis Academy

Location → American University, Dubai	050 655 6152
Hours → 16:00 - 21:00	
Web/email → n/a	Map Ref → 3-A3

The Academy offers professional coaching year-round for aspiring players of all ages and abilities. All coaches are USPTA (United States Professional Tennis Association) qualified professionals. The academy is a world-wide agent for the Florida-based Bollettieri Sports Academy (BSA), and organises international tennis clinics with BSA coaches to tie in with major tournaments on the pro tennis circuit. Plans for 2003 include clinics in Dubai, Melbourne, New Zealand, Sydney and Singapore. The Academy's full-time adult and junior programmes include private lessons, group

Sports

Activities

clinics, competitions and ladies tennis mornings. They also serve up school holiday sports camps for children.

Emirates Golf Club

Location → Jct 5, Shk Zayed Rd	**347 3222**
Hours → 06:00 - 23:00	
Web/email → www.dubaigolf.com	Map Ref → 3-A3

The Emirates Tennis Academy in the Emirates Golf Club is open to members and non-members alike, and offers coaching for all ages and levels of ability. The centre has six courts, and coaching is taught by qualified LTA (Lawn Tennis Association) and USPTR (United States Professional Tennis Registry) professionals.

The programme for adults provides group clinics, individual lessons and club nights, as well as ladies social tennis mornings. The academy has two teams in the ladies Spinneys League and one in the men's Prince League. Every few years, a junior academy trip is planned to the UK to play against London clubs and to the Wimbledon Championships to watch the world's top players in action at the world's most famous tennis tournament.

Triathlon

Other options → Cycling [p.231]
Running [p.257]
Swimming [p.263]

Dubai Triathlon Club

Location → Various locations	**050 654 7924**
Hours → Timings on request	
Web/email → www.dubaitriclub.com	Map Ref → n/a

There are a reasonable number of triathlon enthusiasts in the Emirates and during the winter season (October to April) the Dubai Tri Club committee organises a relatively busy calendar of triathlons, biathlons and aquathons in Dubai and Abu Dhabi.

No membership is required, but all enthusiasts are welcome to send their email address to be registered on the UAE database. For further information, contact Rory McRae on the above number or Adrian Hayes (050 622 4191).

Wadi & Dune Bashing

Other options → Fun Drive – Annual Events [p.52]

With vast areas of rarely visited wilderness to explore, wadi and dune 'bashing' are two of the most popular pastimes in the Emirates, offering a variety of challenging driving.

Dune or desert driving is possibly the toughest challenge for car and driver, but probably the most fun, while in the mountains and wadis the driving is relatively straightforward. Wadis are (usually dry) gullies that follow the course of seasonal rivers and are carved through the rock by rushing floodwater.

One point about the word 'bashing' — while a popular term for this form of entertainment, it can be misleading. Most, if not all, of your journey off-road should be on existing tracks to protect the environment from further damage. Try to avoid the temptation to create new tracks across virgin countryside. Although much of the UAE 'outback' may look devoid of life, there is a surprising variety of flora and fauna that exists in a delicate balance.

For further information and tips on driving off-road, including stunning satellite imagery with 20 superimposed routes, detailed route descriptions and striking photos, refer to the *Off-Road Explorer (UAE)* guidebook, published by Explorer Publishing. This also includes a useful Off-Road Directory.

If you want to venture into the wilderness, but don't want to organise it yourself, contact the tour companies; all offer a range of desert and mountain safaris. See Tour Operators [p.155].

If you don't have a 4 wheel drive, one can be hired from most car hire companies. See Car Hire [p.34].

Wakeboarding

Other options → Beaches [p.150]
Jet Skiing [p.250]
Water Skiing [p.265]

Dubai Water Sports Association

Location → Jadaf · End of Dubai Creek	**324 1031**
Hours → 08:00 - 01:00	
Web/email → dwsa@emirates.net.ae	Map Ref → n/a

Wakeboarding was pioneered by the Dubai Water Sports Association (DWSA) who 'bred' one of the top junior wakeboarders in the world. This is the aquatic equivalent of snow boarding; basically, you strap your feet onto one large board, weigh the

Sports

Activities

back of the boat down to create a bigger wake and then jump over it! Sounds simple? To have a go at this fun, flamboyant and still relatively new sport in the UAE, contact DWSA on the above number.

Water Parks

Other options → Amusement Parks [p.298]

Dreamland Aqua Park

Location → 17km North of UAQ on RAK Rd · UAQ | 06 768 1888
Hours → 10:00 - 20:00
Web/email → www.dreamlanduae.com   Map Ref → UAE-C1

Dreamland Aqua Park brings you the excitement of four million gallons of fresh water and over 60 acres of intense fun! Easily accessible from Dubai and Sharjah, and with 25 aquatic and non-aquatic attractions, Dreamland is one of the largest aqua parks in the world – a truly unique experience for any resident or visitor to the Middle East.

Dreamland combines the best water rides with lush green lawns, which are pleasant places to relax. Alternatively, visit the amusement centre or the 400 metre go-kart track (available without a Dreamland pass). All the excitement may make you hungry ... food stalls and restaurants offer a variety of cuisine; you can even relax and cool down at the jacuzzi bar.

Entrance fees: A visit here is excellent value for money; adults Dhs.40; children Dhs.20.

Opening hours: change according to the season. Fri and public holidays are for families, season pass holders or pre-booked groups only.

SplashLand

Location → WonderLand · Umm Hurair | 324 1222
Hours → 10:00 - 20:00 Closed Sun
Web/email → wonderld@emirates.net.ae   Map Ref → 14-A3

Enter the water filled world of SplashLand, part of the WonderLand Theme & Water Park experience. Try any of the nine water rides, relax by the pool and sunbathe or eat at one of the restaurants. Rides include 'lazy river' (relax on an inner tube on a meandering river), 'shoot the rapids' (slide down a 35 foot ramp on a sled and skip across the water like a pebble), or try the 'speed slides', 'surf hill' and 'twister'. There's an adult swimming pool and a children's activity pool, with slides, bridges and water cannons.

Lockers and changing rooms are available. Various memberships are available for SplashLand only,

the theme park only, or both areas.

See also: WonderLand Theme & Water Park [p.298].

Timings: change seasonally, so check to avoid disappointment. Wed ladies day (boys under 1.25 metres); Thu families and schools.

Wild Wadi Water Park

Location → Wild Wadi · Umm Suqeim | 348 4444
Hours → 11:00 - 21:00
Web/email → www.wildwadi.com   Map Ref → 4-A2

Wonderfully named, Wild Wadi is one of the world's most advanced water adventure theme parks. The park is created around the adventures of Juha, a mythical friend of Sinbad. Spread over 12 acres it offers a variety of water rides, including Jumeirah Sceirah (the tallest and fastest free fall slide outside North America), where speeds of up to 80 km per hour are possible!

For pure relaxation, Juha's Journey allows you to float serenely through a changing landscape, while younger visitors can enjoy Juha's Dhow and Lagoon. For the young and young at heart, this stunning park offers a day of unforgettable fun.

Entrance fees: adults Dhs.99; children Dhs.80.

Lifeguards patrol all water areas and rides are regulated by height restrictions for those under 1.1 metres. To safeguard your wallet, you are given a wrist credit card – what you don't spend is refunded when you leave.

Water Skiing

Other options → Beach Clubs [p.268]
Jet Skiing [p.250]
Wake Boarding [p.264]

Club Joumana

Location → Jebel Ali Htl · Jebel Ali | 804 8058
Hours → 06:30 - 22:00
Web/email → www.jebelalihotel.com   Map Ref → 1-A1

Located on the hotel's beautiful sandy beach and part of Club Joumana, the Aqua Hut offers several types of water sports, from motorised activities such as water skiing (try regular water skis, mono skis, wakeboards or kneeboards) and banana boat rides, to non-motorised windsurfing, catamaran and laser sailing and kayaking. Water skiing costs Dhs.80 for half an hour, with lessons an extra Dhs.40. An additional Dhs.80 entrance fee is charged to the club for non-residents of the hotel.

Sports

Activities

Dubai Water Sports Association

Location ➜ Jadaf · End of Dubai Creek | 324 1031
Hours ➜ 08:00 - 01:00
Web/email ➜ dwsa@emirates.net.ae   Map Ref ➜ n/a

Set along Dubai's Creek, Dubai Water Sports Association is devoted to the promotion of water sports: primarily water skiing and wakeboarding. The association has two tournament ski boats, a slalom course and a full sized jump for hire. The club organises occasional wakeboarding competitions for all levels of ability.

Clubhouse facilities include a lawn with sun loungers, swimming pool, children's playground, barbecue area and jacuzzi. The clubhouse is the site for some very good parties. There's no skiing on Sundays, but the club is still open. Monday is for kids coaching from 3:30pm until dusk.

> *Costs: Yearly and monthly memberships are available and annual members receive a discount on the ski tow. Daily entrance fees for non-members; Dhs.15 weekdays; Dhs.25 Fri and public holidays (free entrance on the first visit). Ski tow Dhs.45 for 10 - 15 minutes for non-members.*

Pavilion Marina & Sports Club

Location ➜ Jumeirah Beach Htl · Umm Suqeim | 406 8800
Hours ➜ 06:30 - 22:30
Web/email ➜ www.jumeirahinternational.com   Map Ref ➜ 4-B2

Water skiing is one of the many water sports available here and the best time to learn is early morning, when the sea is at its calmest. All levels, sizes and ages are catered for when it comes to skiing and lessons are given to those wanting to learn or to improve on their technique. Specialist water skis are used for different abilities, including combos and slalom monos.

Other activities available for those wishing to try some of water skiings 'cousin' sports include wakeboarding and kneeboarding – again, lessons are available.

> *Prices: members water skiing, wakeboarding or kneeboarding Dhs.65 per 15 minutes; day visitors Dhs.75 per 15 minutes. For more details contact Sean harrison on 050 659 3875.*

Windsurfing

Other options ➜ Beach Clubs [p.268]

Fun Sports

Location ➜ Various locations, see below | 399 5976
Hours ➜ 09:00 - 17:00
Web/email ➜ funsport@emirates.net.ae   Map Ref ➜ n/a

Fun Sports is one of the leading water sports companies in Dubai - for information, refer to their review under Fishing.

BEACH, HEALTH & SPORTS CLUBS

Keep fit fans should have no problem finding facilities that suit them among Dubai's excellent range of health clubs, beach clubs and sports facilities. To help distinguish among the various types of facilities available, we have categorised them as follows:

- Health clubs generally offer workout facilities: machines, weights etc, plus classes varying from aerobics to yoga
- Beach clubs are similar to health clubs, but with the added bonus of beach access
- Sports clubs have similar facilities to health clubs, and also offer additional activities such as swimming, tennis, squash and/or golf

Neighbourhood gyms also exist in Dubai. Many of these are filled with 'serious' workout fanatics (mostly beefy men) and the facilities tend to be older and dated. Prices, however, are generally a fraction of health club membership fees.

Refer to the Club Facilities table on [p.277] for full details on the various clubs in Dubai including their membership rates and all amenities offered.

Sun soakers

Beach, Health & Sports Clubs

Activities

You haven't seen Dubai until you've explored Wild Wadi.

f you're looking for fun in Dubai, the Wild Wadi Water Park is it! Welcome to
2 acres devoted to pure exhilaration, with 23 exciting rides to thrill
and delight the whole family. Come once and you're sure to
come again, because... **you just can't get enough!**

Wild Wadi is located between Burj Al Arab and The Jumeirah
Beach Hotel. Telephone: +971 4 348 4444 www.wildwadi.com

WATER PARK
DUBAI

Beach Clubs

Other options → Health Clubs [p.270]

Caracalla Spa & Health Club

Location → Le Royal Meridien · Al Sufouh |399 5555
Hours → 08:00 - 22:00
Web/email → www.leroyalmeridien-dubai.com   Map Ref → 2-E2

This club offers a comprehensive health and beach package for the family. Different levels of membership include different facilities: Gold is for the full club and includes the use of the pool and beach; while Silver is for fitness and includes the gym, sauna, steam room, jacuzzi, hammam pools, tennis and squash courts. The gym offers a good range of cardio and weight machines.

The extensive beachfront and lawn area are covered with shady palm trees with space for activities such as beach volleyball and soccer, the children's club and the water sports centre. The large undulating pool has a swim-up bar with waiter service.

Entrance fees: non-members are charged Dhs.150 (off peak), for use of the pool and beach only.

Club Joumana

Location → Jebel Ali Htl · Jebel Ali |804 8058
Hours → 06:30 - 22:00
Web/email → www.jebelalihotel.com   Map Ref → 1-A1

Drive slowly through the luxurious hotel grounds on your way to this beach and health club with a few 'distinct advantages'. In addition to the gym, jacuzzi, sauna, squash and tennis courts, and numerous other sporting facilities, membership allows access to the hotel's beautiful private beach and discounts at many of the food and beverage outlets. Members can also enjoy access to two freshwater pools with swim-up bars, a seawater and a children's pool. The Resort Golf Course is a 9-hole par 36 course, which offers extensive practice facilities and lessons at the golf academy. Mooring fees in the resort's private marina allows use of all facilities.

Entrance fee: Dhs.80, contact the club for full membership details. Located about 30 minutes drive from Dubai.

Club Mina

Location → Le Meridien Mina · Al Sufouh |318 1901
Hours → 07:00 - 21:00
Web/email → club@lemeridien-minasiyahi.com   Map Ref → 3-A2

Set in beautifully green, split level gardens, Club Mina is an excellent facility offering the requisite swimming pools, long white sandy beach, children's play area and plenty of space to stretch out and enjoy the atmosphere.

For the energetic, there are a variety of activities (tennis, water skiing, volleyball, sailing, etc). Alternatively, if you're in relaxation mode, Club Mina offers a host of bars and outdoor dining areas, so you can sit back on the beach with your favourite beverage, enjoy a poolside shisha or have lunch without bothering to put your shoes on. Individually, the facilities are excellent, but together they create a vacation like atmosphere, which makes for an excellent getaway.

Club Mina also hosts international powerboat racing championships, exhibitions and concerts.

Dubai Marine Leisure Club

Location → Opp Jumeira Mosque · Beach Rd, Jumeira |346 1111
Hours → 07:00 - 22:00
Web/email → www.dxbmarine.com   Map Ref → 6-D2

This all-inclusive complex has been popular for years. Most people know it from the many restaurants located on the premises, but only members and resort guests get to enjoy all that it has to offer. The private beach offers plenty of water sports opportunities. There are also two pools (one with a waterfall) with lounge chairs and bar service. Sports options include tennis, squash, beach volleyball, basketball and table tennis, while for personal fitness, there's a gym, aerobics studio and spinning centre. You can enjoy a steam bath or a trip to the spa to relax after a day of activities. The beautiful landscaping makes this a great getaway in the heart of Dubai.

Hiltonia Health & Beach Club

Location → Hilton Dubai Jumeirah · Al Sufouh |318 2227
Hours → 07:00 - 22:00
Web/email → dbd_jumeirah@hilton.com   Map Ref → 2-D2

You'll enjoy sun, sea, fine white sand and swaying palms at this Jumeira location. The possibilities for

Beach, Health & Sports Clubs

Activities

leisure are seemingly endless; choose from relaxing in the pool or exotic gardens, a wide range of water sports, the gym or the luxurious health club.

Jumeirah Beach Club

Location ➜ Jumeirah Beach Club, The · Jumeira
Hours ➜ 08:00 Sat & Wed
Web/email ➜ www.jumeirahbeachclub.com
| 344 5333
Map Ref ➜ 5-D1

Perhaps the most notable feature of this exclusive club is its spectacular landscaping; wind your way through tropical gardens to reach the many amenities membership offers. The beautiful beachfront is well kept, and there's a very large pool with an island in the middle. You can enjoy a beverage from the bar while soaking up the sun next to the pool or on the beach. For sporty types, there are many fitness options – the health club has a decent variety of muscle-toning equipment and cardio machines, and tennis, squash and basketball courts can also be booked. Fitness and sports lessons, along with special programmes for children are all available at this garden oasis.

Jumeirah Health & Beach Club, The

Location ➜ Sheraton Jumeirah Beach · Al Sufouh
Hours ➜ 07:00 - 22:00
Web/email ➜ sherjum@emirates.net.ae
| 399 5533
Map Ref ➜ 2-D2

Open to all, this beach club offers a range of facilities, including a beautifully kept lawn, pool and a fine sandy beach. A lifeguard is on duty.

The gym is equipped with treadmills, bicycles, rowing machines, steppers and a good selection of Cybex training equipment. Also available are a sauna, steam room, massage and beauty salon with hairdresser. Other facilities include two squash courts, two floodlit tennis courts, volleyball, water sports and a temperature controlled pool, with pool bar. In addition to a small children's play area, there's the Pirates Club, which offers weekly entertainment programmes.

Every Friday visitors can use all the facilities (except the gym) for Dhs.50 per person, which includes a light lunch.

Timings: beach 08:00 - 19:00; pool 07:00 - 19:00. Weekends and public holidays 07:00 - 20:00.

Metropolitan Resort & Beach Club

Location ➜ Metropolitan Resort · Al Sufouh
Hours ➜ 08:30 - 20:00 Gym 08:30 - 22:00
Web/email ➜ www.methotels.com
| 399 5000
Map Ref ➜ 2-E2

Sun, sand and sea! This beach club exudes a holiday feeling that is relaxed to an almost sleepy extreme, which is reflected in its facilities. The sports amenities of gym and tennis courts are basic additions to the main attractions of pool and beach!

The huge mushroom-shaped swimming pool with swim-up bar complements the pretty stretch of beach for sunbathing. Water sports, such as jet skiing, water skiing, windsurfing and charter fishing are run by Fun Sports and are available at an additional cost. This family/holidaymaker beach club offers a refreshingly mellow and laid back environment in which to relax. On Fridays there's a buffet.

Entrance fees: non-members Dhs.100 per adult, Dhs.50 per child.

Oasis Beach Club

Location ➜ Oasis Beach Hotel · Al Sufouh
Hours ➜ 09:00 - 19:30
Web/email ➜ www.jebelali-international.com
| 315 4029
Map Ref ➜ 2-D2

A lively, younger crowd seems to descend on this beach club, mainly to enjoy the large swimming pool complete with swim-up bar, outdoor heated jacuzzi, the beach and the Coco Cabana beach bar and restaurant. Plenty of grassy areas, loungers and umbrellas allow space to relax. Other facilities include a kids pool, gym, steam bath and sauna, outside floodlit tennis court, archery, pétanque, beach volleyball and soccer court, while water sports include water skiing, ringo and banana rides, catamarans, snorkelling and much more.

Daily entrance rates are very reasonable for a beach hotel, as are the annual membership rates, making the Oasis Beach Club definitely worth a visit.

Entrance fee: Dhs.60 weekdays; Dhs.80 on Fri and public holidays.

Pavilion Marina & Sports Club

Location ➜ Jumeirah Beach Htl · Umm Suqeim
Hours ➜ 06:30 - 22:30
Web/email ➜ www.jumeirahinternational.com
| 406 8800
Map Ref ➜ 4-B2

Outstanding facilities and very competent staff set this club ahead of many others in Dubai. It's

Beach, Health & Sports Clubs

Activities

also one of the best options for families. There are three pools; a lap pool, a shallower family pool and a large leisure pool with sunken bar, all set in beautiful surroundings. Sports include tennis, squash, golf and loads of water activities at the private beach. The gym has top-notch equipment, and lots of it! Cardio machine users can enjoy the audio/video system, or simply take in the lovely view of the Gulf. The unisex spa has three hot tubs, jacuzzi, plunge pool, two saunas (scented with eucalyptus or sandalwood) and steam. These, and many other amenities, make this place truly worth the money.

Aviation Club

Ritz-Carlton Beach Club

Location ➜ Ritz-Carlton Dubai · Al Sufouh |399 4000
Hours ➜ 06:00 - 22:00
Web/email ➜ www.ritzcarlton.com   Map Ref ➜ 2-E2

The Spanish hacienda style of the hotel is a perfect backdrop to the classy beach and health facilities at the Ritz-Carlton. Three swimming pools lie hidden between curving walkways and abundant foliage. None of the pools are ideal for serious length swimming, but a large kids water slide is popular (too bad adults aren't allowed to use it!). If the pool isn't your scene, then relax on the large beach or enjoy the range of water sports.

The leisure facilities are extensive and excellently maintained by a team of friendly staff (facilities include tennis, squash, aerobics studio, state-of-the-art gym and a Ritz-Carlton Kids Club). Changing facilities are shared with the spa, so

visitors also have access to the sauna, jacuzzi and steam room.

Health Clubs

Other options ➜ Beach Clubs [p.268]
Sports Clubs [p.279]
Sporting Goods [p.206]
Annual Events [p.48]

Al Nasr Fitness Centre

Location ➜ Al Nasr Leisureland · Oud Metha |337 1234
Hours ➜ 09:00 - 22:00
Web/email ➜ alnasrll@emirates.net.ae   Map Ref ➜ 10-E4

This huge leisure and sports complex houses a great variety of activities for the whole family. Kids will love the children's pool with a boat in the middle, and the regular pool is huge with a really cool water slide! However, the fitness centre is rather basic. Consisting mainly of a few multi-resistance machines, small bikes, treadmills and some free weights, the gyms (separate for men and women) aren't the major attraction here. However, if you do want to get some exercise, swim, bowl, ice skate, play tennis, squash or video games all at the same venue, this is the place for it.

Aviation Club, The

Location ➜ Nr Tennis Stadium · Al Garhoud |282 4122
Hours ➜ 06:00 - 23:00
Web/email ➜ www.aviationclubonline.com   Map Ref ➜ 14-C3

This popular venue offers pretty much everything possible for a health and sports club. There's a par 3 golf course, tennis, squash and basketball courts, volleyball, plus a reasonable sized pool with lots of loungers. Overlooking the pool, the glassed-in gym is equipped with everything needed for a great workout. There are also loads of fitness classes.

The locker rooms are impressive: the steam room and plunge pool are quite big, as is the sauna which even has a TV in it (one of many at the club). There's a healthy café, bars and restaurants for re-energising or relaxing after indulging in all that activity. Membership also includes many event discounts.

Beach, Health & Sports Clubs

Activities

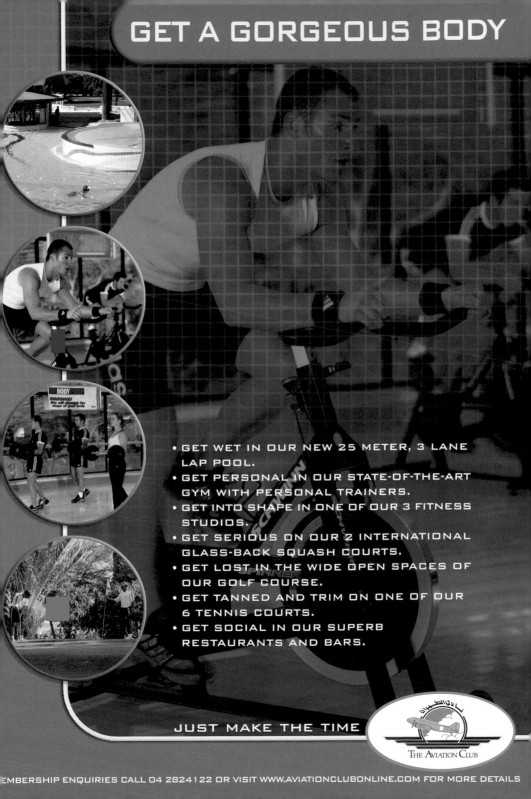

Ayoma Health Club

Location ➜ Taj Palace Hotel · Deira
Hours ➜ 07:00 - 24:00
Web/email ➜ www.tajpalacehotel.co.ae

223 2222

Map Ref ➜ 11-D2

Located in the new and attractive Taj Palace Hotel in downtown Deira, Ayoma is a smallish but adequate health club with reasonable membership rates. Split between two rooms, the workout facilities have equipment for most major muscle groups. Watch the latest videos on MTV while running on the treadmill in a room with stylish dim lighting. Outside, the kidney-shaped pool provides a chance to cool off on hot Dubai afternoons, or you can soak in the jacuzzi to relax those tired muscles. The locker rooms have a small sauna and steam, and the whole place is pleasant and well kept.

Big Apple, The

Location ➜ Emirates Towers · Shk Zayed Rd
Hours ➜ 06:00 - 22:00
Web/email ➜ www.jumeirahinternational.com

319 8661

Map Ref ➜ 9-C2

This club offers no-nonsense workout facilities at a reasonable price. It does not, however, have some of the amenities that other clubs offer (for example, no sauna, steam room, or swimming pool, although from January 2003 annual membership should include use of the Emirates Towers Hotel pool facilities). There are Nautilus resistance machines, a good free weights area and loads of cardiovascular machines in a big open setting. The cardio area has TVs (personal headphones are available), or you can enjoy the latest dance music from the PA system. A separate room hosts a variety of exercise classes, such as spin, varied impact aerobics, step and boxing.

Body Connection Health & Fitness Club

Location ➜ Rydges Plaza Hotel · Al Satwa
Hours ➜ 06:00 - 23:00
Web/email ➜ www.rydges.com.au

398 2222

Map Ref ➜ 7-A4

Compact but adequate, this fitness venue is good for those who want to exercise in relative solitude. The limited Nautilus equipment targets most major muscle groups and there are also a few cardio machines and some free weights to give a well-rounded workout. The gym overlooks the pool and jacuzzi (use of which is included in the membership), and the surrounding seating area is perfect for relaxing with a beverage. The changing facilities offer a small sauna and steam room, and massage services can be booked.

Bodylines

Location ➜ Towers Rotana Hotel · Shk Zayed Rd
Hours ➜ 07:00 - 22:00
Web/email ➜ towers.hotel@rotana.com

343 8000

Map Ref ➜ 9-B2

Located on top of the garage, this club is small but has enough equipment for a decent workout (free weights, cardio and Life Fitness resistance machines). There's also a studio where you can participate in various fitness classes, including self-defence. The locker rooms are clean and have a sauna and steam, and the flower-shaped pool (not really for laps) with attached jacuzzi is good for lounging. There's also a snack bar in case you want

The Big Apple

to munch while getting some sun. The pool area can be rented out for private parties. It's a bit pricey, with discounts offered for Emirates Airline employees.

Bodylines Jumeira

Location → Jumeira Rotana Hotel · Al Satwa | **345 5888**
Hours → 07:00 - 22:00
Web/email → jumhotel@emirates.net.ae   Map Ref → 6-E3

Although memberships are available at this fitness club, it's better suited to hotel guests who don't have to pay extra. Facilities are basically two Vectra machines, a treadmill and an exercise bike, plus a two seater sauna in the locker room –membership fees are fairly steep for what's offered. The rooftop pool is not for laps, but with the surrounding seating area overlooking Satwa is a pleasant spot. You can also play table tennis after taking a dip.

Bodylines Leisure & Fitness Club

Location → Al Bustan Hotel · Al Garhoud | **282 0000**
Hours → 07:00 - 22:00
Web/email → bustnhtl@emirates.net.ae   Map Ref → 14-E3

This is yet another quality fitness centre located in Deira. The gym is fully equipped with Nautilus resistance machines, as well as cardio machines and free weights, and a good variety of aerobics classes are held. Sports options include basketball (single-basket), squash, floodlit tennis courts and table tennis. The hexagonal pool looks cool, but it's probably better for lounging in or around than for swimming laps. A snack and beverage service is available from the pool bar. Relaxation can be had in the sauna, steam and jacuzzi in the locker rooms. Children are welcome and can enjoy their own pool or supervised play area.

Club Olympus

Location → Hyatt Regency · Deira | **209 6802**
Hours → 07:00 - 23:00
Web/email → clubolympus@hytdubai.co.ae   Map Ref → 8-D2

Members here have a full range of fitness options. This is one of the few facilities in town with a circuit track (circling the tennis courts, and fairly small) for those who want a break from the treadmill. There are also squash courts, table tennis, aerobics, and of course a fully-equipped Nautilus gym. The pool

is small for laps, but the surrounding deck is perfect for getting some sun and fresh air while having a snack or beverage. Other relaxation opportunities include a jacuzzi, steam room, sauna (with TV) and plunge pool.

Cardio Equipment

Club, The

Location → Dubai Wrld Trade Ctr Apts · Shk Zayed Rd | **306 5050**
Hours → 07:00 - 23:00
Web/email → info@dwtc.com   Map Ref → 9-D2

A veritable oasis among the buildings and bustle of Sheikh Zayed Road, this place has something for everyone! Racquet sports... got 'em – four tennis courts and three squash courts. Swimming... yep, a pool for laps and a kiddie pool with playground area. Want to play other games... try basketball, indoor soccer, table tennis, or billiards. While for fitness, there's a complete gym with free weights, resistance and cardio machines, and the aerobics studio has fitness and martial arts classes. You can make a day or evening of it by visiting the restaurant, lounge bar or banquet hall. All of this is available in attractively landscaped surroundings.

Creek Health Club, The

Location → Sheraton Hotel & Towers · Creekside, Deira | **207 1711**
Hours → 07:00 - 22:00
Web/email → sheradxb@emirates.net.ae   Map Ref → 11-C1

The facilities here are limited and would probably be more attractive to hotel guests than outside

Beach, Health & Sports Clubs

Activities

members, but there is some variety. There's a big Nautilus multi-machine, some free weights and a few cardio machines. The triangular pool looks good, although lap swimming is not really an option. There's one tennis court and a ping-pong table. The locker rooms have a small steam room and sauna, and you can relax and have a snack in the lounge area or on the pool deck.

Dimension Health & Fitness Club

Location ➜ Metropolitan Hotel · Jct 2, Shk Zayed Rd |407 6704
Hours ➜ 06:00 - 24:00
Web/email ➜ methotel@emirates.net.ae   Map Ref ➜ 5-C4

Catering to hotel guests, apartment residents and members, this club offers excellent facilities for both exercise and leisure. The gym is packed with free weights and cardio machines, plus Nautilus equipment for every muscle in the body (there's even a neck machine). Upstairs there's a studio where a good variety of classes are held (aerobics, kickboxing, step, yoga), or use the punch bag or table tennis when classes aren't on. Membership also includes use of the large pool, complete with sunken pool bar, steam room, sauna or jacuzzi. Alternatively, pay extra for a Chinese massage or check out the treatments at the new Ayurvedic centre.

Fitness Planet

Location ➜ Al Hana Centre · Al Satwa |398 9030
Hours ➜ 06:00 - 23:00 Fri 16:30 - 22:00
Web/email ➜ fitnessplanet@hotmail.com   Map Ref ➜ 7-A4

Fitness Planet isn't just a fitness club, it's a fitness *scene* – very popular among trendy but serious workout buffs. The reasonable and flexible pricing scheme makes membership accessible to most, while qualified trainers can design a programme just for you. Equipment ranges from resistance machines to a well-stocked free weights area and multiple cardio machines to ensure that your fitness programme doesn't get too monotonous. You can also participate in one of the many fitness classes, enjoy a protein smoothie or indulge in the jacuzzi, steam or sauna facilities.

Opened in October 2002 on the same site, Fitness Planet Hers offers the same variety and quality of facilities as Fitness Planet, but is for ladies only: a great option for women who want to get in shape but prefer to do it only with other women.

Griffins Health Club

Location ➜ JW Marriott Hotel · Deira |607 7755
Hours ➜ 06:00 - 23:00
Web/email ➜ marriott@emirates.net.ae   Map Ref ➜ 12-A3

Griffins is a compact health club offering a range of facilities in attractive surroundings, supported by friendly staff. Facilities include Planet Cardio – a dimly lit room packed with STAR TRAC cardio equipment and TV screens. There's also a separate free and fixed weights gym, two squash courts and a fresh juice bar. Fitness classes are held in the main area and coaching is available for squash and swimming. Male and female changing rooms each have sauna, steam and jacuzzi.

The picturesque rooftop swimming pool is a great place to watch planes flying over from the nearby airport, although too short for serious length swimming. On winter evenings, the area is transformed into Awafi, an excellent outdoor Arabic restaurant (the pool can still be used).

Entrance fees: non-members: Sat - Wed Dhs.66; weekends Dhs.82.5.

Gym 2000

Location ➜ Creek Golf Club · Al Garhoud |295 6000
Hours ➜ 07:00 - 22:00
Web/email ➜ www.dubaigolf.com   Map Ref ➜ 14-C2

As befits its location, Gym 2000 is equipped with the latest hi-tech cardio machines, complemented by modular weight stations and free weights. It includes some unique equipment such as a skywalker and treadwall – a rotating climbing wall with varying speeds and slope angles. Personalised fitness programmes, including nutritional advice, can be arranged and these are very popular. Large, luxurious changing rooms are shared with the golfers. The spectacular swimming pool, set on a broad terrace, surrounded by greenery and with its own snack bar, is the perfect place to relax (swimming lessons are a recent addition to existing activities).

Health Club, The

Location ➜ Emirates Towers · Trade Center 1&2 |330 0000
Hours ➜ 06:00 - 22:00
Web/email ➜ www.emirates-towers-hotel.com   Map Ref ➜ 9-C2

This club is more expensive than many, but little extras make it seem worth the money. Friendly staff even come round during your workout with chilled towels to cool you off!

There's a good range of exercise equipment, including plenty of free weights, Nautilus and cardio machines. If you don't feel like using the gym, there's a full-length pool or relax in the jacuzzi or comfortable lounge chairs (food and beverages are available from excellent waiting staff). After your activities, hit the steam and sauna in the locker rooms. If you forget toiletries, don't worry, they've got it covered. So, for serious exercise or serious relaxation, this place is a good bet.

Hiltonia Fitness Centre

Location → World Trade Centre Hotel · | 306 1139
Hours → 07:00 - 22:00 Fri 09:00 - 18:00
Web/email → info@worldtradecentrehotel.com   Map Ref → 10-A2

The World Trade Centre Hotel has been around for a while, and so has the equipment in the gym. It's not bad, but it's not quite state-of-the-art either. However, you can get a workout at a reasonable price (Universal resistance machines, cardio machines, free weights). There's saunas in the locker rooms, and membership includes use of the pool (go early if you want to tan – the building blocks the afternoon sun). Some of their special packages include personal training and massage, and there are swimming lessons available from their Russian 'national champion'.

Hiltonia Health & Beach Club

Location → Hilton Dubai Jumeirah · Al Sufouh | 318 2227
Hours → 07:00 - 22:00
Web/email → dbd_jumeirah@hilton.com   Map Ref → 2-D2

For information on Hiltonia Health & Beach Club, refer to the review under Beach Clubs [p.268].

Inter-Fitness, Dubai

Location → Hotel Inter-Continental · Deira | 222 7171
Hours → 24 hrs
Web/email → dubai@interconti.com   Map Ref → 8-C4

There are numerous hotels in Deira, but surprisingly few of them have adequate health club facilities. Inter-Fitness is one of the better ones. The gym is a bit on the small side, but has a good range of cardio and Icarian resistance machines, along with free weights. Membership also includes use of the pool

(nice view) and the squash, tennis and basketball courts. Sports lessons are available. The spa facilities (sauna, steam, plunge pool) are located between the men's and women's changing rooms and are reserved for each at different times.

Kelly's Health & Fitness Centre

Location → Beh Al Kawakeb Bld, · Trade Center 1&2 | 343 4392
Hours → 08:00 - 21:30
Web/email → khfc@emirates.net.ae   Map Ref → 9-A2

Kelly's is a longstanding fitness establishment with everything you need for a good workout. It's not glamorous or polished (unlike some facilities in the area), but would appeal to the more serious trainer. Although it's not very big, it's packed full of Icarian and Schwinn equipment and lots of free-weights. The pool and locker room (with sauna) are shared by another Dubai institution, Henry Africa's (aka The Bunker), so opportunities for refreshments and socialising can be had. Membership rates are among the more reasonable in town making it good value.

Le Mirage Dubai

Location → Le Meridien Dubai · Al Garhoud | 702 2430
Hours → 06:00 - 22:00 Fri 08:00 - 21:00
Web/email → lemirage@le-meridien.dubai.com Map Ref → 14-E3

This comprehensive facility is open to members and hotel guests. There are two swimming pools – a quieter, less crowded one near the car park, and a more happening one inside the hotel courtyard (complete with sunken pool bar and jacuzzi). Racquet sports players can enjoy the squash and tennis courts, and lessons are available for swimming, tennis and squash.

The fitness facilities are separate and offer a cardio section with top-notch Life Fitness equipment, a good resistance machine area, free weights, aerobics, and a separate personal training room. Most of the prices are reasonable and there are also special children's facilities and activities.

Lifestyle Health Club

Location → Sofitel City Centre Hotel · Al Garhoud | 603 8825
Hours → 07:00 - 23:00 Fri 08:00 - 20:00
Web/email → jp@citycentre/sofitel.com   Map Ref → 14-D1

Here's an opportunity to combine serious shopping (at Deira City Centre Mall) with serious exercising.

Beach, Health & Sports Clubs

Activities

Club Membership Rates

Club Name	Location	Male	Female	Couple	Family	Non-Members (peak)
				Membership Rates		
Beach Clubs & Spas						
Caracalla Spa & Health Club	Le Royal Meridien Beach Resort & Spa	8,000	8,000	11,000	12,500	–
- Fitness only		4,800	4,800	6,000	12500	–
Club Joumana	Jebel Ali Hotel & Golf Resort	3,000	2,000	5,000	3,800	80
Club Mina	Le Meridien Mina Seyahi	5,000	5,000	8,000	8,000	–
Dubai Marine Beach Resort & Spa	Dubai Marine Beach Resort & Spa	3,800	3,000	4,500	6,750	–
Jumeirah Beach Club	Jumeirah Beach Club	7,750	7,750	10,500	12,800	150
Jumeira Health & Beach Club	Sheraton Jumeirah Beach Resort & Towers	4,800	4,800	6,500	On req.	–
Metropolitan Beach Club	Metropolitan Resort & Beach Club Htl	5,000	4,000	6,000	6,500	–
Oasis Beach Club	Oasis Beach Hotel	3,800	3,800	4,500	5,500	70
Pavilion Marina & Sports Club	Jumeirah Beach Hotel	7,000	7,000	9,200	10,800	200
Ritz-Carlton Health Club & Spa	Ritz-Carlton Dubai	10,700	10,700	13,500	16,000	–
Health Clubs						
Al Nasr Fitness Centre (m/f separate)	Al Nasr Leisureland	1,150	920	–	–	#1
Assawan Health Club	Burj Al Arab	On req.	On req.	On req.	On req.	–
Aviation Club	Aviation Club	5,000	3,750	6,500	7,500	–
Ayoma Health Club	Taj Palace Hotel	3,500	3,000	5,250	–	85
Big Apple, The	Emirates Towers Boulevard	2,200	2,200	3,900	–	20
Body Connection Health Club	Rydges Plaza Hotel	2,500	2,500	3,800	4,000	100/3x
Bodylines Jumeira	Jumeira Rotana Hotel	1,900	1,600	2,500	1,850	50
Bodylines Leisure & Fitness	Towers Rotana Hotel	2,800	2,300	3,800	4,300	55
Bodylines Leisure & Fitness	Al Bustan Rotana Hotel	3,250	2,750	4,250	4,750	75
Club Olympus - Peak	Hyatt Regency Hotel	3,500	2,000	4,200	On req.	60
- Off peak		2,000	1,200	2,500	–	50
Club, The	Dubai International Hotel Apartments	3,500	3,000	4,500	5,700	35
Creek Health Club	Sheraton Dubai Hotel & Towers	2,500	2,500	3,400	4,500	50
Dimensions Health & Fitness Center	Metropolitan Hotel	2,400	2,000	3,500	4,000	55
Fitness Centre	World Trade Centre Hotel	2,100	2,100	3,000	–	25
Fitness Planet (mixed & ladies)	Al Hana Centre	2,350	2,350	–	–	30
Griffins Health Club - Peak	JW Marriott Hotel	3,575	2,530	5,060	On req.	83
- Off peak		2,200	1,540	3,025	On req.	88
Gym 2000 (9 months)	Dubai Creek Golf & Yacht Club	2,000	2,000	2,750	3,750	70
Health Club, The	Emirates Towers Hotel	4,000	4,000	6,500	On req.	100
Hiltonia Health Club	Hilton Dubai Jumeirah	4,500	4,500	6,000		
Inter Fitness Dubai	Hotel Inter-Continental Dubai	4,300	3,500	5,800	9,800	50
Kelly's Health & Fitness	Behind Al Kawakeb Residence	1,600	1,600	2,750	–	100/3x
Le Mirage Dubai - Gold	Le Meridien Dubai	4,750	3,600	6,250	7,250	100
- Silver		3,400	2,900	4,600	6,600	100
Lifestyle Health Club	City Centre Residence	2,600	2,600	4,160	4,160	50
Nautilus Academy	Al Mussalla Towers	3,000	2,500	5,000	–	40
Nautilus Fitness Centre	Crowne Plaza	3,200	3,200	4,600	On req.	50
Nautilus Health Centre	Metropolitan Palace Hotel	3,750	2,750	5,000	–	–
Pharoahs (mixed & ladies)	Pyramids	5,500	5,500	8,000	10,000	60
Platinum Club	Atrium Suites	3,000	3,000	4,100	–	–
Willow Stream	Fairmont Hotel	4,500	4,500	7,500	–	150
Golf & Sports Clubs						
Dubai Country Club		3,350	2,200	–	5,350	60
Dubai Creek Golf & Yacht Club		4,500	4,500	6,500	6,500	–
Emirates Golf Club		13,000	10,000	On Req.	17,500	–
Nad Al Sheba Club		*1	*1	*2	*3	–

KEY #1 10 + fees *1 500-11,000 *2 Spouse 50% *3 Juniors Available

Club Facilities

Club Name	Gym						Activity				Relaxation				
	Treadmills	Exercise bikes	Step machines	Rowing machines	Free weights	Resistance machines	Tennis courts	Swimming Pool	Squash courts	Aerobics/Dance Exercise	Massage	Sauna	Jacuzzi	Plunge pool	Steam room
Beach Clubs & Spas															
Caracalla Spa & Health Club	8	6	6	3	✔	16	4FL	✔	2	✔	✔	✔	✔	✔	✔
- Fitness only	8	6	6	3	✔	16	4FL	–	–	–	–	✔	✔	–	–
Club Joumana	1	1	1	1	✔	✔	4FL	✔	2	–	✔	✔	✔	–	✔
Club Mina	8	3	1	1	✔	18	4FL	✔	–	–	✔	✔	✔	✔	✔
Dubai Marine Beach Resort & Spa	5	5	2	1	✔	13	2FL	✔	✔	✔	✔	✔	–	–	✔
Jumeirah Beach Club	8	9	3	2	✔	12	7FL	✔	3	✔	✔	✔	✔	✔	✔
Jumeira Health & Beach Club	3	4	3	2	✔	11	2FL	✔	2	✔	✔	✔	✔	–	✔
Metropolitan Beach Club	3	2	1	1	✔	✔	3FL	✔	2	✔	✔	✔	✔	✔	✔
Oasis Beach Club	2	2	1	1	✔	✔	1FL	✔	–	–	✔	✔	✔	✔	–
Pavilion Marina & Sports Club	9	8	2	3	✔	23	7FL	✔	3	✔	✔	✔	✔	✔	✔
Ritz-Carlton Health Club & Spa	5	7	2	1	✔	9	4FL	✔	2	✔	✔	✔	✔	✔	✔
Health Clubs															
Al Nasr Fitness Centre (m/f separate)	4	5	–	–	✔	4	✔	✔	✔	–	✔	✔	–	–	–
Assawan Health Club	5	8	3	2	✔	15	–	✔	1	✔	✔	✔	✔	✔	✔
Aviation Club	7	4	3	2	✔	14	6FL	✔	2	✔	✔	✔	✔	✔	✔
Ayoma Health Club	5	3	–	1	✔	7	–	✔	–	–	✔	✔	✔	✔	–
Big Apple, The	8	3	4	2	✔	11	–	✔	–	✔	–	✔	–	–	✔
Body Connection Health Club	2	2	2	2	✔	9	–	✔	–	✔	✔	✔	✔	✔	✔
Bodylines Jumeira	1	1	–	–	✔	2	–	✔	1	–	✔	✔	✔	–	✔
Bodylines Leisure & Fitness (Rotana)	2	1	2	–	✔	6	–	✔	–	–	✔	✔	✔	–	✔
Bodylines Leisure & Fitness (Al Bustan)	6	6	2	2	✔	9	3	✔	2	✔	✔	✔	✔	✔	✔
Club Olympus - Peak	7	4	2	2	✔	10	3	✔	2	✔	✔	✔	✔	✔	✔
- Off peak	–	–	–	–	–	–	–	–	–	–	–	–	–	–	–
Club, The	6	3	3	2	✔	12	4FL	✔	3	✔	–	✔	✔	✔	–
Creek Health Club	2	2	2	–	✔	1	1	✔	–	✔	✔	✔	✔	–	✔
Dimensions Health & Fitness Center	6	4	4	2	✔	19	1	✔	–	✔	✔	✔	✔	✔	✔
Fitness Centre	5	6	4	4	✔	10	–	✔	1	–	✔	✔	–	–	✔
Fitness Planet (mixed & ladies)	7	7	5	2	✔	25	–	–	–	✔	✔	✔	✔	✔	✔
Griffins Health Club - Peak	7	6	4	2	✔	✔	–	✔	2	✔	✔	✔	✔	✔	✔
- Off peak	–	–	–	–	✔	–	–	–	–	–	–	–	–	–	–
Gym 2000	4	3	2	3	✔	13	7 FL	✔	3	✔	✔	✔	✔	✔	✔
Health Club, The	8	3	2	2	✔	11	–	✔	–	–	✔	✔	✔	✔	✔
Hiltonia Health Club	4	2	2		✔	2	–	✔	–	–	✔	✔	✔	✔	✔
Inter Fitness Dubai	5	3	2	2	✔	10	1FL	✔	2	✔	✔	✔	✔	✔	✔
Kelly's Health & Fitness	3	4	3	1	✔	11	–	✔	–	–	✔	✔	✔	✔	✔
Le Mirage Dubai - Gold	10	4	2	2	✔	22	5FL	✔	2	✔	✔	✔	✔	✔	✔
- Silver	10	4	2	2	✔	22	–	✔	2	✔	✔	✔	✔	✔	✔
Lifestyle Health Club	4	5	2	1	✔	14	2FL	✔	2	✔	✔	✔	–	✔	✔
Nautilus Academy	16	12	12	6	✔	40	–	✔	2	✔	✔	✔	✔	✔	✔
Nautilus Fitness Centre	3	3	1	2	✔	15	–	✔	2	✔	✔	✔	✔	✔	✔
Nautilus Health Centre	3	2	2	2	✔	13	–	✔	2	✔	–	✔	✔	✔	✔
Pharoahs (mixed & ladies)	7	8	4	2	✔	18	3	✔	2	✔	✔	✔	✔	✔	✔
Platinum Club	10	9	2	2	✔	36	–	✔	–	✔	✔	✔	✔	✔	✔
Willow Stream	5	4	2	2	✔	13	–	✔	–	✔	✔	✔	✔	✔	✔
Golf & Sports Clubs															
Dubai Country Club	4	3	2	2	✔	✔	7FL	✔	3	✔	✔	–	–	–	✔
Dubai Creek Golf & Yacht Club	4	3	2	2	✔	13	–	✔	–	–	✔	✔	✔	–	✔
Emirates Golf Club	3	2	2	2	✔	10	4	✔	2	✔	✔	–	–	–	–
Nad Al Sheba Club	–	–	–	–	–	–	–	–	–	–	–	–	–	–	–

Beach, Health & Sports Clubs

Activities

On the first floor of this three-level club, there's a bright seating area where you can relax and watch TV or sit out on the terrace. There are also two squash courts. Upstairs, there's a good gym with lots of free weights, cardio and resistance machines, plus a decent variety of exercise classes in the studio.

The locker rooms have both sauna and steam, and although the rooftop pool is too small for laps, it has a good view. Massage is offered and an on-site hair salon is available for ladies.

Nautilus Academy, The

Location → Al Mussalla Towers · Bank St, Bur Dubai | 397 4117
Hours → 06:00 - 23:00
Web/email → nautilus@unionproperties.com   Map Ref → 8-A4

This modern, high-energy facility is great for people who need motivational surroundings to get them going. The music, lighting, layout and atmosphere are such that even a couch potato extraordinaire would be moved to give it a try! The Nautilus and cardio machines are plentiful in number and variety, and there's a separate room for spinning and aerobics classes.

The staff are qualified to meet your personal training needs, but if working out isn't your thing, go for squash or swimming. The locker rooms are pleasant and relaxation can be had in the steam room, sauna, jacuzzi or café.

Nautilus Fitness Centre

Location → Crowne Plaza · Shk Zayed Rd | 331 4055
Hours → 07:30 - 22:00 Thu & Fri 09:00 - 20:30
Web/email → nscdxb@emirates.net.ae   Map Ref → 9-D2

As the name implies, this small but well-rounded facility focuses on Nautilus body training techniques. In addition, there are free weights, cardio machines and various aerobic classes to suit most fitness objectives.

The staff are friendly and helpful, and all the standard health club amenities are available – steam room, sauna, swimming pool and squash court. The pool is a little small for laps, but the deck offers a great view of Sheikh Zayed Road. The club's location is ideal for nearby residents or office workers.

Nautilus Health Centre

Location → Metropolitan Palace Hotel · Deira | 227 0000
Hours → 06:00 - 23:00
Web/email → metpalac@emirates.net.ae   Map Ref → 11-D2

This location is a reasonable option for those wishing to workout in Deira. The gym isn't huge, but it's complete. The resistance equipment is of course Nautilus, and there's also a selection of cardio machines and free weights. Members can lounge in the cross-shaped pool (a bit small for laps), sunbathe or have a snack and beverage from the deck bar. The locker rooms are equipped with a small sauna, steam and jacuzzi for relaxing after working out.

Pharaohs Club

Location → Pyramids · Umm Hurair | 324 0000
Hours → 07:00 - 22:00 Fri 09:00 - 21:00
Web/email → www.uae-climbing.com.   Map Ref → 13-D2

Complete luxury... that's what members of Pharaohs can experience. This club should appeal to those who are looking for more than simply a gym to work out in (although there are two excellent, well-equipped gyms; one is ladies-only). However, it's the other amenities that really set this place apart. Alongside squash and tennis courts, Pharaohs offers a gigantic pool with a sunken pool bar and a second pool with a river current to float down. Inside, the plush towels are perfect for wrapping up in while lounging in the dimly lit relaxation room. There are jacuzzis inside and out, and all of it is completed by lavish but tasteful décor and landscaping.

Platinum Health Club

Location → Atrium Suites · Hor Al Anz | 266 9990
Hours → 08:00 - 23:00 Thu 11:00 - 21:00 Fri 13:00 - 23:00
Web/email → getfit@emirates.net.ae   Map Ref → 12-C4

Tucked away on the mezzanine level of the Atrium Suites, the facilities here are well maintained, offering separate areas for men and women. The gym is reasonably spacious but not crowded, and the atmosphere is relaxed and quiet. For a cardio routine there are various bikes and step machines, while for toning there are a good selection of free weights and resistance machines. The locker rooms have a jacuzzi, steam, sauna and massage room.

Platinum has a wide range of additional amenities, such as an aerobics studio, juice bar, a play zone for kids, beauty salon, sports therapy, nutrition programmes, personal training, martial arts classes and babysitting.

Sports Clubs

Other options ➜ Beach Clubs [p.268]
Health Clubs [p.270]

Dubai Country Club

Location ➜ Nr Bu Kidra R/A · Al Awir Rd | 333 1155
Hours ➜ 08:00 - 24:00
Web/email ➜ www.dubaicountryclub.com   Map Ref ➜ 17-B3

If you're looking for a club that caters for all your family needs, Dubai Country Club is worth considering. Sports facilities are excellent with tennis and squash courts, a sand golf course and a fully equipped gym, while the noticeboards are full of clubs to interest all age groups and levels of fitness, from circuit training to aqua aerobics. There's a large pool area with plenty of sun loungers, plus shaded children's play areas. Other activities on offer include badminton, basketball, netball and football.

All activities are available to members, however, the two restaurants (the Windtower and the Oasis) and certain activities are open to all, provided advance notice is given. Entrance fees depend on the activity.

India Club

Location ➜ Nr, Indian High School · Oud Metha | 337 1112
Hours ➜ 06:00 - 24:00
Web/email ➜ www.indiaclubdubai.com   Map Ref ➜ 10-E4

Opened in 1964, this club currently has 6,500 members and its objective is to provide facilities for sports, entertainment and recreation, and to promote business.

Facilities include a gym, with a separate steam and sauna for men and women, badminton, squash and tennis courts, snooker, table tennis, basketball, a swimming pool, a variety of indoor games like hockey, volleyball and cricket, and a bowling alley. Coaching is available in all activities. The club regularly holds sports tournaments and there are frequent quiz nights, ladies evenings, children's parties, and so on. A new feature to be introduced shortly is an air conditioned children's play area. Food outlets include restaurants and a number of bars.

Toning Equipment

InSportz

Location ➜ Nr Gold & Diamond Park · Shk Zayed Rd | 347 5833
Hours ➜ 09:00 - 22:00
Web/email ➜ insportz@emirates.net.ae   Map Ref ➜ 4-C4

InSportz is Dubai's first indoor sports centre – it makes the idea of participating in sport all year a reality! Facilities include five multi-purpose playing courts, a cricket coaching net, changing rooms and cafeteria, all within the comfort of air conditioned surroundings. Sports available include cricket, football, basketball, tennis and fitness, and there's a complete coaching programme for juniors.

Individuals and teams can hire the courts, and various leagues and tournaments are held during the year. Prices start from Dhs.20 per person, inclusive of equipment. InSportz also caters for birthday parties, corporate events, event management, children's holiday sports programmes and summer camps. For further information, contact the above number or (347 0838).

Sharjah Wanderers Sports Club

Location ➜ Nr Sharjah English School · Sharjah | 06 566 2105
Hours ➜ 08:00 - 24:00
Web/email ➜ www.sharjahwanderers.com   Map Ref ➜ UAE-C2

This is an extremely popular and sociable club that's well used by the expat community in Sharjah, Dubai and the Northern Emirates. Facilities include floodlit tennis courts, squash courts, floodlit football, rugby and hockey pitches, a swimming

Beach, Health & Sports Clubs

Activities

pool, gym, library, snooker and a kids play area, as well as classes in aerobics and aqua aerobics. There's a good restaurant and the club holds regular social events, such as a twice monthly quiz night.

Sharjah Wanderers Golf Club is also part of the club and is located out of town on the Airport Road, near Sharjah National Park. Sharjah Diving Club (BSAC) uses the swimming pool for training and has its own on-site lecture facilities and compressor room.

LEISURE

Dubai's booming tourist trade combined with its vast and vibrant expat community make it a natural centre for abundant leisure activities. These can range from the gentle pampering of a beauty salon or health spa to a more energetic Pilates session, a relaxing day at a beach club, or a concert or play. You may even want to take the option of participating in a drama group, dance lessons, or chill to the core with a little meditation guidance. Whichever your leisure pleasure, there's a good chance someone in town is willing to provide it.

Beauty Salons

Other options → Beauty Training [p.286]
Perfumes & Cosmetics [p.204]

Beauty is big business in Dubai! There are a huge variety of salons to visit, offering every type of treatment imaginable. Shoppers can find a range of products including everything from Paul Bryan and Toni & Guy. Services ranging from Manicures, to pedicures. Waxing, to henna, to the latest cuts and styles. Salons here are really popular and busy at night specially for weddings and occassions/functions. As you would expect, the quality and range of treatments vary greatly, so trial and error or word of mouth is probably the best way of finding a good salon.

All Salons are filled with a multitude of cultures. Or, as some prefer, have the stylist come to your home. In the hotels you have female and male stylists but outside hotels you have only female stylists. Independent salons are good for privacy, men are not permitted inside and the windows are blocked out for those nosy pedestrians.

There are also numerous small salons aimed at Arabic ladies. In particular, they offer henna designs — look out for a decorated hand on the signboards in shop windows. The traditional practice of painting henna on the hands and feet, especially for weddings or special occasions, is still very popular with the national population. The intricate brown patterns fade after 2 - 3 weeks. For visitors to the emirates, a design on the ankle or shoulder can make a great memento of a visit here and costs only about Dhs.30.

Bridge

Country Club Bridge

Location → Country Club · Al Awir Rd	**331 8519**
Hours → see timings below	
Web/email → n/a	Map Ref → 17-B3

This group plays on the last Saturday of the month at Dubai Country Club and at a different location every Monday, from 20:00 - 23:00. You don't have to be a member of the club to play bridge here and newcomers are always welcome. For more information, contact Ann Wilkins on the above number.

Dubai Bridge Club

Location → Country Club · Al Awir Rd	**050 658 6985**
Hours → Mon 20:00 - 23:30	
Web/email → olavo786bridge@yahoo.com	Map Ref → 17-B3

Dubai Bridge Club was formed in 1977 with the main objective of promoting the game in the UAE. It has no clubhouse or premises and operates on a non-profit making basis, with committee members serving in an honorary capacity. The club has a multitude of nationalities, with members from the UAE, Poland, Iran, France, India, Syria and the UK, to name a few. Meetings are weekly and trophies are presented to the player of the month and the year. For more information contact Olavo D'Sousa on the above number or Sushil Amin (050 450 0926).

Dubai Ladies Bridge Club

Location → Nad al Sheba · Nad Al Sheba	**395 4070**
Hours → Sun and Wed 08:45 - 13:00	
Web/email → n/a	Map Ref → 17-A3

Ladies only bridge mornings are held at 9am on Sundays and Wednesdays at the Nad Al Sheba

Leisure

Activities

Dhs.100 ~ € 28

millennium stand. For further details, contact Marzie Polad or Jan Irvine (398 0727).

Chess

Other options → Scrabble [p.284]

Dubai Chess & Culture Club

Location → Nr Al Shabab Club · Hor Al Anz | 296 6664
Hours → 10:00 - 13:00 17:00 - 23:00 Fri 17:00 - 23:00
Web/email → www.dubaichess.com   Map Ref → 11-B3

As its name suggests, this club is involved in all aspects of chess and cultural programmes. Members can play chess at the club seven nights a week and competitions are organised on a regular basis. International competitions are also promoted, including the Dubai International Open and the Asian Cities Competition, attracting representatives from up to 41 cities across Asia.

During Ramadan and for National Day, special club events are organised. Members can also take classes with the professional chess school. Facilities at the club include an Internet room, cafeteria and a snooker/billiard room.

Costs: annual membership: Dhs.100 for nationals; Dhs.200 for expats.

Ramadan timings: 20:00 - 02:00.

Drama Groups

Dubai Drama Group

Location → Country Club · Al Awir Rd | 050 658 3981
Hours → Sat, Sun & Tue 20:00
Web/email → www.dubaidramagroup.org   Map Ref → 17-B3

To entertain is the raison d'être for the many members who take to the stage, sing and dance or help behind the scenes with lighting and sewing costumes. Annual membership costs Dhs.100, which entitles you to a monthly newsletter and a lot of hard work and fun. This amateur dramatic society stages four productions each year; a pantomime at Christmas and the other three can be anything from farce to thrillers and one act plays.

Everyone is welcome at rehearsals and they always need help in all areas of stagecraft. Meeting times vary, so contact Janet Yarsley for further information.

Health Spas

Other options → Health Clubs [p.270]
Massage [p.283]

Ayoma Spa

Location → Taj Palace Hotel · Deira | 223 2222
Hours → 10:00 - 22:00
Web/email → www.tajpalacehotel.co.ae   Map Ref → 11-D2

With a focus on Ayurvedic therapy and treatments, Ayoma Spa promises 'total relaxation of the mind, body and soul'. Warm, relaxing surroundings infused with subtle touches like low lighting and soothing aromas, plus a gentle, personalised service, ensure your visit will be memorable. A divine foot therapy at the start of your treatment sets the tone for the rest of your relaxing experience.

Facilities include separate saunas and steam rooms, swimming pool and jacuzzi. Recommended treatments include the Keraliya abhyanga, a traditional oil massage from South India, and the Ayoma abhyanga, Ayoma's signature herbal oil massage performed by two therapists – a unique and addictive experience.

Cleopatra's Spa

Location → Pyramids · Oud Metha | 324 7700
Hours → See timings below
Web/email → www.waficity.com   Map Ref → 13-D2

If you're looking for that extra special something and want to be pampered, then a visit to the magnificent Cleopatra's Spa is a must. The spa offers a range of exotic treatments, from facials to wraps and hydro baths to massages – check out the monthly treatment specials. It has separate areas for men and women and treatments are administered by qualified staff. Whether you are tired, overworked or simply looking for the ultimate 'pick me up', this place is sure to make you feel ready for anything!

Cleopatra's Spa also incorporates a specialised sports injury clinic for the treatment and prevention of sports injuries.

Timings: Female spa Sat - Thu 09:00 - 20:00, Fri 10:00 - 20:00; Male spa Mon - Sat 10:00 - 22:00, Sun 10:00 - 19:00.

Leisure

Activities

Dubai Marine Spa

Location → Dubai Marine Beach · Beach Rd, Jumeira | 346 1111
Hours → 10:00 - 17:00 Closed Fri
Web/email → www.dxbmarine.com   Map Ref → 6-D2

Opened in late 1998, this dimly lit spa specialises in Espa beauty products, with a selection of packages for both men and women. Treatments last from as little as ten minutes to a full day and are designed to combat the environmental, physical and mental stresses of modern living, as well as making you look and feel great.

Located on different levels in one of the villas of the resort, the spa has three qualified therapists and five treatment rooms. Programmes include facials, body treatments, reflexology and special treatments for men. For full-day programmes, a light lunch and use of the facilities at the resort are included.

Oxygen Parlour

Location → The Atrium Centre · Bur Dubai | 352 3500
Hours → 09:00 - 22:00 Fri 16:00 - 22:00
Web/email → www.unitedeuropeltd.com/o2world Map Ref → 8-A4

Catching up with the global trend of oxygen parlours, O2World has landed in Dubai. Offering aromatherapy and electronic massage as well, o2World suggests a minimum of two sessions per week, continuously for three months for 'optimum results'. 20 minutes of 95% pure oxygen along with aromatherapy is Dhs.60, while 15 minutes of electronic massage (body, leg or eye) is Dhs.15.

Willow Stream Spa

Their combined package of oxygen and aromatherapy and full electronic massage is Dhs.100 for 65 minutes of relaxation.

Ritz-Carlton Spa

Location → Ritz-Carlton Dubai · Al Sufouh | 399 4000
Hours → 06:00 - 22:00
Web/email → rcdubai@emirates.net.ae   Map Ref → 2-E2

This very busy spa reflects a Balinese theme throughout – from the treatments to the décor, with much of the wooden furniture and artwork coming from this Indonesian island.

The subterranean facilities include eight treatment rooms, a hair and beauty salon, jacuzzi, sauna, steam room and a ladies' gym, complete with toning tables. The most popular treatment – the Balinese massage – is luxury (tell your masseur how much or how little pressure you'd like). Treatments are deluxe, and this is reflected in the prices.

With easy access between the spa and the health and beach club, the Ritz's extensive facilities ensure that any visit will be one of exquisite pampering.

Royal Mirage Residence & Spa

Location → Royal Mirage Palace Hotel · Al Sufouh | 399 9999
Hours → 09:00 - 21:00
Web/email → www.royalmiragedubai.com   Map Ref → 3-A2

Scheduled to open in December 2002, the Royal Mirage promises an exclusive haven in which pampering is the predominant indulgence. The spa is architecturally impressive, with towering domes and intricate carved arches. It will offer a service dedicated to nurturing beauty and the pursuit of well being, while the traditional Oriental hammam will offer massage, steam baths and jacuzzis within a serene and restful area.

Royal Waters Health Spa

Location → Al Mamzar Centre · Deira | 297 2053
Hours → 09:00 - 17:00 Sat and Wed 17:00 - 00:00
Web/email → therwspa@emirates.net.ae   Map Ref → 12-C4

Opened in January 2002, this quiet spa offers a gym, rooftop swimming pool, café, sauna and steam, plus comprehensive inner and outer healing services for better health. The focus is on holistic healing and they pride themselves on being 'a

Leisure

Activities

haven of peace and tranquillity'. They offer different memberships and programmes, including everything from stress management to nutrition, reiki, Pilates, a range of spa and beauty treatments, and even a consultation with their in-house doctor.

Comfortzone products from Italy are used, along with Lillian Terry complexes – apparently the world's first mix of aromatherapy and homeopathy ingredients.

Timings: ladies 09:00 - 17:00; men 06:00 - 09:00 & 17:00 - 22:00.

Spa Thira

Location ➔ Opp Jumeira Beach Park · Jumeira | 344 2055
Hours ➔ 09:00 - 20:00 Thu 09:00 - 13:00   Closed Fri
Web/email ➔ spathira@yahoo.com   Map Ref ➔ 5-C2

The ultimate one stop beauty shop, Spa Thira is located in a beautifully converted double storey villa. Music filters through the rooms and a sense of peace and well being pervades.

A full range of beauty therapies are offered, with various facials, manicures, semi-permanent make-up and Chinese massage as a start, as well as a hair salon. The most outstanding treatment is the soft-light laser, for safe and lasting hair removal. The atmosphere is open and friendly and your every need is foreseen, including a simple snack menu and a fashion designer to create a new outfit! It's only open to women during normal hours, but men are welcome to make appointments outside these times.

Willow Stream Spa

Location ➔ Fairmont Hotel · Shk Zayed Rd | 332 5555
Hours ➔ 06:00 - 24:00
Web/email ➔ www.fairmont.com   Map Ref ➔ 9-E1

Only open a few months, this new addition to the Sheikh Zayed Road skyline houses quite a luxurious health club and spa. Decorated like a Roman bath, the club wraps around the hotel's light rectangular centre. On the east side, there's the sunrise pool and jacuzzi for morning types, while for afternoon sun, there's the sunset pool on the west side.

The sleek gym has state-of-the-art Technogym equipment and a good cardio area, but the free weights section is a little more limited. The spa areas are extremely relaxing, with cool foot pools, jacuzzi and steam. Fruit and juices are provided, but members can also visit the Sol Café for refreshments.

Massage

Other options ➔ Health Spas [p.281]
Health Clubs [p.270]

Probably the ultimate way to pamper and unwind is by having a massage. Whether it's a regular weekly treat or to get over a particularly trying time at work, it's sure to relax and soothe. Prices and standards vary, so shop around until you find someone that suits you. The cost for a full body massage ranges from Dhs.100 - 220 for one hour of heaven!

Massages, plus a variety of other treatments, are available at Dubai's excellent spas; for further details refer to [p.281].

Meditation & Reiki

Other options ➔ Alternative Therapies [p.98]

Reiki and meditation are excellent for creating a sense of calm and well being. While meditation can be performed at home with even only basic knowledge, reiki is a healing technique based on the belief that energy can be channelled into the patient by means of touch. Translated as 'universal life force energy', reiki can, like meditation, emotionally cleanse, physically invigorate and leave you more focused.

Archie Sharma Reiki

Location ➔ Al Garhoud Residential Area | 282 4468
Hours ➔ 10:00 - 17:00   Closed Fri
Web/email ➔ -   Map Ref ➔ 14-D4

Archie Sharma is a reiki master who has been practising for over six years and is involved in both teaching and healing. He also conducts Zen meditation, is a qualified herbalist and reflexologist and, when time permits, advises on feng shui, the Chinese art of placement.

Holistic Healing & Life Source Energy

Location ➔ Next to Al Wasl Park · Jumeira | 344 9880
Hours ➔ 09:00 - 18:00   Closed Fri
Web/email ➔ vaniola@hotmail.com   Map Ref ➔ 4-D3

Karen Meyer-Reumann is a counsellor, holistic healer and family display practitioner whose aim is to help you 'break your pattern'. With 27 years experience of meditation/monasteries, teaching meditation and being a 'zero point antenna',

Leisure

Activities

licensed to produce Life Source Energy products, she gives you the tools to lift your energy levels through healing, balancing emotion and mind, and allowing you to drop your limitations.

Pookat Suresh Reiki

Location → Various locations
Hours → 08:00 - 13:00 16:00 - 19:00   **285 9128**
Web/email → esbipookat@yahoo.com   Map Ref → n/a

Reiki is one of the simplest forms of natural healing, needing only one or two days to learn its main feature, which is to heal the self and others. The Pookat Suresh Reiki centre offers various degrees of attunement. In the first degree seminar, which also covers theoretical and practical aspects of reiki, a series of four attunements are given by a traditional master to channel a higher amount of universal life force energy. The second degree level teaches powerful absentee healing and the tremendous flexibility of reiki.

For further details, contact reiki master Pookat Suresh Babu (050 453 9643).

Pilates

Other options → Yoga [p.284]

House of Chi & House of Healing

Location → Musalla Towers · Bur Dubai
Hours → Closed Fri   **397 4446**
Web/email → www.hofchi.com   Map Ref → 8-A4

For information on House of Chi & House of Healing, refer to their review under Yoga [p.284].

Pilates Studio, The

Location → Nr Thunder Bowl, Shk Zayed Rd
Hours → 08:00 - 20:00 Thu 08:00 - 14:00 Closed Fri **343 8252**
Web/email → pilates@emirates.net.ae   Map Ref → 5-E3

Pilates is an effective and safe way to tone up and strengthen core muscles. The technique was developed over 70 years ago by German Joseph Pilates and it has since been refined and updated in the light of modern anatomical knowledge. Using over 500 controlled movements, it is a form of exercise for everyone – young, old, fit, not so slim, and especially those in rehabilitation (post illness or injury).

Pilates was introduced to the UAE in 1998 by Catherine Lehmann, a physiologist with many years experience of teaching the Pilates method. This studio opened in September 2000 and offers both mat and reformer classes for absolute beginners through to advanced.

Scrabble

Other options → Chess [p.281]

Dubai Scrabble League

Location → Al Karama
Hours → Mon 20:00   **050 653 7992**
Web/email → lobo1511@emirates.net.ae   Map Ref → 10-D2

If you're looking for a game of scrabble, then this club meets once a week to play friendly games for all levels of players. Members include everyone from beginners to world cup players! Regular competitions are held and players also attend competitions as far afield as Bahrain, Singapore and Bangkok. The *UAE Open Tournament*, held every year in March/April, is the qualifier for the *Gulf Open* in Bahrain, from which the top ranked UAE player goes to represent the country in the World Cup. For more information, contact Selwyn Lobo.

Yoga

Other options → Pilates [p.284]

Al Majaz

Location → Trade Centre Rd · Al Karama
Hours → 09:00 - 14:00 16:00 - 21:00   **335 3563**
Web/email → www.goldenfistkarate.com   Map Ref → 10-D1

Al Majaz offers a variety of self-improvement and fitness classes, plus swimming lessons. For ladies and girls above the age of ten years, there's yoga – the natural way to keep body and mind together, as well as aerobics and self-defence classes. In addition, separate classes for adults, girls and boys are available in karate, kung fu, taekwondo and jiu-jitsu. Transport can be provided.

Gems of Yoga

Location → Wht. Crown Bld · Jct 1, Shk Zayed Rd | 331 5161
Hours → 06:30 - 13:30 15:00 - 22:00 Fri 16:00 - 22:00
Web/email → yoga@emirates.net.ae   Map Ref → 9-D2

Gems Of Yoga integrates yoga and art, bringing increased fitness to an individual's lifestyle. Yogasanas, udras, pranayam, meditation and various stress release techniques are built into the programmes, and these act as a balancer on a physical level, helping to cure minor disorders of the body. On a mental level yoga helps to focus and increase concentration, bringing increased harmony and balance to life. The centre offers classes such as weight-watchers desktop yoga, prenatal and postnatal yoga, therapeutic yoga and animal yoga for children (every Thursday 16:00 - 18:00).

Costs: Packages range from Dhs.550 to Dhs.1,500. Yoga at home packages Dhs.2,500; free beach yoga classes are held every last Thu of the month at Umm Suqeim beach.

House of Chi & House of Healing

Location → Musalla Towers · Bur Dubai | 397 4446
Hours → Closed Fri
Web/email → www.hofchi.com   Map Ref → 8-A4

In perfect balance … mind, body and spirit is the maxim of this alternative therapies outlet. From the start the surroundings inspire peace and well being, while the team of practitioners include professionals in the fields of traditional Chinese medicine, martial arts and yoga.

In Eastern beliefs, strength is drawn from the 'chi'. Through both martial and meditative arts, everything within the House of Chi is geared towards the development of the chi, or central point. The House of Healing offers a variety of methods to alleviate health problems and promote inner harmony. Services include the treatment of physical ailments and stress, weight loss and physical therapy to improve your mind and spirit.

Timings: House of Chi 08:00 - 21:30; House of Healing 10:30 - 22:30.

Karama Natural Massage & Yoga Centre

Location → 109, Karama Centre · Al Karama | 337 8921
Hours → 08:30 - 23:30 Fri 08:30 - 14:00 18:00 - 20:30
Web/email → almadxb@emirates.net.ae   Map Ref → 10-D2

Operating for over 15 years, this centre is run by qualified professionals with expertise in the traditional systems of Ayurveda, herbal beauty care, yoga and meditation. This is a one-stop institution with all the facilities that are necessary for a natural system of healing, rejuvenation and beauty care. Separate areas are available for men and women.

EXPAND YOUR HORIZONS

Other options → Education [p.102]
Support Groups [p.100]

Now that you actually have the time to do it, why not take that painting or flower arranging class you've always dreamed of? Or, since you've come all this way, think about taking a course in Arabic or one of the many other languages available. Dubai has a surprising range of extracurricular activities for eternal students, from workshops or month-long courses to special interest groups, learning opportunities are abundant and flexible enough to fit your schedule.

Art Classes

Other options → Art [p.185]
Art Supplies [p.187]
Café Ceramique [p.381]

Creative Modern Center

Location → Opp Audio Workshop · Al Rashidiya | 285 9925
Hours → 09:00 - 13:00 16:00 - 19:30
Web/email → mdrnart@emirates.net.ae   Map Ref → n/a

Previously known as the Modern Art Center, the Creative Modern Center offers mothers and children the chance to be creative in an arty atmosphere. The centre has a variety of courses, including painting, drawing, calligraphy, sculpture, fabric painting, flower arranging, ceramic flower making and cookery. Mums can also join aerobics, aqua aerobics or karate classes.

For children, the centre offers activities for different age groups. Classes are also given in arts and crafts, cookery, photography, drawing, pottery, ballet, swimming and taekwondo. Special programmes are organised for school holidays. Contact the above number for details on prices and class timings.

Dubai International Art Centre

Location → Opp Jumeira Plaza, Jumeira
Hours → Sat & Thu 08:30 - 16:00 Sun & Wed 08:30 - 19:00
Web/email → artdubai@emirates.net.ae
Map Ref → 6-C2

| 344 4398

Fondly known as the 'Arts Centre', this hub of arty-crafty types is a haven of tranquillity. The arty ones are busy doing, while other visitors are looking at displays, using the excellent art shop or library, or just enjoying a drink in the small garden.

Classes are offered in over 70 subjects, including all types of painting and drawing, Arabic, dressmaking, etching, pottery, photography, and much more. Each course lasts for six or eight weeks and prices vary according to the materials required. Exhibitions of members' work are held twice a year and there are also regular lectures and demonstrations.

Annual membership fees: Dhs.250 allows members to sign up for some of the many classes on offer each term. Family membership Dhs.350; student membership Dhs.50.

Elves & Fairies

Location → Jumeirah Centre · Beach Rd, Jumeira
Hours → 09:00 - 13:00 3:30 - 20:30 Closed Fri
Web/email → jmeadows@emirates.net.ae
Map Ref → 6-C2

| 344 9485

This craft shop for adults and children alike specialises in stencils, rubber stamps and face painting. They also deal in decorative paint effects and stock related paints, glazes, colourwash, varnishes and brushes, as well as cross-stitch, mosaics and decoupage. Elves and Fairies run regular workshops for children and adults on all things crafty – contact Dave for details.

NBM Arts and Crafts

Location → Nr Spinney's Warehouse · Al Quoz
Hours → 09:00 - 13:30 16:30 - 19:30
Web/email → nbmdubai@emirates.net.ae
Map Ref → 4-C4

| 347 5700

The unique and colourful look of NBM Arts and Crafts building lends itself to the art related activities you'll find inside. On offer are a variety of arts and crafts workshops for children and adults. Students and artists are offered a full range of art supplies, as well as knowledgeable staff to guide them with their art projects and purchases.

Other options → Dance Classes [p.287]

Ballet Centre, The

Location → Behind Jumeira Plaza · Jumeira
Hours → 09:00 - 12:30 15:00 - 18:30 Closed Fri
Web/email → balletct@emirates.net.ae
Map Ref → 6-C3

| 344 9776

Located in central Jumeira, this dance and exercise centre offers plenty of classes for adults and children. There is a coffee shop and dance-wear shop on the premises, but more importantly, it has five rooms with wooden sprung floors, vital for dance and aerobics.

Adult fitness covers step, aerobics, Pilates, yoga and jazzercise. For those interested in dance, try ballet, tap, jazz, Irish, salsa, Spanish, ballroom and belly dancing! The centre also offers taekwondo, gymnastics, wing-tsun, guitar, piano and singing lessons, plus specialist classes for expectant mothers, such as antenatal fitness, yoga and baby massage. Contact the centre for a timetable – there's bound to be something that suits your schedule!

Beauty Training

Cleopatra & Steiner Beauty Training Centre

Location → Wafi Residence · Umm Hurair
Hours → 08:30 - 20:00
Web/email → www.cleopatrasteiner.com
Map Ref → 13-D2

| 324 0250

This is the Middle East's first internationally endorsed beauty and holistic training centre. A wide variety of topics are available, from basic make up and teenage grooming to advanced facial treatments and aromatherapy.

The centre provides opportunities for beginners or those pursuing their hobby, as well as those wishing to build on existing qualifications. Lasting from 12 to 250 hours, the courses can help develop career opportunities in beauty salons, sales and consultancy, marketing and management and assist self-employed therapists. On completion, participants are awarded an internationally recognised diploma. For successful students, there may be employment opportunities within the organisation.

Expand Your Horizons

Activities

Belly Dancing

Please see → Dance Classes [p.284]

Dance Classes

Other options → Music Lessons [p.292]
Singing Lessons [p.294]

Sociable, great fun and excellent exercise for all ages and standards, dance has a universal appeal that breaks down barriers and inhibitions (sometimes)! As well as the following organisations that are dedicated to dance, some health clubs, restaurants and bars hold weekly sessions in flamenco, salsa, samba, jazz dance, ballroom, and so on. Keep an eye out for details at places such as Savage Garden. In addition, some health clubs offer dance based aerobic classes that are good fun and surprisingly energetic.

Al Naadi Club

Location → Al Ghurair City · Deira | 205 5229
Hours → 06:00 - 23:00
Web/email → www.alghuraircentre.com   Map Ref → 11-D1

Although mainly for residents of the Al Ghurair apartments, this club does admit outside visitors. Ballet lessons leading to Royal Academy of Dancing examinations are taken by Sally Bigland, a qualified teacher from the UK. She also teaches Latin American dance (cha cha, rumba, jive, etc) to adults at 8pm on a Saturday. Indian dance is taught by Mrs Saraswathi Pathy on Mondays and Wednesdays at 17:00 - 19:00.

In addition, the club offers taekwondo and karate. Taekwondo is taught by Munir Gharwi every Thursday 13:30 - 14:30 for boys and girls aged six and older. Karate is held for an hour at 5pm every Sunday and Tuesday.

> **Costs:** Latin American dance and ballet Dhs.400 per term of 12 sessions. Indian dance Dhs.200 per month. Taekwondo Dhs.240 per term of eight classes. Karate Dhs.200 per month.

American Square Dance Group

Location → Nr American School, Jumeira | 355 4059
Hours → Sat 20:00 - 22:00
Web/email → na   Map Ref → 6-A3

Grab your partner by the hand, get on the dance floor and be ready to heel-toe, heel-toe all evening! This is a lively evening of American square dancing in the old Wild West style. No need to wear check shirts or flouncy dresses, but do wear long sleeves (men) and comfortable shoes, as you will be energetically twirling and moving over every inch of the floor.

Beginners, mainstream and plus levels are taught, and everyone is welcome, whether couples or singles. For further details, contact Marjorie on the above number or Lene (344 2591). Classes are currently held on Mondays.

Ceroc Dubai

Location → Various locations | 050 428 3061
Hours → Timings on request
Web/email → www.cerocdubai.com   Map Ref → n/a

Ceroc is an exiting modern dance from the UK and is a great way to socialise and keep fit. It can be danced to a wide range of music, from the latest club hits to the sounds of yesteryear, and footwork is kept to a minimum, so it's easy to learn. The evening starts with a beginners' class taken by a UK champion instructor, followed by intermediates and finally the freestyle section where you can practice all your moves. Pure dance addiction! There's no need to bring a partner, since everyone rotates to dance with everyone else, and no special footwear or clothing is required. Call Des for further information.

Dance Centre, The

Location → Various locations | 286 8775
Hours → 09:00 - 17:00 Closed Thu & Fri
Web/email → donnad@emirates.net.ae   Map Ref → n/a

The Dance Centre offers classes in ballet, tap, jazz and modern dance to children of all ages and has studios all over Dubai (Jumeira, Umm Suqeim, Mirdif) and in Sharjah. It is affiliated to the Royal Academy of Dance in London and so is able to enter students for their RAD graded examinations each year. For further information contact the above number or (050 624 2956).

Indian Classical Dances

Location → Nr MMI & Pioneer Bld · Al Karama | 335 4311
Hours → 16:30 - 20:00 Closed Fri
Web/email → geekay@emirates.net.ae   Map Ref → 10-C3

Indian classical dances have their own unique style, with fast rhythmic footwork and facial expressions. Mrs Geetha Krishnan, a reputed Bharatnatyam and

Kuchipudi teacher, holds classes for anyone aged six years and up. On completion of the course, which takes around four years, the pupil performs her Arangetam – a presentation in front of reputed maestros and critics.

Mrs Krishnan also choreographs classical and folk dances, plus fashion shows, when her students get a chance to exhibit their talents. She is available for event organising on a freelance basis.

Leaders Dance Club

Location ➔ Btw Mazaya & Safestway, Shk Zayed Rd | 343 3288
Hours ➔ 10:00 - 22:00 Closed Fri
Web/email ➔ leadclub@emirates.net.ae   Map Ref ➔ 5-D3

This ballroom and Latin dance club offers a stylish choice of 15 kinds of dance for everyone. So, everything from a tango or a waltz to rumba, cha-cha, salsa, merengue, paso doble, jive, samba, quick step or belly dancing is covered, as well as a new exercise called dance fitness. Courses can be in groups or privately according to timings and your choice of dance.

Savage Garden

Location ➔ Capitol Hotel · Al Satwa | 346 0111
Hours ➔ 18:00 - 03:00
Web/email ➔ caphotel@emirates.net.ae   Map Ref ➔ 7-A2

Savage Garden is the venue for salsa and merengue dance classes, run by Megda and Liliana, to the sounds of the live Colombian band and DJ. The classes are offered daily from 19:00 - 20:00 for beginners and 20:00 - 21:00 for more advanced salseros. Afterwards you can stay behind and practice your moves at this popular nightclub.

The charge is Dhs.40 per hour, with a package of ten classes offered at a discounted rate of Dhs.350.

Dog Training

Other options ➔ Pets [p.87]

Dog Training Classes

Location ➔ Various locations | 347 2592
Hours ➔ Timings on request
Web/email ➔ bugsy@emirates.net.ae   Map Ref ➔ n/a

OK, so we all yearn to complete the happy family picture – the kids, the parents and the beautiful dog. But so often that harmonious picture is shattered as the four legged mutt crashes onto the domestic scene! No need to give up in despair, and no need for Rufus to rule the roost. Training can change an impossible dog into a wonderful family companion, but it takes patience and understanding.

For details of group or individual dog training classes, contact Anne on the above number or (050 655 8925). Training for deaf dogs is also provided.

Environmental Groups

Other options ➔ Environment [p.11]

Over the last few years, environmental issues have gradually become more important in the UAE; however, as is always the case, far more needs to be done by all sections of the community.

Leading the way, HH Sheikh Mohammed bin Rashid Al Maktoum, Crown Prince of Dubai, has established a prestigious international environmental award in honour of HH Sheikh Zayed bin Sultan Al Nahyan, President of the UAE. The award, which was first presented in 1998, goes to an individual or organisation for distinguished work carried out on behalf of the environment.

On an everyday level there are increasing numbers of glass and plastic recycling points around the city, most notably outside Spinneys supermarkets. The Khaleej Times sponsors bins for collecting newspapers for recycling; these are easily spotted at a variety of locations, but mainly outside shopping centres.

In addition, the government of Dubai is gradually taking action with school educational programmes and general awareness campaigns. However, overall, there seems to be very little done to persuade the average person to be more active environmentally, for instance by encouraging the use of unleaded petrol or by reducing littering.

If you want to do something more active, contact one of the environmental groups that operate in the emirates. These range from the Emirates Environmental Group and the flagship Arabian Leopard Trust to Feline and K9 Friends. They always need volunteers and funds. Go on, do your bit!

Expand Your Horizons

Activities

Dubai Natural History Group

Location → Jumeira English Speaking Sch · Jumeira | **349 4816**
Hours → See timings below
Web/email → na   Map Ref → 5-B3

Dubai Natural History Group (DNHG) was formed in 1986 to further knowledge and interest in the flora, fauna, geology, archaeology and natural environment of the Emirates. Meetings are held on the first Sunday of each month and are free of charge. These usually take the form of lectures by local or visiting speakers on a range of natural history topics, mostly involving the UAE.

Regular field trips are arranged and the group maintains a modest library of natural history publications, which are available for members to use. Members receive a monthly newsletter, *The Gazelle*, which covers news, future activities and those of related groups in Abu Dhabi and Al Ain.

Cost: annual membership is Dhs.100 per family; Dhs.50 for individuals.

Contact: Valerie Chalmers, Vice Chairman and Secretary on the above number; Gary Feulner, Chairman (330 3600); or write to PO Box 9234, Dubai.

Emirates Environmental Group

Location → Various locations | **331 8100**
Hours → Timings on request
Web/email → www.eeg-uae.com   Map Ref → n/a

This is a voluntary, non-governmental organisation devoted to protecting the environment through education, action programmes and community involvement. The group started in September 1991 and has since grown considerably. Its membership includes everyone from individuals to corporate members and schools.

Activities include regular free evening lectures with speakers on environmental topics, and special events such as recycling collections and clean-up campaigns. It brings out a bi-lingual, bi-annual newsletter with a free circulation of 20,000 for the community, and a monthly newsletter for its members. Volunteers are always needed and everyone is welcome.

For further information, phone, fax (332 8500), visit their Website, or email.

Annual membership: adults Dhs.50; students Dhs.10 - 25. Corporate membership is also available.

Flower Arranging

Other options → **Plants & Trees [p.204]**

Ikebana Sogetsu Flower Arranging Classes

Location → Hamriya, Opp Syrian Consulate · Deira | **262 0282**
Hours → 09:30 - 12:30 03:30 - 18:30 Timings on request
Web/email → fujikozarouni@hotmail.com   Map Ref → 11-D1

Ikebana means the art of Japanese flower arranging. It is seen as a way of life; an artistic way to enrich our lives and environment with all the glories of plant life. There are numerous schools of ikebana, each following a particular set of rules and arrangement techniques, but without losing sight of the fundamentals of the art.

Classes in Dubai are held by Fujiko Zarouni, a qualified teacher from Japan. In addition to creating wonderful displays for the home, teachers and students who form the Ikebana Sogetsu group do demonstrations, displays, open days, and so on.

Gardening

Other options → **Plants & Trees [p.204]**

Gardening Workshop

Location → Jumeira | **344 5999**
Hours → First Mon of month 16:00
Web/email → bomi@emirates.net.ae   Map Ref → 12-C3

The Gardening Workshop was established in October 2000, taking over from the Gardening Group, which was dissolved in April 2000. Members of the group aim to share their love and knowledge of gardening in a friendly and informal atmosphere. During the cooler months, trips to greenhouses, nurseries and member's gardens are arranged. Speakers, who are experts in various fields, address the meetings and, where possible, give practical demonstrations. Meetings are generally held on a Monday of every month at 4pm. For further information, contact Deena B Motiwalla on the above number.

Expand Your Horizons

Activities

Language Schools

Other options → Education [p.102]

Alliance Française

Location → Nr American Hospital · Oud Metha | **335 8712**
Hours → 09:00 - 13:00 16:00 - 20:00 Closed Thu & Fri
Web/email → afdxb@emirates.net.ae   Map Ref → 13-D1

Founded in Paris in 1883, the Alliance Française is a non-profit making organisation that promotes French language and culture. Established in Dubai in 1982, it is known as the best place to learn French.

For adults, lessons are on Saturdays, Mondays and Wednesdays, while for children, classes are held on Sundays and Tuesdays. Terms run from September to June, with a summer school during July and August. Students have free access to the on-site library. In addition, Alliance Française organises various cultural events during the year, such as concerts, exhibitions and ballets.

Due to demand, the Alliance has started French language classes for adults at the French School in Sharjah (Lycée Georges Pompidou).

Arabic Language Centre

Location → Trade Centre · Main Strip - Shk Zayed Rd | **308 6036**
Hours → 08:30 - 17:30 Closed Thu & Fri
Web/email → alc@dwtc.com   Map Ref → 10-A2

A division of the Dubai World Trade Centre, this language school was established in 1980 to teach Arabic as a foreign language. Courses for beginners through to advanced levels are run five times a year and each course lasts 30 hours. Sessions are held at 09:00 - 11:00, 13:30 - 15:30 and 18:15 - 20:15. All materials are provided by the centre and included in the course fees of Dhs.1,550.

Specialist courses can be designed to meet the requirements of the hotel, banking, hospital, motor and electronic industries, while private courses offer individual tuition and flexible timings.

Location: halls 5 and 5A of the DWTC exhibition complex.

Berlitz

Location → Nr Dubai Zoo · Beach Rd, Jumeira | **344 0034**
Hours → 08:00 - 20:00 Thu 08:00 - 14:00 Closed Fri
Web/email → www.berlitz.co.ae   Map Ref → 6-B2

For more than a century Berlitz has been operating worldwide and the Berlitz Method has helped more than 41 million people acquire a new language.

A variety of courses are offered and they can be customised to fit specific requirements, such as 'English for banking' or 'technical English'. Instruction is in private or small groups, with morning classes for women and special children's classes (minimum age four years) on Thursdays. Additional training includes translation and interpretation, self-teaching audio and videotapes, books and interactive CD-ROM.

The Sharjah branch is one of the latest of over 500 Berlitz centres in more than 50 countries (06 572 1115).

British Council

Location → Nr Maktoum Bridge · Oud Metha | **337 0109**
Hours → 10:00 - 13:00 17:00 - 20:00 Closed Sun & Tue pm, Thu/Fri
Web/email → www.britcoun.org/uae   Map Ref → 11-A3

The British Council has teaching centres in Dubai, Abu Dhabi, Sharjah and Ras Al Khaimah, offering English language courses for adults, children (3 to 16 year olds) and company groups. There are also business English courses aimed at professionals who need to improve their language skills for the workplace. In addition, the Council offers a range of exam preparation courses from O and A levels to IELTS, Preliminary English Test (PET), First Certificate in English (FCE) and Business English Certificates.

Post-graduate courses are available in partnership with the University of Strathclyde Graduate School of Business, Newcastle University and Glasgow University.Classes: held daily (during the summer or Ramadan), or two or three times a week, depending on ability.

Fees: English courses (36 hours) Dhs.1,550; Arabic courses (24 hours) Dhs.1,100; computer courses (12 hours) Dhs.750. More more details contact on the above number of toll free 800 4066.

Expand Your Horizons

Activities

Dar El Ilm School of Languages

Location → Nr Defence R/A · Trade Center 1&2 | 343 7573
Hours → 09:00 - 17:30 Thu 09:00 - 13:00 Closed Thu pm & Fri
Web/email → darelilm@emirates.net.ae   Map Ref → 9-A2

Now entering its fifteenth year, Dar El Ilm offers language courses to students of all ages and abilities, with the emphasis on making learning fun. The company strives to provide a professional yet personal approach.

Adult tuition is offered in English, French, German, Italian and Spanish. Courses last 21 hours and are run six times during the academic year (fees start at Dhs.1,200). For children, classes are offered in Arabic, English, French, German, Italian and Spanish. Courses are run throughout the year and extra tuition is available for help with schoolwork, etc. There is also a summer school.

Location: Sheikh Zayed Road by Defence roundabout.

Polyglot Language Institute

Location → Al Masaeed Bld, beh Inter-Con · Deira | 222 3429
Hours → 09:00 - 13:00 16:00 - 21:00 Closed Fri
Web/email → www.polyglot.co.ae   Map Ref → 8-C4

Opened in 1969 and located in the heart of Deira, the Polyglot Language Institute offers year-round courses in modern languages, secretarial and computer skills for individuals and companies.

Courses offered include: Arabic, general English, business English, TOEFL preparation, French, German, office skills, typing, secretarial and computer studies. There's also a high quality translation service in four languages. Classrooms are bright and spacious with modern facilities. Each course lasts 6 - 10 weeks and consists of classes three times a week in the mornings or evenings. All books and materials are provided. Call the above number or (222 2596).

Costs: courses are either Dhs.1,350 or Dhs.1,500.
Location: fourth floor, Al Masaeed building, above the Iran Insurance Company.

Libraries

Other options → Books [p.188]
Second-hand Items [p.205]

Alliance Française

Location → Opp. American Hospital · Oud Metha | 335 8712
Hours → 08:30 - 13:30 16:00 - 20:00 Closed Thu (half day) & Fri closed
Web/email → afdxb@emirates.net.ae   Map Ref → 13-E1

The Alliance Française multimedia library has over 10,000 books (including a children's section), plus 50 daily, weekly and monthly French newspapers and magazines, 1,800 videos, 100 CD-ROMs and soon a collection of DVDs. Full membership of the library costs Dhs.650 for the year (books only Dhs.350 per year, videos only Dhs.550 per year). Alliance Française students are allowed free access.

Archies Library

Location → Pyramid Bld, Near Burjuman · Al Karama | 396 7924
Hours → 10:00 - 14:00 17:00 - 22:00 Fri 17:30 - 22:00
Web/email → abcl180@hotmail.com   Map Ref → 10-E1

Forty-five thousand books! Yes, 45,000 all in English and you don't have to buy a single one. Archies has fiction, non-fiction, classics, cookery, health and fitness, management, a vast selection of books and comics for children, plus a wide selection of the latest magazines.

The annual membership fee of Dhs.75 and a Dhs.100 refundable deposit entitles you to borrow any four books for ten days. The renewal fee is Dhs.50. The reading charge varies between Dhs.1 – 4. With their ingenious 'dial-a-book' service, books can be delivered anywhere in the UAE for a mere Dhs.3!

There is now a branch in Sharjah (06 572 5716).

British Council Library

Location → Nr Maktoum Bridge · Oud Metha | 337 1540
Hours → 09:00 - 20:00 Closed Fri
Web/email → information@ae.britcoun.org   Map Ref → 11-A3

The British Council is well known for its English courses and for being the centre for UK-based examinations and assessments. The library is used by the many students who attend the courses, but is also open to the public, and non-members may use the reference collection.

Expand Your Horizons

Activities

The service includes a lending library with a wide selection of fiction and non-fiction materials, as well as videos and CD-ROMs, a self-access centre for students of English and an education information unit for those wishing to study in the UK. An Internet unit is open to the public.

Membership fees: the annual adult membership fee of Dhs.350 entitles you to borrow two books for two weeks, plus one CD-ROM and two videos for one week.

Juma Al Majid Cultural & Heritage Centre

Location → Nr Dubai Cinema · Deira | 262 4999
Hours → 08:00 - 19:30   Closed Fri
Web/email → n/a   Map Ref → 12-A4

Established in 1991, this is a non-profit reference library and research institute. With an emphasis on Islam, the collection includes 500,000 items of cultural media with topics ranging from heritage to current world issues, plus 3,000 periodicals and out of print publications. These are mainly in Arabic, but there are also some items in English, French, German, Persian and other languages.

The library and private collections are open to anyone interested in social and human sciences. Books cannot be taken home, but you are able to use the reading room. There's no fee to use the library.

Old Library, The

Location → Int Art Centre · Beach Rd, Jumeira | 344 6480
Hours → 10:00 - 12:00   16:00 - 18:00   Closed Fri
Web/email → dubailendlibrary@yahoo.co.uk   Map Ref → 6-C2

The Old Library was formerly known as Dubai Lending Library. The new name reflects the fact that the library is independent, created in 1969 to serve the English-speaking expat community, and as such is the oldest English language library in Dubai. It continues to be a non-profit organisation, run by a band of volunteers. New volunteers and donations of books are always welcome. Funds are raised from annual subscriptions and new books are bought as monthly as money allows.

Annual subscriptions: family Dhs.80 (may borrow five books at a time); single Dhs.50 (may borrow two books at a time); child Dhs.20 (may borrow two children's books).

Public Library

Location → Nr St George Htl · Bur Dubai | 226 2788
Hours → 07:30 - 21:30   Thu 07:30 - 14:30   Closed Fri
Web/email → www.dpl.gov.ae   Map Ref → 8-B2

This library was established in 1963, which makes it one of the oldest in the Gulf. It has an English and an Arabic lending section, plus a reading room for magazines and newspapers. Books can be borrowed for two weeks at a time, with a limit of three books per person. For the application form you need one passport sized photo and a copy of your passport and visa.

Fees: Dhs.200 adults (Dhs.150 refundable), no lending fee.

Music Lessons

Other options → Singing Lessons [p.294]
Dance Classes [p.287]

Crystal Music Institute

Location → Al Attar Centre · Al Karama | 396 3224
Hours → 08:00 - 12:00   15:30 - 21:00
Web/email → www.crystalmusicdubai.com   Map Ref → 10-E2

Recognised by the UAE Ministry of Education, the Crystal Music Institute aims to promote fine arts and enhance the cultural horizon of individuals. Courses are mainly for children and are available for a variety of instruments, including piano, electric organ, guitar and violin. Classical Indian singing (Carnatic and Hindustani vocal), Bharatnatyam and Western dance, and arts and crafts are also offered.

Children take periodic examinations, which are conducted by the Trinity College of Music (London), in Dubai. Students have the chance to perform on stage and the institute also arranges musical shows. Transport can be provided.

Dubai Music School

Location → Stalco Bld, Zabeel Rd · Al Karama | 396 4834
Hours → 09:00 - 13:00   15:00 - 20:00   Closed Fri
Web/email → www.glennperry.net   Map Ref → 10-D3

Dubai Music School (DMS) was founded in 1980 by pop star and producer Glenn Perry to encourage the artistic potential of aspiring musicians. One to one classes are offered in guitar, piano, organ, violin, brass, drums, singing and composing for beginners and serious amateurs. Students take the Trinity College of London examination (there's a 100% pass rate). The school has a recording studio and will arrange songs for singers and help them to appear on MTV.

Lessons last for one hour and students are expected to attend two classes a week. DMS also has centres in Deira and Sharjah. Transport can be arranged.

Costs: monthly prices range from Dhs.200 - 395, plus a Dhs.50 registration fee.

Dubai Wind Band

Location → American School · Jumeira | 394 1011
Hours → Tue 19:30 - 21:00
Web/email → www.geocities.com/dubaiwindband2002 Map Ref → 6-A3

This is a group of over 50 woodwind and brass musicians. Abilities range from beginners to Grade 8 plus, and all levels and ages are welcome. The band is in popular demand during December for seasonal singing and music engagements at clubs, malls and hotels. For further information, contact Peter Hatherley-Greene on the above number or (050 651 8902).

Sruthi Music & Dance Training Center

Location → No 14, Sana Fashion Bld · Al Karama | 337 7398
Hours → 08:00 - 12:00 16:00 - 21:00 Closed Fri
Web/email → n/a | Map Ref → 10-C1

Shruthi is dedicated to developing a child's latent talents for music, dance and arts and crafts. Coaching is available for a variety of instruments including piano, electric organ, guitar, drums, violin (Carnatic), accordion, harmonica and tabala, and students can enter the Trinity College of Music (London) examinations held in Dubai.

Lessons are also offered in Carnatic and Hindustani vocals, as well as dance, from Indian styles such as Bharatnatyam or Kathak to Western dance styles, like disco and jive. Within the arts and crafts programme are sketching, watercolours, oils, pastels and pottery painting. Transport can be provided.

Vocal Studio

Location → Al Rostamani Bld. Trade Center 1&2 | 332 9880
Hours → Timings on request
Web/email → doremivs@emirates.net.ae | Map Ref → 9-B2

The Vocal Studio offers a range of singing related activities for adults and youngsters. Lessons are taught by professional teachers and the centre offers exam preparation for the ABRSM and Trinity College London syllabuses; grades range from beginners to advanced. Students are also encouraged to take part in performances, such as recitals and concerts.

Choral singing groups are a popular and fun way to sing with other people. Groups are: The Dubai Youth Choir (Primary school ages 9 - 11), The Viva la Voce Vocal Ensemble (Secondary school ages 14 - 18), and the Dubai Woman's Chorus for adult women. These groups sing a range of music and often incorporate movement and choreography into their pieces.

Salsa Dancing

Other options → Dance Classes [p.287]

Salsa Dubai

Location → Various locations | 050 450 7427
Hours → See timings below
Web/email → www.salsanight.com | Map Ref → n/a

Salsa Dubai introduces the worldwide craze of salsa to Dubai. It's fronted by Phil, who has over seven years of salsa experience, including Cuban, New York and Spanish styles. Classes are tailored to the individual, so everyone can progress at their own speed. Members also have the opportunity to learn the infamous La Rueda (the Cuban salsa class where partners are swapped!). Classes are fun and present an excellent mix of dance, music, fitness and socialising, and afterwards members often stay on to dance for fun. Nights out are organised at local Latin venues to enjoy live Latin bands and dance music.

Classes:

- *Ballet Centre: Mon19:30 - 20:30 (beginners/intermediates)*
- *Cactus Cantina: Satur 20:00 - 22:00 (intermediates/advanced), Sun 20:00 - 22:00 (beginners/advanced)*
- *Pharaohs Club: Tues 20:00 - 22:00 (beginners/intermediate).*

Singing Lessons

Other options ➜ Music Lessons [p.292]

Dubai Harmony Chorus

Location ➜ Various locations
Hours ➜ Tue 19:30 - 22:00
Web/email ➜ holmqvis@emirates.net.ae

348 9395

Map Ref ➜ n/a

Imagine creating exciting choral music and being part of a harmonious blending of voices, barbershop style ... and then do it! Barbershop harmonising is different from other kinds of group singing. Finding the right part for your voice is the initial step, but this is simple as any woman of average singing ability, with or without music or vocal training, will find a part that fits her range.

Dubai Harmony Chorus boasts a membership of 50 women from many different countries who share a love of singing. Rehearsals are held weekly. Call Phyllis Holmqvist or Kathy Young for details.

Dubai Singers & Orchestra

Location ➜ Various locations
Hours ➜ Timings on request
Web/email ➜ http://dubaisingers.tripod.com/

349 1896

Map Ref ➜ 11-A3

This is a well-established group of amateur musicians who meet regularly to make music in a variety of styles, from requiems and serious choral works to Christmas carols, musicals or variety shows. At the moment the orchestra generally only meets when involved in a Dubai Singers production.

Membership is open to all and no audition is required, except for solo parts – tenors are especially welcome! Members pay Dhs.50 per year and enjoy subsidised music, regular social events and after show parties. The choir meets once, sometimes twice a week; venues and days may vary.

Social Groups

Other options ➜ Support Groups [p.100]

With its cosmopolitan population, it's not surprising that Dubai has a large number of social and cultural groups. These are sometimes linked to an embassy or business group and can be an excellent way of meeting likeminded people. However, if your particular interest or background is not covered, now is the perfect opportunity to challenge your

organisational skills and start something new – there'll always be someone out there who'll join in! Refer to the Business Section [p.116].

Dubai Adventure Mums

Location ➜ Various locations
Hours ➜ Timings on request
Web/email ➜ www.dubaiadventuremums.com

349 3147

Map Ref ➜ n/a

This group of women from all over Dubai want the excitement of life and the opportunity to meet new people. Once a month they set off without their children or partners to test themselves in new, challenging and fun ways! The aim of this non-profit group is to offer women (ages range from 17 to 70) a range of recreational activities that they may not have tried before. Instructors offer advice and teach everyone the safest way to enjoy these activities, which all start at beginners level. Contact Debbie Magee for further information. The group also meets for a monthly coffee morning.

Dubai Manx Society

Location ➜ Various locations
Hours ➜ Timings on request
Web/email ➜ www.worldmanxindubai.com

394 3185

Map Ref ➜ n/a

Formed in July 2000 by Gil Costain Salway, the Dubai Manx Society provides a focal point for expats from the Isle of Man and promotes links between the island and Dubai through its culture, history and traditions. Members meet once a month for various cultural events. Membership is primarily for those born on the island or of Manx origin, but the group also welcomes those who have the interests of the island at heart. The society issues a quarterly newsletter and has traditional Manx/Viking gatherings (Cooish) throughout the year.

Dubai Round Table

Location ➜ Country Club · Al Awir Rd
Hours ➜ 1st Mon of every month 20:00
Web/email ➜ www.geocities.com

331 7744

Map Ref ➜ 17-B3

Round Table has been around for over 75 years. It is a descendant of Rotary and is now present in over 60 countries, and is further extending this year to three new countries around the world. In the Arabian Gulf there are 11 Tables with a membership that represents a broad cross section of

professions within your locality. In the meantime take some time to trawl through the pages at the linked Round Tables from this site and find out more about the best young person's fellowship organisation in the world! Also active are Dubai Creek (Indian) Ladies Circle and 41 Club.

Toastmasters International	
Location → Al Futtaim Training Centre · Rashidiya	|268 6000
Hours → 07:15 - 21:30	
Web/email → www.toastmasters.org	Map Ref → n/a

Toastmasters International is the leading movement devoted to making effective oral communication a worldwide reality. Through member clubs, it helps men and women learn the arts of listening, thinking and speaking – vital skills that enhance leadership potential and foster human understanding. The clubs provide a supportive and positive learning environment, which in turn foster self-confidence and personal growth. They have a variety of clubs in the UAE. For further information, contact Ms Saira Ranjith on 050 535 74 35.

KIDS' STUFF

Other options → Children's City [p.138]
Education [p.102]

Dubai has to be one of the best places in the world for kids. It seems like wherever you go, there are numerous play sites and activities devoted specifically to children. From the thrill of 'discovering' dinosaur bones in the sand to visiting a planetarium or the just plain goofy fun of a bouncy castle, amusement for the little ones is never far away

For further details of what there is for kids in Dubai and the Northern Emirates, refer to the *Family Explorer* (formerly *Kids' Explorer*). This handbook offers a wealth of information for the whole family, not only on what there is to do in the area, but also on 'how' to live here. Covering everything from medical care, education and birthday parties to eating out and activities divided into indoor and outdoor sections to make the most of facilities during the hot summer months, the *Family Explorer* has the answers.

Children's City	
Location → Creekside Park · Creekside, Bur Dubai	|334 0808
Hours → 09:00 - 22:00 Fri 16:00 - 22:00	
Web/email → www.childrencity.ae	Map Ref → 14-A1

Opened in 2002, Children's City is an educational project providing kids with their own learning zone and amusement facilities by providing hands-on experiences of the theoretical subjects that they learn at school. Children's City is aimed at 5 - 12 year olds, although items of interest are included for toddlers and teenagers. Highlights include a planetarium with a 180-degree screen, a mock-up of the front of an aircraft in the Flying Gallery, plus natural and cultural galleries nearby.

Gymboree Play & Music	
Location → Al Mina Rd · Satwa	|345 4422
Hours → Timings on request	
Web/email → gymboree_dubai@hotmail.com	Map Ref → 7-A2

Gymboree offers play and music classes, which combine age appropriate parent or carer interaction, for newborn babies to the under fives. Set in a colourful area, filled with state-of-the-art child-safe gym equipment, classes are designed to build confidence, imagination, social skill and physical abilities. The music classes combine rhythm, movement and use of basic musical instruments while exploring styles of music that change every three weeks.

Gymboree is also a new name for parties and events, hosting everything from birthdays or baby showers to theme parties.

Scouts Association (British Groups Abroad)	
Location → Various locations	|344 6186
Hours → See timings below	
Web/email → n/a	Map Ref → n/a

The Scouts Association aims to encourage the balanced development of young boys through weekly activities and outings. In the UAE, the association is represented by various sections that meet in Dubai, Sharjah and Abu Dhabi.

Different groups are for different ages: Beavers core ages 6 - 8 years, Cubs core ages 8 - 10 ½, Scouts core ages 10½ - 14, Explorer Scouts core ages 14 - 18, and the Scout Network core ages 18 - 25. Activities for the three younger groups include

Kids' Stuff

Activities

games, badge activities, sports, competitions, outings, etc. The waiting list for Beavers in particular can sometimes be quite long. All services of the leaders and helpers are voluntary.

Groups: there are three groups operating in Dubai:

The 1st Dubai Scout Group (one Cub pack), meets on Tues 16:30 - 18:00 at The English Speaking School, Dubai (DESS), contact dbcubs@yahoo.com.

The 2nd Dubai Scout Group (one Cub pack), meets on Sun 17:30 - 19:00 at Jumeirah English Speaking School (JESS), contact madscot@emirates.net.ae.

For 3rd Dubai Scout Group (three Beaver Scout colonies, two Cub packs and a Scout troop), contact janette@paradigm-uae.com for meeting times and locations.

In Sharjah, the 1st Sharjah Scout Group (one Cub pack), meets on Mon 17:00 - 18:30 at Sharjah English School, contact jddymock@emirates.net.ae.

For any general issues regarding the organisation, contact District Commissioner UAE Susan Jalili (349 3982).

Shooting Stars

Location ➡ Jumeirah Road · Jumeira | 344 7407
Hours ➡ Timings on request
Web/email ➡ s_stars@emirates.net.ae   Map Ref ➡ 6-A2

Shooting Stars is an adventure video production company that produces keepsake videos of children in imaginative situations. Using the latest digital technology they can turn children into the stars of their own video adventure: a popular choice is 'My Arabian Adventure' (the background tape is filmed in the dunes at Hatta). A unique and rather unusual gift to send back to the grandparents! For more information contact the above number or (050 798 8209).

Amusement Centres

City 2000

Location ➡ Hamarain Centre · Deira | 266 7855
Hours ➡ 10:00 - 23:00 Fri 16:30- 23:00
Web/email ➡ city2000@emirates.net.ae   Map Ref ➡ 12-A4

City 2000 offers video games and rides in an air conditioned environment. From racing on a track or bombing in a fighter plane, young or old can enjoy the simulators and find an outlet for the adventurous spirit! For little ones there are funny videos and the latest rides. The company claims to eliminate the more violent machines that are available in many adult amusement centres.

Entrance is free and food is supplied by the nearby foodcourt. Machines are operated by Dhs.1 tokens

and all machines take two tokens, except for adult simulator games, which take three.

Encounter Zone

Location ➡ Wafi Mall · Umm Hurair | 324 7747
Hours ➡ 10:00 - 24:00 Fri 13:30 - 23:00
Web/email ➡ ezone@emirates.net.ae   Map Ref ➡ 13-D2

Divided into two sections, Encounter Zone offers a range of action packed fun for all ages; Galactica for teenagers and adults, and Lunarland for kids aged 1 - 8 years.

Galactica is based on interactive attractions, like the Crystal Maze, the ultimate mind and body challenge (similar to the TV programme) and The Chamber, a living house of horror. Other features include Galactica Express, a themed inline skates/skateboarding park. Lunarland hosts a galaxy of games and activities especially designed for younger children, such as Crater Challenge, Lunar Express or the Komet, a unique roller coaster ride. Encounter Zone also offers packages for special occasions.

Costs: Sat to Wed an all day pass to play all attractions (except video games) costs Dhs.40 in one area (Dhs.50 to play both sides). Sat to Thu a morning pass (10:00 - 14:00) costs Dhs.20, which entitles you to play all attractions (except for video, arts and crafts activities). Attractions can also be paid for separately, prices range from Dhs.5 - 15 in Lunarland and Dhs.10 - 22.50 in Galactica. Video games range from Dhs.2 - 8.

Fantasy Kingdom

Location ➡ Al Bustan Centre · Al Qusais | 263 2774
Hours ➡ 09:00 - 23:00 Fri 14:00 - 23:00
Web/email ➡ www.al-bustan.com   Map Ref ➡ 15-C2

Themed as a medieval castle, Fantasy Kingdom offers adventure, fun and excitement. The centre is located in the comfort of a 24,000 square feet indoor play area, which is divided into sections for different age groups.

While younger children enjoy the soft play area and merry-go-rounds, or learn in the relaxed atmosphere of the learning corner, older ones can opt for the latest redemption, video, sports and interactive games, bumper cars, pool or air hockey. The updated Horror Cave has the latest scares and thrills – guaranteed to chill the blood of even the bravest!

Refreshments are available from the Stone Age Café or the nearby Al Bustan Foodcourt. The centre also caters for birthday parties.

Cost: Dhs.2 per token with no entrance fee (tokens become cheaper the more you buy).

Kids' Stuff

Activities

Magic Planet

Location → City Centre · Al Garhoud	**295 4333**
Hours → 10:00 - 24:00 Fri 12:00 - 24:00	
Web/email → www.deiracitycentre.com	Map Ref → 14-D1

Magic Planet is one of Dubai's favourite family entertainment centres. Ride the stately carousel or Ferris wheel, swing through Clarence camel's adventure zone, or test your skills on the bumper cars and latest video games. If you prefer a more leisurely route, watch the world pass from the City Express train or take a trip in a safari car. When you need a break, stop at the foodcourt where you can choose from over a dozen outlets.

Entrance is free and you pay as you play, using Dhs.2 cards (they become cheaper the more you buy). Alternatively, for unlimited entertainment buy a Planet All Day Special. For Dhs.50 you can play and play … Magic planet – all the fun in the world!

Amusement Parks

Other options → Water Parks [p.265]

Fruit & Garden Luna Park

Location → Al Nasr Leisureland · Oud Metha	**337 1234**
Hours → 09:00 - 22:30 Closed Fri am	
Web/email → www.alnasrleisureland.ae	Map Ref → 10-E4

This new park offers some great rides, suitable for everyone from 4 years to 60 years old, ideal for a child's birthday party. Rides include go-karts, bumper cars, helicopter, mini bumper and a roller coaster.

Entrance fees: Adults Dhs.10; children under five Dhs.5.

WonderLand Theme & Water Park

Location → Nr Creekside Park · Umm Hurair	**324 1222**
Hours → 15:00 - 21:00 Thu & Fri 12:00 - 21:00 Closed Sun	
Web/email → wonderld@emirates.net.ae	Map Ref → 14-A3

If you've noticed the brightly coloured roofs by Garhoud Bridge, then you've seen WonderLand, the only theme and water park in the Middle East. The park is divided into three areas: Main Street, Theme Park and SplashLand (see entry under Water Parks [p.265]), each offering something different.

There are a huge variety of indoor and outdoor rides for all ages, from the 130 kph Space Shot, which shoots you 210 feet into the air in less than

2½ seconds, to a more sedate ride on a camel, and everything in between! Alternatively, just enjoy the tropical landscape, relax by the pool or visit the food outlets. Parties and events can be catered for and there's also paintballing and go-karting.

Party Organisers

Flying Elephant

Location → Flying Elephant Warehouse , Shk Zayed Rd	**347 9170**
Hours → Timings on request	
Web/email → www.flyingelephantuae.com	Map Ref → 4-D4

Flying Elephant offers everything you would expect from a party planning company: from adding special effects for a product launch or providing a turnkey service for annual family days to entertainment on your little one's first birthday party in your back garden. The company can bring a wide range of products to the occasion, such as balloons and decorations, or the Gulf's largest outdoor confetti blaster (as seen at some of the larger musical concerts).

This is a truly versatile company with a fun and friendly attitude that's willing to work hard to turn your ideas into memorable events.

Gymboree Play & Music

Location → Al Mina Rd · Satwa	**345 4422**
Hours → Timings on request	
Web/email → gymboree_dubai@hotmail.com	Map Ref → 7-A2

For further information on Gymboree Play & Music, refer to the review under Kids' Stuff [p.295].

Gymboree

Kids' Stuff

Activities

The following pages show you where to go out.
This page shows you how to get there

On a hot summer night, you've got a hot date, and a hot destination. Why not drive a cool car?

Going Out
EXPLORER

Going Out - Eating Out / On the Town

EATING OUT

If you're going out and about in Dubai, you will soon find that there is a surprising variety of places to go and things to do. It may not be quite the buzzing city found in other parts of the world, but Dubai is without doubt the Party Capital of the Gulf, with enough choice to keep even the most ardent socialite happy.

The following section has been divided into two; the city's numerous restaurants are listed under Eating Out, while cafés, bars, pubs, nightclubs and 'cultural' entertainment such as theatre, cinema and comedy clubs, are under On the Town.

Eating Out

Eating out is extremely popular across all segments of the Dubai community. As well as offering the chance to enjoy cuisine from all over the world, it gives the opportunity to exchange news and argue the merits of anything from a foreign leader to the latest movie.

Cosmopolitan and vibrant, Dubai has an excellent variety of restaurants. From Austrian to Thai, Indian to Italian and everything in between, there really is something to suit every taste and budget. Most places open early in the evening at around 18:00, but generally aren't busy until about 21:00. As well as dining out, dining in with a takeaway is very popular – it sometimes seems as though no one in Dubai knows how to cook!

Many of Dubai's most popular restaurants are in hotels, and these are virtually the only outlets that can serve alcohol with your meal (if you want booze, check for the Alcohol Available icon in individual reviews). However, remember that there are many superb independent restaurants around town that shouldn't be ignored just because they are unlicensed.

Many restaurants specialise in more than one style of cuisine; for instance, an Indian restaurant may also serve Thai and Chinese food. In addition, many places promote theme nights with different types of cuisine or ingredients, such as Italian or seafood. The choice of what you can eat is dramatically increased by these speciality nights, allowing you to sample some truly international cuisine. Many restaurants also have weekly buffet nights when you can eat, and sometimes drink, as much as you like for a great value, all-inclusive price.

Eating Out

Going Out

Dhs.100 ~ € 28

2003 | DUBAI EXPLORER

Drinks

Although Dubai is about the most liberal state in the GCC, alcohol is only available in licensed restaurants and bars that are within hotels, plus a few non-hotel outlets, such as golf clubs and some government-owned establishments.

The mark-up can often be considerable – it's not unknown for a Dhs.11 bottle of indifferent wine to be charged at Dhs.90 plus. While most independent restaurants aren't able to serve alcohol, don't let it put you off since the food is often just as good, sometimes better.

Like alcohol, a bottle of house water can also be outrageously marked up, especially for premium brands. Imported water can be charged at up to Dhs.30 a bottle and if you object to this, we suggest you send it back and ask for a local bottled water (but not tap water). A standard one litre bottle of water usually costs Dhs.1.50 in a supermarket and is in no way inferior to imported brands.

See also: Alcohol [p.182]

Hygiene

Outlets are regularly checked by the municipality for hygiene and they are strict on warning places to improve and, when necessary, closing them down. Bear this in mind when you consider eating at the 'tatty' little shawarma shop by the side of the road or a small independent restaurant. It is safe to eat there and you're unlikely to get food poisoning. Indeed, you'll probably have an excellent cheap and atmospheric meal.

Tax & Service Charge

On top of the basic bill, there can be a 10% municipality tax and a 15 - 16% service charge. The municipality tax apparently only applies to 'rated' hotels. These taxes are required to be incorporated into the customers' bill, but they are often indicated as being in addition to a price by ++. This information has to be clearly indicated somewhere on the menu. It's unclear whether the latter charge is actually passed on to staff or whether it can be withheld for poor service. When in doubt, give your servers a break.

Tipping

Tipping is another grey area, but following the standard rule of 10% will not be out of line. It's not necessarily expected, but will be appreciated. Few waiters seem to realise that there's a direct correlation between good service and the size of the tip!

Independent Reviews

We undertake independent reviews of all restaurants and bars that we include in this book. The following outlets have been visited by our freelance reporters and the views expressed are our own. The aim is to give a clear, realistic and, as far as possible, unbiased view (that we are permitted to print!). However, if we have unwittingly led you astray, please do let us know. We appreciate all feedback, positive, negative and otherwise. Please email, phone, fax, or snail mail a letter. Your comments are never ignored.

Ratings

Rating restaurants is always a highly subjective business. We asked our reviewers to summarise their experiences (see the bottom of each entry) in terms of **Food**, **Service**, **Venue**, and **Value**. They were also asked to consider their restaurant as compared to other venues in the category and in the same price range. In other words, you may notice that a local cafe has the same summary rating as a premium gourmet restaurant. This is not to say that they are equal to one other. Instead, this is a way of comparing restaurants that are similarly styled and priced to each other. We hope this will help you to make informed choices regardless of your taste or budget.

Each rating is out of four - one blue dot means **poor**, two means **acceptable**, three means **good** and four means **fab**:

Food ●●●○ Service ●●●○ Venue ●●●○ Value ●●●○

Venues scheduled to open later in 2003 received 'n/a' ratings:

Food – n/a   Service – n/a   Venue – n/a   Value – n/a

Restaurant Listing Structure

With over 400 specially selected outlets in the *Dubai Explorer*, the choice can seem daunting. Listed alphabetically by region, then country, or commonly known style of cuisine, this section hopes to add to the variety of your dining experience by giving as much information as possible on the individual outlets. For an 'at a glance' clarification of this listing, refer to the index at the beginning of this section.

As with all good, simple rules, there are exceptions. Restaurants in the international category usually serve such a variety of food that it is impossible to pin them down to one section. While a restaurant that specialises in cooking seafood in styles from all over the world will be found in Seafood, however, a Thai restaurant that cooks a lot of fish Thai style will still be listed under Thai! Makes sense? We hope so!

Where a restaurant specialises in more than one type of cuisine, the review appears under the main category.

In order to avoid any confusion concerning a particular restaurant's listing, as a rule, any non-English names retain their prefix (ie, Al, Le, La and El) in their alphabetical placement, while English names are listed by actual titles, ignoring prefixes such as 'The'. Bon appetit!

Privilege Cards

The table shows a list of privilege or discount cards for use at various establishments. These cards are basically offered to encourage you to return as often as possible. Generally, they can be used at a number of restaurants, so you won't get bored, and most offer incredible discounts and other added benefits, making them excellent value for money.

Icons — Quick Reference

For an explanation of the various symbols or icons listed against the individual reviews, refer to the

Quick Reference Explorer Icons

👆	Explorer Recommended!
100	Average price ± Dhs.25 (3 courses per person)
🚫	NO Credit Cards Accepted
🎸	Live Band
🍷	Alcohol Available
🙂	Have a Happy Hour
🛵	Will Deliver
👶	Kids Welcome
✆	Reservations Recommended
👔	Dress Smartly
🚫	Outside Terrace
Ⓥ	Vegetarian Dishes

Quick Reference Explorer Icons table.

The prices indicated are calculated as the cost of a starter, main course and dessert for two people. This includes any relevant taxes, but excludes the cost of drinks. Another good cost indication is whether the outlet is licensed, the restaurant location (in a hotel or not), type of cuisine, etc. The Dhs.150 icon indicates that an average meal should cost anywhere between Dhs.125 to Dhs.175, ie Dhs.150 ± 25.

Vegetarian Food

Vegetarians may be pleasantly surprised by the range and variety of veggie cuisine that can be found in restaurants in Dubai. Although the main course of Arabic food is dominated by meat, the

Privilege Cards			
Hotel / Company	Includes	**Phone**	**Cost**
Hilton Hotels	Hilton Dubai Creek, Hilton Jumeirah Beach	399 1111	800
Holiday Inn Hotels	Holiday Inn Bur Dubai, Holiday Inn Downtown Deira	336 6000	575
Hyatt Regency Hotel	-	209 1234	610
JW Marriott	-	262 4444	444
Le Meridien Hotels	Le Meridien Dubai,Le Meridien Mina Siyahi, Le Royal Meridien	399 3333	750
Metropolitan Hotels	Metropolitan Beach, Metropolitan Deira, Metropolitan Hotel, Metropolitan Palace	343 0000	500
Ramada Hotel	-	351 9999	350
Rotana Hotels	Al Bustan Rotana, Jumeirah Rotana, Rihab Rotana, Rimal Rotana, Towers Rotana	343 8000	630
Sheraton Hotels	Four Points, Sheraton Deira, Sheraton Dubai Creek, Sheraton Jumeirah Beach	268 8888	595
DNATA	n/a	203 3945	415
Dining Club, The	n/a	335 5656	195
Landmark Group	n/a	338 3683	25

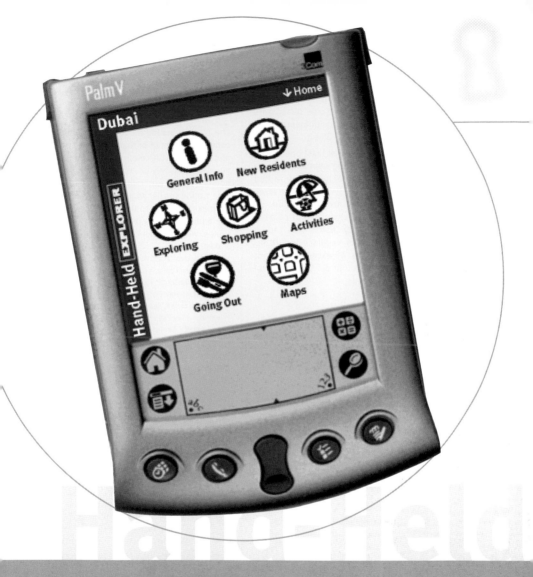

The Insiders' Guide to What's Hot and What's Not in Dubai has Gone Digital!

he **Hand-Held Explorer (Dubai)** is the first of Explorer ublishing's travel guides that can be downloaded onto our Palm Pilot. Now all the information available in the **ubai Explorer** can be accessed with the push of a button. nteractive, informative and innovative... the **Hand-Held xplorer** is easy to install, a breeze to use and packed with seful information - all at your fingertips.

- Seven sections of practical information & recommendations
- 500 independent restaurant, bar and cafe reviews
- Expansive searches for places to go & stay
- Contact & location details for all activities
- Fully referenced, interactive colour maps of Dubai
- Intuitive, user-friendly interface with help at the touch of a button

Available from leading software and electronic stores or directly from Explorer Publishing

xplorer Publishing & Distribution • Dubai Media City • Building 2 • Office 502 • PO Box 34275 • Dubai • UAE
none (+971 4) 391 8060 **Fax** (+971 4) 391 8062 **Email** info@explorer-publishing.com **Web** www.explorer-publishing.com

staggering range of mezze, which are often vegetarian, and the general affection for fresh vegetables should offer enough variety to satisfy even the most ravenous herbivore. A word of warning: if you are strict veggie, confirm that your meal is completely meat-free. Some restaurants cook their 'vegetarian' selection with animal fat or on the same grill as the meat dishes.

Nowadays, most outlets offer at least one or two veggie dishes. However, if you want a little more variety, choices include the numerous Indian vegetarian restaurants, which cater for the large number of Indians who are vegetarian by religion. These offer so many styles of cooking and such a range of tasty dishes that Indian cuisine is hard to beat for vegetarians. Other highlights include loads of excellent Italian, Mexican, Far Eastern and International restaurants all over the city.

RESTAURANTS

American

Other options ➜ American Bars [p.392]
Steak-Houses [p.372]
Tex-Mex [p.376]

Billy Blues

Location ➜ Rydges Plaza Hotel · Al Satwa | **398 2272**
Hours ➜ 18:00 - 23:00
Web/email ➜ cactus1@emirates.net.ae   **Map Ref** ➜ 7-A4

Billy Blues exudes a rich atmosphere of blues and '70s R&B. Navigate over the peanut shells on the floor to the bar to find friendly faces. Original and appealing promotions, like a Dhs.18 lunch buffet or Friday's Dhs.15 deal for food, and 'buy one get one free'. Billy Blues now has live music and a pool table as an added attraction. A popular place to meet before moving on elsewhere, or even to stick around for the whole night to soak up the cool, relaxed vibes.

Food ●●●○ Service ●●●○ Venue ●●●● Value ●●●○

Chili's

Location ➜ Jumeira Beach Centre · Jumeira | **344 1300**
Hours ➜ 11:00 - 23:00 11: 00 - 01:00 Thu Closed Fri am
Web/email ➜ eirae@emirates.net.ae   **Map Ref** ➜ 5-C2

The concept behind the American chain Chili's is a controlled formula of standardised service, menu and ambience. A colourful environment in which you can safely rely on enjoying a family-orientated, good, friendly experience. This is a particularly safe option for birthday parties as the staff really do make an effort to mark the occasion. Despite the name, at Chili's there are dishes to suit most tastes, with a particular emphasis on quantity.

Other Locations:
- *Nr Princeton Hotel, Al Garhoud (282 8484)*
- *BurJuman Centre (352 2900)*
- *Deira City Centre (295 9559)*
- *Dubai Internet City (Opening Soon)*
- *Sahara Centre, Sharjah (06 531 8890)*
- *Dubai Home Delivery (282 8303)*

Food ●●●○ Service ●●●○ Venue ●●●○ Value ●●●●

Chili's

Coco's

Location ➜ City Centre · Al Garhoud | **295 3777**
Hours ➜ 10:00 - 24:00
Web/email ➜ www.deiracitycentre.com   **Map Ref** ➜ 14-D1

Part of the large American chain, Coco's is a simple concept that is passably well-executed: neutral decor, bland food, and ample portions. Outlets offer standardised and familiar fare – burgers, soups, salads, a bit of Mexican, sandwiches, pasta

American

Going Out

Family Time
Kids Time
Lunch Time
Party Time
Fun Time
Free Time
Dinner Time
Hang out Time

Any Time, is Chili's Time!

Bahrain

Egypt

Kuwait

Lebanon

Oman

Qatar

Saudi Arabia

United Arab Emirates

People around the world eat at Chili's

Dubai Jumeirah, (04) 344 1300. Deira City Centre, (04) 295 9559. Garhoud, (04) 282 8484.
Abu Dhabi Al Mariah Cineplex, (02) 671 6300. **Al Ain** Al Jimi Mall, (03) 763 8020.
Opening Late 2002 Sharjah. Sahara Centre. Dubai. BurJuman Centre and Dubai Internet City.

etc – though surprisingly, the service and the quality are definitely hit-or-miss. Popular for breakfast and child-friendly. If in need of a sit-down lunch or a quick dinner without any surprises, the convenience and moderate prices make this a viable option.

Another branch is located in Khalid Al Attaar Tower on Sheikh Zayed Road (332 6333). ⓒⓒ

Food ●●●○ Service ●●●○ Venue ●●●○ Value ●●○○

Fuddruckers

Location → Nr Princeton Htl · Al Garhoud | **282 7771**
Hours → 07:30 - 24:00 Fri 08:00 - 22:00
Web/email → fuddubai@emirates.net.ae   **Map Ref →** 14-D2

Everything at Fuddruckers seems to be bigger (and better) than in other fast food restaurants. With large portions, 'baked on the premises' buns, bottomless beverages (coffee, tea, iced tea and soft drinks) and a large, well organised dining area, it's a favourite for families and anyone looking for simple and reasonable meal. Although famous for their burgers and fries, they also serve a delicious pancake breakfast. Probably one of the few fast food restaurants that people go out of their way to visit. ⓒⓒ

Another branch is located in Town Centre (342 9693).

Food ●●●○ Service ●●●○ Venue ●●●○ Value ●●●○

Go West

Location → Jumeirah Beach Htl · Umm Suqeim | **348 0000**
Hours → 13:30 - 15:30 18:00 - 23:30 Thu - Fri 13:30- 15:30
Web/email → www.jumeirah-beach.com   **Map Ref →** 4-B2

Slap on your chaps and spurs, saddle up the youngsters and hustle on down for an evening of live entertainment and top notch chow. Whether dining in a covered wagon or under the stars, the atmosphere is of family fun. The food, when it finally arrives, is worth the wait, and the wine list is far superior to anything you might expect to find "out on the range". Great venue for American food ... if you've got time on your hands. ⓛⓢ

Food ●●●● Service ●●○○ Venue ●●●● Value ●●●○

Hard Rock Café

Location → Hard Rock Café · Jct 5, Shk Zayed Rd | **399 2888**
Hours → 12:00 - 03:00
Web/email → www.hardrock.com   **Map Ref →** 3-A3

The Hard Rock Café serves up exactly what anyone would expect, and a little bit more. The staff are friendly and obliging, the food comes in American-esque huge portions, and a live band rocks the house six nights a week. Although not exactly health food, they do offer limited vegetarian options along with those nachos, burgers and fries. Friday afternoons are devoted to kids, with balloons, face painting and a clown. A total entertainment and eating family-friendly experience. ⓂⓃⓁ

Food ●●●○ Service ●●●○ Venue ●●●○ Value ●●●○

Harry's Place & The Cigar Room

Harry's Place & The Cigar Room

Location → Renaissance Hotel · Hor Al Anz | **262 5555**
Hours → 18:00 - 02:00
Web/email → rendubai@emirates.net.ae   **Map Ref →** 12-A3

This eclectic venue, with attached (indoor) "terrace," Hollywood-influenced decor, dance floor, and attached cigar room emphasises 'big': gung-ho steaks, pasta and pizzas, world-class cigars, and drinks aplenty. After 21:30, the band and the disco ball overwhelm the main dining area; choose the terrace or cigar room for some peace. Harry's is one of those places where the staff know your name after two visits, so gather up the rat pack and head down to toss

American · *Going Out*

Welcome
to Century Village

A world of choices

**Indoor · Outdoor · Lebanese · Chinese
Portuguese · Japanese · Italian · French**

In the heart of Dubai, located next to the Irish Village
under Dubai Tennis Stadium. Call Dubai 04 2824122

back a T-bone, a couple of pints, and a fine hand-rolled Cuban.

Food ●●●○ Service ●●○○ Venue ●●○○ Value ●●●○

Top Americas

Billy Blues	M's Beef Bistro
Go West	Pachanga
Johnny Rockets	Rodeo Grill
JW Steakhouse	Western Steak House

Henry J. Beans

Location ➔ Capitol Hotel · Al Satwa | **345 8350**
Hours ➔ 12:00 - 03:00
Web/email ➔ www.henryjbeans.com   **Map Ref** ➔ 7-A2

A lively, hip atmosphere with a Tex-Mex oriented menu and a lavish range of cocktails makes this a fun place for Friday brunch with the family, or late night partying. Energetic staff know everything imaginable about libations, and you'll find some of the best burgers in town here. Large TV screens, pool tables, a resident band that gets the place rocking six nights a week, and special guest DJs make for grand diversions. Go early if you want a quiet dinner before the pace heats up.

Food ●●●○ Service ●●○○ Venue ●●●○ Value ●●○○

Johnny Rockets

Location ➔ Opp Jumeirah Centre · Beach Rd, Jumeira | **344 7859**
Hours ➔ 12:00 - 24:00
Web/email ➔ n/a   **Map Ref** ➔ 6-C2

Great for kids and 'mature' burger lovers, this joint elevates lowly fast food to delicious levels. Table jukeboxes and 'performing' staff (you'll either love or hate it) keep the mood light. Best for a quick bite as seats and tables (and paper plates and cups) are not meant to encourage lingering. Great malt shakes, very large portions and a lively, friendly atmosphere most afternoons and evenings (plus a regular Friday afternoon post-beach clientele), make this is a great contender.

Food ●●●● Service ●●●○ Venue ●●●○ Value ●●●○

Planet Hollywood

Location ➔ Wafi City · Umm Hurair 2 | **324 4777**
Hours ➔ 12:00 - 03:00
Web/email ➔ www.planethollywood-dubai.com   **Map Ref** ➔ 13-D2

Planet Hollywood is a good place for a 'fun' meal out. Movie memorabilia covers the walls and ceilings in this sometimes buzzing venue that caters to families, nightclubbers, and kids birthday parties. The menu includes a wide range of American dishes and caters to both veggies and meat lovers. However, be warned – in keeping with the Hollywood theme, portions are larger than life, and if you overindulge yourself early on, you'll miss out on some decadent desserts. Family Friday brunch is very popular here – book ahead.

Food ●●●○ Service ●●●○ Venue ●●●○ Value ●●●○

Americas

Lumping together Central, North and South America may seem strange, but there is a method to the madness. Generally speaking, this cuisine is especially good for meat lovers. Many of the steakhouses and American joints, for example, offer prime quality meat especially flown in from the States to be cooked to your preferred temperature. Desserts vary widely in this category, but often the old favourites like Mississippi mud pie, apple pie or chocolate cake with lashings of ice-cream can be found somewhere on the menu - to the delight of those who like to finish with a dish that is sweet, filling, and calorie laden. In general, this is hearty fare with the emphasis on portion size: steaks, ribs, and burgers in such restaurants usually make dainty eaters cringe with disbelief. Often main courses in this category come with chips, but most restaurants will offer alternatives, such as a baked potato or salad, if you show some concern for your arteries.

Moving south, the cuisine is still meat based - in particular, Argentinean cooking is noteworthy for serving high quality steaks, but Caribbean dishes show a little more interest in fruit, vegetables and chicken. The hotter and spicier Mexican and Tex-Mex cooking usually has a wider choice for vegetarians. Some of the options include refried beans, guacamole, salsa, nachos (small, hard tortillas topped with melted cheese, peppers and chilli), fajitas (a soft tortilla, wrapped around sizzling vegetables and cheese or meat) and enchiladas (a tortilla filled with meat or cheese and served under a rich sauce), plus some great salads. Great if you have the appetite of a bear, but be careful if you like to have room for dessert. Check out the following cuisines:

American, Argentinean, Cajun/Creole, Cuban, Mexican & Tex-Mex and Steak- Houses

American

Going Out

The perfect Hollywood setting...

fun, exciting and absolutely delicious.

GREAT AMERICAN FOOD, AUTHENTIC HOLLYWOOD MEMORABILIA AND THE BIGGEST STARS PERFORMING FOR YOU ON THE BIG SCREEN.

TONS OF FUN FOR KIDS WITH EXCITING ACTIVITIES EVERY MONTH AND AN AWESOME WILD BRUNCH EVERY FRIDAY.

WHAT'S MORE... BRING THIS COUPON WITH YOU AND GET 20% OFF YOUR FOOD BILL. THIS OFFER IS FOR A ONE-TIME USE ONLY AND CANNOT BE USED IN CONJUNCTION WITH ANY OTHER OFFER OR PROMOTION. VALID UP TO 30TH SEPTEMBER, 2003.

LOCATED AT WAFI CITY. FOR RESERVATIONS, PLEASE CALL: 3244777

Rattle Snake

Location → Metropolitan · Jct 2, Shk Zayed Rd | **343 0000**
Hours → 17:00 - 03:00
Web/email → methotel@emirates.net.ae   **Map Ref** → 5-C4

   150

Designed to look like an old Western movie set, with each corner of the restaurant offering a different scene – courthouse, jail, railway station, etc – this is a fun venue. The moody lighting adds to the atmosphere, but is in no way reflected in the attitude of the staff... no surly waiters here. American/Mexican/Tex-Mex fare pleases most, but leaves veggies with limited options. Big portions and cold drinks go down well either at a table near the band or outside on the terrace.⊙

Food ●●●○ Service ●●●○ Venue ●●●○ Value ●●○○

Scarlett's

Location → Emirates Towers · Trade Centre 1&2 | **319 8743**
Hours → 12:00 - 03:00
Web/email → www.emirates-towers-hotel.com   **Map Ref** → 9-C2

   150

The Deep South décor (an "Antebellum mansion") theme is popular with the 'want to be seen' thirty something crowd early, while the younger generation turns up late for the vibrant atmosphere of the upstairs dance floor. A substantial and diverse menu boasts rather bland Mexican food, burgers, steaks, and a lovely cinnamon apple flan. In practice, this is slightly tarted up pub fare. Aggressive service and inflated prices confirm that one is paying for the atmosphere here.⊙

Food ●●●○ Service ●●○○ Venue ●●○○ Value ●●○○

TGI Friday's

Location → Holiday Centre · Trade Centre 1&2 | **331 8010**
Hours → 11:00 - 24:00 Wed & Thu 11:00 - 01:00
Web/email → tgifdxb@emirates.net.ae   **Map Ref** → 9-D2

   150

This large chain restaurant – with loud music, a bar, dance floor, and Hollywood memorabilia – offers American fare: enormous burgers, sizzling Tex-Mex fajitas, as well as speciality salads, appetisers, pasta and ribs. The portions could easily feed two. Sinful desserts as well, from warm carrot cake to a huge Oreo ice-cream sandwich. Unlicensed, but juices, mocktails, and shakes are grand. The extremely helpful – if sometimes manic – staff keep the pace moving. TGI Friday's appeals to many, but is a particular treat for the kids.

See also: A second branch is at the Al Bustan Rotana Hotel, Al Garhoud (282 7674). It offers the same menu and service, plus alcohol, and is open 12:00 - 03:00.⊙

Food ●●●○ Service ●●●○ Venue ●●●○ Value ●●●○

TGI Thursday's

Location → Astoria Hotel · Bur Dubai | **353 4300**
Hours → 10:00 - 01:00
Web/email → www.astamb.com   **Map Ref** → 8-A2

  150

In the style of, but not related to, the well-known TGI Friday's chain, this American knock-off proves that the concept is easy to imitate. Wonderfully located, they serve giant steak sandwiches and burgers, as well as rich desserts. Bar prices are good and the atmosphere is young, noisy and lively. One good point is its proximity to The George & Dragon pub and one of Dubai's favourite nightspots, Pancho Villas, allowing you to continue partying after your meal.⊙

Food ●●●○ Service ●●●○ Venue ●●●○ Value ●●●○

Arabic/Lebanese

Other options → **Dinner Cruises [p.379]**
Arabic Nightclubs [p.411]
Belly Dancing [p.287]
Persian [p.366]

Al Basha

Location → Metropolitan Resort · Al Sufouh | **399 5000**
Hours → 13:00 - 24:00
Web/email → metbeach@emirates.net.ae   **Map Ref** → 2-E2

 150

Copious, well-presented and delicious food is the hallmark of this venue. Although the menu is not extensive, the dishes are consistently very good. An oud player accompanied by traditional drums and sometimes a belly dancer provide entertainment. Shisha is available, but there is also a non-smoking section. The terrace is ideal when the weather cools as it overlooks the beach and has a relaxed, casual, sociable atmosphere. After a satisfying meal, take a stroll around the surprisingly large grounds for even more people-watching.

Food ●●●○ Service ●●●○ Venue ●●●○ Value ●●●○

Al Dar

Location → Above McDonald's · Beach Rd, Jumeira | **342 0990**
Hours → 13:00 - 01:00
Web/email → n/a **Map Ref →** 6-C2

Ignore the tatty front and enter into the plush 'Arabic' décor inside. The menu features traditional Lebanese dishes, such as grilled meats, humous and tabouleh, along with fresh seafood. Beautifully and simply presented, the dishes are surprisingly filling and especially good. On Fridays, a lunch buffet is available, and for those needing a little seclusion, there are private cabins to hide yourself away from the rest of the clientele, which leans towards the young Arab crowd and families.

Food ●●●○ Service ●●●○ Venue ●●●○ Value ●●●○

Al Diwan

Location → Metropolitan Palace · Deira | **205 1336**
Hours → 11:00 - 15:00 19:00 - 01:00 Fri 19:00 - 01:00
Web/email → www.methotels.com **Map Ref →** 11-D2

With its good selection of upscale Arabic food, the Al Diwan is an extremely popular venue in the vicinity of Deira. The friendly staff and festive room make the exotic elements of Arabic dining all the more enticing. Highly aromatic biryani, grills, and decadently sweet desserts make for flavourful traditional choices. Although lurching towards the higher price range, considering the portions and the room, this is not a bad value for money. Great for tourists or new arrivals.

Food ●●●● Service ●●●○ Venue ●●●● Value ●●●○

Al Fardous

Location → Sheraton Deira · Hor Al Anz | **268 8888**
Hours → 18:00 - 03:00 Closed Sat
Web/email → shedeira@emirates.net.ae **Map Ref →** 12-A3

Cosy and dimly lit, this venue offers a flexible menu that is bound to please. The usual suspects are served up with the usual good cheer and playfulness. Live music, belly dancing, and a sociable atmosphere make this a loud

restaurant. As expected in this category, things start late and continue on until early. Very popular on weekends, so reservations are recommended. Not the cheapest option, but the extra price is reflected in the quality of the venue. Closed during Ramadan.

Food ●●○○ Service ●●●○ Venue ●●●○ Value ●●○○

Middle Eastern

There is no one distinct Middle Eastern or Arabic cuisine, but it is instead a blend of many styles of cooking from the region. Thus an Arabic meal will usually include a mix of dishes from countries as far afield as Morocco or Egypt to Lebanon and Iran. In Dubai, modern Arabic cuisine almost invariably means Lebanese food. Typical ingredients include beef, lamb, chicken, rice, nuts (mainly pistachios), dates, yoghurt and a range of seafood and spices. The cuisine is excellent for meat eaters and vegetarians alike.

A popular starter is a selection of dishes known as 'mezze' (meze or mezzeh), which is often a meal in its own right. It is a variety of appetisers served with flat bread, a green salad and 'radioactive' pickles. Dishes can include 'humous' (ground chickpeas, oil and garlic), 'tabouleh' (parsley and cracked wheat salad, with tomato), 'fatoush' (lettuce, tomatoes and grilled Arabic bread), and 'fattayer' (small, usually hot, pastries filled with spinach and cottage cheese).

Charcoal grilling is a popular cooking method and traditionally dishes are cooked with many spices including ginger, nutmeg and cinnamon. An authentic local dish is 'khouzi' (whole lamb, traditionally wrapped in banana leaves, buried in the sand and roasted, then served on a bed of rice, mixed with nuts), which is most often available at Ramadan for the evening meal at the end of the day's fast ('Iftar'). It would also have been served at the 'mansaf'; the traditional, formal Bedouin dinner, where various dishes would have been placed on the floor in the centre of a ring of seated guests. Other typical dishes include 'kibbeh' (deep-fried balls of mince, pine nuts and bulgar (cracked wheat), and a variety of kebabs. Seafood is widely available and local varieties of fish include hammour (a type of grouper), chanad (mackerel), beyah (mullet) and wahar, which are often grilled over hot coals or baked in an oven.

Meals end with Lebanese sweets, which are delicious, but very sweet. The most widely known is 'baklava' (filo pastry layered with honey and nuts) and 'umm Ali' (mother of Ali in English), which is a rich, creamy dessert with layers of milk, bread, raisins and nuts - an exotic bread and butter pudding. Check out the following cuisines.

Arabic/ Lebanese, Egyptian, Emirati, Moroccan, Persian and Turkish

Arabic/Lebanese

Going Out

Al Iwan

Location → Burj Al Arab · Umm Suqeim
Hours → 12:00 - 02:00
Web/email → www.burj-al-arab.com

301 7600

Map Ref → 4-A1

    300

Say yes when your rich uncle asks you to join him at Al Iwan: it delivers all the excess one has come to expect. Delight in the flamboyance of the Burj al Arab and relax with Al Iwan's conservative continental cuisine in Arabic dress. Although you may balk at a bowl of cubed lamb's liver and diced tomatoes, the grilled red snapper and other reliable fish and meat entrees restore equanimity. Desserts draw strength from local recipes, and your uncle's bill will reinforce the hotel's image.

Food ●●●○ Service ●●●○ Venue ●●●● Value ●●○○

Al Khayal

Location → Jumeirah Beach Htl · Umm Suqeim
Hours → 12:30 - 15:00 20:00 - 03:00
Web/email → www.jumeirah-beach.com

348 0000

Map Ref → 4-B2

   200

Elegant, trendy and stylish, Al Khayal offers a tasteful and refined Arabic experience. With its circular hall, artful interiors and smoky atmosphere, this cosy venue exudes Arabian vibes. Start with assorted mezze and proceed to the mixed grill, both signature dishes. Finish decadently by indulging in honeyed desserts. Purposefully leisurely service allows guests to enjoy the band. The lights dim when Sherihan hits the floor... if she stops and asks your name, you may need time to recall who you are, let alone where you are.

Food ●●●○ Service ●●●○ Venue ●●●○ Value ●●●○

Al Khayma

Location → Dubai Marine Beach · Beach Rd, Jumeira
Hours → 19:30 - 03:00
Web/email → www.dxbmarine.com

346 1111

Map Ref → 6-D2

  150

Located in the heart of Jumeirah, the Al Khaimah offers upscale Arabic cuisine, various flavours of shisha, and delightful live Arabic music. As the name suggests, the decor revolves around the khaimah seating with a variety of couches and low chairs. The lively atmosphere is friendly, and the service adequate. In terms of food, no particular surprises: grills, mezze, biryanis, etc that are generally well prepared and tasty. The venue itself,

however, pushes the restaurant into the more interesting category of options.

Food ●●●○ Service ●●●○ Venue ●●●○ Value ●●●●

Al Koufa

Location → Nr Cyclone · Umm Hurair 2
Hours → 18:00 - 01:00 Thu 18:00 - 03:00
Web/email → n/a

335 1511

Map Ref → 10-D4

   100

One of a few places serving some Emirati dishes, Al Koufa offers good Arabic food, great people watching and pretty decent shisha. The venue has evolved over the years from a temporary looking tent into an almost as temporary looking building, complete with polystyrene walls. The food and service are better than the décor. Before 23:00, the place is almost entirely deserted. After that, the loud band starts up and people pack in. An authentic Emirati experience you won't find here, but a window into Dubai's 'prowling' culture you will...

Food ●●●○ Service ●●●○ Venue ●●○○ Value ●●●○

Al Nafoorah

Location → Emirates Towers · Trade Centre 1&2
Hours → 12:30 - 15:00 19:30 - 23:30
Web/email → www.emirates-towers-hotel.com

330 0000

Map Ref → 9-C2

  200

Another authentic Lebanese restaurant with an exhaustive menu; Al Nafoorah starts early and excels in food and presentation. Décor is warm without being over the top. Efficient service keeps things moving and will help the rare few who can't figure out the menu. Start with fish kibbeh; continue with the mixed grill and know that the tantalising desserts are complimentary. The terrace offers a welcome continuation of the evening, where gentle puffs of shisha ensure that any remaining stress goes up in smoke.

Food ●●●○ Service ●●●● Venue ●●●○ Value ●●●○

Al Qasr

Location → Dubai Marine Beach · Beach Rd, Jumeira
Hours → 12:30 - 15:30 19:30 - 23:00 Thu 12:30 - 03:30
Web/email → www.dxbmarine.com

346 1111

Map Ref → 6-D2

     200

Al Qasr offers two dining experiences: come for lunch or an early dinner for a quiet meal, or have a late dinner and enjoy a lively Arabic show. The

Arabic/Lebanese

Going Out

menu includes many Lebanese favourites, and the mezze and grilled prawns are especially good. The audience really gets into the belly dancing show and the live Arabic music, making for a festive night. Continue the experience with shisha in the majlis. Service is generally good, but waiters can be hard to find once the show starts.

Food ●●●○ Service ●●○○ Venue ●●●○ Value ●●●○

crispy shrimps and spicy grilled meat are hard to forget. When the Arabic band and belly dancer begin their show, this restaurant really shines. Although quiet early, Al Tannour gets packed to capacity until late, but the hospitality and service remain genuine. On all counts, a winner for an Arabian night out.

Food ●●●● Service ●●●○ Venue ●●●○ Value ●●●○

Al Safadi

Location → Al Rigga Rd · Deira | **227 9922**
Hours → 08:00 - 12:00 13:00 - 02:00 Fri 08:00 - 02:00
Web/email → n/a | **Map Ref →** 11-D2

 100

Like most of the restaurants in this category, the service is good, the food copious and tasty, and the value for money fantastic. Perhaps a less vast menu than others, but the payback is that what's listed is likely to be very nicely prepared. The meat selection is on view and is grilled in front of you, and they also serve special lunch plates. The lights are bright and the customer turnover high, with a mainly Lebanese clientele, so don't plan to linger.

Food ●●●● Service ●●●○ Venue ●●○○ Value ●●●○

ARZ Lebanon

Location → Trade Centre Rd · Bur Dubai | **396 4466**
Hours → 08:00 - 01:00 Fri 13:00- 01:00
Web/email → abci1@emirates.net.ae | **Map Ref →** 10-E1

 100

This beautifully decorated (Danish run) Lebanese restaurant has seating for about 70, including a romantic little alcove outside. The menu has so much to offer, you'll welcome the help of your friendly waiter in making your choice. If you're not in the mood for Lebanese, ARZ also offers a small range of Italian pastas and continental dishes. The highlight is the piping hot Lebanese bread, freshly baked in an open oven while you watch. Takeaway, home delivery and outside catering available.

Food ●●●○ Service ●●●○ Venue ●●●○ Value ●●●○

Al Shami

Location → Nr Travel Centre · Deira | **269 5558**
Hours → 07:00 - 03:00 Fri 13:30 - 03:00
Web/email → n/a | **Map Ref →** 11-E3

50

Run by a Syrian team, this Arabic restaurant is a very traditional affair, not only in terms of ambience but also in taste. Usually very busy, Al Shami has excellent value lunch buffets everyday for Dhs.20. Choose from over 25 Arabic starters or the daily specials, which are not listed on the menu, so don't forget to ask!

Food ●●●● Service ●●●○ Venue ●●●○ Value ●●●●

Automatic

Location → Beach Centre, The · Beach Rd, Jumeira | **349 4888**
Hours → 12:00 - 01:00
Web/email → n/a | **Map Ref →** 6-B2

50

A perennial favourite place to introduce visiting relatives and friends to Arabic food. Big, fresh portions, a lively cafeteria ambience, and delightfully affordable pricing make this a winner. The extensive menu includes excellent fish, a standard selection of mezze, a mixed grill (an enormous platter of different fish and meats) as well as tempting daily specials and an excellent Friday buffet. In addition, each table gets a complementary vegetable garden "salad." Remember to leave some room for dessert (good luck!).

Food ●●●○ Service ●●○○ Venue ●●○○ Value ●●●●

Al Tannour

Location → Crowne Plaza · Trade Centre 1&2 | **331 1111**
Hours → 20:00 - 03:00 Closed Fri
Web/email → www.crowneplaza.com | **Map Ref →** 9-D2

 200

Al Tannour places quality and style over quantity. The dim candlelit ambience turns smoky when the fragrant shishas get going. A generous three-course meal is offered on twin-sharing basis;

Arabic/Lebanese

Going Out

Awafi

Location → JW Marriott Hotel · Deira
Hours → 21:00 - 02:00 Only open in Winter
Web/email → www.marriott.com

262 4444

Map Ref → 12-A3

If you're seeking the 'highest level' of Arabic dining, look no further than Awafi. Unobstructed views, an authentic Arabian experience and generous servings highlight your experience. Choice of seating is limited only by your mood - dine at a table, Arabic style on the floor, or lounge by the pool. With importance placed on freshness, choices range from mezze to mains that'll satisfy your appetite and wallet. Whether you're dining, chilling out or watching the belly dancers wiggle into the night, this rooftop venue a must.

Food ●●●○ Service ●●●● Venue ●●●○ Value ●●●○

Awtar

Location → Grand Hyatt Dubai · Umm Hurair 2
Hours → 07:30 - 03:00 Closed Fri
Web/email → www.hyatt.com

209 6993

Map Ref → 13-E3

Awtar will be the Grand Hyatt's Arabic venue. It is hard to imagine how it is going to distinguish itself in a very crowded field. They plan to seek the high-end market with their plush setting and upscale décor. The menu will feature the usual favourites – mezze, flat bread, grilled meats, and honeyed sweets – most probably very well executed. Live entertainment will enliven the room, though no word yet as to what sort.

Food – n/a Service – n/a Venue – n/a Value – n/a

Ayam Zaman

Location → Ascot Hotel · Bur Dubai
Hours → 19:30 - 01:30
Web/email → info@centuryhoteldubai.com

352 0900

Map Ref → 8-A3

The menu might be modest but the flavours certainly aren't. Traditional favourites like shish tawook and hummous make up the menu. A popular fixed menu of 21 dishes is a good way to sample various delights. In true Arabic style, things don't get going until late. There is live music every night starting at 21:30 and shisha is on offer. The wine list is decent but pricey. To keep the value for money going strong, go native and drink juice for an evening.

Food ●●●○ Service ●●●○ Venue ●●●● Value ●●●○

Bazerkan

Location → Capitol Hotel · Al Satwa
Hours → 12:00 - 16:00 20:00 - 03:00
Web/email → caphotel@emirates.net.ae

346 0111

Map Ref → 7-A2

Sit on the roof terrace and gaze at the lights along nearby Sheikh Zayed Road as you enjoy delectable Lebanese favourites. The indoor dining area offers more plush seating and a live Arabic band beginning at 22:00. The mezze are mouth-watering and the grilled meats are a delight. Don't miss the tabouleh. Wine and beer choices are limited, but not dire. The considerate staff ensure a pleasant dining experience. Top off the evening with shisha and great coffee, and watch the world scurry below.

Food ●●●○ Service ●●●○ Venue ●●●○ Value ●●●○

Beach Café Restaurant

Location → Beach Centre, The · Beach Rd, Jumeira
Hours → 10:00 - 01:00 Closed Fri am
Web/email → n/a

344 6066

Map Ref → 6-B2

This little gem of a restaurant is a welcoming oasis after a long, hot morning on the beach. The menu combines Arabic and Italian dishes, all freshly and expertly prepared, well presented, and delivered to your table with a friendly smile. It's worth straying off the beaten track to find this venue, tucked away on the first floor of the Beach Centre. Good food, good service and a cool, welcoming environment will reward your efforts, and you will certainly return.

Food ●●●○ Service ●●●○ Venue ●●○○ Value ●●●○

Fakhreldine

Location → Holiday Inn Bur Dubai · Umm Hurair 2
Hours → 12:00 - 15:00 19:00 - 01:00
Web/email → hiburdxb@emirates.net.ae

336 6000

Map Ref → 10-D4

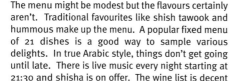

Excellent Lebanese cuisine is what sets Fakhreldine apart from the rest in this very full category. The entrance is easy to miss as it's hidden on the side of the hotel, but once you're in there, there's an impressive list of mezze to choose from, plus mixed grill, lamb and kebab mains. Relatively inexpensive, however drinks can sink deep into your wallet. A live singer adds to the ambience that'll make sure you come back to Fakhreldine for more.

Food ●●●○ Service ●●○○ Venue ●●●○ Value ●●●○

Fakhreldine

L'Auberge

Location → City Centre · Al Garhoud
Hours → 12:00 - 24:00 Fri 13:00 - 24:00
Web/email → www.deiracitycentre.com

295 0201

Map Ref → 14-D1

L'Auberge offers decent Arabic food within the mall. Seating options include social booths, open tables or small alcoves that can be curtained off for private dining. Service is good and not too rushed. Like most Lebanese restaurants, Arabic bread and a huge garden salad arrive at your table first, with which you can enjoy a selection of mezze or other starters. Main meals consist mostly of grills. Overall, a surprisingly pleasant restaurant, particularly suited for an escape from consumer mania.

See also: Hamarain Centre (262 6965).

Food ●●●○ Service ●●○○ Venue ●●●○ Value ●●●○

Majlis Al Bahar

Location → Burj Al Arab · Umm Suqeim
Hours → 19:30 - 24:00
Web/email → www.burj-al-arab.com

301 7777

Map Ref → 4-A1

This small beach restaurant with an imposing view of the Burj Al Arab feels like a slice of balmy paradise. A trio of excellent roaming musicians entertain diners with an eclectic mix of songs. The menu offers casual fare (like burgers) as well as Arabic inspired international cuisine, with the various seafood options making for difficult choices. Relaxing and comfortable, with pleasant, informed waiters, this venue delivers luxury without the usual snobbery: overall an outstanding dining experience.

Food ●●●○ Service ●●●○ Venue ●●●○ Value ●●○○

Mawal

Location → Al Bustan Hotel · Al Garhoud
Hours → 12:30 - 15:30 19:30 - 02:00
Web/email → fb@albustan-rotana.com

282 6530

Map Ref → 14-E3

Fresh, familiar Lebanese food and a welcoming staff make this venue successful. Try the small sausages, goat labneh, or orange peel preserve for something a little different. Both traditional (tabouleh etc) and the more exotic and interesting Lebanese dishes are served. Mawal offers some of the best Lebanese food in Dubai and you certainly won't leave with an empty stomach! Entertainment is offered by a singer and a belly dancer. In a crowded category, this is among the better options.

Food ●●●○ Service ●●●○ Venue ●●●○ Value ●●●○

Mays El Reem

Location → JW Marriott Hotel · Deira
Hours → 12:30 - 15:30 20:00 - 03:00 Closed Sat
Web/email → marriott@emirates.net.ae

607 7823

Map Ref → 12-A3

Good for tourists or if you have visitors from out of town, Mays El Reem delivers all the charm of Arabia in one sitting – as well as linguistic problems, disorganisation and a surprisingly hefty bill. Concoct your own Middle-Eastern feast from a wide selection of hot and cold Arabic mezze and main dishes while a lively music duo sets the tone. Finish with a shisha as you watch the belly dancer shake her stuff. The 'Mays' experience starts and ends late, so arrive after 22:00.

Food ●●●○ Service ●●○○ Venue ●●●○ Value ●●○○

Mays El Reem

Mazaj

Location ➜ Century Village · Al Garhoud   **282 9952**
Hours ➜ 12:00 - 03:00
Web/email ➜ www.aviationclubonline.com   **Map Ref** ➜ 14-C3

    150

Mazaj brings a traditional slice of Lebanese culture and lifestyle to Dubai. Their famous grill selections are paradise for carnivores; vegetarians may feel a little slighted. The helpful and happy staff serves a pleasant Arabian atmosphere with the food, while a roaming musician adds to the fun. A great place for newcomers to try a shisha and talk late into the night. In winter months, the large terrace is a joy for people-watching at the other venues of Century Village.

Food ●●●○ Service ●●●○ Venue ●●●● Value ●●●○

Saj Express

Location ➜ Oasis Tower, Shk Zayed Rd · Shk Zayed Rd   **321 1191**
Hours ➜ 09:00 - 02:00
Web/email ➜ sajxpress@emirates.net.ae   **Map Ref** ➜ 9-B2

   100

Better for takeaway than for eating in and enduring shockingly bright lighting and sometimes 'laughably bad' service, Saj Express offers a menu ranging from their speciality saj (thin bread filled with savoury or sweet ingredients baked on a metal dome), to a good selection of hot and cold dishes – from hommus to grilled meats. Meat lovers are better cared for than veggies; regardless both will appreciate hommus beiruty and 'chocoba extra' – saj filled with chocolate sauce and a mixture of fruits and nuts – divine!

Food ●●●○ Service ●○○○ Venue ●●○○ Value ●●●○

Argentinean

La Parrilla

Location ➜ Jumeirah Beach Htl · Umm Suqeim   **348 0000**
Hours ➜ 12:30 - 15:00   19:00 - 02:00
Web/email ➜ www.jumeirah-beach.com   **Map Ref** ➜ 4-B2

250

Relaxing in the convivial, ranch-house-themed La Parilla, it's easy to forget that it's situated 25 floors up with spectacular views of the Arabian Gulf. This memorable restaurant specialises in extremely tender grilled meats flown in from the US. Limited

alternatives are available for the less carnivorous. The signature dessert, chocolate pancakes with strawberries, is flambéed tableside (you must!). An energetic and entertaining (but loud) Argentinean band lends real authenticity to the venue. Not a cheap night out, but fabulous for an occasion.

Food ●●●○ Service ●●●○ Venue ●●●○ Value ●●○○

Pachanga

Location ➜ Hilton Jumeirah · Al Sufouh   **399 1111**
Hours ➜ 19:00 - 24:00
Web/email ➜ hiltonjb@emirates.net.ae   **Map Ref** ➜ 2-D2

   300

Pachanga combines flavoursome South American cuisine with a lively musical atmosphere. Choose a table with a view of the live entertainment (bordering on the deafening), sit in the air-conditioned tapas bar overlooking the sea, or have a drink and a cigar at the bar. Order perfectly grilled, delicious meats and seafood from the Argentinean, Brazilian, Mexican, or Cuban sections of the menu and finish your meal with the irresistible hot chocolate soufflé. You'll be energised by the music and tempted by the meals here.

Food ●●●● Service ●●●○ Venue ●●●○ Value ●●●○

British

Other options ➜ **Pubs [p.404]**
Fish & Chips [p.326]

Bray, The

Location ➜ Metropolitan · Jct 2, Shk Zayed Rd   **343 0000**
Hours ➜ 19:00 - 23:30
Web/email ➜ www.methotels.com   **Map Ref** ➜ 5-C4

 150

In classic old English style, The Bray offers a truly elegant and memorable dining experience. Candlelight and rich oak tables help set the mood; beef Wellington, old Claret and an impressive array of other options make this one of Dubai's best-kept secrets. Monthly promotions and an 'early bird' option further add to the appeal. For veggies there's a range of choices and the chef will prepare special dishes on request. Anglophiles take note of this one.

Food ●●●○ Service ●●●○ Venue ●●●● Value ●●●○

Cajun/Creole

Other options → Cuban [p.323]
Tex-Mex [p.376]

Oh! Cajun

Location → Emirates Towers · Trade Centre 1&2
Hours → 19:30 - 24:00
Web/email → www.emirates-towers-hotel.com   **Map Ref →** 9-C2

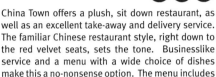 **300**

Oh, what a surprise to find Creole and Cajun cuisine just off the lobby of the Emirates Towers. The menu includes some surprise twists on some of Louisiana's spicy favourite seafood and beef dishes. The selection of seafood dishes, while limited, ranges from spicy to sophisticated. Appetisers, side dishes and desserts are inspired by the roots of Cajun cooking, though authenticity isn't always there. The restaurant with its dark finishes and colourful painting is pleasant venue for couples or friends.●

Food ●●○○ Service ●●●● Venue ●●●○ Value ●●●○

Top Far East

Blue Elephant	**Mr. Chow**
Creekside	**Sakura**
Imperial Garden	**Thai Bistro**
Miyako	

Chinese

Other options → Filipino [p.326]
Malaysian [p.358]
Singaporean [p.372]
Thai [p.377]

China Times

Location → Jumeirah Plaza · Beach Rd, Jumeira
Hours → 12:00 - 15:00 19:00 - 24:00
Web/email → binhendi@binhendi.com   **Map Ref →** 6-C2

 50

This quality restaurant has a relaxed atmosphere and an eclectic décor combining both modern and traditional designs. The variety and quality of food and service are excellent, and the chef will alter the level of spiciness to suit your taste. Chinese style seafood is the speciality, although the menu offers a range of dishes. This is one Chinese restaurant that will not leave you feeling

hungry a few hours later! Conveniently located for the Jumeira shops and beach.●

Food ●●●○ Service ●●●○ Venue ●●●○ Value ●●●○

China Town

Location → Khalid Bin Walid St · Bur Dubai
Hours → 12:00 - 15:00 19:00 - 23:30
Web/email → na   **Map Ref →** 8-A4

 100

China Town offers a plush, sit down restaurant, as well as an excellent take-away and delivery service. The familiar Chinese restaurant style, right down to the red velvet seats, sets the tone. Businesslike service and a menu with a wide choice of dishes make this a no-nonsense option. The menu includes plenty of exciting additions to the old favourites – unfortunately, there's no crispy duck, although the wanton soup is a worthy choice. Generous portions help make this a good value for money.●

Food ●●●○ Service ●●○○ Venue ●●○○ Value ●●●○

China Valley

Location → Nr Sana, Trade Centre Rd · Al Karama
Hours → 12:00 - 15:00 19:00 - 24:00
Web/email → n/a   **Map Ref →** 10-C1

150

This long-standing, competent independent venue is suited to conversational dining. A lengthy, clearly organised menu covers the well-known Chinese dishes that you would expect – quite a few with a 'chilli' designating them as "spicy". The food is generally tasty and ample, and the waiters quietly efficient and in full control, even when the place fills up. Fixed price lunches and dinners give greater flexibility to the already reasonable prices. Book in advance at weekends; good for large parties (in a separate room).●

Food ●●●○ Service ●●●○ Venue ●●●○ Value ●●●●

Chinaman

Location → Hamdan Colony · Al Karama
Hours → 12:00 - 15:00 19:00 - 23:30   Closed Fri am
Web/email → n/a   **Map Ref →** 10-E1

 50

As good or better than most, this tiny and inexpensive venue is a handy secret. No Chinese lanterns or stone dragons clutter the space –

Cajun/Creole | Chinese

Going Out

there's simply no room in this 15-person venue! The menu has all the usual choices at a cheaper price than elsewhere, and dishes are promptly served by the manager. The quantity and quality are good; try the Cantonese roast chicken or the spicy duck in plum sauce. Take-away is available, but can be slow as the restaurant is usually busy.

Food ●●●○ Service ●●○○ Venue ●●○○ Value ●●●○

Chinese Kitchen

Location → Nr Union Co-op · Al Wasl Rd, Jumeira | **394 3864**
Hours → 12:00 - 15:00 18:00 - 24:00
Web/email → n/a   Map Ref → 5-B2

This mainly take-away Jumeira favourite does also offer limited seating upstairs. Sparse but comfortable décor keeps the focus on the food and hospitality. Delivery and in-house dining is fast and efficient. Chef Mr. Chen prides himself on his home-made sauces and individually made spring rolls and wontons. Other Hunan and Szechwan favourites include lemon chicken, garlic prawns and Shanghai rice. An ideal location, outside catering, and free delivery are other good reasons to try this restaurant.

Another branch of Chinese Kitchen is in Khalid bin Waleed Rd, Bur Dubai (393 6984) 12:00 - 15:00 & 19:00 - 01:00.

Food ●●●○ Service ●●●○ Venue ●●●○ Value ●●●○

Chinese Palace

Location → Al Ghurair City · Deira | **228 1043**
Hours → 12:00 - 15:00 18:00 - 23:30
Web/email → www.alghuraircity.com   Map Ref → 11-D1

If you are looking for somewhere to have a cosy dinner without too many people around, this is the place (although the background music can be too loud). Surroundings are bright and spacious, and peppered with 'typical' Chinese red lanterns and dragons. Weekdays, it's not at all crowded for dinner, although lunchtimes are quite busy. They have a selection of clay-pot-dishes served as well as typical Chinese food. There is a buffet every Thursday night and Friday lunch.

See also: Fast food versions in the BurJuman Centre and Deira City Centre Mall.

Food ●●●○ Service ●●●○ Venue ●●●○ Value ●●●○

Dynasty

Location → Ramada Hotel · Bur Dubai | **351 9999**
Hours → 12:30 - 14:30 19:30 - 23:00
Web/email → rhddxb@emirates.net.ae   Map Ref → 7-E3

Dynasty offers an up-market, authentic Chinese food experience in the heart of Bur Dubai. The restaurant is decorated authentically, only diminished by the lounge singer performing (non Cantonese tunes) in the hotel lobby. In addition to a wide range of a-la-carte dishes, Dynasty offers four set menus for about Dhs.120 per person with an excellent selection of traditional (ie. no sweet and sour chicken balls) fare. Chinese tea (and fortune cookies, of course) offer an excellent end to an enjoyable evening out.

Food ●●●○ Service ●●●○ Venue ●●●○ Value ●●●○

Four Seasons

Location → Rydges Plaza Hotel · Al Satwa | **398 2222**
Hours → 12:00 - 15:00 19:00 - 24:00
Web/email → rhrdxb@emirates.net.ae   Map Ref → 7-A4

The little-known Four Seasons is a delight for lovers of Chinese food. The view over Jumeira is lovely, but don't spend too much time watching the Satwa Roundabout: it can be terrifying! Not particularly busy during the week and more suited for quiet conversation, the food arrives piping hot and deliciously fresh. The menu consists of the usual options, and for hearty appetites there are a number of set menu banquets. Familiar fare, but well executed, this venue may be worth a special trip.

Food ●●●● Service ●●●○ Venue ●●○○ Value ●●○○

Golden Dragon

Location → Trade Centre Rd · Al Karama | **396 7788**
Hours → 12:00 - 14:45 19:00 - 23:45
Web/email → n/a   Map Ref → 10-D1

This venerable venue serves superior food in a welcoming environment. A private room seats 14 people for larger parties. The Peking duck is not to be missed (available without 24 hours notice). Try the hot and sour soup and various seafood dishes. Some of the staff have been there for over 20 years (John and Patrick) and all are of Chinese descent. With 80% of the clientele regulars, perhaps this is the best Chinese food outside of a five-star hotel.

Food ●●●○ Service ●●●○ Venue ●●●○ Value ●●●○

Imperial Garden

Location ➜ Capitol Hotel · Al Satwa	**346 0111**
Hours ➜ 12:30 - 15:30 19:30 - 24:00	
Web/email ➜ caphotel@emirates.net.ae	**Map Ref** ➜ 7-A2

  150

The illusion is convincing: the staff are dressed in traditional costume and the décor evokes an imperial garden. The food is good with an extensive choice – meat or fish eaters and vegetarians alike are all well catered for. Dishes are well-executed and generous; the live lobster or crab are particularly nice. The staff are well informed and knowledgeable, and more than happy to help with your choice of food. Not the best value for money, but a decent upscale Chinese choice.

Food ●●●● Service ●●●● Venue ●●●○ Value ●●●○

Long Yin

Location ➜ Le Meridien Dubai · Al Garhoud	**282 4040**
Hours ➜ 12:30 - 15:00 19:30 - 24:00	
Web/email ➜ longyin@le-meridien-dubai.com	**Map Ref** ➜ 14-E3

  300

This interesting, up-market formal venue offers Cantonese and Szechwan dishes from an impressive but rather pricey menu. Black lacquer panels frame beautiful Chinese tapestry figures, whilst a little bridge spans ponds of bright goldfish. Nibble sesame coated cashews when deciding between Chef Sam's famous Peking Duck or prawns in (overly) spicy Cantonese sauce with crunchy vegetables and fried rice. The dim sum are disappointing, but refreshing jasmine tea served by friendly and informative staff add to the Oriental feel of this pleasant (if noisy) restaurant.

Food ●●○○ Service ●●●○ Venue ●●○○ Value ●●●○

Mini Chinese

Location ➜ Al Diyafah Street · Al Satwa	**345 9976**
Hours ➜ 12:00 - 15:00 18:30 - 24:00	
Web/email ➜ binhendi@binhendi.com	**Map Ref** ➜ 7-A3

    100

For a spot of lunch or dinner after shopping, drop into this extremely bright, cheap and cheerful restaurant. Best for families or groups, the atmosphere is friendly and service quick. Simple, clean, and with lots of yellow and black, the decor certainly avoids garish Chinese clichés. The food is plentiful and satisfying, as well as reasonably priced. Try the chicken with tomato and coriander, the shredded vegetables, or the chicken chow mein. Worth a visit if you're in the area and craving Chinese.

Food ●●●○ Service ●●○○ Venue ●●○○ Value ●●○○

Long Yin

Going Out

Chinese

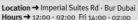

Mr. Chow

Location → Imperial Suites Rd · Bur Dubai | **351 0099**
Hours → 12:00 - 02:00 Fri 14:00 - 02:00
Web/email → openhouse_rest@yahoo.com **Map Ref** → 7-D3

   100

A vast menu and mild Chinese ambience define this restaurant. With around 200 dishes on the menu, it may take a while to decide what to order. Try the Manchurian beef or Schezuan duck for spice, and 'kond chen lobster' or Mongolian lamb for subtler flavours. The staff are friendly, perhaps a little overly attentive and eager, and the gaps between courses can be very short. In a casual restaurant this may be what most prefer. Regardless, a decent choice for value and quality.

Food ●●●● Service ●●●○ Venue ●●●○ Value ●●●●

Nanking Chinese

Location → Beh Regent Palace Htl · Bur Dubai | **396 6388**
Hours → 12:00 - 24:00
Web/email → n/a **Map Ref** → 11-A1

  150

Run by the enthusiastic Mr Errol, this modest looking restaurant offers excellent food. The comprehensive Chinese menu emphasises healthy eating. Garlic chicken with plum sauce wrapped in crispy iceberg lettuce is light and crispy. Spicy tofu is a wonderful vegetarian option. Portions are just right, so you can try a whole range of dishes without feeling as though you've overeaten or burnt a hole in your wallet. A rare example of genuine concern for food and hospitality.

Food ●●●● Service ●●●○ Venue ●●●○ Value ●●●●

Noodle House, The

Location → Emirates Towers · Trade Centre 1&2 | **319 8757**
Hours → 12:00 - 23:30
Web/email → helen@emirates-towers-hotel.com **Map Ref** → 9-C2

 200

This bright, up-market fast food restaurant offers delicious, beautifully presented Oriental dishes from a limited but affordable menu peppered with options. The Cantonese duck is to die for and the fat ribbon-noodle dish (Char Kway Teow) gorgeous. The Gai Lan vegetables are disappointing. Service can be a little spotty, but generally friendly and informative. No reservations necessary here - fast turnover is the key. Watch the chefs working in the open kitchen or sit at the small bar while enjoying good, fast-ish food.

Food ●●●○ Service ●●○○ Venue ●●●○ Value ●●○○

Open House

Location → Nr Pyramid Bld · Al Karama | **396 5481**
Hours → 09:00 - 02:30
Web/email → n/a **Map Ref** → 10-E1

   100

How many days must one reserve for sampling the 200 items on the menu? Whatever the answer, it would be time well-spent. By forgoing the mediocre Chinese options in favour of the Indian fare, the gourmand can save time and ensure enjoyment, unlikely to find a single clunker. Choices ranging from mutton tikka masala to bhindi do piyaza, complemented by some of the best naan in town and served by lovely staff guarantee satisfaction, especially upon examination of the modest bill.

Food ●●●○ Service ●●●● Venue ●●○○ Value ●●●●

Noodle House

Peacock

Location → Sheraton Jumeirah Beach · Al Sufouh | **399 5533**
Hours → 12:00 - 15:00 19:00 - 24:00
Web/email → sherjum@emirates.net.ae | **Map Ref →** 2-D2

   200

Currently under restoration, this hotel lobby restaurant is slated for a complete makeover that will turn the former Chinoisserie décor into a contemporary Chinese fusion outlet. The concept is called "zen ambience", whatever that may be. The hotel's press release assures us that Chef George will remain, though with a new menu. If this is true, the food promises to be good and mostly authentic. The renovation should make this an amusing and relaxing spot for people watching and upscale Chinese fare.

Food ●●●● Service ●●○○ Venue ●●○○ Value ●●●○

Summer Place

Location → Metropolitan · Jct 2, Shk Zayed Rd | **343 0000**
Hours → 12:30 - 14:30 19:00 - 23:30
Web/email → methotel@emirates.net.ae | **Map Ref →** 5-C4

   150

This breath of fresh air may actually be authentic: everything from the chefs to the cutlery to the chairs, has come from Hong Kong. It's spacious, yet cosy, thanks to dim lighting and lots of space between tables. Delicious, interesting, and generous fare does not come cheaply, but quality makes up for cost. Try aromatic crispy duck, or shredded beef chilli. The service is another welcome surprise: attentive but never intrusive; they'll happily assist with making sense of the vast menu.

Food ●●●● Service ●●○○ Venue ●●●● Value ●●●○

Cuban

Other options → **Cajun/Creole [p.319]**
Tex-Mex [p.376]

Cuban Bar

Location → Hilton Jumeirah · Al Sufouh | **399 1111**
Hours → 18:30 - 03:00
Web/email → www.hilton.com | **Map Ref →** 2-D2

  150

Enjoy a sweet Cuban cocktail and a cigar with Hemingway and Bogart watching over you. The dark, panelled walls and plush seats contrast with the open sea view. Order a selection of hot and cold tapas from the pictures on the menu; wash them down with variety of rum drinks or the regular bar selection. The centre bar or the leather chairs and sofa provide a comfortable spot to share the delicious snacks with friends and enjoy the music drifting in from the courtyard.

Food ●●○○ Service ●●●● Venue ●●●● Value ●●●●

El Malecon

Location → Dubai Marine Beach · Beach Rd, Jumeira | **346 1111**
Hours → 19:30 - 03:00
Web/email → dxbmarin@emirates.net.ae | **Map Ref →** 6-D2

    150

This venue remains popular for extended evenings of drinks and salsa dancing (lessons offered on certain days). Fun, for sure, but the food is also not bad. Duck with polenta is divine and the Cuban inspired dishes are bursting with bright flavours and spice. As with any busy venue, service can feel a bit harried, but they do a good job trying to appease everyone. Later, when the band gets going, this is one of the most festive places in town.

Food ●●○○ Service ●●●● Venue ●●●○ Value ●●○○

Egyptian

Other options → **Arabic/Lebanese [p.312]**

Fatafeet

Location → Nr British Embassy · Bur Dubai | **397 9222**
Hours → 09:00 - 02:00
Web/email → n/a | **Map Ref →** 8-C4

     50

Smoking shisha, sipping Arabic coffee, and enjoying a wonderfully atmospheric view of the Creek is the combination that this cafe has to offer. Very pleasant in the cooler months as the setting is delightful. Additional offerings are the usual batch: fruit juices, mezze, salads, and so forth, plus some good Egyptian mezze. Service can be extremely leisurely; consider it part of the "cultural" experience. Although parking seems ample, it does fill up quickly; otherwise park further along the Creek and enjoy the stroll.

Food ●●●○ Service ●●○○ Venue ●●●● Value ●●●●

Chinese | Egyptian

Going Out

Emirati

Other options → **Belly Dancing [p.287]**
Arabic/Lebanese [p.312]

Al Areesh

Location → Al Boom Tourist Village · Umm Hurair 2 | **324 3000**
Hours → 12:00 - 16:00 19:00 - 24:00
Web/email → abt@emirates.net.ae   **Map Ref →** 14-A3

  100

Capturing local traditions and flavours in a pleasant setting, Al Areesh offers a good value for local cuisine. It's the closest Dubai has to an authentic Emirati restaurant, and boasts a tranquil setting on the Creek. Arabic salads and mezze adorn the central buffet, while meat or fish main courses are grilled in the open air. The buffet (lunch & dinner Dhs.45; Dhs.70 for the meat buffet) includes all the food you can eat, although drinks, including the ubiquitous fruit juices, are extra.⊠

Food ●●●○ Service ●●●○ Venue ●●●● Value ●●●○

European

Top Posh

Al Iwan	Tagine
Sahn Eddar	Verre

European

In Dubai, the most dominant of the European cuisines is Italian; there are numerous restaurants around offering the 'best' tiramisu in town, plus the usual selection of pasta and pizzas. The atmosphere of many of these outlets aims for an 'authentic' Italian feel, with whitewashed walls, jars of pasta, wood-fired pizza ovens, checked tablecloths and even singing staff (in Italian of course!).

Within this style of cuisine, there is a growing number of independent restaurants springing up around the city, offering good value for money, but no chance to indulge in a glass of Chianti with your cannelloni. Check out the following cuisines: British, European, Fish & Chips, French, German, Irish, Italian, Mediterranean, Pizzerias, Portuguese, Russian and Spanish.

Cellar

Location → Aviation Club, The · Al Garhoud | **282 4122**
Hours → 12:00 - 15:30 19:00 - 23:30 11:30 - 16:30
Web/email → www.aviationclubonline.com   **Map Ref →** 14-C3

200

Elegant, romantic, stylish, modern and daring to be different, The Cellar stands out as special from the first step into their ecclesiastical sanctum. An innovative menu, superb presentation, delicious meals and an extensive array of very reasonably priced wines prove an irresistible combination. Service still needs work though. The less formal BBQ on the balcony, business lunches and Friday brunches ensure there is something for everyone. Extraneous noise from the Irish Village can occasionally filter through but doesn't detract from the overall experience.⊠

Food ●●●● Service ●●○○ Venue ●●●○ Value ●●●●

Dubai Restaurant

Location → Nad Al Sheba Racecourse · Nad Al Sheba | **336 3666**
Hours → Thu 19:00 - 01:00 Fri 12:00 - 16:00
Web/email → www.nadalshebaclub.com   **Map Ref →** 17-A3

200

With a superb view of the racing and golf courses, the Dubai Restaurant at the Millennium Grandstand arguably serves up the tastiest Friday Roast. Relaxed and casual, diners enjoy a leisurely lunch whilst sitting back and watching some good and not so good golf. The emphasis is on the roasts: succulent beef, lamb and pork with perhaps the best Yorkshire puds ever. A separate kiddies area leaves the restaurant free for you to enjoy the dulcet tones of the singer.⊠

Food ●●●○ Service ●●○○ Venue ●●●○ Value ●●●○

Emirati | European   Going Out

Stylish and relaxed ambience.

International cuisine.

Dubai's best stocked cellar.

Excellent value.

Friendly staff to guide you to the best selection.

For Reservations call 04 - 2829333

Glasshouse - Brasserie

Location ➜ Hilton Creek · Creekside, Deira
Hours ➜ 12:30 - 15:00 19:00 - 24:00
Web/email ➜ hiltonck@emirates.net.ae
227 1111
Map Ref ➜ 11-C2

 200

From London's signature chef, Gordon Ramsey, comes one of the trendiest and wanna-be-hip restaurants in Dubai. With fantastic food set in an funky backdrop, Glasshouse continues to rival fashionable eateries anywhere in the world. The food is clever and imaginative. The carefully contrived menu ranges from homey classics to fusion extravaganzas. Top service, fantastic food and unusual ambience places Glasshouse among the finest in Dubai's vast scope of refined restaurants.▨

Food ●●●○ Service ●●●○ Venue ●●●○ Value ●●●○

Nina

Location ➜ Royal Mirage Arb. Crt. · Al Sufouh
Hours ➜ 19:00 - 23:30   Closed Sat
Web/email ➜ www.royalmiragedubai.com
399 9999
Map Ref ➜ 3-A2

Nina is a new wave Indo-European restaurant newly opened in December 2002 in the Royal Mirage Arabian Court. After descending the staircase, you'll come across funky décor with a lively and colourful backdrop. Flickering candles, cascading beads and vibrant music set the scene for an exotic night out. The food menu promises to enliven the palate with plenty of flavour with mixes of spices.▨

Food – n/a Service – n/a Venue – n/a Value – n/a

Retro

Location ➜ Le Meridien Mina · Al Sufouh
Hours ➜ 19:00 - 01:00 Fri 19:00 - 01:00
Web/email ➜ f&b@lemeridien-minaseyahi.com
399 3333
Map Ref ➜ 3-A2

 300

Ignore the chaos and instead, concentrate on the imaginative menu – continental fusion – including confit duck, honey roasted magret with ravioli of foie gras and choucroute with griottes jus. Any doubts as to ingredients, check with the knowledgeable head waiter, who will also assist with selections from an extensive wine list. For value, select from the 3-course menu. Request seating in the interior dining room. Well presented and perfectly cooked dishes of contrasting flavours entice one to return.▨

Food ●●●● Service ●●●○ Venue ●●●○ Value ●●●○

Filipino

Other options ➜ **Karaoke Bars [p.402]**
Chinese [p.319]
Malaysian [p.358]
Singaporean [p.372]
Thai [p.377]

Tagpuan

Location ➜ Karama Shopping Centre · Al Karama
Hours ➜ 10:00 - 24:00
Web/email ➜ n/a
337 3959
Map Ref ➜ 10-D2

 50

This restaurant lives up to its name ('meeting place' in Tagalog), attracting a regular clientele of Filipino residents and visiting US sailors. Tagpuan is an excellent value for money experience, offering a wide choice of both Chinese and Filipino dishes. A complimentary bowl of soup arrives with each main, and portions are generous. The formica tables, TVs and free karaoke give this workingman's diner an unpretentious and happy atmosphere that genuinely welcomes visitors.▨

Food ●●●○ Service ●●●○ Venue ●●○○ Value ●●●●

Fish & Chips

Other options ➜ **Pubs [p.404]**
Seafood [p.369]
International [p.336]
British [p.318]

Chippy, The

Location ➜ Pink Bld · Trade Center 1&2
Hours ➜ 17:00 - 01:00 Fri 14:00 - 01:00
Web/email ➜ na
343 3114
Map Ref ➜ 9-A2

 50

If you need a fish and chips fix, then this shop is ideal. Resembling a local UK chippy with plastic formica tables and chairs, The Chippy feels and looks authentic. Order the popular haddock and chips or try the haggis, white pudding (very tasty), or macaroni pie. The chips are golden and plump but the mushy peas could have been mushier. If you have room for dessert try the pineapple and banana fritters or decadent battered Mars bars – if you dare!▨

Food ●●●○ Service ●●●○ Venue ●○○○ Value ●●●○

European | Fish & Chips

Going Out

Fryer Tuck

Location → Opp Jumeirah Centre · Beach Rd, Jumeira | **344 4228**
Hours → 12:00 - 15:00 19:00 - 23:00 12:00 - 16:00 Fri
Web/email → n/a   **Map Ref** → 6-C2

  (150)

Fancy good old English fish and chips, served with mushy peas and pickled onions – or how about steak and kidney pie? Eat in the bright, airy, though rather clinical, 50 seat restaurant, or take-away. The standard menu includes sausage in batter, cod, hammour, pies and other easily recognised fare, all deliciously cooked. Since opening in 1976, they have offered authentic chip shop food, and certainly know how to wrap a mean paper package of chips. The real thing, although arteries beware!

Food ●●●○ Service ●●○○ Venue ●○○○ Value ●●○○

Plaice, The

Location → Century Village · Al Garhoud | **286 8233**
Hours → 12:00 - 01:00
Web/email → www.aviationclubonline.com   **Map Ref** → 14-C3

    (100)

Fish and chips the traditional way is the concept behind this 'plaice' (now if they would just wrap them in the Daily Mail…). Fish, more fish, and loads of hot, fresh chips are available for dining in, take-away or delivery. Situated just to the left of the entrance to the Irish Village, The Plaice provides a quick and very casual alternative to the other restaurants in Century Village. Good for those times when nothing but a good chippie will do.

Food ●●●○ Service ●●○○ Venue ●●●○ Value ●●○○

French

Cafe Chic

Location → Le Meridien Dubai · Al Garhoud | **282 4040**
Hours → 12:30 - 14:45 20:00 - 23:45 Closed Fri am
Web/email → cafechic@le-meridien-dubai.com **Map Ref** → 14-E3

(300)

To celebrate pure ingredients classically prepared, this venue is a natural choice. Michel Rostang oversees this French-dominated kitchen that coaxes endlessly rich and subtle flavours out of everything. Lobster bisque, duck carpaccio, saddle of rabbit and chocolate soufflé effortlessly flaunt their charms. Simply elegant decor and a helpful – if a bit overwhelmed – staff help keep the restaurant from becoming outrageously snobby. As one of the premier venues in town, Cafe Chic gracefully rewards diners with immaculately well-executed and balanced dishes.

Food ●●●○ Service ●●●○ Venue ●●●○ Value ●●○○

Cafe Chic

Le Classique

Location → Emirates Golf Club · Jct 5, Shk Zayed Rd | **347 3222**
Hours → 12:00 - 15:00 19:00 - 01:00
Web/email → www.dubaigolf.com   **Map Ref** → 3-A3

    (150)

As the name suggests, the food here is rich and elegantly French-influenced. The extensive table d'hôte is an easy choice, or select from the varied menu. Very well-executed, well-presented fare delights patrons. Dance the night away to the romantic tunes of the resident duo, or for a casual evening take advantage of the terrace. You don't have to be a member of the golf club to be able to visit Le Classique, a venue and experience worth the drive.

Food ●●●○ Service ●●●○ Venue ●●○○ Value ●●●○

Top European	
BiCE	Il Rustico
Bray, The	Ossigeno
Cellar	Retro
Focaccia	Splendido Grill
Hofbrauhaus	Verre

Going Out Fish & Chips | French

St Tropez Bistro

Location → Century Village · Al Garhoud | **286 9029**
Hours → 12:00 - 15:00   19:30 - 23:30
Web/email → sttropez@emirates.net.ae   **Map Ref →** 14-C3

  150

This is a quaint and extremely intimate little restaurant with the ambience of a small French bistro. The atmosphere inside is cosy and friendly, ideal for a small group of friends out for some excellent food. Alternatively, dine alfresco in the Century Village courtyard, especially pleasant and relaxing in the winter months. Service can be leisurely.

On offer are a variety of grilled meats, such as juicy lamb rack or fillet, however, steak, either prime beef or veal, is the house speciality. This is the type of place where you go for a quick bite to eat, only to return home several hours later!

Food ●●●○ Service ●●●○ Venue ●●○○ Value ●●●○

Verre

Location → Hilton Creek · Creekside, Deira | **227 1111**
Hours → 12:30 - 14:30   19:00 - 24:00   Fri 19:00 - 24:00
Web/email → hiltonck@emirates.net.ae   **Map Ref →** 11-C2

   **300**

Verre serves some of the finest European food in town. Understated yet meticulous cuisine is presented in minimalist surroundings, leaving you to concentrate on the flavours. Non-drinkers will find it quite affordable. Get used to the goldfish-bowl atmosphere of plain glass walls, soothed by soft lighting and music. Informed service, especially from the French servers, begins with the expansive wine list and never lets up. Gourmets disappointed by pretence and hollow fanfare elsewhere should come to taste why this restaurant rates so highly.

Food ●●●● Service ●●●○ Venue ●●○○ Value ●●●●

Fusion

Other options → **British [p.318]**
International [p.336]

Al Muntaha

Location → Burj Al Arab · Umm Suqeim | **301 7600**
Hours → 12:30 - 15:00   19:00 - 24:00
Web/email → www.burj-al-arab.com   **Map Ref →** 4-A1

 300

Al Muntaha is a great experience: its panoramic daytime view and modern techno décor become even more dramatic at night. Much thought has gone into the sophisticated menu that lists a dazzling choice of enticingly described dishes, and the wine list is encyclopaedic. Presentation is beautiful, and most dishes live up to expectations, but one or two are lacking in flavour. Al Muntaha pampers its guests with an exceptional venue and professional service, but at these prices needs greater consistency in the food quality.

Food ●●●○ Service ●●●○ Venue ●●●● Value ●●○○

Celebrities

Location → Royal Mirage Palace · Al Sufouh | **399 9999**
Hours → 19:00 - 23:30   Closed Sat
Web/email → sales@royalmiragedubai.com   **Map Ref →** 3-A2

 **300**

The grand marble staircase and elegant, intimate and luxurious dining room make guests feel like coveted celebrities. With views of lantern-lit pools and fountains, and the gentle sounds of live music, this is a romantic setting in which to dine on delicious, perfectly prepared international fare (with an Arabic twist) at reasonable prices. Basil-lobster ravioli, curry-dusted scallops, or steak in pomegranate sauce are but a few of the contemporary fused with traditional options. This gastronomic delight, orchestrated by highly professional, attentive waiters, is memorable.

Food ●●●● Service ●●●○ Venue ●●●● Value ●●●○

Eauzone

Location → Royal Mirage Arb. Crt. · Al Sufouh | **399 9999**
Hours → 12:00 - 23:30   Closed Sun
Web/email → www.royalmiragedubai.com   **Map Ref →** 3-A2

Bathed by the blue of the sky and sea, Eauzone is the place to contemplate the rhythm of ocean tides and the setting sun. Resting peacefully on the

French | Fusion

Going Out

beach, surrounded by swaying palm trees, Eauzone features shaded wooden decks and floating 'majlis' overlooking the Arabian Gulf and pool. The ambience is casual by day and stylish after sunset. Once night transcends, it evokes intimacy in a slick, refined restaurant complemented by modern food with an Asian twist.

Food – n/a Service – n/a Venue – n/a Value – n/a

La Baie

Location → Ritz-Carlton Dubai · Al Sufouh | **399 4000**
Hours → 19:00 - 23:00 Closed Sun
Web/email → rcdubai@emirates.net.ae **Map Ref** → 2-E2

Charm, warmth, elegance, and superior food: it must be the Ritz. Honey/ginger glazed duck breast with celery spatzle and caramelised apples or lemon/herbs marinated lobster salad with warm oxtail terrine encourages high expectations for La Baie's desserts. Like the pianist, the staff, and the baronial comfort of the dining room, the chocolate cake with soft orange centre maintains the ecstasy. The chef has the courage to show how much he knows about food and cooking, priceless knowledge that draws Dubai's wisest diners to the Ritz-Carlton.

Food ●●●○ Service ●●●○ Venue ●●●● Value ●●○○

La Baie

Mystizo

Location → Hotel Inter-Continental · Deira | **222 7171**
Hours → 12:00 - 15:00 19:30 - 24:00
Web/email → www.interconti.com **Map Ref** → 8-C4

Mystizo gives a whole new meaning to fusion, mixing African, Arabian, Oriental and Spanish flavours. The ambience is modern and exotic, but the food is adequate; you're best off with one of their specialities – the seafood combination, lamb shanks or their signature dessert, the Strawberry Kilimanjaro. After your meal, head over to the Mystizo bar/club to dance the calories away. Better as a place to see and be seen, Mystizo still needs time to work out the kinks.

Food ●●●○ Service ●○○○ Venue ●●●○ Value ●●○○

Rotisserie, The

Location → Royal Mirage Arb. Crt. · Al Sufouh | **399 9999**
Hours → 06:30 - 23:30
Web/email → www.royalmiragedubai.com **Map Ref** → 3-A2

The Rotisserie is set in a grand dining room that boasts a courtyard terrace and open veranda overlooking the resort's gardens and fountains. The show kitchen evokes a bygone era, with high vaulted ceilings, voluminous stone and copper chimneys, enamelled cast iron ovens and large wooden tables. Guests can interact with the chefs who will prepare the cuisine that is based on historical recipes from Europe and Arabia, presented with a contemporary approach.

Food – n/a Service – n/a Venue – n/a Value – n/a

Sphinx

Location → Pyramids · Umm Hurair 2 | **324 9603**
Hours → 19:30 - 23:30
Web/email → www.waficity.com **Map Ref** → 13-D2

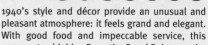

1940's style and décor provide an unusual and pleasant atmosphere: it feels grand and elegant. With good food and impeccable service, this venue rates highly. From the Royal Beluga caviar to the enticing apple pudding, the food can be well matched with appropriate wines. A strong menu of starters; for a lighter meal consider ordering two and skipping the mains. From the over-the-top entrance to the last taste, this is a restaurant worth trying.

Food ●●●● Service ●●●○ Venue ●●●● Value ●●●○

Tamarind

Location → Jumeira Tower · Trade Centre 1&2 | **343 9111**
Hours → 07:00 - 24:00
Web/email → chanels@emirates.net.ae   **Map Ref** → 9-B2

Low key and casual, this venue is ideal for a light dinner or a lunch. Bright and cheerful, the room feels welcoming and warm, and the service generally follows suit. One of the better run independent venues, their menu is simple but delightful. Unusual combinations of sandwiches and soups are the mainstay, with a small array of other options as well. Great mixed fruit juices also, which makes the fact that it is unlicensed easier to swallow. A good value for money.

Food ●●●○ Service ●●○○ Venue ●●●● Value ●●●○

Teatro

Location → Towers Rotana · Trade Centre 1&2 | **343 8000**
Hours → 11:30 - 15:00 18:00 - 24:00
Web/email → na   **Map Ref** → 9-B2

In the mood for an international mix of cuisines? Then Teatro might be for you. With menu options ranging from Japanese to Chinese, Italian to Indian, you're bound to find something you like. Portions aren't enormous and the food is simple here, though the prices don't reflect this... unless there's a special promotion happening. The lively, comfortable atmosphere is enhanced by the open kitchen. Service is a highlight, as are the desserts; recommended is the Chef's Sampler – a taste of each of their delicious desserts.

Food ●●○○ Service ●●●● Venue ●●●○ Value ●●○○

German

Brauhaus

Location → Jumeira Rotana · Al Satwa | **345 5888**
Hours → 18:00 - 01:00 Thu & Fri 12:00 - 24:00
Web/email → jumhotel@emirates.net.ae   **Map Ref** → 6-E3

Devoid of pretense, this hidden venue delivers heavy German food with good cheer. The rustic authenticity begins with the music (cringe!), and continues through the gigantic portions and rich combinations. No-nonsense menu includes sausages aplenty, horseradish-salmon (very nice), peppersteak (excellent), goulash soup, perfect Spätzle, apple strudel, and cheesecake. Vegetarian options are sparse. If you manage dessert, God bless; we couldn't. The bubbly manageress greeting regulars and chatting with tables compensates for the shy, halting waitress. Unlike many joints in town, this one feels genuine.

Food ●●●○ Service ●●●○ Venue ●●○○ Value ●●●○

Der Keller

Location → Jumeirah Beach Htl · Umm Suqeim | **348 0000**
Hours → 18:00 - 23:30
Web/email → www.jumeirah-beach.com   **Map Ref** → 4-B2

Vaulted ceilings, wrought iron chandeliers and russet table linen provide Der Keller with a rustic warmth. From the noisy hubbub of the bar to the more decorous restaurant, the expansive selection of traditional Germanic fare makes this a lively venue. The Swinehaxe (pork hocks) and apple strudel are renowned, though the former must be ordered 24 hours in advance. Children and vegetarians are not forgotten, though hearty appetites are distinctly favoured. Popular for its pleasant atmosphere and good value for money.

Food ●●●○ Service ●●●● Venue ●●○○ Value ●●●○

Hofbrauhaus

Location → JW Marriott Hotel · Deira | **262 4444**
Hours → 12:30 - 16:00 19:30 - 02:00
Web/email → marriott@emirates.net.ae   **Map Ref** → 12-A3

True to Bavarian keller style, this is both a restaurant and a bar. German beer lovers note:

Fusion | German

Going Out

the 1 litre mass glass is sure to satisfy. Cosy alcoves surround the main dining area – perfect for a bit of privacy without feeling exiled. The fare is familiar but extensive: assorted German sausages, authentic Wiener Schnitzel, Sauerkraut, Potato Dumplings and Soups. Side orders, salads and individual sausage orders enable you to mix and match your own mains. Vegetarians beware, most salads also include meat.●KHB

Food ●●●● Service ●●●● Venue ●●●○ Value ●●●○

Indian

Other options → **Pakistani [p.366]**

Al Tandoor

Location → Opp Century Htl · Bur Dubai   **393 3349**
Hours → 12:30 - 15:00 19:00 - 24:00
Web/email → n/a   Map Ref → 7-E2

In the heart of Indian restaurant land, Al Tandoor attracts a mixed crowd of happy eaters. The menu, offering no pork or beef, is extensive and the food unusually subtle and delicate without being bland. Service can be spotty, but always friendly. As expected, the value for money is good. If you are also looking for Indian furniture and wall coverings, Samuel will happily take you to his shop to continue your patronage!●ABH

Food ●●●● Service ●●○○ Venue ●●●○ Value ●●●○

Antique Bazaar

Location → Four Points Sheraton · Bur Dubai   **397 7444**
Hours → 19:30 - 02:30
Web/email → fpshrdxb@emirates.net.ae   Map Ref → 8-A4

Perfectly adequate Indian food complements the pleasing scene at Antique Bazaar. Though not for sale, antique seats – silver, heavily carved, or ivory-inlaid chairs – define the beautifully decorated bazaar. A large troupe of musicians arrives at 21:00 to add authentic sound to sight. Bring out-of-town visitors to this lively, popular venue. Seek the security of thali (two meats, three vegetables, rice, naan, dessert) served on silver trays, and pretend that your intimate knowledge of Mughal cuisine created the memorable evening.●AP

Food ●●●● Service ●●●○ Venue ●●●● Value ●●●○

Asha's

Location → Pyramids · Umm Hurair 2   **324 0000**
Hours → 12:30 - 15:00 19:30 - Late
Web/email → www.pyramidsdubai.com   Map Ref → 13-D2

This attempt to offer Indian cuisine with a difference does distinguish itself from the rest. The creation of Asha Bhosle, the Indian artiste best known for her unmistakable voice, Asha's is a thoughtful and friendly venue. With the plan to franchise its hopefully successful formula, this eatery will have a lot to prove. Asha's menu centres on kebabs with a focus on flavour and spice. Food is good, reasonable, and comprehensible. For a casual meal when in the vicinity, this is a decent choice.●RP

Food ●●●○ Service ●●●○ Venue ●●●○ Value ●●●○

Ashiana

Ashiana

Location → Sheraton Hotel & Towers · Deira   **228 1111**
Hours → 12:30 - 15:30 19:30 - 01:00 Closed Fri am
Web/email → sheradxb@emirates.net.ae   Map Ref → 11-C1

Ashiana (which means 'nest') regularly attracts birds of a feather. Aficionados of upscale Indian

German | Indian

Going Out

cuisine will crow with delight at the wide array of carefully prepared delicacies. Crispy Shami Kebabs and in-house speciality Murgh-e-Ashiana are worth trying. Sweet lovers will need more of the Mithai Shorba (assorted sweets). Tables are small, and some seats may be uncomfortable for enjoying the live band – which may be a blessing in disguise. The justified popularity of this venue creates a lively atmosphere; book ahead if possible.

Food ●●●● Service ●●●○ Venue ●●●○ Value ●●●○

Bombay Brasserie

Location → Marco Polo Hotel · Hor Al Anz |**272 0000**
Hours → 19:00 - 02:00
Web/email → marcohot@emirates.net.ae   Map Ref → 8-E4

   200

Walking into the Bombay Brasserie through a heavy wooden door instantly reveals the appeal of this attractive restaurant. An entertaining live band plays traditional Indian music nightly. Mouth-watering, fresh-cooked food (which takes time to prepare) is served courteously by attentive staff. The menu boasts a wide variety of dishes, listed by province, from all over India. The paneer and vegetable kebabs are more-ish and the prawn curry and dal spectacular. Fragrant meat, seafood and vegetables, with a fusion of Eastern flavours are delicious.

Food ●●●○ Service ●●●○ Venue ●●●● Value ●●●○

Bombay Chowpatty

Location → Trade Centre Rd · Al Karama |**396 4937**
Hours → 08:00 - 13:30 17:00 - 24:00
Web/email → n/a   Map Ref → 11-A1

  50

Good, convenient Indian food makes this pair of casual eateries worth knowing. Bombay Chowpatty's main restaurant is located opposite the BurJuman Centre; its sister is in Lamcy Plaza. To help break the burger habit, consider this Indian alternative. The usual dishes – sometimes inscrutable on the menu – are fresh and tasty. Some preparations are quite spicy, but there is always cool fruit juice or an iced lassi to put out the fire. Great value for money.

Food ●●●○ Service ●●●○ Venue ●○○○ Value ●●●●

Chhappan Bhog

Location → Trade Centre Rd · Al Karama |**396 8176**
Hours → 12:30 - 15:00 19:30 - 24:00
Web/email → n/a   Map Ref → 10-E1

   100

Flash: Chappan Bhog has expanded its vegetarian offerings from 56 to 80, apparently by popular demand from the regulars. If a connoisseur, you will love the variety. Novices will be happy with more familiar fare like crispy Paneer Pakora or Lachcha Paratha (layered bread) . The aromatic Navraton Korma is not to be missed, and when available, do sample the memorable Kesri Rasmalai. Recent renovation has smartened up the venue. Although Dubai offers limited options to vegetarians, Chappan Bhog certainly proves a delicious exception.

Food ●●●○ Service ●●●○ Venue ●●●○ Value ●●●●

Chicken Tikka Inn

Various locations |**396 4600**
Hours → 12:00 - 15:00 18:30 - 24:00
Web/email → na   Map Ref → n/a

100

Still going strong after 30 years, the original outlet has expanded into a small chain of restaurants. Popular favourites include chicken and mutton dishes, kebabs, grills, curries, biryani, plus a variety of vegetable dishes and a few seafood items. Add to these traditional Indian breads and the ubiquitous chips. The restaurants are clean but fairly basic, with ample seating and family rooms. Catering is also available and worth considering. Reasonably priced, friendly, and probably in your neighbourhood, this is an above average cheap eats joint.

Other locations:
• *Deira, Jumeira, Al Karama and Qusais.*
Food ●●●○ Service ●●●○ Venue ●●○○ Value ●●●●

Top Asian Subcontinent	
Antique Bazaar	Handi
Coconut Grove	India Palace

Indian

Going Out

Coconut Grove

Location ➜ Rydges Plaza Hotel · Al Satwa | **398 3800**
Hours ➜ 13:00 - 15:00 19:30 - 24:00
Web/email ➜ coconut@emirates.net.ae **Map Ref** ➜ 7-A4

   (150)

Vibrant colours and tastes combine to form wonderful cuisine in Coconut Grove. The innovative chef prepares unique dishes using spices and a mixture of Indian and Sri Lankan tastes, to combine the best from Kerala, Tamil Nadu, Goa and old Ceylon. Palm trees and huge wooden artefacts create an exotic room. Ensure you taste the cocktails and home-made chutney as well as the pineapple halwa and saffron flavoured rice. Rounding out the experience, a guitarist plays each night.

Food ●●●● Service ●●●○ Venue ●●●○ Value ●●●●

Curry in a Hurry

Location ➜ Al Durrah Tower · Trade Centre 1&2 | **332 3223**
Hours ➜ 12:00 - 15:00 19:00 - 24:00 Fri 19:00 - 24:00
Web/email ➜ www.curryinahurry.jetaime.as **Map Ref** ➜ 9-D2

    (100)

This new venue offers a good compromise between fast food and proper dining. Fine for a quick mall meal. Lunchtimes are quite popular, as the prices are very reasonable (cash only at present), the service is friendly and the range of choices, which include vegetarian dishes, are decent. Break the burger habit with a feisty curry and some naan for a change. Oddly, perhaps, they also do take-away, as well as delivery (though this is not for those in a hurry).

Food ●●●○ Service ●●●○ Venue ●●●○ Value ●●●●

Delhi Darbar

Location ➜ Opp Post Office · Al Karama | **334 7171**
Hours ➜ 11:30 - 15:30 18:30 - 00:30
Web/email ➜ na **Map Ref** ➜ 10-E2

 (100)

Delhi Darbar excels at Mughlai food – in spite of the extensive Chinese options. Subtle colours and simple decor contribute to the pleasant atmosphere. Reshmi paratha or biryani, fish fingers or golden fried prawns, plenty of delicious options are on offer. Free home delivery and takeaway are available. Business sorts frequent the restaurant for lunch as it's light on the stomach and pocketbook. Due to its popularity, service can be slow; just enjoy the paintings on the wall and exercise patience.

Food ●●●○ Service ●●●○ Venue ●●●○ Value ●●●○

Gazebo

Trade Centre Rd, Al Karama | **397 9930**
Hours ➜ 12:00 - 15:30 19:00 - 24:00
Web/email ➜ na **Map Ref** ➜ 10-E1

 (100)

Offering no less than 11 styles of Indian bread and 5 different raithas, Gazebo rises above its

Asian Subcontinent

Asian cuisine covers an enormous range of styles, tastes, cooking methods and ingredients. For some, even religion plays a part in what can be eaten. Dishes are usually heavily spiced, but not necessarily with hot peppers (unless you request it), cooked in a sauce and served with rice and/or bread. Breads vary from the unleavened, deep-fried poppadum (ground lentils fried in oil) or paratha (thick unleavened bread fried on a griddle) to puris or naan (nan) bread, which can be plain, buttered or stuffed with meat, raisins or nuts.

Cooking methods range from curries, kebabs and grills to biryani, tandoor and even steamed food. The most popular meats are chicken and lamb, although fish is widely used in the coastal styles of cooking where it would traditionally have been available. Vegetables are used generously and Indian cuisine is especially good for vegetarians because of the vast numbers of people who are vegetarians as dictated by their religious beliefs.

In Dubai, there is an enormous number of Indian restaurants, with many of the independents (ie, those not linked to a hotel or club, and therefore not serving alcohol) offering incredible value for money.

Service can be tricky: generally it is friendly, but there are often communication difficulties. Take it in good humour and have a laugh: your mistaken order may turn out to be unexpectedly delicious, or that extra portion may make a great lunch the next day. The portions are usually large (often unlimited for buffets) and the quality of food excellent, although the surroundings can vary from sparse with plastic tables and chairs to intricate decorations with live music and dancing.

It's hardly surprising that many people in Dubai rarely cook when they can eat out or buy a tasty takeaway or home delivery meal for as little as Dhs.15. Check out the following cuisines:
Indian and Pakistani

Indian

Going Out

competitors along this busy strip of Bur Dubai eateries. The biryani served in an authentic steaming mud pot is a must and the only place in Dubai to serve it this way. Seafood features heavily along with traditional favourites. The staff are keen to make suggestions to please. If you're after superb quality at affordable prices for lunch, dinner, event catering or home delivery, look no further.

Food ●●●● Service ●●●○ Venue ●●●○ Value ●●●○

Handi

Location ➜ Taj Palace Hotel · Deira   **223 2222**
Hours ➜ 12:00 - 15:00   19:00 - 24:00
Web/email ➜ tajdubai@emirates.net.ae   **Map Ref** ➜ 11-D2

 200

'Fit for a King' - that's what the Mughal cuisine at Handi is all about. The rich blending of spices and curries leads to delicious starters and mains. The main attraction is the open kitchen, where the chef exhibits his tricks of the trade making popular Indian bread. A homely ambience absorbs the richness of the food, and the colourful hues add that little extra touch to the warm atmosphere. An impressive outlet with well-presented, tasty food and great service – recommended.

Food ●●●● Service ●●●● Venue ●●●○ Value ●●●○

India Palace

Location ➜ Nr Princeton Htl · Al Garhoud   **286 9600**
Hours ➜ 12:30 - 15:30   19:00 - 23:45
Web/email ➜ sfcdxb@emirates.net.ae   **Map Ref** ➜ 14-D2

 150

The unassuming exterior explodes into a Mughal fantasy once inside. Musicians play traditional instruments and obsequious staff cater to every whim (at least until it gets busy, then they get flummoxed). Better than average food; the upscale prices mean that the chicken tikka melts in your mouth and the level of spice is as you requested it. For a lark, try a private dining cabin (4 - 10 people) and summon your waiter with a bell (to then have him knock before entering).

Food ●●●● Service ●●●○ Venue ●●●● Value ●●●○

Kamat

Location ➜ Opp Bur Juman · Al Karama   **396 7288**
Hours ➜ 10:30 - 15:30   19:00 - 24:00
Web/email ➜ n/a   **Map Ref** ➜ 10-E1

  100

For the adventurous vegetarian, Kamat offers a splendid array of oriental comestibles. Whilst the decor is basic and the linen past its best, the staff are convivial and the food is exotic enough to tempt even a confirmed carnivore. The combo meals are infinitely more interesting than the fare offered by the surrounding fast food outlets and prove excellent value at just Dhs.12. Kamat offers cheap, tasty, veggie food without any pretence or ostentation.

Food ●●●○ Service ●●●● Venue ●●●○ Value ●●●○

Kitchen

Location ➜ Beh Hardees · Al Diyafah St, Satwa   **398 5043**
Hours ➜ 10:00 - 02:30
Web/email ➜ openhouse_rest@yahoo.com   **Map Ref** ➜ 7-A3

 100

Whether you're in the mood for take-out or you need catering than doesn't cost a fortune, give Kitchen a try. Despite its hidden location behind Pizza Hut on Diyafah Street, its well known in the Satwa community. While their main speciality is Indian, there's an international menu to choose from too, with something to suit everyone, including a range of vegetarian dishes. Grab a take-out menu on your way out; we're betting you'll be hooked after the first bite.

Food ●●●○ Service ●●○○ Venue ●●○○ Value ●●●○

Kohinoor

Location ➜ Sea View Hotel · Bur Dubai   **355 8080**
Hours ➜ 12:00 - 15:00   20:00 - 01:00
Web/email ➜ www.seaviewhotel.co.ae   **Map Ref** ➜ 7-D2

 150

Kohinoor has a muted, warm, comfortable feel that transports you to a Mughal courtyard mansion. The quality of food is excellent; dishes have a clear flavour. Vegetarians are well catered for, while carnivores will rejoice in the choice of meats and sauces. Their signature dish: tricolour paneer, representing the Indian flag, is superb. Mughal cuisine was favoured by royals, and it's easy to see why – it's light, mild and delicious. Classical

Indian

Going Out

musicians (playing quite loudly) help create a superb, unique atmosphere.

Food ●●●● Service ●●●○ Venue ●●●○ Value ●●●○

Kwality

Location → Opp Century Htl · Bur Dubai | **393 6563**
Hours → 13:00 - 14:45 20:00 - 23:45
Web/email → n/a   **Map Ref** → 7-E2

    150

In spite of the orthographic nightmare of its name, this Indian restaurant is highly competent. Popular for many years, Kwality offers a bewildering array of dishes in a friendly setting. Downstairs is for bachelor diners and take-away clients, but upstairs is where family customers sit and savour. Big portions, reasonable prices, and endless options attract hoards. Novice Indian food aficionados may appreciate somewhat westernised flavours. The restaurant is busiest from 21:30 onwards and it is advisable to book on weekends and holidays.

Food ●●●○ Service ●●●○ Venue ●●●○ Value ●●●○

Mohanlal's Taste Buds

Location → Al Karama | **336 2001**
Hours → 12:30 - 15:00 19:30 - 24:00
Web/email → tastbuds@emirates.net.ae   **Map Ref** → 10-D2

  100

Escape to a world of friendly faces and traditional ambience. Soft ethnic music, a Banyan tree trunk supporting the roof, and rustic wooden décor tastefully add to the charm. The menu warmly proposes a variety of Keralite dishes and a limited range of Mughlai and far eastern delicacies, either a la carte or in a buffet. Value for money encourages families to flock here. Courteous service and consistent warmth define this venue that feels like a home away from home.

Food ●●●○ Service ●●●○ Venue ●●●○ Value ●●●○

Nawab

Location → Computer Plaza · Bur Dubai | **359 9884**
Hours → 12:30 - 15:00 18:30 - 24:00
Web/email → nawabs@emirates.net.ae   **Map Ref** → 7-E4

 100

Nawab is just on the positive side of average for Indian diners. Comfortably furnished and even slightly atmospheric, the joint feels friendly enough. The menu is predictably vast, but the

Hyderbad cuisine is noted as the speciality of the house. Indeed some of the curries (ahem, Vindaloo) are wickedly hot. Other dishes can be bland or oily; ask for recommendations, though be warned that while the waiters try hard, there can be miscommunications. Make sure you order the tandoori fries to start.

Food ●●●● Service ●●●○ Venue ●●●○ Value ●●●○

Yoko Sizzlers

Location → Opp Bur Juman Centre · Bur Dubai | **396 8558**
Hours → 12:00 - 15:00 19:00 - 24:00
Web/email → yokodubai@yokosizzlers.com   **Map Ref** → 11-A1

  100

No, it's not a Japanese restaurant, it's a Bombay chain. Yoko is what the management prefers to describe as a 'sizzler' and the food does sizzle, with hot plates of beef, chicken, mutton or seafood steaks. Gigantic portions of Indian (and some Chinese) food are served quickly and efficiently. The décor is reminiscent of a fast food joint, with a few comfortable seats in the corners. A good place to take the kids or to pop in for a quick meal if you're in the neighbourhood.

Food ●●●○ Service ●●●○ Venue ●●●○ Value ●●●○

International

Other options → **Fusion [p.328]**

Academy

Location → Creek Golf Club · Al Garhoud | **295 6000**
Hours → 06:00 - 22:00
Web/email → dubaicreek@dubaigolf.com   **Map Ref** → 14-C2

  200

A good alternative to other terraced outlets, this unobtrusive bar and restaurant serves ambitious dishes with quiet aplomb. Reposing within the golf course, post-game players pause for drinks, yet non-members may also appreciate the setting and menu. TVs could distract in the plush interior, whereas greenery and golfers backdrop the tranquil tables outside. Courses are composed as artfully on the plate as on the palate, and the bill shouldn't upset the calm. Arrive early to dine amongst these greens before their mid-evening closing.

Food ●●●○ Service ●●○○ Venue ●●●○ Value ●●●○

Paul Thuysbaert

PHOTOGRAPHY

Ⓜ 050 6249762   Ⓣ 04 2868802
Ⓔ ptphoto@emirates.net.ae   Ⓦ ptphotography.com

Al Dana

Location → Crowne Plaza · Trade Centre 1&2   **331 1111**
Hours → 24 hours
Web/email → hicpdxb@emirates.net.ae   **Map Ref** → 9-D2

   150

If you don't mind bland décor, the quality of food at reasonable prices makes the trip to Al Dana worth your while. In comparison to the other restaurants on the same floor, Al Dana is easily overshadowed in terms of size and décor, but if you do manage to step in, you'll quickly forgive and enjoy the good food and quick service. An a la carte menu is available to choose from as well, but the buffet tends to be better value for money.◙

Food ●●○○ Service ●●●○ Venue ●●●○ Value ●●●○

Al Dana

Location → Riviera Hotel · Deira   **222 2131**
Hours → 12:00 - 15:00
Web/email → riviera@emirates.net.ae   **Map Ref** → 8-C3

  150

Located in the Riviera Hotel along the Creek, it offers good value for simple fare, and an opportunity for an evening stroll along the wharf after dinner. Small, quiet, and unpretentious, the restaurant's international buffet menu changes daily and includes home-made soups, salads, a variety of meats and fish, and home-made desserts. The service is excellent, the waiters attentive. For some, the unlicensed status may kill the appeal. Perhaps not a destination in itself, but a worthwhile option if in the neighbourhood.◙

Food ●●○○ Service ●●●○ Venue ●●○○ Value ●●●○

Al Dawaar

Location → Hyatt Regency · Deira   **209 1100**
Hours → 12:30 - 15:30 19:00 - 23:30
Web/email → hyattbus@emirates.net.ae   **Map Ref** → 8-D2

 ☺ 📞 V ♟ **150**

Al Dawaar is Dubai's only revolving restaurant – the main reason to go. The imaginative buffet (lunch and dinner) is more varied and better quality than many of Dubai's 'all you can eat' options, but the cost is higher as well (and drinks are extra). Minimalist décor and low lighting allow the city lights to take centre stage at night, while during the day the huge windows afford panoramic views of the sea and the city. A natural choice for those with visitors in town.◙

Food ●●●○ Service ●●●○ Venue ●●●○ Value ●●○○

Al Dawaar

Antigo

Location → Le Meridien Dubai · Al Garhoud   **282 4040**
Hours → 12:30 - 15:30 19:00 - 23:30
Web/email → antigo@le-meridien-dubai.com   **Map Ref** → 14-E3

    300

Compared to the many buffet-themed restaurants in town, this one is adequate. If pressed for time, imitate a footballer and choose several kilos of the 20 hot offerings then sweep through the dozen desserts. If you want to linger in the diner-like setting over Antigo's best fare, sample the 40 items of the cold buffet (don't overlook the cheeses!). The insistent environment and the ordinary, though ever-edible food do not justify the Dhs.120 price.◙

Food ●●●○ Service ●●●○ Venue ●●○○ Value ●●●○

Antigo

Going Out   International

Apartment, The

Location → Jumeirah Beach Htl · Umm Suqeim
Hours → 19:00 - 23:30
Web/email → www.jumeirah-beach.com   **Map Ref** → 4-B2

| 348 0000

 300

The perfect illusion of visiting a (very) well-heeled friend who is a crack chef is achieved at this venue. The space is divided into wonderfully intimate rooms, and Patrick Lenotre's famous cuisine fills this apartment with delight. Foie gras with blackcurrants, salmon & snails, mushroom artichoke soup, tender duck breast – the menu is unbeatable. From the charming hostess to the vigilant if soft-spoken servers, dining here is an utter joy. This temple of marvellously executed cuisine is one of the best restaurants in town.

Food ●●●● Service ●●●○ Venue ●●●● Value ●●●○

Bella Vista

Location → Jumeira Rotana · Al Satwa
Hours → 19:00 - 23:00 Closed Sat
Web/email → jumhotel@emirates.net.ae   **Map Ref** → 6-E3

| 345 5888

150

With a consistently good buffet, attractive views, and reasonable prices, Bella Vista remains a reliable bet for casual dining, and making it a popular stop for Dubai grazers. Each nightly all-inclusive buffet has a different theme, with a full range of meat, fish, vegetable dishes, along with salads and desserts. As the night wears on, Bella Vista gets a bit crowded and noisy, which makes perusing the buffet a bit competitive, so be sure to make a reservation and arrive early.

Food ●●●○ Service ●●●○ Venue ●●○○ Value ●●●○

Boardwalk

Location → Creek Golf Club · Al Garhoud
Hours → 12:00 - 24:00
Web/email → dubaicreek@dubaigolf.com   **Map Ref** → 14-C2

| 295 6000

100

Situated on a boardwalk over the water, this spot remains among the favourite outdoor venues in town. The casual menu includes interesting salads, juicy burgers, 'Thai spicy beef', 'fajitas al carbon' and 'Arabic chicken'. Service seems to depend on luck, and also seems to respect that guests probably wish to linger. The deck seats up to 300 people, or alternatively sit inside in the stylish bar area. Unfortunately, advance bookings are not taken but a waiting list for tables operates once you're there.

Food ●●●○ Service ●●○○ Venue ●●●● Value ●●●○

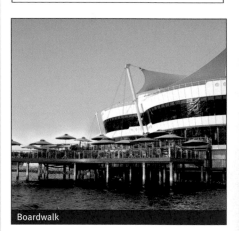
Boardwalk

Californian

Location → Dusit Dubai · Trade Center 1&2
Hours → 12:30 - 14:30 22:30 - 03:00 06:30 - 10:30
Web/email → www.dusit.com   **Map Ref** → 9-A2

| 343 3333

200

The Californian is a posh "coffee shop" restaurant that looks out over Dubai from the 24th floor. The quirky menu consists of buffet breakfasts and an unusual blend of a la carte selections, from Thai to continental to sandwiches and salads. A delicious starter of Mediterranean vegetables in red cabbage leaves or beef with mustard and creamy gorgonzola sauce on polenta are both recommended. Good for private conversation and unobtrusive staff: the view is free.

Food ●●●○ Service ●●●○ Venue ●●●○ Value ●●○○

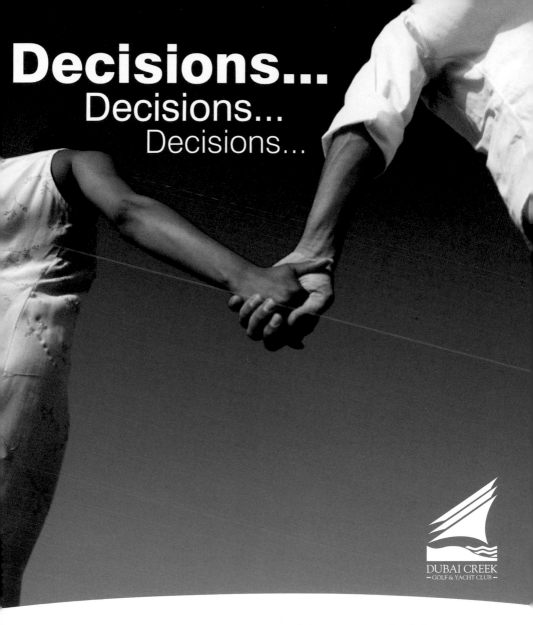

Decisions...
Decisions...
Decisions...

DUBAI CREEK
GOLF & YACHT CLUB

making your decision easy

Whatever the occasion, you'll find an experience to match at the Dubai Creek Golf & Yacht Club. Whether it's that romantic dinner à deux, a casual get together with friends, a friendly business lunch or an evening of music, cocktails and casual chic; you'll find our stunning array of F&B outlets can cater to your every need. Call 04 295 6000 to make your reservation.

Cascades

Location ➜ Fairmont Hotel · Shk Zayed Rd | **332 5555**
Hours ➜ 24 hrs
Web/email ➜ www.fairmont.com **Map Ref** ➜ 9-E1

Engineered into the Fairmont's techno heart, diners at Cascades become part of the complicated kaleidoscope of light and motion. Like the venue, the food is stunning: corn cakes and grilled zucchini, eggplant, and peppers braced with Saint-Mauré cheese and tomato fondue or, perhaps, char-grilled prime sirloin on vegetables and garlic mashed potatoes in a bold balsamic reduction. The optional buffet of appetisers and desserts provides more than mere filler. For a post-modern dinner that is more than fanfare, call in to Cascades.

Food ●●●● Service ●●●○ Venue ●●●● Value ●●●○

Coco Cabana

Location ➜ Oasis Beach Hotel · Al Sufouh | **399 4444**
Hours ➜ 10:00 - 21:00
Web/email ➜ sales.obh@dutcohotels.com **Map Ref** ➜ 2-D2

Sun, sand, clear blue waters and tempting food: Coco Cabana is a great place for a prolonged beach-afternoon. Open-air atmosphere provides a great sea view. Go bananas with Banana Express (sweet banana & corn with smoked salmon) or create your own sandwiches. Mix of Three is sensibly packaged with crispy golden fried prawns, chicken fingers and hammour. Winters offer additional reason to chill out with a barbecue buffet, but you may have to elbow your way in on weekends.

Food ●●●○ Service ●●●○ Venue ●●●○ Value ●●●○

Exchange, The

Location ➜ Fairmont Hotel · Shk Zayed Rd | **311 8610**
Hours ➜ 19:00 - 23:30 Closed Fri
Web/email ➜ www.fairmont.com **Map Ref** ➜ 9-E1

Even devastated naturalists should relish the splendid wild game on offer at The Exchange. Less savage diners will remain delighted with the marvellous cuts of aged U.S. prime beef such as the seven-ounce filet accompanied by eight mustards and a variety of sauces headed by Béarnaise. The kitchen behind the curving dining room, serviced with friendly competence, emphasises quality and takes only fifteen minutes to bake a sunflower cake that illuminates memory. The Fairmont continues to enliven the dining scene with this top-notch carnivorous pleasuredome.

Food ●●●○ Service ●●●● Venue ●●●○ Value ●●●○

Fontana

Location ➜ Al Bustan Rotana Hotel · Al Garhoud | **705 4650**
Hours ➜ 12:30 - 15:00 19:00 - 23:30
Web/email ➜ apothotl@emirates.net.ae **Map Ref** ➜ 14-E3

No matter what you're craving, there's a good chance you can find it at Fontana. The speciality here is theme nights with lavish buffets and decorations to match. Sunday is Seafood Night, Monday is Arabian Night, Wednesday is Curry Night, and Thursday is Mexican Night, with unlimited margaritas and Coronas. The food lacks authenticity (and flavour sometimes), but service is attentive and prompt. Reservations are recommended for theme nights. Continental and American breakfasts are available, and lunch features an international buffet plus a la carte.

Food ●●○○ Service ●●●○ Venue ●●○○ Value ●●●○

La Cité

Location ➜ Sofitel City Centre · Al Garhoud | **603 8890**
Hours ➜ 12:00 - 15:00 19:30 - 23:30
Web/email ➜ cityhotl@emirates.net.ae **Map Ref** ➜ 14-D1

After a hard day's shopping La Cite is a good option if you wish a break from the hustle and bustle in City Centre. A typical hotel outlet, this bright and spacious dining area greets guests with a spectacular ice carving and a live pianist. Theme nights (Seafood, Italian or Mexican buffets) are reasonable but of mediocre quality. Service is friendly, the fare plentiful; the only surprise being a particularly good cheese selection. Not a destination in itself, however it is convenient, pleasant, and adequate.

Food ●○○○ Service ●●○○ Venue ●●○○ Value ●●○○

La Cite

Lakeview

Location → Creek Golf Club · Al Garhoud | **295 6000**
Hours → 06:30 - 23:00
Web/email → dubaicreek@dubaigolf.com | Map Ref → 14-C2

 150

Located at the clubhouse, the Lakeview restaurant has a pleasant feel to it. Offering a breathtaking view of the Dubai Creek and the golf course, this seems a perfect place to spend a few hours on a pleasantly cool night. The food, delicious and diverse, caters particularly to adventurous palates. Well-paced and unobtrusive service lets the food and the venue shine all that much brighter. With its relatively reasonable prices, high quality, and genuinely pleasant ambience, this restaurant merits a visit.

Food ●●●○ Service ●●○○ Venue ●●●○ Value ●●●○

Market Café, The

Location → Grand Hyatt Dubai · Umm Hurair 2 | **209 6993**
Hours → 06:00 - 11:00 12:30 - 15:30 19:00 - 23:00
Web/email → www.hyatt.com | Map Ref → 13-E3

This proposed venue is meant to be the hotel's family restaurant. The setting is planned to be a large 'enchanted garden' – evidently the largest in Dubai. Precisely what this means remains to be seen, but lush tropical foliage will presumably feature prominently. Cuisine is mixed with five open kitchens – Japanese, Asian and Italian cuisine as well as a large grill section – suiting any taste. Probably worth a visit at least just to see what the garden looks like.

Food – n/a Service – n/a Venue – n/a Value – n/a

Market Place, The

Location → JW Marriott Hotel · Deira | **262 4444**
Hours → 19:30 - 23:30 Closed Fri
Web/email → marriott@emirates.net.ae | Map Ref → 12-A3

 250

With an extensive fixed price buffet (and drinks included), this is an excellent venue for large groups, offering variety for everyone without the final bill getting out of control. Set in charming surroundings, every evening there's a different buffet, plus an extensive brunch on Fridays. This is casual dining in a relaxed, informal atmosphere with a tasty and interesting variety of dishes. However, watch out for the waiter who discreetly replenishes your drink –your car may end up being valet parked all night.

Food ●●●○ Service ●●●○ Venue ●●●○ Value ●●●○

Oasis, The

Location → Country Club · Al Awir Rd | **333 1155**
Hours → 08:00 - 21:00
Web/email → dcc@emirates.net.ae | Map Ref → 17-B3

100

The Oasis provides famished diners with a casual location for a bite to eat after that strenuous game of tennis. Serving everything from hearty breakfasts to sumptuous suppers, their menu features freshly made sandwiches along with an array of delicious salads and Mediterranean style main dishes. Poolside seating is recommended over the somewhat unimaginative interior décor. Service is adequate, prices reasonable, portions large and house policy is workout wear friendly. When in the area, a preferable option to fast food.

Food ●●○○ Service ●●●○ Venue ●●○○ Value ●●●●

Wines	
Agency, The	Spectrum On One
Al Muntaha	Sphinx
Cellar	Uptown
Fusion	Verre

Oceana

Location → Hilton Jumeirah · Al Sufouh
Hours → 07:00 - 15:00 18:00 - 24:00
Web/email → hiltonjb@emirates.net.ae
Map Ref → 2-D2

| 399 1111 |

   200

The ideal restaurant if you're looking for a quiet, relaxed brunch, lunch or dinner buffet with family or friends. There's an a la carte menu, but the buffet is the draw here. Veggies can have a feast on the selection of salads on offer, and meat lovers will drool at the sight of the live cooking station making the daily special before their eyes. Make sure you leave enough space for the chocolate mousse – it's nothing short of heavenly.

Food ●●●○ Service ●●●○ Venue ●●●○ Value ●●○○

Palm Garden

Location → Sheraton Jumeirah Beach · Al Sufouh
Hours → 12:00 - 15:00 18:30 - 24:00
Web/email → sherjum@emirates.net.ae
Map Ref → 2-D2

| 399 5533 |

 250

Palm Garden is a wonderfully relaxing restaurant. There is a choice of nightly themed buffet or a-la-carte menu. The Mediterranean buffet offers an extensive range and variety of foods – the Minestrone is to die for and the Floating Islands decadent. A chef prepares pasta dishes to order – deliciously hot and fresh. It is a lovely hotel restaurant with good service and great attention to detail even down to the 'Arabic' motif in the upholstery.

Food ●●●○ Service ●●●● Venue ●●●● Value ●●●●

Promenade

Location → Four Points Sheraton · Bur Dubai
Hours → 12:00 - 15:00 19:30 - 23:30
Web/email → fpshrdxb@emirates.net.ae
Map Ref → 8-A4

| 397 7444 |

  150

Break up your work day and leave behind the hot, dusty streets of Bur Dubai for the cool, marbled, elegance of The Promenade. Starched damask table linen, fresh flowers and highly attentive staff team up to ensure a relaxing environment for business lunches and conference buffets. The all inclusive price (Dhs.78) allows access to a variety of salads, a selection of hot entrees, dessert, plus as much water as you can drink. For those wishing alternative beverages, they are also available.

Food ●●○○ Service ●●●○ Venue ●●●○ Value ●●○○

Pronto

Location → Fairmont Hotel · Shk Zayed Rd
Hours → 07:00 - 23:00
Web/email → www.fairmont.com
Map Ref → 9-E1

| 332 5555 |

   100

The posted prices confronting customers hurrying to Pronto, the Fairmont's new venue aimed primarily at the take-out trade, announce that it is "gourmet" fare. Quality products from sushi to spicy chicken and noodle salad to roasted vegetables to a variety of breads and pastries emphasise Pronto's aspirations. Office-dwellers wishing to distinguish themselves will take away a Pronto sandwich – and buy a jar of preserves for the boss. A way to kick the burger habit...

Food ●●○○ Service ●●●○ Venue ●●●○ Value ●●○○

Sails

Location → Jumeirah Beach Club · Jumeira
Hours → 07:00 - 23:00
Web/email → jbc@jumeirahbeachclub.com
Map Ref → 5-D1

| 344 6222 |

 **150**

Set in the lush heart of the Jumeirah Beach Club gardens, Sails offers a casual dining atmosphere with a free dress code. Dishes range from Western favourites (fish and chips) to Asian curries and for those on diets, a healthy living menu provides more detail on what you are eating than most care to know! With outdoor seating in the cooler months, this is the place to enjoy a lively family Friday buffet brunch or a relaxed candle-lit dinner in a quiet, leafy setting.

Food ●●○○ Service ●●○○ Venue ●●●○ Value ●●○○

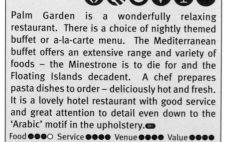

International

Going Out

Spectrum On One

Location ➜ Fairmont Hotel · Shk Zayed Rd | **332 5555**
Hours ➜ 18:00 - 01:30
Web/email ➜ www.fairmont.com   **Map Ref** ➜ 9-E1

A perfect option for those tired of the ubiquitous buffets in town, this world of cuisine is a logistical marvel. Six separate kitchens – Thai, Japanese, European, Indian, Chinese, and pastries – cook dishes to order from the astoundingly vast menu. Mix and match from any kitchen, pray it will all arrive at your table at the same time, and enjoy the stylish rooms (also with different corresponding décors) and helpful service. An upscale solution to the familiar 'who wants what' problem of group dining.

Food ●●●○ Service ●●●● Venue ●●●● Value ●●○○

Spice Island

Location ➜ Renaissance Hotel · Hor Al Anz | **262 5555**
Hours ➜ 19:00 - 23:30
Web/email ➜ rendubai@emirates.net.ae   **Map Ref** ➜ 12-A3

Can't decide between Indian, Chinese, Arabic, Italian, Polynesian, Mexican, European, Japanese or seafood? Why not have them all! Housing the best bites from all corners of the world under one roof, this is one of the most popular all-you-can-eat venues, and for good reason. The spacious venue is self serve, apart from drinks, and has specific areas for each cuisine, some of which have live cooking stations with chefs to customise even the fussiest diner's meal. Buffets range from Dhs.99-Dhs.179; reservations recommended.

Food ●●●● Service ●●●○ Venue ●●●○ Value ●●●●

Villa Beach Restaurant

Location ➜ Jumeirah Beach Club · Jumeira | **348 0000**
Hours ➜ 12:00 - 16:00 19:00 - 23:00
Web/email ➜ info@jumeirahbeachclub.com   **Map Ref** ➜ 5-D1

Intimate, charming, exclusive and affordable – what more do you want from your dining experience? The Villa Beach Restaurant excels in all regards. A warm welcome from informed, discreet and attentive waiters begins a romantic, memorable evening in this delightful chalet on the beach. With a choice of al fresco or indoor dining, soft music complements the sound of waves lapping the shore. Dine on beautifully prepared and delicious international cuisine from an imaginative, vegetarian-friendly menu. Don't skip dessert! Pricey, but worth it.

Food ●●●● Service ●●●● Venue ●●●● Value ●●●○

Waterfront

Location ➜ Jumeirah Beach Htl · Umm Suqeim | **348 0000**
Hours ➜ 08:00 - 21:30 07:00 - 22:00
Web/email ➜ www.jumeirah-beach.com   **Map Ref** ➜ 4-B2

Unequalled views of the Burj Al Arab make this a first choice for a swift after-work drink or a casual weekend lunch. Health buffs will appreciate the high energy, low fat menu which reflects the café's proximity to the hotel's sports pavilion. The Friday buffet is popular. Go early on weekend days to get a table outside, or enjoy a candle-lit dinner at night. Waterfront offers affordable meals, a relaxed, leisurewear dress code and one of the best views in town.

Food ●●●○ Service ●●○○ Venue ●●●○ Value ●●●○

Wavebreaker

Location ➜ Hilton Dubai Jumeirah · Al Sufouh | **399 1111**
Hours ➜ 08:00 - 22:00
Web/email ➜ hiltonjb@emirates.net.ae   **Map Ref** ➜ 2-D2

For a taste of beach resort luxury, visit Wavebreaker. Set on a spacious deck, indulge in alcoholic beverages and snacks such as fish and chips, sandwiches and salads. With theme night buffets including seafood on Monday, Polynesian on Wednesday and Arabic on Friday, it also makes for a great night out. Happy hour is a real treat at two drinks for the price of one every evening from 17.00 to 19.00. A great way to spend a lazy afternoon in the sun.

Food ●●●○ Service ●●●○ Venue ●●●○ Value ●●●○

International

Going Out

Windtower

Location → Dubai Country Club · Al Awir Rd | **333 1155**
Hours → 12:00 - 15:00 19:00 - 24:00 Closed Fri pm
Web/email → dcc@emirates.net.ae | **Map Ref →** 17-B3

  150

Add the Windtower to your list of good-and-reasonable eateries in Dubai. Sit in a pleasant candle-lit room while enjoying a leisurely meal from the eclectic menu. The range of choices bounces from chicken stuffed with apricots and cashew nuts, coated with Thai-spiced sauce to pan-fried beef fillet with blue cheese mousse and red currant butter sauce. The set menu (Dhs.70) is a super choice. Reservations are recommended, if for no other reason than to get by the guard at the gate to the Country Club.◉
Food ●●●● Service ●●●○ Venue ●●●○ Value ●●●●

Italian

Other options → **Pizzerias [p.367]**
Mediterranean [p.358]

Al Fresco

Location → Crowne Plaza · Trade Centre 1&2 | **331 1111**
Hours → 12:30 - 15:30 19:00 - 23:00
Web/email → www.crowneplaza.com | **Map Ref →** 9-D2

200

This intimate little eatery is an ideal choice for a business lunch: a convenient location, delicious food, and quick service. But don't forgo it as a dinner option - the décor is casual yet classy in that uniquely Italian way, as is the food. Pizzas, pastas and other Italian favourites vie for attention on the menu, and there is a small but interesting choice of both starters and desserts. The venue is tiny and fills up quickly, so make a reservation.◉
Food ●●●○ Service ●●●○ Venue ●●●○ Value ●●●○

Andiamo!

Location → Grand Hyatt Dubai · Umm Hurair 2 | **209 6993**
Hours → 12:30 - 15:00 18:00 - 23:30
Web/email → www.hyatt.com | **Map Ref →** 13-E3

Scheduled to open soon, this restaurant is set to challenge the competition in the Italian dining market. Billed as pure Milan chic with an open "theatre" kitchen for culinary dramas, it will serve up the usual Italian dishes. The concept is to be delicious and authentic food at reasonable prices. The décor: lots of funky organic shapes, ceramics, and colours. We'll have to see if they can get the food right, but if so, BRAVO.◉
Food – n/a Service – n/a Venue – n/a Value – n/a

Bacchus

Location → Fairmont Hotel · Shk Zayed Rd | **311 8000**
Hours → 11:30 - 23:30
Web/email → www.fairmont.com | **Map Ref →** 9-E1

200

Forget fast food and take time to relax and enjoy a really good pizza. Bacchus is a popular venue for classic Italian fare with a few novel additions; not everyone is accustomed to eating caviar and salmon on pizza! The wine list is not as extensive as the name might imply, but it is reasonably priced. Colonnades, marbled tables and the adjacent pool create the impression of a Roman bath, whilst live entertainment is provided by a panoramic view of the Sheikh Zayed Highway.◉
Food ●●●○ Service ●●●○ Venue ●●●○ Value ●●●○

BiCE

Location → Hilton Jumeirah · Al Sufouh | **399 1111**
Hours → 12:00 - 15:00 18:30 - 24:00
Web/email → hiltonjb@emirates.net.ae | **Map Ref →** 2-D2

200

BiCE continues to live up to its reputation as one of Dubai's leading Italian restaurants. It simply feels suavely Italian, with crisp white linen, plush banquettes, and a roaming manager who makes every guest feel a regular.

Effective communication solutions.

Brochures

Guidebooks

Catalogues

Prestige art books

Branding

pmdesign

The menu is loaded with Italian specialities, some familiar and some more avant garde. The pasta is fresh, the meat cooked to perfection, and the pizzas large and crunchy. Factor in the highly talented pianist as entertainment, and BiCE becomes a top choice for a superior evening.

Food ●●●● Service ●●●● Venue ●●●● Value ●●●○

Best Business Dinners

Al Iwan	La Cité
BiCE	Long Yin
Boston Bar, The	Miyako
Fusion	Shabestan
Glasshouse - Brasserie	Taverna

Biella Caffé Pizzeria Ristorante

Location → Wafi Mall · Umm Hurair 2 | **324 4666**
Hours → 10:00 - 23:30
Web/email → www.pyramidsdubai.com   Map Ref → 13-D2

Stylish European décor and mostly flavourful food make for an enjoyable, relaxed dining experience or quick shopping break. The wood burning oven cranks out thin crust pizzas decorated with fresh ingredients beyond the basic Margarita. A good choice of simple pasta dishes (including great lasagna verdura), seafood and meat dishes, caters to every taste. Juices, coffees, and desserts are recommended, especially the coconut torta. Service is not rushed. Opt for the outdoor terrace on cooler days.

Food ●●●○ Service ●●○○ Venue ●●●○ Value ●●●○

Capanna Nuova

Location → Dubai Marine Beach · Beach Rd, Jumeira | **346 1111**
Hours → 19:30 - 23:30
Web/email → www.dxbmarine.com   Map Ref → 6-D2

It's easy to imagine you're dining on the Italian coast at this beachside restaurant. The prime dining areas are on a deck with a great ocean view. Many Italian favourites grace this menu, and local seafood is used nicely in many of the dishes. Don't miss the pasta stuffed with hammour in a rocket cream sauce with prawns. Spotty service and some average dishes, but with such a setting who can complain? Reservations are advisable, especially in the cooler months. A good place to bring out-of-town guests.

Food ●●○○ Service ●●○○ Venue ●●●● Value ●●○○

Carnevale

Location → Jumeirah Beach Htl · Umm Suqeim | **348 0000**
Hours → 12:30 - 15:00 19:00 - 23:00
Web/email → www.jumeirah-beach.com   Map Ref → 4-B2

Carnevale gives the ubiquitous hotel Italian the five star treatment. While not unique, what it does is done to the highest standard. An extensive wine list complements the fish-orientated menu, where appetisers are kept light alongside more robust main courses. Presentation is exquisitely faultless, especially desserts, which unfortunately promise more than they deliver. Candlelight, soft music and romantic scenes adorning the walls make for an intimate dinner venue that leaves little to chance.

Food ●●●○ Service ●●●○ Venue ●●●○ Value ●●○○

Casa Mia

Location → Le Meridien Dubai · Al Garhoud | **282 4040**
Hours → 12:30 - 15:00 20:00 - 24:00
Web/email → casamia@le-meridien-dubai.com Map Ref → 14-E3

Casa Mia offers quality Italian fare in an al fresco setting. The terrace seating surrounds a fountain, and the restaurant interior is a simple combination of white walls and wood. The food is good and unpretentious, with fresh ingredients used throughout, most notably in the pizzas from the wood-fired oven. Service is excellent. This restaurant is definitely a cut above the average Italian experience in Dubai, plus its outdoor location makes it an especially attractive option, but expect to pay accordingly.

Food ●●●○ Service ●●●● Venue ●●●○ Value ●●●○

Ciao Ciao

Location → Nr White Crowne Bld · Trade Centre 1&2 | **332 3310**
Hours → 11:00 - 01:00
Web/email → n/a   Map Ref → 9-D2

One of the better independent Italian venues in town, Ciao Ciao continues to gain popularity. Generous, if familiar and sometimes bland, appetisers, pastas, pizzas, and mains may not be entirely authentic but are well-rendered nonetheless. With friendly management and servers, dinner in the funky upstairs "vineyard" dining room will delight. The terrace is another

Going Out

Italian

SPOILT FOR CHOICE WITH A VARIETY OF RESTAURANTS & BARS!

A culinary haven of restaurants & bars awaits you at Le Meridien Dubai.
Be it dining in a cosy or trendy setting, indoors or al fresco, *the choice is yours!*

Hotel Lobby

ANTIGO Global cuisine
GOURMANDISES Pastry shop
PEARL BAR Lobby bar

La Promenade

LONG YIN Chinese cuisine
CAFÉ CHIC French cuisine operated by
Michel Rostang 2 star Michelin chef
M'S BEEF BISTRO International selection of beef
KIKU Japanese cuisine
SEAFOOD MARKET Fresh seafood the
Far Eastern way

Meridien Village

AL MIJANA Lebanese cuisine
SUKHOTHAI Thai cuisine
CASA MIA Italian cuisine
THE DUBLINER'S Irish Pub
JULES International bar with live entertainment
MERIDIEN VILLAGE TERRACE Theme nights

Where the world's
great cuisines meet

CALL FOR RESERVATIONS: (04) 7022500

Le MERIDIEN
DUBAI

P. O. Box 10001 Dubai, U. A. E., Tel: (04) 2824040 Fax: (04) 2824672
www.lemeridien-dubai.com
www.lemeridien.com

Vertical labels: ANTIGO · GOURMANDISES · PEARL BAR · LONG YIN · CAFE CHIC · M's BEEF BISTRO · KIKU · SEAFOOD MKT. · AL MIJANA · SUKHOTHAI · CASA MIA · THE DUBLINER'S · JULES · M.V. TERRACE

option for cool evenings and Sheikh Zayed Road traffic watching. Although not licensed, this restaurant still feels festive. Great for parties, and generally a good value for money.⬚

Food ●●○○ Service ●●●○ Venue ●●○○ Value ●●●○

Come Prima

Location → Al Bustan Hotel · Al Garhoud
Hours → 12:00 - 15:00 19:00 - 24:00
Web/email → fb@albustan-rotana.com
Map Ref → 14-E3

| 282 0000

Come Prima is notable for outstanding food, service to match, and an excellent value for money Dhs.95 all-you-can-eat and drink antipasti night. The décor is upmarket 'Manhattan', with understated, elegant and trendy, but not at all stuffy surroundings. The menu's attention to detail and creativity are subtle, and can be superb. There are monthly special menus and lunch specials offer an opportunity to try a variety of dishes. Reservations are advisable, especially on Wednesdays.⬚

Food ●●●○ Service ●●●○ Venue ●●●○ Value ●●●○

Cucina

Cucina

Location → JW Marriott Hotel · Deira
Hours → 12:30 - 15:30 19:30 - 23:30
Web/email → www.marriott.com
Map Ref → 12-A3

 | 262 4444

The concept of singing waiters may be misguided, but dinner at Cucina remains delightful. Dough slapping and kitchen orders enliven this pleasant faux-rustic Italian piazza. The persuasive menu dutifully offers well-executed familiars. Superior pizzas, home-made pasta, and hearty mains like juniper/rosemary roasted lamb loin. Desserts seemed gimmicky: GIANT tiramasu draws raves; Ice Cream "spaghetti" is a whimsical novelty. Well-trained and genuine staff pace the meal perfectly. Ignore the singing; the food and service are worthy of attention.⬚

Food ●●●○ Service ●●●○ Venue ●●●● Value ●●○○

Da Vinci's

Location → Airport Hotel · Al Garhoud
Hours → 12:00 - 24:00 Thu 12:00 - 01:00
Web/email → apothotl@emirates.net.ae
Map Ref → 14-D3

| 703 9123

It's reassuring to know that in an ever-changing Dubai, some things remain the same. Da Vinci's always offers a warm welcome, like dropping into a friend's house for supper. An easy dining experience, with a wide choice including old favourites such as three coloured pasta with salmon and cream sauce and Caesar salad. This venue delivers quality (though sometimes bland), affordable food and drink in a homely, yet lively, atmosphere. Always busy, the restaurant continues to be a popular choice.⬚

Food ●●○○ Service ●●●○ Venue ●●●○ Value ●●●○

Gelato

Location → Al Kawakeb Bld C ·Trade Center 1&2
Hours → 12:00 - 02:00
Web/email → -
Map Ref → 9-A2

| 343 3435

Gelato is a casual, easygoing restaurant/café, specialising in generic pizza, somewhat bland pasta and Italian coffee, plus a range of salads and soups for the health conscious (so long as you ask for the dressing on the side). They also serve home-made ice-cream, for the not so health conscious, made with fresh cream. There are three

Italian

Going Out

seating areas — downstairs, upstairs or the outside terrace, which is ideal for a quiet coffee. Very popular at lunchtime, especially among flight crew. For free home delivery, call (800 4501).

Other Locations:
- Al Diyafah Street (343 8464);
- Grand Cineplex (324 3313).

Food ●●○○ Service ●●○○ Venue ●●○○ Value ●●○○

Il Rustico

Location → Rydges Plaza Hotel · Al Satwa
Hours → 12:00 - 15:00 18:00 - 23:30
Web/email → rhrdxb@emirates.net.ae

398 2222

Map Ref → 7-A4

 200

Cosy and authentic, Il Rustico serves up the usual Italian fare. Fresh ingredients are the order of the day and everything, including the pasta, is made on the premises. Stick to one of the many choices of pasta or pizza and you won't go wrong. Service is efficient and not hovering, though the pace can be a bit too hurried at times. Perfect for a relaxed meal, especially given that the overall noise level is not too high (unless a large party arrives).

Food ●●●● Service ●●●○ Venue ●●●○ Value ●●●●

Italian Connection

Location → Nr Lamcy Plaza · Oud Metha
Hours → 08:00 - 23:00
Web/email → n/a

335 3001

Map Ref → 10-D4

 150

Italian Connection is an impressive little modern café that's a good option for informal dining or a snack. The extensive menu makes decisions difficult, but it always delivers a smile with its well-presented dishes and happy staff. Great for food on the run, business lunches or a sit down meal. A new Italian chef ensures the food is once again tasty and authentic. It doesn't have the best location in town but is worth the visit.

Food ●●●○ Service ●●●○ Venue ●●●○ Value ●●●●

La Moda

Location → Hotel Inter-Continental · Deira
Hours → 13:00 - 15:00 20:00 - 02:30
Web/email → intercon_bc@itcdubai.co.ae

205 7333

Map Ref → 8-C4

 250

La Moda is a buzzing, modern venue offering quality Italian food in a central location. The food in this stylish restaurant is beautifully presented, and the menu is extensive, going well beyond workaday Italian selections — wild asparagus and ricotta ravioli with almonds, for example, or herbed monkfish on lemon risotto. The pizzas are delightfully crispy and thin. Although on the expensive side, the distinctive ambience and variety of superior dishes on offer ensure La Moda merits repeat visits from its eclectic clientele.

Food ●●●○ Service ●●●○ Venue ●●●○ Value ●●○○

La Vigna

Location → Century Village · Al Garhoud
Hours → 11:30 - 01:00
Web/email → www.aviationclubonline.com

282 0030

Map Ref → 14-C3

 150

This Italian venue finds its alfresco seating booked solid most winter nights. For the quieter summer months, dining is moved inside to the two-level interior decorated to resemble a rustic Italian vineyard. The open plan kitchen displays the restaurant's traditional pizza oven. Prices are moderate and this is reflected somewhat in the menu and quality of food. However, the staff are friendly and helpful and the atmosphere is genial. Although licensed, the wine selection is rather slim.

Food ●●○○ Service ●●○○ Venue ●●●● Value ●●○○

Luciano's

Location → Metropolitan Resort · Al Sufouh
Hours → 19:00 - 01:00
Web/email → metbeach@emirates.net.ae

399 5000

Map Ref → 2-E2

300

If you are in the neighbourhood, Luciano's is a pleasant, mid-range Italian restaurant that offers quiet, unhurried food in rustic-style surroundings. The menu includes well-executed standard Italian dishes (a good, fiery Putanesca for example), alongside some more unusual combinations, such as grilled snapper on black squid's-ink risotto. Dessert, unfortunately, may prove slightly disappointing. Service is efficient without being intrusive. Modest prices, and the added attraction of its leafy poolside terrace, make Luciano's a good, low-key venue.

Food ●●●○ Service ●●●○ Venue ●●●○ Value ●●○○

Mosaico

Location → Emirates Towers · Trade Centre 1&2 | **319 8754**
Hours → 24 hrs
Web/email → sales@emirates-towers-hotel.com   Map Ref → 9-C2

 300

A stunning mosaic floor welcomes you to this modern yet sophisticated and airy restaurant overlooking the hotel pool. In the tranquil and relaxed setting, enjoy the large bread sticks with tasty tapenade, freshly-made pasta, scrumptious tiger prawns and moist tiramisu, all at reasonable prices. The well-selected wine list offers great choice, and knowledgeable, professional staff give welcome advice whilst being extremely courteous. Open 24 hours, Mosaico is perfect for a late-night dinner al fresco amongst fairy lit trees.

Food ●●●○ Service ●●●○ Venue ●●○○ Value ●●●○

Ossigeno

Location → Le Royal Meridien · Al Sufouh | **399 5555**
Hours → 18:00 - 24:00
Web/email → f&b@leroyalmeridien-dubai.com   Map Ref → 2-E2

   200

Wonderful dining at Ossigeno justifies the journey to Dubai's outskirts. The best ingredients in the hands of a skilled chef make for outstanding mains like veal liver in balsamic reduction or tuna as it should be (rare!). Primi, however, define the excellent authenticity of Ossegino. One could subsist on the hand-made fettuccine with buttery mushroom sauce or the risotto fully stocked with shrimp and calamari. Though some guests look to be expecting a one-course trattoria, no one should leave this sleekly elegant ristorante disappointed.

Food ●●●● Service ●●●● Venue ●●●○ Value ●●●●

Pax Romana

Location → Dusit Dubai · Trade Center 1&2 | **343 3333**
Hours → 19:30 - 01:00 Closed Fri
Web/email → info@dusit.com   Map Ref → 9-A2

   250

Pax Romana has made its peace with Italian cooking. Under the influence of Roman traditions, the chef capitalises on first-class ingredients — for example, fresh mesclun, bold cheeses, sea bass, and veal shanks — to present handsome creations that please even a timid palate. True to form, the service staff dawdle. Yet the chocolate of the splendid cassata

speaks emphatically to the truest of faux Romans and concludes a curious musical duel between the reassuring hotel pianist and the recorded opera heard in the imperial hall isolating nonsmokers.

Food ●●●○ Service ●●○○ Venue ●●●○ Value ●●○○

San Lorenzo

Location → Metropolitan Palace · Deira | **205 1333**
Hours → 12:30 - 15:30 19:30 - 23:30
Web/email → metpalac@emirates.net.ae   Map Ref → 11-D2

  250

Some say tacky, others say camp; either way the mood of this restaurant is funky. The voluptuous violinist/guitarist provides entertainment, and the décor is shabby (ironic?) Italian. The surprisingly enticing menu, with good selections of risotto, pastas, etc oversells the less-than-perfectly executed cuisine. Pan-seared salmon was greasy and a bit dry; asparagus risotto with some truffles was sticky. A shame, because San Lorenzo had a good reputation, but may now be a bit past its prime in more ways than one.

Food ●●●○ Service ●●○○ Venue ●●●○ Value ●●○○

Venezia

Location → Metropolitan · Jct 2, Shk Zayed Rd | **343 0000**
Hours → 12:00 - 15:00 19:00 - 24:00
Web/email → www.methotels.com   Map Ref → 5-C4

   250

This amazing faux piazza, replete with a canal and gondolas, is pure Dubai (or Las Vegas). A good variety of starters and main courses includes risotto, pasta, meat dishes and seafood. The food, like the service, is adequate. There's no wine list: instead pop into the cellar where a member of staff helps you select your wine (you can even taste a few). The main restaurant is restricted to those over 12, although children are welcome in the Ombra (pizza) Bar upstairs.

Food ●●●○ Service ●●●○ Venue ●●○○ Value ●●○○

Verdi

Location → Taj Palace Hotel · Deira | **223 2222**
Hours → 12:00 - 15:00 19:00 - 24:00 Fri 12:00- 24:00
Web/email → tajdubai@emirates.net.ae   Map Ref → 11-D2

 200

Worth a visit, Verdi is a modern, open plan restaurant partnering old style Italian cooking with

Italian

Going Out

new age flair. Quiet, undoubtedly owing to the no alcohol rule in the hotel, but more emphasis is placed on the food and service, which are excellent. Attentive, smiling waitresses have time to converse and explain the varied menu and nightly promotions offering outstanding value. The setting is bright and colourful with small, intimate touches, which, with the open fired oven, infuse a real taste of Italy.

Food ●●●○ Service ●●●○ Venue ●●●○ Value ●●○○

Vivaldi

Location → Sheraton Hotel & Towers · Deira | **207 1717**
Hours → 06:30 - 01:30
Web/email → sheradxb@emirates.net.ae **Map Ref** → 11-C1

 **200**

If you love Italian food you'd be doing yourself a disservice not to pay Vivaldi a visit. The décor is stunning and you'd struggle to find better views of the Creek. Even if you don't get a table by the window, you can watch the chefs making all your favourite Italian treats in the open kitchen around which the restaurant is structured. The food is delicious and beautifully presented, and the service is friendly and professional. Well worth a visit, but reservations are essential.

Food ●●●○ Service ●●●○ Venue ●●●● Value ●●●○

Japanese

Other options → **Karaoke Bars [p.402]**

Benihana

Location → Al Bustan Hotel · Al Garhoud | **282 0000**
Hours → 12:00 - 14:45 19:00 - 23:30
Web/email → fb@albustan-rotana.com **Map Ref** → 14-E3

 200

Benihana is easily one of Dubai's liveliest Japanese restaurants, especially during theme nights (Sunday: teppanyaki, Saturday & Tuesday: sushi). Hard-core Japanese fans won't be overly impressed with the quality or authenticity of food though; Benihana caters more to those not particularly familiar with Japanese cuisine. Novice eaters, on the other hand, will appreciate elastic bands tied around the ends of chopsticks and the "Americanised" Japanese menu. One of the six

teppanyaki tables is your best bet for the evening, but book ahead.

Food ●●●○ Service ●●○○ Venue ●●○○ Value ●●○○

Bento-Ya

Location → Al Kawakeb Bld D · Trade Center 1&2 | **343 0222**
Hours → 12:00 - 15:30 18:30 - 22:30 Fri 17:30 - 22:30
Web/email → na **Map Ref** → 9-A2

 150

Bento-Ya is an unassuming, unpretentious, compact Japanese restaurant good for a quick lunch or a casual dinner. Specialising in bento boxes (lunch or dinner) – decent value for the amount of food provided – this is a 'no-frills' neighbourhood restaurant offering a slightly less expensive option than a hotel outlet. Though atmosphere, superior quality, and refined service are somewhat lacking here, the Japanese chef does serve up a decent variety of home-style Japanese cooking to a good mix of patrons.

Food ●●○○ Service ●●○○ Venue ●●○○ Value ●●○○

Creekside

Location → Sheraton Hotel & Towers · Deira | **207 1735**
Hours → 12:30 - 15:30 18:30 - 24:00 Closed Fri am
Web/email → sheradxb@emirates.net.ae **Map Ref** → 11-C1

 100

Creekside offers the best deals in town for all you can eat sushi (Sunday, Dhs.70++) and all you can eat Japanese (Thursday, Dhs.98++). This unassuming restaurant is very popular with those who have tried it once and can't stop going back. Unlike other places with special buffet nights, the quality of food and service remains excellent here, no matter what special is on offer. Highly recommended for fresh, traditional Japanese food and attentive, friendly service any night of the week.

Food ●●●● Service ●●●● Venue ●●●○ Value ●●●○

Sushi

Italian | Japanese

Going Out

Teppanyaki

ET Sushi

Location → Emirates Towers · Trade Centre 1&2 **330 0000**
Hours → 12:30 - 15:00 19:30 - 24:00
Web/email → www.emirates-towers-hotel.com **Map Ref** → 9-C2

  150

ET Sushi's main attraction is its conveyor belt, snaking through the small, modern, minimalist single-room restaurant. Those with a penchant for freshness may choose to sit close to the chefs to grab fresh, tasty sushi as it's placed on the belt. Bargain lovers and novices will prefer this to the a la carte menu, where portions are larger, but priced almost 50% higher. Dress warmly – the a/c is set on high to 'keep the fish fresh'! Great for parties and large groups.

Food ●●●○ Service ●●○○ Venue ●●●○ Value ●●●○

Hana

Location → Riviera Hotel · Deira **222 2131**
Hours → 12:00 - 15:00 19:00 - 23:00
Web/email → riviera@emirates.net.ae **Map Ref** → 8-C3

 **150**

Hana is often filled with Japanese guests – a good sign when you enter. The ageing décor: "Polynesia meets Japan" is inviting, and two menus (Japanese and "A Taste of Asia") offer an array of different East Asian dishes. Japanese fare dominates: teppanyaki action entertains, nigiri and sushi are recommended, udon isn't. South Asian specialities like Pad Thai, Singapore Noodles, Chinese spring rolls and Malaysian curries tempt. Two cosy tatami rooms offer privacy and respite from the air conditioning. A good value for an early night out.

Food ●●●○ Service ●●●○ Venue ●●○○ Value ●●●○

Japengo Cafe

Location → Palm Strip · Beach Rd, Jumeira **345 4979**
Hours → 10:00 - 01:00
Web/email → binhendi@binhendi.com **Map Ref** → 6-D2

 150

Fish is the order of the day in this trendy café/restaurant. Sushi, sashimi, seared fish, fresh tuna, and salmon are complemented by plenty of other options – pizzas, salads, sandwiches, stir-fries and lamb, and several delicious choices for veggies. Pleasantly decorated in a 'fusion' of natural wood, rattan, bamboo and hard wooden tables, which contrast interestingly with steel and glass. Dine inside or outside on the terrace. If you have room to spare, try the Japengo chocolate cake or cheesecake.

Food ●●●○ Service ●●○○ Venue ●●○○ Value ●●●○

Kiku

Location → Le Meridien Dubai · Al Garhoud **282 4040**
Hours → 12:30 - 15:00 19:00 - 23:30 Fri 19:00 - 23:30
Web/email → kiku@le-meridien-dubai.com **Map Ref** → 14-E3

300

This is the Japanese restaurant for those 'in the know'. Packed with a great mix of nationalities, Kiku hums with activity. The Japanese chef prepares dishes to perfection and the sushi is not to be missed. Fresh, delicious and of perfect consistency, maki rolls and nigiri are a delight to devour. For something different, try the tempura ice cream served on a bed of fresh fruit. Ideal for either a business dinner, or a casual evening out, Kiku will more than satisfy expectations, despite slow service.

Food ●●●● Service ●●○○ Venue ●●●○ Value ●●●●

Minato

Location → Hotel Inter-Continental · Deira **205 7333**
Hours → 19:00 - 23:00
Web/email → intercon_bc@itcdubai.co.ae **Map Ref** → 8-C4

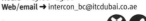

300

Minato offers an authentic Japanese dining experience in traditional surroundings, combined with warm Filipino hospitality. All the standard Japanese dishes are present, plus many more. Sushi and sashimi is fresh, cut flawlessly, and highly recommended. For the more price-conscious, Monday's sushi and Saturday's teppanyaki buffets are a great option at Dhs.99 net.

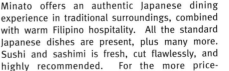

Japanese

Going Out

WITH ELEVEN *success*
STORIES,
IT'S THE *perfect* SETTING
FOR DINING OUT.

There are many restaurants in Dubai. But only a few can claim to be the best in their class. You'll find them at Emirates Towers - your first choice for world class cuisine. **To reserve your table, simply call 04 319 8711.**

The Agency • ET Sushi • Harry Ghatto's • Mosaico • Al Nafoorah • The Noodle House
• oh! cajun • The Oyster Lounge • Scarlett's • tokyo@thetowers • Vu's

EMIRATES TOWERS
hotel

JUMEIRAH
INTERNATIONAL
www.jumeirahinternational.com

Service is both efficient and discreet, but the semi-private rooms are far from private – try to book one of the two tatami rooms if you have a romantic or quiet meal in mind.

Food ●●●○ Service ●●●● Venue ●●●○ Value ●●●○

Miyako

Location → Hyatt Regency · Deira
Hours → 12:30 - 15:00 19:00 - 23:00
Web/email → hyattbus@emirates.net.ae   **Map Ref →** 8-D2

| 209 1234 |

 ... 300

This upscale restaurant exudes a feeling of tranquillity and a sense that you've arrived in Japan. The menu is extensive, the service impeccable and the décor traditional. Dishes are prepared to perfection by the Japanese chef. The sushi and nigiri are highly recommended, particularly the unagi. Teppanyaki and box sets are also favourites with guests. A sushi bar, tatami room and teppanyaki tables add to your authentic experience. This "refined dining" venue is ideal if you are out to impress.

Food ●●●● Service ●●●● Venue ●●●● Value ●●●○

Sakura – Crowne Plaza

Location → Crowne Plaza · Trade Centre 1&2
Hours → 12:00 - 15:00 19:00 - 23:00 Fri 19:00 - 23:00
Web/email → www.crowneplaza.com   **Map Ref →** 9-D2

| 331 1111 |

 300

Sakura is a quiet, low-key restaurant decorated in typical Japanese black lacquer. Besides the usual teppanyaki tables and sushi bar, Sakura has two cosy, private tatami rooms, one overlooking Sheikh Zayed Road. Service is pleasant here, albeit elusive. Soba noodles are highly recommended; the sushi isn't. Sushi rice was the wrong consistency, the seaweed stale, and some types of fish previously frozen. That said, with a new Japanese chef coming on board shortly, things are bound to look up for Sakura.

Food ●●○○ Service ●●○○ Venue ●●●○ Value ●●○○

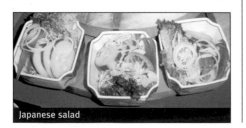

Japanese salad

Sakura

Location → Taj Palace Hotel · Deira
Hours → 12:00 - 15:00 19:00 - 23:30 Fri 12:00 - 16:00
Web/email → tajdubai@emirates.net.ae   **Map Ref →** 11-D2

| 223 2222 |

200

If you are in search of a zen-like Japanese experience, the Taj Palace's Sakura is your best bet. From the food to the chopsticks and pottery dishes, and even the modern, open-plan décor – details are key and everything's a work of art. The menu is extensive; some offerings are so authentically Japanese, they aren't found on other menus in town. Vegetable garnishes shaped like flowers complement fresh, delicious sushi and teppanyaki – both are recommended. For a cosy dining experience, book the sofas in advance.

Food ●●●○ Service ●●●● Venue ●●●● Value ●●●○

Sho Cho

Location → Dubai Marine Beach · Beach Rd, Jumeira
Hours → 19:30 - 00:30
Web/email → www.dxbmarine.com   **Map Ref →** 6-D2

| 346 1111 |

   300

This chic (some say terminally hip) Japanese-inspired restaurant rates highly as a cocktail venue The very fashionable room can outshine the sometimes holier-than-thou staff, but the menu has a few moments of brilliance. Seared salmon skins, prawn salad, and of course decent sushi make dining here a pleasure. Later in the evening, the noise level can be impossible, and weekends are very busy, so book in advance. With all the good drinks on the menu, beware the skyrocketing bill syndrome.

Food ●●●○ Service ●●○○ Venue ●●●○ Value ●●○○

Sumo

Location → Pink Bld · Trade Center 1&2
Hours → 11:00 - 23:00 Fri 16:00 - 23:00
Web/email → sumodxb@emirates.net.ae   **Map Ref →** 9-A2

| 343 5566 |

  150

Sumo is a healthy fast food lover's best option for good, fast, inexpensive Japanese cuisine. While eating in is an option, the atmosphere is a bit cold; takeaway is recommended. Specialising in bento boxes, the menu has a limited selection of sushi and sashimi as well. The Banzai Roll (avocado and BBQ eel) and the California Roll are excellent. Traditional Japanese food or an extensive menu you won't find here, but good value for money and a quick fix for a non-adventurous sushi craving you will.●

Food ●●●○ Service ●●○○ Venue ●●○○ Value ●●●●

Sushi

Location → Grand Hyatt Dubai · Umm Hurair 2
Hours → 12:00 - 15:00 19:00 - 23:30
Web/email → www.hyatt.com

209 6993

Map Ref → 13-E3

No surprise here: this will be the Grand Hyatt's sushi venue (spring 2003). This restaurant is planning to use small details to lend tranquillity and pleasure to the dining experience. Careful attention to food and an intimate setting should contribute to making this a popular restaurant, if they can keep the quality high and the prices reasonable. The sushi market in Dubai is already tough; we shall see if Sushi is up to the challenge.●

Food – n/a Service – n/a Venue – n/a Value – n/a

Sushi Sushi

Location → Century Village · Al Garhoud
Hours → 12:30 - 01:00
Web/email → www.aviationclubonline.com

282 9908

Map Ref → 14-C3

Fresh, funky décor and the best al fresco option of all the Japanese restaurants in Dubai. Die-hard Japanese aficionados may frown at Sushi Sushi's food and service; this is a place to see and be seen rather than a temple of Japanese cuisine. Grilled and non-traditional dishes are recommended over the sushi, which can comprise stodgy rice and meagre quantities of fish. The 'all you can eat' Dhs.39 lunch and Dhs.89 dinner (Tuesdays) draw crowds. A pleasant, Japanese-inspired venue.●

Food ●●○○ Service ●●○○ Venue ●●●● Value ●●○○

tokyo@the towers

Location → Emirates Towers · Trade Centre 1&2
Hours → 12:30 - 15:00 19:30 - 24:00
Web/email → www.emirates-towers-hotel.com

330 0000

Map Ref → 9-C2

Minimalist décor belies a cornucopia of dishes here. The staff will readily sort through the range of average sushi as well as teppanyaki, which you can have entertainingly prepared in front of you at the teppanyaki table. For a touch of seclusion, try the tatami room behind sliding wooden doors. This is a good restaurant for friends, families and business people (excellent business lunches) rather than a romantic night out – Harry Ghatto's karaoke next door can get intrusive.●

Food ●●●○ Service ●●●○ Venue ●●●○ Value ●●○○

Yakitori

Location → Ascot Hotel · Bur Dubai
Hours → 12:30 - 15:00 18:30 - 23:30
Web/email → info@centuryhoteldubai.com

352 0900

Map Ref → 8-A3

One of Dubai's diamonds in the rough, Yakitori is an unexpected pleasure for Japanese food lovers. The Japanese sushi chef caters to any request, and the results are superb. The asparagus and bacon wraps are also highly recommended. The décor is stylish, but don't plan for a romantic meal; the bright lights won't allow you to hide anything from your date. While service can be sporadic, the food in this gem is definitely worth braving Computer Street's traffic for.●

Food ●●●● Service ●●○○ Venue ●●●○ Value ●●●●

Korean

Silla

Location → Ramada Continental · Al Hamriya
Hours → 11:00 - 15:00 18:00 - 23:00
Web/email → ramadadb@emirates.net.ae

266 2666

Map Ref → 12-B4

Silla is one of Dubai's few Korean restaurants, providing good value in authentically East Asian surroundings. Patronised by Koreans, its strength is Korean dishes, though there are Japanese and Chinese options too. A selection of tasty starters is included in the price of main courses, catering mostly to carnivores. The drinks menu is somewhat limited, and service elusive, perhaps in keeping with the venue's unassuming nature. However, for affordable Korean food and a change of pace, Silla is a good choice.●

Food ●●○○ Service ●●○○ Venue ●●○○ Value ●●●●

Japanese | Korean

Going Out

Malaysian

Other options → **Chinese** [p.319]
Filipino [p.326]
Singaporean [p.372]
Thai [p.377]

Fusion

Location → Le Royal Meridien · Al Sufouh
Hours → 19:00 - 24:00
Web/email → f&b@leroyalmeridien-dubai.com **Map Ref** → 2-E2

399 5555

An elegant combination of service, fresh ingredients, artistic presentation and tranquil surroundings, this Malaysian/Indonesian restaurant rates highly. The tasty and creative selection of seafood dishes is offered with the option of spicy or mild, plus there is a wide choice of vegetarian and meat dishes. The ultra chic décor, with the choice of bar, terrace or indoor dining affords plenty of options. The staff are discreet and unassuming, mirroring the minimalist nature of the surroundings. A fab introduction to the region's cuisine.
Food ●●●● Service ●●●○ Venue ●●●○ Value ●●●○

Lagenda Malaysia

Location → Mayfair Hotel · Deira
Hours → 24 hrs
Web/email → mayfair@emirates.net.ae **Map Ref** → 11-D2

228 4444

Hidden away in the busy Deira shopping area, this undiscovered little place seats only 30. Primarily attracting lunchtime diners sampling authentic Malaysian cuisine, the interior is adorned with a collection of traditional handicrafts. A variety of traditional cooking styles are used for the main courses such as rendang, sambal, goreng-goreng and panggang, and dishes come with vegetables, rice or noodles. The food is delicately spiced and full of flavour, and if you're unfamiliar with the cuisine, the staff will make recommendations – you won't be disappointed.
Food ●●●○ Service ●●●○ Venue ●●○○ Value ●●○○

Far Eastern

For lovers of light, generally healthy food with an emphasis on steamed or stir-fried cooking methods, Far Eastern cuisine is an excellent option either for dining out or takeaway. Seafood and vegetables dominate the menu, but the staples are rice and noodles, with dishes enhanced by the use of delicate and fragrant herbs and spices like ginger, lemon grass, and coconut milk. Dishes can be spicy, but generally less so than a fiery, denture melting Vindaloo curry.

The décor of Thai, Malaysian and Polynesian restaurants often reflects a stereotypically exotic view of the Far East, with bamboo, beach huts and 'demure' oriental waitresses. Sometimes this combines to create a tasteful, relaxing and classy ambience and sometimes it doesn't quite make it. With the exception of Chinese outlets, Far Eastern restaurants are generally located in hotels in more upmarket surroundings, with prices that match.

Japanese restaurants generally offer a choice of seating options, from teppanyaki tables where the entertainment is provided by the chefs as they juggle, dice and slice, to private tatami rooms or the sushi option, where dishes pass before your eyes on a conveyor belt. Any way you like it, the standard of Japanese food in Dubai is high, with prices to match.

Dubai has a great number of Chinese restaurants and standards vary greatly from monosodium glutamate-laden taste killing dishes to light, nourishing and delicious cuisine. Many of the independents (ie, those not linked to a hotel or club) offer good value for money, with large portions and quality food. As with Indian outlets, many Chinese restaurants offer tasty takeaway and home delivery, giving Dubai residents even less incentive to learn how to use their wok. Check out the following cuisines:

Chinese, Filipino, Japanese, Korean, Malaysian, Polynesian, Singaporean, Thai and Vietnamese

Mediterranean

Other options → **Italian** [p.346]
Pizzerias [p.367]

Cafe Insignia

Location → Ramada Hotel · Bur Dubai
Hours → 06:00 - 23:30
Web/email → rhddxb@emirates.net.ae **Map Ref** → 7-E3

351 9999

While you may not be immediately impressed with Cafe Insignia, don't give up too soon. Unimaginative decor and quietude fail to suggest the fabulous food. Feast your eyes on the victuals

Going Out

Malaysian | Mediterranean

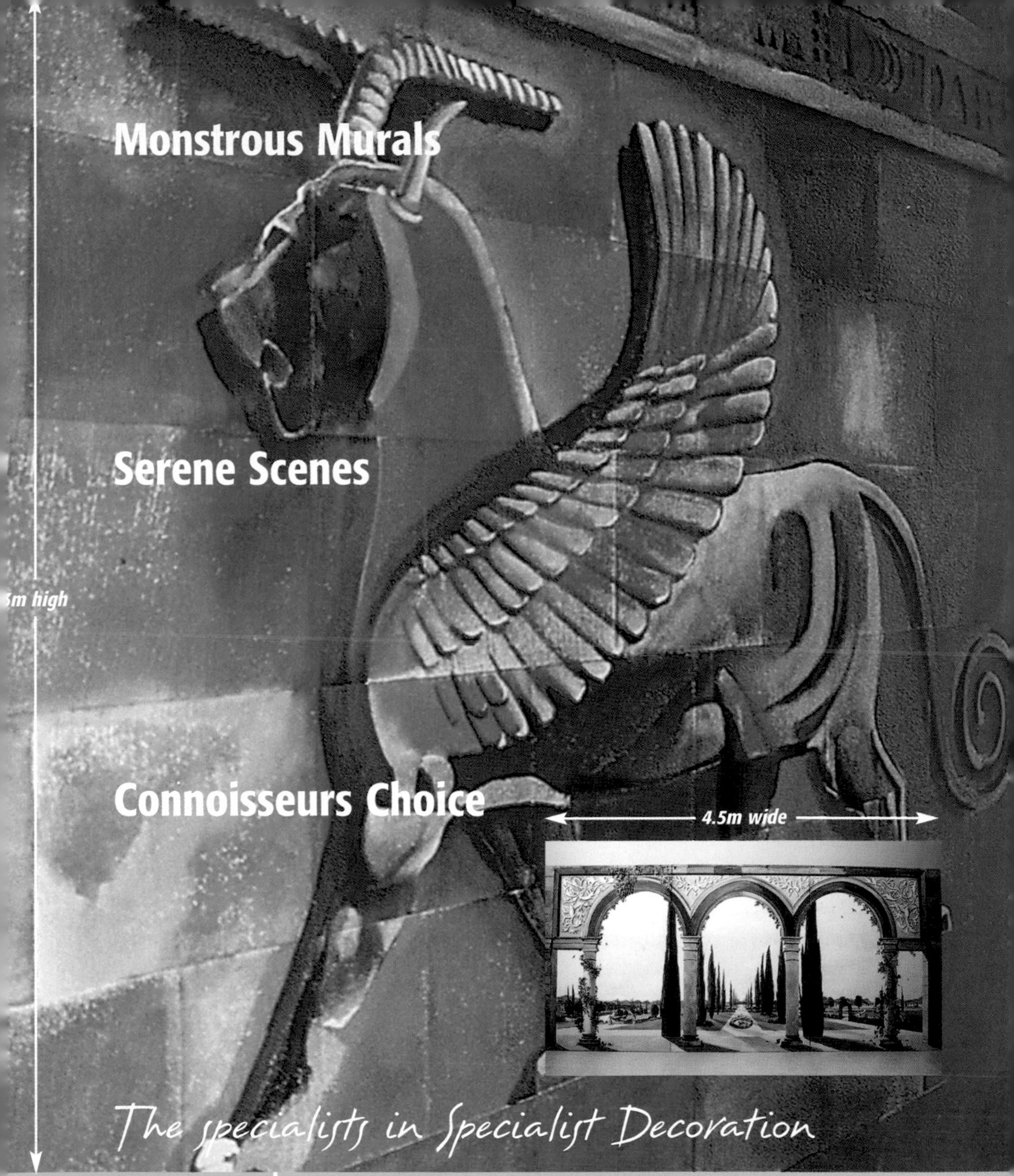

Monstrous Murals

Serene Scenes

5m high

Connoisseurs Choice

4.5m wide

The specialists in Specialist Decoration

Mackenzie Associates

TROMPE L'OEIL, MURALS AND CREATIVE COMMISSIONS

PO Box 34275, Dubai, United Arab Emirates
Tel: +(971 4) 396 2698 Fax +(971 4) 3422812 email: mackenziea1@yahoo.com

rather than the environs and experience an epicure's delight of exciting colours, flavours and textures. The set menu, while providing absolutely no choices, represents excellent value at Dhs 65 for 3 courses plus a glass of house wine; alternatively select your own food from the more expensive a la carte menu. A restaurant with great potential.

Food ●●●○ Service ●●●○ Venue ●●●○ Value ●●○○

Focaccia

Location → Hyatt Regency · Deira
Hours → 12:30 - 15:00   19:30 - 23:30
Web/email → hyattbus@emirates.net.ae
Map Ref → 8-D2

   250

This beloved restaurant has earned a great reputation over the years. The design imitates a large Mediterranean villa with several different rooms: kitchen, conservatory, library, cellar and courtyard, all with seating options. A perfect atmosphere and setting for a quiet romantic dinner; or book the whole library for a large party (20ish). A particularly good antipasti bar and divine desserts bracket the numerous and excellent Spanish and Italian mains. Service is professional and helpful and prices are reasonable. Indeed, little room for criticism here.

Food ●●●● Service ●●●○ Venue ●●●● Value ●●●○

Gozo Garden

Location → Airport Hotel · Al Garhoud
Hours → 12:30 - 15:30   20:00 - 23:30
Web/email → apothotl@emirates.net.ae
Map Ref → 14-D3

| 282 3464

 150

From this garden modelled on a Mediterranean courtyard, embark upon a culinary circumnavigation of the globe. Enjoy theme nights like 'The Best of British', 'Aromas of Arabia', 'Spices From the Orient' or 'Tropical Delights of Hawaii'. In Gozo, the world really is your oyster. Animated clientele and a genial duet combine to keep the place bustling with music and laughter. Fixed price buffets include beer, spirits and soft drinks. A chance to savour a fun world of food without breaking the bank.

Food ●●●○ Service ●●○○ Venue ●●●○ Value ●●●○

La Villa

Location → Sofitel City Centre · Al Garhoud
Hours → 12:30 - 15:30   19:30 - 24:00   Fri 19:30- 24:00
Web/email → cityhotl@emirates.net.ae
Map Ref → 14-D1

| 294 1222

 150

Hearty and generous Mediterranean food is featured on the menu of this quiet restaurant located next to the lively City Centre. Try delicacies from the antipasti buffet, home-made pasta or something from the grill. For Dhs.99, the Latin Grill dinner includes the antipasti buffet, your choice of grilled meat (chicken, pork, veal, kangaroo, fish, ostrich, or duck) and the dessert and cheese cart. A pianist/singer performs in the adjacent bar nightly (except Saturdays). Convenient after a long day of shopping.

Food ●●●○ Service ●●●○ Venue ●●●○ Value ●●●○

La Villa

Medzo

Location → Pyramids · Umm Hurair 2 | **324 0000**
Hours → 12:30 - 15:00 19:30 - 23:30
Web/email → www.pyramidsdubai.com   Map Ref → 13-D2

    200

For remarkable modern Italian fare with a touch of the Mediterranean, visit the stylish Medzo. It's tempting to just order everything on the imaginative antipasti menu, but consider it a starting point to be followed with the lobster and tomato broth with mussels, forest mushroom risotto, or roasted helwayoo with spinach gnocchi. The sublime – and affordable - dishes are presented artistically on unusual tableware. With plenty of grown-up appeal and fantastic flavours, Medzo is ideal for a date or dinner with friends.
Food ●●●○ Service ●●●○ Venue ●●●● Value ●●●○

Olives

Location → Royal Mirage Palace · Al Sufouh | **399 9999**
Hours → 06:30 - 24:00
Web/email → royalmirage@royalmiragedubai.com Map Ref → 3-A2

 150

Olives is an atmospheric, relaxed and friendly Mediterranean environment perfect for enjoying some excellent food. The menu offers possibly the best pizza in town, plus some unusual combinations of ingredients. The buffet has a good selection of salads, seafood, cold cuts and warm plates. The dessert table warrants more than one visit. Service is genuine and friendly. With its relaxed and open setting and view of the hotel gardens, Olives makes an extremely pleasant night out – a meal here is definitely worth the trip.
Food ●●●○ Service ●●●○ Venue ●●●● Value ●●●○

Oregano

Location → Oasis Beach Hotel · Al Sufouh | **399 4444**
Hours → 18:00 - 24:00 Closed Mon
Web/email → foodbeverage.obh@dutcohotels.com   Map Ref → 2-D2

   150

Tantalise your taste buds with a home-style blend of provincial Mediterranean cuisines. Oregano specialises in succulent southern French and northern Italian delights. With rustic interiors, a jovial accordionist, great food and wines, you'd be excused for forgetting where you are. Beautiful menus tell the story of the cuisine's origins, and the friendly staff offer guidance: duck confit or pasta, risotto or vegetarian; prawns or grilled fish?

Deserts are great – the tiramisu is delicious, but the selection of French cheeses is simply divine.
Food ●●●○ Service ●●●○ Venue ●●●○ Value ●●●○

Prasino's

Location → Jumeirah Beach Club · Jumeira | **344 5333**
Hours → 12:30 - 15:00 19:30 - 23:30
Web/email → info@jumeirahbeachclub.com   Map Ref → 5-D1

  300

Prasino's, overlooking the Gulf, features Mediterranean food and strives for an ambience to reflect it, with tiled floors, muted earth tones and tea-lights. The food succeeds beautifully – perfectly cooked and modishly presented with a bias towards seafood. There is plenty of choice for carnivores but a limited vegetarian selection. A separate bar area is great for lounging with a drink and taking in the view. Music is live but subtly jazzy, making Prasino's more stylish than your average beach club cafe.
Food ●●●○ Service ●●●○ Venue ●●●○ Value ●●●○

Seabreeze

Location → Le Royal Meridien · Al Sufouh | **399 5555**
Hours → 12:00 - 01:00
Web/email → f&b@leroyalmeridien-dubai.com   Map Ref → 2-E2

 **200**

As the name suggests, this venue is refreshing and relaxing. When the weather is fine, the spacious outdoor terrace is preferable to the maritime styled interior. The compact menu includes contemporary cuisine, including some exciting and original dishes. Well-presented and well balanced dishes like stuffed salmon with crab meat and avocado or grilled US beefsteak with crispy fried onions and peppercorn sauce were delivered with smiling, genuine service. The result is good value for money from this quality eatery.
Food ●●●○ Service ●●●● Venue ●●●○ Value ●●●○

 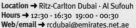

Splendido Grill

Location → Ritz-Carlton Dubai · Al Sufouh | **399 4000**
Hours → 12:30 - 16:30 19:00 - 00:30
Web/email → rcdubai@emirates.net.ae   Map Ref → 2-E2

   300

Splendido offers Mediterranean cuisine abundantly flavoured with fresh herbs. Risotto, pasta and pizza are complemented by a variety

Our philosophy on food is simple.

The Ritz-Carlton, Dubai

Lobster with sweet pea purée

At The Ritz-Carlton, Dubai we believe that diners should be allowed to appreciate the natural flavours of each ingredient. In our signature restaurant **La Baie** we have put this philosophy to work with a new menu exquisite in its fresh simplicity. We would like to share this vision with you.

THE RITZ-CARLTON®
DUBAI

P. O. Box 26525, Dubai, United Arab Emirates. Tel: (971) 4 3994000, Fax: (971) 4 3994001, Website: www.ritzcarlton.com
Call toll-free from: Bahrain 800 995 • Istanbul 00 800 44 91 1137 • Jordan 800 22 010 • Kuwait 245 28 57
Qatar 0800 97 115 • Saudi Arabia 800 89 71 435 • UAE 800 4789

of grilled meats, fish and freshly prepared salads. While the food is tasty, you're paying for a 'Ritz experience' – venue, service, and presentation. For a romantic evening, request a table on the terrace where you can dine over flickering candlelight and enjoy expansive views of the Gulf. From 20:00 a Spanish band plays soulful background music or lively American blues, according to requests.

Food ●●●○ Service ●●●● Venue ●●●● Value ●●●○

Splendido Grill

Vu's

Location → Emirates Towers · Trade Centre 1&2 | **330 0000**
Hours → 13:00 - 15:00 19:00 - 23:00
Web/email → www.emirates-towers-hotel.com **Map Ref** → 9-C2

High in the Dubai sky, Vu's staff values efficiency as it serves the best of terra firma and the seas beyond. The chef's innovative fare – flaky anchovy bread, pumpkin basil soup, eggplant ravioli – deserves noticing, though the view can be distracting. Main courses like baked grouper with dill and cucumber, allow an idle glance out the windows, but the epaisse cheese, running gently toward fruits and nuts stuck sweetly in place, transfixes attention. Chic, modern, and delicious, the restaurant is excellent... did we mention the view?

Food ●●●○ Service ●●●○ Venue ●●●● Value ●●●○

Moroccan

Other options → **Arabic/Lebanese [p.312]**
Persian [p.366]
Turkish [p.378]

Al Khaima

Location → Le Royal Meridien · Al Sufouh | **399 5555**
Hours → 20:00 - 24:00 20:00 - 01:00 Thu
Web/email → www.leroyalmeridien-dubai.com **Map Ref** → 2-E2

Walk past immaculately manicured lawns and palm trees to Al Khaima ('The Tent'). Try for the tables on the patio – a delightful setting right on the beach. Start with the well-presented, flavoursome mezze and go no further; mains can be a disappointment. The fresh Arabic bread, cooked while you watch is delicious. Shisha options are plentiful and the Arabic band entertain, while the service is outstanding. While reasonable value for money, the romantic beach setting is the main draw here.

Food ●●●○ Service ●●●● Venue ●●●○ Value ●●●○

Tagine

Location → Royal Mirage Palace · Al Sufouh | **399 9999**
Hours → 19:30 - 23:00 Closed Mon
Web/email → royalmirage@royalmiragedubai.com **Map Ref** → 3-A2

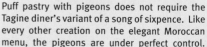

Puff pastry with pigeons does not require the Tagine diner's variant of a song of sixpence. Like every other creation on the elegant Moroccan menu, the pigeons are under perfect control.

Going Out Moroccan | Mediterranean

Welcome to the Magic of Arabia

Royal Mirage

JUMEIRA BEACH, DUBAI

ARABIAN COURT   THE PALACE   RESIDENCE & SPA

Royal Mirage, Jumeira Beach, PO Box 37252, Dubai, UAE. Tel: (971-4) 399 99 99, Fax: (971-4) 399 99 98.
www.royalmiragedubai.com

Succulent New Zealand lamb honours the tagine stew. Fluffy couscous features spicy, juicy chicken, handfuls of raisins, almonds, and chick peas. Flaky pastries, heavenly creams, and delicate cinnamon sing with Tagine's gentle musicians – a reprise that insists on a swift return. A Moroccan fantasy of the highest order, Tagine is seamlessly excellent.

Food ●●●○ Service ●●●● Venue ●●●● Value ●●○○

Pakistani

Other options ➜ **Indian [p.332]**

Karachi Darbar

Location ➜ Various locations
Hours ➜ 11:00 - 24:00
Web/email ➜ na

334 7272

Map Ref ➜ n/a

50

A top option for tasty, friendly, and cheap Indo-Pakistani fare, this restaurant chain is a perennial favourite in Dubai. The simple décor, plain menus, and utilitarian settings may not pull visitors off the street: this is a shame. The no-nonsense but very welcoming service, the range of high-quality food, and the generous portions make these restaurants exceptional. Amazingly, service and food are consistently good across the various branches, which further confirms that this is one local eatery that is worth seeking out.

Other Locations:

- *Karama Shopping Centre, near the large car park (334 7272)*
- *Bur Dubai, near HSBC (353 3177)*
- *Al Qusais, Qusais Road (263 2266)*
- *Al Mussalla, Naif Road, near Hyatt Regency Hotel (272 3755)*
- *Hor Al Anz, behind Dubai Cinema (262 5251)*
- *Al Qusais, Sheikh Colony (261 4131)*
- *Rashidya (285 9454).*

Food ●●●○ Service ●●●○ Venue ●●○○ Value ●●●●

Ravi's

Location ➜ Nr Satwa R/A · Al Satwa
Hours ➜ 24 hours
Web/email ➜ n/a

331 5353

Map Ref ➜ 6-E4

 50

Near the Satwa roundabout, opposite Union Co-operative at the end of Satwa's one way shopping street is Ravis, an unpretentious, local Pakistani restaurant that is worth a visit. Popular with Jumeira residents as well as Asian bachelors

tucking into a hearty lunch, the food is good and cheap. For an ethnic breakfast, try dhal and chapattis. A large, separate dining section caters for families, or those who prefer carpeted floors and an attempt at decor. A great antidote to the prices and pretense of hotel venues.

Food ●●○○ Service ●●●● Venue ●●○○ Value ●●●●

Persian

Other options ➜ **Arabic/Lebanese [p.312]**
Moroccan [p.364]
Turkish [p.378]

Al Borz

Location ➜ Al Durrah Tower · Trade Centre 1&2
Hours ➜ 11:00 - 16:00 19:00 - 01:00
Web/email ➜ n/a

331 8777

Map Ref ➜ 9-D2

 100

Tucked away on the mezzanine floor, Al Borz is a real surprise: great fun and value for money. Iranian décor sets the tone; cordial service picks it up from there. A variety of succulent kebabs and stews served with fragrant rice make a good introduction to this cuisine. Make sure you leave room for dessert as the 'pastany' (traditional ice-cream) and 'faloodeh' (unique iced dessert) are delicious. Book in advance, especially to secure a romantic table tucked away in a private alcove by the fountain.

Food ●●●○ Service ●●●○ Venue ●●●○ Value ●●●●

Pars Iranian Kitchen

Location ➜ Al Diyafah Street · Al Satwa
Hours ➜ 12:00 - 15:30 19:00 - 24:00 Fri 13:00 - 16:00
Web/email ➜ n/a

398 4000

Map Ref ➜ 7-A3

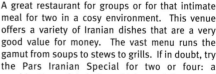 100

A great restaurant for groups or for that intimate meal for two in a cosy environment. This venue offers a variety of Iranian dishes that are a very good value for money. The vast menu runs the gamut from soups to stews to grills. If in doubt, try the Pars Iranian Special for two or four: a combination of kebabs, chicken, shrimps and potato, with different types of steamed, flavoured rice. For Dhs.450 have a full 'quzi' (whole lamb) cooked for your party at home.

Food ●●●○ Service ●●○○ Venue ●●●○ Value ●●●○

Pakistani | Persian

Going Out

Shabestan

Location → Hotel Inter-Continental · Deira | **205 7333**
Hours → 13:00 - 15:00 20:00 - 23:00
Web/email → intercon_bc@itcdubai.co.ae **Map Ref** → 8-C4

    300

It may not be the cheapest Persian restaurant in town, but it's by far the classiest and best tasting one we've come across here. Candlelit with a Persian band and a view overlooking the Creek, the ambience itself is worth the trip. The starter selection is limited; it might be better to skip them and keep room for the generous mains, the majority of which are lamb dishes. There's also a separate family menu for four or more, but bring a full wallet.

Food ●●●○ Service ●●●○ Venue ●●●● Value ●○○○

Shahrzad

Location → Hyatt Regency · Deira | **209 1200**
Hours → 12:30 - 15:30 19:30 - 23:30
Web/email → hyattregency@hytdubai.co.ae **Map Ref** → 8-D2

200

Step into the text of 1001 Arabian Nights: Shahrzad promises 1001 flavours for your delight. Fanoos (glass-covered lamps) and lanterns complement vibrantly coloured walls and curtains which evoke the glories of Persian culture. Courtly service makes guests feel like sultans. Specialities include Iranian charcoal-grilled kebabs, stews cooked with vegetables, herbs and fruits. Crisp Iranian cookies and Faloodeh are worth trying as well. Escape from the daily drag: Shahrzad has 1001 ways to please you.

Food ●●●○ Service ●●●● Venue ●●●● Value ●●●○

Pizzerias

Other options → **Italian [p.346]**
Mediterranean [p.358]

Ciro's Pomodoro

Location → Le Meridien Mina · Al Sufouh | **399 3333**
Hours → 12:00 - 16:00 19:00 - 03:00
Web/email → f&b@lemeridien-minaseyahi.com **Map Ref** → 3-A2

     150

Ciro's Pomodoro offers an interesting range of pizzas in a lively atmosphere. Live music, a small dance floor and capable and efficient staff all make for a buzzing venue. As well as pizzas, there are pastas, grills and a number of salad options. They do a decent pizza, although the starters are somewhat less inspiring. You might not go to Ciro's Pomodoro for fine dining, but it has all the ingredients for a convivial night out.

Food ●●○○ Service ●●●● Venue ●●●○ Value ●●○○

La Fornace

Location → Le Royal Meridien · Al Sufouh | **399 5555**
Hours → 18:00 - 01:00
Web/email → f&b@leroyalmeridien-dubai.com **Map Ref** → 2-E2

  250

Pizza lovers of the world take note: La Fornace ("the furnace") offers a huge choice (two whole pages of the menu) of your favourite flat, round, cheesy delicacy, as well as some other Italian classics. As expected from a good Italian kitchen, the food is delicious, hot and wholesome, and it's all served up with a smile by super-friendly waiters. The setting is full of rustic charm and romantic little corners – a great "first-date" restaurant. Not open for lunch.

Food ●●●○ Service ●●●○ Venue ●●●○ Value ●●●○

Pizza Corner

Location → Nr Riviera Htl, Baniyas St · Deira | **228 4330**
Hours → 11:30 - 24:00 Fri 13:30 - 01:00
Web/email → n/a **Map Ref** → 8-C3

   100

Pizza Corner is a cosy place with a manager who has been here since 1974, and knows just how to make you feel at home. The upstairs dining area has a dark and casual feel, while the terrace allows you to relax and eat in a pavement café type atmosphere. Pizzas can be customised and generously spread with your favourite toppings. In addition, there's a good range of salads from which you can make your own combinations. Good value for money and quick.

Other Locations: Another branch of Pizza Corner is located near Century Hotel, Bur Dubai (393 1889).

Food ●●●○ Service ●●●○ Venue ●●●○ Value ●●●○

Pizza Express

Location → Opp Four Points Sheraton · Bur Dubai | **324 7324**
Hours → 11:30 - 24:00 Fri 13:30 - 01:00
Web/email → jordanas@emirates.net.ae
Map Ref → 8-A4

  150

The Bank Street branch of this famous pizza chain offers all the predictable favourites. The pizzas don't disappoint; they are tasty, not greasy and with decent crusts. If you're not in the mood for one of the 20 pizzas, other menu choices include salads and (bland) pasta dishes. Surroundings are modern and spacious and service is friendly and quick. Unusually for Dubai, the service charge is not included in the bill, and all gratuities actually go to the servers.

Other Locations: Another branch of Pizza Express is in Park N Shop, Jumeira (800 4067).

Food ●●●○ Service ●●○○ Venue ●●○○ Value ●●●○

Polynesian

Other options → **Chinese [p.319]**
Filipino [p.326], Malaysian [p.358]
Singaporean [p372], Thai [p.377]

Bamboo Lagoon

Location → JW Marriott Hotel · Deira | **262 4444**
Hours → 19:00 - 24:00
Web/email → www.marriott.com
Map Ref → 12-A3

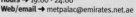 200

Enjoy a fusion of oriental cuisines in bamboo huts on stilts surrounded by a flowing stream. Impressive, but lacking in terms of Asian hospitality. This restaurant has something for everyone; tiny tots to grandparents will be thrilled by the sizzling Mongolian BBQ and the rhythmic drums of the Polynesian band. A la carte or themed buffet, seafood market or teppanyaki tables, choose culinary delights from China, Thailand, Japan and Indonesia. Exotic cocktails complete the impression of a

tropical idyll. Book early to avoid disappointment - it's popular.

Food ●●●○ Service ●●●○ Venue ●●●● Value ●●●○

Beachcombers

Location → Jumeirah Beach Htl · Umm Suqeim | **348 0000**
Hours → 12:00 - 01:00
Web/email → www.jumeirah-beach.com
Map Ref → 4-B2

 300

Lovers of romantic settings should not miss Beachcombers. Overlooking a breathtaking view of the beach and the Burj Al Arab, diners relax in faux-rustic Polynesian surroundings and sample quality international cuisine. By day, the menu is a la carte; by night, a buffet. Theme nights with live entertainment take place regularly, dramatically changing the atmosphere of the restaurant and providing fun for everyone. The waiters are attentive and well-trained. Though the food is good, the venue itself is the main attraction.

Food ●●●○ Service ●●●○ Venue ●●●○ Value ●●●○

Tahiti

Location → Metropolitan Palace · Deira | **205 1364**
Hours → 19:00 - 24:00
Web/email → metpalac@emirates.net.ae
Map Ref → 11-D2

 250

Original, lively, and great for a group of people looking for value for money on drinks, this venue offers a regular all-inclusive buffet. It is the sort of place that everyone seems to mention the next day at work, though one wonders how much repeat business they receive. Decent, pan-Asian fare, and an entertaining floor show that can be annoying for serious conversationalists. For a party evening, this is a good one-stop choice.

Food ●●●○ Service ●●●○ Venue ●●●● Value ●●●○

Trader Vic`s

Location → Crowne Plaza · Trade Centre 1&2 | **331 1111**
Hours → 12:00 - 15:00 19:00 - 02:30 Fri 19:00 - 23:00
Web/email → www.crowneplaza.com
Map Ref → 9-D2

   200

Please see review under Cocktail Lounges - On the Town [p.396].

Food ●●●○ Service ●●●○ Venue ●●●○ Value ●●○○

Going Out | Pizzerias | Polynesian

Portuguese

Other options → **Spanish[p.372]**

Da Gama

Location → Century Village · Al Garhoud | **282 3636**
Hours → 12:30 - 01:00
Web/email → www.aviationclubonline.com | Map Ref → 14-C3

  150

Situated in a prime outdoor location, Da Gama offers the unusual combination of Portuguese and Mexican food. The leafy outside seating is in buzzing Century Village; the restaurant interior is beautifully decorated, with red velvet and icy blue sections (it does double duty weekend nights as the VIP Lounge). The menu includes standard Mexican fare, Portuguese dishes (including Goan curries) – Portuguese wine, too – and a number of prawn specials, but you need a big appetite to do these heavy and somewhat disappointing offerings justice.

Food ●●○○ Service ●●●○ Venue ●●●○ Value ●●○○

Russian

Troyka

Location → Ascot Hotel · Bur Dubai | **359 5908**
Hours → 12:00 - 15:00 19:00 - 02:45
Web/email → www.centuryhoteldubai.com | Map Ref → 8-A3

   150

Visit Troyka for a truly authentic Russian experience that will include mouthwatering food, live music and Russian girls performing Russian dance. Let the traditionally dressed waiters recommend dishes or try the Borscht soup, the Strosvetskaya (salmon, buckwheat, egg, and cheese) or the beef stroganoff (rich, mushroomy and accompanied by an enormous plate of mashed potatoes), all of which were excellent. While the décor is somewhat uninspired, this restaurant is popular for its food and entertainment; reservations are highly recommended.

Food ●●●● Service ●●●○ Venue ●●○○ Value ●●●●

Seafood

Other options → **Fish & Chips[p.326]**
Dinner Cruises [p.379]
International [p.336]

Al Bandar

Location → Heritage & Diving Village · Al Shindagha | **393 9001**
Hours → 11:00 - 16:00 19:00 - 01:00
Web/email → haribbin@emirates.net.ae | Map Ref → 8-B1

  150

Good international seafood and an idyllic setting keep this venue popular. Monkfish, billed as the house speciality, vies with live lobster. The food is simply delicious and excellent value for money. Various specials sweeten the offer: Sunday's special includes soup, starter and special seafood dish for Dhs.35; Tuesdays, ladies receive a free starter; Fridays, children under 10 are given a free child's meal. Group offers (minimum four) include a starter, soup, main and soft drink for Dhs.39. A great reasonable evening.

Food ●●●○ Service ●●○○ Venue ●●●○ Value ●●○○

Al Mahara

Location → Burj Al Arab · Umm Suqeim | **301 7600**
Hours → 12:30 - 15:00 19:00 - 24:00
Web/email → restaurants@burj-al-arab.com | Map Ref → 4-A1

    300

Plutocrats, mafiosi, and 'entrepreneurs' will feel right at home at this Burj extravaganza. Calculated to impress with excess, the restaurant curls around an enormous aquarium. As expected, the mostly seafood menu is meticulously interesting – every dish seems to have truffles, caviar, champagne and lobster worked into it somehow. Truly well-executed food, in most cases, does distract from the mesmerising aquarium. Formal but not offensively snobby service makes the evening elegant. Worth the whopper of a bill? You decide.

Food ●●●● Service ●●●○ Venue ●●●● Value ●●●○

Aquarium

Location → Creek Golf Club · Al Garhoud | **295 6000**
Hours → 12:30 - 15:00 19:30 - 23:00
Web/email → dubaicreek@dubaigolf.com | Map Ref → 14-C2

     300

With a great view overlooking the Creek, and another great view to the centre of the venue at their famous (and giant) aquarium, the food needs to be spectacular to compete. Mostly it is, with a strong emphasis on seafood (no, it does not come from the fish tank centrepiece). Lobster thermadore and chocolate fondant are divine, if heavy. Slightly lacking in atmosphere – it doesn't have the charisma of many of the new eateries in Dubai – but the stunning views of the city more than compensate.●

Food ●●●○ Service ●●●○ Venue ●●●○ Value ●●●○

Aquarium

Beach Bar & Grill, The

Location → Royal Mirage Palace · Al Sufouh | **399 9999**
Hours → 12:00 - 15:00 19:00 - 23:00
Web/email → royalmirage@royalmiragedubai.com Map Ref → 3-A2

 **250**

Surrounded by turquoise water, lush gardens and golden sands, The Beach Bar & Grill aims for a casual atmosphere during the day, but something more elegant in the evening. Fresh linen, flickering candles and the dark wood of the interior, offset by loads of cream and white, add to the stylish experience. The creative menu includes a selection of fresh fish, charbroiled shellfish, paella and mixed grills. This is a cool spot, but decide for yourself!●

Food ●●●○ Service ●●●○ Venue ●●●● Value ●●●○

Far East Seafood Market

Location → Regent Palace Hotel · Bur Dubai | **396 3888**
Hours → 12:00 - 15:00 19:00 - 23:45
Web/email → www.ramee-group.com   Map Ref → 11-A1

150

Living up to its name, the Far East Seafood Market serves delicious seafood with a Thai accent. Start with the complimentary appetisers and then let one of the knowledgeable waitresses guide you over the wooden bridge to the seafood "market". To complete your main course, choose from a variety of vegetables, rice and noodles. A selection of wines is available and, if you can manage, a small dessert menu. For seafood cooked "just right" and a pleasant ambiance, this eatery is worth a visit.●

Food ●●●● Service ●●●○ Venue ●●○○ Value ●●●○

Fish Bazaar

Location → Metropolitan · Jct 2, Shk Zayed Rd | **407 6867**
Hours → 12:30 - 15:00 19:00 - 24:00
Web/email → methotel@emirates.net.ae   Map Ref → 5-C4

    150

Perched atop the Metropolitan Hotel, this Thai-seafood restaurant overlooks the lights of Sheikh Zayed Road and Dubai city beyond. Another market-style restaurant, the selection of iced fishes can be daunting – don't hesitate to ask the staff to help you avoid disasters. The three chilli sauce is delightful, though rather spicy. Complimentary tom yum soup as a starter is a nice touch. More reasonable than other similar venues, this is a good value for money and a nice alternative to buffets.●

Food ●●●○ Service ●●●○ Venue ●●●○ Value ●●○○

Fishmarket, The

Location → Hotel Inter-Continental · Deira | **205 7333**
Hours → 13:00 - 15:15 20:00 - 23:30
Web/email → intercon_bc@itcdubai.co.ae   Map Ref → 8-C4

 300

Fish Market is more of a concept than just another seafood restaurant. Expert servers help diners select raw ingredients from an inspirational spread of seafood and vegetables, all priced by weight. Ingredients are then whisked off to the kitchen to be transformed into heavenly fare according to your cooking instructions: shark curry, langostines in garlic butter, the sky's the limit. Superb food, knowledgeable (if slow at times) service and views of lights dancing over the Creek make for a delightful (if pricey) "special occasion" dinner.●

Food ●●●● Service ●●●○ Venue ●●●○ Value ●●○○

Seafood

Going Out

Golden Fork

Location → Various locations | **na**
Hours → 08:30 - 03:00
Web/email → na   **Map Ref** → n/a

   (100)

This chain offers an extensive range of Filipino, Indian, Chinese and continental dishes. The rooms are sterile and the waiters adequate, but the food can be quite good. Fresh fish specials are on display, and portions are large with a complimentary soup as a starter. Burgers, Indian curries, stir-fries and sweet and sour dishes also are available. It's not gourmet food but, for the money it is a bargain.

Other Locations:

Golden Fork and Cindy's restaurants:
- *Nasr Square (221 1895)*
- *near Astoria Hotel (393 3081)*
- *Dune Centre, Satwa (398 3631)*
- *Al Riqqa Street (222 9802)*
- *Satwa (345 9846)*

Food ●●●○ Service ●●●○ Venue ●●○○ Value ●●●●

Marina Seafood Market

Location → Jumeirah Beach Htl · Umm Suqeim | **348 0000**
Hours → 12:30 - 14:30 19:00 - 01:00
Web/email → www.jumeirah-beach.com   **Map Ref** → 4-B2

    (300)

Overlooking the Gulf and the Jumeirah Beach Hotel marina, with large aquariums inside, this spectacular venue feels like part of the sea. Options are abundant, from sushi to grills to stir fry. Singapore-style shrimp, the chef's special, is a joy of flavours. Aspiring gourmets can compose their own combinations, though the staff are quick to advise against culinary disasters. Save space for the chocolate soup with walnut pudding before strolling or catching a ride back to the mainland.

Food ●●●● Service ●●●● Venue ●●●● Value ●●●○

Mi Vida

Location → Le Royal Meridien · Al Sufouh | **399 5555**
Hours → 19:00 - 24:00
Web/email → f&b@leroyalmeridien-dubai.com   **Map Ref** → 2-E2

(200)

A restaurant for food, not frills: choose you own fare from a well-stocked fresh seafood market,

then select your cooking style and sauces from a wide choice of options. A creative antipasto bar offers tasty starters. Fresh breads and scrumptious stuffed olives ready the palate. Seafood is cooked to perfection, including the peculiar "Italian" spring rolls (mussels, cream and vegetables). Attentive, efficient waiters, and excellent wine and beverage options. The ambience needs more soft touches to match the prices; nonetheless, for seafood lovers it is heavenly.

Food ●●●● Service ●●●○ Venue ●●●○ Value ●●●○

Sea World

Location → Above Safest Way · Trade Center 1&2 | **321 1500**
Hours → 12:00 - 00:15
Web/email → www.seaworld-dubai.com   **Map Ref** → 5-D3

 (150)

This venue attempts to brings the novelty of a seafood market to a mass audience. Browse live and iced seafood, place selections in your trolley, add vegetables, and select your preferred cooking method and sauce. Cheery staff advise on the prolific options. Stick to the simplest preparation to avoid spoiling your fish, and avoid the msg. Not being part of a hotel means no alcohol, but slightly better prices. A good place for the biggest party to chomp crustaceans in this vast, family-friendly restaurant.

Food ●●○○ Service ●●○○ Venue ●●○○ Value ●●○○

Seafood Market

Location → Le Meridien Dubai · Al Garhoud | **282 4040**
Hours → 12:30 - 15:00 19:30 - 23:30
Web/email → seafoodmkt@le-meridien.dubai.com **Map Ref** → 14-E3

 (200)

The Seafood Market is a blend of casual dining, superb fresh seafood and excellent service; if you eat here, go with a strategy. The smart diner will skip the overpriced, forgettable appetisers and go for a bigger fish (or better yet, lobster). Meals are ordered "market-style" at a long counter of seafood and vegetables, and can be steamed, sautéed, fried or grilled – all to perfection. For dessert, splurge on the "Strawberry Kilimanjaro" and all eyes (and mouths) will turn your way with envy.

Food ●●●● Service ●●●○ Venue ●●○○ Value ●●○○

Seafood

Going Out

Singaporean

Other options → **Chinese [p.319]**
Filipino [p.326], Malaysian [p.358], Thai [p.377]

Peppercrab

Location → Grand Hyatt Dubai · Umm Hurair 2 | **209 6993**
Hours → 19:00 - 23:30 Closed Sun
Web/email → www.hyatt.com   **Map Ref →** 13-E3

The Hyatt's seafood outlet will feature Singaporean cuisine. The concept is a South East Asian fish market, and their signature dish will be shared Peppercrabs, a speciality of Singapore. The open plan kitchen will allow diners to watch the chef do his magic, and the planned menu does sound delicious. Seafood dominates the menu, and includes dishes like stingray and chilli crab that are not often found around town. One to watch – we hope it will turn out to be a winner.⊚

Food – n/a Service – n/a Venue – n/a Value – n/a

Singapore Deli Café

Location → Nr. Bur Juman Centre · Bur Dubai | **396 6885**
Hours → 09:00 - 15:00 19:00 - 23:30
Web/email → delimd@hotmail.com   **Map Ref →** 11-A1

When it comes to noodles, Singapore Deli is as authentic as they come. This small restaurant may look like a deli with pink walls and flower prints, but it serves up crispy deep-fried wontons and spring rolls, and generous portions of steaming noodles. For noodle fans, the "Hawker noodles" are not to be missed. The menu includes brunch items such as muffins, waffles, sandwiches, cookies and speciality coffees as well. Those who discover Singapore Deli are likely to return for a regular (and reasonable) fix.⊚

Food ●●●○ Service ●●●○ Venue ●●●○ Value ●●●●

Singapura

Location → Oasis Beach Hotel · Al Sufouh | **399 4444**
Hours → 18:00 - 24:00 Closed Sun
Web/email → foodbeverage.obh@dutcohotels.com **Map Ref →** 2-D2

You'll find a relaxed, comfortable, authentic Singapore atmosphere with ocean views here. Tables are decorated with taste, and a basic menu

suggests the tone of the restaurant. There's an excellent fresh seafood bar, and seafood is cooked perfectly to order. Food presentation fits with the oriental concept, though the waiters can be overly attentive at times. Dessert options are very rich. Decent, if slightly pricey wine list, and all the usual house drinks are available. Worth a visit for something a bit different.⊚

Food ●●●○ Service ●●○○ Venue ●●●○ Value ●●●○

Spanish

Other options → **Tapas Bars [p.404]**

Seville's

Location → Planet Hollywood · Umm Hurair 2 | **324 7300**
Hours → 12:00 - 15:30 16:00 - 24:00
Web/email → www.planethollywood-dubai.com **Map Ref →** 13-D2

 150

This reasonably good tapas bar has a warm and dark atmosphere; it's an inviting space to share a variety of Spanish dishes with friends and to listen to the excellent guitarists. Particularly sociable on weekends, the terrace can get rather full. Moderately priced and tasty (though oily), hot and cold tapas are joined by a selection of speciality dishes. Although the staff are friendly, service is somewhat reluctant after the main course has been served. A good place to congregate early before plunging into the late nightlife nearby.⊚

Food ●●●○ Service ●●○○ Venue ●●●● Value ●●●○

Steak-Houses

Other options → **American [p.306]**

49'ers

Location → Sea Shell Inn · Bur Dubai | **393 4477**
Hours → 18:00 - 03:00
Web/email → sshelinn@emirates.net.ae   **Map Ref →** 7-E2

    100

Casual American-style eating and drinking with a DJ or live band playing most nights of the week is 49ers' appeal. Tuesdays and Sundays offer two free drinks for the ladies. Cowboy and cowgirl waiters are efficient though not personable. The open kitchen displays a

Singaporean | Steak-Houses

Going Out

selection of steaks, fish, chicken, prawns and even a veggie burger option, barbecued to your choice of temperature. A simple concept, but pleasant for a casual dinner or drinks (followed by dancing).

Food ●●●○ Service ●●●○ Venue ●●○○ Value ●●●○

Beach Comber Bar & Carvery Grill

Location → Metropolitan Resort · Al Sufouh |**399 5000**
Hours → 13:00 - 15:00 19:30 - 24:00 Fri 13:00 - 24:00
Web/email → metbeach@emirates.net.ae   **Map Ref** → 2-E2

   (150)

Not a bad place for a clandestine meeting as the tables outside are dimly secluded and there are very few Dubai residents present! Good barbecued meats and large portions of unusual meats like kangaroo and kudo ought to appeal to someone. Service is not particularly speedy and remember to self-serve the first course, since no instructions are given by the staff. The clientele are mainly hotel guests, and prices are reasonably good value, especially the fixed menu.

Food ●●●○ Service ●●○○ Venue ●●○○ Value ●●●○

Grill Room, The

Location → Sheraton Jumeirah Beach · Al Sufouh |**399 5533**
Hours → 12:00 - 15:00 19:00 - 24:00
Web/email → sherjum@emirates.net.ae   **Map Ref** → 2-D2

(200)

Newly refurbished and redesigned, the Grill Room offers a vast array of fresh Australian meat, including ostrich, lamb, and beef. A low-key setting of brick and wood make the restaurant feel unpretentious, but elegant nonetheless. The split-level design keeps the noise level reasonable and makes the already small venue feel even more intimate. As with any new restaurant, the staff may take some time to settle in. A promising addition to the concept of upscale grill restaurants.

Food – n/a Service – n/a Venue – n/a Value – n/a

JW's Steakhouse

JW's Steakhouse

Location → JW Marriott Hotel · Deira |**262 4444**
Hours → 12:30 - 15:00 19:30 - 23:30
Web/email → www.marriott.com   **Map Ref** → 12-A3

   (300)

The JW's Steakhouse really does live up to its reputation as one of, if not the best, steakhouses in town. With its unique blend of superb food and service, it stands apart from other dining experiences in Dubai. Only for serious carnivores, prime Angus beef is cooked to melt in your mouth. You'll feel you've arrived in another era, with its refined feeling of a gentlemen's club (but including women), complete with wing-back leather chairs. Surroundings are cosy, discrete and intimate, and the clientele, for good reason, quite devoted.

Food ●●●● Service ●●●● Venue ●●●● Value ●●●○

Legends

Legends

Location → Creek Golf Club · Al Garhoud |**295 6000**
Hours → 19:00 - 23:30 Closed Fri
Web/email → dubaicreek@dubaigolf.com   **Map Ref** → 14-C2

   (300)

Great steak with a view! The large roof terrace overlooks the Creek and the shadow of the impressive clubhouse; the setting doesn't get much better than this (make sure you get a table outside – make the most of it). A steakhouse by genre, the menu is great and the steaks divine – if you like meat. Don't bother if you are a vegetarian. Enjoy over-large steaks while soaking up the stunning view of Dubai by night.

Food ●●●○ Service ●●●○ Venue ●●●○ Value ●●●○

Steak-Houses

Going Out

M's Beef Bistro

Location ➜ Le Meridien Dubai · Al Garhoud | **282 4040**
Hours ➜ 12:30 - 14:45 20:00 - 23:45
Web/email ➜ beefbistro@le-meridien-dubai.com **Map Ref** ➜ 14-E3

Hot, chic and trendy: this is the place to eat meat. Black, glass-topped tables and glamorous furnishings, candle light and quiet conversations, this bistro exudes style. The diminutive menu concentrates on beef: cattle from New Zealand or steers from the USA, carpaccio, tartar, char-grilled or fondue – take your pick. The latter is only available on the terrace, so it's not a viable option for those sizzling summer months. Crepes Suzette flambéed at the table provide a splendid spectacle to finish a memorable repast.
Food ●●●○ Service ●●●● Venue ●●●● Value ●●●○

Manhattan Grill

Location ➜ Grand Hyatt Dubai · Umm Hurair 2 | **209 6993**
Hours ➜ 19:30 - 23:30 Closed Sat
Web/email ➜ www.hyatt.com   **Map Ref** ➜ 13-E3

Steak houses are apparently all the rage here these days. This one is proposed to be on par with anything other international cities have to offer. Furnished with dark, sumptuous wood and comfortable chairs, Manhattan Grill's menu will revolve around aged, grilled beef. Wine, oysters, some fish options round out the options. Billed as a sophisticated, confident venue, it should be perfect for Rat Pack fantasies and impressing dates with big...martinis! (open spring 2003)
Food – n/a Service – n/a Venue – n/a Value – n/a

Prime Rib

Location ➜ Le Royal Meridien · Al Sufouh | **399 5555**
Hours ➜ 19:30 - 24:00
Web/email ➜ www.leroyalmeridien-dubai.com **Map Ref** ➜ 2-E2

Selective carnivores with a particular passion for US Angus beef take note. An elegantly stylish and welcoming atmosphere features the kitchen as an energetic centrepiece. Simplicity and quality are hallmarks of the limited menu, and the service is notable for its no-nonsense efficiency. An impressive wine list caters to the wealthy aficionados as well as mere mortals.

All told, for red meat and red wine, this venue has it right.
Food ●●●● Service ●●●○ Venue ●●●● Value ●●○○

Rodeo Grill

Location ➜ Al Bustan Hotel · Al Garhoud | **705 4620**
Hours ➜ 12:30 - 15:00 19:00 - 24:00
Web/email ➜ fb@albustan-rotana.com **Map Ref** ➜ 14-E3

Rodeo Grill is a meat lover's paradise that feels like a romantic escape with dim lighting, candles, fine china, and impeccable service. House specialities include perfectly grilled steaks and fish, Caesar salad made tableside, foie gras, and a daily vegetarian option. Patrons seated opposite the glass-enclosed kitchen delight in watching chefs skilfully practising their art. Servers encourage a tranquil mood with efficient orchestration. A rich selection of desserts, liqueur-coffees, and digestifs perfectly finish the meal. Carnivores and lovers alike will delight in Rodeo Grill.
Food ●●●● Service ●●●● Venue ●●●○ Value ●●●○

Shooters

Location ➜ Jebel Ali Shooting Club · Jebel Ali | **883 6555**
Hours ➜ 13:00 - 15:00 19:00 - 22:30 Closed Tue
Web/email ➜ www.jebelalihotel.com   **Map Ref** ➜ 1-A2

Although Shooters is out of town, its location at the shooting club makes a visit a unique experience. In keeping with its surroundings, the restaurant has a Western theme. The focus of the menu is on US imported steaks, which are cooked to a high standard. One feature of the restaurant that you'll either love or hate is its panoramic view of the clay shooting area – although there's obviously soundproofing, shotgun blasts are still audible in the background.
Food ●●●○ Service ●●●○ Venue ●●●○ Value ●●○○

Western Steak House

Location ➜ Crowne Plaza · Trade Centre 1&2 | **331 1111**
Hours ➜ 12:00 - 15:00 19:00 - 23:30
Web/email ➜ www.crowneplaza.com   **Map Ref** ➜ 9-D2

Mouth-wateringly tender beef from the USA, courteous waiters, and a decent wine list add up to a nice experience. The easy set menu includes

OVER 180 CHEFS, EVERY ONE PASSIONATE ABOUT FOOD

Each of our 14 restaurants and bars brings together a team of gifted chefs who love to create food you'll be passionate about. Representing all corners of the globe, each brings a particular style based on their local traditions and each guarantees a grand dining experience, wherever it is you choose to tantalize your taste buds.

Fresh ingredients, authentic dishes, good company - the recipe for a Grand experience.

Call 04 317 1234 to reserve your table now.

www.grandhyattdubai.com

dining companion. Sukhothai also offers an outdoor terrace, but some of the charm is lost as the atmosphere blends with the other restaurants in the Meridian Village, and as a result, can get quite noisy.
Food ●●●○ Service ●●●○ Venue ●●●○ Value ●●●○

Sukhothai

Thai Bistro

Location ➜ Dubai Marine Beach · Beach Rd, Jumeira │ **346 1111**
Hours ➜ 18:30 - 23:30
Web/email ➜ www.dxbmarine.com   Map Ref ➜ 6-D2

This popular Thai restaurant rates highly for its wonderfully elegant setting: al fresco seating overlooking the pool/cove. Unfortunately, the service, while friendly and knowledgeable, tends to be quite slow. The food is pleasing enough, featuring a diverse selection of seafood items, but does not rival the best of the increasingly competitive Thai restaurants. That said, few diners seem to leave hungry or unhappy, so when seeking ambience and a generally elegant evening, Thai Bistro is a good choice.
Food ●●●● Service ●●●○ Venue ●●●● Value ●●●○

Thai Chi

Location ➜ Pyramids · Umm Hurair 2 │ **324 4100**
Hours ➜ 12:00 - 15:00 19:00 - 24:00
Web/email ➜ www.pyramidsdubai.com   Map Ref ➜ 13-D2

Save Thai Chi's bargain luncheon buffet for yourself and splurge with your guests at night, a more exotic time for entering a Wafi City

pyramid. Settle into the restaurant's comfortable Thai area on the theory that the Chinese section might be a rhyming afterthought. The exotic-feeling menu delights; try the tasty texture of kale leaves with dried shrimp, roasted peanuts, ginger, and lemon with tamarind sauce. This venue's version of Thai cooking seeks subtle, not fiery, effects, perfect for aficionados of pure Asian flavours.
Food ●●●○ Service ●●●○ Venue ●●○○ Value ●●○○

Turkish

Other options ➜ **Arabic/Lebanese [p.312]**
Persian [p.366], Moroccan [p.364]

Topkapi

Location ➜ Taj Palace Hotel · Deira │ **223 2222**
Hours ➜ 12:00 - 15:00 19:00 - 24:00
Web/email ➜ tajdubai@emirates.net.ae   Map Ref ➜ 11-D2

A tiled fountain murmuring in the background welcomes you to Topkapi, where traditionally attired staff escort you to elegant tables. The ethnic furniture, covered in embroidered cushions is emphasised by Turkish-tile walls. The menu offers a wide range of Turkish delicacies at reasonable prices. Choose from soups, mezze, kebabs, grills and authentic lamb stews. An excellent, relaxed dining choice for Turkish food enthusiasts as well as those wishing to feel like a sultan for the night.
Food ●●●○ Service ●●●○ Venue ●●●○ Value ●●●●

Vietnamese

Other options ➜ **Chinese [p.319]**
Malaysian [p.358]
Singaporean [p.372]
Thai [p.377]

Indochine

Location ➜ Grand Hyatt Dubai · Umm Hurair 2 │ **209 6993**
Hours ➜ 19:00 - 23:30 Closed Mon
Web/email ➜ www.hyatt.com   Map Ref ➜ 13-E3

Another new one scheduled to open soon, as the name suggests, this restaurant will offer a blend of authentic Vietnamese, Cambodian, Laos and Thai cuisine. The décor promises skylights, timber and bamboo, and lots of green combining to evoke the oriental splendour of Indochine. When in the mood for the exotic scents and tastes of lemongrass, lime and mint, fish sauce, and galangal, this should become one of the top choices. Perhaps this will help shake up Dubai's sometimes passive pan-Asian food market.

Food – n/a   Service – n/a   Venue – n/a   Value – n/a

DINNER CRUISES

Other options → Creek Tours [p.160]
Boat, Dhow &
Yacht Charters [p.162]

Al Boom Tourist Village

Location → Nr Al Garhoud Bridge · Umm Hurair 2 | **324 3000**
Hours → 20:30 - 22:30 daily
Web/email → abt@emirates.net.ae   Map Ref → 14-A3

  200

Al Boom Tourist Village is the largest dhow operator on the Creek, currently with five dhows catering to capacities of 20 - 150 passengers. Cruises depart from the Tourist Village for a two-hour dinner cruise daily from 20:30 - 22:30. The menu consists of a seafood and meat barbecue buffet, with some Emirati dishes and all grilled food items cooked on board. The cost is a very reasonable Dhs.100, including soft drinks, mineral water and tea or coffee.

Food ●●●○   Service ●●○○   Venue ●●●●   Value ●●●○

Al Mansour

Location → Hotel Inter-Continental · Deira | **205 7333**
Hours → 20:30 - 22:30
Web/email → intercon_bc@itcdubai.co.ae   Map Ref → 8-C4

  250

Indulge in a nicely prepared Arabic buffet while cruising along the Creek. The views are spectacular; the food adequate. Friendly, almost overly-eager staff cater to all whims. Diners board the well-maintained, traditional wooden dhow at set sailing times in the afternoon and evening, and relax upstairs on the open-air deck or down below in the windowed buffet area. The dhow comes complete with live Arabic music, a majlis, and shisha. A fantastic option for neophytes or for when out-of-town guests appear.

Food ●●●○   Service ●●○○   Venue ●●●●   Value ●●●○

Creek Cruises

Location → Creekside, Deira | **393 9860**
Hours → 09:00 - 18:00   Closed Fri
Web/email → www.creekcruises.com   Map Ref → 11-C2

   300

This air conditioned dhow departs nightly at 20:30 for dinner Creek cruises. Complimentary welcome drinks and a decent international buffet do nothing to distract from lovely views of the city slipping by. Seek out a seat on the upper deck majlis in good weather. Better yet, cater a private party (from 20-200) and design a genuinely remarkable evening.

Food ●●○○   Service ●●○○   Venue ●●●●   Value ●●○○

Creekside Leisure

Location → Opp Dubai Municipality HQ · Deira | **336 8406**
Hours → Timings on request
Web/email → www.tour-dubai.com   Map Ref → 11-C1

   300

For a different Creek cruise experience, try the 'Romantic Cruise for Two' which includes a limousine pick up and drop off, flowers and a Cuban cigar on arrival, butler service, a choice of two four-course menus, an open bar or a bottle of champagne, a choice of music and an intimate two-hour dining cruise. Expensive, yes, but certainly impressive!

Food ●●●○   Service ●●○○   Venue ●●●●   Value ●●○○

Danat Dubai Cruises

Location → Nr British Embassy · Bur Dubai | **351 1117**
Hours → 08:00 - 18:30
Web/email → www.danatdubaicruises.com   Map Ref → 8-C4

   300

Danat offers daily cruises of the Dubai Creek or farther into the Arabian Gulf on a modern catamaran. Fully licensed evening cruises (1 hour+) depart daily in the late afternoon, while the heartier dinner cruise sails from after 20:00. If you're looking for a non-traditional Arabian Creek dhow cruise experience, this is the one to choose. Dance party events are occasionally held on the later cruise – call for details of upcoming events.

Food ●●●○   Service ●●○○   Venue ●●●○   Value ●●●○

Vietnamese | Dinner Cruises

Going Out

Royal Tours

Location → Nr Sheraton Htl · Creekside, Deira |**223 1567**
Hours → Timings on request
Web/email → www.royaltours-dubai.com   **Map Ref →** 11-C1

  300

Every evening Royal Tours offers a dinner cruise along the Creek aboard their air conditioned dhow. You'll take in great views of Dubai's skyline as you journey to the Hyatt Regency Hotel, then return along the Creek, up to the golf club and back. Dine on an average buffet dinner accompanied by live Arabic music, then after your meal, sit back and be entertained by the belly dancer. The cruise starts at 20:30, returning at 22:30. Dhs.195 per person.▣

Food ●●●○ Service ●●○○ Venue ●●●● Value ●●●○

CAFÉS & COFFEE SHOPS

Dubai is a wonderful city for those who love a café culture – take a break from work or shopping, relax with the newspapers, a cup of tea and a cake, or simply enjoy the chance to catch up on gossip with friends.

The numerous cafés around the city vary from outlets that border on being a restaurant and serve an excellent variety of cuisine, from cake to a full blown three course meal, to those that have more of a cake and coffee with a few sandwiches coffee shop approach. Because of the limitations on opening a restaurant serving alcohol outside of a hotel or in certain clubs, plus a high number of people who do not drink alcohol, cafés enjoy a popularity here that they do not perhaps have in other parts of the world.

The following section on cafés encompasses cafés, coffee shops, ice-cream parlours, Internet and shisha cafés.

Al Nakheel Lounge

Location → Grand Hyatt Dubai · Umm Hurair 2 |**209 6993**
Hours → 24 hrs
Web/email → www.hyatt.com   **Map Ref →** 13-E3

Situated in the grand lobby area, this sophisticated lounge offers guests the best view of the Grand Hyatt's lobby. This café serves continental breakfasts, a selection of sandwiches and salads, a wide variety of freshly brewed coffees, teas, herbal infusions, homemade French pastries, freshly baked biscuits, as well as delicate truffles and pralines. There's also live entertainment to accompany your people watching.▣

Food – n/a Service – n/a Venue – n/a Value – n/a

Basta Art Café

Location → Al Faheidi St, Bur Dubai |**353 5071**
Hours → 10:00 - 22:00 Closed Fri
Web/email → na   **Map Ref →** 8-B3

Recently opened in the historical Bastakiya area, the Basta Art Café is a place to view some art, have a quick, healthy snack and unwind. Best to visit in the cooler months, when the peaceful courtyard of the 70 year old restored windtower house appeals. Food is 'home style' and simple: fresh juices, coffee, salads, sandwiches and pancakes. Art exhibitions rotate, interspersed with private art and theatre functions. A change from the typical Dubai café, this place is still 'undiscovered'.▣

Food – n/a Service – n/a Venue – n/a Value – n/a

Basta Art Cafe

Bocadillo Cafe

Location → Khalid Al Attaar Tower · Trade Centre 1&2 |**331 3133**
Hours → 11:00 - 00:30
Web/email → n/a   **Map Ref →** 9-C2

 50

If you are a crêpe fan, this is the place for you. Small, cosy, and with a tavern-like feel, the main seating area is upstairs beyond the open plan kitchen. Here you'll find tables plus some relaxing sofas. The menu is

Mediterranean in style, but favours a good selection of savoury and sweet crêpes. Generous portions may have you needing a siesta before returning to work. Popular with the younger office set and busy at lunch, arrive early, or enjoy a take-away.

Food ●●●○ Service ●●○○ Venue ●●○○ Value ●●○○

Brewster's Café

Location ➜ Al Dhiyafa St · Satwa   **345 4345**
Hours ➜ 10:00 - 23:00
Web/email ➜ na   **Map Ref** ➜ 6-E3

Brewster's adds a wide choice of bagels to the successful formula followed by other specialist coffee shop chains. Like them, it provides a smart, crisp, (if a little formulaic) outlet in which you are encouraged to spend time over a (allegedly) superior coffee, and in this instance, a superior bagel. Choose a sandwich and assorted toppings for a filling; they have salads too, and various cakes. Bagel fans will help make this cafe find its own niche in a crowded market.

Food ●●●○ Service ●●○○ Venue ●●○○ Value ●●○○

Café Ceramique

Location ➜ Town Centre · Beach Rd, Jumeira   **344 7331**
Hours ➜ 08:00 - 24:00
Web/email ➜ tast4art@emirates.net.ae   **Map Ref** ➜ 5-E1

Amateur artisans paint pots over coffee while others take in a bagel and the sea view. Customers can decorate crockery with paints, brushes and help supplied; creations are glazed in-house and collected later. The staff genially assist adults and kids with the decorating, though food service can be a bit more leisurely. The draw is certainly the novelty and activity rather than the somewhat bland food. This is a fun place for enthusiasts who enjoy workshops and creches combined.

Food ●●○○ Service ●●○○ Venue ●●●○ Value ●●○○

Café Havana

Location ➜ Spinneys (Umm Suqeim) · Umm Suqeim   **394 1727**
Hours ➜ 10:00 - 01:00
Web/email ➜ binhendi@binhendi.com   **Map Ref** ➜ 5-A3

Café Havana boasts three equally popular venues catering for quite different clientele. All outlets serve fantastic smoothies and milkshakes, and run daily specials. The menu is straightforward: pizzas, burgers, salads, pastas and sandwiches. The Umm Suqeim and Deira City Centre branches provide a pleasant lunch or post-shopping break, especially for families. The Lamcy Plaza outlet is situated in the foodcourt and caters to fast food clientele looking for quality. In all three cases, a superior option to bland international chains.

Food ●●●○ Service ●●○○ Venue ●●○○ Value ●●○○

Cafe Mozart

Location ➜ Nr Carlton Tower Htl · Deira   **221 6565**
Hours ➜ 08:00 - 23:00
Web/email ➜ n/a   **Map Ref** ➜ 8-C4

Relaxed and calm, Cafe Mozart is a handy retreat from the busy streets of Deira. Set up by Austrian-born Suzan nine years ago, it's quaint and welcoming – if a little kitsch with Mozart-o-rama adorning the walls. Curiously, it also serves Thai food from a comprehensive menu, somewhat skewing the Vienna-theme. Otherwise there's a typical cafe range of sandwiches, salads, some main courses and cakes etc, the latter being most tempting. The café also undertakes private parties and outside catering.

Food ●●○○ Service ●●●○ Venue ●○○○ Value ●●○○

Cafe Renoir

Location ➜ Wafi Mall · Umm Hurair 2   **324 6407**
Hours ➜ 08:30 - 24:00 Fri 14:30 - 24:00
Web/email ➜ www.waficity.com   **Map Ref** ➜ 13-D2

Step inside Cafe Renoir and you enter a bright and interesting French farmhouse-themed cafeteria with wooden floors, big pillars and a cobbled courtyard. It also has a patio with wrought iron tables for shisha smokers. Healthy and generous salads, savoury pancakes, omelettes, or onion soup and a sandwich at Dhs.25 make this a bargain dining option. Alternatively, sit and enjoy a cappuccino with one of their delicious pastries. The food here is consistently excellent.

Food ●●●○ Service ●●○○ Venue ●●○○ Value ●●●○

Cafe Wien

Location ➔ Beach Centre, The · Beach Rd, Jumeira | **344 8001**
Hours ➔ 08:00 - 24:00
Web/email ➔ binhendi@binhendi.com   **Map Ref** ➔ 6-B2

  100

Dominating the mall, Cafe Wien is divided into two sections: an indoor area providing more of a restaurant feel, and a relaxing open section in the mall itself, surrounded by trees. Whilst offering the usual café catering of pizza, sandwiches, pasta, etc., Cafe Wien also sells a variety of cigars. The clientele is varied depending on the time of day. In the evenings, patrons are serenaded by the tinkling sounds of the grand piano.⊚

Food ●●○○ Service ●●○○ Venue ●●●○ Value ●●○○

Coffee Bean & Tea Leaf

Location ➔ Corporate Centre, Al Raffa Rd · Mankhool | **398 4333**
Hours ➔ 07:30 - 00:30
Web/email ➔ www.coffeebean.com   **Map Ref** ➔ 7-D3

V 50

Guess what...they specialise in coffee and tea. The full range of hot and cold variations on the theme are available, in some cases in enormous portions. Food is limited, and not the tastiest around, and includes breakfast (muffins, scones, eggs) with tea or coffee, which includes free refills until 11:00. All breakfasts are priced at under Dhs.20. There are also a few sandwich options on the menu. Inside feels a little claustrophobic but the outdoor seating is relaxed and comfortable.⊚

> *Other locations: Bank Street, Bur Dubai (352 2225); La Plage, Jumeirah (342 9992); World Trade Centre, Shk Zayed Road (332 6655)*

Food ●○○○ Service ●●○○ Venue ●●○○ Value ●●○○

Coffee Bean, The

Location ➔ Aviation Club, The · Al Garhoud | **282 4122**
Hours ➔ 07:00 - 23:00
Web/email ➔ aviation@emirates.net.ae   **Map Ref** ➔ 14-C3

V 100

This small, but bright and modern café makes a great stop before or after a workout at the Aviation Club. Simple, but tastefully decorated, they offer coffee drinks as well as light meals (sandwiches, jacket potatoes, salads, etc) and pastries. High speed DSL connections are available for Internet access, often with daily specials including surfing and java. Friendly staff help keep the place informal yet efficient. Not a first date kind of place, but a popular venue and a great option when in the club.⊚

Food ●●●○ Service ●●●○ Venue ●●○○ Value ●●●○

Cosmo Café

Location ➔ Union Property Tower · Shk Zayed Rd | **332 6569**
Hours ➔ 13:00 - 02:00
Web/email ➔ na   **Map Ref** ➔ 9-C2

 V 150

Newcomer Cosmo does its best to cater to the hip and trendy crowd. The décor inside is modern and warm, with touches of chrome, glass and concrete. However, chips called 'Golden Sticks' cross that fine line between 'cool' and 'trying too hard'. Menu items range from simple starters to sandwiches, pizzas, and some mains. Unfortunately, food and service don't mirror the surroundings or high prices. Seems most of the clientele already know that, and go for the shisha and people watching on the terrace instead.⊚

Food ●●○○ Service ●●○○ Venue ●●●○ Value ●●○○

Costa

Location ➔ Century Village · Al Garhoud | **209 5000**
Hours ➔ 08:00 - 01:00 Fri 10:00 - 24:00
Web/email ➔ costa@mmi.co.ae   **Map Ref** ➔ 14-C3

  V 50

There are now six branches of this popular chain in town. The familiar formula – simple, comfy seating and low coffee tables inside, and (sometimes) outside terraces with basic tables and chairs – works to varying degrees. Only the Century Village and City Tower II branches have an outside terrace. The usual upscale coffee shop menu offers reasonable and tasty sandwiches and sweets. For an added kick, note that the Century Village outlet is licensed to cure what ails you.⊚

> *Other locations:*
> • *City Tower II, Sheikh Zayed Road (331 2499) 07:00 - 24:00*
> • *Deira City Centre (294 0833) 09:00 - 24:00, Fri 10:00 - 24:00*
> • *DNATA Airline Centre, Sheikh Zayed Road (321 0978) 07:30 - 20:00*
> • *Internet City (391 8896) 07:30 - 20:00*
> • *Spectrum Building, next to Lamcy Plaza (335 0814) 08:00 - 19:00, Closed Fri.*
> • *Dubai International Airport, (220 0179)*

Food ●●●○ Service ●●○○ Venue ●●●○ Value ●●●○

Take a Break with

COSTA COFFEE
passionately
ITALIAN

making coffee is
not only science
its an art

ITALIANS
KNOW
HOW

COSTA
total passion

Favoloso!

COSTA BEANS – SLOW ROASTED FOR FULLER FLAVOUR

Dome Cafe

Location → BurJuman Centre · Bur Dubai | **355 6004**
Hours → 07:30 - 23:30 Fri 13:00 - 23:30
Web/email → www.burjuman.com   **Map Ref →** 11-A1

    100

An Australian franchise with a lively atmosphere: business meetings on one table and gossip on the next. Service can be haphazard especially at busy times. The diverse menu ranges from Far Eastern specials, pizzas, pies, and a selection of gourmet sandwiches on various fresh breads. Excellent home baked cakes, ice creams and pastries satisfy a sweet tooth. They also have an excellent children's menu and a segregated smoking section. Open early until late, this café caters for a quick coffee or a leisurely light meal.

Other locations:
- *Jumeirah Plaza on the Beach Road (349 0383)*
- *Bin Sougat Centre (284 4413).*

Food ●●●○ Service ●○○○ Venue ●●○○ Value ●●○○

Fountain Café

Location → Btn City Tower 1 & 2 · Trade Centre 1&2 | **331 1502**
Hours → 07:30 - 00:30 Fri 18:00- 24:00
Web/email → n/a   **Map Ref →** 9-D2

  100

The Fountain Café boasts an outside terrace amid the skyscrapers. Traffic noise may bother some though. The menu consists of the usual café favourites: sandwiches, salads and jacket potatoes with several choices of fillings, etc. There are daily specials, and a small selection of cakes (in particular, a yummy banana cake). This is a busy café, so if you time it wrong (middle of the lunch break) you may have to wait a while for your meal. Shisha is offered in the evening.

Food ●●○○ Service ●●○○ Venue ●●●○ Value ●●○○

French Connection

Location → Wafa Tower - Trade Centre 1&2 | **343 8311**
Hours → 07:00 - 24:00
Web/email → n/a   **Map Ref →** 9-A2

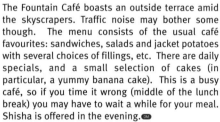 100

A tantalising display of gateaux, pastries and breads welcomes you when you enter French Connection. The trendy décor of this café gives it a light atmosphere, though with the arrival of numerous other cafes on the scene, French Connection's popularity and buzz have waned somewhat. Coffees and croissants, quick snacks, lunches (salads and sandwiches), and many patisserie items are on offer, though not light on the wallet. There's also a bakery section with a variety of French breads, baked fresh daily.

Food ●●○○ Service ●●○○ Venue ●●○○ Value ●●○○

Gerard

Location → Magrudy Shopping Mall · Jumeira | **344 3327**
Hours → 07:30 - 23:00 Fri 07:30 - 22:30
Web/email → www.magrudy.com   **Map Ref →** 6-C2

   50

One of the first European style cafés to be established in Dubai, Gerard is popular with all nationalities, who come to people watch, chat or read the papers. There's a very pleasant atmosphere, created in part by the shaded terrace. Enjoy coffee and delicious freshly baked croissants, or try the various freshly made cakes and sandwiches. It's especially popular on Friday mornings for a gentle awakening after a hard night out.

Other locations:
- *Al Ghurair City. & Sharjah*

Food ●●●○ Service ●●○○ Venue ●●○○ Value ●●○○

IKEA

Location → City Centre · Al Garhoud | **295 0434**
Hours → 10:00 - 22:00 Fri 14:00 - 22:00
Web/email → www.ikeadubai.com   **Map Ref →** 14-D1

 50

In the middle of epic IKEA excursions, don't forget the calm cafe nestled inside the IKEA universe. Reasonable, tasty, and most of all relatively quiet, this self-service food bar offers dozens of food options, including a daily vegetarian special. Fresh "Swedish" food is the theme: try the prawn mayonnaise open sandwich or the heartier Swedish meatballs. Surprisingly good cappuccino and hot chocolate, though in this climate, why bother? A clearly superior option to the chaos of the food court within the mall.

Food ●●●○ Service ●●○○ Venue ●●○○ Value ●●●○

Issimo

Location → Hilton Dubai Creek · Creekside, Deira | **227 1111**
Hours → 07:00 - 23:00
Web/email → hiltonck@emirates.net.ae | **Map Ref →** 11-C2

Doubling as a Milanese espresso bar and chic urban drinks venue, Issimo is sleek modernism exemplified. Lounge in the black leather chairs over a light lunch or coffee and sweet, or sip a pre-dinner drink at the curved stainless steel bar. The menu changes daily, with treats such as polenta and lemon torta, panini, ciabiatta, salads, and focaccia. The bar has a fine list of wine, brandy, scotch, and grappa. Time spent in this cosmopolitan spot is sure to up your coolness level.

Food ●●●○ Service ●●●○ Venue ●●●○ Value ●●●○

La Brioche

Location → Jumeirah Centre · Beach Rd, Jumeira | **349 0588**
Hours → 08:00 - 23:30
Web/email → binhendi@binhendi.com | **Map Ref →** 6-C2

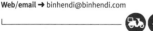

This trendy, relaxed café is pleasantly decorated, and tables are generously spaced for privacy. The menu is all encompassing, consisting of an interesting, varied mix to suit all tastes. Breakfast items are served throughout the day. Other fare includes soups, salads, sandwiches, pasta and pizza, and some regulars like fish and chips. The steak is excellent value at just Dhs.28, and the caesar salad is deliciously garlicky and spicy; don't expect to see any friends the next day!

Food ●●○○ Service ●●○○ Venue ●●○○ Value ●●●○

La Gaufrette

Location → City Centre · Al Garhoud | **295 0073**
Hours → 08:00 - 23:00 Fri 09:00 - 23:00
Web/email → www.deiracitycentre.com | **Map Ref →** 14-D1

The specialities at this chain of coffee shops are waffles and salads (no, not together!), which are usually very fresh and healthy. There's a range of in-house baked pastries and cakes, ice-creams, Belgian chocolates and other light meals. The prices are reasonable and the atmosphere acceptable. Some outlets are very popular, while others are somewhat neglected, hence the standard of service and food varies. But where else can you get fresh waffles if you've got the craving?

> *Other locations:*
> • *Bur Juman Centre (351 8688)*
> • *Hamarain Centre (269 9554)*
> • *Metropolitan Hotel (343 3776)*

Food ●●○○ Service ●●○○ Venue ●●○○ Value ●●○○

La Marquise

Location → Palm Strip · Beach Rd, Jumeira | **345 8433**
Hours → 08:00 - 24:00
Web/email → frbakery@emirates.net.ae | **Map Ref →** 6-D2

This upmarket café provides high quality café food and a good view of Jumeira Mosque. Attractively presented and flavourful salads and sandwiches, as well as a small selection of pasta, omelettes, soups and breakfasts are on offer. They also have shisha and a special fruit cocktail menu. Service is friendly and the food arrives quite rapidly at your table. A wide choice of French pastries and exceedingly good gateaux are available in the café or via their free home delivery service.

> *Other location:*
> • *Sheikh Zayed Road branch (343 3320).*

Food ●●●○ Service ●●○○ Venue ●●○○ Value ●●○○

Fresh bread

Le Café

Location → Sheraton Deira · Hor Al Anz
Hours → 06:30 - 02:00
Web/email → www.starwood.com

268 8888

Map Ref → 12-A3

  100

Situated in the lobby, Le Café serves as a comfortable rendezvous venue. The experience is what you expect from a five-star hotel: tidy décor, friendly and efficient service, and comfort. The menu has a selection of soups, salads and sandwiches, as well as an extensive range of ice cream and coffee. Drinks are relatively pricey, while the food is reasonable, if unexceptional. The clientele are a mix of hotel guests and locals, slipping down a drink or meeting for business. 🔘
Food ●●○○ Service ●●●○ Venue ●●○○ Value ●●○○

Lime Tree

Location → Nr. Jum. Mosque · Beach Rd, Jumeira
Hours → 07:30 - 20:00
Web/email → limetree@emirates.net.ae

349 8498

Map Ref → 6-D2

   100

A pleasant little oasis, the Lime Tree is a refreshingly well-conceived café. Located in a funky-coloured, minimalist villa, the setting is just right. There are two outdoor seating areas (the upstairs one is recommended) as well as the cosy interior to choose from. Build your own meal from an extensive deli; veggies beware of the 'hidden' animal products. Coffees, juices (lime soda is excellent), salads, pastas, daily specials, and the best carrot cake in town, are all on offer for reasonable(ish) Jumeira prices. 🔘
Food ●●●○ Service ●●○○ Venue ●●●○ Value ●●○○

Lobby Lounge, The

Location → Ritz-Carlton Dubai · Al Sufouh
Hours → 14:00 - 18:00
Web/email → rcdubai@emirates.net.ae

399 4000

Map Ref → 2-E2

 150

Afternoon tea at the Ritz is relaxing, decadent and very, very civilised. Set in plush, elegant surroundings reminiscent of a tropical colonial setting, this is the perfect place to while away an afternoon. The terrace, with its stunning view, is not to be missed in the cooler months. The 'Royal Tea' includes champagne, finger sandwiches, scones, home-made jams and clotted cream (and arteries!), delicate pastries and tea. The experience is pure

Ritz and a great way to enjoy the good life (or entertain colonialist fantasies) on a budget. 🔘
Food ●●●○ Service ●●●○ Venue ●●●● Value ●●●○

More

Location → Nr. Welcare Hospital, Al Garhoud
Hours → 08:00 - 24:00
Web/email → infomore@emirates.net.ae

283 0224

Map Ref → 14-D4

100

MORE is what Dubai has needed for a long time – a good dose of industrial chic. While lacking the 'hard edge' of similar places in the West, MORE works, and well. Wholesome dishes are prepared with fresh ingredients; the salads and catch of the day are excellent and highly recommended. Seating options are wide-ranging, from a small coffee bar, to lots of private tables, a couple of sofas and two enormous wooden tables. For a place packed with personality, MORE has got it all. 🔘
Food ●●●○ Service ●●●● Venue ●●●● Value ●●●○

Panini

Location → Grand Hyatt Dubai · Umm Hurair 2
Hours → 14:00 - 18:00
Web/email → www.hyatt.com

209 6993

Map Ref → 13-E3

This planned cafe will open next to Andiamo! in spring 2003. The plans are for an Italian bakery that specialises in oven fresh crusty breads, homemade cakes, pastries, praline chocolates, freshly baked biscotti and homemade Italian ice cream. This will likely be a lively venue to people watch over coffee, and, perhaps more importantly, it is planning to do significant take-away business. As better bakeries are always a good thing, we await their opening. 🔘
Food – n/a Service – n/a Venue – n/a Value – n/a

Sahn Eddar

Location → Burj Al Arab · Umm Suqeim
Hours → 15:00 - 19:00
Web/email → www.burj-al-arab.com

301 7600

Map Ref → 4-A1

   300

Afternoon tea is one of life's little luxuries, and taking it in one of the worlds most luxurious hotels, turns a treat into a memorable experience. The 'Traditional Afternoon Tea' (Dhs.115) resembles a four-course meal: finger sandwiches, scones, pastries, sweet meats and a choice of 16 varieties of tea. These delicacies can be ordered individually, but the scones with home-made strawberry and rose petal jams are a must. It's hard to imagine a more magnificent setting in which to enjoy this civilised repast. ●

Food ●●●● Service ●●●● Venue ●●●● Value ●●●○

Shakespeare & Co.

Location → Kendah House · Trade Centre 1&2
Hours → 07:00 - 24:00
Web/email → n/a

331 1757

Map Ref → 9-B2

●🖐 Ⓥ **100**

The only thing that this venue shares with its namesake in Paris is a truly eclectic concept. Not wildly promoted, they rely on word of mouth... and they have succeeded. Something of an insider haunt, the food is good and the ambience relaxing. Choosing between the charmingly rustic interior and the terrace is the first challenge; choosing a meal from the diverse, creative menu is another. Arabic, Moroccan, and some continental dishes appear (sometimes slowly) out of the smallish kitchen, bound to delight. ●

Other location:
* *Shakespeare & Co. is located in Gulf Towers (335 3335).*

Food ●●○○ Service ●○○○ Venue ●●●○ Value ●●○○

The Lobby Lounge

Spot Cafe

Location → Nr Four Points Sheraton · Bur Dubai
Hours → 08:30 - 24:00 Fri 12:00 - 24:00
Web/email → spot_cafe@hotmail.com

352 1215

Map Ref → 8-A4

   🚫 **50**

This bright café is popular with the local business lunch crowd for hip and healthy French and Italian food. Particularly busy at lunchtimes, it's also open for breakfast and dinner, and serves up a decent Friday brunch of Mediterranean and continental cuisine. For a quick snack or a light meal, this is a good choice, though service can be spotty. Perhaps not the best choice for a quiet cup of coffee and a book, however. ●

Food ●●●○ Service ●●○○ Venue ●●○○ Value ●●○○

Square, The

Location → Wafi City · Umm Hurair 2
Hours → 10:00 - 22:00 Fri 14:00 - 22:00
Web/email → www.waficity.com

324 2543

Map Ref → 13-D2

Ⓐ Ⓥ **150**

In spite of its slightly off-putting name and casual appearance, this Wafi Mall café offers diverse international dishes and attentive service in addition to prime people watching. The menu features everything from rich lobster bisque and California clubs to focaccia sandwiches and Vietnamese Summer Rolls. The decadent milkshakes, a house speciality, are not to be missed. While more expensive than a typical mall café, the food is well worth the money and portions are generous. It's well suited to the spiffy surroundings. ●

Food ●●●○ Service ●●●○ Venue ●●●○ Value ●●●○

THE One

Location → Nr Jumeira Mosque · Beach Rd, Jumeira
Hours → 09:00 - 21:30 Fri 14:00 - 22:00
Web/email → purchase@theoneme.com

342 2499

Map Ref → 6-D2

   100

This is a popular spot for a quick coffee or bite to eat if in the area. The dozen or so bright and airy tables are neatly divided from the main shop by curtains. Offerings include tasty sandwiches, mezze, pastries and a wide range of shakes and juices. A different home-made soup is available each day, often in unusual flavours such as aubergine. The cakes (carrot, walnut, chocolate) are excellent, but order them when you spot them in the display counter; they disappear quickly. ●

Food ●●●○ Service ●●○○ Venue ●●○○ Value ●●●○

On The Town | Cafés & Coffee Shops

West One

Location → Jumeirah Centre · Beach Rd, Jumeira
Hours → 07:30 - 21:30
Web/email → www.dubaishoppingmalls.com

349 4500

Map Ref → 6-C2

This sandwich bar is a good choice if you fancy a quick sandwich or light meal on the run, but it's a little short on atmosphere. However, the food is tasty and fresh; the service fast and friendly, and with a set lunch starting from Dhs.25, it's good value. There is also a kiddies menu to keep little ones happy. West One's speciality is outside catering – from corporate functions to private parties and even sandwich-hawking to hungry office workers around the city. 🅙🅤🅡

Food ●●○○ Service ●●●○ Venue ●●○○ Value ●●●○

Zyara Café

Location → Nr Al Salam Tower · Trade Centre 1&2
Hours → 08:00 - 24:00
Web/email → zyara@emirates.net.ae

343 5454

Map Ref → 9-B2

Don't visit if you're in a hurry! The relaxed atmosphere, eclectic décor and laissez-faire service are all conducive to taking your time over a drink or light meal. 'Zyara' is Arabic for visit, and there is a wide variety of magazines, books and games to help you pass the time while you wait for your order. The mainly Arabic buffet attracts a largely Lebanese clientele, whereas the predominantly sandwich and salad menu is popular for business lunches. 🅓🅜

Other location:
• *Dubai Media City (391 8031).*

Food ●●○○ Service ●○○○ Venue ●●●○ Value ●●○○

Internet Cafés

If you want to surf the Web, visit a chat room, email friends or play the latest game, but want to be a little bit sociable about it, or perhaps do not have your own facilities for being online, Internet cafés are a perfect location to visit. Over the last few years, this type of café has become a common feature throughout Dubai. The mix of coffee, cake and technology has proved an irresistible draw, and this particular niche of café will doubtless continue to expand.

As always, facilities, ambience, prices and clientele vary considerably, so poke your head in the door and then make your decision. Prices are typically Dhs.5-15 per hour. Happy surfing!

Shisha Cafés

Other options → **Arabic/Lebanese [p.312]**
Persian [p.366], Morocccon [p.364]
Turkish [p.378]

Shisha cafés are common throughout the Middle East, offering relaxing surroundings and the chance to smoke a shisha pipe (aka Hubble Bubble or Narghile) with a variety of aromatic flavours. They are traditionally the preserve of local men who meet to play backgammon and gossip with friends. However, these cafés are popular with locals and visitors alike, especially in the cooler winter evenings.

Most outlets offer a basic menu; generally Arabic cuisine and a few international options, plus coffees, teas and fruit juices. So, choose your flavour of shisha and sit back – this is what life is all about!

Prices are typically around Dhs.15 - 25, and loads of cafés continue to spring up around town. Many literally offer door to car door service, so you can roll up, wind down your window or smoke on the pavement next to your car – especially good if you want to impress that date on the back seat!

Shisha	
Ahram	Metropolitan Hotel
Al Hakawati	Sheikh Zayed Rd
Al Khayma	Dubai Marine
Al Koufa	Nr American Hospital
Apple Café	Twin Towers
Aroma Garden	Nr Maktoum Bridge
Awafi	JW Marriott
Calypso Pool Bar	Sofitel City Centre Hotel
Cosmo Café	Sheikh Zayed Rd
Courtyard	Royal Mirage Hotel
Fakhreldine	Holiday Inn Bur Dubai
Fatafeet	Next to Dubai Creek
Istikana	Sheikh Zayed Rd
Kotchina	Sheikh Zayed Rd
Moods	Sheraton Jumeirah Beach

If you get 'hooked' (pun intended), and wish to have your own, Carrefour Hypermarket in City Centre and Al Karama (see [p.138]), among many trinket shops all over the city, are particularly good places to get started, offering a variety of pipes and some of the basic tobacco flavours. It can be a very

Going Out · Cafés & Coffee Shops | Shisha Cafés

satisfying experience, puffing on a pipe around a campfire in the desert, watching the stars.

FOOD ON THE GO

Bakeries

Other options → **Arabic/Lebanese [p.312]**

In addition to bread, bakeries offer a wonderful range of pastries, biscuits and Lebanese sweets. Arabic foods include 'borek' (flat pastries, baked or fried with spinach or cheese) and 'manoushi' (hot bread, doubled over and served plain or filled with meat, cheese or 'zatar' (thyme seeds)). Biscuits are often filled with ground dates.

Fruit Juices Etc.

Fresh juices are widely available, either from the shawarma stands or juice shops. They are delicious, healthy and cheap, and made on the spot from fresh fruits such as mango, banana, kiwi, strawberry and pineapple (have the mixed fruit cocktail if you can't decide).

Yoghurt is also a popular drink, often served with nuts, and the local milk is called 'laban' (a heavy, salty buttermilk that doesn't go well in tea or coffee). Arabic mint tea is available, but probably not drunk as widely as in other parts of the Arab world; however, Arabic coffee (thick, silty and strong) is extremely popular and will have you buzzing on a caffeine high for days!

Shawarma

Other options → **Arabic/Lebanese [p.312]**

Throughout the city, sidewalk stands sell 'shawarma', which are made from rolled pita bread filled with lamb or chicken carved from a rotating spit and salad. Costing about Dhs.3 each, these are inexpensive and well worth trying, and are an excellent alternative fast food to the usual hamburger. The stands usually sell other dishes, such as 'foul' (a paste made from fava beans) and 'falafel' (or ta'amiya), which are a small savoury balls of deep-fried beans.

While most shawarma stands offer virtually the same thing, slight differences make some stand out from the rest. People are often adamant that their particular favourite serves, for example, the best falafel in town. These can often be the first place you eat when you come to the UAE, however, look around – every restaurant has its own way of doing things and you might find that the best is, surprisingly, the smallest, most low-key restaurant you happen upon by chance.

Al Mallah

Location → Al Diyafah St · Al Satwa | **398 4723**
Hours → 17:30 - 04:00
Web/email → n/a | Map Ref → 6-E3

   50

Among the throngs of small Arabic joints, this one stands out from the rest. Situated on one of the busiest streets in the city, it mainly offers outside seating on the pavement with a few tables and chairs inside. Food-wise, the shawarmas and fruit juices are excellent, the cheese and zatar manoushi good, and they have possibly the biggest and best falafel in Dubai! Watch the world drive by and have an evening snack, or stay a while longer and order a bigger meal.

Other location
• Al Mateena Road, Deira (272 3431).

Food ●●●● Service ●●●○ Venue ●●○○ Value ●●●●

Al Shera'a Fisheries Centre

Location → Nr Marks & Spencer · Deira | **227 1803**
Hours → 10:00 - 01:00
Web/email → n/a | Map Ref → 11-E1

100

We all know the lovely but ubiquitous shawarma that spins on spits everywhere in town. Do you think you've tried them all? Guess again! This venue takes a winning concept and, well, let's say, adapts it. This is the only joint in town that serves fish shawarma. Actually, quite tasty and a pleasant change. Worth a visit to this very casual shop, if only for the novelty. What's next, date hummous?

Food ●●●● Service ●●●○ Venue ●●○○ Value ●●●●

Bakeries | Shawarma

On The Town

FRIDAY BRUNCH

An integral part of life in Dubai, Friday brunch is a perfect event for a lazy start or end to the weekend, especially once the hot weather arrives. Popular with all sections of the community, it provides Thursday night's revellers with a gentle awakening, and much needed nourishment. For families, brunch is a pleasant way to spend the day, especially since many venues organise a variety of fun activities for kids, allowing parents to fill themselves with fine food and drink and to simply relax.

Different brunches appeal to different crowds; some have fantastic buffets, others are in spectacular surroundings, while some offer amazing prices for all you can eat.

CATERERS

A popular and easy way to have a party, special occasion or business lunch, in-house catering allows you to relax and enjoy yourself, or to concentrate on… anything but the cooking. Numerous outlets offer this service, so decide on the type of food you want – Indian, Chinese, Italian, Lebanese, finger food, etc, and ask at your favourite or local restaurant, or café to see if they do outside catering.

Alternatively, most of the larger hotels have an outside catering department, usually capable of extravagant five-star functions. There are also specialist companies who provide a variety of services at very reasonable prices. You don't even

Friday Brunch

Restaurant	Location	Phone	Buffet	A La Carte	Breakfast	Lunch	Kid Friendly	Alcohol	Outside Terrace	Cost Adult	Child	Timings
Al Muntaha	Burj Al Arab	301 7777	y	n	y	y	y	y	n	240	120	11:00 - 15:30
Alamo	Dubai Marine	346 1111	y	n	y	y	y	y	n	60	30	11:00 - 15:00
Antigo	Le Meridien Dubai	282 4040	y	y	y	y	y	y	y	98	50	12:30 -15:30
Aquarium	Creek Golf & Yacht Club	295 6000	y	n	n	y	y	n	y	75	35	11:30 - 15:00
Biggles	Airport Hotel	282 3464	y	n	y	y	y	y	y	39	19	11:00 - 15:00
Brasserie	Le Royal Meridien	399 5555	y	y	n	y	y	y	y	120	110	12:00 - 15:30
Café Boulvar	Hotel Inter-Continental	222 7171	y	n	n	y	y	y	n	99	50	12:00 - 16:00
Cafe Insignia	Ramada Hotel	351 9999	y	n	y	y	y	y	n	55	~	12:00 -15:00
Carter's	Pyramids	324 9601	y	n	y	y	y	y	y	60	30	11:30 - 15:00
Cascades	Fairmont Hotel	332 5555	y	n	y	y	y	y	y	95	45	09:00 - 15:15
Dubai Restaurant	Nad Al Sheba Racecourse	336 3666	y	n	n	y	y	n	y	60	30	12:00 - 16:30
Finnegans	Dubai Park Hotel	399 2222	y	n	y	y	y	y	n	59	30	12:00 - 15:00
Fontana	Al Bustan Rotana Hotel	282 0000	y	n	n	y	y	y	n	99	50	12:00 - 15:00
Gozo Garden	Airport Hotel	282 3464	y	y	y	y	y	y	y	38	19	12:00 - 15:30
Henry Afrika's	Sheikh Zayed Road	343 0501	y	n	y	y	y	y	y	50	25	12:00 - 17:00
La Fontana	Jebel Ali Golf Resort & Spa	883 6000	y	y	y	y	y	y	y	140	70	12:30 - 15:30
Long's Bar	Towers Rotana Hotel	343 8000	y	n	y	y	y	n	n	49	m	12:00 - 16:00
Market Place	JW Marriott Hotel	607 7901	y	n	y	y	y	n	n	88	m	12:30 - 15:00
Mosaico	Emirates Towers Hotel	330 0000	y	y	n	y	y	y	n	85	u	11:00 - 15:00
Oceana	Hilton Dubai Jumeirah	399 1111	y	y	y	y	y	y	n	75	45	12:30 - 15:30
Planet Hollywood	Wafi City	324 4777	y	y	y	y	y	y	y	65	33^	11:30 - 15:00
Prasino's	Jumeirah Beach Club	344 5333	y	y	n	y	y	y	y	110	55	12:00 - 15:00
Spice Island	Renaissance Hotel	262 5555	y	y	y	y	y	y	y	91	75	12:00 - 15:00
Splendido	Ritz-Carlton	399 4000	y	n	n	y	y	y	y	140	70	12:30 - 15:30

m-metre (charged by height)   ~5% off   u-under 12 is free   ^1st child is free

Friday Brunch | Caterers

Going Out

have to stay at home to get in-house catering – how about arranging a party in the desert with catering?

Depending on what you require, caterers can provide just the food or everything from food, crockery, napkins, tables, chairs and even waiters, doormen and a clearing up service afterwards. Costs vary according to the number of people, dishes and level of service, etc, required.

In-house Catering	
Dubai World Trade Centre	308 6944
Emirates Abela	282 3171
Intercat	334 5212
Sandwich Express	343 9922
West One	349 4500

For a list of hotel numbers, check out the hotel table in General Information [p.28]. For restaurant and café names browse the Going Out section of the book. You can also refer to the catering section in the telephone books, especially the Hawk A – Z business pages, or www.yellowpages.co.ae.

Room Service Deliveries	
Location → Nr. Capitol Htl · Satwa	**345 5444**
Hours → Anytime you want it...	
Web/email → www.roomservice-uae.com	Map Ref → 7-A2

The concept, successful in most international cities, is to deliver food from your favourite restaurant. Peruse the directory of participating restaurants, make a selection from the menu, and call it in: food should be on its way in an hour. Minimum orders are Dhs.40 lunch and Dhs.60 for dinner with a Dhs.10-20 delivery charge. Deliveries can be made anywhere in central Dubai and Jebel Ali anytime between 11:00 - 23:00, with deliveries to Sharjah and 'Greater Dubai' outside rush hour times.

Food – n/a   Service – n/a   Venue – n/a   Value – n/a

Top Trendy Venues	
Apartment, The	Noodle House, The
Ginseng	Tangerine
More	Vintage

ON THE TOWN

Other options → **Leisure [p.280]**

If you're on the town in Dubai, you will soon find that there are a good many places to go and things to do. It may not be quite the buzzing city found in other parts of the world, but Dubai is without doubt the 'Party Capital of the Gulf', with enough choice to keep even the most ardent socialite happy. The following section covers the 'cultural' entertainment such as theatre and comedy clubs, as well as cafés, bars, pubs and nightclubs.

In Dubai, people tend to go out late, usually not before about 21:00. Even on weeknights, kick off is surprisingly late and people seem to forget, after about the tenth drink, that they really ought to be at work the next day. If you're venturing out to Arabic nightclubs or restaurants, you're likely to find them almost deserted before 23:00.

Wednesday and Thursday, being the start of most peoples' weekend are obviously busy, but you will also find that during the week many bars and restaurants offer promotions and special nights to attract customers, hence creating a lively atmosphere. Particularly popular is Ladies Night, which is traditionally on a Tuesday (and the busiest night of the week for some places). Women are given tokens at the door offering them free drinks – the number varies from one to an endless supply and it may be limited to certain types of drink. This ploy certainly seems to attract male customers too. With men outnumbering women in Dubai (by two to one), it's an unbalanced world where women, for once, can take full advantage.

Below are the main places that have a Ladies Night/s at some point during the week:

Generally cafés and restaurants close between 23:00 and 01:00, with most bars and nightclubs split between those who close 'early' at 01:00 and those who stay open 'late' until 02:00 or 03:00. Few are open all night.

To complement the Bars and Nightclubs, refer also to the information on Eating Out [p.302]. Many restaurants have a very good bar and some also have a dance floor which kicks in towards midnight. However, they are usually reviewed only once – as a restaurant. In this section, you will also find further information on, for instance, the alcohol laws.

Caterers | On the Town

On The Town

BARS

Other options → **Pubs [p.404]**
Nightclubs [p.409]

Dubai has an excellent number of bars with a good variety of different styles. Most are located in hotels, and while many bars come and go, the more popular ones are always busy.

In addition to the bars reviewed here, there are plenty of others (usually in the smaller hotels) which do not attract the regular crowds of the more popular venues. If you're looking for somewhere different... get out there and explore!

The city's more upmarket locations range from terminally hip cocktail lounges to decadent wine bars, from jazz bars to cigar bars – all providing salubrious surroundings for those opulent and self-indulgent moments.

For more details on where and when people in Dubai go to drink, refer to the start of the "On the Town" section. For information on the individual bars read on...

Door Policy

Even amongst the mix of nationalities in the cultural melting pot that is Dubai, there are certain bars and nightclubs that have a selective entry 'policy'. Sometimes the 'Members Only' sign on the entrance needs a bit of explaining. Membership is usually introduced to control the clientele frequenting the establishment, but is often only enforced during busy periods. At quieter times, non-members may have no problem getting in, even if unaccompanied by a member. Basically, management uses the rule to disallow entry if they don't like the look of you or your group, and they will point to their sign and say 'Sorry'. Large groups (especially all males), single men and certain nationalities are normally the target. You can avoid the inconvenience, and the embarrassment, by breaking the group up or by going in a mixed-gender group.

If you find yourself being discriminated against, don't get mad – get even! In most cases it's not worth trying to discuss this rationally with the doorman – it won't work. Most companies hate bad publicity – try taking the issue up with some of the local media.

Other solutions include taking out membership for that particular club, shamelessly trying to bribe the doorman, getting there early (around 19:00), going with Bruce Willis, or staying home.

Dress Code

Most bars have a reasonably relaxed attitude to their customers dress sense. Some places, however, will insist on no shorts, jeans or sandals, while others require at least a shirt with a collar. Nightclubs generally have a dressier approach – dress to impress. As Dubai is well on its way to becoming the trendy tourist destination, the dress code will continue to lean towards the latter extreme.

Specials

Many places have occasional promotions with different themes and offers. These run alongside special nights, such as Ladies Night, which are usually held weekly. For the promotions, you can find out what's coming up in the weekly and monthly entertainment publications and from the venues concerned. Special nights such as the popular quiz nights, are mainly promoted in the bar or pub, and many attract quite a following. Delightfully, the prizes are often fab.

American Bars

Billy Blues

Location → Rydges Plaza Hotel · Al Satwa | **398 2272**
Hours → Fri 18:00 - 02:00
Web/email → cactus1@emirates.net.ae | **Map Ref** → 7-A4

   150

Please see review under American [p.306] .
Food ●●●○ Service ●●●○ Venue ●●●● Value ●●●○

Boston Bar, The

Location → Jumeira Rotana · Al Satwa | **345 5888**
Hours → 12:00 - 02:00
Web/email → jumhotel@emirates.net.ae | **Map Ref** → 6-E3

   150

Serving a multitude of purposes, the busy and efficient Boston Bar appeals to a broad crowd. It's a watering hole/eating venue for the lunch, 'after work' and dinner crowd, and then it's the place to be for the younger weekend crowd when a DJ spins five nights a week. Offering everything from salads, to soups, burgers, steak and lamb chops, Boston Bar gets busy during the week and truly springs to life on Ladies' Night, weekends, and for major sporting events.
Food ●●●○ Service ●●●○ Venue ●●●○ Value ●●●○

Going Out | Bars | American Bars

Goodfellas

Location ➜ Regal Plaza Hotel · Bur Dubai | **355 6633**
Hours ➜ 12:00 - 03:00
Web/email ➜ regaldxb@emirates.net.ae **Map Ref** ➜ 8-A4

 150

Goodfellas caters to your Sopranos fantasies! Plenty of seating, and a good variety of beverages, plus USA-sized portions. The menu offers mainly American fare (steaks, soups, and fries with most dishes), plus traditional English grub – enormous pies! Tuesday is Cocktail Night and the music certainly helps evoke 1920's America. A big TV and macho ambience makes this a bar for the boys. Centrally located, it's great for a drink before heading into town.

Food ●●○○ Service ●●○○ Venue ●●○○ Value ●●○○

Henry J. Beans

Location ➜ Capitol Hotel · Al Satwa | **345 8350**
Hours ➜ 12:00 - 03:00
Web/email ➜ www.henryjbeans.com **Map Ref** ➜ 7-A2

150

Please see review under American [p.310].
Food ●●●○ Service ●●○○ Venue ●●●○ Value ●●○○

Rock Bottom Cafe

Location ➜ Regent Palace Hotel · Bur Dubai | **396 3888**
Hours ➜ 12:00 - 15:00 18:00 - 03:30
Web/email ➜ www.ramee-group.com **Map Ref** ➜ 11-A1

 100

The rough and ready ending to any big night out, this joint rocks at full volume. The resident band is among the town's finest, belting out cover songs until the DJ takes over. Quieter early on, steak and burgers hog the all-American menu. The smoky pool tables and Harley Davidson Motorcycles parked outside kick-start the rock'n'roll atmosphere, and the 'too late in the evening to care' revellers do the rest. Over 21's only and ID may be required. The door 'policy' is very strict here (i.e. favours Westerners).

Food ●●○○ Service ●●○○ Venue ●●●○ Value ●●○○

Merry Zoos

Agency, The	Kasbar
Antique Bazaar	Noodle House, The
Boston Bar, The	Planetarium
Gozo Garden	Savage Garden
Henry Africa's	Scarlett's
Henry J. Beans	Seville's
Irish Village	Spice Island
Jules Bar	

Scarlett's

Location ➜ Emirates Towers · Trade Centre 1&2 | **319 8743**
Hours ➜ 12:00 - 03:00
Web/email ➜ www.emirates-towers-hotel.com **Map Ref** ➜ 9-C2

 150

The decadence of the Deep South lives on in the club section of Scarlett's. A festive mood and consistent crowds testify to the popularity of the venue. Tuesday and Sunday Nights are ladies nights, and Emirates cabin crew receive a 50% discount. Mediocre dining downstairs gives way to a genial meat-market bar and dance floor upstairs. Arrive late and stay until early to experience the full effect. Music tends to be top 40 and a strict dress code is in effect.

Food ●●●○ Service ●●○○ Venue ●●○○ Value ●●○○

Ladies Nights

BiCE	Wed
Boston Bar	Tue
Cactus Jacks	Wed
Carters	Wed
Champions	Thu
Harry's Place	Tue
Henry J Beans	Wed
La Moda	Thu
Long's Bar	Tue/Wed
Marbles	Tue
Pancho Villa's	Sun/Tue
Planeterium	Wed/Fri
Rockafellas	Wed
Scarlett's	Tue/Wed
Seville's	Tue
Vivaldi	Tue

American Bars

On The Town

Zinc

Location ➜ Crowne Plaza · Trade Centre 1&2
Hours ➜ 20:00 - 03:00
Web/email ➜ www.crowneplaza.com

331 1111

Map Ref ➜ 9-D2

  150

This fresh, modern newcomer to Dubai's nightlife targets the younger crowd. The band plays upbeat covers of 70's disco and current pop tunes, and between sets the DJ spins disco house and R&B. The spacious metallic interior features a central neon bar, sizeable dance floor, punchy sound system and several styles of seating. An over-complicated bar system renders the service poor, and drinks follow customary hotel prices. Especially with its late licence, Zinc should become a high profile nightspot.

Food ●●○○ Service ●●○○ Venue ●●●○ Value ●●○○

Beach/Waterfront Bars

Barasti Bar

Location ➜ Le Meridien Mina · Al Sufouh
Hours ➜ 08:00 - 02:00
Web/email ➜ f&b@lemeridien-minaseyahi.com   **Map Ref** ➜ 3-A2

    150

Try the Barasti at sunny 14.00 when the sea breezes conspire with damp 40-degree air to provide relief. Discover shade under sturdy umbrellas, cloth napkins that don't blow away, and casually efficient staff. Standard fare includes superb french fries, ersatz Caesar salad, and a remarkable sandwich of chicken salad, pressed turkey, cheese, and a fried egg, reminder of club sandwiches long forgotten. Oh, yes, and this is a perfect place for a drink. Barasti should attract crowds for that endeavour alone.

Food ●●○○ Service ●●●○ Venue ●●●● Value ●●○○

Sunsets

Al Iwan	Pax Romana
Barasti Bar	Prasino's
Beachcombers	Splendido Grill
Boardwalk	Sunset Bar
Dhow & Anchor	Uptown
Horizon	Vu's
Oh! Cajun	Waterfront

Wavebreaker

QD's

Location ➜ Creek Golf Club · Al Garhoud
Hours ➜ 17:00 - 01:00
Web/email ➜ dubaicreek@dubaigolf.com   **Map Ref** ➜ 14-C2

  100

Relaxed, casual yet fun and lively, QD's is a trendy open-air bar that is ideal for pre or post-dinner drinks. Sit back and enjoy the views of the Creek while listening to the upbeat tunes played by the resident DJ. QD's will not be offering a snack menu this year, however it's a great place to meet friends and while away the evening hours. Open from 17:00 till 01:00, October to May or June, depending on the temperature.

Food ●●○○ Service ●●○○ Venue ●●●○ Value ●●○○

Cabaret Bars

Other options ➜ **Arabic Nightclubs [p.411]**

Bollywood Cafe

Location ➜ Regent Palace Hotel · Bur Dubai
Hours ➜ 19:00 - 03:00
Web/email ➜ www.ramee-group.com   **Map Ref** ➜ 11-A1

   100

Although they offer acceptable Indian food and a full bar, the real draw is the live show. Ignore the florid décor, jazzy posters of Bollywood stars, and garish artwork. Spicy prawns or tender chicken tikka will easily fill you up while you watch the entertainment. The waiters do their best to accommodate large parties of diners near the stage. The acts might be a band miming to a Bollywood hit, or one-man stand-up drama. Take a chance, have a laugh.

Food ●●○○ Service ●●○○ Venue ●●●○ Value ●●○○

Yarba

Location → Dubai Park · Jct 5, Shk Zayed Rd | **399 2222**
Hours → 18:00 - 03:00
Web/email → www.dubaiparkhotel.com | Map Ref → 3-A3

 150

This hidden treasure for Indian music lovers is not the place for a quiet, romantic evening. Loud and flashy, the music and the show are great fun, particularly if you like kitsch. Mainly Arab and Indian men patronise the venue. Decent drinks and a good, if modest, menu encourage settling in for the evening. Great for a change of pace, but be warned, if you arrive before 22:30 you'll be the only one there.

Food ●●○○ Service ●●○○ Venue ●●○○ Value ●●○○

Cigar Bars

Cigar Bar

Location → Fairmont Hotel · Shk Zayed Rd | **332 5555**
Hours → 18:00 - 02:00 Closed Fri
Web/email → www.fairmont.com | Map Ref → 9-E1

300

For cigar lovers, or for those who want to figure out the trend, this is a treat. The clubby and intimate room overlooking Sheikh Zayed Road has only five seating areas, each one with comfy sofas and leather chairs. Delightfully unpretentious, the staff are thrilled to initiate novices to this adult pleasure. The cigar menu is a greatest hits of Cubans that range from reasonable to obscene in price. Good champagne, port, and wine by the glass, and a full bar.

Food ●●●○ Service ●●●● Venue ●●●● Value ●●●○

Harry's Place & The Cigar Room

Location → Renaissance Hotel · Hor Al Anz | **262 5555**
Hours → 12:00 - 02:00 Fri 18:00 - 02:00
Web/email → rendubai@emirates.net.ae | Map Ref → 12-A3

 150

Please see review under American [p.308].

Food ●●●○ Service ●●○○ Venue ●●○○ Value ●●●○

Library & Cigar Bar, The

Location → Ritz-Carlton Dubai · Al Sufouh | **399 4000**
Hours → 16:00 - 01:00
Web/email → rcdubai@emirates.net.ae | Map Ref → 2-E2

 **100**

Modelled after a traditional Gentleman's Club, awash in wood and leather, the luxurious Library Bar feels posh. Sit in comfortable splendour, gaze at the spectacular chandeliers in the adjacent coffee shop, and listen to the gentle harmonies from the live piano. Food selection is not a priority here; this is an ideal, although somewhat expensive, location for pre or post dinner drinks, or to sit and chat the evening away. Caviar and cigars are available for connoisseurs.

Food ●●●○ Service ●●●○ Venue ●●●○ Value ●●●○

Cocktail Lounges

Other options → **Nightclubs [p.409]**

Ginseng

Location → Planet Hollywood · Umm Hurair 2 | **324 4777**
Hours → 19:00 - 02:00
Web/email → www.planethollywood-dubai.com | Map Ref → 13-D2

 200

Ginseng is about as far as you can get from the ersatz English pubs which abound. This quality cocktail bar, with its minimalist decor and Asian touches, attracts a style-conscious crowd, but it is not nauseatingly trendy. Resident DJs play suitably chilled sounds and party vibes. There is an extensive (and pricey) drinks list, administered by expert staff, and the menu includes exquisite "Asian tapas" like blackened tuna sashimi or sake mussels. Ginseng fills up quickly, but it is a deservedly popular venue.

Food ●●●● Service ●●●○ Venue ●●●○ Value ●●○○

Cocktail Lounges

Cabaret Bars | Cocktail Lounges

On The Town

Moods

Location → Sheraton Jumeirah Beach · Al Sufouh
Hours → 11:00 - 03:00
Web/email → sherjum@emirates.net.ae

399 5533

Map Ref → 2-D2

    150

Formerly named Sirroco, this renovated bar is now somewhat disappointingly called Moods. Aiming to compete as a jazz cocktail bar, the venue remains a good meeting place. For drinks, snacks or shisha, the terrace is pleasant and leads into an air conditioned tent. The mostly Arabic menu has some international additions that help to round out the options. The mélange of concepts makes Moods feel slightly schizophrenic.

Food ●●○○ Service ●●○○ Venue ●●●○ Value ●●○○

Trader Vic`s

Location → Crowne Plaza · Trade Centre 1&2
Hours → 19:00 - 02:00
Web/email → www.crowneplaza.com

331 1111

Map Ref → 9-D2

    200

Step into the (familiar) South Pacific at Trader Vic's, start with one of their signature cocktails, and nibble on Polynesian and Chinese snacks from the finger food menu. Choices abound for delicious mains: wok dishes, meats from the Chinese wood-fired oven, and lots of seafood. The macadamia nut crusted snapper is sinfully good, as is the crispy duck. Desserts range from basic to exciting tableside flambé dishes. This is a good place for groups out for festive occasions – reservations are absolutely necessary.

Food ●●●● Service ●●●○ Venue ●●●○ Value ●●○○

Uptown

Location → Jumeirah Beach Htl · Umm Suqeim
Hours → 18:00 - 02:00 18:00 - 02:00
Web/email → www.jumeirah-beach.com

348 0000

Map Ref → 4-B2

   100

The piano doesn't actually stop as you walk in, but heads will turn. Ideally, get there for happy hour between 18:00 – 19:00 or you'll find your bill climbing as high as your breathtaking vantage point over the city and sea from the generous terrace. The wine list is extensive and the cocktails plentiful and well-chilled. Food comes only as bar-snacks with a Far-Eastern slant. More smart and stylish than pretentious, Uptown remains one of Dubai's great relaxed meeting spots.

Food ●●●○ Service ●●●○ Venue ●●●● Value ●●○○

Alamo, The

Location → Dubai Marine Beach · Beach Rd, Jumeira
Hours → 12:00 - 15:30 19:00 - 00:45
Web/email → www.dxbmarine.com

349 3455

Map Ref → 6-D2

   150

Please see The Alamo review under Tex-Mex [p.376].

Food ●●○○ Service ●●○○ Venue ●●●○ Value ●●○○

Bridges

Location → Fairmont Hotel · Shk Zayed Rd
Hours → 21:00 - 02:00
Web/email → www.fairmont.com

332 5555

Map Ref → 9-E1

300

Separated from the lobby with a polished metal, sweeping half-wall, Bridges is a stunning venue. Seating to accommodate various sized groups in comfortable contemporary chairs creates a great lounge for any time of the day or night. The menu is fun to read with a history and anecdotal notes on the selections of teas, coffees, and alcohol. A snack menu offers caviar, oysters, Arabic and vegetarian selections. Knowledgeable bartenders, excellent service and a dramatic interior help soften the prices of Bridges.

Food ●●●○ Service ●●●○ Venue ●●●● Value ●●○○

Calypso Pool Bar

Location → Sofitel City Centre · Al Garhoud
Hours → 10:00 - 22:00
Web/email → cityhotl@emirates.net.ae

603 8811

Map Ref → 14-D1

 100

Situated on the rooftop, well away from the hustle and bustle of Dubai, Calypso offers a typical poolside lunch and dinner menu, with ample portions of salads, sandwiches, burgers and grilled items. The reasonably priced, popular poolside BBQ is both comfortable and relaxed, with shisha and great views over the Creek. If a dip in the pool tempts, the charge is Dhs.50, (this also allows you use of the facilities at the Lifestyle Health Club).

Food ●●○○ Service ●●○○ Venue ●●●○ Value ●●○○

Going Out | Cocktail Lounges | General Bars

Carbon Lounge & Bar

Location ➜ Hilton Dubai Creek · Creekside, Deira | **227 1111**
Hours ➜ 10:00 - 01:00 Closed Sat
Web/email ➜ hiltoncck@emirates.net.ae   **Map Ref** ➜ 11-C2

   150

A very fortunate location in a notable hotel provides the Carbon Lounge with its primary assets. It is brushed with the same sparking steel and glass as the rest of the hotel, albeit a little darker. More importantly, neighbours Verre and Glasshouse have an enviable wine selection, and attract discerning diners, which means the bar welcomes pre or post-dinner guests with a pricey drinks menu and exotic nibbles. For an extravagant cocktail before a fine meal, the Carbon Lounge fits the bill.

Food ●●●○ Service ●●○○ Venue ●●○○ Value ●○○○

Carter's

Location ➜ Pyramids · Umm Hurair 2 | **324 9601**
Hours ➜ 12:00 - 02:00 12:00 - 03:00 Thu
Web/email ➜ www.waficity.com   **Map Ref** ➜ 13-D2

150

Without pretense, full of life, and deeply satisfying to food lovers, Carter's is a rare hybrid of fine restaurant and nightspot that works well on both counts. Endless events and drink specials appeal to the cocktail crowd while divine food, like seared scallop salad, monkfish with crab couscous, and pear tatin delight foodies. Immaculate service, friendly – if sometimes singles-oriented – ambience, no-nonsense but pleasant décor, and spacious, comfortable tables complete the experience. Value for money, and conveniently located, Carter's is a consistent winner.

Food ●●●○ Service ●●●○ Venue ●●●○ Value ●●●○

Cooz

Location ➜ Grand Hyatt Dubai · Umm Hurair 2 | **209 6993**
Hours ➜ 18:00 - 03:00
Web/email ➜ www.hyatt.com   **Map Ref** ➜ 13-E3

Soon to open, Cooz is planned to be a stylish, elegant bar serving premium whiskeys, cognacs, smooth martinis from around the world, and a selection of Cuban cigars. Sounds like a great concept. For food, they are planning to offer a fine selection of deluxe canapés, balik salmon, Iranian caviar and foie gras, with a pianist providing background music. This bar promises to be an upscale and elegant option in the increasingly large category of posh drinking.

Food – n/a Service – n/a Venue – n/a Value – n/a

Happy Hours

Barasti	Hofbrauhaus
Beach Bar	Irish Village
Carter's	Jules Bar
Dubliner's	Long's Bar
Finnegans	Seville's

Gulf Pavilion, The

Location ➜ Ritz-Carlton Dubai · Al Sufouh | **399 4000**
Hours ➜ 09:00 - 23:00
Web/email ➜ rcdubai@emirates.net.ae   **Map Ref** ➜ 2-E2

   150

Elegant, stylish and rich in quality: the Ritz Carlton always makes you feel special. Situated between twin pools, surrounded by palms and lush, manicured lawns, it is reminiscent of a Riviera café with panoramic views of the Gulf. For informal lunches or casual star-lit dinners, the food, presentation and service are top notch. There is a kids menu and the wine lists vary according to the time of day. Perhaps pricey for simple café fare, but careful attention to detail never comes cheaply.

Food ●●●○ Service ●●●● Venue ●●●○ Value ●●●○

Henry Africa's

Location ➜ Nr Al Kawakeb Blds · Trade Center 1&2 | **343 0501**
Hours ➜ 10:00 - 01:00
Web/email ➜ n/a   **Map Ref** ➜ 9-A3

    100

Henry Africa's is a somewhat dingy and no-frills hangout. 'The Bunker,' as it is known to regulars, is a colourful nightspot for expats and a great place to indulge in pub grub. Jungle motif decor suggests Africa, but Wednesdays feature karaoke, and Thursdays a live jam session. A favourite for hangover Friday brunch. This 'come as you are' affair is definitely worth visiting if you know what to expect.

Food ●●●○ Service ●●●○ Venue ●●●○ Value ●●●●

On The Town | General Bars

Horizon

Location → Le Meridien Mina · Al Sufouh
Hours → 11:00 - 19:00
Web/email → www.lemeridien-minaseyahi.com **Map Ref →** 3-A2

| **399 3333** |

Kick back, soak up the sun and sample the cocktail menu at this relaxed poolside bar with spectacular views of the beach and Palm Island on the horizon. Less hip than its neighbour, the Barasti Bar, Horizon offers snacks, shisha and a live Tandoori cooking station, primarily for the lunchtime trade. A popular venue for hotel guests and club members. You'll be tempted to pay the weekend entry fee to take advantage of the facilities and make a day of it. ◉

Food ●●○○ Service ●●●○ Venue ●●●○ Value ●●●○

Jules Bar

Location → Le Meridien Dubai · Al Garhoud
Hours → 11:00 - 03:00
Web/email → julesbar@le-meridien-dubai.com **Map Ref →** 14-E3

| **282 4040** |

Not one of the jewels in the culinary crown of Le Meridien, Jules Bar nonetheless offers tolerable liners for beverage-obsessed stomachs. The enchiladas, fajitas, burritos, and chimichangas dominating the menu may come as a surprise, but the thirty or so dishes themselves have travelled far enough from their origins to be non-threatening. In daylight, scars on interior surfaces framed by rival TV sets bespeak rollicking good times with bands and beverages at night when, despite its food, Jules Bar shines. ◉

Food ●●○○ Service ●●●○ Venue ●●●○ Value ●○○○

Lindbergh's

Location → Sheraton Deira · Hor Al Anz
Hours → 18:00 - 02:00
Web/email → shedeira@emirates.net.ae **Map Ref →** 12-A3

| **268 8888** |

Lindbergh's combines an Art Deco-style cocktail lounge on one side of the room with a comfy bird's eye view of Deira on the other. The proximity to the Airport's flight path might interest a few aviation fans, otherwise the pianist and the TV screens entertain. Drinks and bar food do not tread far from 'club sandwich' hotel fare and prices. A congenial hang-out, but being far from the action means no-one is beating a path to the door. Beware: parking can be tricky. ◉

Food ●●○○ Service ●●○○ Venue ●●●○ Value ●●○○

Long's

Location → Towers Rotana · Trade Centre 1&2
Hours → 12:00 - 23:45
Web/email → www.rotana.com **Map Ref →** 9-B2

| **343 8000** |

Long's is a fashionable and popular port of call on weekends on promotion nights like Wednesday's Ladies Night. Based on Raffle's in Singapore, the decor is nicely tasteful. Early on, the scene is quiet; the cosier dark wood restaurant adjacent can serve quite sophisticated European dishes at reasonable prices. When quiet, this substantial venue feels desolate, but when it's hopping, the mood is charged. Catch up with friends, the crowd circling the bar, or settle in the restaurant for a more intimate stay. ◉

Food ●●●○ Service ●●○○ Venue ●●○○ Value ●●○○

Marbles

Location → Hotel Inter-Continental · Deira
Hours → 18:00 - 02:30
Web/email → intercon_bc@itcdubai.co.ae **Map Ref →** 8-C4

| **205 7333** |

In the neighbourhood and fancy a quick, quiet drink on the way home from work? Try Marbles Bar. Happy hour daily from 18:00-21:00 for the usual tipple, premiums not included. A cosy venue – sofas, plush armchairs or tables if you prefer – with a small but decent snack menu. Beef & chicken satay come on a mini-grill, sizzling enticingly. The band begins at 21:30 nightly (except Saturdays), but there are several comfy corners if you prefer more intimacy. Service is both courteous and efficient. ◉

Food ●●○○ Service ●●●○ Venue ●●○○ Value ●●○○

MoMo

Location → Hilton Jumeirah · Al Sufouh
Hours → 19:00 - 03:00
Web/email → www.hilton.com **Map Ref →** 2-D2

| **399 1111** |

Scheduled to open some time in the new year, MoMo will be located on the ground floor of the Hilton Dubai Jumeirah, replacing the Studio One cocktail bar. MoMo will tap into the current vogue for lounge experiences, and will be offering cocktails along with Asian food such as sushi and dim sum. Music (including live bands), karaoke, and sports TV are all planned for this new venue. ◉

Food – n/a Service – n/a Venue – n/a Value – n/a

Patrick's Bar & Grill

Location → York International Hotel · Bur Dubai
Hours → 19:00 - 02:00
Web/email → www.dubaiyorkhotel.com   **Map Ref** → 7-E2

  100

Patrick's is an oasis of open-air informality in a seedy part of town. Outside, the mishmash of furniture cobbled around the tiny rooftop pool allows for conversation with easy-listening music for a back garden barbecue feel. A small menu of beverages and barbecue snacks cooked nearby are very good value. The soon-to be-completed inside, and sports bar above, will continue the relaxed ambience. Strictly barring the working girls, Patrick's faces a difficult task in this location.

Food ●●○○ Service ●●○○ Venue ●●○○ Value ●●●●

Piano Bar, The

Location → Le Royal Meridien · Al Sufouh
Hours → 17:00 - 01:00
Web/email → f&b@leroyalmeridien-dubai.com   **Map Ref** → 2-E2

 100

From fresh roses on the table to the muted tones of the pianist, the Piano Bar exudes a certain sense of style. Chic and elegant, it's a popular place for aperitifs or a quiet drink with friends. The staff are efficient and friendly, and well trained in the art of mixing cocktails. There is a good selection of spirits, beers and soft drinks on offer, and if the variety of nuts provided is not enough, you can always order a snack.

Food ●●●○ Service ●●●● Venue ●●●○ Value ●●●○

Al fresco at Century Village

Pool Bar

Location → Le Meridien Dubai · Al Garhoud
Hours → 06:30 - 20:00
Web/email → www.lemeridien-dubai.com   **Map Ref** → 14-E3

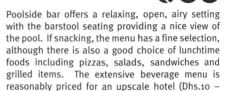 150

Poolside bar offers a relaxing, open, airy setting with the barstool seating providing a nice view of the pool. If snacking, the menu has a fine selection, although there is also a good choice of lunchtime foods including pizzas, salads, sandwiches and grilled items. The extensive beverage menu is reasonably priced for an upscale hotel (Dhs.10 – Dhs.15) but service and food delivery is a little too relaxed - making this an enjoyable lunch retreat only if you're not in a rush.

Food ●●●○ Service ●●○○ Venue ●●●○ Value ●●●○

Pool Bar & Restaurant

Location → Grand Hyatt Dubai · Umm Hurair 2
Hours → 10:00 - 24:00
Web/email → www.hyatt.com   **Map Ref** → 13-E3

This landscaped tropical garden bar is designed to cater to guests basking in the sun around the pool and pavilion area. When it opens in spring 2003, it will offer a scenic, tropical setting with views of landscaped gardens, water features and the Dubai Creek. Guests can choose from a variety of fresh crisp salads, platters of tropical fruit with honey and lime granite, Balinese tums, Malay satays, Indian samosas, Vietnamese spring rolls and much more.

Food – n/a Service – n/a Venue – n/a Value – n/a

Rainbow Room

Location → Aviation Club, The · Al Garhoud
Hours → 11:00 - 15:00 19:00 - 01:00
Web/email → aviation@emirates.net.ae   **Map Ref** → 14-C3

  100

This sober setting is right for a business lunch or quiet drink - good value and the atmosphere is relaxed. Order from the varied snack menu (prices range from Dhs.20 - 40), meet for a quick drink, or watch major sports events on the large TV. The lounge accommodates 200 and an additional 200 can be catered for on the wooden deck around the outdoor swimming pool, making this a good location for special functions.

Food ●●○○ Service ●●○○ Venue ●●○○ Value ●●●○

Satchmo's

Location → Le Royal Meridien · Al Sufouh **399 5555**
Hours → 17:30 - 02:00
Web/email → f&b@leroyalmeridien-dubai.com **Map Ref →** 2-E2

Satchmo's is a stylishly happening place to visit. Whether you're ready to burst after a meal at the adjoining prime rib restaurant, want a late night jaunt, or just pre-dinner drinks, this place reminiscent of an underground jazz venue is a good choice. The modern yet warm atmosphere is complemented by a split-level interior, allowing good views of the great live band. After midnight, everything livens up when the DJ starts playing dance music. Keep an eye open for visiting DJ's and special promotions.

Food ●●●○ Service ●●●● Venue ●●●○ Value ●●●○

Siam

Location → Dusit Dubai · Trade Center 1&2 **343 3333**
Hours → 17:00 - 03:00
Web/email → info@dusit.com **Map Ref →** 9-A2

Siam is a good meeting place for a warm-up tipple before an energetic night on the town. The Thai-style décor exudes colonial charm: wicker chairs and wooden shutters look out onto the hurly-burly of Sheikh Zayed Road. The bar (impressively long) is well stocked and an interesting menu of bar snacks will help you pre-empt the munchies. The pool table and big screen TV keep sports fans happy; with Ladies Night on Tuesdays, and Karaoke Night on Wednesdays, there's something for everyone.

Food ●●○○ Service ●●●○ Venue ●●●● Value ●●○○

Spectrum Bar

Location → Fairmont Hotel · Shk Zayed Rd **332 5555**
Hours → 18:00 - 01:30
Web/email → www.fairmont.com **Map Ref →** 9-E1

This modern and trendy bar on the first floor of the dazzling Fairmont Hotel ranks highly as a plush and pleasant venue. The glass-fronted cellar tempts wine aficionados with the goodies on offer, while the staff are matchless with their efficiency, courtesy and genuine interest when advising enthusiastically about cocktails. Perhaps this is the perfect mellow place for a cocktail before your

meal, as it's located between all the other hotel restaurants. Go easy on the cocktails or order a taxi in advance.

Food ●●●○ Service ●●●● Venue ●●●● Value ●●○○

Spike Bar

Location → Emirates Golf Club · Jct 5, Shk Zayed Rd **347 3222**
Hours → 06:30 - 23:00
Web/email → egc@dubaigolf.com **Map Ref →** 3-A3

Although mainly catering to golfers, this bar is open to all who wish to enjoy its relaxed and friendly atmosphere. Located on the ground floor of the clubhouse, this is a busy outlet offering a wide-ranging menu from breakfast through to dinner. The terrace, running alongside the Majlis practice putting green, is an ideal way for golfers to complete a day on the course, particularly during the cooler months. Probably not worth a special visit if you loathe golf.

Food ●●○○ Service ●●○○ Venue ●●●○ Value ●●○○

Spikes Bar

Spikes Bar

Location → Nad Al Sheba Club · Nad Al Sheba **336 3666**
Hours → 06:30 - 01:00
Web/email → www.nadalshebaclub.com **Map Ref →** 17-A3

Relaxed and casual, this bar remains open until midnight with the floodlit golf course as a backdrop. Comfy seating and multiple TV's result in a homey feeling. The nightly buffet (except Fridays) is adequate and particularly convenient if at the complex for other events. The a la carte menu is available all day, and there is a 'stable visit' breakfast that caters to those

who want to tour the equestrian facilities. A convenient spot to know about.

Food ●●●○ Service ●●●○ Venue ●●●○ Value ●●●○

Sunset Bar

Location → Jumeirah Beach Club · Beach Rd, Jumeira | **344 5333**
Hours → 17:00 - 23:00
Web/email → www.jumeirahbeachclub.com **Map Ref** → 5-D1

If tranquility and relaxation rate high on your list, then Sunset Bar could be your permanent Friday hangout. Carpets and cushions placed on the private beach, a great happy hour, complimentary snacks and excellent service combine to make this place unbeatable. The chillout experience begins just before sunset and it's wise to arrive early. The super mix of relaxing fusion/lounge music, cheap cocktails and shishas galore will take away the gloom of going back to work the next day.

Food ●●●○ Service ●●●○ Venue ●●●● Value ●●●○

Vu's

Location → Emirates Towers · Trade Centre 1&2 | **330 0000**
Hours → 13:00 - 15:00 19:00 - 23:00
Web/email → www.emirates-towers-hotel.com **Map Ref** → 9-C2

On the 51st floor, this outstanding venue has a spectacular view. Cutting-edge modern design, deluxe cocktails, and the inimitable view give patrons a feeling of 'not being in Dubai' (which can be a lifesaver at times!). An awe-inspiring room, with prices to match. Posh snacks are on offer for late night nibbles. The staff too have loads of personality and add to the ambience. This is a very cool spot and quite unlike any other venue in Dubai; great for special occasions or dates.

Food ●●●○ Service ●●●○ Venue ●●●● Value ●●●○

Karaoke Bars

Other options → **Filipino [p.326]**
Japanese [p.353]

Harry Ghatto's

Location → Emirates Towers · Trade Centre 1&2 | **330 0000**
Hours → 09:30 - 03:00
Web/email → www.emirates-towers-hotel.com **Map Ref** → 9-C2

This upscale sing-along bar is small and very noisy, but then again, that's exactly how it should be. Ever popular with a very mixed crowd, it's cosy and modern with a full bar and (mediocre) food. The staff energetically keep things rolling. Although the song selection is not the widest, they'll sing with you if you need support. Self-conscious karaoke neophytes may appreciate the private room that can be reserved. Go for a laugh and a change of pace, and have dinner beforehand.

Food ●●○○ Service ●●○○ Venue ●●●○ Value ●○○○

Hibiki Karaoke Lounge

Location → Hyatt Regency · Deira | **209 1234**
Hours → 19:30 - 03:00
Web/email → hyattbus@emirates.net.ae **Map Ref** → 8-D2

This Japanese karaoke bar invites all prima donnas to take the stage. More reserved crooners may prefer to hire a private room with a group of friends. The service is exceptional, and a vast range of expensive cocktails brings an elegant executive feel to a fun evening's entertainment. Happy hour is a real attraction for good value. The cosy atmosphere attracts more singles, but if it's a fine Cuban you prefer, have a look at the cigar menu.

Food ●●●○ Service ●●○○ Venue ●●●○ Value ●○○○

Deliciously Unpretentious

ARZ Lebanon	Henry Africa's
Carpenter's Bar	Irish Village
Fusion	Ossigeno
George & Dragon	Troyka

Sports Bars

Other options → **Activities [p.224]**
Television / Satellite TV [p.92]

Aussie Legends

Location → Rydges Plaza Hotel · Al Satwa
Hours → 15:00 - 03:00 Thu 12:00 - 03:00
Web/email → rhrdxb@emirates.net.ae   Map Ref → 7-A4

398 2222

Aussie and like-minded revellers frequent this easy-going bar mainly when big sports games are screened. With TV's tuned to the rugby, and space to jump around, the atmosphere can be rip-roaring – yet at times, the regulars and pool players sparsely populate the big bright gaudy venue. Waitresses adeptly totter by with huge but not hugely-priced casual dining creations in the seated area; a crispy calorific 'Aussie Wedges' starter fills a prop-forward. Theme nights can buzz but the fashion-conscious crowd doesn't regularly call.

Food ●●○○ Service ●●○○ Venue ●●○○ Value ●●●○

Champions

Location → JW Marriott Hotel · Deira
Hours → 12:00 - 02:00 Fri 18:00 - 02:00
Web/email → www.marriott.com   Map Ref → 12-A3

262 4444

Champions is an American sports bar striving to be the most lively in town. There are the usual TV's, sports memorabilia, table football, and a pool table. This bar/restaurant is the champion of theme nights varying each month and continuing throughout the year – best to call for details. The restaurant serves large portions of bar snacks, as well as main courses including burgers, chicken wings and steaks. The food isn't exactly weight-watcher fare – definitely intended for the armchair sports fan!

Food ●●○○ Service ●●○○ Venue ●●●○ Value ●●○○

Cricketers Sports Bar

Location → Ramada Continental · Al Hamriya
Hours → 12:00 - 16:00 18:00 - 02:00
Web/email → ramadadb@emirates.net.ae   Map Ref → 12-B4

266 2666

Pop into the Cricketer for a quick drink on the way home from work. A casual bar is served by welcoming staff and decorated with assorted cricket paraphernalia: photos, bats, shirts and shields. The menu is varied with BBQ and fried options dominating; the veggie selection is limited. The chicken curry with rice or naan is just right – spicy and a good filler after a hard day. Unwind and listen to the (loud) band with a free pint accompanying the BBQ meal.

Food ●●○○ Service ●●●○ Venue ●●○○ Value ●●○○

Sports Bar

Location → Emirates Golf Club · Jct 5, Shk Zayed Rd
Hours → 08:00 - 23:00
Web/email → www.dubaigolf.com   Map Ref → 3-A3

347 3222

The Sports Bar is a grand place to catch up on all the latest sports action from around the world. This comfortable little bar runs half a dozen TV's simultaneously so guests can keep up to date with plenty of different events, including international golf, football, rugby, cricket and motor racing. A casual outlet, the Sports Bar also offers a choice of passable snacks and more substantial dishes, as well as a full bar.

Food ●●○○ Service ●●○○ Venue ●●●○ Value ●●○○

Winners

Location → Sea Shell Inn · Bur Dubai
Hours → 12:00 - 03:00
Web/email → sshelinn@emirates.net.ae   Map Ref → 7-E2

393 4777

Winners is for losers. Satellite sports channels, a range of beverages and an ample, reasonably priced menu including pasta, kebabs and curries cater to the clientele at Winners. Its sporting theme is weak, relying on a tired looking mountain bike over the bar and an upside down table-tennis table on the ceiling. With a male-dominated clientele, this is not a place most unaccompanied women would feel comfortable. Whatever sport you're a fan of, there are plenty of other venues in Dubai that score better in all categories.

Food ●●○○ Service ●●○○ Venue ●○○○ Value ●●○○

Tapas Bars

Other options ➜ **Spanish [p.372]**

Tapas Bar

Location ➜ Hilton Jumeirah · Al Sufouh | **399 1111**
Hours ➜ 18:30 - 03:00
Web/email ➜ www.hilton.com **Map Ref** ➜ 2-D2

   150

Please refer to the Pachanga review under Argentinian restaurants [p.318].
Food ●●●○ Service ●●●○ Venue ●●●○ Value ●●●○

Wine Bars

Agency, The

Location ➜ Emirates Towers · Trade Centre 1&2 | **330 0000**
Hours ➜ 12:30 - 01:00 Fri 15:00 - 01:00
Web/email ➜ www.emirates-towers-hotel.com **Map Ref** ➜ 9-C2

   100

As a wine bar The Agency is out there on its own, if only for the number of wines on offer – over 50 from Europe, the Americas and Australasia at prices to suit any budget. The décor, lighting and music are classy, sassy and subtle – a relief from the glare and noise elsewhere. There's a short but imaginative, tasty and well-priced menu, focusing mainly on tapas, served all day. The Agency is a great place to wind down and catch up with friends.
Food ●●●○ Service ●●●○ Venue ●●●○ Value ●●●○

Vinoteca

Location ➜ Grand Hyatt Dubai · Umm Hurair 2 | **209 6993**
Hours ➜ 12:00 - 15:00 18:00 - 23:30
Web/email ➜ www.hyatt.com **Map Ref** ➜ 13-E3

Vinoteca is another new entry into the wine bar market, scheduled to open in spring 2003.

As with other similar venues in town, this one is slated to offer a wide selection of wines by the glass or by the bottle. The plans specify an upscale and friendly environment in an intimate room (around 20 seats). Snacks will be offered,

but no word yet as to specific varieties. Knowing the Grand Hyatt, it will probably be worth a visit.
Food – n/a Service – n/a Venue – n/a Value – n/a

Wines

Agency, The	**Sphinx**
Cellar	**Uptown**
Fusion	**Verre**
Spectrum On One	**Vintage**

Vintage

Location ➜ Pyramids · Umm Hurair 2 | **324 0000**
Hours ➜ 12:30 - 01:00
Web/email ➜ www.pyramidsdubai.com **Map Ref** ➜ 13-D2

  200

One of a slew of wine bars finding favour in town, newly opened Vintage succeeds brilliantly. Casually elegant, with a wine list to make grown men weep, this is a venue for adults. Food is simple and fresh: heavenly cheeses, sausages, and small nibbles aplenty make it perfect for a light supper or a snack before a late dinner. Promotions often take the already reasonable wine prices very low indeed. Presently rather quiet, but as word gets out, Vintage threatens to become quite popular.
Food ●●●○ Service ●●●○ Venue ●●●○ Value ●●●○

PUBS

Other options ➜ **Bars [p.392]**

Pubs in Dubai generally look close enough to the real thing to transport you from the brown desert to the green, green grass of home – not most people's vision of the Middle East.

Some of these pubs, the English ones especially, are very well established and were among the first places for socialising in Dubai. The Irish pubs are some of the favourite and best drinking venues around town.

Popular with all nationalities, a good number of pubs manage very successfully to recreate the warm, friendly atmosphere of a typical hostelry. Thousands of miles from their proper location, these places have become genuine locals for many people, offering just what they've always done – good beer, tasty food and great crack.

Biggles

Location → Airport Hotel · Al Garhoud |282 3464
Hours → 12:00 - 01:30
Web/email → apothotl@emirates.net.ae   Map Ref → 14-D3

A quirky theme, good buffet (especially for brunch) and plenty of noise make Biggles a good place for a family outing or a quick drink with mates. The décor is reminiscent of a Churchill-esque era, which goes well with this British pub. TV's adorn every corner, showing the latest football league matches, and the live band does a good job of drowning out all form of conversation. Food is on the average side here, though prices aren't.●●

Food ●●○○ Service ●●●○ Venue ●●○○ Value ●●●○

Carpenter's Bar

Location → Hyatt Regency · Deira |209 1400
Hours → 12:00 - 15:00 18:00 - 02:00 Thu 18:00 - 02:00
Web/email → hyattbus@emirates.net.ae   Map Ref → 8-D2

Carpenter's Bar has a classy – if dated – feel: subdued lighting and comfortable armchairs make this a relaxed and discreet venue in which to meet friends and unwind. Whether sipping an aperitif before dinner or whiling away the evening in the bar, a range of drinks is available, as well as imaginative cocktails, all at the usual hotel prices. Complimentary bar snacks are disappointingly stark. Chat in comfort before the noisy Filipino band commands attention, at which point the bar rather loses its appeal.●

Food ●○○○ Service ●●●○ Venue ●●○○ Value ●●●○

Chelsea Arms

Location → Sheraton Hotel & Towers · Deira |207 1721
Hours → 12:00 - 16:00 18:00 - 24:00
Web/email → sheradxb@emirates.net.ae   Map Ref → 11-C1

The Chelsea Arms is a typical 'English style' pub. Small by Dubai standards, its staff are cheery and welcoming. The menu includes the usual pub fare, such as bangers and mash, fish and chips, and other hearty meat-based dishes, although these are more functional than memorable. The Chelsea Arms sits at the smarter end of the generic pub experience, and for this reason, the atmosphere is perhaps closer to that of a hotel lounge than that of a bustling pub.●

Food ●●○○ Service ●●●○ Venue ●●○○ Value ●●○○

Churchill's

Location → Sofitel City Centre · Al Garhoud |603 8400
Hours → 12:00 - 02:00
Web/email → cityhotl@emirates.net.ae   Map Ref → 14-D1

Handily near the busiest shopping centre this side of Mars, Churchill's pulls in a few punters with the tried and tested (but not to the limit) 'English' pub formula. This synthetic Dubai 'pub' includes wood panelling, pints of lager, pub games and fish-and-chip food with football on the telly and a duo playing cover songs. Perhaps too much fanfare and too little by way of authentic food and beverages, or even a real bar, but still acceptable, particularly to escape the shopping frenzy.●

Food ●●○○ Service ●●○○ Venue ●●○○ Value ●●○○

Churchill's

Pubs

On The Town

Dhow & Anchor

Location → Jumeirah Beach Htl · Umm Suqeim | **348 0000**
Hours → 12:00 - 00:30
Web/email → www.jumeirah-beach.com **Map Ref** → 4-B2

    300

Popular with beachgoers, this small pub/restaurant with an outdoor terrace provides a calm oasis in which to eat, drink and relax with friends. Stand at the bar or take a table to sample the affordable traditional English and European fare. Vegetarians are catered for; although the mushrooms lacked flavour, the camembert was richly creamy. The seafood pie was stuffed with plump pink prawns, the summer pudding scrumptious. Served by friendly, helpful staff, this pub will fulfil your expectations.

Food ●●○○ Service ●●●○ Venue ●●●○ Value ●●○○

Dubliner's

Location → Le Meridien Dubai · Al Garhoud | **282 4040**
Hours → 11:00 - 01:00
Web/email → dubliners@le-meridien-dubai.com **Map Ref** → 14-E3

   150

Fancy great food at fabulous prices in a traditional Irish pub? Then pull up a pew or pose at the bar with a pint of your favourite libation in character-rich Dubliner's. Try the home-made soup or excellent Irish stew loaded with tender lamb from a select, very reasonably priced menu. Happy, helpful staff (mostly genuine Irish artifacts), lively piped music, big screen TV, a regular live band, al fresco dining on cosy courtyard - what more could you want?

Food ●●●○ Service ●●○○ Venue ●●●○ Value ●●●○

George & Dragon

Location → Ambassador Hotel · Bur Dubai | **393 9444**
Hours → 12:00 - 16:00 18:00 - 01:00 Fri 18:00 - 01:00
Web/email → ambhotel@astamb.com **Map Ref** → 8-A2

100

Nestled within Dubai's oldest hotel, the George and Dragon is the closest thing in town to a traditional English pub, complete with a wide range of "honest to goodness" pub fare, a great range of beers, sports TV channels, a pool table and a decent darts board. The staff are efficient and refreshingly friendly without all the formality and stuffiness so common in other venues. For a down

to earth, unpretentious trip to the pub, you can't do much better than the George and Dragon.

Food ●●○○ Service ●●●○ Venue ●●●○ Value ●●●○

Humphrey's Tavern

Location → Trade Centre Hotel · Trade Centre 1&2 | **331 4000**
Hours → 12:00 - 24:00
Web/email → information@worldtradecentrehotel.com **Map Ref** → 10-A2

 200

The English pub atmosphere here is complete with a dartboard, bar and big screen TV. A good place to have a drink or a lunch buffet of shepherd pie and other English-style fare. The buffet is best described as hearty, which makes it a favourite for the Trade Centre crowd. The center bar, wood panelling, small size and convenient location make it a good place for intimate conversations over pub grub.

Food ●●●○ Service ●●○○ Venue ●●○○ Value ●●○○

Irish Village

Location → Aviation Club, The · Al Garhoud | **282 4750**
Hours → 11:00 - 02:00 Thu 11:00 - 03:00
Web/email → www.aviationclubonline.com **Map Ref** → 14-C3

     100

Although stuck alongside the tennis stadium, this may be the mother of all Dubai pubs. The mock Dublin façade, (mostly) friendly service, lively crowds, ample outdoor seating, and surprisingly good food all combine to make this venue a winner. Bands entertain inside while people watching and drinking rule outside. Don't go if looking for a quiet evening as it's busy most nights, especially on weekends. Parking is ample and the beer never runs out at this legendary watering hole.

Food ●●●○ Service ●○○○ Venue ●●●● Value ●●●●

Pubs

Going Out

GUARANTEED
IRISH

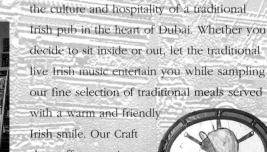

The Irish Village restaurant and bar recreates the culture and hospitality of a traditional Irish pub in the heart of Dubai. Whether you decide to sit inside or out, let the traditional live Irish music entertain you while sampling our fine selection of traditional meals served with a warm and friendly Irish smile. Our Craft shop offers genuine superior quality Irish art and crafts.

Casual and comfortable, The Irish Village is the place to be.

The Irish Village
Dubai

P.O. Box 55400, Dubai, United Arab Emirates. Tel: 04 2824750   Fax: 04 2824759

Top Al Fresco

Academy	Horizon
Beachcombers	Sails
Boardwalk	Seville's
Capanna Nuova	Splendido Grill
Dhow & Anchor	Villa Beach Restaurant
Gulf Pavilion, The	

Old Vic

Location ➜ Ramada Hotel · Bur Dubai **351 9999**
Hours ➜ 12:00 - 15:00 19:00 - 23:30
Web/email ➜ rhddxb@emirates.net.ae   **Map Ref** ➜ 7-E3

Satisfy burger and pint cravings with a stop at The Old Vic. Many regulars enjoy the numerous theme nights, daily happy hour, and hearty pub fare. Favourites include mixed grill, cottage pie, curries, and bangers and mash. The bar separates the dining from the drinking area, so you can enjoy conversation and still hear the live music. Lots of televisions make this a lively spot to watch sports. Other diversions include a pool table and darts. Lively and homey, this pub blissfully lacks pretense.

Food ●●○○ Service ●●○○ Venue ●●●○ Value ●●●○

Pub, The

Location ➜ Hotel Inter-Continental · Deira **205 7333**
Hours ➜ 12:00 - 24:00
Web/email ➜ intercon_bc@itcdubai.co.ae   **Map Ref** ➜ 8-C4

The Pub is everything you'd expect from a British pub. The bar and walls gleam with dark finished wood, TV's show sporting events, and service is efficient. Portions are large and choices extend beyond British fare to include international and vegetarian cuisine. If you want to fill up on tasty starters, and you're not worried about cholesterol, try the combination platter. The Pub's compact size makes it a cosy retreat and an ideal place to enjoy a pint, watch sports, and have a quick meal.

Food ●●●○ Service ●●●○ Venue ●●○○ Value ●●○○

Red Lion

Location ➜ Metropolitan · Jct 2, Shk Zayed Rd **343 0000**
Hours ➜ 10:00 - 01:00
Web/email ➜ methotel@emirates.net.ae   **Map Ref** ➜ 5-C4

This fairly average pub seems to survive on the business of residents from the neighbourhood and people who happen to drop in. The result is a rather cosy and intimate ambience, though it can feel alienating to newcomers. Standard bar menu offers decent grub, and drinks are in the normal price range. Check the board for nightly specials. Darts, snooker, sports TV, and quiz nights make this feel like a British local hangout. Perhaps that is reason enough to make a visit.

Food ●●○○ Service ●●○○ Venue ●●○○ Value ●●○○

St. Andrew's Snug

Location ➜ Rydges Plaza Hotel · Al Satwa **398 2222**
Hours ➜ 12:00 - 01:00
Web/email ➜ rhrdxb@emirates.net.ae   **Map Ref** ➜ 7-A4

One of the smallest in Dubai, St Andrew's is a warm, cosy pub, providing a pint and a meal in quiet and comfortable surroundings. Although the décor could definitely do with some improvement, you're made to feel as welcome as your local back home. The bar has a reasonable (pricey) selection of beers, however the menu is limited and rather than traditional British pub grub, it has a more international flavour with dishes such as curries, pasta, burgers and nachos.

Food ●●●○ Service ●●○○ Venue ●○○○ Value ●●○○

Swan, The

Location ➜ JW Marriott Hotel · Deira **262 4444**
Hours ➜ 18:00 - 24:00
Web/email ➜ www.marriott.com   **Map Ref** ➜ 12-A3

The smallest pub in Dubai, it's a refuge for the few traditionally dressed locals who watch sports on the TV and anyone else who wants to feel like they've stepped into someone's dark wood-panelled living room. When the TV is off it can be a cosy and almost secret place to have a quiet conversation. You are unlikely to bump into a colleague, or to be disturbed by a big party of revellers – there simply isn't enough room.

Food ●●○○ Service ●●○○ Venue ●●○○ Value ●●○○

Going Out · Pubs

Thatcher's Lounge

Location → Ascot Hotel · Bur Dubai
Hours → 10:30 - 02:00
Web/email → www.centuryhoteldubai.com | **352 0900**

Map Ref → 8-A3

 150

Thatcher's Lounge is an unusual venue, an upmarket pool-room and quiet bar - perhaps a good place to come for an intimate meeting. Two large pool tables dominate a room of understated elegance. A tasty mix and match selection of food is available from some of the hotel restaurants, and is reasonably priced and very good, despite being carried down from the other restaurants. Happy hour runs from 15:00 - 20:00 daily, when the average drink is reduced from Dhs.16 to Dhs.13.

Food●●●○ Service●●○○ Venue●●○○ Value●●●○

Viceroy, The

Location → Four Points Sheraton · Bur Dubai
Hours → 12:00 - 02:00
Web/email → www.fourpoints.com | **397 7444**

Map Ref → 8-A4

100

The Viceroy combines all the nuances of an Olde English Tavern with the big screen entertainment of a sports bar. The smoky air, friendly service, and bustling tables exude an atmosphere of contentment. Cheap, palatable pub grub is the order of the day with a few Indian specialities thrown in for good measure. However, don't leave space for puddings. Daily promotions of beer and spirits, lunchtime specials and Monday quiz nights make this a popular venue with the local business community.

Food●●●○ Service●●○○ Venue●●●○ Value●●●○

Exchange Lounge, The

NIGHTCLUBS

Other options → **Belly Dancing [p.287]**

Packed with all nationalities, Dubai's nightclubs are very popular from about 23:00 until well into the small hours. Even on weeknights, there's a good scene and at the weekend many places are full to overflowing.

There's a reasonable number of dedicated nightclubs, as well as numerous other venues with schizophrenic personalities that are bars or restaurants earlier in the evening, then later turn into the perfect place to cut loose and shake your thang. For authentic club nights, look out for the increasingly common visits by international DJs and the special nights held all over Dubai by various event organisers.

Additionally, since you're in the Middle East, don't forget the option of Arabic nightclubs. Here you can sample a wide variety of Arabic food and enjoy a night of traditional Arabic entertainment, usually with a belly dancer, a live band and singer. These venues only start getting busy very late in the evening, and can still be empty when most other nightspots are packed, reflecting the Arabic way of starting late and finishing, well... later.

For information on door policy and dress code, refer to the introduction to Bars [p.392].

Cyclone

Location → Nr American Hospital · Umm Hurair 2
Hours → 12:00 - 15:00 19:30 - 03:00
Web/email → cyclone@emirates.net.ae | **336 9991**

Map Ref → 10-D4

 150

Cyclone has remained famous as a late night spot because its clientele consists mainly of men out to meet the many "international" girls who seem to fancy the place. Once past the strict doormen (who may relieve you of Dhs.50), the large oval bar anchors the action, although there is also a good-sized dance floor. The Cyclone is an interesting venue for an adult night out in varied company that may find you waking up not quite in the circumstances you expected.

Venue●●●○ Value●○○○

Kasbar

Location → Royal Mirage Palace · Al Sufouh | **399 9999**
Hours → 22:00 - 03:00 Closed Sun
Web/email → www.royalmiragedubai.com | **Map Ref →** 3-A2

   250

With an expansive cocktail menu and wine list, three levels of entertainment, and an almost romantic ambience, Kasbar redefines nightclubs as we know them. Featuring an Arabian theme, candles make up the majority of the venue's lighting, giving it a warm appeal. Catering to all moods, the main level consists of a dance floor and tables; climbing up the spiral staircase takes you to a mezzanine overlooking the dance floor, while downstairs offers an Arabian lounge style area. The well-balanced theme and ambience make this a venue that shouldn't be missed.
Venue ●●●● Value ●●○○

Kasbar

Mix

Location → Grand Hyatt Dubai · Umm Hurair 2 | **209 6993**
Hours → 18:00 - 03:00
Web/email → www.hyatt.com | **Map Ref →** 13-E3

Billed as 'outrageous fun', this nightclub/entertainment complex promises to be vast and amusing. Although not open till spring 2003, Mix is described as a split level compound with private rooms, a stage for live music, an 'island bar', and funky, innovative cocktails. With a capacity of 300 guests, this may become one of the hot spots in town. With many other large clubs in town, it remains to be seen who makes the cut and who does not.
Venue n/a Value n/a

Planetarium

Location → Planet Hollywood · Umm Hurair 2 | **324 0072**
Hours → 22:00 - 03:00 Closed Mon
Web/email → www.planethollywood-dubai.com **Map Ref →** 13-D2

  150

Drawing international DJs the likes of Claude Challe, Ravin and Roger Sanchez to name a few, it's not hard to see why Planetarium has established itself as THE central hangout for clubbers in Dubai. With six theme nights each week, no less than four major events per month, and resident DJ Charlie C's versatility with house, rave, R'nB and latino, you can almost forgive the limited capacity of the venue. Drinks are on the pricey side. Planetarium has strict entrance rules; dressing like a slob will keep you from experiencing one of Dubai's better nightclubs.
Venue ●●●● Value ●●●○

Premiere, The

Location → Hyatt Regency · Deira | **209 1333**
Hours → 22:00 - 03:00
Web/email → hyattbus@emirates.net.ae | **Map Ref →** 8-D2

200

Stuck with a tired 80's feel and severe decor scarcely altered in 15 years, this bar/club may have seen better days. Still extremely popular with the late night singles crowd, who at nearly 01:00 are clearly more interested in 'people watching' than in dancing. The well-situated, central dance floor sees little use until very late. Patrons prefer to gather around the edges of the room chatting and drinking. Couples and groups are discouraged as seating is limited, and the ambience hungry.
Venue ●●○○ Value ●○○○

Nightclubs

Going Out

Rockafellas

Location → Regal Plaza Hotel · Bur Dubai | **355 6633**
Hours → 20:00 - 23:00
Web/email → regaldxb@emirates.net.ae   **Map Ref** → 8-A4

Rockafellas provides a typical nightclub atmosphere with low lights, music (DJs and live bands) and basic decorations. The two bars offer an extensive drink menu and quick service. The food is a mix of Arabic and Mexican snacks, and Cajun food and salads. While popular as a night club venue, the dining service is slow and the food basic and not well prepared – making Rockafellas a great place for fun and drinks but not for dining out.

Venue ●●○○ Value ●●○○

Rocky's Café

Location → Regent Palace Hotel · Bur Dubai | **396 3888**
Hours → 19:00 - 03:00
Web/email → rameedex@emirates.net.ae   **Map Ref** → 11-A1

Hollywood themed and glitzy, this venue is dominated by a huge stage and dance floor upon which nightly competitions (karaoke, Miss Filipino UAE, Mr Calendar Man, etc) and live music run. TV screens replay movie action, while deeper inside the café are pool tables. Spirits, beer and cocktails are on offer, along with a limited selection of oriental dishes on the menu, and no desserts. This is a good place to party, particularly given the warm Asian hospitality.

Venue ●●●○ Value ●●○○

Savage Garden

Location → Capitol Hotel · Al Satwa | **346 0111**
Hours → 18:00 - 03:00
Web/email → caphotel@emirates.net.ae   **Map Ref** → 7-A2

It may become Savage Garden late at night, but early it is quite tame. Though a limited menu, there are interesting choices of Mexican and Chilean food, some quite pricey. Excellent starters set high standards. Try the prawn, spinach and sesame salad or sautéed mushrooms to whet your appetite, but choose carefully from the mains and don't bother with dessert. Service is adequate in this jungle setting with nightly salsa lessons. A live band and DJ after 22:00 ensures a lively, buzzing atmosphere – open till 03:00.

Venue ●●○○ Value ●○○○

Tangerine

Location → Fairmont Hotel · Shk Zayed Rd | **332 5555**
Hours → 20:00 - 03:00
Web/email → www.fairmont.com   **Map Ref** → 9-E1

This rich red underworld maintains exclusivity with strict bouncers and stiffer prices. Torch-glow lit and A/C draught, the heavy-set Arabic decor invokes cavernous comfort. Bar staff proffer superior beverages and can tailor rich cocktails to individual tastes. Lounge over cushion-clad sofas and behind curtained alcoves or sway to insistent music, strafed by blobs of light. The guest-list door policy and very high prices should ensure that Tangerine attract a certain crowd – for a while at least.

Venue ●●●○ Value ●○○○

Arabic Nightclubs

Other options → **Dinner Cruises [p.379]**
Belly Dancing [p.287]

Abaya Nightclub

Location → Dubai Park · Jct 5, Shk Zayed Rd | **399 2222**
Hours → 10:00 - 03:00
Web/email → dxbprkht@emirates.net.ae   **Map Ref** → 3-A3

Families dine early, but after 22:30, the entertainment begins, and from then on the majority of the customers are Arab men. Decent food, attentive waiters and full-on entertainment have built the club a regular clientele, despite the Dhs.150 cover charge (includes mezze and a full menu) and high drink prices. Keep on drinking, sit back and enjoy a succession of singers and dancers backed by a four-piece band. The madness will either drive you out or draw you in, but you certainly can't ignore it.

Venue ●●○○ Value ●●○○

Arabic Nightclubs
Nightclubs
On The Town

Amnesia

Location → Dubai Park · Jct 5, Shk Zayed Rd
Hours → 20:00 - 02:00
Web/email → www.dubaiparkhotel.com

399 2222

Map Ref → 3-A3

  150

Previously called Atlantis, this young, happening place offers reasonably priced drinks and a limited Arabic menu, but people are here more to dance, chill out and meet other singles. The door policy is very strict, though more so for men than women. A singer accompanied by a keyboard player, and DJ later on, entertain with popular Arabic songs, attracting people onto the small central dance floor. The gallery area at bar level is good for people watching.

Venue ●●○○ Value ●●○○

El Khan

Location → Ramada Continental · Al Hamriya
Hours → 20:00 - 03:00
Web/email → ramadadb@emirates.net.ae

266 2666

Map Ref → 12-B4

100

A lively, very late night venue, El Khan offers an evening with a distinct Arabic flavour. From the ageing furnishings to the varied shisha, this nightclub caters to a specific clientele. An Arabic band and singer entertain. The club has a limited menu featuring Lebanese style mixed grills and mezze, including a variety of beverages at very premium prices. Being both expensive and well below average in quality, the cuisine is definitely not the draw.

Venue ●○○○ Value ●●○○

Layalina

Location → Metropolitan · Jct 2, Shk Zayed Rd
Hours → 22:30 - 03:00 Closed Fri
Web/email → methotel@emirates.net.ae

343 0000

Map Ref → 5-C4

   150

Layalina nightclub purports to provide traditional Arabic culture – at a price. The club doesn't open until 22:30, and the band plays familiar Arabic songs using traditional and modern instruments. As the evening develops, the belly dancer begins to wriggle. The food and menu are great, as they should be for such high prices, with a strong range of traditional cuisine. Service is helpful and courteous – unlike in most clubs where you're lucky to get a smile with your change.

> *Entrance fees:* Dhs.178 per person weekdays, Dhs.205 at weekends.

Venue ●●○○ Value ●○○○

ENTERTAINMENT

Cinemas

Other options → **Theatre [p.417]**

A trip to the cinema is one of the most popular forms of entertainment in the Emirates and movie buffs here are reasonably well catered for, although showings are generally limited to the latest Arabic, Bollywood or Hollywood releases. At present there are four cinemas in Dubai and three in Sharjah showing English language films, with another few showing Indian and Arabic films, including the unique Rex Drive-In cinema at the Mirdif Interchange, Airport Road.

Most of the newer cinemas are multi-screen mega sites, while the older cinemas tend to be larger, with fewer screens and a traditional, crowded cinema atmosphere.

Dubai has seen an explosion in the number of screens available over the past couple of years, with the opening of an twelve screen complex near Wafi City and another eleven screen outlet as part of Deira City Centre Mall. These two sites alone have a capacity of 6,000 seats. These will be added to with multi screen cinemas as part of the expansion of both Al Ghurair City and BurJuman Centre. All sites offer a wider range of all the latest Arabic, Asian and Western films.

Cinema timings can be found in the *Weekly Explorer (Dubai)* – contact Explorer Publishing if you would like to register as a free subscriber. Alternatively, timings are in the daily newspapers, as well as in an entertainment special in the Gulf News every Wednesday.

Release dates vary considerably, with new Western films reaching the UAE anything from four weeks to a year after release in the USA. New movies are released every Wednesday. Films often don't hang around for too long, so if there's something you really want to see, don't delay too much or it will be gone!

The cinemas tend to be cold, so make sure you take a sweater. During the weekends, there are extra shows at midnight or 01:00 – check the press for details. Tickets can be reserved, but usually have to be collected an hour before the show and sales are cash only. With so many screens around now, you will often find cinemas half empty, except for the first couple of days after the release of an eagerly-awaited blockbuster.

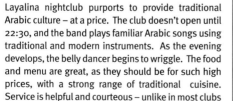

Cinemas

Dubai Cinemas

Name	Tel No.	Map	Location	No. of Languages	Screens	Prices Normal	Special
Al Nasr	337 4353	10-E3	Nr Al Nasr Leisureland	M, T	1	15.00	20.00
Al Massa	343 8383	5-C4	Metroplex	A, E	8	25.00	30.00
Century Cinemas	349 9773	5-E1	Mercato Mall	A, E, H	7	30.00	-
CineStar	294 9000	14-D1	Deira City Centre	A, E, H	11	30.00	40.00
Deira	222 3551	11-D1	Deira	M, T	1	15.00	20.00
Dubai	266 0632	12-A3	Deira	H	1	15.00	20.00
Galleria	209 6469/70	8-D2	Hyatt Regency	H	2	20.00	-
Grand Cineplex	324 2000	13-D3	Nr DEWA / Grand Hyatt	A, E	12	25.00	30.00
Lamcy	336 8808	10-D4	Lamcy Plaza	H	2	20.00	-
Plaza	393 9966	8-A2	Bur Dubai	H	1	15.00	20.00
Rex Drive-In	288 6447	Overview	Madinat Badr	H	1	15.00	-
Strand	396 1644	11-A2	Al Karama	H	1	15.00	20.00

Key: A = Arabic; E = English; H = Hindi; M = Malayalam; T= Tamil

Comedy

Other options → **Theatre [p.416]**

The regular comedy scene in Dubai is unfortunately limited, however, there are regular visits from the Laughter Factory and Jongleurs, as well as the occasional comical theatre production or one-off event. Comedy shows tend to be aimed at the British population; other nationalities may not find the sense of humour as funny as the Brits in the audience do.

Events are often promoted only a short time before they actually take place, so keep your ears to the ground for what's coming up.

Laughter Factory, The	
Location → Hyatt Regency · Deira	**355 1862**
Hours → Check press for dates	
Web/email → www.dubai.hyatt.com	**Map Ref** → 8-D2

Based on the successful concept of 'alternative' comedy (meaning an alternative to sexist and racist jokes), this option is a great opportunity to see established as well as up-and-coming talent. Acts from the UK; each comedian selected to suit the Middle East expat market. The unique feature is that it offers three different styles of comedy in one show, providing a broad spectrum of humour. Call for details as shows run bi-monthly and may have differing timings or pricings.

Concerts

Throughout the year, Dubai hosts a variety of concerts and festivals, with visits from international artists, bands and musicians. Most events are held in the winter, as well as during the Dubai Shopping Festival and international sporting events. Ticket prices are around the same, or a bit higher, than you would expect to pay elsewhere.

There's no regular calendar of events for music lovers, so for details of what's going on, check out the *Weekly Explorer (Dubai)* – contact Explorer Publishing if you would like to register as a free subscriber. You can also check the daily press, magazines, and listen for announcements and adverts on the radio. Promoters may be able to supply information on events, but usually no long-term programmes exist, and details are only available about a month in advance. Tickets go on sale at the venues and through other outlets, such as Virgin Megastore. Tickets for some concerts can also be purchased online at www.ibuytickets.com or www.itptickets.com.

Classical Concerts

There is only a small number of classical music events held each year in the city. Most notably, the Crowne Plaza Hotel hosts visiting orchestras, musicians and singers from all over the world. Other venues have performances by musical groups or artistes, mainly during special events such as the gala dinners of large trade exhibitions.

In addition to musicians of an international stature, some hotels have a lobby musician or restaurant

www.factoryproduct.com

Factory Productions
04 355 1862
Music
Comedy
Parties
Djs

00% entertainment

that feature classical accompaniment from a pianist. These are often of an excellent standard.

Classical Concert Venues

Classical Concert Venues	
Ajman Kempinski Resort Hotel	06 745 1555
Al Bustan Rotana Hotel	282 0000
Crowne Plaza Hotel	331 1111
Dubai Creek Golf & Yacht Club	295 6000
Nad Al Sheba Club	336 3666
Ritz-Carlton Hotel	399 4000
Sheraton Hotel & Towers	228 1111

Dance Events

Dubai is building itself a surprisingly good club scene, offering some great nights on a fairly regular basis. Different themed nights are organised by international promoters at various clubs around the city, as well as special events like the 'In The Mix' and Ministry of Sound events, which bring in international DJ's for epic line-ups and non-stop action. Previous names include Ravin, Sash!, Grooverider, Ian Van Dhal, Judge Jules, Alister Whitehead, Claude Challe, and Roger Sanchez.

Like many events in Dubai, dance events are often announced at short notice, and while the main action is widely publicised, other events can sometimes be promoted in a more underground sort of way.

Pop Concerts

Cynics could say that Dubai, and the Gulf in general, are only honoured by visits from Western bands that are 'on their way down'. However, recently there have been improvements in the standard of performer. Over the last few years, 'big' names have included Elton John, Jamiroquai, Deep Purple, Roger Waters, UB40, Bryan Adams, Rod Stewart, Tom Jones, Sting, Maxi Priest, and James Brown.

Dance Event Organisers

Dance Event Organisers	
Atlantis	399 2222
Aviation Club	282 4122
Dubai International Marine Club	399 5777
Dubai Watersports Association	324 1031
Planetarium	324 0072

Concerts are usually held at venues such as Dubai Tennis Stadium, Irish Village and the Dubai International Marine Club (DIMC). Smaller venues have hosted the likes of Bad Manners or Leo Sayer, as well as Abba or Madness tribute bands. Good fun, if not exactly cutting edge stuff.

For Asian and Arabic music lovers, there is a range of concerts and musical programmes held in venues like Al Nasr Leisureland and DIMC. These feature some of the biggest names from the Middle East, India, Pakistan and Sri Lanka.

See also: Nightclubs.

Concert / Dance Event Venues

Concert / Dance Event Venues	
Al Nasr Leisureland	337 1234
Aviation Club, Tennis Stadium	282 4122
Crowne Plaza	331 1111
Cyclone	336 9991
Dubai Country Club	333 1155
Dubai Creek Golf & Yacht Club	295 6000
Dubai International Marine Club	399 3333
Hard Rock Cafe	399 2888
Hyatt Regency Hotel	209 1234
Irish Village	282 4750
Jumeirah Beach Club	344 5333
Metropolitan Hotel	343 0000
Rock Bottom Cafe	396 3888
Virgin Megastore (for tickets only)	295 8955

Fashion Shows

Complementing Dubai's reputation as one of the best places to shop for clothes in the Middle East, there are regular fashion shows in Dubai, though very little is arranged on a long term basis. Check out the *Weekly Explorer* or keep an eye out in hotels, local newspapers, etc, for what's happening in the month to come. During the Dubai Shopping Festival, there are up to 30 fashion shows held in hotels and shopping malls; the press during the Festival carries information on dates and times.

Theatre

Other options → Drama Groups [p.281]
Cinemas [p.412]

The theatre scene in Dubai is rather limited, with fans relying chiefly on touring companies, and the occasional amateur dramatics performance. One regular highlight is the British Airways Playhouse, which tours the world.

The amateur theatre scene always welcomes new members, either on stage or behind the scenes. There are also the occasional murder mystery dinners where you are encouraged to display your thespian skills by being part of the performance.

Good news for theatre lovers: the first community theatre for amateur and professionals groups is due to be built in Dubai in 2003. It will be located near Nad Al Sheba with tiered and gallery seating for 500.

Going Out | Concerts | Theatre

Found out-of-date information?

Then let us know!

Whether it's an idea, a correction, an opinion or simply a recommendation – we want to hear from you. Log on and become part of the Explorer Community – let your opinions be heard, viewed, compiled and printed...

www.explorer-publishing.com

Explorer Publishing & Distribution • Dubai Media City • Building 2 • Office 502 • PO Box 34275 • Dubai • UAE
Phone (+971 4) 391 8060 Fax 391 8062 Email info@explorer-publishing.com Web www.explorer-publishing.com

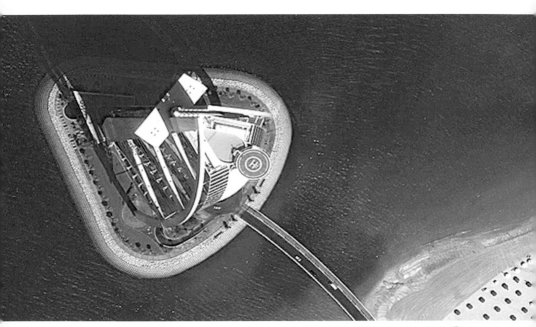

Maps

EXPLORER

Maps

Map Overview

The maps in this section are all colour aerial photographs taken in late 2002 by the QuickBird satellite. All of these aerial images have been digitally rectified and are called "orthoimages".

To make it easy to find places on the maps, they have all been orientated parallel to Dubai's coastline, rather than the customary north orientation. While the overview map on this page is at a scale of approximately 1:180,000 (1cm = 1.8km), all other maps range from 1:12,000 (1cm = 120m) to 1:48,000 (1cm = 480m).

To also help you locate your destination etc, we have superimposed additional information such as main roads, roundabouts, and landmarks on the maps. Many places listed throughout the Dubai Explorer also have a map reference listed alongside so you can know precisely where you need to go (or what you need to tell the taxi driver).

Map Legend

The colours for each landmark, or point of interest are colour coded to tie in with the most relevant section. For example, all hotels follow the General

DIGITALGLOBE

MAPS geosystems

Information colour, likewise any restaurants that appear under the Going Out section follow that colour. In addition, the pull out map has its own legend explained on the map.

QuickBird, Maps & Photographic Images

The QuickBird satellite was launched in October 2001 and is operated by DigitalGlobe™, a private company based in Colorado (USA). Today, DigitalGlobe's QuickBird satellite provides the highest resolution, largest swath width and largest

on-board storage of any currently available or planned commercial satellite.

MAPS geosystems are the Digital Globe Master resellers for the Middle East, West, Central and Eastern Africa. They also provide services for data processing and application development. For more information on QuickBird, email quickbird@maps-geosystems.com. For additional information on other photographic maps, aerial enlargements or detailed maps in general, please contact MAPS geosystems (06 572 5411).

Intro

Maps

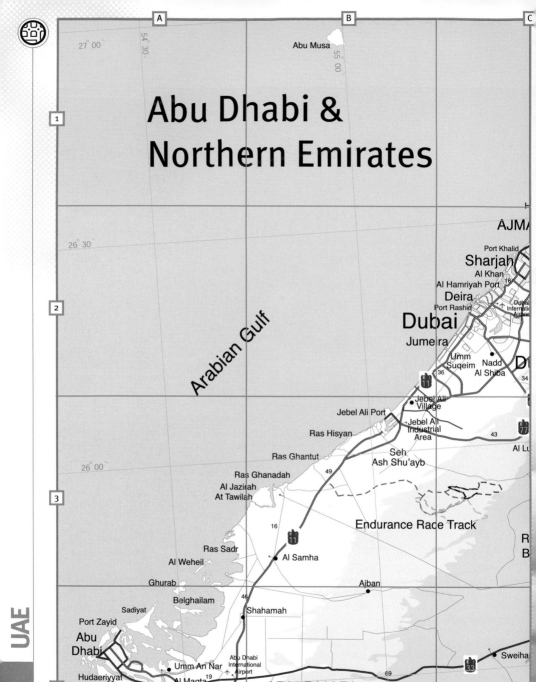

Abu Dhabi &
Northern Emirates

Abu Musa

Arabian Gulf

AJMA

Port Khalid
Sharjah
Al Khan
Al Hamriyah Port
Deira
Port Rashid
Dubai Internatio Airport
Dubai
Jumeira

Umm Suqeim
Nadd Al Shiba
D

Jebel Ali Village
Jebel Ali Port
Jebel Ali Industrial Area
Ras Hisyan
Seh Ash Shu'ayb
Al Lu

Ras Ghantut
49
Ras Ghanadah
Al Jazirah At Tawilah

Endurance Race Track

R B

16
Al Samha

Ras Sadr
Al Weheil
Ghurab

Aiban

Belghailam
Sadiyat
46
Shahamah

Port Zayid
Abu Dhabi
Umm An Nar
Al Magta
19
Abu Dhabi International Airport
69
Sweiha

Hudaeriyyat
Feteisi
Musaffah

ABU DHABI

UNITED ARAB EMIRATES

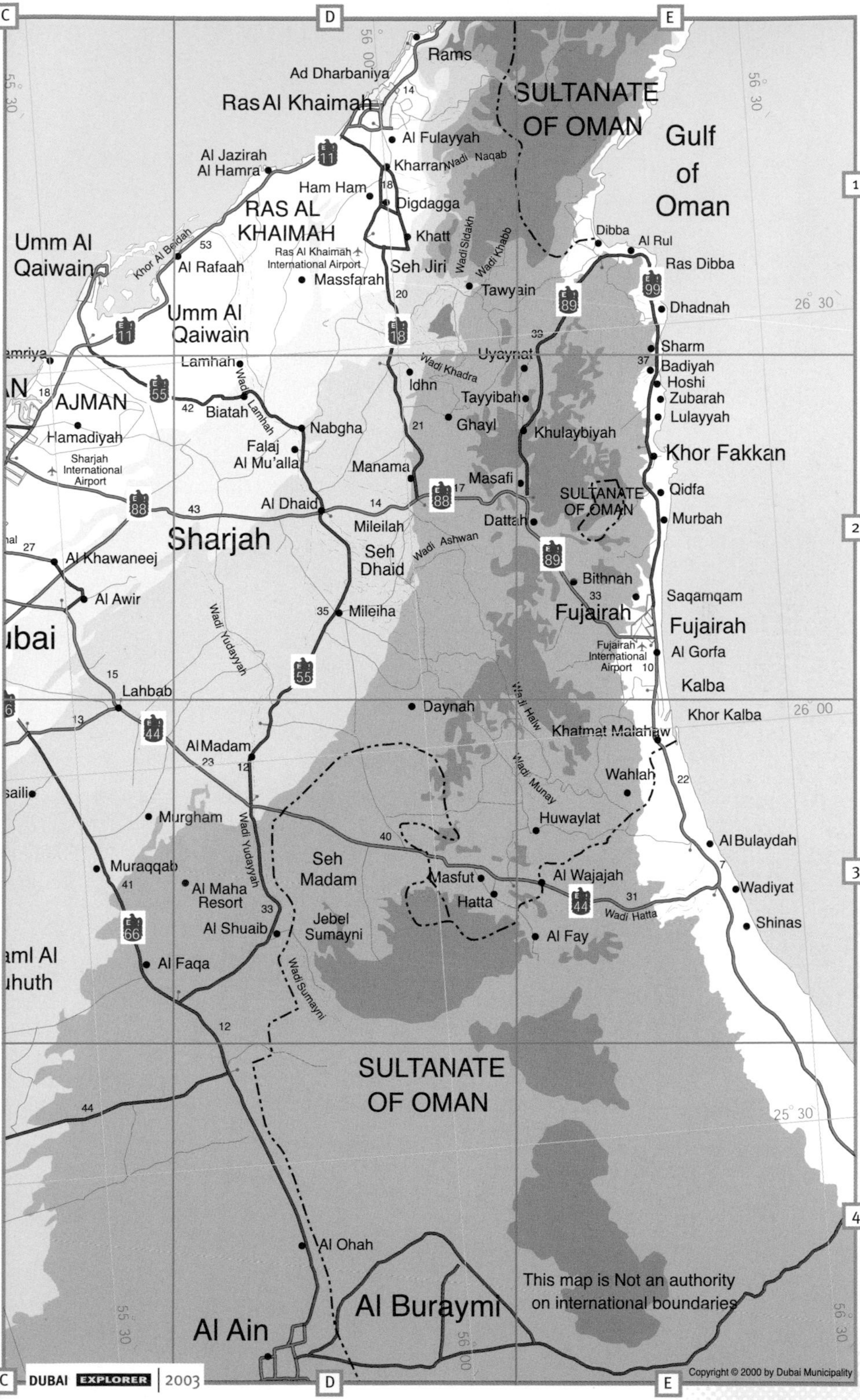
C
D
E
1
2
3
4
Rams
Ad Dharbaniya
Ras Al Khaimah
Al Fulayyah
Al Jazirah
Al Hamra
Kharran
Wadi Naqab
Ham Ham
Digdagga
RAS AL
KHAIMAH
Khatt
Ras Al Khaimah International Airport
Seh Jiri
Wadi Sidakh
Wadi Khabb
Massfarah
Tawyain
Khor Al Beidah
Al Rafaah
Umm Al
Qaiwain
Umm Al
Qaiwain
SULTANATE
OF OMAN
Gulf
of
Oman
Dibba
Al Rul
Ras Dibba
Dhadnah
Sharm
Badiyah
Hoshi
Zubarah
Lulayyah
Khor Fakkan
Qidfa
Murbah
Lamhah
Wadi Lamhah
Uyaynat
Wadi Khadra
Idhn
Tayyibah
Ghayl
Khulaybiyah
AJMAN
Biatah
Nabgha
Hamadiyah
Falaj
Al Mu'alla
Manama
Masafi
Sharjah
International
Airport
SULTANATE
OF OMAN
Al Dhaid
Mileilah
Dattah
Sharjah
Seh
Dhaid
Wadi Ashwan
Al Khawaneej
Bithnah
Saqamqam
Al Awir
Mileiha
Fujairah
Fujairah
Wadi Yudayyah
Fujairah International Airport
Al Gorfa
Kalba
Lahbab
Daynah
Wadi Halw
Khor Kalba
Khatmat Malahaw
Al Madam
Wahlah
Wadi Munay
Murgham
Huwaylat
Al Bulaydah
Wadi Yudayyah
Seh
Madam
Muraqqab
Masfut
Al Wajajah
Wadiyat
Al Maha
Resort
Hatta
Wadi Hatta
Shinas
Jebel
Sumayni
Al Shuaib
Al Fay
Al Faqa
Wadi Sumayni
SULTANATE
OF OMAN
Al Ohah
This map is Not an authority
on international boundaries
Al Buraymi
Al Ain
Copyright © 2000 by Dubai Municipality

Jebel Ali Beach

Jebel Ali Hotel & Golf Resort

Dubai Kart Club

Jebel Ali Shooting Club

Jebel Ali Free Zone

Interchange No-9

Interchange No-8

1

Maps

DIGITALGLOBE

D   E

Arabian Gulf

1

2

2

DUBAL

Interchange
No - 6

Interchange
No - 7

Jebel Ali Village

3

2

4

1

Maps

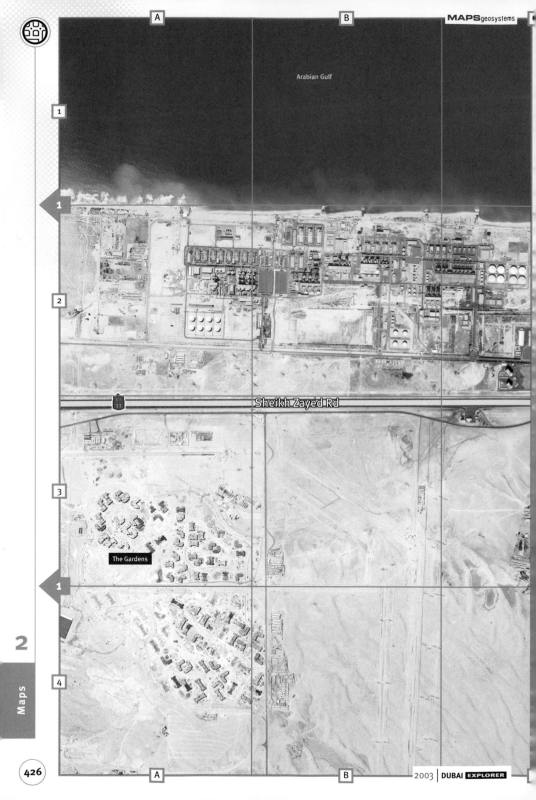

Arabian Gulf

Sheikh Zayed Rd

The Gardens

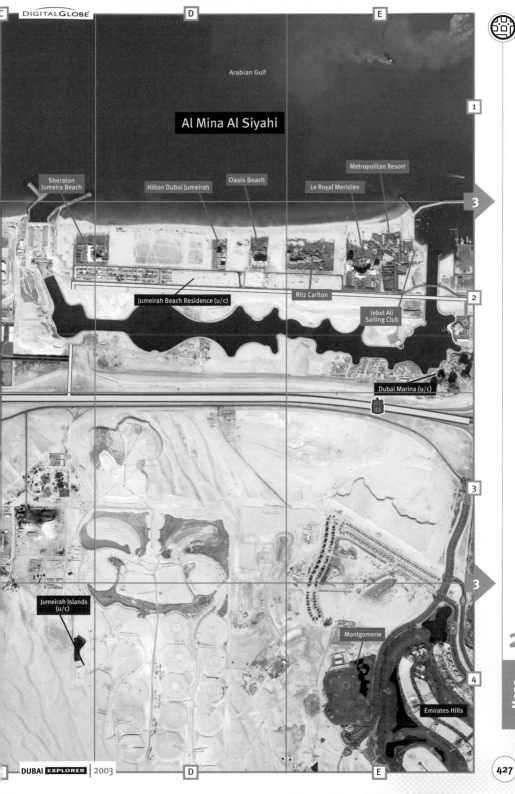

DIGITALGLOBE

Arabian Gulf

Al Mina Al Siyahi

Metropolitan Resort

Sheraton
Jumeira Beach

Hilton Dubai Jumeirah

Oasis Beach

Le Royal Meridien

Jumeirah Beach Residence (u/c)

Ritz Carlton

Jebel Ali
Sailing Club

Dubai Marina (u/c)

Jumeirah Islands
(u/c)

Montgomerie

Emirates Hills

Maps

2

427

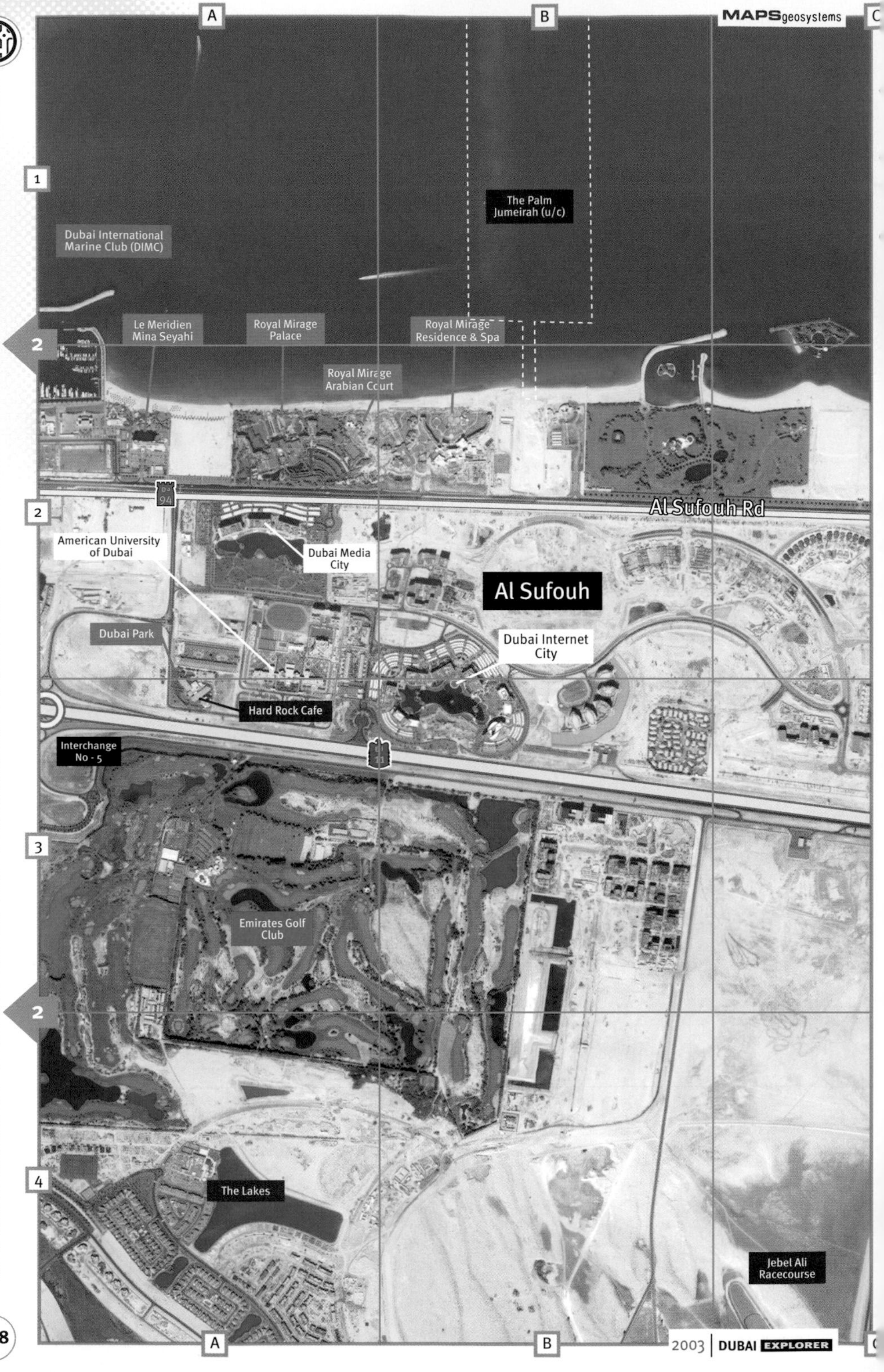

1

The Palm
Jumeirah (u/c)

Dubai International
Marine Club (DIMC)

2

Le Meridien
Mina Seyahi

Royal Mirage
Palace

Royal Mirage
Residence & Spa

Royal Mirage
Arabian Court

Al Sufouh Rd

2

9A

American University
of Dubai

Dubai Media
City

Al Sufouh

Dubai Park

Dubai Internet
City

Hard Rock Cafe

Interchange
No - 5

3

Emirates Golf
Club

2

3

Maps

4

The Lakes

Jebel Ali
Racecourse

C   D   E

1

4

2

Dubai College

Al Sufouh

3

Desert Springs Village

Al Barshaa

11

4

Souk Al Nakheel
(u/c)

3

Maps

4

D   E

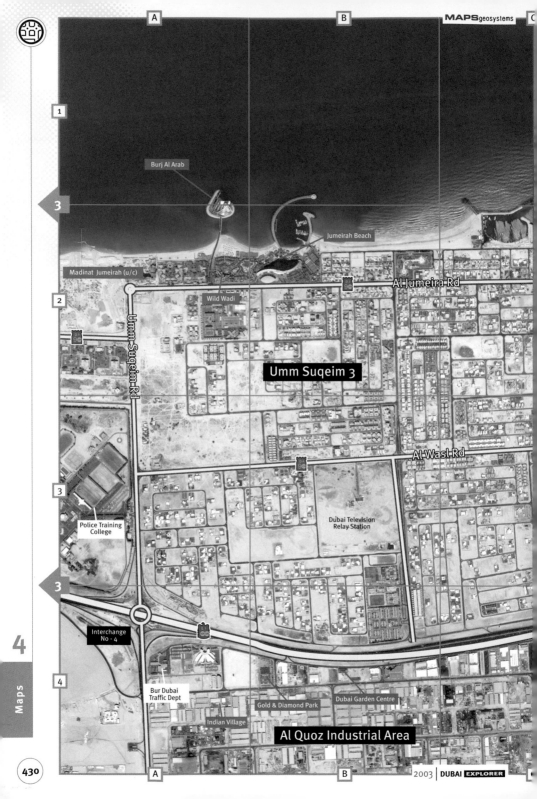

A

B

C

1

Burj Al Arab

3

Jumeirah Beach

Madinat Jumeirah (u/c)

Al Jumeira Rd

2

Wild Wadi

Umm Suqeim Rd

Umm Suqeim 3

Al Wasl Rd

3

Police Training
College

Dubai Television
Relay Station

3

Interchange
No - 4

Bur Dubai
Traffic Dept

4

Indian Village

Gold & Diamond Park

Dubai Garden Centre

Al Quoz Industrial Area

A

B

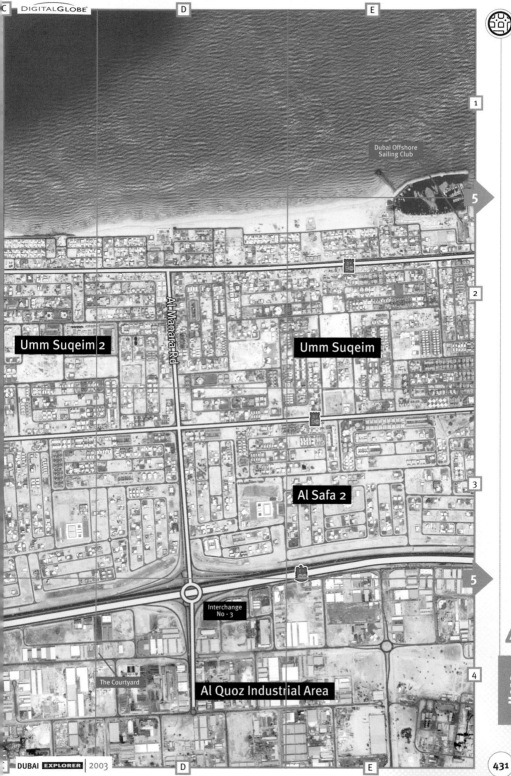

C D E

1

5

Dubai Offshore
Sailing Club

2

Al Manara Rd

Umm Suqeim 2

Umm Suqeim

Al Safa 2

3

5

Interchange
No - 3

The Courtyard

Al Quoz Industrial Area

4

Maps

D E

1

4

D4
94

2

Jumeira 3

Union Co-op / Choithram

D7
92

Spinneys Centre   Park N Shop

Al Safa

Safa Park

3

Jumeira English
Speaking School

11

4

Ace Hardware

Interchange
No - 2

Metroplex
Cinema

Oasis Center

Muscat Rd

5

Maps

4

Al Quoz

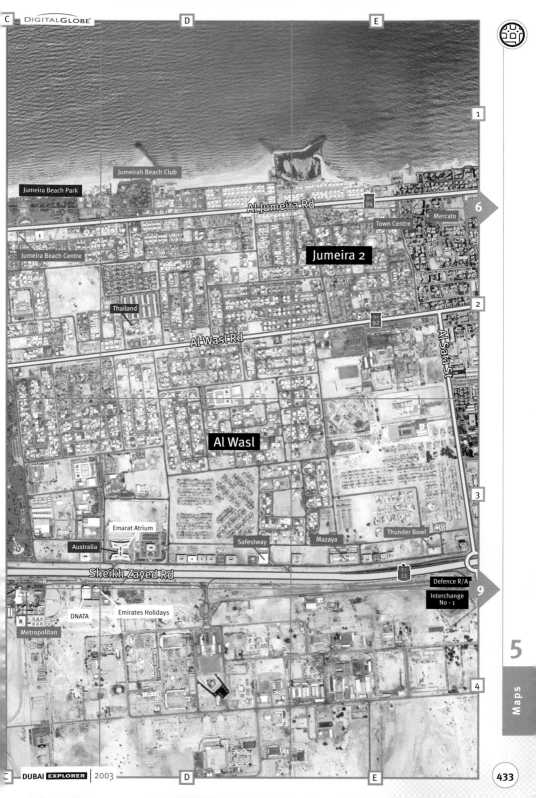

1

Jumeirah Beach Club

Jumeira Beach Park

Al Jumeira Rd   D4 94

6

Town Centre   Mercato

Jumeira Beach Centre

Jumeira 2

Thailand

2

Al Wasl Rd   D4 92

Al Safa St

Al Wasl

3

Emarat Atrium

Australia

Safestway   Mazaya   Thunder Bowl

Sheikh Zayed Rd   E1 11

Defence R/A

9

Interchange No - 1

DNATA   Emirates Holidays

Metropolitan

4

5

Maps

A

B

C

1

5

2

Dubai International
Art Centre

Al Jumeira Rd

Beach Centre

Century Plaza

Dubai Zoo

Jumeirah Plaza

Jumeira

3

American School

Al Wasl Rd

5

Al Wasl

6

Maps

4

Al Satwa Rd

A

9

B

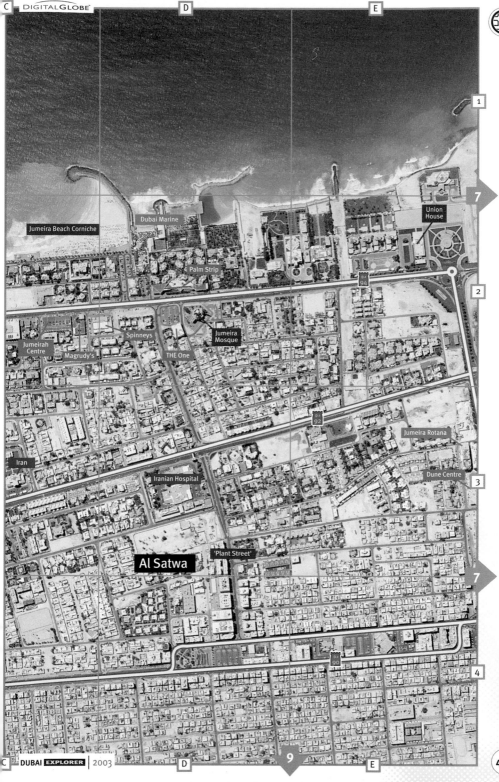

DIGITALGLOBE

1

7

Union House

Jumeira Beach Corniche

Dubai Marine

Palm Strip

2

Jumeirah Centre

Spinneys

Jumeira Mosque

Magrudy's

THE One

Jumeira Rotana

Iran

Iranian Hospital

Dune Centre

3

Al Satwa

'Plant Street'

7

4

6

Port Rashid

Dubai Port Police
Head Quarters

Capitol

Al Mina

Sri Lanka

Al-Adhid

Al Dhiyafah

Al Mankhool

Al Satwa RA

Al Hana Centre

Rydges Plaza

Al Satwa East

Al-Adhid

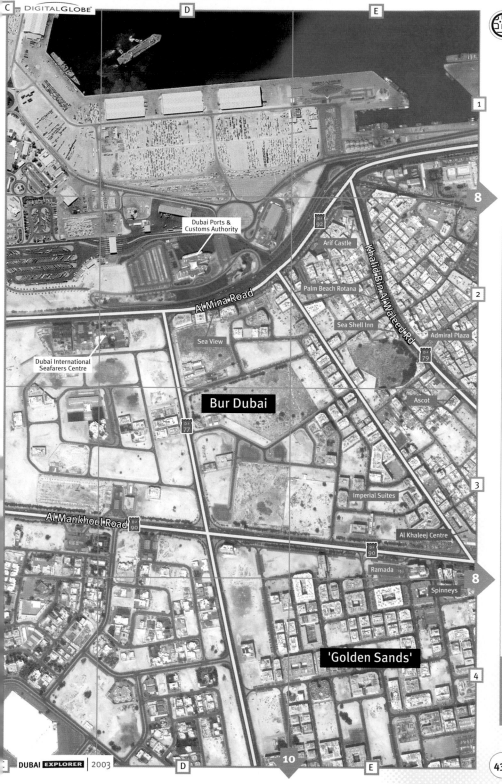

C D E

1

8

Dubai Ports & Customs Authority

Arif Castle

Palm Beach Rotana

Khalid Bin Al Waleed Rd

Sea Shell Inn

2

Admiral Plaza

Al Mina Road

Sea View

Dubai International Seafarers Centre

Bur Dubai

Ascot

3

Imperial Suites

Al Mankhool Road

Al Khaleej Centre

Ramada

8

Spinneys

'Golden Sands'

4

7

Maps

D E

10

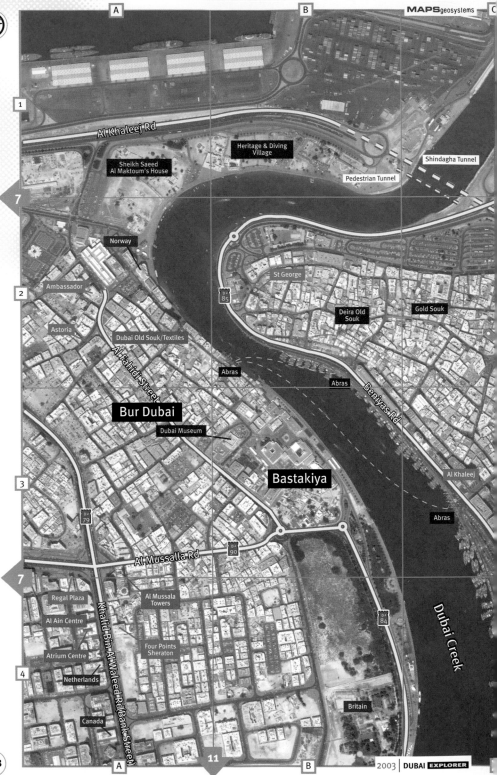

A · B · C

1 · 2 · 3 · 4

7 · 7

8

Maps

Al Khaleej Rd

Heritage & Diving Village

Sheikh Saeed Al Maktoum's House

Pedestrian Tunnel

Shindagha Tunnel

Norway

St George

Ambassador

Deira Old Souk

Gold Souk

Astoria

Dubai Old Souk/Textiles

Al Fahidi Street

Bur Dubai

Abras

Abras

Beniyas Rd

Dubai Museum

Bastakiya

Al Khaleej

Abras

Al Mussalla Rd

Regal Plaza

Al Mussala Towers

Al Ain Centre

Khalid Bin Al Waleed Rd (Bank Street)

Atrium Centre

Four Points Sheraton

Dubai Creek

Netherlands

Canada

Britain

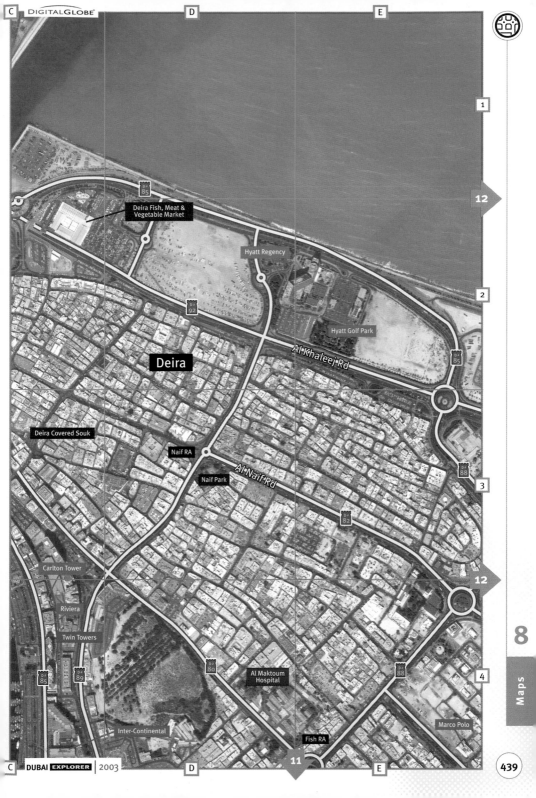

Deira Fish, Meat & Vegetable Market

Hyatt Regency

Hyatt Golf Park

Al-Khaleej-Rd

Deira

Deira Covered Souk

Naif RA

Naif Park

Al-Naif-Rd

Carlton Tower

Riviera

Twin Towers

Al Maktoum Hospital

Inter-Continental

Marco Polo

Fish RA

8

Maps

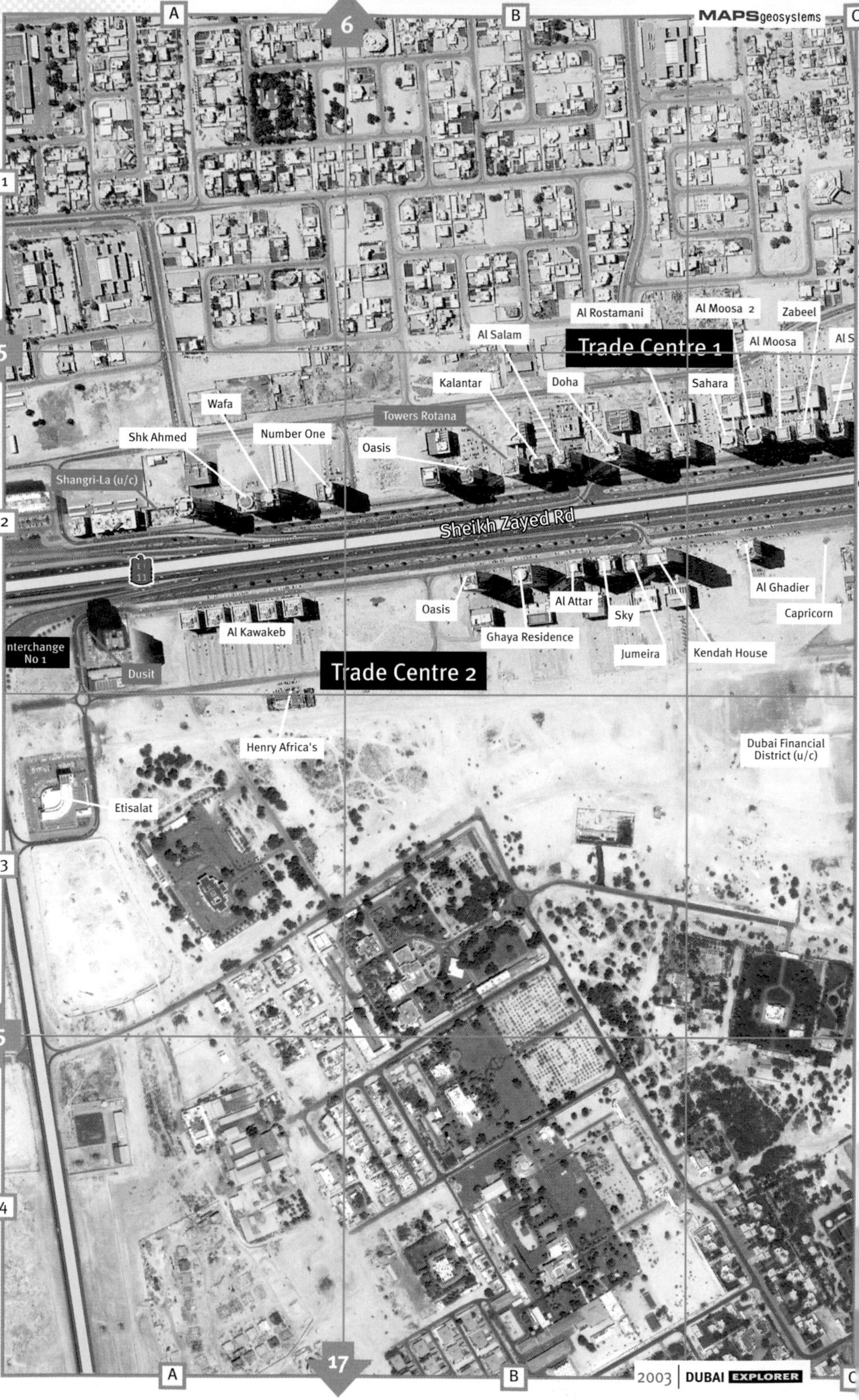

A   6   B   C

1

Al Rostamani
Al Moosa 2   Zabeel
Al Salam
Al Moosa
Trade Centre 1   Al S
5
Kalantar   Doha   Sahara
Wafa   Towers Rotana
Shk Ahmed   Number One   Oasis
Shangri-La (u/c)
2   Sheikh Zayed Rd

Al Ghadier
Oasis   Capricorn
Al Attar   Sky
Al Kawakeb   Ghaya Residence   Kendah House
Interchange   Jumeira
No 1   Dusit   Trade Centre 2

Henry Africa's   Dubai Financial
District (u/c)
Etisalat

3

5

9

Maps

4

A   17   B   C

Al Satwa

Khalid Al Attaar

City 2

White Swan

API World Tower

Fairmont

Safa

Al Wasl

City

Al Durrah

Saeed

White Crowne

France

Crowne Plaza

Sheikh Zayed Road

Dubai World Trade Centre

Trade Centre Apartments

Italy | Japan
Switzerland | USA

The Tower

Dubai International
Exhibition Centre

Emirates Towers

Dubai International
Conference Centre (u/c)

Emirates Towers
Office

Ibis (u/c)

Novotel (u/c)

6

D

E

1

10

2

3

10

4

9

Maps

D

17

E

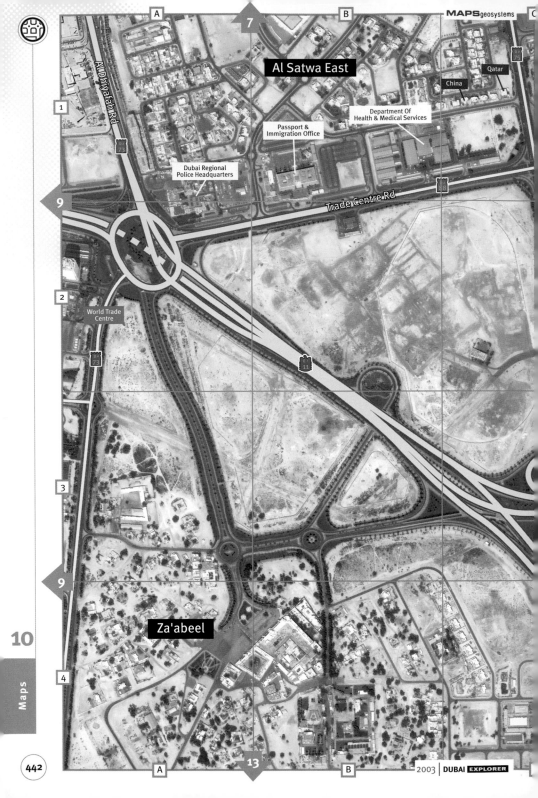

Al Satwa East

Al Dhiyafah Rd

China

Qatar

Department Of
Health & Medical Services

Passport &
Immigration Office

Dubai Regional
Police Headquarters

Trade Centre Rd

World Trade
Centre

Za'abeel

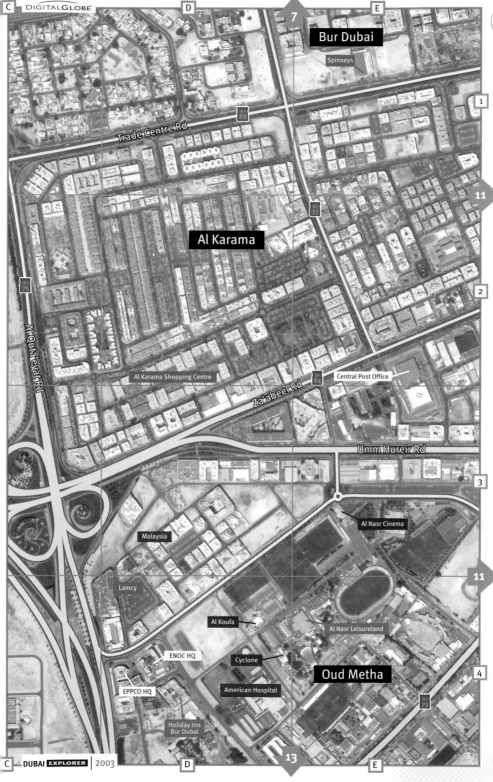

Bur Dubai

Spinneys

1

Trade Centre Rd

88

11

Al Karama

2

75

Al Karama Shopping Centre

Za'abeel Rd

84

Central Post Office

Umm Hureir Rd

3

Al Nasr Cinema

Malaysia

11

Lamcy

Al Koufa

Al Nasr Leisureland

ENOC HQ

Cyclone

Oud Metha

4

EPPCO HQ

American Hospital

79

Holiday Inn
Bur Dubai

10

Maps

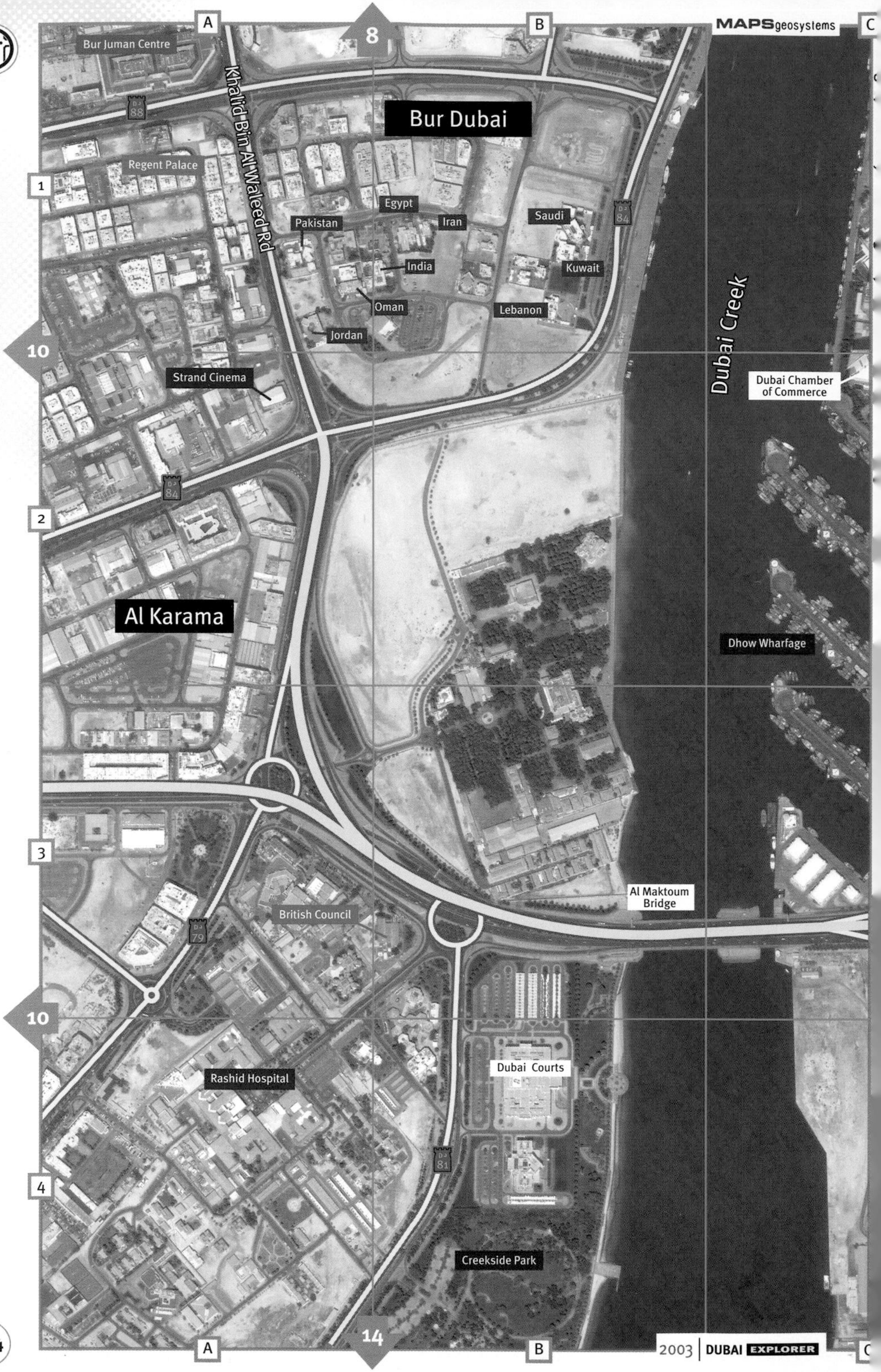

MAPSgeosystems

8

Bur Juman Centre

Khalid Bin Al Waleed Rd

Bur Dubai

Regent Palace

1

Egypt

Pakistan

Iran

Saudi

India

Kuwait

Oman

Lebanon

Jordan

10

Strand Cinema

Dubai Creek

Dubai Chamber
of Commerce

2

Al Karama

Dhow Wharfage

3

British Council

Al Maktoum
Bridge

10

Rashid Hospital

Dubai Courts

11

Maps

4

Creekside Park

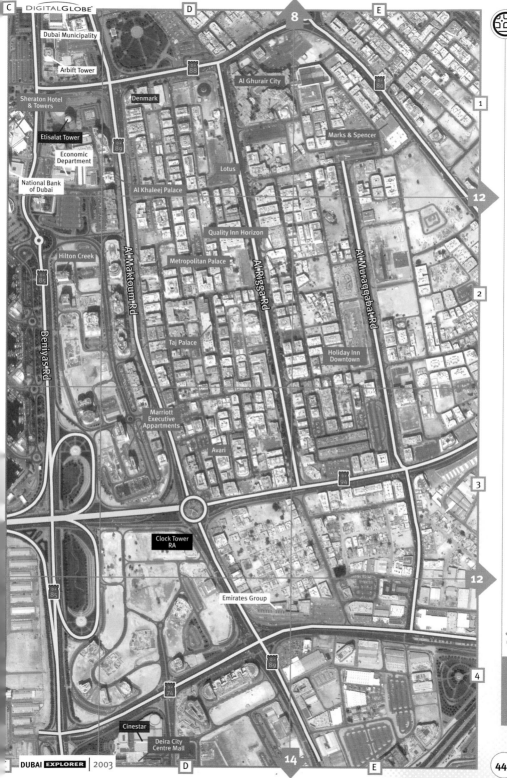

DIGITALGLOBE

Dubai Municipality

Arbift Tower

Al Ghurair City

1

Sheraton Hotel & Towers

Denmark

Marks & Spencer

Etisalat Tower

Economic Department

Lotus

12

National Bank of Dubai

Al Khaleej Palace

Quality Inn Horizon

Hilton Creek

Metropolitan Palace

2

Al-Maktoum-Rd

Al-Rigga-Rd

Al-Muraqqabat-Rd

Taj Palace

Holiday Inn Downtown

Beniyas-Rd

Marriott Executive Appartments

Avari

3

Clock Tower RA

12

Emirates Group

11

4

Cinestar

Deira City Centre Mall

MAPSgeosystems

1

8

Fruit & Vegetable Market

Al Khaleej Rd

Al Baraha Hospital (Kuwait)

New Dubai Hospital

2

92

Al Hamriya

Al Mateena Street

Sheraton Deira

Al Rasheed Rd

3

Renaissance

JW Marriott

Dubai Cinema

Hor Al Anz

Al Hamriya Shopping Centre

11

Hamarain Centre

Abu Hail Rd

12

Salah Al Din Rd

Ramada Continental

4

82

Al Ittihad Rd

Galadari Interchange

Police HQ

15

Airport Terminal - 2

Maps

C

D

E

1

Al Hamriya Port

Al Mamzar

Al Mamzar
Beach Park

2

Khor Al Mamzar

3

12

4

Maps

Sharjah

Al Mulla Plaza

Dubai-Sharjah Highway

D

15

E

447

Za'abeel

Oud Metha Rd

Al Wasl
Hospital

Al Wasl
Club

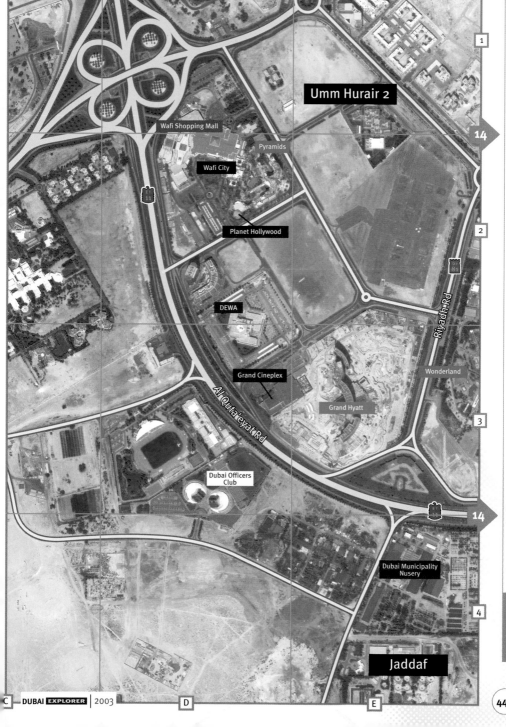

DIGITALGLOBE

Alliance
Francaise

Umm Hurair 2

Wafi Shopping Mall

Pyramids

Wafi City

Planet Hollywood

DEWA

Grand Cineplex

Al Qutaeyat Rd

Riyadh Rd

Wonderland

Grand Hyatt

Dubai Officers
Club

Dubai Municipality
Nusery

Jaddaf

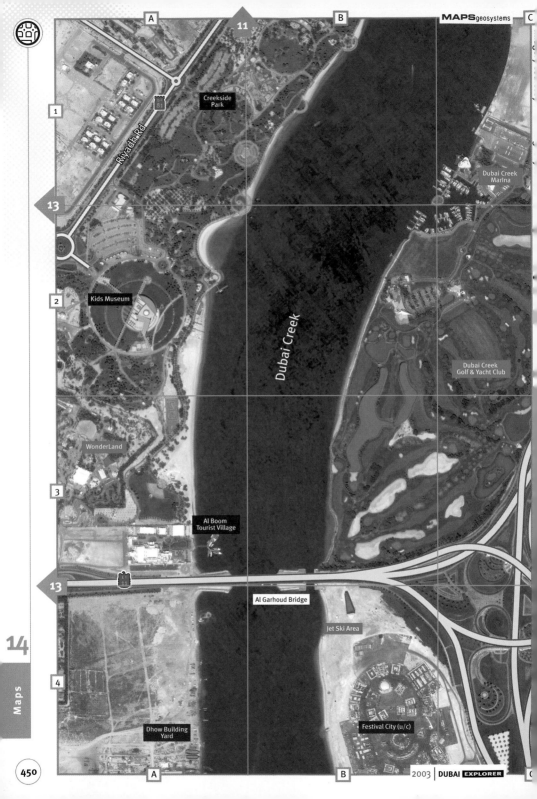

MAPS geosystems

A

B

1

13

Riyadh Rd

Creekside Park

Dubai Creek Marina

2

Kids Museum

Dubai Creek

Dubai Creek Golf & Yacht Club

WonderLand

3

Al Boom Tourist Village

13

Al Garhoud Bridge

Jet Ski Area

4

Dhow Building Yard

Festival City (u/c)

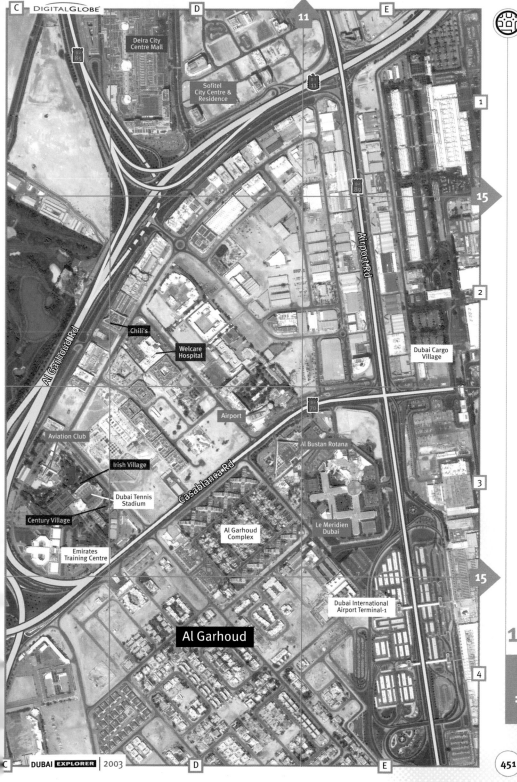

DIGITALGLOBE

Deira City
Centre Mall

Sofitel
City Centre &
Residence

11

1

15

Airport Rd

2

Dubai Cargo
Village

Chili's

Welcare
Hospital

Al Garhoud Rd

Airport

Casablanca Rd

Al Bustan Rotana

3

Aviation Club

Irish Village

Dubai Tennis
Stadium

Century Village

Al Garhoud
Complex

Le Meridien
Dubai

Emirates
Training Centre

15

Al Garhoud

Dubai International
Airport Terminal-1

4

14

Maps

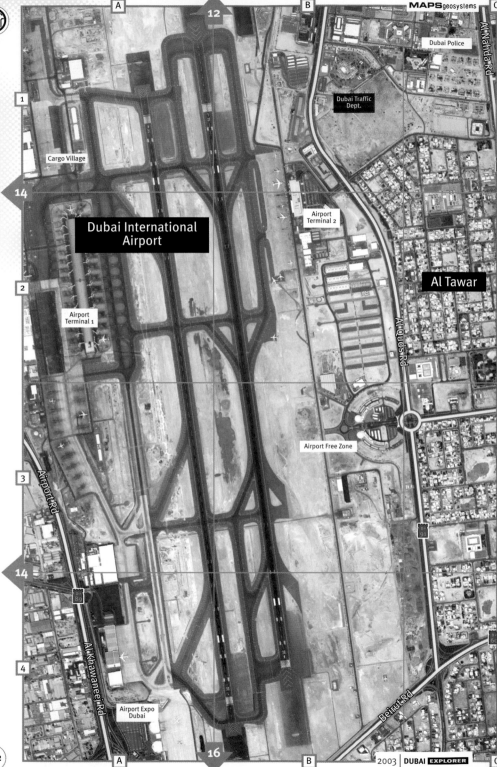

MAPSgeosystems

Dubai Police

Dubai Traffic
Dept.

Cargo Village

**Dubai International
Airport**

Airport
Terminal 2

Al Tawar

Airport
Terminal 1

Al Quds Rd

Airport Rd

Airport Free Zone

91

89

15

Maps

Al Khawaneej Rd

Al Nahda Rd

Airport Expo
Dubai

Beirut Rd

Higher Colleges
of Technology

Al Bustan Centre

Emirates Driving
School

Al Qusais

Damascus Rd

Baghdad Rd

Al Nahda Rd

**Al Qusais
Industrial Area**

Muhaisnah

Beirut Rd

1

2

3

4

15

Maps

16

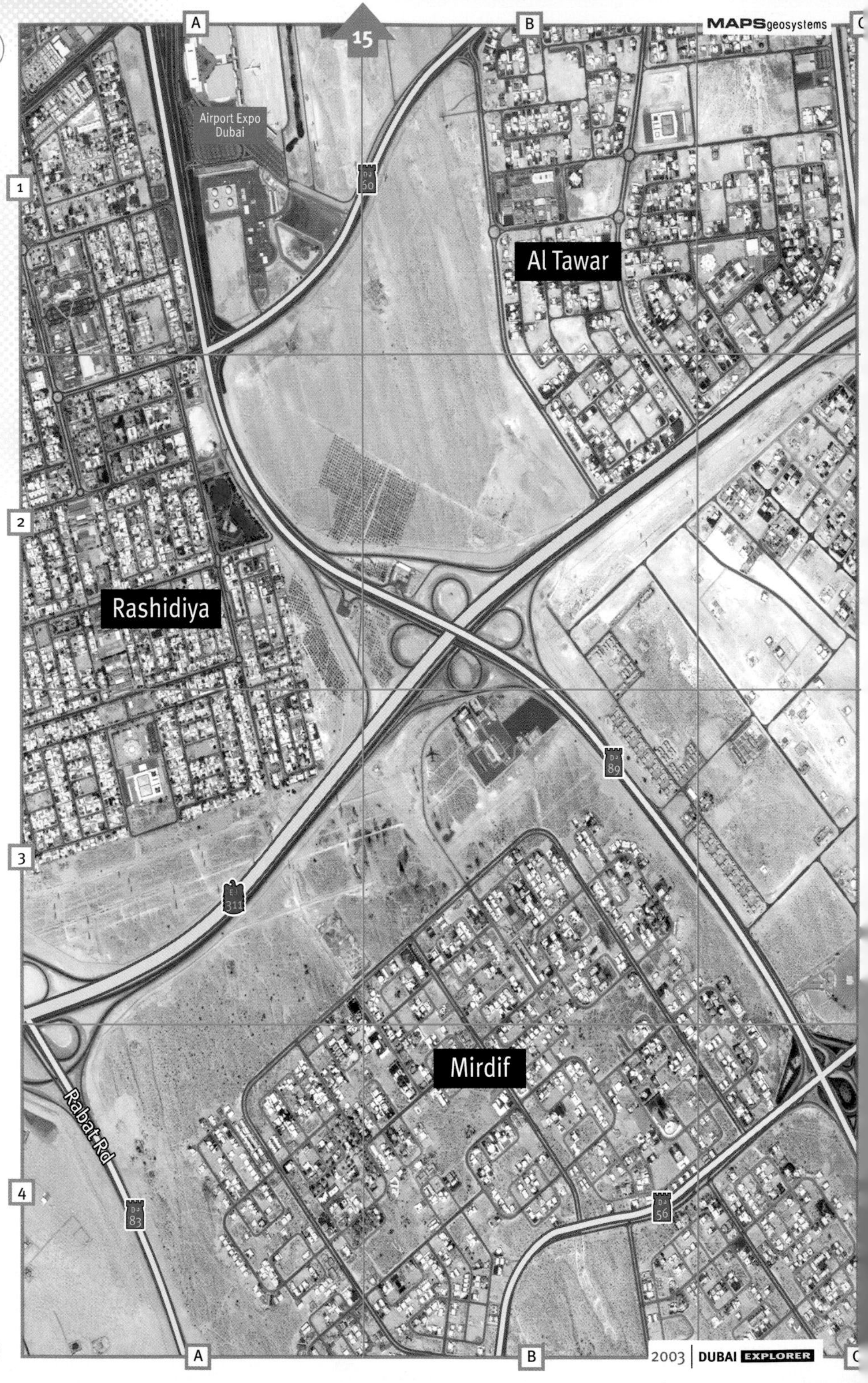

15

Airport Expo
Dubai

1

Al Tawar

2

Rashidiya

3

89

211

Mirdif

16

Maps

Rabat Rd

4

83

56

A

B

C

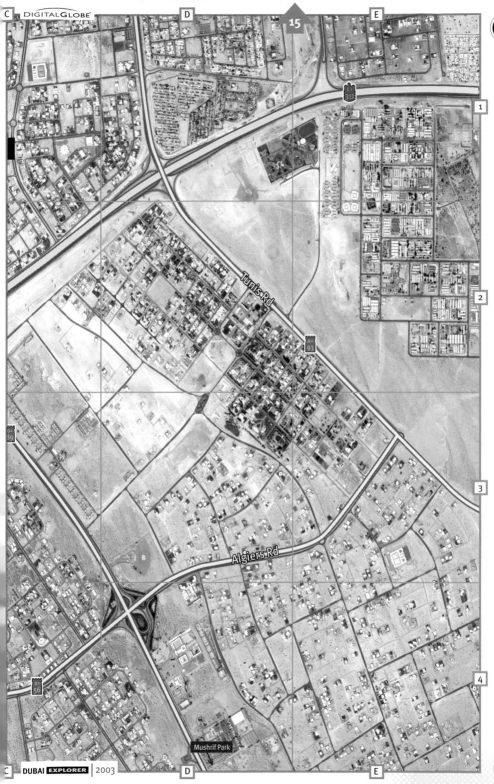

Tunis Rd

Algiers Rd

Mushrif Park

16

Maps

9

Doha Rd

2nd Zabbel Rd

1

66

2

Nad Al Sheba
Camel Racetrack

Khor Dubai
Wlidlife Sanctuary

Godolphin
Gallery

Bu Kidra /
Country Club Int.

Horse Racing
Stadium

Dubai Exiles
Rugby Club

Ras Al Khor Rd

3

Nad Al
Sheba Club

Dubai Country Club

66

Dubai Polo Club

Dubai - Al Ain Rd

Nad Al Sheba

**Al Awir
Industrial Area**

4

Index

EXPLORER

Index

Index